W9-BZI-160

THE RISE AND FALL OF
THE SOVIET EMPIRE

THE RISE
AND FALL
OF THE
SOVIET EMPIRE

BRIAN CROZIER

Published in Association with NATIONAL REVIEW

FORUM
An Imprint of Prima Publishing

© 1999 by Brian Crozier

FORUM
An Imprint of Prima Publishing
3875 Atherton Road
Rocklin, California 95765

PRIMA PUBLISHING, FORUM, and colophons are trademarks
of Prima Communications, Inc.

Library of Congress Cataloging-in-Publication Data
Crozier, Brian
The rise and fall of the Soviet Empire / Brian Crozier.
p.   cm.
Includes bibliographical references and index.
ISBN 0-7615-2057-0
Soviet Union—History. I. Title
DK266 .C758 1999
947.084—dc21   99-34314
                                                   CIP
99 00 01 02 HH 10 9 8 7 6 5 4 3 2
Printed in the United States of America

How to Order
Single copies may be ordered from Prima Publishing, P.O. Box 1260BK, Rocklin, CA 95677; telephone (916) 632-4400. Quantity discounts are also available. On your letterhead, include information concerning the intended use of the books and the number of books you wish to purchase.

Visit us online at www.primalifestyles.com

To Barbara and Amy,
gratefully and affectionately

CONTENTS

LIST OF DOCUMENTS

AUTHOR'S NOTE

———➤●◄———

THE RISE AND FALL OF THE SOVIET EMPIRE is a history of the beginning, middle, and end of the Soviet Empire, from 1917 to 1991 and following. In this book, I aim to describe the means by which the Soviet regime gained control over new territories; how it reasserted control when challenged; and in what circumstances it lost control, not only of outside territories but of itself: how the imperial regime finally collapsed.

Lenin, the founder of the regime, reconquered the territories of the Tsarist Empire by military force. After World War II, Lenin's successor, Joseph Stalin, added the East European satellites to the Empire by the "liberation" and occupation of territories from which Hitler's *Wehrmacht* had been expelled by the Soviet Red Army.

From 1959 to 1983, a new "peripheral" empire was added, using new techniques, best described as "teleguided" coups, initiated and supported from Moscow. During this long and protracted course, there were a number of failures. The most decisive failure of all came with the Soviet Union's unsuccessful attempt to conquer Afghanistan.

Between 1988, when the Soviet forces pulled out of Afghanistan, and the end of 1991, the whole system collapsed. This book ends with six epilogues, outlining the chaos and rebirth of ruling parties in the former USSR; the return of Communist parties to power in Eastern Europe under different names; the evolution of Communist governments in Asia; the survival of Fidel Castro's weakened regime in Cuba; and some "reflections" on Lenin's legacy to the world.

ACKNOWLEDGMENTS

M Y THANKS ARE owed to a number of people for their help during the three years and three months, from January 1, 1996, to the end of March 1999, that I was researching, writing, and editing this history of *The Rise and Fall of the Soviet Empire*.

To my long-serving assistant Barbara Rose, whose editorial skills were invaluable; to my other long-serving assistant Amy Wade, who collated the large collection of Appendixes; to Molly Molloy, Research Librarian at the Hoover Institution on War, Revolution, and Peace at Stanford University, California, whose knowledge and skills in finding whatever source I needed were outstanding; to Lora Soroka, whose handling of the vast collection of archives at the Hoover Institution was very helpful; to Charles Palm, Deputy Director of the Hoover and his assistant Lois Christopherson, who made all arrangements for my recurring visits; to Martin Dewhirst of Glasgow University, a leading Sovietologist, who translated the relevant Hoover archives; to Leonid Finkelstein, a leading Soviet dissident, whose advice was very useful; and not least to Richard Mellon Scaife, who endowed the "Distinguished Visiting Fellowship" that made this work possible. My thanks are also due to the Woodrow Wilson International Center for Scholars, whose Cold War International History Project greatly enriched the archival appendixes.

INTRODUCTION

THE SEMANTIC MAZE

THE HISTORIES OF the Soviet imperial expansion and of the Cold War overlap, but they are not identical. The "imperial imperative" first came with Lenin's reconquest of the Tsarist Empire between 1918 and 1920. It was Lenin's ambition to incorporate the whole world into the Communist Empire he was establishing, but that was not how he expressed it. He had adopted Marxism as his guiding principle, and he proclaimed it his revolutionary duty to help History by spreading Communism all over the world. Marxism-Leninism thus became the instrument with which he expanded his world empire.

To this end, in 1919 he set up the Third International, better known as the Comintern. Lenin died, however, in January 1924 after a long period of incapacitation, and it was left to his followers to attempt to implement his vision.

The term "Cold War" was of Western coinage; its original connotation was never accepted on the Soviet side. What the Western "enemy" called the Cold War, the Soviet camp called "peaceful coexistence." The term "Cold War" was first used in 1947, when the American financier and presidential adviser Bernard Baruch described the mutual hostility between the Soviet and U.S.-led Western camps. As the 1975 *Encyclopaedia Britannica* put it, this was "a war fought on political, economic and propaganda fronts, with limited recourse to weapons, largely because of fear of a nuclear holocaust." (The Soviet Union's "limited recourse to weapons" did not, however, rule out non-nuclear wars, as would happen in Vietnam—twice—or in Afghanistan, or Soviet-backed transnational terrorism or guerrilla wars in many countries.)

In Western eyes, the Cold War initially consisted of hostile words and deeds from the Soviet camp, to which, at least for the first two decades, the West responded with considerable reluctance. Thereafter, from the mid-1970s, the Western side significantly moderated its response, especially in the field of counter-propaganda.

The expression "peaceful coexistence" was coined by Lenin's foreign commissar, G. V. Chicherin, and was first applied to the undefined period between the Russian Revolution and the world revolution that was supposed to have followed, but had been inexplicably delayed.

Lenin had forecast between the "capitalist" and "Socialist" powers an inevitable world war, which (of course) the capitalists would lose. The word *peaceful* in "peaceful coexistence" referred to the (temporary) absence of armed hostilities between the two groups of powers. However, the lesson of nuclear power, as demonstrated by the United States with the destruction of Hiroshima and Nagasaki in the closing stages of World War II, was in time absorbed into Soviet strategic thinking, and the connotation of "peaceful coexistence" was revised during the reign of Nikita Khrushchev. A world war between the Communist and capitalist countries was no longer seen as inevitable (although later Soviet strategic plans, not intended for dissemination, provided for the possibility of a nuclear war that would end with a Soviet victory).

Accordingly, when Communist parties from all over the world (including China, for the last time) met in Moscow at the end of 1960, it was unanimously agreed that henceforth peaceful coexistence meant "the intensification of the international class struggle." In other words, of what the West called the "Cold War": the sum total of hostile words and deeds on both sides of the former Iron Curtain.

In the eyes of many, the Cold War was symbolized by the Iron Curtain, which in turn was symbolized by the Berlin Wall. This was misleading, since the term *Iron Curtain* (ironically first coined in a totally different context by Hitler's propaganda chief, Joseph Goebbels) had been popularized by Winston Churchill in a speech in 1946; the Berlin Wall was not built until 1961. So strong was the symbolism, however, that the destruction of the Wall in 1989 was widely hailed as "the end of the Cold War."

It would be more accurate to see it as the *beginning* of the end. Only when the Soviet system collapsed at the close of 1991 could the Cold War be truly said to have ended.

Did the Soviet collapse mean that the Cold War had ended in victory for the West? Understandably, many of those involved in this protracted struggle claimed that it had. In my view, such a claim was mistaken. The West had not won the Cold War; *the Soviet side had lost it*. True, President Ronald Reagan, in particular, had imposed intolerable strains on the Soviet system, notably by his Strategic Defense Initiative (SDI), misleadingly labeled "Star Wars": the purpose of the SDI was purely defensive, its object being to destroy any Soviet intercontinental weapons that were targeting the United States before they could hit their targets.

The best way to see the problem clearly is to consider the analogy of the two World Wars. After World War I, the victorious Allies imposed their terms on the defeated Germans with the Treaty of Versailles; after World War II, not only were the Allies able to impose their terms on the defeated Nazis, they could bring the major war criminals to the imposed justice of Nuremberg. At the end of the Cold War, the West was not able to impose either terms or retribution on the defeated Communists. The West was therefore robbed of a true victory, even though the Communists had lost.

Moreover, within a few years of the Communist defeat, Communist parties, many of them under different names, came back to power over most of Eastern Europe; in China and in several other Communist countries, including Cuba, the Communists stayed in power, even when they appeared to have abandoned the Marxist economic ideologies that had been their original *raison d'être*. The West's "victory" was far from total.

The Rise and Fall of the Soviet Empire is not a history of the Cold War, but a history of the beginning, middle, and end of the Soviet Empire. I touch on the Cold War and peaceful coexistence only in that context.

Historically, the rise falls into three stages:

Stage 1 (1918–1924): The restoration of the Tsarist Empire and its extension to include Outer Mongolia.

Stage 2 (1945–1975): The satellization of adjacent territories in Central Europe and the Far East, including China for some years (1950–1960) and North Korea (1948), North Vietnam (1954) and Laos, and later South Vietnam and Cambodia (1975).

Stage 3 (1959–1979): The birth and growth of the peripheral empire, starting with Fidel Castro's takeover of Cuba, the Seychelles, Grenada, Nicaragua, and Ethiopia, and the Soviet-engineered coups in Afghanistan, followed by the Soviet invasion of Afghanistan at the end of 1979.

Stage 1 was of course preceded by the Bolshevik Revolution and followed by Stalin's reign of terror and consolidation of existing gains. This period, already very widely covered by earlier historians, is treated in this volume only to the extent that it relates to the imperial theme.

Stages 2 and 3 overlap, and were marked by many Soviet-supported attempts, ending in failure, to take over a large number of target countries by subversion, terrorism, or guerrilla wars. The examples include the 1948 outbreaks in Southeast Asia (Indonesia, Malaya, Burma, and the Philippines); the wars in the former Portuguese territories of Angola and Mozambique (which started in 1959 and 1962 respectively); and failed coups, terrorism, or insurgencies in many other countries, including Argentina and Uruguay, Tunisia and Sudan, Sri Lanka and Turkey, and many others.

The American occupation of Grenada in 1983 was a turning point for the Empire. Five years later, the then-Soviet president, Mikhail Gorbachev, ordered the withdrawal of Soviet forces from Afghanistan, and of Cuban forces from Angola. The imperial collapse had begun.

The text here has been enriched by vitally important archives released in Moscow before and since the collapse of the Empire. In nearly all cases, these archives confirm intelligence that had already been secured by Western secret services (see my 1993 memoirs, *Free Agent: The Unseen War, 1941–1991*).

PHASE I

— ❦ —

IMPERIAL TAKEOFF
1917–1924

CHAPTER ONE

LENIN SEIZES HIS MOMENT

MARCH–DECEMBER 1917

H AVING SEIZED POWER in Petrograd in November 1917, Lenin launched what would become the greatest imperial expansion in world history. Unlike most of the great conquerors before him (such as Alexander the Great, Julius Caesar, Genghis Khan, Napoleon), Lenin himself never led troops into action. Instead, he incited them. The instruments with which he created his imperial legacy were, first, his own ideology and, second, the Comintern. The ideology was Marxism-Leninism, his own interpretation of the philosophy of Karl Marx. The Comintern, or Communist International—a Soviet-controlled association of national Communist parties—was Lenin's device for spreading the ideology to all countries of the world.

Lenin did not live to see the full fruits of his efforts. When he died, physically and mentally incapacitated, in January 1924, Russia's hold extended only to the limits of the Tsarist Empire he had restored—from the Ural Mountains in the west to the Bering Sea in the Far East. It was left to his successors—Joseph Stalin, Nikita Khrushchev, and Leonid Brezhnev—to impose Moscow-controlled regimes, first upon neighboring countries and later to the further reaches of the globe.

BORN IN 1870 at Simbirsk—a city on the Volga river—Lenin's original name was Vladimir Ilich Ulyanov. (In his honor, his birthplace was later renamed Ulyanovsk.) His father was a schoolteacher, later promoted to schools inspector. Vladimir Ilich did well at school and seemed destined for an academic career, but a family tragedy in 1887 turned him into a revolutionary. That year, his beloved eldest brother, Aleksandr, was executed for joining a terrorist group plotting to assassinate Tsar Aleksandr III. In the fall of that year, Vladimir Ilich was expelled from the University of Kazan, where he had enrolled only three months earlier, for participating in an illegal student assembly. Banished to the nearby village of Kokushkino, where his older sister Anna had already been "deported," he was allowed back to Kazan a year later, but was denied readmission to the university. While in his village exile, he had read Karl Marx's *Das Kapital*. By 1889, he called himself a Marxist, which signaled to the authorities that he blamed "capitalism" for his country's problems and looked to "communism" for their solution.

Four years later, the Ulyanov family moved to St. Petersburg where Vladimir Ilich resumed his studies. He graduated in law and began to practice, at the same time meeting with other Marxists to discuss the need for revolution. In 1895, he broadened his circle of conspirators by traveling in Western Europe. The most important of the political exiles he met was Georgy Plekhanov, who became a formative influence in his intellectual life. On Vladimir's return to St. Petersburg, he and other Marxists formed what might be seen as the first pre–Marxist-Leninist political group: The Union for the Struggle for the Liberation of the Working Class.

In December 1895, he was arrested with other conspirators, jailed for fifteen months, then sent to Siberia for three years. There he was joined by his fiancée, Nadezhda Krupskaya, a fellow member of the Union. Because civil marriages were not recognized, they were married in church (to their shared ideological embarrassment); thereafter his wife served as his secretary.

In January 1900, his Siberian exile over, Vladimir went back to Western Europe and joined Plekhanov and others in launching a newspaper named *Iskra (The Spark)* in the hope of unifying the Russian Marxist groups at home and abroad into one party calling itself Social Democratic: an early contribution to the "semantic maze." Vladimir Ilich Ulyanov changed his name to Lenin in 1901.

By all accounts, Lenin was the ultimate political fanatic. A most convincing portrait of the man appears in a chapter of Richard Pipes's monumental work, *The Russian Revolution: 1899–1919*.[1] In personality, Lenin combined two seemingly incompatible characteristics: a disagreeable first impression and a magnetic charisma. Stockily built, he had slanting eyes and prominent cheekbones, suggestive of the Siberian East. Those meeting him found him "provincial." By age thirty, he was almost completely bald. He made no attempt to charm those he met, spoke harshly, and preferred a sarcastic laugh to a friendly smile.

The charismatic force made its appearance on further acquaintance. Most of those who knew him agreed that in Lenin's mind the only thing that mattered was "the cause," meaning *his* cause. Those who agreed with the cause (as he saw it) were called "we" and "us." Those who did not were "they" or "them"—the enemy. Tolerance of the enemy was out of the question and was not even to be contemplated. The only satisfactory fate for "them" was obliteration.

The number of "enemies," thus interpreted, was virtually limitless. Within his Social Democratic Party, however (and its Communist successor), Lenin did tolerate dissent, but only as a temporary phase to be eliminated as soon as possible by the force of his personality and by his arguments. And yet, unlike the totalist* dictators who succeeded him (Mussolini, Hitler, Stalin, Mao), Lenin never sought a cult of personality. It would be wrong to interpret this as modesty. It simply meant that Lenin and his cause were inextricably one. As Pipes points out, he left less biographical material than any other leader of the Russian Revolution.

Lenin's cruelty was limitless and arose from a total indifference to the sufferings of "them." The Revolution had to triumph, and if the price was the elimination of those who disagreed, so be it. "They" did not count. Interestingly, he was not personally sadistic. As the ex-Soviet historian Dmitri Volkogonov puts it, "His was more the social, philosophical cruelty of a leader. His main argument for the use of terror was that it was in the interests of the proletariat."[2]

Another passage from the same author helps to explain the workings of Lenin's ruthless revolutionary mind: "Lenin took every opportunity to ram home the message that terror was inevitable. . . . In effect, Lenin believed

---

*The words *totalist* and *totalism* will be used throughout this book, except when quoting other authors. The original words *totalitarian* and *totalitarianism* are usually credited (in their Italian equivalents) to Mussolini's adviser Giovanni Gentile, who used the first of them in a speech on March 8, 1925. There is nothing sacrosanct about them, and I have always found them inelegantly and unnecessarily polysyllabic.—BC

that terror would save the country from starvation. The food 'must be taken from the rich.' Black marketeers must be shot."[3]

This callousness cohabited, surprisingly, with physical cowardice. If in personal danger, Lenin's instinct was not to fight, but to flee. The needs of his country and of his compatriots were not of the slightest importance to this fanatical Russian. The one thing that mattered was world revolution. He was bothered by Marx's insistence on capitalism and capitalists as the enemy—enemies to be eliminated—because capitalism was weak in Russia. Marx would not have chosen Russia as the place to start a revolution.

In the theories of Karl Marx and Friedrich Engels, revolution would start in one of the advanced capitalist countries, such as England or Germany. In Marxian class terms, the proletariat would annihilate the bourgeoisie, meaning the capitalists.

The trouble with this theory, in Lenin's mind, was that the country of his birth had only an embryonic capitalism and lacked both a substantial capitalist class and a proletariat. What it did offer was a vast peasantry and a considerable aristocracy. The accepted view in the minds of Marxists was that, of course, revolution would come to Russia in time, but not now. First it would be necessary for capitalism to develop, and with it a working class to rise against capitalism and triumph.

Perhaps it came down to definitions of terms. If according to the accepted definitions, Russia was not ripe for revolution, it would be necessary to change the definitions. Accordingly, Lenin redefined the relatively rich peasants as "petty bourgeois" capitalists and the landless peasants as a rural proletariat. Russia had been industrializing itself fast. Therefore, Lenin believed, conditions were ripe for revolution now, not in some hypothetical future.

In his key work, *What Is to Be Done?*, published in 1902, Lenin defined his proposed revolutionary party (at that time still the Social Democrats) as the organization that would carry out political agitation, guide the economic struggle of the working class, and give the proletariat its revolutionary training. Thus, three years before the failed revolution of 1905 against the Russian Tsar, and fifteen years before the Russian revolutions of 1917, Lenin had made it clear that all power would be concentrated in the hands of a revolutionary party acting in the name of the proletariat. There was no question of asking the proletariat whether it agreed with this proposed monopoly of power, and still less of consulting other parties or sections of the population.

Lenin already had his revolutionary party, called Bolsheviks, meaning "majority," from the Russian word for "more": *bol'she*. This party had emerged in 1903, at the close of the Second Congress of the Russian Social Democratic Labor Party when Lenin obtained a majority after the departure of several disgruntled Jewish delegates. The defeated Social Democrats became known as the Mensheviks or "minority" (from *men'she,* meaning "fewer"). Essentially, the Mensheviks remained Social Democrats while the Bolsheviks became Communists. However, they continued to call themselves the Social Democratic Labor Party (Bolsheviks).

In January 1905, the first Russian Revolution broke out, and went on till the end of the year. Frustratingly, no doubt, for Lenin, he played no part in this largely spontaneous outbreak of serial violence because he was in Geneva when it started. In October, he wrote a series of articles for publication in St. Petersburg, adding illuminating details to his pre-revolutionary work *What Is to Be Done?* (mentioned earlier). This time, he advocated violent methods, including: "pour boiling water from top storeys, . . . throw acid over the police, and steal government money." *

Lenin returned to Russia in November 1905, a few weeks before the unorganized Revolution was finally suppressed. In 1907, he was again driven out of Russia, and spent most of his further exile writing revolutionary texts and combating the Mensheviks. In 1912, he convened a Bolshevik Party conference at Prague, where he denounced the Mensheviks as "schismatics". When the Great War broke out in 1914, he was briefly in Russia, but he and other Bolsheviks returned yet again to Switzerland, to avoid arrest while they plotted to overthrow the Tsarist regime. The Great War was not yet over, but by the end of 1916, the Russian Army had been utterly defeated by the Austro-German forces, with the loss of at least a million men—half of them dead, the rest prisoners. The Tsarist troops mutinied, and the old regime was collapsing. And now, in February and March 1917, strikes and riots broke out in St. Petersburg. Lenin watched events from afar with restless envy: he was in the wrong place at the right time. The Tsar, Nicholas II, abdicated on

---

*Quoted from Dmitri Volkogonov, *Lenin: Life and Legacy* (HarperCollins, London, 1994), pp. 70–71.

March 15, and a provisional government headed by Prince George Lvov as president took over. In Lenin's mind, events were taking a wrong turn: There was no point to the collapse of the Tsarist empire unless the revolutionary regime he had envisioned took its place.

The new government, in which the only Socialist, Alexander Kerensky, served as minister of justice, had proclaimed civic liberties for all: the equality of all citizens, without social, religious, or racial discrimination. This was not the revolution Karl Marx had been calling for, and which Lenin and his followers had been plotting—rule by a revolutionary elite in the name of the workers. At all costs, Lenin had to get back to Russia.

In secret talks with German officials and military officers, Lenin reached a deal—a purely Machiavellian one on both sides. The German High Command rightly calculated that Lenin and Bolshevik exiles would undermine the provisional government, which wanted to fight on: and Lenin wanted to opt out of the war, whatever the price, to concentrate on the more important matter of seizing power and holding on to it. The practical outcome was a German decision to support the Bolsheviks financially to the tune of more than 50 million marks in gold, estimated at that time to be worth between US $6 and $10 million.[4] Lenin and his little group of fellow-exiles in Switzerland would be transported through Germany to Russia in a sealed train. In the event, nineteen Bolsheviks, including Lenin and his senior allies (Gregory Zinoviev, Karl Radek, and Anatoli Lunacharski),* left Zurich on March 27, 1917 (or April 9 under the Western calendar) on a train provided by the German government. Four days later, via Sweden and Finland, they reached Petrograd. Lenin's success was not immediate. In mid-May, Kerensky became war minister, and appealed to the defeated troops to fight on in a new spirit. A new Russian offensive was launched; it collapsed in total defeat. Seizing what he thought was his moment, Lenin and his Bolsheviks tried to take power in mid-July. The attempt was premature. Leon Trotsky, who had joined Lenin and the others from his own exile in America and London, was arrested, and Lenin, branded a German agent by Kerensky, fled to neighboring Finland.

---

*Zinoviev and Radek were both executed during Stalin's show trials in the 1930s. Lunacharski, who had served as the Soviet ambassador to Spain, died a natural death in France at the end of 1933.

During his brief exile in Finland, Lenin wrote one of his key works: *The State and Revolution.* In it, he outlined his plan for a "proletarian revolution." The existing parliamentary republic, which he denounced as a dictatorship of the propertied minority, would yield to the dictatorship of the propertyless majority.*

I know of no evidence that Lenin saw the irony of replacing a non-dictatorship with a real one. A sense of humor was not one of his personal characteristics. Nor did he see the irony of demolishing the existing "imperialism," which he described as "the highest stage of capitalism," with the imperialism of the new Russia as the nascent center of the world Communist order he envisioned.

WHEN LENIN'S ATTEMPT to seize power in mid-July 1917 collapsed, Prince Lvov resigned as president and Kerensky took over. Unlike Lenin, who wanted to negotiate a peace deal with the Germans, whatever the cost, Kerensky had decided to fight on—before the aborted coup. As war minister, he had launched an offensive against the Austro-German forces. By July 7, the offensive had collapsed, leaving the remnants of the Russian forces totally demoralized. Kerensky lost the will to carry on fighting, but his newly appointed commander in chief, General Lavr Kornilov, decided to resume the fight against the invaders.

Thereupon Kerensky fired him, but General Kornilov ignored the dismissal and ordered his troops to march on Petrograd. He had made his aims clear: to destroy the Petrograd Soviet (or Council) and rid the provisional government of its Socialist elements. Kerensky found himself in an impossible crossfire. Kornilov's ambitions were thwarted, however, when his troops deserted *en masse.*

Which way could Kerensky turn? By then, the Bolsheviks seemed to be winning. The civilian "masses" were turning increasingly to them. The people had had enough of war, and the Bolsheviks appeared to be offering peace. Petrograd's factory workers were turning their way, as were soldiers of the Petrograd garrison.

**The State and Revolution* was not published until early 1918. In a postscript dated December 13, 1917, Lenin revealed that he had planned a seventh and final chapter but never wrote it because it clashed with the actual "October Revolution." As he put it, "It is more pleasant and useful to go through 'the experience of the revolution than to write about it.'"

In mid-September 1917, a desperate Kerensky freed Trotsky and other jailed Bolshevik leaders. In October, the Bolsheviks found themselves in a majority in the Petrograd Soviet, with Trotsky as chairman. Back from Finland, Lenin was ready for his long-planned revolution. On November 6 (24 October in the old calendar), the Bolsheviks, the Petrograd soldiers, the sailors from Kronstadt, and the workers' Red Guards (self-appointed by the Bolsheviks) stormed the Winter Palace and arrested whichever members of the provisional government they could find. For Kerensky the game was up, but he was still unwilling to admit it. He escaped, made an abortive attempt to retake Petrograd with an inadequate force of loyal troops, then vanished and took refuge abroad.

Lenin headed the new government, with Trotsky as commissar for foreign affairs and Joseph Stalin as commissar for nationalities. For all three, this was their first taste of power. In the initial revolutionary hierarchy of 1917, Lenin was Number 1, Trotsky Number 2, and Stalin Number 3 (a hierarchy that Stalin would modify to his own benefit after Lenin's death).

Trotsky, born Lev Davidovich Bronstein, was the son of a prosperous Russified Jewish farmer. Like Lenin, he had spent some years in jail, in Siberian exile, and in conspiratorial freedom abroad. A fluent writer and a mesmerizing orator, he had worked with Lenin on the revolutionary newspaper *The Spark*. His main contribution to revolutionary theory, in his book *Results and Prospects* (written in jail in 1906), was his vision of "permanent revolution." Whereas Lenin had opted to redefine the bourgeoisie and the proletariat, Trotsky advocated maintaining a continuing state of revolution to build up a genuine, party-led unrest in Russia, in the belief that this would lead not only to the development of a revolutionary urban working class but also to a permanent revolutionary state internationally.

Stalin was the son of an alcoholic Georgian cobbler; his baptismal name was Iosef Vissarionovich Dzhugashvili. The revolutionary pseudonym "Stalin," by which he became known, meant "man of steel." Ironically, he had read Marx while training to be a priest in the Theological Seminary at Tiflis. He, too, had his period of Siberian exile, from 1913 to 1917.

On November 25, elections for a Constituent Assembly (whose purpose, of course, was to draw up a new constitution) were held, and the Bolsheviks were heavily defeated, winning only 225 seats to 420 for the Social Revolutionaries (an anti-Marxist party that stood as the main alternative to the Marxist Social Democratic Workers' Party in the last few years of Tsarist rule). Lenin, however, was not going to let election results hold up his revolution. When the Assembly met in Petrograd on January 18, 1918, he called in the Red Guards, who dispersed the members.

Lenin immediately initiated his revolutionary program, which included the repudiation of the national debt, the nationalization of the land and of all banks and factories, obligatory membership of trade unions without the right to strike, and the confiscation of all Church property.

The Marxist revolutionaries were in power, but their hold on it was still precarious. It would be necessary to enforce and perpetuate it with suitable ruthlessness. To do so, on December 20 Lenin made a decision of major and enduring importance: he set up the ancestor of what would become the KGB, under the cumbersome title of All-Russian Extraordinary Commission for the Struggle against Counter-Revolution and Sabotage. It was thereafter known as the *Cheka*, from two of its lengthy set of initials. There are varying reports on whether the *Cheka* recruited ex-members of the Tsarist secret police, the *Okhrana*. As a leading authority puts it: "The Chekas had no scruples about using former Okhrana agents, well practised in the business of reporting on revolutionary organizations." Most of the *Okhranniki*, however, ended up in concentration camps.[5]

On the preceding day, December 19, Lenin had picked his man—the Polish-born Felix Dzerzhinsky, at that time the commandant of Smolny—to run what would become the most ruthless and pervasive instrument of repression in the world.

The ultimate fanatic was now firmly in power, with his hand-picked enforcer to keep him there.

CHAPTER TWO

THE RECONQUEST

1917–1924

———⟫•⟪———

F ROM THE FIRST days of Lenin's victory, the "semantic maze" conditioned all official pronouncements. Thus, on November 15, 1917, Lenin's revolutionary government, in a "Declaration of the Rights of Peoples," proclaimed that all the peoples living in territories of the former Tsarist empire (from Ukraine in the West to Caucasia in the South and Siberia in the East) were henceforth equal and sovereign. As such, they had the right to secede and set up independent states.[1] Not surprisingly, at that early stage, he was taken at his word.

The first nation to take advantage of Lenin's apparent readiness to yield sovereignty was Finland. For five hundred years, since 1154, the Finns had been under Swedish domination, but the Russian Tsars had taken over in a series of wars that culminated in Sweden yielding what was left of Finland to Aleksandr I in 1809. Finland, however, kept its ancient constitution until 1899, when the Russians declared their right to legislate on Finnish affairs. By 1902, Finnish forces had been incorporated into the Russian Army.

After the Russian Revolution of March 1917, things changed. The "ancient political rights" of Finland, where Lenin had found refuge, had been restored by the Russian provisional government. What did these "rights" mean? Both countries now had provisional governments, and the two now met to define the terms, but they had not reached agreement when the Bolsheviks seized power. So, on December 6, 1917, the Finnish parliament, known as the Diet, proclaimed Finland the Republic of Finland. Lenin had more pressing matters to attend to, and his government formally recognized Finland's independence on January 4, 1918. There was a small snag, however: the Russian troops in Finland were not brought home. They would soon try to crush Finland's infant independence.

Next to proclaim independence was the Baltic Republic of Lithuania, on December 11. Four days later, Moldavia followed suit, and on January 10, 1918, the independent Republic of the Don—home to the fighting Cossacks—was announced.

Lithuania's example was soon followed by the other two Baltic countries, Latvia and Estonia. As early as November 17, 1917, only two days after Lenin's Declaration of the Rights of Peoples, the new Provisional National Council of Latvia claimed the right of self-determination. On January 5, 1918, it informed the Lenin-controlled Russian Constituent Assembly that Latvia had decided to separate itself from Russia. On February 24, Estonia's National Council also proclaimed independence.

Two other important national entities had chosen the moment of the March 1917 Revolution to move toward independence: Ukraine and Belorussia. That month, a Ukrainian Central Rada, or Council, was formed. The proximity of the Russian giant was intimidating, and instead of proclaiming independence, the Rada, backed by the Ukrainian National Congress, merely expressed the aspirations of the Ukrainian "masses" (a suitably Socialist term) for national independence. There were two such statements, on June 23 and November 20.

As with Finland, Ukrainian discussions with the first Russian provisional government proved difficult. When Lenin's Bolsheviks took over in November, the Rada, now losing patience, refused to recognize the authority of the new regime. On January 22, 1918, it proclaimed Ukraine's complete independence. It had what appeared to be grounds for such boldness, in that the new Soviet government had officially recognized Ukraine's right to separate from Russia in a note to the Central Ukrainian Rada on December 17, 1917. The Soviet statement included these words: "Everything that touches national rights and the national independence of the Ukrainian people, we, the Soviet of People's Commissars, accept clearly without limitations and unreservedly."[2]

Never were true intentions more specifically obscured. In case the Ukrainians should fail to recognize the falsity of the words used, the

Soviet government delivered a forty-eight-hour ultimatum to the Rada, threatening to declare war on Ukraine if the Ukrainians failed to assist the Bolshevik forces against the White Russian military in the Don region, together with a guarantee of unfettered Soviet troop movements.

On February 1, 1918, less than three months after the Bolshevik takeover, the Central Powers (Germany and Austria) recognized the independence of Ukraine. On February 9, a peace treaty with Ukraine was signed at Brest-Litovsk. The next day, Trotsky misguidedly interpreted the treaty as the end of Russia's war with the Central Powers and declared it to be over. Thereupon the Germans resumed hostilities, seized several towns and, by March 4, arrived at a point 100 miles from Petrograd. By then, Lenin had renewed peace negotiations with the Central Powers, which culminated in Russia's own devastating Treaty of Brest-Litovsk.

Belorussia went through much the same process as Ukraine, with the formation of a National Committee at Minsk shortly after the March 1917 Russian Revolution. In July 1917, the committee changed its name to Central Rada of Belorussian Organizations. In October, the Rada claimed the right to represent the Belorussian people. Two months later an elected all-Belorussian Congress passed a resolution calling for the creation of the Belorussian National Republic.

In the Transcaucasian territories of Georgia, Azerbaijan, and Armenia, the independence process went through two distinct phases. In the first, after the March Revolution, revolutionary committees seized control from the demoralized Russian authorities, but the committees were pro-Menshevik, that is, social-democratic and anti-Bolshevik. There was no clamor for independence, and no opposition was manifested when the Russian provisional government set up a Special Committee for Transcaucasia in Tiflis, Georgia's capital.

However, when the Bolsheviks took over in November, the local committees refused to recognize Lenin's government. Instead, they proclaimed a Transcaucasian Federation, consisting of loosely linked independent republics in Georgia, Armenia, and Azerbaijan. A Georgian National Council, set up on November 22, 1917, went on to proclaim independence and secession from Russia in April 1918: a short-lived triumph, as it happened. As for neighboring Armenia, Lenin had specifically promised full secession rights in a statement in October 1917, on the eve of the Bolshevik takeover, but appeared to forget his promise thereafter. By then,

Stalin had been given authority over the "nationalities" and was against independence for any of the Caucasian peoples (including of course the Georgians, of whom he was one). The Transcaucasian Federation collapsed on May 26, 1918, because of dissension between the three countries. Three days later, the Azeris proclaimed their independence, and on December 7, 1918, the first Azerbaijan parliament was elected by universal suffrage.

BACK NOW TO Lenin's ideological thinking, which took absolute precedence over any legal or historical conventions. On the question of national claims to independence and secession, as indeed on the questions of Russian society and the legitimacy of the Bolshevik seizure of power, Lenin's guiding principle was simply Marxism as he interpreted it: in other words, Marxism-Leninism. Nothing else counted. Russia itself was important only because developments there had given Lenin his chance to ignite the "proletarian" revolution that he would extend to all other countries of the world.

Therefore, when Lenin had called for the right of the peoples of the former Tsarist Empire to secede from Russia and set up independent governments, the absent word *proletariat* was uppermost in his mind. So long as those claiming independence were demonstrably Communists acting in the name of the proletarian revolution, and were ready therefore to accept guidance from the world's first "proletarian" government, there was no problem. But the notion that the peoples of the former Tsarist empire should claim independence on grounds of ethnic identity and sovereignty was totally foreign to Lenin's intellectual guiding principles.

In that context, the glaring contradiction between his apparently open "offer" of independence and his real aim of control from Moscow, where he happened to be in power, was nonexistent. As he had put it, as early as 1913, "Social Democracy has as its fundamental and principal task to assist the self-determination, not of peoples or of nations, but of the proletariat of every nationality. We must always and unconditionally strive toward the unification of the proletariat of all nationalities. . . ."[3]

Stalin, after his appointment by Lenin as commissar for nationalities, wrote an essay on "Marxism and the National Question," which Richard Pipes dismisses (rightly) as superficial and logically inconsistent.[4] Stalin defined the nation as a "historically evolved, stable community arising on the foundations of a common language, territory, economic life, and psychological make-up, manifested in a community of culture." Lenin, however, clung to his earlier view that nationalism was essentially a capitalist phenomenon that was bound to vanish with the forthcoming death of capitalism.

He dismissed rival definitions. For example, the Social Revolutionaries had been calling for a federalist approach on the basis of national self-determination. Here, we are once again deep into the semantic maze. Nations could exercise self-determination, but only on lines dictated by "democratic centralism," meaning the unity of action as determined by the ruling party. In Lenin's view, a federalist solution to Bolshevik Russia's problem of national self-determination would result in the creation of undesirable mini-states.

In some respects, Lenin's arguments were caught in an ideological web of his own making. He publicly supported self-determination for the oppressed colonies of the western empires in Africa and Asia. But the provisos he attached to self-determination within the numerous nations of the former Tsarist Empire gave precedence to class imperatives over national aspirations. In other words, the nations concerned could have "self-determination," but only if they adopted "Socialism" as defined by the Communist parties.

Having seized power in the wartime chaos of November 1917, however, Lenin's government was in no condition to deal with the imperial problem until he had rid Russia of the German and Austrian military presence—until he had, in effect, repaid the considerable debt he had incurred by accepting Germany's readiness to transport him and his closest colleagues from Switzerland to Russia.

The debt was repaid, with massive interest, under the Treaty of Brest-Litovsk, at the expense of the defunct Tsarist Empire.

At the turn of the year, 1917–1918, the geographical limits of Bolshevik authority were very restricted. The revolutionaries faced multifarious challenges: from the armies of the Central Powers, from White Russians (as Belorussians are known), and from local nationalists. In Finland, for example, civil war broke out at the end of January between the Socialists and conservative nationalists. The Socialists were aided by troops loyal to the Bolsheviks, while the Germans helped the conservatives. In May, the Right could claim victory.[5]

Regardless of independence claims, the Germans were still occupying the Baltic provinces, and the local German residents gave the orders. In Minsk, capital of Belorussia, the situation was particularly fluid. The local Bolsheviks, supported by Communist troops, formed a government at the end of 1917. Its authority beyond Minsk extended only to such cities as Vitebsk and Bobruisk, and lasted merely one hundred days. In February 1918, the Soviet authorities started pulling out of Minsk, with the advancing German forces at their backs. To add to the confusion, the German forces were supported by forces of the Polish Legion and even of the Russian-sponsored Polish Army, which had opted to join forces with the Germans following the Bolshevik coup in Russia.[6] The Germans went on to set up a puppet White Russian administration in Minsk.

Further south, in Bessarabia, on the borders of Romania, a Council of the Land had been set up at the end of 1917. When, in January, its authority was challenged by pro-Bolshevik local forces, the council appealed to the Romanian government for protection. On April 9, 1918, the council voted for Bessarabian union with Romania. By then, Lenin's government had accepted Germany's terms for total defeat.

A new factor in this confused equation was the intervention of Turkey in the wake of the German defeat of the Russian armies. In the campaigns of 1915 and 1916, the Tsarist armies had seized various Turkish towns. Now, in the first three months of 1918, the Turkish forces took them back: Erzinjan in mid-January, Erzerum at the end of February, and Trebizond in early March. At this stage, the Bolsheviks simply lacked the capacity to resist the Turkish advance.

In early December 1917, the Bolsheviks had signed an armistice with the German Command, the peace terms to be decided later. These negotiations took place at the headquarters of Prince Leopold of Bavaria in the Polish town of Brest. In military and political terms, the resulting treaty, signed on March 3, 1918, was a disaster for Lenin and his Bolsheviks. Although Germany agreed to evacuate certain parts of Russia then under military occupation, the Russians had to agree to cede independence to all the western and southern borderlands, including Ukraine and Transcaucasia.

Russia would have to evacuate the Eastern Anatolia territories of Turkey, as well as the districts of Kars, Ardahan, and Batum. The Bolsheviks were also forced to demobilize completely and keep all warships within Russia's harbors. They recognized the peace treaty between the Ukrainian People's Republic and the Central Powers. Under Article II of a supplementary "German-Russian Financial Agreement," Russia also agreed to pay Germany 6 billion marks to compensate Germans "who shall have suffered damage by reason of Russian measures."*

CIVIL WAR BEGINS

BY THE TIME the Treaty of Brest-Litovsk was signed in 1918, the great Russian Civil War had already begun. As with all events involving the Bolsheviks, this appalling conflict can be defined and understood only if one grasps the ideological dimension. In Lenin's mind, civil war was an inevitable, indeed an *indispensable,* component of the revolution. Forty-six years before the "October" Revolution of 1917, the Paris Commune of 1871 had provided a perfect example of how not to conduct a "proletarian" uprising. In a letter dated April 12 of that year,[7] Karl Marx had commented that the Parisian Communards had been defeated because they "did not want to start a civil war." Lenin agreed wholeheartedly and had no time for pacifist Socialists who called for an end to fighting. Peace was "a slogan of philistines and priests. The proletarian slogan must be: Civil war." Trotsky was even blunter: "Soviet authority is organized civil war." As Pipes rightly puts it, "From such pronouncements, it should be evident that the Civil War was not forced on the Communist leaders by the foreign and domestic 'bourgeoisie': it lay at the heart of their political programme."

As is the rule of civil wars, the great Civil War of 1918 to 1920 was a catalog of horrors. There are no accurate statistics, but the estimated deaths ran into millions, whether from acts of war or atrocities or famine. It was also, owing to the vastness of the contested territories, a conflict of exceptional complexity. Professor Pipes divides it into three major phases.[8] *Phase 1* began almost immediately after the Bolshevik coup and mostly involved small units. For that reason, it became known as the "partisan" war and lasted one year. The Red Army was not formed until

---

*As history decided, the Treaty of Brest-Litovsk was in effect rendered null and void by the total defeat of the Central Powers in November 1918. The Soviet Union did not regain control over the Baltic Republics, however, until Stalin's pact with Hitler in 1939.

the autumn of 1918, when *Phase 2* began. Phase 2 lasted seven months, from March to November 1919, and assured victory for the Bolsheviks. *Phase 3* was essentially a mopping up in the Crimea, but was slowed down on the Bolshevik side when the Polish Army invaded Ukraine. It ended in November 1920, with the evacuation of the remnants of the anti-Bolshevik White Army by the British and French navies. Phases 2 and 3 were further complicated by foreign interventions.

Such was the picture in strategic terms. Each phase, however, divides naturally into two or three geographic sections: Phase 1 consisted of the war with the Cossacks, the war for Ukraine, and, hundreds of miles to the southeast, the war with the independent-minded Muslims of Transcaspia. Phase 2 consisted of the war in White Russia and the Baltic region, plus the Western intervention in northern Russia. Phase 3 was marked in the Siberian Far East by a war against the Japanese invaders, followed by a further war between the Bolsheviks and the White forces, and, thousands of miles to the southwest, by a campaign for control of Transcaucasia.

Phase 1: 1918

In the first phase, the anti-Bolsheviks enjoyed the participation of a number of able generals. The label "White" (apart from its Belorussian connotation) was a Bolshevik creation, designed to associate those on the opposite side with the French Bourbon monarchy. But the label stuck. In fact, the Whites were not monarchists; they had no desire to restore the Tsarist regime. Their first military leader, General Mikhail Vasilevitch Alekseev, was sixty years old when Lenin's Bolsheviks took over. He was a pure professional soldier with no special political aims other than to prevent the Bolsheviks from consolidating their hold on power. For him, this aim was less political than patriotic. He saw the new revolutionaries as fanatics who had no interest in preserving what was left of the defeated Russian forces or in honoring the pledges made by Russia before the collapse of the old regime.

He traveled south to Don Cossack region, where he set up his headquarters at Novocherkassk, then rounded up and enlisted several hundred officers who had been made idle by the routing of the Tsarist forces. One of those who joined him was a younger officer, General Lavr Kornilov (mentioned in the previous chapter). Where Alekseev was quiet and reserved, Kornilov was loud and flamboyant. They soon clashed, and Kornilov got his way: he would lead the emerging White army as commander in chief, while Alekseev would handle the financial side and relations with the Don Cossacks. The White army, initially known as the "Alekseev Organization" was renamed the "Volunteer Army."

Two other Russian generals rose to brief prominence during this first phase of the Civil War. One was General Alexis Kaledin, whom the Don Cossack contingent of the Tsarist army elected as their chief when they made their way home after the Imperial defeat. The other was General Anton Denikin. A plump man with a darkish twirled mustache and a pointed, whitening beard, Denikin had considerable charm and intellect, reflected in the five volumes of memoirs he left.

This first phase of the Civil War was a period of confusion. The first loyalty of the generals was to Mother Russia, but their troops, and the civilians, gave precedence to the Don region and Cossack population. The lines of communication were no less confused, and the fighting partisans on both sides often had to cross enemy-held areas to convey messages to friendly units.

To further complicate the situation, a Czechoslovak Legion revolted against the revolutionaries and set up two anti-Bolshevik "governments": one in Samara, the other in Siberia. To the west, however, Latvian fighters joined forces with the Bolsheviks. In this first phase of the Civil War, the Russians were in a minority among those who did the fighting.

Two of the White generals—Kaledin and Kornilov—died tragic deaths. Although the Don Cossacks had picked Kaledin as their chief, they wavered in their support as the Bolsheviks pressed on, regardless of desertions and lack of discipline. Local Cossacks were speaking out against him for his own loyalty to those other Russian officers, Kornilov and Alekseev. Depressed by these attacks, Kaledin committed suicide on February 11, 1918, leaving the Cossacks without a military chief for about three months.

Ten days later, in bitter weather, 2,000–3,000 troops of Alekseev's Volunteer Army, with nearly as many civilians, pulled out of Novocherkassk and Rostov, in what became known as "the Ice March." During that period, Kornilov was directing local resistance from a farmhouse near the Kuban Cossack capital, Ekaterinodar. With some 7,000 men, the Cossacks were heavily outnumbered by 17,000 Bolsheviks. Kornilov was killed while studying a map when an enemy shell burst on the farmhouse.

He cracked his skull on a stove and was buried under the collapsed roof. The Cossacks were demoralized by his death, and the less flamboyant General Denikin took over.

Better news followed when a brigade of 2,000 Russians from Romania reached the Don and joined Denikin's force. In April 1918, as the Ice March was ending, anti-Bolshevik uprisings broke out. With some help from local Germans, the Bolshevik forces were expelled from the Don region. In May, Denikin's White Volunteers (as he called them) recaptured both Rostov and Novocherkassk.

Another front in Phase 1 was Ukraine, where Lenin's main concern was to prevent a German takeover. As mentioned earlier, Germany and Austria had recognized Ukraine's independence from Russia, which the Ukrainians had proclaimed on January 28, 1918. However, when the Central Powers signed a peace treaty with a moderate Socialist government in Kiev on February 9, Lenin sent a force of nearly 7,000, commanded by V. A. Antonov-Ovseenko, into Ukraine to rally as many pro-Bolshevik elements as he could and forestall the Central Powers. But the Germans were ready to move in. On March 3, 1918—the very day the Treaty of Brest-Litovsk was signed—they sent an expeditionary force that occupied Kiev, then Odessa on March 13 and Kharkov on April 8, before invading the Crimea, where on May 1 they seized Sevastopol. Under German protection, General Paul Skoropadski was named *hetman* (leader) of Ukraine.

Until the signature of the Russo-German Treaty of Brest-Litovsk on March 3, Trotsky had been Lenin's foreign affairs commissar. Now the job went to Georgy Chicherin, and Trotsky was appointed war commissar. As such, he faced the daunting task of creating a professional army, as distinct from the rabble that was being trounced by the Whites. In the life-or-death crisis that now faced the Bolsheviks, ideological analysis had to cede the way to hard realities. Some 250,000 ex-officers, more than 80 percent of them of peasant origin, were available, but the Bolsheviks had cut off their pensions and treated them as class enemies. Shunned by civilians and in fear of the Cheka, they eked out a miserable existence. And they were the relatively lucky ones. In October 1918 more than 8,000 others were in jail, hostages to Lenin's Red Terror (as it was now known, not to his displeasure).[9] By the end of the year, thousands of ex-officers were being recruited, either as volunteers or under duress.

Some months earlier, an incident had taken place that would weigh heavily on the future history of the revolution. On August 18, 1918, as Lenin was about to enter his limousine in front of the Michelin works in Moscow, a woman named Feiga Roidman, but known as Fanny Dora-Kaplan, shot and seriously wounded him. Although initially he made a rapid recovery, fragments of the bullets are believed to have contributed to the three paralytic strokes that, in effect, removed him from the leadership of the revolution after May 1922.[10]

Phase 2: 1918–1919

Foreign intervention added a new, though temporary, dimension to Phase 2 of the Civil War. On June 23, 1918, a British force landed at Murmansk, near the northern frontier of Finland. Its primary objective was to hold German forces in the east and prevent Allied stores from falling into German hands. On August 2, a joint British-French force captured the port of Archangel and started backing a puppet government of northern Russia. Soon afterward, an American force also landed, and there was much fighting between the three-nation Allied forces and the Bolsheviks.

Only the French, however, advocated serious intervention to oust the Bolsheviks, but the Great War Armistice of November 11, 1918, put a stop to any such plans, other than financial assistance to the Whites. On September 30 and October 12, respectively, the Allies abandoned Archangel and Murmansk. The Bolsheviks moved in forthwith.

In Ukraine, White Russia, and the Baltic Region, the Bolsheviks suffered further initial reverses in 1918, but achieved lasting military and political victories in 1919 and 1920. The Ukrainian situation was particularly volatile. On November 15, 1918, only four days after the Armistice in the west, the Ukrainian Socialists, led by General Simon Petliura, ousted the German-installed government of General Skoropadski.

On December 18, a French force occupied Odessa, but in the spring of 1919 Trotsky's Bolshevik forces struck back, ousting the French on April 8. Already, in February, the Bolsheviks had taken Kiev. Thereupon Ukraine became a Soviet republic, but not for long, for in August General Denikin's White Army took it back. Then he, too, was ousted by the returning Bolsheviks on December 17. A further complication came on May 7, 1920, when a Polish force occupied Kiev. Once more, the Bolsheviks struck back, and on December 28 of that year, they formally reiterated their recognition of Ukraine as a Soviet Republic, nominally independent but ultimately under Moscow's control, as with the other Soviet Republics, such as Georgia and Armenia. Lenin's concept of nominal independence would be perpetuated by Stalin after Lenin's death.

What they meant by "independence" was revealed only two days later when Ukraine joined the other Soviet republics to form the Union of Soviet Socialist Republics (USSR).

Meanwhile, the Germans had been holding on to the Baltic region and most of White Russia, even well after the Armistice that had ended the Great War. Seizing their opportunity, on October 19, 1919, the Whites sent an army, commanded by General Nicholas Yudenitch, to march on Petrograd. He was driven back by the Bolsheviks.

At this stage, however, the Bolsheviks were prepared to leave the Baltic countries in relative peace, and in 1920 they recognized the independence of Estonia, Lithuania, and Latvia, on February 2, July 12, and August 11 respectively. Finland's turn for recognition came on October 14. Unlike Ukraine and Belorussia, the Baltic Republics were not immediately incorporated into the USSR. All three of them retained their independence until the Second World War. As for White Russia, it united with the other Soviet republics in 1922.

The Bolshevik campaign to crush the Muslims of Transcaspia and Transcaucasia illustrates the extraordinary diversity of the Russian empire and its Soviet successor. As early as November 15, 1917 (old Calendar), a few days after the Bolshevik seizure of power, the Third Session of the Supreme Soviet in Petrograd issued a Declaration of Rights to the Peoples of Russia and the East, the key passages of which read:

> Muslims of Russia, Tartars of the Volga and the Crimea, Kirghiz, Kazakhs and Sarts of Siberia and Turkistan, Turks and Tartars of Transcaucasia, Chechens and Mountaineers of the Caucasus, and all those whose Mosques and Oratories have been destroyed, whose beliefs and customs have been trampled under foot by the Tsars and oppressors of Russia. Your beliefs and usages, your national and cultural institutions, are henceforth free and inviolate. Organize your life in complete freedom. You have the right. Know that your rights,

like those of all the peoples of Russia, are under the powerful safeguard of the revolution and its organs, the Soviet of Workers, Soldiers and Peasants.

Lend your support to this revolution and its government.[11]

Acting on this apparent invitation to take matters into their own
hands, a group of Turkistan Muslims called a congress in the city of
Kokand, in the Ferghana Valley, and elected a provisional assembly and
government. Two-thirds of the seats were allocated to the local Turkic
Muslims and one-third to Russians, and Turkistan was proclaimed an autonomous region, leaving it to the All-Russian Constituent Assembly to
define the terms of its autonomy.

The Muslim triumph was short-lived. In Turkistan's capital, Tashkent, power had been seized by a mixed Soviet, consisting not only of
Bolsheviks, but Mensheviks and Socialist Revolutionaries. All the revolutionaries were Russians, consisting largely of railway workers and returned soldiers. From Tashkent they moved on to seize other ethnically
Russian centers, including Merv, Ashkhabad, and Krasnovodsk.

The new Soviet, whatever its commitment to Leninist ideas, was viru-
lently anti-Muslim, which in the context of Turkistan's ethnic composition, meant harsh intolerance of more than 90 percent of the population.
In mid-February 1918, they sent a "Red Guard" from Tashkent to Kokand to oust the rival government, as they saw it. The Red Guard consisted of Russian soldiers, plus a number of forcibly recruited prisoners of
war from the German and Austro-Hungarian armies. It had been given a
license to loot as well as kill. Many hundreds of the local population were
massacred, and after the looting, the town was drenched in petrol and
burned to the ground.[12]

Many of the inhabitants, having fled to the nearest mountains,
formed bands of horseback guerrillas, known as the Basmachis, who
combined brigand holdups with anti-Russian ambushes.

During this time of trouble, Lenin's new Bolshevik government was
powerless to intervene because the White armies separated them from
Transcaspia. After the Red Army's victories in Transcaucasia, they were
able to impose their authority in Turkistan. Initially, they wooed the local
Muslims by encouraging them to reopen bazaars closed down by the

overzealous Tashkent Soviet. Many of them joined the Communist Party, which was the guaranteed road to official jobs.

While these measures took the fire out of the Basmachis, later measures reignited it. In Turkistan as elsewhere, Communist economic policy involved the expropriation of local agricultural produce; so the Basmachis revived.

More volunteers flocked to the Basmachis after the capture of Khiva and Bukhara in early 1920 by the Turkistani Red Army, commanded by Mikhail Frunze, a brilliant young officer (aged thirty-five at the time) who went on to win Stalin's backing and replace Trotsky as war commissar. In all, it took the Bolsheviks nearly a decade to subdue the Muslim guerrillas.

It was not until December 30, 1922, that the Transcaspian republics of Turkmenistan, Uzbekistan, Kazakhstan, Tadjikistan, and Kirghistan were formally incorporated into the new Union of Soviet Socialist Republics—a status that was reconfirmed under the new "democratic" Constitution of the USSR promulgated by Stalin on December 5, 1936.

Phase 3: 1919–1922

The third and last phase of the Civil War began in the Far East in 1919 and in the Caucasus in 1920. In both sectors, foreign intervention played a part. Japanese forces had landed at Vladivostok on December 30, 1917, within weeks of the Bolshevik coup. At that time, the so-called Czech Legions, consisting largely of Austrian war prisoners, had begun to march toward Vladivostok, with the long-term aim of eventually joining the Allied forces many thousands of miles away in Europe. They clashed with Bolshevik units in June 1918, seized control of the Trans-Siberian Railway, and found allies among the local anti-Bolshevik forces. Meanwhile, an autonomous Siberian government had been set up at Omsk. They were soon joined by moderate Socialists who had formed a Directory—in effect, a rival Soviet—at Ufa.

The Czechs, meanwhile, were extending their operations into the Volga region and Ekaterinburg on July 26. The conservative and anti-Bolshevik forces had been biding their time, and they struck in a raging storm on the night of November 17–18, 1918, capturing Omsk and ousting the Socialists from the government. The fall of Omsk brought total though short-lived power to Admiral Aleksandr Kolchak, former commander of the Tsarist

Black Sea fleet, who had become war minister in the anti-Bolshevik government in Western Siberia. Under pressure from land forces involved in the capture of Omsk, the admiral, who was not keen to take up a higher political post, took the optimistic title of "Supreme Ruler of Russia."

Admiral Kolchak would soon find out that he had been right at first to decline the power that had been offered him. He had no interest in administration, and no experience in commanding ground forces. He led his Siberian White Army into eastern Russia, capturing Perm on December 24 and Ufa, but his triumph was short-lived. In a vigorous counteroffensive, the Bolsheviks took Orenburg and Ekaterinburg on January 25 and 27, 1919, respectively. Over the next few months, they forced Kolchak and his White Army back until, on November 14, they recaptured Omsk, while Kolchak's forces fell back on Irkutsk. Depressed by his failure, Kolchak handed over his command to General Nicholas Semënov on December 17. Kolchak would suffer the fate Lenin's Bolsheviks reserved for the defeated: he was captured and executed on February 7, 1920, and his body was thrown into the Angara River.

By then, Lenin's Red Army had attempted to take over Vladivostok, but the more numerous Japanese troops forced them back. In realistic self-defense, the Soviet government on April 6 announced the creation of a Far Eastern Republic, with Chita as its capital—in effect a buffer state. The Bolsheviks bided their time. When the Japanese decided to pull out of Vladivostok on October 25, 1922, the Red Army troops stationed in the "Far Eastern Republic" moved in. Following the pattern established elsewhere, the new Soviet Union simply annexed the buffer republic on November 19 of that year.

BY OCTOBER 1919, the initial success of General Denikin's White forces in Ukraine and the Caucasus had come to a halt. Earlier in the year, he had gained control of the mountainous northern Caucasus and in May he launched a major offensive, advancing through the Ukraine toward Moscow. In October, however, the Red Army defeated him at Orel, some 250 miles from Moscow. It was a major reversal. His disintegrating army retreated to the Black Sea port of Novorossisk, and the retreat turned into a rout, with a mass of displaced civilians joining his rabble of defeated troops. By then, Denikin had come under heavy criticism from General Peter Wrangel, the commander of the Caucasian White forces.

Typhus reigned in Novorossisk, and the local hospital was overwhelmed. In his book *The White Armies of Russia*,[13] George Stewart paints a vivid picture of Denikin standing on the bridge of the French warship *Capitaine Saken* watching men and women kneeling on the quay and appealing to Allied naval officers to take them aboard. Some 50,000 refugees were indeed accepted aboard Allied ships. A few days later, on April 2, 1920, Denikin, by this time in Sevastopol, announced his resignation. On the same day, the remaining White officers immediately and unanimously invited Wrangel to take over as commander in chief. Undaunted by Denikin's failures, the new commander in chief, starting from a base north of the Sea of Azov, invaded southern Russia. Between June and November, his forces seized a wide area, at a time when the Bolshevik forces were heavily involved in repulsing the aggressive thrust from Poland mentioned earlier, which had started on May 7, 1920.

The best detachments of the Red Army, such as the cavalry under General Semyon Budenny, and four infantry armies under General Mikhail Tukhachevsky, were in action. Soon, the Poles were outnumbered 2 to 1. On June 11, they were driven out of Kiev and on July 15 out of Vilna.

At the time, the Polish president was Marshal Joseph Pilsudski, whose ambition was to revenge Poland for past humiliations at the hands of the Russians. On July 30, the Polish Revolutionary Committee had announced that it was about to proclaim a Polish Soviet Socialist Republic. In Moscow, Lenin's appetite for revolutionary carnage was stimulated, and he fed his agents in Poland with visions of a "merciless liquidation of landlords and peasants." Each class enemy killed would bring a reward of 100,000 rubles.[14] By mid-August, Pilsudski's dream was in tatters, as the Red Army stood outside Warsaw.

In response to an appeal from Pilsudski, France sent several hundred officers under General Maxime Weygand to train and advise the Polish forces. The French aid does not, however, appear to have played a significant part in the sudden change of military fortunes that followed. For obscure reasons, instead of storming Warsaw, which was there for the taking, General Tukhachevsky sent his forces northward to prevent Western supplies from Danzig from reaching the Polish capital.

This was the opportunity President Pilsudski was waiting for. He had been assembling a secret force of 20,000 troops south of Warsaw, and on August 16 they attacked the Red Army from the rear, taking nearly

100,000 prisoners. Lenin had assumed that the Polish proletariat would rise as one in support of the revolution. Instead, patriotic fervor outweighed revolutionary dreams, and Lenin found himself having to sue for peace. An armistice followed on October 18. Under the Treaty of Riga, signed on March 18, 1921, the Red Army had to surrender to Poland all its territorial gains, and indeed the towns of Vilno and Lvov east of the Curzon Line.* Lenin's bloodthirsty revolutionary fantasy remained just that.

After the armistice, Trotsky transferred his main fighting contingents to the south, and forced Wrangel's White armies back to the Crimea on November 1. For Wrangel and for Caucasian independence, this was the end. On November 14, he evacuated the remnants of his army to Constantinople.

A Soviet government was set up in Georgia on February 25, 1921, and another in Armenia on April 2. This was the penultimate stage of Phase 3. A year later, on March 22, 1922, the new Soviet governments plus Azerbaijan merged to form the Transcaucasian Soviet Socialist Republic. There was one more formality: on December 30 of that year, the new Republic joined the USSR.

Thus, on all fronts, the Leninist victory was complete. Despite the duration of the conflict, its complexity and its intensity, the consensus among historians of the Civil War is that the Communist victory was inevitable, for a variety of reasons:

1. The Bolsheviks controlled the Russian center of the vast Tsarist Empire, whereas their White, Muslim, and other enemies were scattered. The White armies, in contrast, operated in ethnically alien territories.
2. The Red Army, once it was organized by Trotsky, was a single, united force, whereas the White armies were disparate.
3. From the start of hostilities, the population of Communist-controlled Russia outnumbered that of the White-controlled areas by more than 4 to 1.
4. The strength of the competing armies was even more disproportionate: nearly 3 million in the Red Army against no more than 250,000 in the various White armies.

---

*The Curzon Line defined the eastern frontier of Poland recognized by the Allies in December 1919 on the suggestion of Britain's then-Foreign Secretary, Lord Curzon.

5. Not only were most of the defense industries located in Russia, but the Red Army also disposed of the vast pile of weapons and other military material left behind by the collapsed Tsarist forces.
6. The railway system was mainly centered in Moscow, which made it decisively easier for the Red Army to transport forces and supplies than for the Whites.

The one exception to this catalog of advantages was in food supplies and coal. Shortages of both caused deep, but ultimately bearable, hardship to the population in the Bolshevik-controlled areas.[15]

The view that the Bolsheviks were bound to win has nothing to do with the rightness or otherwise of Leninist doctrine. Victory was simply inherent in the built-in advantages enjoyed by the Bolsheviks.

CHAPTER THREE

WORLD REVOLUTION

ADJOURNED

1918–1924

L ENIN AND HIS followers were prisoners of his dogma. They saw the successful Revolution of 1917 as merely a starting point—the first in a wave of similar revolutions that would inevitably follow, spreading in due course to all countries of the world. There must have been a nagging doubt in Lenin's own mind, not about the inevitability of world revolution, but about the liberties he himself had taken with Marxian dogma, since by all normal social criteria, Russia was clearly not the place where the proletariat could successfully overthrow the capitalist system. As we saw in Chapter 1, since Russia did not meet the Marxian criteria, Lenin had found it necessary to tamper with the definitions of such crucial terms as "proletariat," "peasant," and "capitalist."

Having taken these dogmatic liberties, he appears to have been even more motivated to spark a revolution wherever the opportunity seemed to present itself. He seized or created opportunities in Poland and the Baltic countries, in the German cities of Berlin and Munich, and in Hungary. All of them failed. Though dismayed, Lenin was not thrown off his chosen revolutionary path. The failures were followed by a political development that transcended the failures in importance: the creation of the Communist Third International, or Comintern, as Lenin's instrument for world revolution.

A closer look at these failures throws light on the weaknesses of the Marxist-Leninist doctrines. The doctrinal case for impending revolution seemed strong in Germany. Just as Tsardom had collapsed in the wake of Russia's catastrophic military defeat, so did Germany's imperial regime, after the Allied victories in the West. The first sign of popular rebellion came on October 28, 1918, as the German sailors at Kiel mutinied when ordered by the admiralty to take to sea and fight the British. By November 4 and 5, the mutiny had spread elsewhere, and, ominously, councils (the equivalent of Soviets) of workers and soldiers were springing up at Kiel and elsewhere.

By then the Kaiser, William II, alarmed by calls from the Reichstag for his abdication, had left Berlin for Army headquarters at Spa. Then came a revolt in Munich, where an Independent Socialist, Kurt Eisner, proclaimed a Bavarian Republic. On November 8, three days before the Armistice, the new chancellor, Prince Max of Baden, advised William II to abdicate, to save the nation from civil war; but the Kaiser refused. He changed his mind the next day, and a Republic was proclaimed.

In his special Imperial train, the ex-Emperor fled to Holland. He did not sign his abdication until November 28. By then, all of Germany's minor monarchs had abdicated. Thereupon, two rival Socialist groups rose to prominence: the Social Democrats, led by Friedrich Ebert and Philipp Scheidemann, and the Communists who called themselves "Spartacists" and were led by Karl Liebknecht and Rosa Luxemburg.

For Lenin in Moscow, the news from Berlin sounded tantalizingly like reports of the events in St. Petersburg almost exactly a year earlier. Surely all that needed to be done was to send the right agents to the German capital to make sure that the Spartacists seized their moment, as the Bolsheviks had done. The *real* proletarian seizure of power was bound to succeed the bourgeois revolution that had taken over from the defunct monarchy.

Lenin, however, had failed to allow for the fact that the Social Democrats now in office had learned from the catastrophic developments in Russia, and were determined to stay on. In October, before they had taken over, Germany had closed down the Soviet embassy that had sheltered German revolutionaries and fostered their subversive activities.

In the chaos of Germany at that time, it was nevertheless possible for Lenin to act. He did so by sending a team of professional revolutionaries to turn events in the desired direction. The team was headed by Karl Radek, a confidant of Lenin's who had accompanied him in his Swiss exile and back to Russia on the German train. An Austrian by birth, he also had the assets of language and of useful contacts in Germany. Others in the group included Adolf Ioffe, an ex-Menshevik and close friend of Trotsky's; Nicholas Bukharin, who had wanted to break off talks with Germany leading to the Brest-Litovsk Treaty; and Christian Rakovsky, a Bulgarian-born revolutionary and founder-member of Lenin's Bolshevik party.[1]

There were two obvious targets. One was the newly formed German Communist Party, run by Paul Levi. The other, which appeared more likely to succeed, was the Spartacus League. Karl Liebknecht's father, Wilhelm, had been a founding member of the German Social Democratic Party, which was committed to Karl Marx's view of social change. Rosa Luxemburg, brought up in Poland, had been involved in underground activities there. She moved to Berlin and her book, *Sozialreform oder Revolution (Socialism or Revolution,* 1889), had caused a stir. Her answer to her own question, implicit in the book's title, was unequivocal: Revolutionary mass action.

On January 5, 1919, the Spartacists turned Luxemburg's theory into reality with a mass demonstration by intellectuals and workers. The date they chose for the demonstration was designed to preempt elections to a National Constituent Assembly. They announced the creation of a Military-Revolutionary Committee and "deposed" the government. Their model was, of course, the Bolsheviks' seizure of power in November 1917, but the Spartacists went on to commit a deadly error by appealing to Army veterans of the *Freikorps,* who started arresting the revolutionaries instead of the ministers. Karl Radek was one of those arrested. On January 15, 1919, Rosa Luxemburg and Karl Liebknecht were assassinated. A charge that Russian officials and Russian money had been behind the uprising was made in a note to Moscow from the German government.

Undeterred by the Spartacist failure, the Communists made further attempts to seize power in Berlin and Munich, in February and March 1919. Both revolutions were suppressed. On April 4, however, the Communists proclaimed a Soviet Republic of Bavaria. It was short-lived: the German Federal Army overthrew it on May 1.

BÉLA KUN'S HOUR

IN HUNGARY, THE Communists came closer to success. Their leader, Béla Kun, had been living in Russia and was a protégé of Lenin. The defeat of the Central Powers in the Great War had led to the collapse of the former Austro-Hungarian Empire, and on October 17, 1918, the Hungarian parliament had declared its independence from Austria. On November 16, a Hungarian Republic was proclaimed, and on January 11, 1919, a liberal-minded aristocrat, Count Michael Károlyi, was appointed president. His tenure of power was short: he resigned ten days later in protest at the Allied decision to transfer Transylvania to Romania.

This was Béla Kun's opportunity. A Socialist-Communist government was formed, with the Socialist Alexander Garbai as president and himself as foreign minister. He soon ousted the Socialists and set up a Communist dictatorship. Two wars in quick succession shortened his taste of power. On March 28, his government declared war on Czechoslovakia and his newly proclaimed Red Army soon reconquered most of Slovakia. On April 10, however, Romania invaded Hungary to forestall the planned seizure of Transylvania.

Béla Kun's government proclaimed a Communist Constitution, but his Red Army failed to stop the Romanian advance. On August 1, he fled to Vienna, and three days later the Romanians occupied Budapest, which they held until mid-November.*

The total failure of these early attempts to export revolution, however disappointing to the instigators, did not discourage their long-term vision of world revolution. On March 2, 1919, Lenin and his associates launched the Third International, which became known as "the Comintern" (short for Communist International), the organization that would run subversive activities, such as unattributed propaganda or false news items provided for the local press, and especially the penetrating of national trade unions. Until then, the international subversive activities of

---

*Back in Russia and appointed by Lenin as one of the leaders of the Comintern, Béla Kun made several further unsuccessful attempts to start revolutions in Germany and Austria. Accused of "Trotskyism" under Stalin, he was executed in 1939.

the Soviet Communists had been launched and controlled by the ruling party itself. Henceforth, such activities would be run by the Comintern, which, in turn, would be controlled by the Soviet Communist Party. The Comintern's stated aims were "the overthrow of the international bourgeoisie and the creation of an international Soviet republic." The immediate tactical aim, however, was to fight and defeat Social Democracy, which the Soviet leaders (rightly) saw as the main challenge to their own doctrinal purity and obstacle to their strategic goal of world revolution. When, in December 1919, an All-Russian Congress of Soviets was convened, the Comintern was described as "the greatest event in world history." There is no need for non-Communists to go so far, but it would be fair to say that, next to the Bolshevik Revolution itself, the creation of the Comintern was the most important event in Soviet history, for it undoubtedly went on to demonstrate that it was an effective, though not infallible, instrument of Soviet imperialism on a world scale.

Lenin had appointed Gregory Zinoviev as chairman to run the Comintern in its initial phase. Zinoviev's euphoric optimism, if anything, outmatched his master's. On the second anniversary of the Bolshevik Revolution, in November 1919, Zinoviev expressed the hope that the Communist International would "triumph in the entire world" by the time of its third anniversary.[2]

The important Second Congress of the Comintern opened in Petrograd on July 19, 1919, then moved its session to Moscow for security reasons. One-third of the participants were Russians: 69 out of 217. The 148 other participants represented the dozens of other Communist parties already set up in many countries. Echoing Lenin, Zinoviev's speech was rich in semantic oxymorons. The principle of "democratic centralism," which would be the guiding principle of all future Communist regimes based on the original Soviet model, was defined in an example of what the British anti-Communist satirical writer George Orwell would describe as "Newspeak": "the unconditional and requisite obligatory force of all instructions of the superior instance for the subordinate one."[3] In other words, the Soviet Communists would give the orders, and the other Communist parties would carry them out, unconditionally. As for the Soviet Party, the orders would come from Lenin, whose sole concession to democracy as that word is understood outside the Communist world would be to listen to the views expressed by others (if he so wished) until he made his own unchallengeable decisions.

THE INTERNAL EVENTS of the Lenin period are mostly not of direct relevance to this history. One of them, however, deserves attention: the virtually total economic collapse of the world's first "workers' state" in 1921, followed by Lenin's New Economic Policy, or NEP.

To be fair, Lenin's Russia and its restored Tsarist Empire were just emerging from possibly the most vicious and costly civil war in history. But the rigorous imposition of Marxian Socialism had made conditions even worse than they need have been. Petrograd was particularly badly hit by the breakdown of transport, the closing of factories for want of fuel, the hoarding of foodstuffs by the peasants, and the consequent sufferings of the city dwellers. On January 22, 1921, the government announced a cut in bread rations by one-third, for ten days, in various cities, including Moscow and Petrograd. Protest marches and strikes erupted, growing in scale and intensity by late February.

When news of the unrest reached the naval base on the small island of Kronstadt, off Petrograd, the crew of the battleship *Petropavlosk,* hitherto regarded as a Bolshevik stronghold, passed a sweeping anti-Bolshevik resolution, calling for freedom of the press, of speech, assembly, and trade unions, and for the reelection of the Soviet by secret ballot. The resolution was publicly adopted by an assembly of soldiers and sailors, and on March 2, the sailors formed a provisional revolutionary committee.

Under Trotsky, a force of 50,000 was assembled in Petrograd to crush what, by now, amounted to an insurrection. The defenders of Kronstadt were outnumbered by about 4 to 1. On March 18, the Communists stormed the island across its frozen approaches and slaughtered the hundreds of prisoners they had taken.[4]

In the face of these shattering problems, Lenin demonstrated for the first time that this most rigid of dogmatists was capable of a pragmatic decision—by launching the NEP.

While it lasted, the NEP was a partial return to private enterprise. Instead of helping itself to the peasants' food surplus, the government introduced a grain tax, which enabled the landworkers to keep some of the surplus for themselves. A new land statute was passed, which permitted small farms to be run privately, and even sanctioned the use of hired labor. Private citizens were allowed to start new enterprises, and selected small industrial plants were returned to their former owners. In the cities, private commercial establishments were also permitted, and the financial system was reorganized, on semi-capitalist lines.

Despite these appearances to the contrary, the changes did not amount to the jettisoning of the recently imposed Socialism, since large-scale industries remained nationalized. Moreover, foreign trade remained a state monopoly. Yet even this limited return to a market economy produced dramatic results. Output rapidly reached prewar levels, in both industry and agriculture, and the collapsed living standards in both town and country returned to a supportable level.

There has been much speculation about whether or not Lenin, had he survived and remained in good mental health, would have abandoned the utopian and brutal Socialism that had been the guiding principle of his revolution.* To a non-Communist observer, this seems to have been a highly unlikely course for a doctrinaire fanatic to take.

The attempted assassination of Lenin in 1918 was followed by a marked intensification of his Red Terror. Arbitrary executions mounted, along with the ubiquity of police informers and the total clampdown on free speech. The ruling party's newspaper, *Pravda*, called for "ten bullets pumped into every single enemy." The late Dmitri Volkogonov's biography of the founder of the USSR, *Lenin: Life and Legacy*,[5] records the delayed effects of Fanny Kaplan's bullets. Lenin experienced the first of three strokes in May 1922, and his mental as well as his physical condition rapidly deteriorated. He contemplated suicide, and his wife, Nadezhda Krupskaya, reportedly asked Stalin to provide him with a lethal dose of potassium cyanide, which Stalin declined to do.[6] According to Volkogonov, Lenin's speech rapidly became incomprehensible. There were frequent outbursts of rage and uncontrolled cruelty, and in his rare periods of relative lucidity, he would order mass liquidations of opposition Socialists and bourgeois. Lenin's commissar for "justice," Nikolai Krylenko, is re-

---

*One of the ideological "speculators" on these lines was of course Mikhail Gorbachev. In a veiled reference to the NEP (not mentioning it by name) in his book *Perestroika* (1987), he wrote, "Gravely ill, Lenin was deeply concerned for the future of Socialism. He perceived the lurking dangers of the new system" (p. 26).

ported to have said, "We must execute not only the guilty. Execution of the innocent will impress the masses even more."[7]

THE SIGNATURE, ON April 16, 1922, of the Treaty of Rapallo between Germany and Soviet Russia just preceded Lenin's final decline. Germany's Weimar Republic and the new Soviet regime had one shared grievance: Though in no way similar, they were both outcast powers. The treaty was revealed to an astonished world at an international conference that opened on that day in Genoa. On the surface, the main point of the treaty was commercial, in effect amounting to an exchange of Russian raw materials for German technology. A deeper and more worrying aspect emerged later, on April 24, 1926, with the Treaty of Berlin enshrining friendship and neutrality between the two countries. The Treaty enabled subsequent secret arrangements between the German and Soviet High Commands, under which the Germans were able to manufacture armaments and carry out training on Soviet soil. This was a clear violation of the Treaty of Versailles, signed on June 28, 1919, by the victorious Western Powers and the defeated Germans and Austrians, marking the end of World War I. Technically, the 1926 Treaty was still in force when the Hitler-Stalin Pact was signed in August 1939, and remained valid until Nazi Germany invaded the Soviet Union in June 1941.

LIFE AFTER LENIN

LENIN DIED ON January 21, 1924, precipitating a struggle for power between Trotsky and Stalin. The latter won, despite a codicil to Lenin's will dated a year earlier, which urged Stalin's removal as general secretary of the Communist Party.

The year of Lenin's death was marked by two events that are related to the theme of this book: the incorporation of Outer Mongolia into the Soviet Empire and the adoption of the Program of the Comintern.

Imperial Russia had already built a dominant interest in Mongolia, although traditionally, Chinese influence had been preponderant. Early in 1921, a group of Mongolian revolutionaries had taken refuge in the Far Eastern Republic, at that time a kind of buffer state between Soviet Russia and China. The leaders of the group were Sukhe Bator and Khorloghiyin Choibalsan. In March 1921, they met at Kyakhta near the border and founded the Mongolian Revolutionary People's Party, following the Bolshevik model. They went on to form a "people's government" and appealed to the Bolsheviks for aid from the Red Army. In May, Baron Ungern-Sternberg, a White Russian officer, who, with Japanese help, had led a private army into Mongolia, attacked the Soviet-controlled area. The attack was a mistake on his part, for he was arrested by the Russians and shot. His misadventure gave the Red Army a good excuse to invade Mongolia, with the Mongolian revolutionaries. On reaching the then-capital, Urga, on July 6, the Mongolian group set up a government with a Lamaist monk named Bodo as prime minister and Sukhe Bator as war minister.[8] The Mongolian Treaty of November 5, 1921, was in fact a friendship pact between Soviet Russia and the Mongolian People's Republic. Encouraged by the friendly welcome from the anti-Chinese local population, the Soviet Communists started fighting Buddhist influence by inciting war against the lamas and the nobility. In April 1922, the Bolsheviks arrested Premier Bodo and other Mongolian leaders, accused them of conspiring with the Chinese (rival claimants to the territory seized by the Mongolian revolutionaries), and executed them. Bodo's successor as prime minister, Danzan, though doctrinally a revolutionary, was mainly motivated by patriotism, specifically by the ambition to unite the Mongolian territories, at that time under Russian and Chinese control. When Sukhe Bator died in 1923, Danzan became commander in chief, but he was overthrown in May 1924 and executed. This left the pro-Soviet Choibalsan in charge, and his advent to full power in effect, though not in words, amounted to the emergence of Mongolia as the Soviet Union's first satellite.

A STILL MORE important event in 1924 was the adoption, at the Fifth Congress of the Comintern, of a program enshrining, in suitably semantic ambivalence, the expansionist imperial plans of the governing Soviet Communist Party. What follows is a selection of key paragraphs of the Program, together with related quotations from Lenin's important work, *Left-Wing Communism: An Infantile Disorder* (1920), which was his definitive statement of how foreign Communist parties should interpret the Russian Revolution:*

---

*These passages appeared in my shorter work, *Strategy of Survival* (1978), together with my non-ideological rewording of the original.—BC

[1.] The ultimate aim of the Communist International is to replace the world capitalist economy by a world system of Communism (*Program of the Communist International,* 1924).

[2.] The successful struggle of the Communist International for the dictatorship of the proletariat presupposes the existence in every country of a compact Communist Party, hardened in the struggle, disciplined, centralized and closely lined up with the masses (*Program*).

[3.] It is most important to have the strictest international discipline in the Communist ranks. This international Communist discipline must find expression in the subordination of the partial and local interest of the movement to its general and lasting interests and in the strict fulfillment, by all members, of the decisions passed by the leading bodies of the Communist International (*Program*).

[4.] Every sacrifice must be made, the greatest obstacles must be overcome, in order to carry on agitation and propaganda systematically, stubbornly and patiently, precisely in all those institutions, societies and associations to which proletarian or semi-proletarian masses belong, however ultra-reactionary they may be. And the trades unions and workers' co-operatives (the latter, at least sometimes), are precisely the organizations in which the masses are to be found (*Left-Wing Communism*).

[5.] Revolutionaries who are unable to combine illegal forms of struggle with every form of legal struggle are very bad revolutionaries . . . (*Left-Wing Communism*).

Let me summarize these five points in non-ideological language:

1. Non-Communist regimes everywhere must be overthrown, and Communist regimes approved by Moscow set up in their place.

2. The revolution will be made everywhere by disciplined Communist parties.

3. These parties will obey the directives of the Communist International, that is, of Moscow.

4. Communists must penetrate democratic organizations and use them for agitation and propaganda.

5. They must work both within and outside the law.

*   *   *

BY THE TIME the epoch-making Program of the Comintern appeared in 1924, thirty-seven Communist parties already existed in the world—all of them nominally independent, but in fact taking orders from Moscow. The earliest of all, intriguingly, was founded in Chile in 1912, some years before Lenin's own party, under the name Socialist Workers' Party (*Partido Obrero Socialista*); the name was changed to Communist Party of Chile in January 1922. Nine more had been founded before World War II broke out in 1939, and ten more by 1946. The grand total of CPs by the mid-1960s was ninety-two.[9] The movement inspired by Karl Marx and set in motion by Lenin thus became a worldwide instrument of revolution (to use Communist terminology) or (more realistically) of the Soviet Union's imperial policy.

PEACE AND WAR

1921–1941

CHAPTER FOUR

THE COMINTERN AT WORK

1921–1939

———

J OSEPH STALIN HAD gained control of key positions by May 1922, when Lenin became incapacitated from the delayed after-effects of the attempt on his life four years earlier (see Chapter 2). Whereas Lenin, leader of the Bolshevik Revolution, had given himself the title of "Chairman of the Council of Commissars" (in substance, prime minister), Stalin contented himself, for the rest of his life, with the more modest-sounding title of "General Secretary of the ruling Communist Party of the Soviet Union." This was a realistic approach, since control of the sole ruling party gave him supreme power.

Inner Party struggles went on, however. In the early post-Leninist phase, the main contenders were, on one side, Stalin and his main allies— Gregory Zinoviev and Lev Kamenev—and on the other side, Leon Trotsky, who later persuaded Kamenev and Zinoviev to switch to his side. In 1927, Trotsky was expelled from the party and banished to Central Asia. Two years later, he was sent into permanent exile from the USSR.

In the new USSR, Stalin imposed his Leninist terror-based tyranny. His Five-Year Plans destroyed the fragile prosperity brought on by Lenin's NEP. Stalin's massacres were probably the worst in history until then: almost certainly, Mao's later massacres, though less systematic than Stalin's, would be even greater. Stalin's show trials were widely accepted as genuine, or at least were spared from attacks by many of the Communist-leaning "intellectuals" in the West.

For sound propaganda reasons, Stalin encouraged the view that henceforth the world's first Communist state would content itself with "Socialism in one country," whereas his rival Trotsky, before and after his forced exile in 1927, continued to preach "world revolution." Lenin's original team—including Zinoviev, Kamenev, Karl Radek, and Nicholas Bukharin—were executed under Stalin's orders between 1935 and 1938. So were Marshal Mikhail Tukhachevsky, by general consent the most gifted of the Soviet military leaders, who had led the Soviet invasion of Poland (see Chapter 2), and seven other high-ranking generals. Thus Stalin had deprived himself of the flower of the Red Army not long before the German invasion of Russia in 1940.

Trotsky, who had opted for refuge in Mexico, would be assassinated by Ramón Mercader, a Spanish Communist wielding an Alpine ax, on August 20, 1940. A modified version of Trotsky's revolutionary views survived him through the Fourth International, which he had formed at a conference in Périgny, France, in September 1938.

Between 1924, when Lenin died, and 1939, when World War II began, the Soviet Empire remained geographically static. The fact that the Soviet empire did not expand in the fifteen years after Lenin's death does not mean that his Third International, or Comintern, was inactive. Far from it. Not only did the number of Communist parties expand, so did their subversive activities in many countries. Of these, the most relevant to our purposes were China, Vietnam, and Spain. The key dates were 1921 (birth of the Chinese Communist Party); 1930 (birth of the Communist Party of Indochina); and 1936 (outbreak of the Spanish Civil War).

THE CHINESE DIMENSION

MOSCOW PLAYED A critical role in the early political life of the Chinese Nationalist leader, Generalissimo Chiang Kai-shek, and simultaneously in the formation and ideological education of the Chinese Communist Party in 1921. Chiang later abandoned the doctrine but retained some of the organizational methods. In ideological terms, the Communist leader, Mao Tse-tung (later Mao Zedong), was a heretic, but in 1949 he would achieve total power, no less than Stalin in his prime, and exercise it in a comparably bloodthirsty and tyrannous manner.

* * *

LENIN'S INTEREST IN China predated the creation of the Chinese Communist Party by three years. On July 4, 1918, Lenin's foreign affairs commissar, Georgy Chicherin, announced that Russia renounced the Tsar's "unequal treaties" with China, along with Russo-Japanese and other agreements that had been negotiated at China's expense. On September 27, 1920, Lenin's government sent a conciliatory note to Peking; however, it was ignored by the Chinese government under pressure from Japan and the Western embassies. Lenin decided to seek links with the Nationalist leader, Sun Yat-sen, and his Kuomintang (Nationalist) Party (KMT).

Sun, a southerner from Kwangtung province, had been the absentee leader of the anti-imperial revolution of October 10, 1911 (still celebrated by the Nationalists in Taiwan and elsewhere as the "Double Tenth"). Sun was in Denver, Colorado, when the news reached him. Back home in December 1911, Sun was elected president of "the United Provinces of China" by a revolutionary provisional assembly. In the confusion that reigned, the title was meaningless. The boy emperor, P'u-I, abdicated on February 12, 1912, and a senior court official, Yüan Shih-k'ai, was elected provisional president of the Chinese Republic two days later. As a gesture toward national unity, Sun Yat-sen resigned.

Although not initially attracted to Communism, Sun was depressed at his failure to attract international support, and at the chaos caused by the rivalries between warlords in various provinces.[1] A full-scale but complex civil war had broken out in 1920 and went on for six years. Sun Yat-sen was therefore in a receptive mood when the Comintern sent its first representative to China in the spring of 1921. In line with Comintern policy, the man chosen by Lenin's team was neither Russian nor Chinese; he was a Dutchman called H. Sneevliet, traveling under the alias of Maring. Sun Yat-sen deeply impressed him. While Maring was in Shanghai, a seamen's strike broke out in Canton and Hong Kong, and Maring was impressed by the discovery that the Kuomintang was already active in the rising Chinese trade union movement.

Back in Moscow, Maring suggested that the best policy for the Chinese Communists would be to infiltrate the Kuomintang, and eventually to control it. The suggestion made sense. At that time, the Chinese Communists had not yet founded a party. This happened shortly afterward, and the inaugural First Congress was held on July 1, 1921.

Accounts of this important occasion differ, mainly because a number of the dozen Chinese who attended were later purged or disgraced by Mao Tse-tung, then age twenty-eight, who was himself present. According to Jacques Guillermaz, a leading French historian of the Chinese Communist Party (CCP), the site chosen for the congress was a girls' school in the French Concession in Shanghai.[2]

The French connection was indeed very strong, and although not one of the original members spoke Russian, several of them did speak French, for they had been studying in Paris at the Sorbonne. Significantly, two Comintern envoys were also present: the Dutch agitator Maring and a Russian, Gregor Voitinsky.

A year later, in July 1922, a "French Section" of the CCP was formed in Paris at a meeting attended by some of the best-known names of later times: Chou En-lai (later prime minister), Ch'en Yi (later a marshal in the Communist People's Army) and Teng Hsiao-p'ing (later Deng Xiaoping), who in his old age would launch Communist China on a major capitalist experiment.

In August 1922, a few weeks after the Paris meeting, Maring was back in China and had a further meeting with Sun Yat-sen, at which he formally proposed that each member of the CCP should also join the Kuomintang. Sun went along with this curious proposal, at least part of the way: he would welcome CCP members who joined the KMT "as individuals."

The Politburo followed up this undoubted progress by sending one of its best diplomats, Adolph Ioffe, to China. Ioffe (who had done useful revolutionary work in Germany in 1918–1919, under diplomatic cover) was initially frustrated in his attempt to set up diplomatic relations with China. He went on to Shanghai for a meeting with Sun Yat-sen. The outcome was a joint communiqué on January 26, 1923, which recorded mutual agreement that at that time conditions did not exist in China either for Communism or for a Soviet system. There was a clear understanding, however, that the KMT would let the Soviet Communists reorganize the party on Communist lines.[3]

There was a follow-up from Moscow, on October 6, 1923, when the Politburo sent Michael Borodin to do the reorganizing. As usual in those conspiratorial times, Borodin was not his real name: he was a Russian of Lithuanian Jewish descent originally called Michael Gruzenberg.

Although Sun Yat-sen, perhaps unwisely, had agreed to the Soviet proposals, Sun decided that he needed a personal report on what was really happening in Moscow. The man he chose for the task was Chiang Kai-shek, who had risen to prominence as a soldier in China's civil war.

Chiang discussed arrangements with Maring and reached Moscow on September 2, 1923. He stayed in Russia until November 29, returning to Shanghai on December 15 after the "interminable" railway journey. Chiang's mission was an eye-opener. He had hoped to meet Lenin, but the leader was already in his long and fatal coma. He did meet Trotsky, with whom he had several long exchanges, as well as Chicherin, Kamenev, Zinoviev, and Radek. However, to his disappointment, he did not meet Stalin.

Thirty-four years later, in 1957, Chiang Kai-shek published his own account of his stay in Moscow, in a book of memoirs.[4] His views of Soviet Communism were negative. Several of the Chinese Party members he had met there spoke slanderously of Sun Yat-sen. He added,

> The Russian Communist Party, in its dealings with China, has only one aim, namely to make the Chinese Communist Party its chosen instrument. It does not believe that our Party can really cooperate with it for long for the sake of ensuring success for both parties. It is the policy of the Russian Communist Party to turn the lands inhabited by the Manchus, Mongols, Moslems and Tibetans into parts of the Soviet domain; it may harbor sinister designs even on China proper.

Chiang's words were spread around the KMT's Standing Committee, but fell on blind eyes and deaf ears. The prevailing mood was euphoric about cooperation with the Communists. Sun Yat-sen had fallen uncritically for Borodin's undoubted charm. Rebellious and full of foreboding, shortly after his return from Moscow Chiang attended the First Congress of the Kuomintang in Canton in January 1924. By then, following Communist lines, the Party had a Central Executive Committee that met every two months, and a small Standing Committee (equivalent to the Soviet Politburo). Mao Tse-tung was one of eight Communists elected to the Central Executive committee, and the Congress adopted the Constitution that had been drafted by Borodin, on orders from the Comintern.

In the ensuing years, deep differences of view and clashes of personality festered within the Chinese Communist Party. The two main contenders were Li Li-san and Mao Tse-tung. Unlike Li, Mao had never been out of China, whereas Li had studied in France and had attended meetings in Moscow, in the process falling heavily under Soviet influence. Indeed, he had been elected secretary-general of the CCP at its Sixth Congress in Moscow, which (by design) coincided with the Sixth Congress of the Comintern, from July 17 to September 1, 1928.

On Li's return, there was a major clash between Li Li-san and Mao. Although Li was probably as Sinocentric as Mao, in the sense that he thought China as a center for world revolution was far more important than Russia, he practiced unquestioning acceptance of Moscow's views on revolutionary techniques. Marxist-Leninist theory laid down that the revolution could only be based on the urban proletariat. No matter that there was hardly any such thing in China. Mao, on his side, was convinced that success could only come through mobilization of the overwhelming peasant population. He was not yet senior enough, however, to disobey Moscow's instructions. In late 1928 and early 1929, Li Li-san's orders to Mao were to seize Wuhan and other large cities. Reluctantly, Mao obeyed. He seized Changsha easily on July 27, 1930, but held it for only ten days before the Nationalists drove the Reds out.

A halfhearted attempt to take Wuhan followed, but the city was heavily guarded, and Mao's forces could only look at the target from afar. In the end, the local Communist groups were driven out of all the target cities. That was it for Li. Accused of Trotskyism, he was brought back to Moscow in disgrace and ousted from his party's Politburo. Perhaps to his own surprise, and certainly to his relief, he escaped liquidation in Stalin's monumental purges, but remained under surveillance. After Mao's victory in 1949, he was allowed to return to China, having duly recanted his "errors." He even became minister of labor in 1958, but was harassed to suicide during Mao's Great Proletarian Cultural Revolution (1966–1976).

HO CHI MINH'S PARTY

IN THE HISTORY of the Soviet Empire, few dates are as important as October 1930, which saw the birth, on orders from the Comintern, of the

Communist Party of Indochina. Many such parties, though not all, are closely associated with the name of their founder, none more so than the CP of Indochina. On the model of Lenin, Stalin, and Trotsky, the leader was known to the world as Ho Chi Minh, meaning "the Enlightened One," but his original family name was Nguyen Tat Thanh. During his long years of revolutionary secrecy, he used no fewer than twenty names, of which the best known to his followers and the French police was Nguyen Ai Quoc, meaning "Nguyen the Patriot."

This choice of *nom de guerre* was significant. He was undeniably a patriot who aspired above all to independence for his country: independence from French rule, which had barely been formally established (in 1887) when he was born in 1890. He was also determined to keep his country free of domination by China, the great imperial neighbor, which had occupied Vietnam for 1,000 years. His road to independence and leadership was Communism, and in the context of his time, this made sense. For most of Ho's life, France showed no signs of granting independence to its colonies in Southeast Asia or elsewhere. Communism seemed to be the only solution.

Born in the village of Kim Lien in Nghe An province, he had been brought up in indignant awareness of the racist humiliations inflicted on his people by the occupying power. His father, a peasant who became a minor official of the imperial court at Hué, had been dismissed for failing to hide his hatred of the French colonialists.[5]

Ho left Vietnam in 1911, at age twenty-one, working as a cabin boy on a French merchant ship. He saw Dakar, Port Said, Alexandria, and New York. In 1914, with the Great War looming, he left the ship and spent some months in the French port of Le Havre, working as a gardener. His next stop was London, where he started off sweeping snow or leaves off the streets before becoming an assistant to the prestigious French chef Escoffier at the Carlton Hotel. More significantly, he joined a clandestine political group for Asians, known to the Vietnamese as *Lao dong hoi ngai* (Workers Overseas). He became an ardent supporter of the Irish revolt against British rule, attended meetings of the Socialist Fabian Society, and read voluminously.[6] In the early fall of 1917, a few weeks before Lenin's October Revolution, Ho decided that Paris was the best place to be for a young revolutionary.

The future Ho Chi Minh spent about six years in Paris,* eking out a living as a photographer's retoucher, but most of his time and energy was devoted to politics. His friends and acquaintances of that period all described him as emaciated, with eyes of burning intensity but, at the same time, having an undeniable charm.** His conversion to Leninism dated from the Second Congress of the Comintern in July–August 1919, when (still in Paris) he read Lenin's *Theses on the National and Colonial Questions,* which called for "the closest possible union between the communist proletariat of Western Europe and the revolutionary peasant movement of the East and of the colonial and subject countries."

Ho joined the French Socialist Party and later became a founding member of the French Communist Party. He had attended the Eighteenth Congress of the Socialists at Tours in December 1920, when the Party split into Socialist and Communist wings. Ho was indeed the first Vietnamese Communist, plunging immediately into Party activities. Under guidance from the French CP, he formed the *Union intercoloniale* and went on to be the editor and publisher of the *Union*'s newspaper, *Le Paria* (the *Outcast*). He also wrote a pamphlet, *Le Procès de la colonisation française* ("The Trial of French Colonialism"), which brought him prestige within the Comintern.[7]

At the end of 1923, Ho Chi Minh went to Moscow as a delegate of the French Communist Party to the Congress of the Peasant International, known as the Krestintern. He stayed on in Moscow for eighteen months under the name of Song Man Tcho, studying Marxism and revolutionary techniques at the University of Toilers of the East. In 1925, the Comintern sent him to southern China under yet another name (Ly Thuy), officially as interpreter to Michael Borodin. Ho's main mission, however, appears to have been rallying groups in Southeast Asia who would be willing to work with the Comintern. He set up the Association of Revolutionary Vietnamese Youth and ran a newsletter entitled *Youth.*

---

*Accounts of his sojourn in Paris differ. According to the German Communist Ruth Fischer (in her book *Von Lenin zum Mao,* 1956), he settled in Moscow in 1922, but Lacouture declares that this was a brief visit to attend the Fourth Congress of the Comintern. He settled in Moscow in 1923 (Jean Lacouture, *Hô Chi Minh,* Paris, 1967, p. 36).

**My own impressions of Ho Chi Minh when I interviewed him in 1956, when he was sixty-six, were much the same. (See Brian Crozier, *The Morning After,* London: Methuen, pp. 22–23.)

Ho Chi Minh reportedly used some of his time in south China and Southeast Asia to betray the leaders or members of potential rival nationalist groups to the French authorities, who in turn paid for these services, thus contributing to the funding of Ho's own activities.[8]

In 1928, Ho turned up in Thailand, where he started organizing the Vietnamese minority on Leninist lines. Banned from his native country by the French Sûreté, Ho was alarmed when a message reached him late in 1929 from Vietnam to inform him that members of his Revolutionary Vietnamese Organization had decided to set up a Communist Party. Ho could not bear the thought that he might be absent from so important a meeting. Having conveyed his views to them, he went to Hong Kong in March 1930, summoned his followers and talked them into unity under his own authority. The outcome was the Communist Party of Indochina, a title that made the range of its activities clear: They would extend not only to the three segments of Vietnam (Tonking in the north, Annam in the center, and Cochinchina in the south) but also to neighboring Laos and Cambodia, which were under French rule as well, thus covering the whole of what was then French Indochina.

Some 6,000 Vietnamese members of the new party went on a rampage on September 12, 1930. Many of them were peasants who attacked landlords and tried to break up large estates. Although no attacks on French nationals were reported, there was a strong and ruthless French reaction.[9] Hundreds of militants were arrested, and most of them were executed. Ho was not among them, since he had spent most of his time in Thailand, heading the Southeast Asian Department of the Comintern's Orient Bureau.[10]

By now, the French had tired of Ho, despite his useful earlier betrayals of rival revolutionaries. On June 6, 1931, in response to a French request, the British authorities in Hong Kong jailed him for two years. On his release in 1933, he went back to the Soviet Union, where he enlisted at the Lenin Institute, the specialized training center for Communists worldwide.

As happened with Lenin's Bolsheviks in 1917, a world war gave Ho Chi Minh's Communist Party the opportunity it had been waiting for. Almost simultaneously, France was invaded by Germany in 1940 and Tonkin was invaded by Japan. The French authorities in Indochina were in no condition to resist the Japanese, who initially were not asking for complete powers. They were content to leave the administration in French hands, in return for the free use of airfields and naval bases. At the time Ho Chi Minh's authority over his party was far from absolute, and the Communist Party, in defiance of Ho, launched revolts in all three regions of Indochina, evidently with the object of unifying them under Vietnamese Communist control. Clearly, in Ho's political wisdom, this was a wildly premature maneuver. The Japanese left the suppression of these revolts to the French, who acted with their usual cruelty.

The Comintern sent its instructions: The Communist Party of Indochina was to create "national liberation fronts" with non-Communist elements, and launch a general movement against "Fascist imperialism." Early in 1941, Ho went to south China, where he obtained the cooperation of the authorities in the provinces of Yunnan and Kwangsi. In May, he carried out the Comintern's instructions, obediently and skillfully, by convening a congress of Vietnamese Nationalists among whom the Communists constituted the hard core. The congress took place in a town in Kwangsi about sixty miles from the Tonkin border. The outcome was the Vietnam *Doc Lap Dong Minh Hoi,* or League for the Independence of Vietnam, usually shortened to Vietminh.

In the forthcoming First Indochina War, five and a half years later, the Vietminh's program was carried out systematically and ruthlessly. It consisted of three points:

1. To drive out the French and the Japanese Fascists;
2. To make Vietnam independent; and
3. To build a "democratic republic" of Vietnam.

The other groups involved in the Vietminh had no trouble with the first two points in the program. They went along with the third, leaving it to the dominant Communist Party to lay down the rules.

Younger Vietnamese Communist leaders were first seen and heard at the congress of the Vietminh. The most prominent of those who achieved later fame were Vo Nguyen Giap, who became the victorious military leader of the Communist forces in both the Indochina wars; Pham Van Dong, later prime minister of the Democratic Republic of Vietnam; and Dang Xuan Khu who, under the name of Truong Chinh, later became the foremost Vietnamese theorist of revolutionary war.

By mid-1941, then, the Comintern had a fully working instrument of Lenin's imperialist policy in what was still, at that time, French Indochina.

SPAIN'S BATTLEFIELD

THE SPANISH CIVIL WAR (1936–1939) was one of the most traumatic episodes of the twentieth century. It was a battlefield for clashing ideologies, a dress rehearsal for World War II. Until April 1931, Spain had been a monarchy. Municipal elections that month brought an overwhelming victory to republican candidates, and King Alfonso XIII went into voluntary exile, without resigning. A provisional Republican government came to power in general elections on June 28, and the new government outlawed the monarchy.

In the five years that followed, Spain sank into political chaos, with its Republican coalition under attack from extremists of the Left (Communists and Anarchists) and Right (the Fascist *Falange* and outraged monarchists). Mobs set fire to many churches and convents, without any reaction from the government. Anarchy continued during those five years.

At the end of 1933, Moscow launched its new "Popular Front" policy in favor of coalitions between Communist and Socialist parties. This new line produced Popular Front governments in France and Spain. The Spanish Popular Front was swept into power in the general elections of February 1936.

Moscow's instrument, during the Republican years and the Civil War, was the Spanish Communist Party which, as in China, Vietnam and elsewhere, had been set up in 1920 by Comintern agents: the Russian Mikhail Borodin (of Lithuanian Jewish origin) and the Indian M. N. Roy.[11] Its original name was simply the *Partido Comunista de España*. But when, the following year, a rival party was announced under the name of *Partido Comunista Obrero de España,* Moscow ordered them to merge, which they promptly did. In April 1933, a new Central Committee of the Party, set up after Moscow-directed purges, met in Madrid and took Moscow's orders from two more Comintern agents: the physically bloated Italian Argentino Vittorio Codovila, and the sinister Hungarian Ernö Gerö who, in 1956, was running his country's ruling party when the Hungarian people made their ill-starred bid to overthrow their Stalinist rulers. By the mid-1930s, the Spanish Communist Party was run by José Díaz, an unconditionally obedient plodder, and Dolores Ibarruri, whose impassioned oratory earned her the nickname of *La Pasionaria*. Probably the decisive voice in policymaking, however, was that of the Italian Palmiro Togliatti, who spent many years in Moscow and used the pseudonym Ercole Ercoli.[12]

Disorders and violence continued to escalate during the first few months of the Popular Front government. In the *Cortes* (Parliament) on June 16, José-María Gil Robles, a moderate Right former war minister, denounced government complacency in the face of events since the February elections, including 160 churches destroyed, 269 murders, 1,287 wounded, and 138 serious assaults. The turning point came on July 13, with the kidnapping and murder of José Calvo Sotelo, a Monarchist former finance minister.

High-ranking Army officers had been following the situation in a state of mounting unrest. Among them was General Francisco Franco, at that time stationed in the Spanish-ruled Canary Islands as the local commander. On July 17—the day after Gil Robles's speech—the General issued a Manifesto calling on the Army to restore order. The next day, the Civil War began.

Franco flew to Tetuan in Spanish Morocco. From there, he sent an emissary to ask for help from Italy's Premier Benito Mussolini, who rebuffed him. A second emissary, sent from the Spanish mainland by General Emilio Mola, who was commanding the uprising, persuaded Mussolini to change his mind. Mussolini sent 12 three-engined Italian Savoia-Marchetti-81s to Morocco. Only nine reached their destination. Franco then explained his needs to two local Nazis, who left for Berlin on July 22. Four days later, Hitler received them at Bayreuth, where he was attending a Wagner festival. He too responded to Franco's request, and within days twenty JU-52 maximum capacity transports and six Heinkel-51 fighters landed in Morocco. Within a few weeks, some 15,000 men of Franco's Army of Africa had crossed the Strait of Gibraltar and were ready for action against the Spanish Republic.

The main pro-Soviet influences in the republican government in power in September 1936 were the prime minister, Francisco Largo Caballero, who, though a Socialist, had been flattered into unquestioning compliance; and two crypto-Communists, Julio Élvarez del Vayo (Foreign Affairs) and the outwardly Socialist Juan Negrín (Finance). There were two members of the Communist Party in the government (at Education and Agriculture), but their roles were relatively unimportant.

In the spring of 1937, while the Civil War was going from bad to worse for the Republicans, the internal political war to give the Communists complete control over the government made rapid progress. From the Comintern's standpoint, there were two main left-wing targets for destruction: the anarchist trade union organization known as the *Confederación Nacional del Trabajo* (CNT), and the Trotskyist *Partido Obrero de Unificación Marxista* (POUM). This war within the Civil War took place mainly in Catalonia, at that time run by the joint Socialist-Communist Party of Catalonia *(Partido Socialista Unificado de Cataluña)*.

One of the Party's leaders was the police chief, Rodríguez Salas, who ordered a raid on the telephone buildings, at that time controlled by the anarchist CNT. He gained his objective at a cost of 500 dead on both sides and about 1,000 wounded.[13]

By 1937, the Comintern agents were tired of Largo Caballero, who had served his initial purpose but was too self-assertive for their needs. A former trade union leader and a magnetic orator, he had been dubbed the "Lenin of Spain" in Soviet propaganda. Now, in early 1937, he fiercely resisted demands, both from the Spanish Communists and from the Soviets, for the unification of Spain's Socialist and Communist parties. On April 17, 1937, he issued a decree bringing the mainly Communist commissars of the Republican Army under his personal control, and dissolved the Communist-controlled Madrid defense *Junta.* For good measure, he had Marcel Rosenberg, the Soviet ambassador, recalled to Moscow.

This was one step too far. The Comintern and its Spanish comrades made overtures to Largo's great rival, the relatively moderate Indalecio Prieto, the naval and air minister. On May 13, the two CP ministers in the Largo cabinet called on him to dissolve the POUM. He refused, and they stormed out. The Comintern men let it be known that they would not make aircraft available for an offensive in Estremadura that Largo had been planning. The moderate Socialists sided with the Communists, and Largo Caballero was forced out as prime minister. The successor the Soviets wanted was not Prieto, but Juan Negrín, the minister of finance and a moderate Socialist, who was known to see the salvation of his side only in close cooperation with the Soviet Union. On May 17, 1937, Negrín replaced Largo Caballero as prime minister. (Negrín's most memorable service to Stalin was to arrange the transfer to Moscow of more than 510 metric tons of Spain's gold, worth at that time $518 million.[14]) A savage persecution of the POUM was launched, which culminated in the murder of its leader, Andrés Nin.

On April 1, 1939, the Spanish Civil War ended in total victory for General Franco and his Nationalist, Monarchist, and Fascist followers. He celebrated his victory with a parade of 120,000 soldiers in Spain's capital, Madrid.

Franco had accepted considerable military aid from Germany and Italy, but he had kept far greater political freedom of action with respect to the Soviet Union. Despite pressure from the Nazi side, he delayed a decision to join the anti–Comintern Pact until the Spanish Civil War was nearly over. The pact had started with an alliance between Germany, Italy, and Japan to consult in the event of an international crisis, with the object of defending their interests against the Comintern. The Spanish cabinet, under Franco's chairmanship, had already agreed on February 20 to join the pact, but only on condition that this decision must be kept secret until the Civil War had ended. Accordingly, it was not publicly disclosed until April 7, six days after the announcement of the Nationalist victory.[15]

According to Hugh Thomas, British historian of the Spanish Civil War, Italy provided some 38,000 men and Germany 5,000, most of whom manned aircraft or tanks.[16] The military hardware was impressive: 806 planes, mostly fighters, 362 tanks, 120 armored cars, 1,555 cannon, and half a million rifles. In contrast, the Soviet Union provided virtually no military hardware to the Republican side, giving priority to political influence and penetration. Only 3,000 "volunteers" were sent to Spain, but the Comintern organized the International Brigades, which totaled some 35,000 volunteers from fifty-four countries.[17] In this complex situation, the role of the International Brigades was never of great military importance: their purpose was primarily to burnish the image of Stalin's USSR as the major prop of democracy, at a time when the "capitalist" Western democracies were "non-intervening," uninvolved outsiders, unwilling to fight for their professed beliefs.

In his short but impressive book, *Heroic Victims* (about the U.S. share of the Communist International Brigades), Herbert Romerstein makes it clear, from his access to Soviet archives, that

> those seeking a socially acceptable history can find it by looking at
> the young volunteers who faced the dangers of combat made far

worse by incompetent and uncaring leaders, inadequate training and inferior weapons. They had also been lied to about the length of time they would have to serve in Spain. If they complained, they ran the risk of attracting the attention of André Marty [a French Communist who oversaw the Brigades operation on behalf of the Comintern] or of the little Martys who were hunting those with deviationist ideas.

The cynical men in Moscow who made the political decisions, and those in New York who made sure they were carried out, cared little for the young victims. They were tools to be used on behalf of the Soviet Union and the international Communist movement.[18]

Romerstein also and rightly recalls the key role played by the German disinformation expert Willi Münzenberg in the vast deception exercise launched and controlled by the Comintern. Although military victory over Franco's *Alzamiento* or *Cruzada* (as the Nationalists liked it to be known) was denied to the Comintern, the distorted view it spread so skillfully in the Western democracies still carries weight in academia and the media.

WHEN, ON OCTOBER 16, 1936, the Spanish Communist Party wrote to "our dear comrade Stalin" to thank him for Soviet support, Stalin replied, "The toilers of the Soviet Union are only fulfilling their duty by rendering every assistance within their power to the revolutionary masses of Spain. They realize that the liberation of Spain from the oppression of the fascist reactionaries is not the private affair of the Spaniards but the common cause of all advanced and progressive mankind."[19]

For obvious reasons, several senior members of Stalin's secret services were closely involved in the Soviet action in Spain. The leading one was Alexander Orlov, who headed the NKVD (*Narodnyi Kommissariat Vnutrennikh Del:* People's Commissariat for State Security, forerunner of the KGB) team in that country. Another was General Walter Krivitsky, who headed Soviet military intelligence, the GRU (*Glavnoye Razvedyvatelnoye Upravelniye:* Chief Intelligence Directorate of Soviet General Staff, that is, Soviet Military Intelligence) in Western Europe.

Both men later defected to the West: Krivitsky in 1937 and Orlov the following year. In 1941, Krivitsky would be found dead in his Washington hotel room with a bullet through his right temple and a revolver nearby: a favorite "set-up" liquidation job by his former employers. Other Soviet officials who served in Spain and were later executed in Stalin's purges included Generals Jan Berzin, the overall Soviet military adviser to the Republican forces, and Vladimir Gorev. In Orlov's book, *The Secret History of Stalin's Crimes,* he notes that General Gorev was arrested only two days after being presented with the Order of Lenin for his outstanding services in Spain: yet another sign of Stalin's egregious power. Russian President Mikhail Kalinin, who had pinned the medal on Gorev's chest, knew nothing of the fate Stalin was reserving for the man he had just honored. Apart from Stalin, only one other man knew: Yezhov, head of the NKVD.[20]

In retrospect, Stalin's decision to intervene in the Spanish Civil War can be seen as having had four objectives: (1) to give the Republican government the means to defeat the Nationalist uprising; (2) to spread the international image of the Soviet Union as a champion of democracy; (3) to neutralize the rival activities of the Trotskyites and anarchists; and (4) to bring the Republican government under Communist control. The second, third, and fourth were attained; but not the first.*

---

*The first fully documented study of the Soviet intervention in Spain was by a Welsh-born United Press correspondent in Spain, Burnett Bolloten: *The Grand Camouflage: The Communist Conspiracy in the Spanish Civil War* (London: Hollis & Carter, 1961). A much revised and enlarged version appeared in 1991, entitled *The Spanish Revolution: The Left and the Struggle for Power during the Civil War.* A factual and objective account by José Manuel Martínez Bande was published by the Spanish Information Service in 1961, under the title *La Intervención Comunista en la Guerra de España.* My own account, in *Franco: A Biographical History* (Boston: Little, Brown, 1967), drew heavily on Bolloten's first version and on Martínez Bande, as well as my own sources. The first account of the International Brigades to draw on the Moscow archives is by a leading American expert on international Communism, Herbert Romerstein: *Heroic Victims: Stalin's Foreign Legion in the Spanish Civil War* (Washington, DC: Council for the Defense of Freedom, 1994).

CHAPTER FIVE

"Totalist"
Rivalries

———>•◦•<———

I N THE SPACE of sixteen years, from 1917 to 1933, the first three
totalist regimes of a troubled century came into power. The first was
Lenin's in Russia, in 1917; the second was Benito Mussolini's in Italy, in
1922; and the third was Adolf Hitler's in Germany, in 1933. Despite mutually hostile propaganda between Fascists or Nazis on one side and
Communists on the other, the three forms of totalism had far more in
common with each other than any of them had with the Western democracies.[1] Like Lenin, Mussolini started as a Marxist; in a modified way, so
did Hitler: *Nazi* is of course short for "National Socialist."

Although Lenin was the first of the three to build (or rebuild) an empire, in the 1930s both Fascist Italy and Nazi Germany were more imperi-
ally active than was Soviet Russia. Italy conquered Ethiopia during 1935–
1936. Hitler was determined to annul the treaties imposed by the Western
Allies on defeated Germany after World War I, namely the Treaty of Versailles and the Treaties of Locarno. Versailles came first, on January 18,
1919. It imposed severe financial penalties on Germany and created the
League of Nations (predecessor to the the United Nations, which followed World War II). The Locarno Treaties—four of them—were signed
on December 1, 1925, and covered a wide range of issues, aimed mainly
at protecting various countries from Germany.

As a first move, Hitler decided to test the situation. He began by re-
claiming the Saar area, on the German side of the river of that name

(*Sarre* in French) dividing Germany from France. Under the Treaty of Versailles the Saar area, rich in coal, had been detached from German rule and placed under the authority of the League of Nations. Hitler made effective use of the Nazi propaganda machine, controlled by Josef Goebbels, his Minister for Propaganda and Information. In a plebiscite in January 1935, 90 percent of the voters on the German side came out in favor of joining the German Reich. Two months later, Hitler sent his troops in to occupy the Saarland. There was no reaction from the French side.

Hitler went on to denounce and repudiate the Treaties of Versailles and Locarno, and on March 7, 1936, his Army occupied the demilitarized Rhineland zone without provoking a reaction from either France or Britain. In September 1936, Hitler threatened war with Czechoslovakia unless the German-speaking Sudetenland was handed over to him. On September 28, at a meeting in Munich, Mussolini and the British and French prime ministers, Neville Chamberlain and Edouard Daladier, conceded to Hitler's demands, thus confirming the "appeasement" policy of the Western Powers. German troops occupied the Sudetenland and took over the Czech fortifications.

In March 1939, Germany set up a protectorate incorporating some 6 million Czechs into the Third Reich, while a Republic of Slovakia was created under German control. On January 26, 1934, Germany had signed a ten-year Non-Aggression Pact with Poland, which the Poles interpreted as an assurance that the Nazis would not attempt to seize an area of Poland along the German border known as "the Polish corridor." The guarantee was shown to be worthless when, in a bellicose speech in the Reichstag (Parliament) on April 28, 1939, Hitler denounced the Non-Aggression Pact. He also repudiated the Anglo-German Naval Agreement of June 18, 1935, under which Germany pledged itself not to expand its fleet beyond 35 percent of the British one. He set up a Berlin-Rome Axis to counter a nonexistent encirclement of Germany by Britain, France, and Poland. The Chamberlain government promised to support Poland's independence.

Then came the great bombshell: the Nazi-Soviet Pact of August 23, 1939, which turned the mutual animosity between Berlin and Moscow into a mutual pledge of non-aggression and neutrality by either government if the other were attacked by a third power. In a desultory way, the Chamberlain and Daladier governments had been negotiating with the Soviet Union since April for a "peace front" to block further Nazi expansion. At the same time, Britain had been sounding out the Germans in secret in search of a security guarantee. The main purpose of Britain's foreign policy at the time was to divert Hitler's aggression from the West to the East, more precisely to the Soviet Union, leaving Britain and France unthreatened. Not entirely without reason, the Soviet side became increasingly suspicious of the West's motives.

A startling piece of news on May 3 should have alerted Britain's Foreign Office and even Neville Chamberlain and his foreign secretary, Lord Halifax: That day, the Jewish and strongly anti-German Soviet foreign affairs commissar, Maxim Litvinov, was removed from office. Nobody was deceived by the alleged detail that his removal was "at his own request." In his stead, Stalin appointed Vyacheslav Molotov; the immediate consequence was a considerable stepping up of Soviet-Nazi diplomatic exchanges.

At that time, the British General Staff and Winston Churchill (who held no official post in the Chamberlain government) were pressing for an unconditional Anglo-French-Soviet military alliance. But neither the British nor the French showed much sense of urgency. A joint delegation arrived in Moscow, apparently at their leisure, by boat on August 11, and immediately ran into unacceptable Soviet conditions for the defensive pact they had in mind. Stalin and Molotov insisted on the Soviet right to send forces through Poland in the event of German aggression. The Poles had publicly made it clear that such a plan was totally unacceptable.

A further alarm signal came on August 20, when the signing of a trade treaty between Germany and Soviet Russia was announced. The day before, Stalin had already made up his mind about the treaty, and on the signing day Stalin and Hitler exchanged friendly telegrams. Hitler warned Stalin, in a convoluted way, that Germany was about to invade Poland ("The tension between Germany and Poland has become intolerable"). He suggested that a German delegation, to be headed by Foreign Minister Joachim von Ribbentrop, should go to Moscow forthwith. Stalin agreed, and Ribbentrop arrived on August 23. That same day, the Non-Aggression Pact between Germany and the Soviet Union was announced. Glass in hand at a celebratory reception, Stalin said, "I know how much Germany loves its Führer. I would therefore like to drink to his health."[2]

Was Hitler seeking an alliance with Stalin, or was it the other way around? It is now clear, from recently discovered top secret Soviet archives, that although the proposal for a non-aggression pact came from Hitler, the original overtures came from Stalin. In a speech to the Politburo Plenum on August 19—the day before the trade treaty—the Soviet leader coolly analyzed the options. In the event of a Treaty of Mutual Assistance with France and Britain, Germany would renounce its claim to Poland and seek a *modus vivendi* with the two Western powers. This would weaken the Communist parties in Britain and France; whereas a pact with Germany would provoke a major war that would enormously strengthen the French Communist Party and to a lesser degree the British party. It was in the Soviet interest that war should break out and that it should last as long as possible. (See Appendix A: Document 1 for the full text of Stalin's speech.)

Other recently discovered top secret Soviet archives confirm Stalin's views.[3] As two former Red Army officers put it, "The Communist dictator had . . . plans for the future connected with dominating Europe with the help of Hitler's war machine and then later eliminating Germany as a rival for total hegemony over the continent."[4] The eleven weeks before the signature of the Nazi-Soviet Pact were occupied by intensive behind-the-scenes talks between officials of the two countries. The Secret (or Secret Supplementary) Protocols to the Treaty spelled out the reciprocal allocations of territories in the Baltic States (Finland, as well as Estonia, Latvia, and Lithuania) to the two signatories. For example, Germany renounced its claim to a delineated area of Lithuania to the USSR on payment of 31.5 million marks (at that time, US $7.5 million) in gold, with the balance in the form of a reduction of German debts to the Soviet Union.[5]

Relieved of anxiety on the Eastern front, Hitler launched a land and air offensive against Poland on September 1, 1939; two days later, Britain and France declared war on Germany. World War II had begun.

DOUBLE INVASION OF POLAND

SECRET CLAUSES OF the German-Soviet Treaty, unrevealed at the time, had paved the way for Stalin's first attempt at imperial expansion. On September 17, sixteen days after the German invasion, the Red Army invaded Poland from the east. Ten days later, Warsaw surrendered to the Germans, and on September 29 the conquering powers divided Poland between them. In area, the Soviets took slightly more than the Germans

(77,620 square miles, to 72,866), but in population, the Germans' victory spoils were considerably greater (22,140,000 to 13,199,000). That same day, the Soviet government acquired naval and air bases under a treaty with Estonia; similar facilities were acquired in Latvia on October 5 and in Lithuania on October 10.

Emboldened by these unequal treaties, Stalin put similar demands on Finland, which turned them down on November 26. Three days later, the Red Army launched attacks on three fronts: on the Karelian Isthmus, in Central Finland, and on the Arctic Sea below Petsamo. Unlike Hitler's highly trained German forces, Stalin's Army was ill trained and weakened by purges and executions. (As mentioned earlier, among those executed, on a flimsily based charge of high treason in June 1937, was Marshal Mikhail Tukhachevsky, by general consent the most gifted and professional of the Red Army's officers.) The Soviet rabble ran into effective and determined resistance from the Finns. It was not until March 12, 1940, that the Red Army breached the main defenses of Finland along the Mannerheim Line. It was by no means a complete victory for the Soviet side, although the Soviets acquired the Karelian Isthmus, the city of Viipuri, a naval base at Hangoe, and territories with a population of 450,000 covering 16,173 square miles.[6]

The effect of these events on the foreign member-parties of the Comintern was traumatic. For more than six years they had dutifully echoed the systematic denunciations of Hitler's regimes from Moscow. Now, suddenly, came a personal directive from Stalin to stop the anti-Nazi campaign and switch to attacks on Anglo-French imperialism. Harry Pollitt, leader of the small but active British Communist Party (CPGB), had enthusiastically condemned Nazi aggression and now had to eat his words, recognizing that the British and French governments were the main obstacle to peace.[7] In the Reichstag, on October 6, 1939, Hitler made an impassioned appeal for peace to Britain and France. Claud Cockburn, interviewed in the Moscow-aligned *Daily Worker,* greeted the Führer's words with enthusiasm as opening the way to "a genuine peace."[8] These sentiments were in tune with the paper's current views.

In Germany, too, in the non-Communist daily *Die Welt,* which was sanctioned by Nazi censors, the Communist leader Walter Ulbricht wrote an article expressing the opinion that those who "intrigue against the friendship of German and Soviet people are enemies of the German people and are branded as accomplices of British imperialism."[9] It is apposite to recall that German Communists, in their thousands, joined the Nazi Party when Hitler came to power, not to undermine it from within but because of the natural affinity between totalists.

In the United States, as in Britain and Germany, the small Communist Party (CPUSA), as early as September 19, 1939, took the line that this was an imperialist war, to be opposed by the workers—while Hitler's invaders were slaughtering Polish soldiers and civilians. As Nikolai Tolstoy points out, "Communist trade unionists set out to sabotage production in munitions factories, lest any aid reach Britain or France."[10]

In France, the large and weighty Communist Party (PCF) was declared dissolved on September 27, 1939. Its organ, *L'Humanité*, was closed down, and thirty-five Communist deputies were arrested. An order was issued for the arrest of the party leader, Maurice Thorez, who by that time had been conscripted into the Army. He beat the system by deserting and fleeing to Moscow, where he stayed until the end of the war, directing anti-Allied propaganda for the French branch of the Comintern.* Between 1935 and 1939, the PCF had been in the vanguard of the struggle against Fascism and the appeasement of Hitler's regime. The Nazi-Soviet Pact turned its members overnight into activists in favor of the Nazis, since Hitler and Stalin were now "friends."[11]

In the spring of 1940, while the German armies were overrunning the Low Countries in preparation for their invasion of France, the PCF stepped up its clandestine propaganda in favor of capitulation to Germany. At the same time, its trade unionists were committing acts of sabotage in French munitions factories. When France collapsed before the German onslaught in June, PCF leader Thorez and his deputy Jacques Duclos publicly rejoiced. (At that time, Thorez was still in Paris; in September, having been conscripted into the French armed forces, he deserted and fled to Moscow.) On June 18, a holy date in the annals of Gaullism, when the general broadcast an appeal to his countrymen from the BBC's

---

*General de Gaulle, on the eve of his departure for Moscow on November 24, 1944, granted Thorez a free pardon for his earlier desertion, whereupon Thorez returned to France. The General's motives appear to have been to gain favor with Stalin, and to mollify the Communists who, at that time, represented a real challenge to his leadership. See Brian Crozier, *De Gaulle: The First Full Biography* (London and New York: Scribner, 1973), pp. 86 and 326.

London studio, the PCF asked the German censorship for permission to publish *L'Humanité*. The party members involved were arrested by the French police but were freed a week later by the Gestapo. The Nazis were rewarded by anti-British articles and other useful propaganda.[12]

STALIN'S GREAT TERROR

IN MILITARY STRATEGIC terms, Stalin wasted the fifteen months following his unimpressive victory over Finland. In terms of paranoid tyranny and mass murder, he excelled in his self-made objective: Lenin's perfect disciple wielding state terror.

His first concern, on gaining control over Finland and the Baltic States, was to import the Great Terror (as Robert Conquest aptly called it) into these new territories of the Soviet Empire. The Red Army's tanks symbolized the invaders' authority; Lavrenti Beria's NKVD demonstrated its true meaning. Tolstoy quotes from a captured document in Lithuania, calling for the liquidation of all Nationalists, Trotskyists, and Christian and Social Democrats, among others. Selected victims were atrociously tortured:

> Others had their testicles kicked to pulp, were seated on red-hot stoves, had needles rammed under their fingernails, were scalped, had their jaws ripped down to their necks, and had their eyes gouged out and their tongues torn out. Executions took place in specially equipped death cells. Elsewhere, . . . victims were bound to trees with iron hoops before being burned alive. Others had been buried alive, some after having had their scalps and hands skinned.[13]

The most notorious of Stalin's wartime atrocities was falsely attributed to Hitler through a scarcely credible but widely believed piece of Soviet disinformation. In April 1940, nearly 22,000 Polish prisoners were rounded up, transported to various sites, and executed. They included officers, civil servants, landowners, policemen, intelligence officers, gendarmes, ordinary soldiers, and prison officers. They were lined up, made to dig their own mass graves, and shot in the back of the neck. The lineup was neat, as each corpse automatically buried itself. There was no trial, and the executions were ordered personally by Stalin in an (unsigned) memorandum dated March 5, 1940 to Beria, the NKVD chief. The relevant decision had been taken that day by the Central Committee of the CPSU.

The whole ghastly episode was to be kept secret, and therefore had no propaganda value. The fact that a mass execution had taken place was unearthed (literally) by the advancing Nazi forces when they reached the Katyn Forest, in the Smolensk region, in 1943. The number of corpses exhumed exceeded 4,000. Not surprisingly, the German propaganda machine made the most of the discovery, broadcasting it to the outside world. The news was of course embarrassing not only to Stalin's government but also to his main allies, the United States and Britain. Roosevelt was quoted dismissing the Nazi claims as "German propaganda and a German plot," while Churchill merely said, "The less said about that the better."[14]

The full truth was not revealed until 1997, when the relevant Soviet archival documents were released to me by the Hoover Institution. (See Appendix A: Documents 2–14.) The document enshrining the decision of March 5, 1940, was sent in February 1959 to the then-head of the NKVD, Aleksandr Shelepin. It referred to the decision to shoot 14,700 Poles, and specified that the victims were not to be tried or presented with any charges.

Further details, which gave the precise numbers of those shot, were sent to Nikita Khrushchev (Stalin's successor) on March 6, 1959. Until then, and indeed until many years later, the only details about the shootings available in the West concerned the Katyn massacre—which had not left the greatest number of corpses. The details were as follows:

- Total shot: 21,857
- In Katyn Forest: 4,421
- In Starobelsk camp, near Kharkov: 3,820
- In Ostashkovo camp in the Kalinin region: 6,311
- In other camps or prisons, in Western Ukraine and Western Belorussia: 7,305

The memorandum made it clear that the relevant documents had been kept secret, and commented:

> For the Soviet organs, none of these cases possesses either any operational interest or any historical value. *It is unlikely that they can possess any real interest for our Polish friends.* (Italics added)

... All the Poles who were liquidated there [in the Katyn Forest] are regarded as having been exterminated by the German invaders. The materials of the investigation at this time were widely covered in the Soviet and foreign press. The conclusions of the commission [set up in 1944] have taken firm root in international public opinion.

Proceeding from the above account, it would appear to be advisable to destroy all the records of the persons who were shot in 1940 during the previously mentioned operation.

In other words: "We did it, but the world believes the Germans did. Therefore, leave the story as it stands."

To lend credence to their disclaimer, the Soviet Union broke off diplomatic relations with the Polish government-in-exile in London. In the interests of solidarity with their Soviet allies, the British and Americans ignored the Polish protests.*

TWO OTHER EVENTS stand out in the wartime spring of 1940. On June 4, leaving their equipment behind, 200,000 British and 140,000 French troops were rescued, mainly by "little boats" at Dunkirk. Britain's losses, including prisoners, totaled about 30,000. The other fatal date

---

*Britain's Foreign Office refused for many years to admit that it was Stalin, not Hitler, who had ordered the Katyn massacre. It was not until 1990, with President Mikhail Gorbachev still in office but with the collapse of the Soviet system looming, that Moscow released the order for the killings, countersigned by Stalin. Six years later, the Hoover Institution acquired a collection of nearly 8 million sheets of Soviet secret documents, known as "Fond-89," which had been handed over by President Boris Yeltsin to the post-Soviet Constitutional Court early in 1992, some months after the collapse of the regime, in an attempt to outlaw the Communist Party (in which he, of course, as well as the deposed leader Mikhail Gorbachev, had made his career) as a "criminal organization." At first, the initiative appeared to succeed, but on appeal, it failed. Some of the most revealing of these documents confirmed the fact that the massacre had indeed been ordered by Stalin, not Hitler; and also that the Foreign Office had yielded to diplomatic pressure from Moscow. Reference is made to an unofficial British plan to erect a monument to the Katyn victims in the important London borough of Kensington and Chelsea, a major tourist attraction. This initiative was taken by the National Association for Freedom (later the Freedom Association) of which I was a founder-member. After representations from the Foreign Office, the borough withdrew the permission it had granted orally, and the monument was built on the outskirts of London, in the Gunnersbury cemetery. Pressure was also put on the Ministry of Defense, which banned the wearing of uniforms by ex-servicemen involved in the unveiling ceremony: a ban which the ex-servicemen ignored without further consequences. Translations of the relevant documents appear as Appendix A: Documents 2–14. BC

was June 22, when France signed an Armistice at Compiègne, under which all French forces were to be disarmed and three-fifths of French territory would be occupied by the Germans. From the Kremlin, Stalin watched these events, unperturbed.

Exactly a year later, the dictator's complacent assumptions would be shattered when a massive German force, assembled for an obvious purpose, crossed the Soviet border along a 2,000-mile front on June 22, 1941. In retrospect, the most astonishing aspect of the invasion was Stalin's stubborn refusal to believe the mounting evidence that it was about to happen. The NKVD's agent in Tokyo, Richard Sorge, who had gained access to files at the German embassy, had reported on Hitler's preparations in considerable and precise detail in May and again in June. It was all there: the size of the assembled forces, the operational plans, the precise timing. But these were not, at that time, facts that Stalin was ready to believe. Maintaining his faith in Hitler's loyalty to the Nazi-Soviet Pact, he marked the Sorge reports "For the archives" or "To be filed."[15]

Likewise, Stalin refused requests from his surviving senior officers to put Soviet troops on full alert and move them into defensive positions. His purges had removed many of the Red Army's best personnel. Moreover, as the invading German forces were driving the Red Army back headlong, Stalin resumed a wholesale removal and murder of senior officers.[16] His refusal to believe the overwhelming evidence that Hitler was about to strike nearly handed victory to his former ally.

POSTWAR AGGRANDIZEMENT

1943–1956

CHAPTER SIX

THE EXPANSIONIST
MACHINE

—⟫●⟪—

I N MAY 1943, Joseph Stalin announced the dissolution of the Comintern. On October 5, 1947, at the close of a lengthy meeting of the Communist Party of the Soviet Union (CPSU) and eight European parties, held in Poland, the birth of the Communist Information Bureau, to be known as the Cominform, was announced. The other Communist parties present were those of Bulgaria, Czechoslovakia, Hungary, Poland, Romania, Yugoslavia, France, and Italy. The headquarters of the new organization would be Belgrade. In combination, the death of the Comintern and the birth of the Cominform constituted one of Stalin's most successful exercises in disinformation (in Russian, *dezinformatsiya*).

The purpose of disinformation was to persuade non-Communists (political leaders, government officials, journalists, academics, or members of the public) that something had happened, even though it had not. The Comintern was "dissolved" to reassure Moscow's wartime capitalist allies that the Soviet Union had abandoned its earlier commitment to world revolution. The "dissolution" of the Comintern was accompanied by a subsidiary deception, namely that unlike the disgraced Trotsky, who had continued to preach world revolution, Stalin, more modestly, was now presented as committed to "Socialism in one country." The early postwar years would soon demonstrate that while Trotsky (and Lenin) had merely *preached* world revolution, Stalin was actually on the road to achieving it.

The main targets of the 1943 "dissolution" ploy were President Franklin D. Roosevelt of the United States and British Prime Minister Winston Churchill. Both targets were bull's-eyed. Roosevelt demonstrated his acceptance of Stalin's word at the Big Three conferences—involving President Roosevelt, Prime Minister Churchill, and Marshal Stalin—of Teheran (1943) and Yalta (1945), devoted respectively to Allied wartime strategy and to post-victory policies. Roosevelt did not live to reap the consequences of his gullibility. Even Churchill, a longtime opponent of Communism, was taken in—in other words, "disinformed." The ultimate demonstration of this unpalatable truth was made manifest by Churchill's statement to the House of Commons on his return from Yalta in February 1945:

> The impression I brought back from the Crimea, and from all my other contacts, is that Marshal Stalin and the Soviet leaders wish to live in honorable friendship and equality with the Western democracies. I feel also that their word is their bond. I know of no government which stands to its obligations, even in its own despite, more solidly than the Russian Soviet government. I decline absolutely to embark here on a discussion about Russian good faith.[1]

Stalin could not have asked for better proof of his skill at *dezinformatsiya*.

The birth of the Cominform in 1947 was no less successful. The object of this exercise was to persuade the West that Stalin, for specific reasons, had decided to revive the Comintern on a much smaller scale: The Cominform was simply a device to keep certain European CPs aligned with Moscow. The Kremlin's target area would no longer be the whole world. The list of parties attending the inaugural meeting made the point: Apart from the Soviet party, the other delegations represented the Italian and French parties (the two largest West European parties), and those installed or about to be installed in power by Moscow in Poland, Hungary, Romania, Czechoslovakia, Bulgaria, and Yugoslavia.

The inaugural meeting of the Cominform, in 1947, was addressed by Andrei Zhdanov, at that time Stalin's right-hand man, in charge of ideology and in particular the ideological content of culture (that is, ensuring that creative writers, painters, and musicians worked within guidelines set by the ruling party). For the Communists present, Zhdanov had an exhilarating message. The world, he said, was now split into two hostile blocs;

the time had come for the colonial peoples "to expel their oppressors." The Soviet Union was committed to peace and was "a foe of national and racial oppression and colonial exploitation in any shape or form."[2]

The very fact that Zhdanov's main theme was the expulsion of the colonial "oppressors" contributed to the Western belief that the Cominform, despite its purely European member parties, was a modified resurrection of the defunct Comintern. And indeed, the follow-up to his speech was a series of insurgencies in South and Southeast Asia, discussed in Chapter 13.

Not only were the Western governments taken in by the Cominform ploy, journalists and academics were also, including the specialists whom I term "Communologists," myself included. The truth did not become known until the early 1970s, from the revelations of Soviet and Soviet Bloc defectors. Immediately after World War II—to be precise, in 1946—Stalin had in fact revived the Comintern simply by incorporating it into the International Department of the Central Committee (ID) of the ruling CPSU. Until it became aware of these revelations, the West had naively accepted the official role of the ID as the body liaising with foreign *non*–Communist parties, whereas the ID's real role had been to transmit Moscow's orders and guidance, as well as funds, to Communist Parties worldwide.

Contrary to the West's immediate postwar perception, it was also the ID that gave the strategic guidance to the KGB and its military counterpart, the GRU. This is not to say that these secret services had no freedom of maneuver: they did, especially in the field of espionage. But in the field of subversion, the KGB's First Chief Directorate—concerned with operations abroad—worked essentially within the guidelines determined by the ID.[3]

Interestingly, the man Stalin chose to run the ID was Boris Ponomarev, who had served under him on the Executive Committee of the original Comintern. Ponomarev would hold this key job until 1986, when Mikhail Gorbachev retired him, at age eighty-one, and replaced him with Anatoly Dobrynin, at that time the Soviet ambassador in Washington.[4]

Since 1917, international subversion had played a major role in Lenin's concept of the new Soviet entity as the center for world revolution. And subversion took varied forms. It included overt as well as covert propaganda; there was a covert dimension even to overt propaganda. For example, there was a covert element in such relatively minor newspapers as the British and American *Daily Worker* (the British one later changed its title to the *Morning Star*), in that both were overtly on sale but were secretly subsidized by Moscow. Truly covert propaganda, however, was truly secret. It involved the recruitment (usually by the KGB) of "agents of influence" in non-Communist countries, forgeries on pilfered official letterheads, and the dissemination of disinformation. This was indeed the major purpose of agents of influence, who themselves fell into two categories: "conscious" (that is, those who were aware of what they were doing and were possibly being paid for it) and "unconscious" (that is, those naive recipients of Soviet disinformation who believed it to be true or were flattered into believing that they were being given privileged access to official secrets). The corresponding professional terms in the CIA (the Central Intelligence Agency, the American equivalent of Britain's Secret Intelligence Service or SIS, better known as MI-6) were "witting" and "unwitting."[5]

A related subversive Soviet activity was the gathering of biographical details to be used for the blackmailing of potential recruits, including spies; and the penetration and disruption from within of enemy intelligence agencies and other government departments. Classic examples include Harold Philby in the 1930s and the CIA officer Aldrich Ames in the 1980s.

The subversive apparatus of the Soviet Union grew exponentially in the postwar period, as Stalin ordered the creation of a huge web of international front organizations. The main ones were

- the World Federation of Trade Unions (WFTU), World Federation of Democratic Youth (WFDY), and Women's International Democratic Federation (WIDF), all in 1945;
- the International Organization of Journalists (IOJ), International Union of Students (IUS), World Federation of Scientific Workers (WFSW), International Association of Democratic Lawyers (IADL), and International Radio and Television Organization (OIRT, from initials in French), all in 1946;
- the International Federation of Resistance Movements (FIR, also from the French), in 1947; and
- the World Council of Peace (later World Peace Council, or WPC), in 1948.[6]

The most important of the international fronts were the WFTU and the WPC. The former infiltrated various national trade unions, including: the French CGT *(Confédération Générale du Travail),* the Italian GCIL *(Confederazione Generale Italiana del Lavoro),* the British TUC *(Trades Union Congress),* and the American AFL-CIO *(American Federation of Labor-Congress of Industrial Organizations).* The World Peace Council provided a platform of pacifist organizations and individuals in western countries. In the United States in particular, it worked to denounce such policies as containment, nuclear parity, and in the last phase of the Cold War, President Ronald Reagan's Strategic Defense Initiative (SDI), better known by the adversarial term, Star Wars.

The postwar creation of these major fronts followed pure Leninist orthodoxy. The great revolutionary himself had called such devices "transmission belts to the masses." In 1972, the CPSU issued a book entitled *The International Communist Movement,* which quoted Lenin as saying that the essence of internationalism is support of revolutionary struggle "through propaganda, sympathy or materially . . . in all countries without exception."

In furtherance of this doctrine, Moscow sent large sums of money to the striking British miners in 1926, would again in 1974, and yet again in 1980. In distant Australia, Soviet money was transmitted secretly to the Communist Party, as the defecting KGB spy V. M. Petrov revealed in 1954.[7]* He would have known; after all, *he* was the "transmitter." Such examples were multiplied by the thousands. Further front organizations were set up in the 1950s and 1960s, and will be mentioned later.

Along with its nonviolent instances of subversion, designed to disseminate disinformation and to support and broaden "industrial action," mainly in Western countries, the Soviet "expansionist machine" also

---

*Petrov had made his career in the MVD (Ministry of Internal Affairs), which was renamed the KGB (Committee of State Security) in March 1954, a few days before his defection on April 3 of that year. For a full account of his activities, see Michael Bialoguski, *The Petrov Story* (Melbourne, London: Petrov, 1955). The Polish-born author knew Petrov and posed as a Communist sympathizer, while liaising with the Australian Service. On May 3, the (British) governor-general of Australia, Sir William Slim, appointed a Royal Commission on Espionage. Appearing as a witness, Petrov revealed that he had given US $25,000 to Lance Sharkey, secretary of the Communist Party in Australia, "to assist in fighting the anti-Communist legislation which the Government wished to put on the Statute Books." The figure quoted by Bialoguski is $20,000.

indulged in violent forms of subversion, including aid to terrorism, guerrilla warfare, and outright war. For decades, the Soviet machine recruited both Communists and non-Communists for violent action, trained them in Moscow or in other centers, including Odessa, Baku, Simferopol, and Tashkent, armed them, and sent them back to their native countries to gain power by violent means.[8] In some cases, of which Vietnam is the most successful, terrorism turned to guerrilla warfare, then to outright war.

The ultimate purpose of all forms of subversion was imperial in the sense that those backed by the machine were expected to set up Communist regimes that owed their ultimate allegiance to Moscow. The attribution of "anti-imperialist" or "anti-colonialist" motives to such movements was in itself an example of disinformation, designed in most cases to disinform the terrorists or guerrillas as well as those designated to be overthrown.

It is broadly fair to say that in all or nearly all the targeted Western countries, nonviolent Soviet subversion was ultimately unsuccessful, in that not one of the countries targeted was in fact taken over by Communist parties. It is also fair to add that despite these ultimate failures, considerable political and/or security disruption was caused in a number of these countries, including at different times the United States, Britain, France, Italy, and Germany. It is not, however, our purpose to dwell on these failures in detail. Of greater relevance are the successes.

The Cominform, which had been transferred from Belgrade to Moscow, was dissolved on April 17, 1956. Ironically, although the first headquarters of the Cominform had been set up in Belgrade, Yugoslavia was expelled from that body on June 28, 1948, for "doctrinal errors" and alleged hostility to the Soviet Union. Stalin did not crush the Yugoslav leader, Marshal Josip Broz Tito, who maintained his defiance and sought a special "non-aligned" role for his country. He got away with it.

A year earlier, on May 26, 1955, Stalin's successor, Nikita Khrushchev, had arrived in Belgrade with an apology to Tito for the earlier treatment of Yugoslavia. Tito accepted the apology but maintained his non-aligned stance.

THE PASSIVE ARMED FORCES

WITH RELATIVELY FEW exceptions (the major one being the Russian Civil War), the armed forces were seldom actively involved in the expansion of the Soviet Empire. During World War II (excepting the unimpressive attempt to overrun Finland), the main role of the Soviet forces was to resist and ultimately to repulse the German invaders. The Baltic States and eastern Poland were absorbed as a direct consequence of the 1939 Nazi-Soviet Pact.

However, the fortunes of war, plus the partition of Europe agreed upon by the Big Three at Yalta and extended at Potsdam in 1945, in effect brought East Germany under direct Soviet control and Central Europe within Moscow's sphere of intimidation. Thus, with relatively little military force, the Communist parties were put in power and their respective countries absorbed into the new satellite empire. There were short-lived exceptions to this rule, such as the crushing of the Berlin revolt in 1953 and of the Hungarian uprising in 1956 (both dealt with in separate chapters).

The formidable buildup of the Soviet military machine, including its nuclear wing, was intended mainly for intimidatory purposes. Its intimidatory power was supplemented and, to some extent, magnified by the parallel role of the subversive machine, in this case primarily executed by the most important of the international fronts, the World Peace Council.

Throughout the postwar imperial expansion, most of the military campaigns were conducted by the surrogate forces of the Soviet Union. During the period from 1945 to 1954, an unacknowledged "theory of contiguity" prevailed among Western observers of the international Communist machine. In other words, it was assumed that territorial accretions were made only under the proximate presence of the Soviet armed forces. This was true of the European satellites, but later events (the Vietnamese Communist victory of 1954 against the French) demonstrated that surrogate military forces, massively supplied with Soviet weapons, could defeat Western powers.

THE MACHINE IN ACTION

MUCH WAS KNOWN about the Comintern, the Cominform, and the International Department before the collapse of the Soviet system; but nothing available in the West before the collapse can compare, in interest and authenticity, with the vast collection of relevant Soviet archives that came into Western hands *after* the collapse. The most relevant material had been assembled, on the orders of President Boris Yeltsin, with the objective of declaring the former ruling Communist Party of the Soviet Union illegal. The attempt failed. A selection of the documents appear in transla-tion as Appendixes.* Examples follow, in chronological sequence.

In Stalin's Time, and Beyond

On January 17, 1950, the CPSU decided to set up a fund to be handled by the All-Union Council of Trade Unions "with the purpose of providing financial assistance to leftist parties and progressive workers' and social organizations abroad that are being repressed and persecuted." The deci-sion was enshrined in a Top Secret draft resolution submitted to Stalin, and later approved by him, with copies addressed to Georgy Malenkov, Vyacheslav Molotov, Lavrenti Beria, Anastas Mikoyan, and Lazar Ka-ganovich, all members of the Politburo. (See Appendix B: Document 1.)

On July 19, 1950, a further Top Secret resolution was approved, pro-viding that the proposed fund be established in Budapest. The sum to be made available would be $2 million: $1 million would come from the So-viet Communist Party; $200,000 from the Chinese Party; and $160,000 each from the ruling parties of East Germany, Poland, Czechoslovakia, Romania, and Hungary. (See Appendix B: Document 2.)

Reporting to Stalin in a Top Secret memorandum on January 20, 1951, V. Grigorian, Chairman of the Politburo's Commission for Foreign Policy, stated that the fund had been overspent by $59,000. The biggest beneficiaries had been the French Party ($300,000, plus an equal amount paid earlier) and the Italian Party ($400,000). (See Appendix B: Docu-ment 3 for further details.)

Under a Top Secret Resolution dated February 8, 1951, the total sum to be allocated to the fund by the Soviet Party was reduced to $1.5 mil-lion. (See Appendix B: Document 4.)

By January 1963, nearly ten years after Stalin's death, the fund had grown to $14,650,000, more than seven times the original allocation. A Top Secret report gave details of allocations to twenty-five Communist parties ranging from Italy's ($5 million) at the top end to the CP of Réu-nion ($8,000). (See Appendix B: Document 5.)

---

*A fuller background is covered by Arnold Beichman, a leading U.S. specialist on Commu-nism, and a research fellow at the Hoover Institution, in "Moscow's Secret Gold" (*The Weekly Standard,* New York, March 4, 1996) and in "Q & A: The Power of Moscow's Se-cret Gold" (*Hoover Newsletter,* Spring 1996). See Chapter 5, footnote**.

Terrorism Plus . . .

Some months after Stalin's death (on September 17, 1953), a memorandum from Stalin's successor, Nikita Khrushchev, established a special department designed to "lead terrorist operations on the territory of the capitalist States." The Twelfth (Special) Department under the Second Main (Intelligence) Administration of the USSR Ministry of Internal Affairs (MVD) would carry out assassinations of the "enemies of the USSR, leaders of émigré organizations. . . ."[9]

In mid-1966, the Soviet Party's Politburo extended financial assistance to the CPs or other "friendly" parties of Bolivia, Paraguay, Madagascar, Sudan, and Sierra Leone.[10]

At the end of January 1968, the list of recipient parties was further extended to Congo (Brazzaville) and the (ex-Belgian) Republic of Congo.[11]

CHAPTER SEVEN

TRANSITIONAL ACCRETIONS

1944–1946

———⊱⊰———

HAVING TAKEN STALIN by surprise in June 1941, Hitler's invading Army made spectacular gains in the first seventeen months, overrunning most of Ukraine and laying siege to Leningrad in the north and Stalingrad in the south. Between September and December 1942, the Soviet launched a major counteroffensive, relieving Leningrad in January 1943 and Stalingrad a month later. In July that year, massive military supplies from the United States and Britain started reaching the Soviet Union. The United States in particular shipped 4,100 planes, 138,000 motor vehicles, and supplies of machinery for Soviet arms factories.

By January 1944, the tide of war had turned irreversibly in favor of the Soviet Union. The Germans were in full retreat, and by February the Soviet forces had reached the prewar borders of Poland. On January 17, ten German divisions, trapped near Cherkassky, were wiped out, with the few survivors left in Soviet hands. Between March 26 and May 9, the Soviets had taken Odessa and Sevastopol, clearing Ukraine and the Crimea.

In the military parlance of that time, Hitler's war with the Soviet Union was seen as the "first front." The landing of Western forces in Normandy, France, on June 6, 1944, constituted the "second front." The immediate effect of it was to deprive Hitler of his last chance of reinforcing his armies in the East. On August 24, 1944, the Soviet forces reached the mouth of the Danube, and Romania capitulated, trapping the German naval forces in the Black Sea.

Meanwhile, thousands of miles to the east, Stalin's men seized the small Turkic country of Tannu Tavu on the Mongolian border, with its agricultural and cattle breeding population of around 100,000, and incorporated it into the Russian federation, as an autonomous *oblast* or administrative region. (In 1961, eight years after Stalin's death, its status would be raised to that of an "autonomous republic.")

This marginal imperial accretion passed seemingly unnoticed by the nations that were at war in the West. Of greater import and news value were the Soviet declaration of war on Bulgaria on September 5, and the savage battle of Budapest in November, in which the Hungarians held out for more than two months before capitulating to the Soviets on February 13, 1945.

Tallinn and Riga, the capitals of Estonia and Latvia, fell on September 22 and October 13, 1944, respectively, and in January the Red Army began its final drive into Germany.

TITO AND HIS RIVAL

OF SPECIAL RELEVANCE to this history was the Soviet capture of Belgrade on October 20, 1944. The German forces had invaded Yugoslavia (and Greece) on April 6, 1941, and twelve days later the Yugoslav government had capitulated. On May 4, 1941, Hitler had proclaimed that the state of Yugoslavia had ceased to exist.

The Führer had spoken too soon, for on May 10, 1941, an unknown colonel in the Yugoslav Army, Drazha Mihailovich, hoisted the flag of his "nonexistent" state on the Serbian mountain of Ravna Gora and announced that the war against the German invaders would go on.[1]

For two years, Mihailovich was a Resistance hero in the eyes first of the British, and later of the Americans when they entered the war in the wake of Japan's bombing of the U.S. fleet at Pearl Harbor on December 7, 1941. By the end of 1943, however, the Allied attitude toward Mihailovich had radically changed. In Washington and in London, the revised assessment was that Mihailovich was collaborating with the Nazis. The man to support in Yugoslavia had become the Communist leader, Marshal Tito.

Accordingly, Allied aid was switched to Tito, whose partisans he turned into a national army. Starved of supplies, Mihailovich was isolated and reduced to inactivity. Although Tito had spent most of the war years in his country, he had been trained in Moscow, and at this time, he was still on good terms with the ruling Soviet party. He was thus invited to enter the Serbian capital, Belgrade, in triumph with the Soviet Red Army, on October 20, 1944. On March 7, 1945, he became the leader of a new Communist government of Yugoslavia, as well as commander in chief of the Yugoslav armed forces.

A year later—on March 13, 1946—Mihailovich was arrested. Charged with treason, he was executed on July 17 after a trial that recalled Stalin's purge trials of the 1930s.

These bare facts, however, need to be supplemented by the known story of Tito's early life, and by the hidden story that was brought to light by the Canadian-born American writer David Martin.* Tito, a Croat by birth, whose real name was Josip Broz, had served in the Austro Hungarian Army during the Great War and was captured by the Russians in 1915. Between 1917 and 1923, he served in Lenin's Red Army. Back in Yugoslavia, he became the leader of the Communist Party. Jailed in 1928 for a six-year sentence, after his release he spent two years in Moscow before being sent to Paris by the Comintern in 1936 to organize the travel arrangements of the International Brigades on their way to Spain.

As did other Communist leaders in the West, Tito remained inactive between the signing of the Nazi-Soviet Pact in 1939 and the German invasion of Russia in 1941 (see Chapter 6). When he went into action, as did the Communist parties in France, Britain, and elsewhere, the Comintern mounted a secret and highly effective operation to discredit Mihailovich in the eyes of Churchill, who had been Mihailovich's enthusiastic supporter. The operation was conducted mainly by a British Communist, James Klugmann, through the Yugoslav Section of Britain's Special Operations Executive (SOE) based in Cairo. In service to the Comintern, Klugmann systematically suppressed vital dispatches, or incorporated material into falsified reports that were destined to reach the eyes of Winston Churchill.

In sum, the evidence assembled by Martin establishes beyond reasonable doubt that James Klugmann was one of Stalin's most successful

---

*A friend of mine for the last twenty years of his life (he died in 1995), David Martin conducted a protracted personal investigation that resulted in four books, only three of which had been published when these lines were written: *Ally Betrayed: The Uncensored Story of Tito and Mihailovich* (1946), *Patriot or Traitor: The Case of General Mihailovich* (Hoover Institution, 1978) and *The Web of Disinformation: Churchill's Yugoslav Blunder* (1990). Shortly before his death, he completed a fourth and definitive version, *The Yugoslav Tragedy: Aftermath of Britain's Wartime Tragedy*, which remains unpublished.—BC

agents of influence. Relevantly, he was one of the group of Cambridge Communists recruited by the NKVD in the 1930s, who included the better known Kim Philby, Guy Burgess, Donald Maclean, and Anthony Blunt. "Indeed [writes David Martin], by common consent he was the most brilliant member of the group."[2]

The extent to which Churchill had been disinformed becomes clear from his account of the meeting he had with Tito in Naples on August 12, 1944: "Tito assured me that, as he had stated publicly, he had no desire to introduce the Communist system into Yugoslavia. . . . The Russians had a mission with the Partisans, but its members, far from expressing any idea of introducing the Soviet system into Yugoslavia, had spoken against it."[3]

Although Tito had shown himself to be an obedient executant of Stalin's policy before and during the war, he would soon demonstrate that, like Ho Chi Minh but more so, he was a Nationalist as well as a Communist. As mentioned in Chapter 6, he defied Stalin over the Cominform; and, exceptionally, he got away with it. Thereafter, he successfully pursued a neutralist policy, better known as "non-alignment" between the power blocs of West and East. Thus, Yugoslavia was the first exception to the rule that newly anointed Communist countries became part of the Soviet Empire (see Appendix C: Document 1).

ITALY INVADES GREECE

IN GREECE, USUALLY considered with Yugoslavia to be part of "the Balkans," Communism simply failed to establish itself, although not for want of trying. The Greek Communist Party or KKE *(Kommunistikon Komma Hellados)* was one of the earliest, founded in November 1918. Although not a mass party, its membership of around 20,000 was not negligible within a total population of some 8.5 million. World War II gave it an opportunity to bid for power. Alternatively, it could be said that Italy's Fascist leader, Benito Mussolini, created the opportunity through his reckless desire to show Hitler that he and his country were also capable of waging war. In this he was soon shown to be mistaken.

Mussolini made no attempt to disguise the envy and alarm with which he had noted Hitler's early military successes in Poland and in the Low Countries (Holland and Belgium) and France. Although Mussolini was the original Fascist leader, he had been tacitly relegated into the role of junior partner in the Berlin-Rome Axis, mainly because he simply did not carry military weight comparable to Hitler's, and was therefore not feared to the same degree by the Western Powers. He had, in fact, got into belligerent action early by occupying Albania (probably the easiest of potential targets) in April 1939. He declared war on France on June 10, 1940, by which time the German armies had already defeated the French.[4]

This was embarrassing for the Italian dictator, and on October 28, 1940, without warning Hitler of his intentions, Mussolini launched an invasion of Greece with seven of the Italian divisions that occupied Albania. If self-humiliation had been his aim, he could not have acted to better effect. Within a few days, the Greek Army, under General Alexandros Papagos, had halted the Italian advance. On November 14, the Greeks launched a devastating counteroffensive. By mid-December, not only had they driven the invaders out, but they had also taken possession of one-third of Albania.

To complicate the situation, British forces had landed on the Greek island of Crete, and British aircraft had set up bases near Athens. Hitler's forces were otherwise engaged at the time, and the German forces could not be deployed in Greece until April 1941. On April 6, Hitler sent twenty-four divisions, with 1,200 tanks, into action in both Yugoslavia and Greece. By May 11, the whole of mainland Greece was under German occupation, and by the end of the month, the Allied commander in Crete, the New Zealand General Bernard Freyberg, was forced to evacuate the island.

It took the Greek KKE somewhat longer than it had taken Tito of Yugoslavia to tackle the German occupation force. It was not until March 1942 that a Communist Resistance apparatus began to make itself felt. The political organization that emerged was named the National Liberation Front (*Ellinikó Apeleftherotikó Métopo* or the EAM), and its armed guerrillas operated under the initials ELAS (*Ethinikó Laïkó Apeleftherotikó Sóma,* People's National Liberation Army). There was a more moderate rival pair of Resistance bodies: the National Social Liberation League and the Greek National Democratic Army, which played a relatively minor role.[5]

What followed was a bitter, intermittent, but prolonged and confusing struggle, part resistance to a foreign enemy, part civil war. The Communists murdered men, women, and children in the thousands, and took hostages in large numbers, driving them along the roads but leaving the exhausted ones to die.

Initially, Greece's foreign enemy was Germany, and in 1942–1943, the Greek population joined the EAM-ELAS guerrillas in large numbers until, on March 10, 1944, they felt strong enough to proclaim a Provisional Committee of National Liberation under a leader named Svolos, of whom little is known. A few weeks later, in April 1944, a Communist-led mutiny in the Greek Navy took place in Alexandria Harbor (an event which, in the view of the distinguished American intellectual James Burnham, marks the beginning of the Cold War[6]). In Greece itself and in neighboring countries, the situation changed in late August, when the advancing Soviet forces invaded Romania. The Germans were faced with an awkward decision: whether to stay on in Greece or switch to the eastern front. In early October, they opted for the switch, and on October 14, British forces landed at Piraeus, the port of land-bound Athens. Five days earlier—on October 9—Churchill had arrived in Moscow for a meeting with Stalin; also present were Churchill's Foreign Secretary, Anthony Eden, and Stalin's equivalent, Vyacheslav Molotov. It was clear to Stalin that the British were better placed than the Soviets to intervene in Greece. Accordingly, he made an oral agreement with Churchill, to the effect that Greece fell within the British sphere of influence. Not surprisingly, however, Stalin did nothing to discourage the Greek Communists from fighting the British, and after the Greek landing, the "enemy" of the Greek Communist Resistance became Britain instead of Germany. ELAS started an offensive against the British on December 3, 1944.

From his exile in Cairo, King George II of the Hellenes appointed the Orthodox Metropolitan of Athens, Mgr. Damaskinos, as regent to a provisional government headed by General Nikolaos Plastiras, a leader of earlier abortive coups, who had taken refuge in France. On February 12, 1945, EAM-ELAS agreed to a truce with the new royalist government. However, the Communists boycotted the free elections that were held on March 11, 1946. The royalist winners organized a plebiscite, which came out in favor of the monarchy by 69 percent. The king returned, but the Communists, led by a man whose *nom de guerre* (literally) was "General Marcos," reopened the civil war, initially in the northern mountains. This phase of the civil war would last nearly three years.

The international situation changed dramatically on March 12, 1947, when the American president, Harry Truman, proclaimed the "Truman Doctrine" (in essence a policy of aiding countries threatened by, and eager to resist, Communism), in effect a warning signal to Stalin to keep his hands off Greece and Turkey, both of which would benefit from a massive economic aid program.

By then the British had left, and the United States was the new "foreign enemy" of the Communist Resistance. On Christmas Eve, 1947, Marcos proclaimed the "First Provisional Government of Free Greece" with the backing of the Soviet Union (despite the Truman Doctrine). The EAM base was at Konitza, in Epirus.

On December 27, the Greek government "dissolved" the KKE and the EAM, but that was a meaningless gesture. The civil war went on until October 16, 1949, when the rebel forces were defeated.

The anti-Communist victory had been made possible by two unrelated circumstances: American aid and Tito's break with the Cominform, which closed the channel of military support to the Greek rebels. Thus a combination of power politics and national defiance deprived Stalin of yet another victory in his imperial expansionism. He appears to have accepted this situation, adhering to the terms of the oral agreement he had made with Churchill in Moscow in October 1944,[7] that Greece fell within the British sphere of interest.

STALIN'S "LAST-MINUTE" OFFENSIVE

UNTIL GERMANY'S COLLAPSE on May 8, 1945, the Soviet Union's share of the fighting in World War II had been entirely concentrated on various European fronts. In the Far East, the United States had borne the brunt of the fighting, with relatively minor contributions from Britain, Australia, and New Zealand. However, on August 8, 1945, exactly three months after Germany's unconditional surrender, the Red Army went into action against the Japanese forces, despite a Neutrality Pact that had been concluded on April 13, 1941, between the Soviet Union and Japan.

There is an important difference between Stalin's motives for launching what might be called a last-minute offensive against the Japanese on the one hand, and on the other, for his massive and prolonged offensives in Europe. There is no reason to believe that Stalin would have entered the war if Hitler had not ordered an invasion of Soviet territory without warning and in violation of the Nazi-Soviet Pact. As Stalin's gigantic Army went on to conquer more and more territories outside the Soviet Union's borders, another motive came into play: the Leninist goal of spreading the Communist revolution over countries that came under Soviet control by right of conquest. In the Far Eastern offensive of August 1945, the spread of Communism was only one aspect. Another was the patriotic one of revenge for the humiliations suffered by Russia in the Russo-Japanese war of 1905. Ignoring Japanese protests at Russian imperialist expansion in the Far East, the Russians seized territories in China, Manchuria, and Korea, provoking military and naval retaliation from Japan, and resulting in a major defeat for the Russians: about 400,000 Russian deaths, compared with 170,000 on the Japanese side.

Stalin said as much in his victory address to the Soviet people on September 2, 1945, the day the representatives of Japan's government and imperial headquarters signed the Instrument of Surrender on board the USS *Missouri* in Tokyo Bay:

> Our defeat in the war of 1904–05 with Japan left a bitter memory in our minds, for it stained our name. Convinced that some day Japan would be beaten and this stain removed, we have been waiting for that day. . . . Now this day has come. Today, Japan has admitted defeat and signed an instrument of unconditional surrender. This means that Southern Sakhalin and the Kurile islands have been transferred to the Soviet Union and will serve . . . as a means for linking the Soviet Union with the Ocean and as a base for our defense against the Japanese aggression.[8]

Alone, this frankness, unusual in Stalin, would probably not have been sufficient to explain his decision to launch the offensive against Japan. But power politics also came into play. In the week of February 4 to 11, 1945, the Big Three—President Roosevelt, Prime Minister Churchill, and Marshal Stalin—had met at Yalta in the Soviet Crimea to discuss the spoils of war in East and West.

On the afternoon of February 8, Roosevelt and Stalin met privately at the Livadia Palace. When Roosevelt pressed him to enter the war against Japan, Stalin said he could do so only if certain conditions were met. Two days later, he spelled out those conditions on paper, in a "Draft of Marshal

Stalin's Conditions for Russia's Entry into the War against Japan." These comprised a guarantee of the status of the Mongolian People's Republic, the restoration of Russian territories seized by Japan in 1904, including southern Sakhalin and adjacent islands, a handover of Port Arthur and Dairen on lease to the Soviet Union, and the unconditional transfer of the Kurile Islands to the Soviet Union.[9] These conditions were accepted by Roosevelt and (at a separate meeting with Stalin) by Churchill; but they were not made public at the time.

A sequel to Yalta was the last Big Three meeting of the war, at Potsdam outside devastated Berlin, from July 17 to August 2, 1945. Initially, the Big Three were President Harry Truman (following Roosevelt's death on April 12), Prime Minister Churchill, and Marshal Stalin. Halfway through the conference, however, Churchill's place was taken by the Labor leader, Clement Attlee, who had come to power on July 26 after the defeat of Churchill's Conservative Party in Britain's first postwar elections. That same day an ultimatum to Japan was delivered from Potsdam in the names of Roosevelt and Stalin, and of both British prime ministers. The Chinese Nationalist leader, Generalissimo Chiang Kai-shek, who had been contacted by radio, also joined in the ultimatum. (In November 1943, Churchill and Roosevelt had held a summit with Chiang in secret "somewhere in North Africa" to discuss the war with Japan. Since the Soviet Union was not yet at war with Japan, Stalin had not been invited.)

In the event, Stalin sent his forces into action in the nick of time on August 8, for on August 6 and 9, the U.S. Air Force dropped the first atomic bombs to be exploded in war, on Hiroshima and Nagasaki. Had Stalin waited another week or two, he might have missed his chance of territorial gains at Japan's expense.

Once again Leninist revolutionary theory played a part in Stalin's motivation. Having overrun Manchuria, he was able to hand over a massive pile of Japanese weapons to the Chinese Communist leader Mao Tse-tung, which, more than any other factor, enabled Mao to defeat Chiang Kai-shek and create the Chinese People's Republic. This major victory for Communism, the most important of all, next to Lenin's Revolution, belongs to a future chapter.

*   *   *

YET ANOTHER IMPERIALIST move by Stalin should be mentioned at this point. At Yalta, and again at Potsdam, Stalin had advanced claims on Turkish and Iranian territories, without success. The Turks had been neutral for most of the war and, with backing from the United States and Britain, stood firm against Soviet demands for joint defense arrangements in the Dardanelles and for a military base on Turkish soil.

The situation in Iran was more complex. In a preventive action against the Germans, Britain as well as the Soviet Union had occupied Iranian territory. The Soviet-held areas in particular became one of the main supply routes for American aid to the Red Army. Both powers had agreed to pull out their forces within six months of the end of hostilities. The British complied, but the Soviet forces stayed on. Stalin had his own covert forces there: Iran's Tudeh or "Masses" party, whose name concealed its Communist allegiance. In response to Stalin's directives, they set up two separate police states on the Soviet model: the "Autonomous Republic of Azerbaijan" and the "Kurdish People's Republic." Both were short-lived. In November 1945, the Iranian government tried to send troops into Azerbaijan to oust the Tudeh rebels, but they were frustrated by the Soviet forces. In March 1946, Iran appealed to the United Nations Security Council against the Soviet presence, and on April 5, the Soviet Union agreed to withdraw.* This was, in fact, the first open clash between the Soviet Union and the Western powers before the UN. President Truman strongly insisted on a Soviet withdrawal, and the publicity was distinctly unfavorable to the Soviet side. The Soviet withdrawal was sudden, and the Tudeh was left to its own devices.

Iran was thus an exception to the general rule that whatever Stalin seized, he held on to. Stalin's reasons for giving in were never spelled out. In speeches in America, Churchill had cited Iran as a testing ground of Soviet intentions. This alone would probably not have caused Stalin to pull out of Iran. But he may well have feared a threat by Truman to move U.S. forces into the area.[10] The countries of Eastern Europe were less fortunate than Iran and Turkey.

---

*In April 1949, the Tudeh party was outlawed, following an attempt on the life of Shah Reza Pahlavi.

CHAPTER EIGHT

SATELLIZATION BEGINS

1945–1948

By the war's end, Stalin's armies occupied Poland and the Baltic States, Czechoslovakia and Hungary, Bulgaria and Albania, Berlin and East Germany; and in the Far East, North Korea as well as the minor Kurile Islands and southern Sakhalin. Let us take a closer look at North Korea and the individual East European countries.

KIM IL-SUNG'S CAREER

THE FIRST LEADER of North Korea, Kim Il-sung, was linked to Moscow throughout his career; he made himself the object of a personality cult that rivaled and perhaps surpassed that of Stalin and of the Chinese leader Mao Tse-tung. He also led his half-country into an international war, with Stalin's special authority.

Japan had taken over Korea in August 1910 as a delayed sequel to its victory in the Russian-Japanese War of 1904–1905. Kim was born nearly two years later on April 15, 1912, with the name Kim Song-ju. His father, a schoolmaster, took his family to Manchuria to join a group of anti-Japanese Koreans in exile when Song-ju was eleven. In 1930, aged eighteen, Kim-ju joined a group of Chinese Communist guerrillas who called themselves the Northeast Anti-Japanese Army, and took the name of the man who had led the anti-Japanese Koreans. Henceforth, he was known as Kim Il-sung. In 1931, he joined the Korean Communist Party (which had been founded in 1925). His circle of comrades-in-arms would later fill the top jobs in his ruling hierarchy.[1]

During World War II, Kim went to the Soviet Union and joined a brigade of the Red Army stationed at Khabarovsk. He is reported to have gone one step further than that other Asian Communist leader, Ho Chi Minh, and was granted Soviet citizenship, retaining it until the end of the war.

When the Soviet Army moved into Korea in late August 1945, Kim followed in its wake. By then, the division of Korea into Communist and non-Communist zones had been decided, in a curiously ad hoc manner. At midnight on the night of August 10–11, two young American colonels had been given half an hour to define the surrender zones in all theaters of the Pacific War. (One of the colonels, Dean Rusk, would later be named secretary of state in President Harry Truman's government.) The two young men hastily drew an imaginary line along the 38th parallel across Korea on a small-scale map of the Far East. The initiative was in their hands, and the line they drew left Seoul, the capital of Korea, in the American zone.[2] On August 24, the Soviet forces, with Kim Il-sung in the rear, entered Pyongyang, soon to become the capital of Communist North Korea.

In January 1946, with Soviet backing, Kim-Il-sung became head of the new North Korean branch of the Korean Communist Party. In February, he headed an Interim People's Committee, in effect a provisional government. Over the next two years, he would gradually but ruthlessly rid himself of both Communist and non-Communist rivals. When the Korean People's Democratic Republic (KPDR) was created on September 9, 1948, Kim Il-sung was its first prime minister: "an oriental carbon copy of Stalin."[3] North Korea thus emerged as the Soviet Union's second Far Eastern satellite (after the Mongolian People's Republic); that is, a nominally independent state ultimately under Soviet control and therefore part of the growing Soviet Empire.

The proclamation of the KPDR had been preceded in South Korea by general elections, under American supervision, which resulted in the proclamation of the Republic of South Korea. Significantly, in the light of the war that followed within two years, Kim's KPDR claimed authority over the whole of the Korean peninsula.

THE EAST EUROPEAN SATELLITES

Albania

Much the same process was occurring in Eastern (formerly known as Central) Europe, at much the same time, in half a dozen countries "liberated" by the Red Army, plus the special cases of East Germany (which did become a satellite) and Austria (which did not). If the criterion of satellization is the advent of a Communist state controlled from Moscow, the chronological order is Albania, Bulgaria, Poland, Czechoslovakia, Romania, and Hungary; East Germany's turn came last, in October 1949.

The poorest and least important of the East European satellites was Albania, but the career of its Communist leader, Enver Hoxha, is perhaps the most interesting. Hoxha was born in October 1908 in Argyrocastro, in the hills of central Albania, an area claimed by Greece but ceded to Albania after the Great War. He was one of a middle-class Bektashi Muslim family, appropriately in a town renowned for its mosques and their minarets. His education was French, starting with the French Lycée in the southern Albanian city of Korçë, followed by higher studies at Montpellier University in southern France. His university career was, however, cut short in 1931, when his government scholarship was withdrawn, presumably because of his unacceptably leftist opinions. Destitute, Hoxha joined the French Communist Party that year, as Ho Chi Minh had done eleven years before, and wrote for the Party organ, *L'Humanité*. He moved to Brussels and found a job as a secretary at the Albanian legation. Adopting the pen name Lulo Malessori, he attacked both Fascism and King Zog of Albania in various articles.

In 1936, he was back in Albania, making a living as a teacher. But tenure was incompatible with the views he was expressing, and once again he was expelled. By 1939, in Tirana, he was running a humble tobacco kiosk, which soon grew in importance as a center for Communist and other anti-Fascist groups looking to Hoxha for leadership.[4]

Then came the Italian invasion in 1939, and Hoxha disappeared. In October 1941, he was sentenced to death in absentia. Not long after, on November 8, he became a founder-member of the clandestine and illegal Albanian Communist Party. Soon he was elected a member of its provisional Central Committee, then was named provisional secretary-general. The party did not hold its First National Congress until March 1943, when his position was confirmed. Some months earlier, in September 1942, at the so-called "Peza Conference," he had set up a National Liberation Movement in which he took on the grandiloquent title of Chief Political Commissar on the General Staff of the Albanian Army of National Liberation (ANLA). He made contact with the Western powers who supplied the ANLA with arms, while military personnel joined it from Yugoslavia. In typical Communist fashion, Hoxha used this army to dispose of rival Nationalist leaders as well as to fight the Germans, who by this time had supplanted Mussolini's failed Italians.

By the spring of 1944, he was the uncontested leader of his Communist-Nationalist movement. His followers bestowed on him the titles of President of the Anti-Fascist Committee and Commander in Chief of the Resistance. In October, a conference was held at Berat, where he was named as prime minister and war minister. By then, his National Liberation forces controlled the whole of his native country.

After standard Communist-controlled elections on January 11, 1946, Albania was proclaimed a People's Republic. In its first government, announced in March, Enver Hoxha remained prime minister, as well as minister of defense and of foreign affairs. Satellization was complete. Until June 1948, Albania had maintained close political and economic links with Yugoslavia. That month, however, Stalin expelled Tito's Yugoslavia from the Communist bloc (see Chapter 6) for his defiance of Moscow's orders, and Albania sided with Moscow. Hoxha became a reliable and outspoken anti-Tito spokesman. He took advantage of the Tito crisis to execute his main rival, a man named Xoxe, and systematically purge pro-Tito elements (real or so labeled) over the next few years. Stalin responded by sending Soviet advisers to Albania and making credits available to replace those that had been coming from Yugoslavia. As we shall see, however, Hoxha sided with China when the great Sino-Soviet split developed in 1960.

Bulgaria: The Easy Satellite

Bulgaria seemed destined to be dominated by Russia, by geographical proximity, Slavic ethnicity, a shared Eastern Orthodox religion, and linguistic similarity. History, however, played a trick on the Bulgars, who, like their occasional enemies the Greeks, were overrun by the Turks and became part of the Ottoman Empire for some five centuries. Communist

Russia, however, had little trouble satellizing the Bulgars at the end of World War II.

Wisdom did not characterize Bulgarian policy during the war. On September 3, 1939, the kingdom, as it was at that time, declared itself neutral. But on April 6, 1941, Bulgaria joined Germany and Italy in an attack on Yugoslavia, parts of which it annexed. In September of that year came a warning from Stalin's government that its unfriendly behavior had been noted. On November 25, as though opting for defiance, the Bulgarians joined the Rome-Berlin-Tokyo alliance, and on December 13 went further by declaring war on the United States. President Roosevelt must have trembled at the thought.

King Boris III of Bulgaria died suddenly on August 29, 1943, ushering in a troubled period. His son Simeon II was only six years old, and a Council of Regency took over. A year later, the Russian bear was at the door. On September 5, 1944, the Soviet Union declared war on Bulgaria, and three days later the Regency government asked for an armistice. Stalin had already approached his British and American allies, and armistice terms were ready. Bulgaria was in no position to argue. On September 18, Soviet forces marched through Sofia.

By then the government had resigned, and a Communist named Kimon Georgiev was premier, though few of his ministers were members of the Party. The new government formally capitulated on October 28, and the Soviet forces stayed on.

Over the next year, under Soviet sponsorship, the Communists spread their membership net, growing rapidly. The outcome was the Fatherland Front, a Communist-controlled coalition that took over after sweeping to victory in a general election. Over the next few weeks, with Soviet approval, the Communists launched a reign of terror in which some 15,000 people with links to the monarchical regime were killed, about one-tenth of them high-ranking figures.

On March 31, Georgiev formed a Communist-dominated government. The events that followed were predictable. On September 8, 1946, a referendum abolished the monarchy, a week later the young king was sent into exile, and on September 15 Bulgaria was proclaimed a People's Republic. A heavily rigged general election followed on October 27, predictably yielding a Communist majority.

Georgiev was a relatively minor figure who did as the Soviets told him. The stage was now set for the return to Bulgaria on November 21 of the veteran Communist leader, Georgi Dimitrov, who with so many others, from East and West, had spent the war years in Moscow. Indeed, he had taken refuge there in 1920 after serving two years in a Bulgarian jail (1915–1917) for revolutionary activities. He had ingratiated himself with the Bolshevik leaders and came home to do his share of revolutionary agitation. For his pains he was exiled, and turned up in Germany, where he burst into the world's headlines in 1933 when the Nazis arrested him, shortly after Hitler's advent to power, on a charge of having set fire to the Reichstag.

A controversy long raged over this dramatic incident. Was the fire started by the Nazis themselves, by the Communists (as the Nazis alleged), or by some dimwit arsonist for the sake of an inadequate ego? The distinguished American journalist and historian William L. Shirer concluded after much research that, although the full truth would never be known, "there is enough evidence to establish beyond a reasonable doubt that it was the Nazis who planned the arson and carried it out for their own political ends."

What were those ends? Clearly, the aim was to put the blame on the Communists, to give the Nazis a pretext to execute as many of them as possible. Shirer quotes Hitler's Number 2 man, Hermann Goering, as shouting at the new Gestapo chief, Rudolf Diels: "This is the beginning of the new Gestapo revolution! We must not wait a minute. We will show no mercy. Every Communist official must be shot, where he is found. Every Communist deputy must this very night be strung up."

As it happened, there was a dim arsonist as well, described by Shirer as a Dutch "feeble-minded pyromaniac" named Marinus van der Lubbe who, as luck would have it, happened to be a Communist and who entered the darkened building and started some small fires of his own. After a trial, he was beheaded.

The main catch, however, was Dimitrov who, with two of his fellow Bulgarian Communists, was arrested and brought to trial before the Supreme Court in Leipzig. Dimitrov acted as his own lawyer, kept his head (in both senses), and provoked Goering to fury. According to the verbatim court record, Goering screamed at Dimitrov, "Out with you, you scoundrel!"

As Dimitrov was led away, he said, calmly, "Are you afraid of my questions, Herr Ministerpräsident?"

Another scream of rage from Goering: "You wait until we get you outside this court, you scoundrel!"

All three of the Bulgarians were acquitted.[5]

This incident gave Dimitrov an international aura. He returned to Moscow, was granted Soviet citizenship, and was appointed general secretary of the Comintern, until its (fictitious) closure in 1943. At the end of World War II, he arrived in Bulgaria with the Red Army and became a ruthless dictaor. Stalin suspected him of Titoism and summoned him to Moscow, where he died in 1949, reportedly of diabetes.[6]

Poland: The Poignant Satellite

There is a special poignancy about the satellization of Poland. The war had begun there, and the country had been invaded by two totalist States: Nazi Germany and the Communist Soviet Union. Nearly 22,000 Polish prisoners had been massacred, and the fact that the Soviets had blamed the Nazis for this atrocious crime was no consolation to the Poles. Then there was the question of who should represent the Polish nation during the war and, on "liberation," who should form a government. In London, a government-in-exile, headed by Stanislaw Mikolajczyk, had been established, but under Stalin's aegis a group of Polish Communists, soon known as "the Lublin Committee," were being kept in reserve.

A tragic episode began in Warsaw in the summer of 1944. On July 31, a 400-mile German line between Riga in Latvia and Warsaw seemed on the point of breaking down before the Red Army. Seizing the moment, General Tadeo Bor-Komorowski, leader of the Polish Resistance, known as the Home Army, started an insurrection in Warsaw. He is believed to have hoped for support from the Soviets, but he had not counted on Stalin's imperial policy. On the dictator's orders, the Lublin Committee and the Red Army simply camped on the banks of the Vistula and left it to the Nazis to destroy Warsaw and with it, the Polish Home Army. At that time, General Wojciech Jaruzelski, who many years later would head a Communist government, is reported to have been in the USSR.

Despite Britain's commitment to Poland and British support for Mikolajczyk, Churchill's government deferred to Stalin's wishes and failed to provide support to the Home Army. By October 2, the Nazis had smashed the Resistance. On January 1, 1945, the Lublin Committee was reorganized into a provisional government, and on April 21 the Soviet Government and the Provisional Polish Government agreed on a twenty-year treaty of mutual assistance.

The British and their French allies had simply been bypassed by the Soviets. In June, however, they persuaded Moscow to agree to a tripartite commission, designed primarily to give a voice to the Mikolajczyk government-in-exile. By then, the Yalta conference had agreed to reduce Poland's eastern territories to the Curzon Line of 1919 (thus leaving the occupied area in Soviet hands) while the western border was extended to the Oder-Neisse Line (where two rivers of those names meet), at Germany's expense, pending a final settlement. On June 28, a government of national unity was agreed, under the Socialist Eduard Osubka-Morawski of the Lublin Committee.

The creation of a satellite regime proceeded in due course. On January 6, 1946, Osubka-Morawski announced the nationalization of all industries employing more than fifty workers. Over the ensuing months, Stanislaw Mikolajczyk, who had been given the post of deputy prime minister, was increasingly marginalized. On June 30, a Communist-organized referendum approved the government's program of nationalization and land reform and the Communist plan for a one-house parliament.

Predictably, rigged elections followed on January 19, 1947. Already, the Communists (known in Poland as the Polish Workers' Party or PZPR, *Polska Zjednoczona Partia Robotnicza*) dominated the scene with their Socialist allies. The governing bloc came out with 394 seats to a mere 28 for Mikolajczyk's Peasant Party. The United States and Britain complained that the Yalta provisions for honest elections had been violated. Bearing in mind the mass allegiance of the Polish people to the Church of Rome, a significant affront to the voters came on September 14, 1947, when the government denounced Poland's Concordat with the Vatican. In March 1950, Church lands would be confiscated.

By late October 1947, a relentless campaign against the Peasant Party bore fruit, and its leader, Mikolajczyk, fled to London on October 24. A purge of his party followed.

Full satellization came in stages over the next three years (1948–1950), marked by the fusion of the Peasant Party with the Communists and Socialists, to form a "United Workers' Party"; a five-year trade agreement with the Soviet Union, in compensation for Poland's predictable decision to follow Stalin's line and reject the American Marshall Plan for postwar recovery; the decision to join the Moscow-controlled Council for Mutual Economic Assistance (better known as "Comecon"); the denunciation of Poland's Treaty of Friendship with Tito's rebellious Yugoslavia; and the appointment of the Polish-born Soviet Marshal Konstantin Rokossovsky as defense minister and commander in chief of the Polish Army. On June 6, 1950, the Soviet Union formally recognized Poland's precarious western border with the East German Democratic Republic, defined by the Oder-Neisse Line, thus further enshrining the principle that satellite frontiers were decided in Moscow.

Not content with the almost total cooperation of the new regime with Moscow, Stalin ordered the arrest of Wladyslaw Gomulka, secretary-general of the Polish United Workers' Party, for "rightist-nationalist deviationism." He and others of the same alleged views were in custody for more than a year (September 1948 to November 1949). During his absence, the governing group was run by the prime minister, Boleslaw Bierut, and the president, Josef Cyrankiewicz.

The grand climax came on July 22, 1952, with the adoption of a new constitution proclaiming a People's Republic. Satellization was complete.

Romania in the Crossfire

As with other countries of Eastern Europe, Romania was caught in the crossfire of German and Soviet warfare, and of the conflicting (though in certain respects similar) ideologies of Fascism and Communism. The first signs of trouble came as early as September 21, 1939, when the pro-Fascist Iron Guard assassinated the premier, Armand Calinescu. The man who replaced him, General George Argeseanu, lasted only a week (from September 21 to 28), and two others came and went in quick succession.

Whither the kingdom of Romania?

With its oil wealth, Romania was a natural strategic target for Hitler. The Soviet Union was not short of oil, but had a long-term interest in denying Germany access to the Romanian wells. In May 1940, Hitler forced Romania into signing an oil and arms pact.

In return, the Romanians asked for a German military mission and guarantee for its frontiers. That request fell on deaf ears. Already, in June, Romania had been forced by a Soviet ultimatum to cede Bessarabia and northern Bukovina to the USSR. Indeed, it was Romania's misfortune that under the Secret Protocol to the Molotov-Ribbentrop Pact the respective spheres of influence of Germany and Russia cut Romania in two.

The Soviet ultimatum came on June 26, 1940, three days after Foreign Minister Vyacheslav Molotov had informed the German ambassador that the Soviet government intended to act on the secret clause, which the latter reported in these words: "The solution to the Bessarabian question brooked no further delay. The Soviet government was still striving for a peaceful solution, but it was determined to use force, should the Romanian government decline peaceful agreement. The Soviet claim extended likewise to Bukovina, which had a Ukrainian population."[7]

On June 1, 1940, not long after Hitler's Blitzkrieg in France, Romania had renounced the (admittedly worthless) Anglo-French guarantee of its territorial integrity. On September 6, King Carol II abdicated and fled the country, leaving the throne to his young son Michael. On November 23, Hitler forced Romania (along with Hungary and Slovakia) to join the tripartite pact between Germany, Italy, and Japan. The Iron Guard basked in this new alignment, and on November 27, it executed sixty-four of King Carol's former officials. Widespread rioting followed.

At that time, Hitler had other problems on his mind, and was still thinking in terms of invading Russia, but not until 1943. He therefore recommended to the Romanians that they should comply with Soviet demands. When the Soviet forces poured into Bessarabia, they indulged in their habitual pillaging and rape. Thousands were deported to the Soviet Union, and many more thousands fled into Romania across the newly imposed frontier.[8]

In October it was Germany's turn to invade Romania, and by February 1941, 680,000 German soldiers were in occupation. On December 7 came a meaningless gesture of compliance with the Nazi occupiers, when Romania declared war first on Great Britain, and five days later on the United States.

In the spring of 1944, the tide of war had changed, and King Michael sent an emissary in secret to Cairo to declare his country's readiness to discuss armistice terms with the Allies. On April 3, Molotov made the kind of statement that disarms potential resistance to forthcoming actions: "The Soviet government declares that it does not pursue the aim of acquiring any part of Romanian territory, or of changing in whatever manner the existing social order in Romania."[9] He returned to the theme on August 25 with an assurance that the Soviet Union had no intention of limiting Romania's independence.

Duly reassured by the first of Molotov's statements, King Michael announced his country's withdrawal from the war on August 23. During the years of Nazi occupation, Romania's premier had been General Ion Antonescu. To mark the change, the king had him arrested, and appointed a pro-Allied government. The Germans did not take this change of allegiance passively: for three days they bombarded Bucharest intensively.

On August 28, the first Soviet troops arrived in the mauled capital, and (as Jan Librach put it), "although greeted as friends, behaved in their usual fashion."[10]

Moscow then gave with one hand and took away with the other. For his service to the Allied cause, King Michael was awarded the Soviet Order of Victory. But the armistice convention, announced in Moscow on September 12, imposed crippling reparations on Romania and returned Bessarabia and Northern Bukovina to Soviet rule. Transylvania, however, was handed back to Romania.

There was worse to come. Like Albania, Bulgaria, and Poland, Romania had to be turned into a Soviet satellite. At that time, the local Communist Party was weaker than elsewhere, with no more than 1,000 members.

The process took three years. The Communists set up a National Democratic Front, which included the left-wing Ploughman's Front, led by Petru Groza. The pressure on the king was relentless, and on March 2, 1945, he called on Groza to form a government. The West exerted its weight as the British and Americans called for a more representative government. In semi-response, opposition parties were offered minor portfolios on January 7, 1947.

The Nazi collaborator, Antonescu, had been sentenced to death in May 1946, and on November 19, after systematic violence against the opposition, a general election gave the National Democratic Front a majority. The pressures continued to mount through 1947. In July, the leader of the National Peasant Party, Julius Maniu, was arrested, as were about 100 other opposition deputies, on charges of treason and espionage. He was sentenced to solitary confinement for life.

On July 28, the National Peasant Party was dissolved, and on December 30, King Michael learned the hard way that the Soviet Order of Victory was no protection for a pro-Western monarch: he was forced to abdicate.

In 1948, two events in particular marked the trend. On March 28, the People's Democratic Front (the revised name of the National Democratic Front) swept the board in fresh elections, with 91 percent of the vote. Petru Groza stayed on as prime minister. A fortnight later, a new constitution, on the Soviet model, was adopted.

As elsewhere, show trials were needed, and they came in abundance through 1949. Political opponents were purged, and so were alleged "deviationists" within the Communist Party. All Catholic bishops were arrested and their congregations "dissolved." Agriculture and industry were nationalized, and all offenses against the state, including minor ones, were made punishable by death.

An example of satellite obedience concerned Romania's relations with Yugoslavia. On December 19, 1947, the two countries had signed a Treaty of Friendship and Mutual Assistance. Barely two years later, on October 21, 1949, Romania denounced the treaty, ostensibly because Tito had been expelled from the Cominform. The unconditional obedience to Moscow's directives that characterized a satellite had been demonstrated.

CHAPTER NINE

THE CZECHOSLOVAK TRAGEDY

1939, 1948–1952

———⟫⦁⟪———

DURING WORLD WAR II, the Czechs and Slovaks suffered less
than the Poles in terms of the number of lives lost, but equally in
national humiliation from the successive violations of their sovereignty,
first by Hitler's Germany, and later by Stalin's Soviet Union. The large minority of ethnic Germans in the Sudeten region provided, by their very existence, a ready-made pretext for Hitler's threats and for the expansionism
which he called Germany's *Lebensraum.*

A Nazi campaign of denunciations began in September 1936, and
worsened a year later when the Czech police suppressed a meeting of the
Sudeten German Party at Teplitz. The Sudeten leader, Konrad Henlein,
demanded complete autonomy for the German minority. On February 20,
1938, Hitler made a speech promising protection for German minorities
outside the Reich. On March 13, Germany annexed Austria, and although the German government gave assurances to Prague of a desire to
improve German-Czech relations, the tension rose rapidly.

It peaked in September, culminating in the Munich conference on
September 29, when the British and French prime ministers, Neville
Chamberlain and Edouard Daladier, "appeased" Hitler, in effect giving
the Führer a free hand in Czechoslovakia. He responded by occupying
and dismembering the Czechoslovak state in March 1939.

World War II ended with the full retreat of the German forces from
Czechoslovakia on May 7, 1945, but not with full independence for the

Czechs and Slovaks. The president, Eduard Beneš, had taken refuge in London, where he established a provisional government. Unlike Mikolajczik of Poland, Beneš favored friendly relations with the Russians. Toward the end of 1943, Beneš had gone to Moscow, where he negotiated a Treaty of Friendship, Mutual Assistance, and Postwar Collaboration, signed on December 12. While in Moscow, Beneš also reached agreement with the exiled leader of the Czechoslovak Communist Party, Klement Gottwald, on the basic principles of a postwar state. These principles were incorporated into a document known as the "Kosice Program," which in effect was "a blueprint for the Sovietization of the country."[1]

On May 9, 1945 (two days after Germany's surrender), Soviet troops marched into Czechoslovakia. Zdenek Fierlinger, an unconditionally subservient Soviet stooge, was appointed prime minister. That same month, Beneš returned to Prague from his wartime exile, and a sweeping purge of pro-Nazi collaborators followed. The wartime Czech president, Emil Hacha, died in prison, and the Sudeten leader Konrad Henlein committed suicide. Two years later, on April 16, 1947, Josef Tiso, the collaborationist Slovak president, was executed.

On June 29, 1945, the Soviets exacted a price for having "liberated" Czechoslovakia, forcing President Beneš to cede Sub-Carpathian Ruthenia to the Soviet Union. With every passing day, Soviet power increased as more and more Czechs and Slovaks joined the Communist Party. Beneš's government launched a major program of industrial nationalization and agricultural reform. By the time general elections were held, on May 26, 1946, the Communists attracted 2.7 million votes out of 7.1 million cast, giving them 114 of the 300 seats in the new Constituent Assembly. Although this was considerably short of an absolute majority, they were the most numerous group in the assembly and would be supported by other left-wing groups, who commanded a further thirty-eight seats, yielding a joint majority of four over the right-wing groups. Beneš, who had been unanimously reelected president, had no option but to call on the Communist leader, Klement Gottwald, to form a government.

Born into a peasant family, Gottwald was an apprentice carpenter when he joined the Social Democratic Party in 1912. Its outlook was too mild for him, and in 1921 he became a founder-member of the Czech Communist Party. In 1930, aged thirty, he became its general secretary. Not surprisingly, he attacked the Munich capitulation in 1938 and, like many other Communist leaders, took refuge in Moscow, where he stayed until 1945.

July 1947 brought a clash of wills between Moscow and Washington and a decisive demonstration of the ultimate authority of the new Soviet superpower. On June 5, in a speech at Harvard University, General George Marshall, recently appointed U.S. secretary of state by President Harry Truman, had launched the European Recovery Program (ERP), better known as the Marshall Plan: a sweepingly generous program of American financial and economic assistance to the European countries that had been ruined or weakened by World War II. The original offer extended to the Eastern Bloc as well as Western Europe.

Considerable new evidence on the Soviet and Eastern Bloc reactions to the Marshall Plan became available after the collapse of the USSR at the end of 1991.* Stalin himself appears to have hesitated in his response to the plan, before turning decisively against it after critical advice from his ambassador in Washington, Nikolai V. Novikov; from a prominent economist, Academician Evguenii Varga; as well as from his foreign minister, Vyacheslav Molotov; and his right-hand man, Andrei Zhdanov.

The plan must of course be seen in the context of contemporary events. America had begun to demobilize immediately at the end of the war, whereas the Soviet Union maintained its wartime forces at full strength. By the end of 1946, the U.S. Army (including its Air Force) was down to 1.5 million men and the Navy to 700,000, from a wartime peak of 15 million for both services.[2]

The Soviet policy of satellizing the East European countries it had "liberated" from German occupation was already clear, and President Truman's policy of "containment," though passive in that it did not involve plans to free the countries under Soviet occupation, was at least a step in the right direction. The Truman Doctrine (warning the Soviet Union to drop plans to take over Greece and Turkey, see Chapter 7) and the Marshall Plan were both part of this "containment."

---

*This material was gathered by the Woodrow Wilson International Center for Scholars in Washington, D.C., and was issued in March 1994 as part of its "Cold War International History Project" in the form of two reports: by Scott D. Parish of the University of Texas at Austin, and Mikhail M. Narinsky of the Institute of Universal History, Moscow. The reports were published as "Working Paper No. 9." The account that follows is based largely on this material.—BC

America's West European Allies—Britain and France in particular—were in dire economic straits, and West Germany was devastated. In France and in Italy (the ex-junior partner in Hitler's Axis) mass Communist parties were making life difficult for democratic politicians and the parties they led. As Jan Librach put it, "The very principle of massive American assistance to Europe went against the grain of Soviet policy: Communism thrived on the economic depression in Western Europe, and American economic assistance to Eastern Europe was bound to revive the issues of political freedoms and national independence."[3]

A major conference in Paris to discuss the Marshall Plan was due to open on June 26, 1947. As late as June 22, Foreign Minister Molotov cabled the Soviet embassies in Poland, Czechoslovakia, and Yugoslavia to say that the Soviet government "thought it desirable" that they should participate. The Czechoslovak and Polish governments, in particular, expressed their enthusiasm to take part.[4]

However, two days later, in a cable to Moscow, Ambassador Novikov interpreted Marshall's Harvard speech as a tactic, "politically acceptable" to the West Europeans, to involve them in support of American policies directed against the Soviet Union. He went further by concluding that the Marshall Plan was the first stage of a coordinated plan to create an anti-Soviet alliance in Europe.

Despite this advice, Molotov did attend the Paris Conference, with a delegation numbering more than 100. Initially, Molotov and his delegation appeared to be accommodating. It soon clashed, however, with the British and French delegations, who had called for a multinational committee to examine and coordinate the aid requests of all European states. Molotov objected to this proposal on two grounds: that it would infringe the sovereignty of individual states, and that it would jeopardize German reparations to the USSR. His counterproposal was that all the individual aid requests should be sent, uncoordinated, to Washington. When his proposals went unsupported, he denounced the West's attitude and walked out of the conference with his delegation.

Despite the walk-out, on July 5 Molotov urged the Czechoslovak government to participate in the next Marshall Plan conference, not with the object of cooperating with the American plans, but to "demonstrate at the conference itself the unacceptability of the Anglo-French plan, prevent adoption of a unanimous decision, and then leave the conference, taking [with them] as many delegates of other countries as possible."[5]

Having digested and approved Molotov's initiative, Stalin summoned Klement Gottwald to Moscow. With Gottwald was a small delegation that included the non-Communist foreign minister, Jan Masaryk. Initially, Gottwald took the line that although Czechoslovakia had accepted the invitation to a further meeting in Paris, it had done so "with serious reservations." The government "was resolved to withdraw its delegation immediately if this should turn out to be necessary." This was not enough for Stalin, however. He argued that the Western Powers were "attempting to form a Western bloc and isolate the Soviet Union." If the Czechoslovak delegation went to Paris, Stalin went on, it "would show that you want to cooperate in an action aimed at isolating the Soviet Union." This would be a "break in the front" of the Slav states and "a success for the Western Great Powers."

Thereupon the Czechoslovak delegation decided not to attend the Paris meeting. In Warsaw, the Poles had the same change of mind. On July 9, the U.S. ambassador to Poland, Stanton Griffis, was twice summoned to meetings. The first was in the morning, with President Boleslaw Bierut, who told him that the Polish government had not yet made a final decision whether to attend the Paris conference. In the evening, he was summoned to the Foreign Ministry, where he was told that Poland would not, after all, attend. One of the arguments used by the Polish foreign minister, Modzelewski, was that the British, French, and Americans apparently placed a higher priority on rebuilding Germany than on helping Poland. In a cable to Washington, Griffis surmised that the change of plan was the result of Soviet pressure.

In both countries, the change of decision resulting from Soviet pressure marked a point of no return in the satellization process. In Czechoslovakia, over the next few months, the Communists relentlessly pursued their infiltration of government departments and the trade unions. The climax came in the four days between February 22 and 25, 1948. Under pressure, twelve non-Communist members of the Gottwald government resigned, as the Communists staged street demonstrations, culminating in a threat of a coup d'état that in fact was more than a mere threat. In a speech on February 24, Gottwald declared, "Today, more than ever, we are tightening the bonds which unite us to the Soviet Union. The destiny of our popular democracy, the very existence of the nation, and the liberty of our State are closely linked to our alliance with the Soviet Union."[6] The last few words were more than mere rhetoric. The Communists went on to conduct house searches and to make arbitrary arrests, while mobs occupied non-Communist newspaper offices and printing works. On February 25, Beneš, under duress, accepted the new Gottwald government, which excluded non-Communists. There was a sad sequel on March 10, when Foreign Minister Jan Masaryk fell to his death from a third floor window in the Foreign Ministry. Suicide or defenestration? Probably the latter, but either is an acceptable hypothesis. By then, Masaryk, who had worked hard to reconcile the irreconcilable views of democrats and Communists, was totally disillusioned.

On May 9, a new constitution was adopted by the Constituent Assembly, and on May 30, the Communist-controlled National Front's single list won all the seats in national elections. On June 7, President Beneš resigned on grounds of ill health: the truth, for he died three months later, on September 3. On September 14, he was succeeded by Klement Gottwald.

As in Poland, but in a different way, the Communist government took control over Roman Catholic affairs, forcing the clergy to swear an oath of loyalty to the state. The lower clergy mostly complied.

As in all other Communist regimes, new and old, a long series of political trials followed. Of these, by far the most sensational, distasteful, and revealing was the Slansky trial. Next to Klement Gottwald, Rudolf Slansky had become the most powerful figure in Czechoslovakia. Indeed, he was secretary general of the ruling party. He had paid, in full measure, the acts of obeisance to Stalin that were required of all satellite leaders. On the Soviet dictator's seventieth birthday in 1949, Slansky delivered the required eulogy before the CPCS Central Committee. The April 1951 issue of the Cominform journal carried a violent attack by Slansky on Western imperialism, which included praise for Stalin's "genius." Three months later, the party organ, *Rude Pravo,* heaped praises on Slansky, on the occasion of his award of the Czechoslovak Order of Socialism.

Perhaps the personality cult of Slansky had gone too far for Stalin's taste. After all, *he*—not some relatively insignificant satellite leader who owed his promotion to Stalin—was the "genius." Whatever the reason, on September 7, 1951, Slansky lost his job as secretary general, and was demoted to the relatively unimportant post of deputy premier. In his own party and country, praise continued to be heaped on him, but only until November 23 of that year, when Slansky was arrested by the security police. It took a year to bring him to trial, along with thirteen others. Slansky himself and ten of the others were of Jewish extraction. All were charged with trying to undermine Socialism, conspiracy against the state, espionage activities, trying to restore capitalism, and dragging the Republic into the imperialist camp.

The trial opened on November 20, 1952, and lasted a week. All fourteen defendants were sentenced to death, although three were reprieved and given life sentences. Slansky was not one of the lucky ones. He was executed with the other unlucky ones, and their collective ashes (according to Frantisek August and David Rees) were scattered on an icy road outside of Prague.[7]

One of the survivors was Eugen Loebl, who was later rehabilitated, in 1963. In his memoirs, he painted a gruesome picture of the physical and mental torture inflicted on the accused before the trial. For months on end, the accused were forced to rehearse approved answers for all the questions put to them. For the benefit of NKVD officials in attendance, everything said was simultaneously translated into Russian. All defendants were required to give the same answers, individually and as a group. Those who got it right were rewarded with better food. Before the actual trial, all the defendants were well fed, and they appeared in clean and well tailored clothes.[8]

The main beneficiary of Slansky's trial and execution was of course Gottwald, but it could easily have been the other way around. Appropriately, Gottwald's last public appearance was as a mourner at Stalin's funeral in Moscow in March 1953. He died on his return to Prague, perhaps unable to face life without the leader he had unconditionally obeyed.

CHAPTER TEN

HUNGARY'S
"SALAMI" REVOLUTION

———◆———

O F ALL THE East European satellites, Hungary was the only one that had already known a Communist regime, albeit briefly, under Béla Kun in 1919 (see Chapter 3). Was that why the satellization of Hungary took longer than elsewhere? This is, of course, an unanswerable question.

Was it because the German occupation of Hungary took place later than elsewhere, and was therefore shorter? That, too, is unanswerable, though not without interest.

German troops, though long on Hungary's border with Czechoslovakia, did not move in until March 22, 1944. During the previous war years, Hungarian governments had shown remarkable skill in appearing to back Nazi Germany while secretly seeking links with the Western Allies. The Molotov-Ribbentrop Pact of 1939 had placed Hungary in Germany's sphere of influence: an understandable situation in the light of the Austro-Hungarian commitment on the side of the Kaiser's armies in the Great War. Some months earlier (on February 24, 1939), Hungary had signed the anti-Comintern Pact, and would sign the Tripartite Pact (which stretched the Berlin-Rome Axis to Tokyo) on November 20, 1940.

Indeed the Hungarians went further, actually fighting against Russia (though without noticeable enthusiasm) and, on December 13, 1941, a few days after Pearl Harbor, declaring war on the United States and Britain. And yet, despite these gestures to appease the Nazis, the Hungarians allowed 50,000 Polish troops to cross their country to join the anti Nazi

Polish forces in the West, while giving asylum to many Jews escaping from Nazi persecution.[1]

As early as 1941 Hungarian as well as Polish representatives in London sounded out the British about their country's hopeful plans to join the Western Allies.[2] In 1943, the Hungarians raised the question of possible terms for an armistice with the British and Americans.

The crunch came later: on March 22, 1944, German troops occupied Hungary, and set up a puppet regime. Yet that same month a U.S. military mission was parachuted in. As Librach points out, "Because of a lack of appropriate political decisions on the part of the Western Allies, none of these efforts yielded tangible results." It is fair to add that they did have other preoccupations on their collective mind at that time. On October 1 of that year, a Hungarian delegation to Moscow signed a tentative armistice with the Soviet High Command.

For many years (since 1919, after the Béla Kun interlude) the dominant figure in Hungarian politics had been Admiral Nicholas Horthy. In February 1920, Horthy had been elected regent of Hungary by the National Assembly. Now, on October 15, 1944, he was removed to Germany for not consulting the Germans when he discussed terms for an armistice with America and Britain.* They replaced him with a Hungarian Nazi leader, Fezenc Szálasi, who immediately introduced a reign of terror. Hundreds of thousands of Hungarians were deported to Germany, many of them Jews destined for the death camps.

Despite all their efforts, the anti-Nazi Hungarians were unable to avoid the outcome they feared most: being caught in the crossfire of the belligerents on the Eastern front. In August 1944, Soviet and Romanian troops crossed the border, and in late December they laid siege on Budapest. The Germans did not abandon the capital until February 13, 1945, by which time much of it was in ruins. They did not move out of Hungary until April, when the Communist regime replaced the Nazi one.

As usual, the Soviet "liberators" had come well prepared politically. The 2d Hungarian Army had joined the Soviet forces, and on December 21, its leader, General Miklós, was made president of a provisional government

---

*Captured by the Allies in 1945, Admiral Horthy was soon released and retired to Portugal, where he died in 1957, at age eighty-nine.

at Debrecen. Other returnees included a group of Communists who had served in Béla Kun's short-lived regime.

Soon the "Bélaknists" had moved into key positions, in charge of the police, the transport system, and agricultural reform: under a decree of March 15, 1945, 3 million hectares of land were confiscated. Another reign of terror followed, with mass arrests and seizures of property. Although an armistice agreement had been signed on January 20 by the Allied Control Commission, the Russians simply ignored the British and American representatives who had been their co-signatories. For having, however unwillingly, fought on Hitler's side, the Hungarians were severely punished. Their country reverted to its 1920 frontiers and was landed with heavy reparations to the Soviet Union, Czechoslovakia, and Yugoslavia. They were allowed, however, to take revenge on the invaders, by expelling the German community of about 500,000.

Despite Soviet de facto control, postwar elections on November 4, 1945, brought the Communists only 17 percent of the votes. The Smallholders' Party came out with 57 percent, and in early February 1946 a Republic was proclaimed, with Zoltan Tildy, leader of the Smallholders, as president, and his colleague Ferenc Nagy as premier. Only one portfolio was allocated to the Communists, but it was the key one of the Interior, which gave them control of the police.

A year later, on February 10, 1947, a Hungarian Peace Treaty was signed in Paris, calling for a slight rectification of the frontier in favor of Czechoslovakia and the return of Transylvania to Romania. But the important happenings were on the home front. On February 25, Béla Kovécs, secretary general of the Smallholders' Party, was arrested on a trumped-up charge of plotting against the occupation forces, thus marking the start of a purge of that party's anti-Communist wing.

The next target was the premier, Nagy, who was accused of conspiracy and was forced to resign on May 31. He was replaced by another Smallholder, Lajos Dinnyes. Meanwhile, within the government and from the occupying power, pressure was mounting in favor of pro-Marxist legislation. On August 1, a three-year plan was announced, calling for nationalization of the banks and a planned economy. By the end of August, the Communists felt they were strong enough to risk another general election, which this time gave them the largest number of seats. In the new coalition, Dinnyes stayed on as premier. Five of the fifteen members of his cabinet were Communists.

On January 12, 1948, the Communists stepped up the pressure, forcing a merger of their party with the Social Democrats to form the United Workers' Party. On July 30, President Tildy was forced to step down, and was replaced by the Chairman of the new United Workers' Party, Arpéd Szakasits. The next target was Premier Dinnyes, who on December 9 was forced to resign by his own party, purged of its anti-Communists. His place was taken by a pro-Communist, Istvén Dobi. By then, however, the real power was wielded, in the background, by the Communist deputy premier, Métyés Rékosi, who would acquire a special notoriety for describing his party's methods as "salami" tactics: small groups in coalition parties to be "cut off in slices" one at a time.

As in Poland and Czechoslovakia, the Roman Catholic Church became a collective target. Cardinal Josef Mindszenty refused to bow to Communist pressure to make concessions to the government. He was jailed along with other Church dignitaries.

Meanwhile, the "salami" tactics went on. On May 15, 1949, a general election with open balloting gave complete victory to the now Communist-controlled National Independence Front. Next came a purge of *Communists*—doubtless inspired by Stalin's lengthy practice in this field. One of the many Party members arrested for allegedly deviating from the pro-Soviet line was the Communist foreign minister, Laszlo Rajk, soon executed for treason and Titoism.

The time had come for a new constitution, which was proclaimed on August 7. Not unexpectedly, it was closely based on the misleadingly "democratic" Soviet Constitution of 1936, specifically designed to please fellow-travelers. At the end of the year, all major industries were nationalized, and a five-year plan was launched, again on the Soviet model.

By then, satellization had been formally accomplished, but a small omission remained to be rectified. In a new purge in May and June 1950, all remaining ex-Socialists, among them Arpéd Székasits, were dismissed from the government. Satellization was complete.

CHAPTER ELEVEN

STALIN'S GERMAN PLOY

1944–1949

———

O F ALL STALIN'S spoils of victory, the seizure of East Germany was by far the most threatening to his erstwhile allies in the West. Not one of the other countries occupied by his forces and kept under Soviet control was, or had been, a Great Power. In Germany, the defeated Great Power, the Soviet and three Western occupation forces confronted each other, leading in 1948 to a major military crisis and later, in 1961, to the building of the Berlin Wall to halt the mass exodus of East Germans to West Germany.

Such was the speed of the American and British advances from West to East that it would have been militarily possible for the Western forces to reach Berlin before the Red Army. However, it had been agreed at the Yalta conference that the symbolically important final assault on the German capital should be left to the Soviets. Under the Protocol of September 12, 1944, the Soviet occupation zone extended to the Elbe and southward to the Bavarian border.

Stalin played his victory cards with cunning skill. As late as December 10, 1944, he had received France's wartime leader, General Charles de Gaulle, in Moscow, where the two men had signed a Treaty of Alliance and Mutual Assistance. As Librach rightly remarks, this did not prevent the Soviet dictator, when the Big Three (minus France) met at Yalta in 1945, from belittling the French role. "France," he said (correctly), "opened the gates to the enemy . . . [and] had not done much fighting in the war."[1] This enabled him to strike a generous pose at Yalta, by agreeing, however grudgingly, that the French should be allocated an occupation zone in Germany (to be carved out of the U.S. and British, but not the Soviet, zones).

Stalin also agreed to French participation in the Allied Council for Germany. Jan Librach goes on to make a valid point, the full significance of which was certainly not known to him (or to others) at the time. Referring to the Russians' success "in creating an aura of friendly collaboration," he added, "It was best illustrated by Hopkins' note to Roosevelt during the final meeting at Yalta: 'Mr President, the Russians have given in so much at this conference that I don't think we should let them down.'"*

Later, when Harry Truman assumed the presidency after Roosevelt's death, Stalin became increasingly intransigent and demanding. As Librach puts it,

> The reasonable explanation [of Stalin's behavior]—that the Soviet government wanted to grab as much of Europe as it could without an open clash with England and the United States—was generally rejected as too simple.
>
> In this situation of uncertainty, President Truman decided to send Harry Hopkins to Moscow once more, a suggestion immediately accepted by Stalin.[2]

To this, a fair comment in the light of later revelations about Harry Hopkins's double role, might be, How else would Stalin react?

THE METHODS USED to incorporate East Germany into the Soviet Empire were similar to those used elsewhere in Eastern Europe, but with one important addition: the recruitment of ex-Nazis into the new police force. The other "tools" of the job were the same: a military presence; building up a party unconditionally obedient to Moscow's will; gradually reducing

---

*The reference is of course to Harry Hopkins, Roosevelt's special envoy to Moscow (Librach, *The Rise of the Soviet Empire,* p. 126). It was learned in the 1990s that Hopkins was an agent of the NKVD (later the KGB), though unpaid. It is important to understand that he had been recruited as an "agent of influence" rather than as a spy, although he is known to have reported to Stalin on White House discussions as well. See Brian Crozier, *Free Agent* (New York and London: HarperCollins, 1993), p. 11, n. 4. In 1996, Hopkins's role was confirmed in the "Venona Documents" (consisting of wartime cable intercepts) released by the U.S. National Security Agency (NSA).

the influence of any competing parties; show trials and purges; and a new constitution on the Soviet model—in two words, state terror—enforced initially by the Soviet presence, and later by the ruling party.

As the British historian David Pryce-Jones puts it, "Forcible conversion from Nazi enemy into Communist satellite made East Germany a special case."[3] This was not the first example of the essential compatibility of two totalist systems commonly held to be antithetical: the Nazi version of Fascism and the Soviet version of Communism.* Hitler himself would declare, in 1934, "I have always . . . given orders that former Communists are to be admitted to the Party at once."[4] And in fact more than half of the 50,000 Brownshirts recruited in 1933—the year of Hitler's advent to power—were former Communists.[5]

And now, in 1945, Stalin was in effect returning the compliment. However, the fact that the Soviet-controlled regime was recruiting Nazis did not mean that it was not executing many of them, just as vast numbers of Communists were executed in Stalin's purges and in the new terror that came with satellization all over Eastern Europe.

Like Communist leaders from Western Europe and other East European countries, Germany's leading Communists had sought refuge in the Soviet Union during the war, and were brought back, thoroughly indoctrinated, when the Red Army "liberated" their part of the Fatherland. The most important of the German party bosses were the secretary-general, Walter Ulbricht, and the future head of the East German *Staatssicherheitsdienst* (State Security Service, better known as the STASI), Erich Mielke.

When the Red Army moved into Berlin, they took over an immense heap of rubble, largely caused by the British and American bombing. None of the essential services was working: gas, electricity, or water. The underground tunnels were flooded, and there was no public transport system. The population had dropped from 4.4 million to 3 million.[6]

It could be argued that the occupying force itself had created the need for an efficient police, regardless of the ideological and political roles allocated to it. As Kurt L. Shell put it, "The Soviet troops took the city of Berlin, and for two months ruled as its sole masters. This two months'

---

*This summary description is derived from the Woodrow Wilson International Center for Scholars, Washington, D.C.: "Cold War International History Project," Paper 10, by Norman M. Naimark of Stanford University, issued in August 1994.

period of exclusive Soviet rule had far-reaching consequences: most important, the Soviets alienated a large part of the city's population by the wave of indiscriminate looting and raping and created a lasting identification . . . of 'Russian' with 'barbaric.'"[7]

In those early months of brutal chaos, the only policing was done by remnants of the former police force, over which the only political control appears to have been exercised by members or former members of the Social Democratic Party (*Sozialdemokratische Partei Deutschlands,* or SPD). There was much extortion and corruption, and clashes with armed bandits, some of them Germans, others Red Army deserters.

During the period from May 1946 to the end of the year, the German Communist Party took over and absorbed the SPD under the new name of "Socialist Unity Party" or SED *(Sozialistische Einheitspartei Deutschlands)* with Ulbricht as its leader. On June 30, 1946, a semi-secret German Administration of the Interior (*Deutsche Verwaltung des Innern,* or DVdI) was set up under Erich Reschke, a Communist who had been jailed by the Nazis. Reschke reported directly to the Soviet Military Administration in Germany, known as the SVAG from its Russian title *(Sovetskaia Voennaia Administratsija v Germanii).* In day-to-day matters, however, Reschke appears to have been under the authority of Erich Mielke, who in turn was responsible to the SVAG.

In Saxony, in the summer of 1945, an East German equivalent of the KGB internal security organ was set up: the fifth department of the Criminal Police *(Kripo).* Known thereafter as K-5, the new department would keep tabs initially on all police officers, and eventually provide surveillance of all officials in the judicial department. Eventually, K-5 came under the authority of DVdI, compiling a central information file with detailed biographical notes on all Interior Ministry employees from the whole of the Soviet occupation zone. Dossiers were systematically passed on to the Soviet Ministry of State Security (MGB, from the Russian *Ministerstvo Gosudarstvennoy Bezopasnosti*) and the Soviet Internal Affairs Ministry (MVD from *Ministerstvo Vnutrennikh Del*).

In August 1947, the Soviet occupation authorities issued Order No. 201 on de-Nazification, which made K-5 responsible for eliminating all former Nazis from the state administration and leadership in society and the economy. Simultaneously, K-5 was instructed to recruit new cadres in large numbers from the East German "working class." In effect, Order No. 201 fully politicized the police.

Under an organizational chart issued on January 8, 1948, K-5's authority was itemized under five headings: (1) violations of SVAG orders, (2) violations of Control Council orders, (3) sabotage of reconstruction, (4) "anti-democratic" (that is, anti-Communist) activities, and (5) technical (meaning surveillance methods, data collection, and postal interference).

As in all Communist regimes, control of information played a central role in the ripening East German state. At a conference of ministers of the Interior, Ulbricht proposed the creation of an information service within the DVdI, to be supervised by Mielke. By then, Mielke controlled K-5 and several other police branches. After receiving Soviet approval, Mielke launched a new Department for Intelligence and Information on November 11, 1948. The new department was soon charged with Soviet-style disinformation as well as maintaining a state monopoly in the selection and dissemination of information. The mandate of the new department extended to the collection of information on any activity by individuals or groups working against "democratic developments," in other words, Communist policies at any time. In an effort to differentiate such activities from the role of similar state organizations in Hitler's time, Mielke insisted that reporting on other people's activities was simply "anti-Fascist vigilance."

By the summer of 1948, Soviet political control over the German occupation zone was total. Between December 1 and 14, the East German Communist leaders—Walter Ulbricht, Wilhelm Pieck, Otto Grotewohl, and Fred Ölssner—went to Moscow, where they reported directly to Stalin about the successes of their multiple police force. They maintained that they were about to purge the criminal police and improve its "ideological quality." To this end, K-5 would be dissolved and replaced by a Chief Directorate for the Defense of the Economy and the Democratic Order, within the DVdI. In fact, as Professor Norman Naimark reports, K-5 continued to exist as an instrument to control personnel issues throughout the East German government. Both K-5 and the Chief Directorate remained under Mielke's personal supervision.

By the middle of 1949, Stalin evidently felt that the control apparatus in East Germany now met his exacting requirements. The outcome, on

October 7, was the foundation of the German Democratic Republic or DDR *(Deutsche Demokratische Republik)*. Satellization was complete.

On the constitutional side, elections for a People's Congress had been held throughout the DDR on May 16, 1948. Despite official pressure, they had yielded only 66.1 percent support for the single list of Communist-approved candidates: a high percentage by Western standards, but not nearly close to the over 95 percent expected in Communist countries. It was enough, however, for the congress to adopt the Communist-drafted Constitution of the DDR without a further poll. The president was Wilhelm Pieck, and the post of prime minister (minister president) went to Otto Grotewohl.

CHAPTER TWELVE

THE FIRST INDOCHINA WAR

1946–1954

———⟶◦⟵———

S TARTING IN LATE 1946, Ho Chi Minh became a leading figure in the expansion of Communism under Moscow's ultimate control. He spent his early career as a Moscow-trained Comintern agent (see Chapter 4). The French military defeat—in France by the Germans, and in Indochina by the Japanese—gave him the opportunity he had been waiting for to set up a Communist state independent of France.

The postwar situation in Indochina, however, was far from straight-forward. No fewer than six nations were involved, half of them Far Eastern and the other half Western: Japan, China, and Vietnam; and France, Britain, and the United States.[1]

The Japanese, heading for defeat in the Pacific, presented an ultimatum—to hand over power unconditionally or face a military takeover—to the collaborationist French government in Vichy on March 9, 1945. By then, Vichy had lost its authority, and within twenty-four hours the Japanese overwhelmed all French garrisons in the peninsula; that is, in Tonking, Annam, and Cochinchina; in Laos; and in Cambodia. On the day of the ultimatum, they arrested the hereditary emperor of Annam, Bao Dai, and ordered him to proclaim the independence of Vietnam and form a govern-ment. Their idea, of course, was a puppet government, but Bao Dai wanted *real* independence. To this end, on August 18, he appealed to French General Charles de Gaulle, who (doubtless with other things on his mind) ignored his approach.

By then, Ho had already set up a provisional government of his own, and on August 7 (the day after the U.S. Air Force had dropped an atom bomb on Hiroshima) he had launched a Vietnamese People's Liberation Committee, with himself as chairman. Never one to neglect whatever opportunities presented themselves, Ho saw the potential utility of Bao Dai in that, as the hereditary emperor, he carried the "Mandate of Heaven" in the eyes of his people. He persuaded Bao Dai to abdicate, hand over the Imperial Seals, and join his committee as Ho Chi Minh's Supreme Adviser. The committee, having served its purpose, was dissolved on August 28, and this time Ho set up a new provisional government, with key posts in Communist hands.

As always with Ho Chi Minh, he combined Nationalist aspirations with Communist methods. On September 2, he proclaimed the independence of Vietnam. The supporting document he issued invoked both France's revolutionary Declaration of the Rights of Man and America's Declaration of Independence. There was no mention of the Communist Manifesto.

As if to complicate the situation, Chiang Kai-shek's Kuomintang forces started occupying Indochina north of the 16th parallel, as provided by the Potsdam conference, from which France had been excluded. China had ruled Vietnam for about 1,000 years (from 111 B.C. to A.D. 939), and went on to try again, not always successfully, to impose its domination on the Vietnamese. Thus, Vietnamese ancestral memories were stirred—a situation in line with Ho's ambition for independence and therefore suiting him well.

The French, however, were determined not to be bypassed. A young Resistance leader, Jean Sainteny, had spent time in Kunming, China, heading a French intelligence network known as M5, and had been given a new mission: to regroup French forces scattered in the Tonking region on the Chinese border. Unexpectedly, he found himself up against multiple resistance: not only from the Vietnamese, but also from the Chinese and from the Americans. By then, President Roosevelt was dead, but his anti-colonial policies were continued under Harry Truman. The local consequence, along the Sino-Vietnamese border, was a secret war between France's M5 and America's Office of Strategic Services or OSS, the precursor of the CIA. The policy entrusted to the OSS was to prevent the French from reasserting their colonial authority, and to this end the

Americans were in close touch with the Vietminh (Ho Chi Minh's League for the Independence of Vietnam, created in 1941)—in other words, with Ho Chi Minh.

Despite this attitude of resistance, Sainteny used his considerable charm to persuade the Americans to fly him and four companions to Hanoi in a U.S. Dakota. With them was the regional chief of the OSS, named Major Archimedes L. Patti. In Hanoi, Sainteny and his friends lost no time, and immediately took possession of the French governor-general's palace. By that time, the Vietminh's commander, Vo Nguyen Giap, already had 10,000 trained men, who had gained experience by fighting the Japanese, under arms.

On August 27, the day before announcing his second provisional government, Ho sent Giap, with a Vietminh delegation, to confer with Sainteny. Not to be outdone, the American Patti persuaded the Vietminh to stand firm against French proposals, with an assurance of full American support. (In later years, the United States would have plenty of time and opportunities to regret this early encouragement of Ho Chi Minh's Vietminh, but in all fairness it has to be said that Ho's strong Nationalist stance, without a spoken word [at that time] in favor of Communism, must have been convincing. This indeed was the object of his exercise.)

Enter the last complicating factor: the British. Under the Potsdam agreements, British forces were to occupy southern Indochina, and in the first week of September, a mixed British-Indian contingent landed in Saigon, under Major-General Douglas Gracey. The British, in contrast to the Chinese and Americans, had no desire to keep the French out of their Far Eastern colony. Indeed, a French force under General Philippe Leclerc was due, but did not start arriving until October 3.

By then, the situation was more confused than ever. Gracey freed French prisoners of war who had been seized by the Japanese and gave them arms. The Vietminh reacted with a taste of what was to come, massacring French civilians and emerging as a group of guerrilla bands. Thereupon, the French set about reconquering "their" territory from South Vietnam northward. The very thought of giving independence to the peoples of Indochina was far from the minds of the returning colonial authorities and of de Gaulle and his government.

In these unpromising circumstances, Sainteny held prolonged negotiations with Ho Chi Minh, with whom he had established cordial relations.

These were followed by even more protracted negotiations between Ho and the French authorities, held mainly at Fontainebleau, near Paris, from June to September 1946. Ho had stuck to his demands for unity (of the three provinces of Vietnam) and full independence. Neither was offered by the French, and Ho went back to Vietnam (by sea) empty-handed apart from a worthless *modus vivendi* agreement.[2]

By prolonging his negotiations with the French, and being absent for four months, Ho Chi Minh had risked his leadership as well as his reputation. Giap had indeed taken advantage of Ho's long absence to stir up as much anti-French sentiment as he could. By the time Ho returned to Tonking, Giap had built up his military force from 10,000 to 60,000 men, although there was a shortage of weapons, especially of rifles. He was almost ready to take on the French colonialists. However, it was the French who started the war, on November 23, with a naval bombardment of the Tonkingese port of Haiphong that left 6,000 dead.

Ready or not, Giap felt the time had come to hit back, and on December 19, 1946, under his command, the Vietminh launched an all-out offensive against the French in Tonking. This first attempt ended in failure, however, and the French pursued the Vietminh forces northward, where they took refuge in the hills along the China border. During the next three years, little happened, but in November 1949, when Mao Tsetung's Chinese People's Liberation Army reached the Tonking border, the strategic situation changed dramatically, in the Vietminh's favor and in the Soviet imperial context. Logistically, this meant that Soviet weaponry, ultimately in decisive quantities, could now be delivered to the Vietminh. International Communist needs outweighed the long history of mutual antagonism between Vietnamese and Chinese, and henceforth the Vietminh enjoyed an ever-ready sanctuary across the border.

At this point, the international political context must intrude. On March 8, 1949, the French recognized the independence of Vietnam under the former Emperor Bao Dai as chief of state. The "independence" they granted, however, was less than complete, as the weight of French officialdom remained heavy and while France reserved the right to maintain military bases in the country. Less than a year later, in January and February 1950, both the Soviet Union and the newly triumphant Communist regime in China recognized Ho Chi Minh's government as the legitimate authority in Vietnam; almost simultaneously, the United States and Great Britain recognized Vietnam, Laos, and Cambodia as associated states within the French Union: a significantly realistic assessment of the limited "independence" conferred by the French colonial power.

THE WAR GIAP waged was both military and revolutionary. It was mainly military in the north, whereas in Cochinchina, in South Vietnam, terrorism was the Communist weapon, used to subjugate the peasants in the villages and unnerve the French in the towns and especially in the southern capital, Saigon. On the Vietminh side, the theoretician of revolutionary war was not Giap but his Party colleague Truong Chinh.

After the failure of his initial offensive, Giap's surviving soldiers licked their wounds, while he planned his next move. His planning was protracted: he did not strike again until October 1, 1950, nearly a year after the arrival of the Chinese forces. The long delay lulled the French into complacency. At this stage, they were still Maginot-minded, even though the original Maginot Line that was to protect them from a German invasion had simply been bypassed when the Germans attacked through France's unfortified northern neighbor, Belgium. In Vietnam, their substitute for the Maginot Line was a string of French-held fortresses along the China border: Lao Kay, Ha Giang, Cao Bang, Lang Son, and Mon Cay.

By October 17—just over a fortnight later—all five of the forts were in Vietminh hands. Giap's rubber-soled infantry had cut off the French garrisons by infiltrating into the 100-mile wide strip of jungle to the south. Giap could chalk up a major victory, with 6,000 French dead to match the dead in Haiphong, and enough captured arms to equip a whole division.

Evidence from documents captured by the French and from Giap's published works indicate that Giap's spectacular victory had worried him. How could it have been so sudden and so complete? Could it turn out to be a strategic error? There was much heated debate on this issue within the Vietminh High Command. In the end, however, in the light of reported sagging morale in France and of the ease with which the French had been dislodged from their strongpoints, Giap decided that the time had come to push them back into the Gulf of Tonking.

The date he chose was January 13, 1951, by which time he had eighty-one fully equipped battalions under arms and highly trained. He soon found out, however, that he had miscalculated the odds. By now, he was up against a French military leader who matched him in strategic ability. During World War II, General Jean de Lattre de Tassigny had led the First French Army from Provence in the south of France to the Rhine, then eastward to the Danube. A flamboyant and dynamic personality, he had arrived in Vietnam in mid-December 1950 as supreme commander of the French forces. His men called him *le Roi Jean,* and such was his charisma that in no time the dejected forces were galvanized into faith in victory under his leadership.

Not for him the "opt out" of delegation: he took personal command, and his defending forces clashed with Giap's at Vinh Yen, a mere thirty miles northwest of Hanoi, the capital of Tonking. Giap's human wave tactics were countered by de Lattre's high explosives and napalm. That fateful figure of 6,000 came up again: 6,000 Vietminh dead, and 500 taken prisoner, in contrast to only 700 French killed.[3]

The war then took a turn that the French could not have foreseen. To follow up on his Vinh Yen victory, General de Lattre decided to take back Hoa Binh, a strongpoint thirty miles southwest of Hanoi, thus cutting the Vietminh's north–south supply line. He captured it easily enough, in November 1951, but the French garrison found itself surrounded by Vietminh troops and under permanent attack. At this point, fate dealt a literally mortal blow to the French side. De Lattre fell seriously ill with cancer and was flown back to France, where he died in January 1952, at age sixty.

The French commander in Tonking, General de Linarès, was of the defensive mold. He pulled out of Hoa Binh and retreated without serious losses, boasting later that this had been "a maneuver of perfect military orthodoxy." But he also said of General Giap: "I wish I had him on my side."[4]

It is of course impossible to know how the war would have progressed if de Lattre had lived on, although it is safe to say that in the long run it was not a war the French could win, with France's reservoir of fighting men 8,000 miles away and against an enemy determined to win back its own country. It is fair to add that the death of de Lattre shortened a struggle that nevertheless had lasted more than eight years.

De Linarès's successor, General Raoul Salan, was a colorless defeatist, better known in later years for his part in a failed attempted coup against General de Gaulle. Up north, some able French officers, still inspired by the late de Lattre's example, tried hard to lure the Vietminh into another defeat that might match Vinh Yen. Time and again, they thought they had surrounded Vietminh units, only to find a void at the center of their iron circle as it closed.

This further stalemate went on until May 1953, when a new supreme commander arrived. General Henri Navarre seemed an odd choice for this crucial posting. He had made his career in military intelligence, and his personality was bland and diffident where de Lattre's had been flamboyant and inspirational. His only previous connection with Indochina was the surveillance of Ho Chi Minh, which he had organized during the Fontainebleau negotiations.

The situation Navarre found was less than encouraging. He had more than 100,000 French Union troops (including Foreign Legion men, Algerians, and other French-ruled Africans). Yet the Vietminh controlled 5,000 of the 7,000 villages in the Red River Delta, Tonking's ricebowl. He came out with the "Navarre plan": to seek American aid and build up his forces in numbers, but especially in firing power. He would then fight the elusive enemy to a standstill and a negotiated truce, on the Korean model.

The Vietminh, meanwhile, had not stood idly by. Their regular army had invaded Laos, the smallest and least developed country of French Indochina. Reaching the outskirts of the Laotian royal capital, Luang Prabang (the administrative capital was Vientiane), they had withdrawn but left their pro-Communist nominee, Prince Souphannouvong, in charge of the two northernmost Laotian provinces. "The Red Prince," as he was known, now headed a rudimentary administration known as the Pathet Lao (Lao state) and claiming to be the only legitimate government of Laos. In distant France, it was decided that, whatever the cost, Laos must be defended.

This strange situation seems to have dominated Navarre's thinking when he decided on a showdown with the Vietminh at Dien Bien Phu, a potential strongpoint in Tonking only a few miles from the Laotian border. There, he decided, he would build up a powerful garrison to draw enemy fire. The French Union garrison was just that: one-third Vietnamese, one-quarter Foreign Legionaries (many of them Germans), 20 percent Africans, mostly from Morocco, and a mere 22 percent metropolitan Frenchmen. The garrison moved in on November 20, 1953.

Ironically for a man who had made his career in military intelligence, the reports reaching him turned out to be catastrophically inaccurate. His briefing officers told him that the Vietminh lacked heavy guns and would be unable to maintain more than two divisions and 20,000 coolies in the area. The reality was less encouraging. For months on end, while the French Union forces were strengthening the Dien Bien Phu garrison, some 80,000 coolies were wheeling bicycles laden with food and arms through the jungle. When the battle began, at a time chosen by Giap, the Vietminh had four well-supplied divisions in battle order.

Moreover, Dien Bien Phu was painfully isolated and vulnerable. Hanoi was 200 miles away, and the French Union garrison could only be fed and supplied by air. Surrounded by hills, it was wide open to artillery fire. On one point, military intelligence had only partially misled General Navarre. They had told him to expect a fresh Vietminh attack in Laos, and it came, but turned out to be a planned diversion. By January 1954, Giap's buildup was menacing, and Navarre was said to be losing his earlier confidence. In March, the Vietminh onslaught began in earnest, and the heroism and later the agony of the mixed garrison made headlines the world over.

When the assault began, the French appealed to the United States for help, but on March 24, President Eisenhower responded with a self-contradictory statement. On the one hand, he declared that the defeat of Communist aggression in Indochina and elsewhere in Southeast Asia was of crucial importance to the United States. On the other hand, he declined to use the American Air Force to relieve the besieged garrison in Dien Bien Phu.

Contrary to Navarre's intelligence, the weapons reaching the Vietminh from China included heavy guns that fired to deadly effect. On the night of May 6, 1954, the last human wave of the besiegers stormed Dien Bien Phu, bringing the First Indochina War to its military end.

Despite their defeat at Dien Bien Phu, the French could have fought on, but the government and the French people had lost the will to do so. In the true sense, this had been a war of attrition, lost as much through press and radio coverage in France as through the speeches in the French National Assembly.

Truong Chinh, the theoretician of the Vietminh, played an important part in the conflict. Like Ho Chi Minh, Lenin, and Stalin, he had changed his name, which was originally Dang Xuan Khu. His choice of *nom de guerre* was significant, for Truong Chinh means "long march" and was a complimentary gesture to Mao Tse-tung, whose Long March with his guerrillas, through 12,000 kilometers from southwest to northwest China, had lasted a year, from October 1934 to October 1935. Unlike many of his compatriots, Truong Chinh never wavered in his advocacy of friendship between the Chinese and the Vietnamese (known in popular history as the Greater and the Lesser Dragons).

Two short works by Truong Chinh made him in effect the doctrinal guru of the Vietminh: *The August Revolution* (1945–1946) and *The Resistance Will Win* (1947). He stressed the primacy of politics over tactics in revolutionary war. In fact, revolutionary war is a struggle for the minds and bodies (rather than the hearts and minds, as Western commentators have tended to stress) of the people. The guerrillas were also terrorists. They terrorized the villagers into feeding them and harboring them. Village headmen were "executed" as an example to others, who were forced to join the guerrillas. Once they had joined, they were outlaws, subject to official reprisals unless they stayed under Vietminh protection.

The lessons of the First Indochina War applied equally to the second (which will be discussed in Chapter 25). The losing enemies, whether French or American, were "foreign imperialists." The Vietminh were Vietnamese patriots, while the many Vietnamese who held a rapidly diminishing power in the cities, especially Saigon and Hanoi, were presented as traitors and collaborators. This simplified image gained credibility from the fact that the combined logistical help of the Russians and Chinese, which had made the Communist victory possible, had not played a visible role in the actual fighting.

With Truong Chinh as the ideological and political guide, Vo Nguyen Giap was the strategic guide as well as the military commander. He elaborated his theory of victorious war in his *La Guerre de Libération et l'Armée populaire* (1950) and in a later collection of essays, *Guerre du Peuple, Armée du Peuple* (1961). He envisaged certain conditions for victory: The People's Army would have to establish absolute moral superiority in its own eyes and those of the people; it must have improved its supplies and material resources; and the international situation must be favorable (that is, help from China and Russia).

In the first Indochina war, Giap had committed one serious error: he "jumped the gun" by launching a "final offensive" in 1951 before conditions were ripe. He made up for this error later.

THE FULL SIGNIFICANCE of the Communist victory in Indochina became clear only during the final phase of the Geneva Conference of 1954. The leader of the French Radical-Socialist Party, Pierre Mendès-France, had come to power in Paris, having pledged to end the war within a month or resign. He lived up to his pledge with, it is said, some help from the fact that the clocks in Geneva's Palais des Nations had been obligingly stopped at midnight on July 20. The core of the peace terms was that Vietnam was to be partitioned along the 17th parallel, into two roughly equal halves, Communist to the north, Nationalist to the south.

This agreement, essentially between Mendès-France and the Soviet foreign minister, Vyacheslav Molotov, came as a bitter disappointment to the Vietminh delegation, and especially to Ho Chi Minh in North Vietnam. Although the Vietnamese Communists had never been led to believe that they would gain control over the whole of the country, they had hoped that the dividing line would be considerably further south, along the *13th* parallel, which would have handed them two-thirds of Vietnam instead of half.

At the core of the Franco-Soviet agreement was a completely extraneous problem: the project for a European Defense Community (EDC)—in essence, a Franco-German military pact—which was to be debated in the French National Assembly in August. Until Mendès-France arrived in Geneva, the French delegation had been headed by the foreign minister in the outgoing government, Georges Bidault, who had flatly refused even to discuss the EDC question with Molotov. Mendès-France had no such reservations. Contrary to what some of his enemies said later, he was by no means pro-Communist. However, as a Jew, he could not bear the thought of French and German soldiers serving and fighting side by side, as would have happened had the EDC project been adopted. After all, the conference was taking place less than a decade after World War II, and Hitler's massacre of the Jews weighed heavily on his mind.

He was therefore ready to use the EDC as a bargaining counter, which persuaded Molotov to give the Soviet Union's Vietnamese satellite less than they had hoped for. When the EDC question was debated in the French Assembly on August 30, Mendès-France let it be known that he would ignore the Communist votes. He simply allowed the proposed treaty to be thrown out on a point of procedure. His pro-European political opponents never forgave him, and voted him out of office six months later.[5]

As a result of the Franco-Soviet bargain, the ex-Comintern agent, Ho Chi Minh, now presided over a half-country that was part of the Soviet Union's peripheral empire.

CHAPTER THIRTEEN

OTHER ASIAN VENTURES

1947–1954

———

THE FIRST INDOCHINA War was by no means the only attempt to extend the Soviet Empire in Southeast Asia. There were four other insurrections in the area: in the Philippines, Burma, Malaya, and Indonesia. All of them arose from Andrei Zhdanov's directive, at the 1947 inaugural meeting of the Cominform, to expel colonial oppressors. All of them failed eventually, possibly because simultaneous uprisings would not have started spontaneously in the absence of a Soviet directive. In contrast, the Indochina War, although undoubtedly approved by Stalin, was a true Nationalist insurrection launched by a leader—Ho Chi Minh—who happened to have joined the world Communist movement at a time when no other path toward independence could be discerned.

The Zhdanov directive was translated into concrete policy at a major conference in Calcutta that took place from February 19 to 28, 1948, convened by two of the postwar Leninist fronts: the World Federation of Democratic Youth (WFDY) and the International Union of Students (IUS). There were 900 delegates from various Communist parties or organizations, plus an uncounted number of "observers." Messages of greetings came from some world-famous non-Communist personalities who were well past the qualifying "youth" requirement: Pandit Nehru of India and his "guru" Mahatma Gandhi (the greetings arrived posthumously, Gandhi having been assassinated shortly before the start of the conference); U Nu, independent Burma's first prime minister; and Mrs. Eleanor Roosevelt,

widow of the deceased president. As J. H. Brimmell, the most authoritative
Western writer on the occasion, put it, they "had obviously been inveigled
into sending greetings under false pretences."[1] There were also messages
from less extraneous personalities, including Klement Gottwald of Czechoslovakia, Ho Chi Minh of Vietnam, and Palme Dutt of the British Communist Party.

Clearly, the objectives of the Calcutta Youth Conference were varied.
They included the stimulation of enthusiasm for the Communist cause, a
demonstration of the wide-ranging influence and power of the world
Communist movement, and favorable publicity derived from the supportive messages of the non-Communist celebrities mentioned previously.

Just as clearly, the conference was too unwieldy and too visibly divided to have been capable of working out strategies, let alone tactics, for
the insurgencies envisaged by Moscow. These would have been determined
by the non-youthful leaders of the relevant parties represented there. In
any case, the methods to be used, as distinct from the ultimate objectives,
were left to the individual parties behind the WFDY and the IUS.

The divisions within the conference were many. For instance, two
mutually antagonistic Burmese delegations turned up: one supporting the
newly independent Burmese government, the other (the Communist one)
dedicated to its overthrow. There was a similar conflict between two Indian delegations. (Strictly speaking, Southeast Asia begins to the east of
India, but the Indians were hosts to the conference.) The deepest impression appears to have been made by the Vietminh delegation, which could
claim, rightly, to be ahead of the pack in the key matter of the struggle
for independence; the Communist view of such newly independent ex-
colonies as Burma, India, and the Philippines was that they could achieve
genuine independence only under Communism: a neat ideological and semantic reversal of the truth.

IT IS USEFUL to summarize the background of the independence movements of Southeast Asia. The Japanese imperial forces had swept through
the whole area during World War II in pursuit of their "Greater East Asia
Co-Prosperity Sphere." Unlike European countries occupied by the Germans, collaboration with the invaders was not a dirty word in Southeast
Asia. The Europeans were citizens of free countries; except for Thailand,
the Asian countries were colonies, and collaboration made sense, at any

rate initially. The Japanese, however, alienated the local populations by their arrogance and brutality, thus discrediting collaboration. The outcome was a wide swathe of resistance and independence movements.

THE PHILIPPINES

AN "INDEPENDENT" PHILIPPINE Republic was proclaimed under Japanese auspices in September 1943. Eighteen months earlier, in March 1942, the local Communist Party had set up a resistance movement that called itself the People's Anti-Japanese Resistance Army, usually known as the Hukbalahap from its initial syllables in Tagalog, the Philippine national language: *Hukbong Bayan Laban Sa Hapon,* or "Huk" for short. A Huk training school was set up in Central Luzon (the main northern island), under Chinese instructors from Mao Tse-tung's Eighth Route Army. The leader of the Huks was Luis Taruc. When the American colonial power returned in October 1944, Taruc started to set up a "People's Democratic Government." But when General Douglas MacArthur captured Manila in February 1945, he had other ideas. He disbanded the Huks and had Taruc arrested, though not detained for long.

The United States, however, lived up to its pledge of independence for the Philippines, in fulfillment of which free elections were held in April 1946. A complicating factor was that the Filipino Communist Party had split between rival pro-Soviet and pro-Chinese wings. Well before the Zhdanov call for rebellions, the Moscow line favored Communist participation in a coalition government that would be persuaded to adopt a Marxist or semi-Marxist program. The pro-Chinese wanted to set up a "People's Democratic Government," using Maoist methods. As it turned out, the elections were won by a political group that had collaborated with the Japanese, which in practice made both the Moscow-line and the Chinese-line policies irrelevant. The two factions decided to bury the hatchet and to opt for insurgency.

This gave Luis Taruc his chance to emerge again. With his supporters he dug up his hidden cache of arms. By early 1948, they were in control of a number of rural districts in eastern and central Luzon. At this stage, Taruc had not told his followers that he was a Communist. Circumstances had isolated him from access to international news, and he does not appear to have heard of the Zhdanov-Calcutta directive until mid-

April, when he negotiated a deal with the new Philippine president, El-pidio Quirino. When Quirino called on the Huks to surrender their arms in return for an amnesty, Taruc agreed. It must be presumed that Mos-cow's instructions reached him almost immediately after that, for he sud-denly reneged on the deal, withdrew to the hills with his followers, and intensified his insurgency. Indeed, it was only then that he revealed him-self as a Communist, instead of simply a defender of peasant rights.

This attitude made sense in the Philippines, whereas (in contrast to Vietnam) an appeal to nationalism would not have, since independence had come to the Philippines two years earlier. However, independence had brought nothing to an oppressed peasantry. This was a land where absentee landlords grew rich on the peasants' crops. The Quirino admin-istration was showing no more concern over the plight of the peasants than had its predecessor under President Manuel Roxas—the first post-independence head of state, who had died suddenly in April 1948.

Quirino was reelected in 1949, thanks to a political machine in which money and armed men played leading roles. Official corruption went from bad to worse with falling copra prices and dwindling foreign ex-change reserves. Officials went unpaid for months, and public works were halted. Faith in government, already low, sank further. Taruc thought the time had come to change the name of his rebel organization. He dropped "Hukbalahap" and opted for *Hukbong Mapagpalaya ng Bayan* (People's Liberation Army). Soon the new Huks were overrunning provincial capitals as well as the ricebowl areas.

In 1950, Luis Taruc's run of success ended, almost abruptly. By 1951, the Huks themselves were in retreat. A year later their military power was broken, and on September 17, 1954, Taruc himself surrendered. This as-tonishing reversal of fate was due to the work of two men: the new Filipino defense minister, Ramón Magsaysay; and his American adviser, Colonel (later Brigadier) Lansdale. When Magsaysay was appointed, in September 1950, the Huks seemed to be heading for complete victory. Barely a month later, however, a number of leading Communists were ar-rested in Manila, and a takeover of the capital was frustrated. Those arrested included José Lava, secretary-general of the Party.

Magsaysay's guiding slogan was "All-out force and all-out friend-ship." He became immensely popular for his honesty, forthrightness, and immense energy. Rightly, he was convinced that, for all Taruc's successes,

most of his followers were not Communists in the true sense. With encouragement from Lansdale, he launched a rural rehabilitation program
for surrendered Huks. To those not guilty of specific crimes, he handed
over land and a loan to develop it. He purged the army and constabulary,
not in the Stalinist sense, but by removing the corrupt and the lazy. When
landlords tried to prosecute the peasants who had received land, Magsaysay provided Army lawyers to defend them. Not only did he rally ex-
enemies to his banner, he galvanized his whole country. When he ran for
the presidency in November 1953, he swept into power. As I put it, many
years ago, "His life had shown that it was possible to defeat the Communists by removing the grievances on which their appeal rested."[2] Tragi-
cally, for his people as well as for his career, Magsaysay died in an
airplane crash in March 1957. But his main self-appointed task had been
accomplished.

BURMA

COMMUNISM, AS A doctrine and as a movement, came late to Burma.
In its early days, the Comintern seems to have been only vaguely aware of
the country, and tended to think of it as an extension of India, and therefore to be dealt with by the Indian and British Communist parties.[3]

In due course a Burmese Communist Party was formed, but not until
1939, and very much under Indian influence. As elsewhere in Southeast
Asia, this negative situation changed rapidly when the Japanese embarked
on their amazingly rapid conquest of Southeast Asia. They had shown
particular interest in Burma, and in 1940 (before their own entry into
World War II) they had had the foresight to smuggle thirty Burmese
Nationalists into Japan. The Nationalists called themselves Thakins or
"masters" to show that they were equal to the British colonial oppressors.
Among them were two formidable personalities: Aung San* and Ne Win.
The thirty Thakins were trained by the Japanese military to be the officers
of an anti-British Burma Independence Army.

---

*Aung San's daughter, Suu Kyi, led her National League for Democracy to victory in elec-
tions in 1988 after years of military rule, but the Burmese Army seized power again and
placed her under house arrest in 1989. She was released in 1995, but not allowed to campaign and was later re-arrested.

The Japanese invaded Burma in 1942 and proclaimed its "independence" under a puppet government led by Ba Maw, whose Fascist measures, together with Japanese excesses, alienated the other Thakins. Most of them rallied around Aung San, who organized a resistance force in which a possible dividing line between Communists and Nationalists was blurred, since all the resisters called themselves "Marxists." Aung San was not in the true sense a Communist but was ready to work closely with those who were. He turned his Japanese-trained Independence Army into a People's Freedom League. One of the other Thakins was the Communist leader Thakin Soe, who formed an Anti-Fascist Organization. In 1944, the two organizations merged to form the Anti-Fascist People's Freedom League (AFPFL).

Aung San and Thakin Soe quarreled and parted in 1946. By then, Aung San and another "comrade" called Ba Swe had left the Communist Party. Both of them wanted immediate action against the Japanese, whereas Thakin Soe argued in favor of postponing any rising, thereby toeing the international Communist line. In February 1946, shortly after the parting of the ways, Soe walked out of the Communist Party with his followers and set up a rival CP along Trotskyist guidelines: in other words, no longer responsive to Moscow's directives. The main Communist Party was led by Than Tun (who, in 1937, had helped to launch a book club calling itself "Red Dragon"). The party remained in the AFPFL, but caused much dissension and embarrassed the AFPFL by fomenting labor troubles and disseminating anti-government and anti-Buddhist propaganda. The AFPFL saw itself as the forthcoming government party, with a mission to unite all Burmans of whatever ethnic origins.

In 1947, however, Than Tun made reconciliatory gestures to the AFPFL at a time when Zhdanov had already issued his call for anti-colonial uprisings, which had evidently not yet reached the Burmese Communists. October 1947 brought the agreement between British Prime Minister Clement Attlee and U Nu that paved the way to Burma's independence.

By now, the Zhdanov directive of 1947 had reached the Burmese Communists, and Than Tun performed the kind of political somersault that characterized Communist parties everywhere when Moscow changed its orders. Than Tun denounced the Attlee-Nu agreement: Burma, he said, was being fobbed off with a false independence. By March 1948, Zhdanov's follow-up message from the Calcutta Youth Conference also reached him, and he led his followers into active dissidence, calling themselves the White Flags. Thakin Soe's Trotskyists were already fighting under the banner of the Red Flags, thus preempting the usual label of militant Communists and leaving the orthodox Communists to use a less exciting one.

A prolonged period of multiple militancy followed, as various non-Burmese ethnic groups, such as the Karens, the Kachins, and the Shans, took to arms to combat the dominant Burmese.

There were realistic hopes at this time that Aung San had the makings of a statesman who might have united Burmans of all groups. In May 1945, he had gone to Ceylon (now Sri Lanka) to meet Admiral Lord Mountbatten, at that time the supreme allied commander in Southeast Asia. Under the resulting arrangement, Aung San's guerrillas would help the returning British forces to drive out the Japanese. Eighteen months later, he had gone to London to negotiate independence with Prime Minister Attlee. Independence duly came on January 4, 1948, but minus Aung San, who, with most of his pre-independence cabinet, was assassinated on July 19, 1947, by gunmen hired by the prewar prime minister, U Saw, in a fit of political envy.*

The Communist insurgencies failed, but Burma's taste of democracy was short-lived. U Nu's AFPFL won elections in 1956, but General Ne Win, one of the original Thakins, seized power two years later. Although he relinquished it in 1960, he seized it a second time on March 2, 1962, and the Army was still holding on to power when these lines were written, thirty-six years later.

MALAYA

IN THE WORLD WAR II victory parade in London in 1945, one of the smaller contingents was led by a Malayan Chinese called Chin Peng, who went home after the event adorned with the Order of the British Empire (OBE). In the context of the times, this made sense. In the context of later

---

*Brimmell points out that at the time the Soviet press was denouncing Aung San as a tool of British imperialism, and spread the disinformation that he had been assassinated on British orders because he had been thinking of welcoming the Communist Party back into the AFPFL (Brimmell, *Communism in South-East Asia*, p. 192).

times, it carried a heavy irony. Chin Peng, a Malayan Chinese, was a member of the Malayan Communist Party (MCP), and the leader of the Malayan People's Anti-Japanese Army (MPAJA) and the Malayan People's Anti-Japanese Union (MPAJU). (All three of the organizations mentioned, although they used the term "Malayan," were overwhelmingly of ethnic Chinese membership.) Three years after the war's end, he would lead the MCP in what became a protracted insurgency against British rule.

In 1943, at the height of the war against the Japanese invaders, Admiral Lord Mountbatten's Southeast Asia Command organized Force 136, a secret initiative to help the resistance groups in the whole area. One of them was the MPAJA, which did indeed fight the Japanese, but only as a secondary priority. The first was to terrorize the mainly Malay villagers, with the usual executions of "traitors." The MPAJU organized the procurement of food and intelligence, as Communist authority became absolute. The terror had a name: the Dog Extermination Campaign, and the Communists' political instrument was a network of People's Councils. The Communists also levied contributions from the mainly Chinese business community, brought out the first postwar newspaper in Malaya, the *People's Voice News (Min Sheng Pao)*. At war's end, they seized as many Japanese weapons as they could, to add to the stockpile of armaments provided by the British.[4] In 1943, the MCP had issued a program calling for the establishment of an independent Malayan Democratic Republic, which they reissued on the day of the announcement of Japan's surrender. The Malays at this stage seemed apathetic about independence, and the large Indian minority was marginalized. Nevertheless, as Brimmell pointed out, the Japanese had "awakened the Malays from their political quiescence" by setting up a Malay Youth Movement complemented by the Special People's Union of Peninsular Malaya and promising independence for Malaya and Indonesia in an entity to be known as Greater Indonesia.

After Japan's defeat, however, the British, although ready to confer independence on Burma and India, did not feel that Malaya was ready for it.

The timing of the Malayan Communist Party's forthcoming insurgency was delayed by a financial scandal, unusual in the Communist world. In March 1947, the secretary-general of the MCP vanished with the Party's (by then) considerable funds. Not much is known about him. His name was either Lai Tek or Loi Tak, and he was rumored to be a Vietnamese. He was never found, and his place was taken by the then-youthful Chin Peng.

The Party had been thinking in revolutionary terms before the Calcutta conference, which it had attended, and in 1947 its strength within the trade unions was such that it was able to spark off a wave of strikes. The Australian Communist leader, L. L. Sharkey, spent two weeks in Singapore on his way home from the Calcutta conference, and discussed the plan for Malaya in detail. With the Russians and Chinese united, the hour was ripe, and the MCP produced an impressive plan inspired by Mao Tse-tung: an uprising in three stages. In the first stage, they would set up "liberated areas" as recruitment bases. In the second, the liberated areas would be broadened; and in the third, the whole country would be "liberated," that is, taken over by the Communists.

For a start, Chin Peng remobilized the MPAJA, then went on to change its name twice. In 1947, it became the Malayan People's Anti-*British* Army; and at the end of 1949, when Mao had won his war against Chiang Kai-shek's Nationalists, it was restyled the Malayan Races' Liberation Army (echoing Mao's "People's Liberation Army," while disguising the fact that its "soldiers" were nearly all Chinese).

A look at the wider political and international background may help to place the Communist rebellion into perspective. London's plans for the future of the colony made sense in Whitehall but not in Malaya or in Singapore. A complicating factor was the power of the Malay sultans, some of whom had collaborated with the Japanese. London's answer was to reduce their power in a proposed Malayan Union. Under an agreement negotiated in August 1945, the sultans, anxious because of their war record, agreed to transfer to Britain all their rights to sovereignty over their individual sultanates. This deal infuriated the Malay community, who felt they were being bulldozed into an agreement without proper consultation. Moreover, they also objected to the British proposals for citizenship, which was to be made available to all persons born in Malaya or Singapore, and also to immigrants who had lived in either area for ten of the past fifteen years. The immediate beneficiaries would of course be the Chinese, who were in a large majority in Singapore but to a lesser degree outnumbered by the Malays in the Malayan peninsula. To the Malays, this looked like a recipe for what they saw as the nightmare of Chinese domination.

On publication of Britain's proposals in January 1946, this apparent impasse in March sparked a new Malay-oriented political movement, which called itself the United Malays' National Organization, or UMNO.*

Two years later, in March 1948, the MCP issued new orders, clearly based on the Zhdanov directive. The former line of "peaceful struggle" was blamed on the vanished thief Lai Tek and was condemned as "right-wing opportunism." Instead, the new policy of "mass struggle against British imperialism" took over. Violence broke out in May, and in early June the new British commissioner-general in Southeast Asia, Malcolm MacDonald, proclaimed a state of emergency. Henceforth, the long war against Malayan Chinese Communists was simply known as "the Emergency." At this early stage, full independence was nowhere near the agenda for either Malaya or Singapore.

Initially, the British authorities underestimated the challenge of the "Communist Terrorists," as they were officially known. Malcolm MacDonald saw the true situation more clearly and arranged for the creation of a special constabulary of 25,000 to 30,000 men to guard threatened estates and mines. In September 1949, General Sir Harold Briggs was brought in as director of operations and introduced drastic methods to resettle Chinese villagers who had been terrorized into helping the Communists into New Villages protected by armed guards and barbed wire. Another general, Sir Gerald Templer, took over in February 1952, with the title of High Commissioner, bringing with him a plan for an accelerated constitutional advance toward independence. By the time his successor, Sir Donald MacGillivray, took over two years later, the Communist terrorists were dwindling in numbers from their peak of 8,000.

As fortune had it, the situation produced a natural leader in Tunku Abdul Rahman, whose Alliance Party swept the board in Malaya's first general election in July 1955, winning fifty-one of the fifty-two seats. The Tunku, as he was generally known, became chief minister. By then the Communists, down to a few hundred, were morally defeated. On August 31, 1957, the Alliance government, still in office, and by now representing Indian as well as Chinese communal interests, won another

---

*For a fuller analysis of the political situation, see Brimmell, *Communism,* pp. 200 et seq. On p. 201, however, Brimmell incorrectly identifies UMNO as the "United Malay National Association."

victory, this time with 74 seats out of 104. In 1960, twelve years after Chin Peng's attempt to carry out Zhdanov's orders, the end of the Emergency was proclaimed.

INDONESIA

OF ALL THE Communist insurgencies in Southeast Asia, the only one that deserves the description *fiasco* was the attempted rising in Indonesia. Unlike the rebel groups in Burma, Malaya, and the Philippines (and of course in Indochina), the Indonesian Communists started off without even the kernel of a "people's army." There were elements of farce in the "rising."

A Communist Party of the Indies had been set up in 1920 by Dutch Communists—one of the many products of Lenin's Comintern. Four years later, an Indonesian named Tan Malaka became the Comintern's principal organizer in Southeast Asia. He was, in fact, a political adventurer, dynamic but unscrupulous. He turned up in Manila, calling himself a musician and using the name of Jorge Fuentes. He had the engaging charm of a con man. The Filipinos took to him, but not the Americans, who deported him in 1927.

After activities in Malaya and Singapore, Tan Malaka became in turn a Japanese agent and a kind of freelance Communist, no longer linked with Moscow. In 1944 the Japanese, having promised Indonesia its independence, set up schools "for the study of nationalism and Marxism." One of the lecturers was Tan Malaka.

In August 1948, Moscow's designated Indonesian Communist leader, called Musso, arrived in Sumatra and was immediately elected secretary general of a new Communist Party, which absorbed two other Marxist-Leninist groups: the Sjarifuddin Socialists and the Independent Labor Party. Although Sjarifuddin had been describing himself as a Socialist, he now revealed that he had been a Communist since 1935. As for Musso, he had lived in the Soviet Union since 1936, including the war years. The outcome of the merger was a new, authentic (that is, Moscow-controlled) Communist Party of Indonesia, henceforth known as the PKI *(Partai Kommunis Indonesia).*

When the Japanese brought Tan Malaka back to Indonesia, they had earmarked him as the leader of a Nationalist movement that would look after Japanese interests from within. He soon revealed that he was his own nominee, not anybody else's. For example, he drew up a document transferring all powers to himself in the event of the deaths of President Sukarno and his deputy, Muhammad Hatta, and forged both their signatures to "prove" it. Achmed Sukarno had proclaimed the independence of the *Republik Indonesia* in 1945 and taken up residence at Jogjakarta, but the Dutch authorities did not recognize his government as legal until 1950.

Tan Malaka tried to talk the Socialist leader Sutan Sjahrir into joining him in a coup d'état to be followed by the expropriation of all foreign properties without compensation. Sjahrir proved resistant, and Tan Malaka circulated rumors that Sukarno and Hatta had been killed by the British, whose forces had reached Indonesia ahead of the Dutch returning after World War II. This time Tan Malaka had gone too far. In March 1946, the new republic's authorities had him jailed.

Musso, meanwhile, had been trying to work precisely to Moscow's orders. In his new role as leader of the PKI, he set up headquarters at Madiun, in Java, and started a Red Army School. Unfortunately for him, his overenthusiastic and inexperienced followers started antigovernment disturbances, and the new Indonesian Army marched on Madiun. By that time, Musso only had 3,000 or 4,000 inadequately trained men under arms. He saw no choice but to issue a premature "call to arms" on September 18, 1948. It took Sukarno's Army only a fortnight to crush the PKI's rebellion. Sjarifuddin and most of the other PKI leaders were executed. Musso himself was killed in action.

Another farcical turn came from Tan Malaka, who had been released from jail on September 16, just two days before Musso's call to arms. He went on to form a Nationalist Communist group, independent of Soviet or Chinese orders, under the name of the Murba (Proletariat) Party. Whatever qualities Tan Malaka lacked, charisma was not one of them. In a short time he built up a huge following and, in retrospect, might well have achieved his unscrupulous plan to take over from Sukarno and Hatta. Fate decided differently. In April 1949, he was captured by the Indonesian Army, and on April 16, he was executed.

Although the PKI, under the leadership of D. N. Aidit, went on to grow into one of the biggest Communist parties in the world, with a membership of around 3 million, Moscow's attempt to create an Indonesian satellite had failed utterly.

CHAPTER FOURTEEN

CHINA:

THE TEMPORARY SATELLITE

1946–1950

━━━━◆━━━━

D URING THE EARLY years of the Chinese civil war (1927–1928) between Mao Tse-tung's Communists and Chiang Kai-shek's Nationalists, Stalin did nothing to help the former defeat the latter. After his "last minute" intervention against Japan in August 1945, in the Pacific war, however (see Chapter 7), Stalin changed his mind. Although he had, in effect, deprived the Chinese Communists of an industrial base by ordering a massive looting of capital equipment in Manchuria, he facilitated a Communist takeover of the conquered territory from the Soviet armed forces. In the late spring of 1946, vast quantities of seized Japanese arms and equipment were handed over to Mao's Chinese People's Army (CPR).

According to one account, the handover comprised 1,226 cannon and 369 tanks, 300,000 rifles, 4,836 machine guns, and 2,300 motor vehicles.* This weaponry and equipment had been used by 594,000 Japanese and 75,000 Manchukuo (Manchurian) soldiers. Stalin also arranged for the transfer of 100,000 trained North Korean troops into the forces of

---

*See Brian Crozier, *The Man Who Lost China* (New York: Scribner's, 1976), p. 291. The figures cited were originally given by the Kuomintang and were officially confirmed by Peking in 1957. Eric Chou, quoting a Moscow broadcast in Chinese in his book *Mao Tse-tung: The Man the Myth* (London: Cassell, 1982), p. 170, gives even higher figures: 700,000 rifles, 11,000 light machine guns, 3,000 heavy machine guns, 1,800 artillery pieces, 2,500 mortars, 700 tanks, 900 airplanes, 800 ammunitions depots. These details also appear in Richard C. Thornton, *China: The Struggle for Power, 1917–1972* (Bloomington, IN, 1973).

Mao's military commander, General (later Marshal) Lin Piao. This unexpected bonanza did not have immediate results, since the Communist soldiers needed time to be trained in the use of unfamiliar equipment. In due course, however, the new weaponry in effect handed victory to the Communist side three years later.

By mid-July 1949, the Nationalist forces had been routed, against a background of runaway inflation and complete demoralization. On August 5, the United States announced the cessation of all aid to Nationalist China, and Chiang Kai-shek's Supreme Council pressed on with its plans to withdraw from the mainland to Formosa (as Taiwan was then more commonly known). The withdrawal was completed by December 8.

Already, in a mass celebration in Peking on October 1, Mao, as Chairman of the Central Administrative Council, had proclaimed the new People's Republic of China (PRC). At his side was Chou En-lai, his premier and foreign minister. It was a carefully staged historic occasion, with Mao standing above the Gate of Heavenly Peace, the main entrance to the Forbidden City. More than a million people had gathered in the marble square below to hear and see the new master of China.[1]

Immediate recognition of the new Communist regime came from the Soviet Union and its East European satellites, and soon afterward from Burma and India. Britain's recognition did not come until January 6, 1950; and America's was delayed until 1972, when the new president of the United States, Richard Nixon, visited Peking.

Although Mao (according to his own interpretation of the ideology) was a Communist, he was also deeply steeped in the traditions of the Middle Kingdom and in the Chinese Confucian heritage of respect for age and central power. In effect, he was now the "Emperor" of his post-imperial nation and the leader of the most populous country in the world, which had an estimated population of some 600 million. This did not, however, make him the senior Communist leader in the world: in this respect he had to defer to Stalin. Moreover, although the Soviet leader had been late in coming to Mao's aid, he had done so decisively. Mao had a debt to be paid to Stalin. Moreover, he knew he would need Soviet support in the years ahead.

As Eric Chou put it

His pronounced allegiance to the Soviet Union was not as natural as it seemed. Behind all the talks about Communist solidarity and political ideology, Mao was realistic enough to see the need for accepting Moscow's leadership of the Communist world. With the industrial installations in Manchuria stripped and taken away by the Russians, he had to find some way of getting them back. Nor could he afford to be ungrateful to the Russians who had helped him secure the victory in Manchuria, the turning point in the civil war. But most important of all, he knew that without the seal of approval from Moscow, he could not hope to control the whole party. Apart from the dormant International Faction, there was a dominant Pro-Soviet force in the party machine. Having not always been high in Moscow's favour, he realised that the Russians might be tempted to influence China through his rivals if he were less than convincing in his pro-Soviet gesture. Although it was not in his nature to play a submissive part, he had no alternative but to defer to Moscow. Fortunately for him, Stalin seemed quite prepared to accept him more or less as his equal.[2]

Already, on April 4, 1949, Mao had startled the world by announcing that in the event of a third world war, the Chinese Communists (still only in sight of final victory) would side with the Soviet Union against the United States. Now, after victory, Stalin invited him to Moscow, to join in the celebrations of his seventieth birthday on December 21. Unexpectedly, Mao spent about nine weeks there. Accounts differ as to why he spent so much time in Moscow. Was it because the Soviet dictator kept his visitor waiting, possibly with the aim of humbling him by demonstrating who was "boss" of the Communist world? Verbatim accounts of two conversations between Mao and Stalin recently released in Moscow suggest that, on the contrary, Stalin went out of his way to be friendly and helpful.[3] Although there is no reason to doubt the accuracy of the Soviet record of these particular meetings, they clearly do not tell the whole story. Moreover, according to Stalin's authoritative biographer, the late Soviet historian Dmitri Volkogonov, most of the Stalin-Mao conversations were not recorded.[4] (The recorded accounts of these conversations appear in Appendix D of this book.)

Let us, however, consider the released accounts first.

The first conversation took place on December 16, 1949, and the second on January 22, 1950. On the first occasion, apart from a Russian and a Chinese interpreter, also present were four of Stalin's closest surviving followers: Vyacheslav Molotov, Georgi Malenkov, Nikolai Bulganin, and

Andrei Vishinsky. After routine greetings, Mao started by saying that China needed three to five years of peace to rebuild its economy "back to prewar levels and to stabilize the country in general."

Stalin's reply was reassuring. He pointed out that the Soviet Union had already had four years of peace, and opined that there was no immediate threat at present: "Japan has yet to stand up on its feet and is thus not ready for war; America, though it screams war, is actually afraid of war more than anything; Europe is afraid of war."

On a humorous note, Stalin added, "In essence, there is no one to fight China, not unless Kim Il Sung decides to invade China?"

He went on to foresee not only five to ten years of peace, but twenty to twenty-five years or longer.

Referring to a recent visit to Moscow by Liu Shao-chi (the ruling party's leading ideologist and the PRC's first president), Mao raised the question of a treaty of friendship, alliance, and mutual assistance between China and the USSR. Perhaps to his surprise, Stalin raised a more controversial issue: whether to continue the existing treaty of 1945 between the USSR and (Nationalist) China, under which the then-Nationalist government agreed to the independence of Outer Mongolia, to Soviet ownership of the Manchurian railway and the port of Dairen for thirty years, and to the conversion of Port Arthur into a joint Sino-Soviet naval base. Stalin went on to say that he was in favor of maintaining this treaty, because "a change even on one point could give America and England the legal ground to raise questions about also modifying the Treaty's provisions concerning the Kurile Islands, South Sakhalin, etc." He added, however, "If, on the other hand, the Chinese comrades are not satisfied with this strategy, they can present their own proposals."

Mao, in his apparently concessionary mindset, had no objections to raise, and indeed remarked that the continued presence of Soviet troops in Port Arthur served Chinese interests, since "Chinese forces are inadequate to effectively fight against imperialist aggression."

If Mao was being concessionary, Stalin could hardly have been more conciliatory. He offered to assist China and said that "we, as Communists, are not altogether comfortable with stationing our forces on foreign soil, especially on the soil of a friendly nation": surely a splendid example of hypocritical humor, given the fact that at that time Soviet forces were stationed in all the East European satellites. Unless, of course, Stalin felt hypocritically guiltless for his saving reference to a friendly nation, for none of the East European nations *wanted* to be Soviet-occupied, even if their Soviet-installed governments did.

Stalin went on to offer to withdraw the Soviet forces in Port Arthur if so requested by China, although, if it suited the Chinese, they could stay as long as twenty years. Mao went on to sound Stalin out on the possibility of a Soviet credit of $300 million, to which Stalin responded with an offer to formalize a deal on those lines, "now," if Mao so wished. Mao accepted: "Yes, exactly now, as this would resonate well in China."

Encouraged, Mao had further requests to make: equipment and assistance for air routes, a naval force and "volunteer pilots or secret military detachments to speed up the conquest of Formosa." Stalin said yes to the air routes and a naval force. As regards a possible assault on Formosa, he demurred: "What is most important here is not to give (the) Americans a pretext to intervene."

He went on, however, with illuminating allusions to Moscow's disinformative skills regarding not only Formosa but also American and British alarm at possible Chinese incursions into Burma and Indochina. On Formosa: "One could select a company of landing forces, train them in propaganda, send them over to Formosa and through them organize an uprising on the isle." On Burma and Indochina: "One could create a rumor that you are preparing to cross the border and in this way frighten the imperialists a bit."

Before Mao took his leave, he asked Stalin for help in preparing an edited Russian translation of his (Mao's) works; to which Stalin replied, "It can be arranged, if indeed there is such a need."

If the first Mao-Stalin meeting had dealt with general principles, the second meeting on January 22, 1950, got down to details. This time, the attendance was larger. Molotov, Malenkov, and Vishinsky were present again, but not Bulganin. Anastas Mikoyan was there, and two lesser members of the Soviet team: N. V. Roshchin and Nikolai Fedorenko (Stalin's Russian-Chinese interpreter). On the Chinese side, Chou En-lai was present, together with the Chinese ambassador to the USSR, Wang Chia-hsiang, and Chen Po-ta, a senior member of the Chinese ruling party's central committee.

Stalin started by saying that on further thought, he felt that the existing treaty between the USSR and China "has become an anachronism."

He asked for Mao's opinion on a treaty of friendship and alliance. Perhaps to his surprise, Mao replied that he and his associates had only worked on an outline, not on a draft. The two men agreed that there was no point in saving Article 3 of the existing treaty, which called for the United Nations to be given responsibility for preventing any further Japanese aggression.

On Stalin's suggestion, Mao agreed that the preparation of the draft should be entrusted to the respective foreign ministers, Vishinsky and Chou En-lai. They also agreed that the existing arrangements for Port Arthur should stand until a peace treaty with Japan was signed.

When Stalin remarked that the existing agreement on Port Arthur was not equitable (from China's standpoint), Mao observed, "But changing this agreement goes against the decisions of the Yalta Conference?"

In jocular mood, Stalin responded, "True, it does and to hell with it! . . . We will have to struggle against the Americans. But we are already reconciled to that."

There was, however, some disagreement over Mao's request for a Soviet credit. He asked whether the shipment of arms would count as part of the monetary loan, pointing out that if so, "then we will have little means left for industry." He inquired, therefore, whether the duration of the loan could be shortened from five years to three or four.

Once more, Stalin's reply was conciliatory. "We must examine our options," he said, but he offered to make the agreement retroactive to January 1 and asked Mao to speed up the Chinese list of requirements for industrial equipment.

Mao then raised a point that gave Stalin another chance for a teasing response. "Under [the terms of the credit agreement] we pay only 1 percent interest."

Stalin's reply: "Our credit agreements with people's democracies provide for 2 percent interest. We could, says comrade Stalin jokingly, increase this interest for you as well, if you would like. Of course, we acted under the premise that the Chinese economy was practically in ruin."

He went on to mention the key role of the Army in economic recovery, thus giving Mao a cue to drop any further discussion of interest rates.

Toward the end of the meeting, Mao thanked Stalin for the use of a Soviet air regiment that had transported 10,000 people and asked whether it could stay on and help transport troops for an attack on Tibet.

Stalin, the "man of steel," responded, "It's good that you are preparing to attack. The Tibetans need to be subdued." He promised to raise the question of the air regiment with the military personnel.

Despite the friendly tone of these two conversations (as released in the post-Soviet period), it is clear from other signs that Mao's protracted visit to Moscow both irritated and humiliated him. Volkogonov stresses Stalin's ignorance of Chinese history and the "politically very primitive" passages about China in his collected works. "While Stalin watched his guest with curiosity and carefully concealed mistrust" (writes Volkogonov), "Mao would suddenly shift from talking about current problems and regale his host with parables from the mysterious and magical world of Chinese folklore." In fact, Mao's ignorance of Russian history may well have surpassed Stalin's corresponding ignorance of China. As for Stalin's mistrust of Mao, it rested on Mao's breach with the Chinese comrades who had opted for the Moscow line rather than his own special brand of Communism. It rested as well on Stalin's contempt for Mao's attempt to build his version of Communism on peasants instead of industrial workers, as had been advocated by Marx and Lenin.

In a later conversation, also released in Moscow, with the Soviet ambassador to Peking, P. F. Yudin,[5] Mao complained of Stalin's "serious mistakes" on the Chinese question, not least by exaggerating the revolutionary capabilities of Chiang Kai-shek's Kuomintang. He went on to complain that Stalin at one stage had cut off communications with him. As reported by Yudin:

> From my side, there was an attempt to phone him in his apartment, but they responded to me that Stalin is not at home, and recommended that I meet with Mikoyan. All this offended me . . . and I decided to undertake nothing further and to wait it out at the dacha. Then an unpleasant conversation took place with [I. V.] Kovalev and [N. T.] Fedorenko, who proposed that I go on an excursion around the country. I sharply rejected this proposal and responded that I prefer "to sleep through it at the dacha."

Despite such difficulties, Sino-Soviet relations reached their logical climax on February 14, 1950, when Mao and Stalin signed a thirty-year Treaty of Friendship, Alliance, and Mutual Assistance. Under the treaty, the Soviet Union assured China of Soviet support against attack by Japan or any other state cooperating with Japan. It also transferred Soviet interests in the formerly Chinese Eastern railway in Manchuria to China, without compensation, as well as in Port Arthur and Dairen, "immediately on the conclusion of the peace treaty with Japan, but not later than the end of 1952." As Stuart Schram points out, however, Stalin did not keep his word on Port Arthur and Dairen, and the ports were returned to China only after his death.[6]

Article 3 of the treaty provided for the transfer to China of all property in the port of Dairen "now provisionally administered to or leased by the Soviet Union." A deeper blow to Mao's Chinese pride was his yielding to Stalin on recognition of the independence of the Mongolian People's Republic: he had made it clear more than once (as Schram points out) that he regarded Mongolia as part of a greater China. To recognize its "independence" implied recognition of Mongolia's de facto status as a Soviet satellite.

Although the terms of the treaty clearly favored Communist China's needs, it undoubtedly placed Mao's new regime in a state of considerable dependence upon the Soviet Union's good will—which, at that time, meant Stalin's. On his return to Peking, Mao praised the Soviet leader as "the greatest leader of humankind" and (with perhaps deliberately excessive optimism) declared that the "Sino-Soviet friendship will last thousands of years." (In actuality, it lasted a mere ten years or less, depending on the interpretation of the beginning of the great Sino-Soviet rift that loomed ahead.) Mao repeated his extravagant praise of Stalin on many occasions. In return, Stalin authorized a loan of US $300 million to China, spread over five years. Thousands of Soviet experts, most of them engineers and other technicians, were sent to China.

In gratitude, Mao ordered the formation of Sino-Soviet Friendship Associations throughout his immense country. His decision to enter the Korean War (see Chapter 15) was the culminating sign of his voluntary subservience to Stalin, in other words, of Communist China's acceptance of satellite status, short-lived though it was. (See Appendix D: Document 3, Mao's Conversation with Yugoslavian Communist Union Delegation.)

CHAPTER FIFTEEN

KOREA:
THE SATELLITE WAR

———⋙⚫⋘———

THE KOREAN WAR of 1950–1953 was waged against South Korea with Stalin's approval by two of Moscow's satellites: North Korea first and later, China. It would probably have been won by the Communist side had it not been for a crass error on Stalin's part. Since January 1950, Jacob Malik, the Soviet representative on the UN's Security Council, had been boycotting its proceedings because China's seat was still occupied by Formosa (known now as Taiwan). The Soviet Union was therefore unable to veto President Harry Truman's moves to commit the UN (primarily, of course, the United States) to the defense of South Korea against the Communist aggression.

The mass of relevant Soviet archives released since the collapse of the Soviet Union make it clear that, contrary to the mistaken perceptions of the international Left, Stalin did indeed fully approve Kim Il Sung's invasion plan as well as Mao Tse-tung's decision to intervene on North Korea's behalf when the UN military intervention began to look threatening. Moreover, Stalin not only sanctioned Kim's plan to invade South Korea, but provided the North with considerable economic and military assistance, including manpower.

On January 10, 1950, the Soviet ambassador in Pyongyang, T. F. Shtykov, reported to Stalin on a conversation with Kim Il Sung during a reception at the Chinese embassy. Whereas the Chinese were advising the North Koreans not to invade the South, Kim wanted to visit "Comrade Stalin" to ask his permission to "liberate" South Korea. Stalin immediately cabled Shtykov to say he was ready to receive Kim.

In Moscow on January 22, the meeting between Stalin, Mao Tse-tung, and Chou En-lai (described in Chapter 14) went on to discuss plans for a North Korean invasion of the South in considerable detail. Stalin agreed to send not only food and other supplies including weapons, but also Soviet military contingents, instructors, advisers, and interpreters.[1]

On January 31, 1950, Ambassador Shtykov reported to Stalin on a meeting with Kim Il Sung the previous day:

> Kim Il Sung received my report with great satisfaction. Your agreement to receive him and your readiness to assist him in this matter made a particularly strong impression. Kim Il Sung, apparently wishing once more to reassure himself, asked me if this means that it is possible to meet with Comrade Stalin on this question. I answered that from this communication it follows that Comrade Stalin is ready to receive you.

Further ciphered telegrams from Shtykov, mainly addressed to the Soviet foreign minister, Andrei Vishinsky, followed on February 7, 10, and 23, and on March 9, 12, and 16. These dealt with Kim's request for armaments for three additional infantry divisions, his readiness to send a specific quantity of lead to Moscow, and North Korea's readiness to deliver a total of 133,050,500 rubles' worth of gold, silver, and monazite concentrate to the Soviet Union.

On March 18, 1950, Stalin sent a message to Kim Il Sung via Shtykov:

> First, I received your communication of 4 March about agreement to send the indicated amount of lead to the Soviet Union. I thank you for the assistance. As regards the equipment and materials you request, and also the specialists in lead industry, the Soviet government has resolved to fully satisfy your request.
>
> Second, I have also received your proposal of 9 March about the delivery to you of arms, ammunition and technical equipment for the People's Army of Korea. The Soviet government has decided also to satisfy this request of yours.
>
> With respect, J. Stalin[2]

Thus reassured, Kim Il Sung visited Stalin in Moscow in March–April and went on to visit Mao in Peking in May. (For further details, see Appendix E: Documents 1–8.)

THE NORTH KOREAN attack came as a complete surprise in Washington, as well as in Seoul and Tokyo. In the interests of Communist disinformation, Kim Il Sung claimed in a broadcast that the South Koreans ("the Syngman Rhee clique") had been the aggressors.[3]

Although caught unawares, Truman and his administration acted speedily and decisively. The U.S. ambassador in Seoul, John Muccio, cabled the news to the State Department on Saturday, June 24. It was received by Dean Rusk, the assistant secretary of state, who telephoned it to his superior, Dean Acheson, who in turn rang President Truman at his home in Independence, Missouri. Their first move was to convene the UN Security Council, which met on Sunday afternoon, June 25, in the absence of the Soviet representative. At 6 P.M. a resolution was passed 9 to 0, with Yugoslavia abstaining, calling for a cease fire and a North Korean withdrawal from South Korea.

In the face of steadily worsening news and appeals from President Rhee, General Douglas MacArthur (still in command in Japan), was instructed to use his air and naval forces to aid the South Koreans and to send the U.S. 7th Fleet to the Formosa Straits to prevent Communist action "that might enlarge the area of conflict."

A further UN resolution was passed on Tuesday, June 27, calling on nation-members to "furnish such assistance to the Republic of Korea as might be necessary to repel the armed attack and to restore the international peace and security in the area." The resolution made history, in that this was the first time an international body had approved the use of force against an aggressor. It was passed by seven votes in favor (United States, Britain, France, Nationalist China, Cuba, Ecuador, and Norway), one against (Yugoslavia), and two abstentions (Egypt and India). On July 7, a South Korean command was set up under American control; next day President Truman appointed General MacArthur as commanding general of the UN forces in Korea.

THE NEXT RELEVANT event was the intervention of the Chinese Communist forces in October–November 1950. The archival prehistory to this key development was included in a mass of documents presented by Boris Yeltsin of Russia to Kim Young Sam of South Korea in June 1994 (see note 2).

Although there were still gaps in the Moscow-Peking exchanges when this book was in press, the evidence is clear that every step in Mao Tse-tung's mobilization of China's "People's Volunteers" was personally approved by Stalin. For instance, in a ciphered telegram to Chou En-lai on July 5, 1950, "Filippov" (Stalin) said, "We consider it correct to concentrate immediately 9 Chinese divisions on the Chinese-Korean border for volunteer actions in North Korea in case the enemy crosses the 38th parallel. We will try to provide air cover for these units."[4]

A few days later (on July 13), "Filippov" sent a message to "Chou En-lai or Mao Tse-tung," via the Soviet Ambassador in Peking, N. V. Roshchin, to complain about an appeal from "the English" to persuade North Korea to withdraw its troops to the 38th parallel, which "could hasten a peaceful solution to the Korean question." Stalin commented, "We consider such a demand to be impertinent and unacceptable."

The message went on:

> It is not known to us whether you have decided to deploy nine Chinese divisions on the border with Korea. If you have made such a decision, then we are ready to send you a division of jet fighter planes—124 pieces for covering these troops.
>
> We intend to train Chinese pilots in two to three months with the help of our pilots and then to transfer all equipment to your pilots. We intend to do the same thing with the aviation divisions in Shanghai.
>
> Communicate your opinion.
>
> Filippov

In a further message to Chou on August 27, Stalin said that ten military specialists in anti-aircraft defense and twenty-eight Air Force advisers would be sent to China. On the diplomatic front, on October 25 Andrei Gromyko instructed the Soviet Ambassador in Washington to protest against the use by the United States of Japanese servicemen in military operations in Korea, which he described as "a gross violation of the Potsdam declaration."

By that time, the Chinese People's Army's preparations for military intervention were nearing completion, but there were still gaps to be filled. On October 27, Mao sent "Filippov" a "TOP PRIORITY" message, via Roschin, spelling out further requirements: "We urgently need to acquire from the Soviet Union the following armaments for the navy: high-speed torpedo boats, floating mines, armoured ships, small patrol boats, mine-sweeping equipment, coastal fortress artillery and torpedo bomber planes."

A more detailed list of further requirements was sent to "Filippov" by Mao on November 8, complaining of "a great variety in the caliber of infantry rifles," which caused a problem with cartridges. Although thirty-six divisions of the People's Liberation Army were in action, only six battle sets of "rifle-machine gun cartridges" were available. A long list of requirements followed, to be delivered if possible in January–February 1951. The listed items included 140,000 Soviet rifles and 58 million cartridges; 26,000 Soviet submachine guns and 80 million cartridges; and 1,000 tons of TNT. Mao's message ended: "I ask you to communicate to me the results of your review of my request. I wish you health."

In a further message to Stalin on November 15, Mao expressed "gratitude to the Soviet pilots for the heroism and effort they have displayed in battle, and for the fact that over the last 12 days they downed 23 invading American planes. . . . I congratulate you on the successes!"

Meanwhile, on October 9, General MacArthur had ordered his UN forces to cross the 38th parallel. Within three weeks, they were nearing the Manchurian border. On November 1, however, a North Korean offensive halted them, and on November 26, the first major Chinese offensive started. On December 1, Stalin cabled Mao to congratulate him on the initial successes of the People's Liberation Army: "Your successes gladden not only me and my comrades in the leadership but also all Soviet people. Allow me to greet from the soul you and your friends in the leadership and the entire Chinese people . . . in their struggle against the American troops."

ALTHOUGH THESE EXCHANGES confirm the satellite status of the Chinese People's Republic in the context of the Korean War, it would be wrong to conclude that Sino-Soviet relations, even in the year of the Friendship and Alliance Treaty of February 1950, were consistently harmonious. In the wake of the UN forces' successful landing at Inchon on September 15, 1950, the Chinese Communist leadership had decided to intervene in the war, even if their Soviet friends and allies proved reluctant to support them. However, Stalin's initial reaction was helpful, and an understanding emerged after initial Chinese feelers that the Soviet Union would provide an air umbrella to the Chinese land forces.[5]

On October 1, 1950, the day after the South Korean Army had crossed the 38th parallel, General MacArthur issued an ultimatum to Kim Il Sung demanding unconditional surrender. Later that day, Kim appealed to the Chinese for assistance. Next day, Mao and his Politburo decided to enter the war around November 15. Mao immediately cabled Stalin to inform him of that decision. On October 8, Mao ordered his "People's Volunteers" to enter the war, and Chou En-lai flew to Moscow to discuss the situation with Stalin.

The two met at a dacha on the Black Sea at 7 P.M. on October 9, and their talk lasted until 5 A.M. next morning. To Chou's disappointment, Stalin now seemed to renege on earlier promises to provide air support for the Chinese. He promised to deliver military equipment for twenty divisions, but declared that the Soviet Air Force would need more time to get ready. Unable to persuade him to stick to earlier promises, Chou sent an urgent cable to Mao pressing him to reconsider the decision to enter the war. On the evening of October 12, Mao cabled General Peng Teh-huai, recently appointed to lead the People's Volunteers, to stop all troop movements and return to Peking immediately for an emergency Politburo meeting.

Despite Stalin's unhelpful attitude, the meeting decided (or, more accurately, Mao did) to go ahead with military intervention. According to Chen Jian (see note 5), "Mao had no other choice but to swallow the fruit of the Russian betrayal. Mao, however, would never forgive it. We have every reason to believe that a seed of the future Sino-Soviet split had thus been sowed in the process of China's intervention in the Korean War."

ONE OF THE most interesting of the revelations by the ex-Red Army coauthors of *Alien Wars** is about the performance of the Soviet units allocated to the North Korean side. So concerned was Stalin to keep the Soviet intervention secret that the aircraft used carried Chinese identification

---

*Oleg Sarin and Lev Dvoretsky: See Chapter 5, n. 3 of the present volume. See also note 1 to this chapter.

marks and at first the pilots wore Chinese uniforms. They had been warned to stay silent, and were given notes with Chinese or Korean phrases written in Russian. This precaution soon proved counterproductive, however, when American pilots started reporting that they were hearing Russians talking to each other in their own language and noticed that their features appeared to be neither Korean nor Chinese, but "Caucasian."

It might have been assumed that American officials, apprised of such evidences of Soviet involvement, would wish to exploit the situation for their own counterpropaganda, but they decided to ignore the evidence, for fear of provoking high indignation among the American public, thus raising the specter of a major war between the United States and the USSR. This was the view expressed in a secret document by Paul Nitze, who at that time headed the Policy Planning Division of the State Department.[6]

Although the early squadrons of Soviet pilots included many highly experienced veterans of World War II, the quality of later and less experienced arrivals inevitably dropped. Discouraging reports on their performance greatly irritated Stalin, who raised the issue at a meeting of the Politburo on December 12, 1951, going so far as to say the war must be ended. The authors of *Alien Wars* report the following exchange:

STALIN: What is the reason that our troops look so helpless in Korea? Maybe our generals have lost their qualifications or become so lazy that they are unable to accomplish their missions.

Marshal of the Soviet Union ALEKSANDR VASILEVSKY (Stalin's Defence Minister): The Theatre of operations is very difficult, geographical conditions are complicated, and the enemy is displaying stubborn resistance. Nothing can be done here with tanks and armoured personnel carriers. Everything is decided in local fights.

S: You, Comrade Vasilevsky, always manage to justify your passiveness. Maybe it is time for you to retire; or can you reverse the course of the war?

V: I am ready to retire if you think I am out of place.

S: The war should be ended. Don't you see how deeply involved we are now? We are ready to take any measures, to replace the entire command element, to increase military supplies by two or three times if need be. We shall do anything necessary. The problem must be solved. Decisive success must be achieved in the near future.[7]

*   *   *

THE WAR ENDED in stalemate. Aiming at victory, General MacArthur had advocated bombing and blockading China and bringing in a substantial force of Chinese Nationalist troops from Formosa. This far transcended the American commander in chief's vision from the White House, and on April 10, 1951, President Truman dismissed MacArthur and replaced him with General Matthew Ridgway, who in turn was succeeded by General Mark Clark a year later.

After much fighting and diplomatic wrangling, an armistice was signed at Panmunjom on July 26, 1953, providing for a demilitarized zone along the North-South boundary, henceforth known as the DMZ (Demilitarized Zone). Discussions on peace took place at Geneva in June 1954, along with the parallel talks marking the end of the First Indochina War. The latter succeeded, at least for a few years; but not the former. Truman's policy of containment, however, had prevailed.

TROUBLE
IN THE SATELLITES
1953–1963

CHAPTER SIXTEEN

THE BERLIN RISING

1952–1955

———

RIOTS BROKE OUT in East Berlin on June 17, 1953, but by that
time the rumblings of discontent had been building up for nearly a
year. In terms of Party organization, the years 1949–1952 had been very
successful—in Stalin's eyes, not least the assimilation of the Nazi police
and security services into their Communist successors. (See Part III, Chapter 11.) But as a whole the Berliners, however disillusioned they were
with their defeated Nazi rulers, saw no reason to enthuse over the new
tyranny of the Soviet invaders. Released East German documents* make
it clear that the riots of 1953 were merely the visible face of a much wider
and deeper popular protest against the Soviet-sponsored regime in the
German Democratic Republic (GDR).

A determining event in the rise of public discontent was the Second
Party Convention of the ruling East German Socialist Unity (Communist)
Party, the SED, which met in East Berlin from July 9 to 12, 1952, and de-
cided on a crash socialization program. The convention was of course

---

*Although the East Berlin riots of June 1953 made big headlines in the Western press, their
full significance was not clear until East German archival documents emerged after the collapse of the Soviet system at the end of 1991. A detailed examination and analysis of this
new material by Christian F. Ostermann, of Hamburg University, was issued in December
1994 by the Woodrow Wilson International Center for Scholars, as *Working Paper No. 11*,
in its Cold War International History Project. Henceforth, Wilson, *Paper 11*. I have drawn
heavily on this material in this chapter.—BC

held under Soviet direction, and the program was inaugurated by Walter Ulbricht, first secretary of the SED, and as such the executant of Soviet will in the East German satellite.

Above all, socialization meant a state offensive against the middle classes: in Marxist-Leninist dogma the main enemy and obstacle to Communism. In the East German context, the middle classes consisted of the private sector in trade and industry, among whom the owners of small businesses were the most vulnerable (and therefore easily targetable) element. Prohibitive taxes were announced, and small business owners were forced to surrender ration cards, which in turn forced them to buy food at the deliberately exorbitant prices fixed by state shops.

Independent farmers, too, were targeted under a collectivization program that forced them into "agricultural production cooperatives." Many of the farmers refused to obey the new rules, and the SED retaliated by setting exorbitantly priced delivery quotas designed to force them out of business.[1] The predictable outcome was a severe shortage of foodstuffs throughout East Germany. In mid-May, industrial working hours were raised by 10 percent.

The churches were also targeted under the new program. In particular, pressures mounted on Protestant Church youth organizations. Conscription and a general military buildup worsened East Germany's economic problems. Thousands of those who resisted the new program were summarily jailed. Many thousands more opted for flight to the more promising world of West Germany, slipping through the border controls from East to West.

The innate fanaticism of the regime ruled out any concessions to the dissenters. Trials and purges multiplied.

This increasingly volatile situation was clearly building up to a possibly disastrous climax in early 1953, while Stalin was fatally ill, and after his death on March 5, when the inevitable succession struggle was in progress. On April 18, in response to appeals from Ulbricht and his senior colleagues, the Soviet Politburo granted a fresh economic aid package to East Germany, reduced the outstanding reparations debt, cut obligatory shipments to the Soviet Union by 25 percent, and extended the allotted time of debt settlement.

On April 22, Vladimir Semyonov, an authority on German affairs and political adviser to the Soviet Control Commission, was recalled to

Moscow for consultations. As Christian Ostermann (see footnote on page 161) aptly observes, "The [Soviet] eagerness to seize the initiative on the German question . . . reflected the fact that Soviet Foreign Ministry officials did not comprehend the gravity of the crisis that was brewing in East Germany." Indeed, the comments and measures proposed at this time were in some senses contradictory and self-defeating.

There were optimists and pessimists. Among the former was Semyonov, who on May 2 in a memorandum to his political chief, Foreign Minister Vyacheslav Molotov, averred that because the SED and other "democratic forces" in the German Democratic Republic were already strong enough to manage their affairs, Soviet "overt political control" could be sharply reduced.

However, the Soviet Foreign Ministry was far from unanimous in its appraisal of the Berlin crisis. When the Presidium of the Soviet cabinet met on May 25, sharp differences of opinion emerged. As Ostermann puts it, on "still fragmentary" evidence, the NKVD's chief, Lavrenti Beria, supported by the first post-Stalin premier, Georgi Malenkov, apparently opposed any further development of "socialism" in East Germany. Possibly in possession of intelligence not released to the relatively junior Foreign Ministry, Beria is reported to have gone perilously out of line by supporting the idea of a renovated united German state, neutral, democratic, and (the ultimate ideological heresy) bourgeois in character. Against this, further socialization in East Germany was supported by Nikita Khrushchev (at that time one of the aspirants to succeed Stalin), Molotov, and his deputy foreign minister, Andrei Gromyko. It cannot be ruled out, however, that the Beria-Malenkov line may have been intended mainly to confuse the Western "enemy." The fact that the Council of Ministers did not issue an agreed resolution until June 2 no doubt reflected the deep divergences of view that prevailed in the Presidium in the wake of apparently threatening moves by the Western Powers, especially the signing of the European Defense Community (EDC) Treaty in May 1952, providing for the creation of a joint Franco-German force.*

The resolution harshly criticized the policy of forced socialization in East Germany, and realistically described the mass exodus of East Germans

---

*The EDC was in fact killed in a French National Assembly vote in August 1954 (see Chapter 12).

to West Germany as "a serious danger to the continued political existence of the German Democratic Republic." In line with Beria's reported views, the resolution called for an end to forced collectivization and the war on private enterprise. The plan for the development of heavy industry under state control was to be revised, and the regimentation of the population relaxed. Coercive measures against the Protestant Church were to be dropped, and "the cold exercise of power" by the Ulbricht regime was denounced. There was, however, no mention of the increased working hours—a significant omission. Instead of concentrating on socialization, the resolution called for a new policy of putting "the political battle for national reunification and the conclusion of a peace treaty at the center of attention of the German people." Since the prerequisite of a peace treaty included reunification on terms acceptable to the Soviet Union and the Western Allies (the United States, Britain, and France), the chances of agreement were still remote at that time.

The East German leaders, Ulbricht and Otto Grotewohl, president of the GDR, had been summoned to Moscow on June 2, 1953, to be given their new policy orders. The Soviet leaders expressed "grave concern about the situation in the GDR," and Malenkov warned them that "if you do not correct the situation now, a catastrophe will happen." The two leaders were ordered to accept the reversal of the previous policy and to assume publicly the blame for the virtual collapse of forced socialization. If this was the "stick," there was a "carrot" too: Soviet promises of substantial aid and easier reparation payments. Moreover, the Soviet Control Commission was to be disbanded: in its place a new Soviet High Commission for German Affairs would be set up, to be headed, however, as the defunct SCC had been, by Vladimir Semyonov.

As before, the East German leaders did as they were told. Back in East Berlin on June 5, the two men listened to orchestrated attacks on Ulbricht's "dictatorial" and "myopic" leadership. On June 11, a "New Course" was announced. Its provisions were sweeping. They included a general amnesty for all East Germans who had sought refuge in West Germany, a more liberal policy on interzonal travel and residence permits, an easing of the campaign against the Protestant Church, assistance to small and medium private enterprises, and the reissue of ration cards to the middle classes. Enough, surely, to provoke comparisons with Lenin's New Economic Policy.

The New Course came as a deep shock, not only to Party members but to the unprepared general public, which greeted it as confessional proof of the SED's final bankruptcy. Not only were the former "class enemies" in effect rehabilitated, but the working class, on whose supposed behalf the harsh earlier measures had been taken, would continue to suffer under the higher work norms imposed earlier. One of Ulbricht's harshest critics within the SED's Politburo, Rudolf Herrnstadt, had called on Semyonov on June 10 to plead for a postponement of the New Course announcement, so that the population could be prepared for the drastic changes envisaged. But Semyonov, faithfully reflecting Malenkov's warning to Ulbricht and Grotewohl, turned down Herrnstadt's plea, warning him that "in fourteen days, you may not have a State any more." As an internal SED report, now available, put it, "Broad segments of the population did [. . .] not understand the party's new course, viewed it as a sign of weakness, or even as a victory by the Americans or the Church."

Curiously, in view of the suddenness and comprehensiveness of the change of course, the authorities seem to have been taken aback by the revolt that followed. This is especially true insofar as they had lifted official curbs on public protests: almost an invitation to the oppressed workers to vent their spleen. This they did on June 16, when hundreds of East Berlin building workers demonstrated, calling for a general strike the next day. The SED's first reaction was conciliatory: an announcement was made to the effect that any increase in work norms would henceforth be "voluntary."

The popular response duly came on June 17, when demonstrations and riots against the regime took place not only in East Berlin, but in major towns throughout the GDR. It is now known that similar protests had been taking place all over East Germany for some time. According to the newly released material, these popular protests had taken place in more than 400 towns or cities, and in many rural areas, whereas at the time, only the manifestations of June 16 and 17 had been publicized. Indeed, it would have been impractical to conceal these in particular, since the Soviet Union sent in tanks and infantry on June 17 to crush the East Berlin rioters, whose number was estimated at 30,000. The death toll was 125, including nineteen in East Berlin.

Moreover, despite the brutal repression of June 17, the disorders continued sporadically throughout the summer. Although Ulbricht had been humiliated within the ruling SED, he remained general secretary and indeed was given enhanced bargaining powers. This is perhaps less surprising than it may appear: after all, Ulbricht had simply carried out policies ordered by the Soviet leadership, and he had been blamed, unjustly, both for inaugurating them and for dropping them.

THE RESPONSE OF the Western Allies to the East German disorders was far from united. In the White House, President Dwight Eisenhower and his team were committed to West German rearmament and to the expected ratification, by France and West Germany, of the proposed European Defense Community (EDC). The initial American response to the dramatic increase in the flow of East German refugees into West Berlin had been that it showed a lowering of morale and a desire to opt out rather than resist. A parallel view was that the flood of refugees must be a deliberate psychological warfare ploy rather than a genuine expression of popular discontent. On February 27, 1953, the American High Commissioner in Germany, James B. Conant, reported to Secretary of State John Foster Dulles that space in West Berlin was "bound to become tight," and the fast mounting arrivals were bringing a danger of epidemics, with the possibility of riots and disturbances.[2]

Conant therefore proposed plans for a "crash evacuation" of refugees using military aircraft and supplemented by a loan to West Germany. Nothing came of Conant's idea, and the Eisenhower Administration, at least initially, was apprehensive about a "peace offensive" launched in Moscow after Stalin's death, and calling for Four-Power talks. Any such development, in Washington's view, might halt progress toward European unity and weaken France's already ambiguous attitude toward possible West German rearmament.[3]

The White House specialist on psychological warfare, C. D. Jackson, proposed that the President should make a speech emphasizing the U.S. desire to "negotiate all the major outstanding issues between the free world and the Soviet Bloc, including the unification of Germany and disarmament."[4] What Jackson was suggesting, in effect, was that the president should call the Soviet bluff by seizing the "peace" initiative from the Kremlin. Dulles was outraged and predicted that such a speech would bring about the fall of the governments of Italy (Alcide de Gasperi),

France (René Mayer), and West Germany (Konrad Adenauer) within a week, thus postponing if not destroying the EDC.[5]

Dulles won the argument, and Eisenhower, in a "Chance for Peace" speech on April 16, made any improvement in Soviet-U.S. relations conditional upon Kremlin concessions, such as free elections in Eastern Europe and the signing of an Austrian peace treaty.

Winston Churchill, back in office as prime minister since October 1951, in effect reclaimed the limelight from Eisenhower in a speech in the British House of Commons on May 16, in which he called for a "conference on the highest level . . . between the leading powers without delay." He envisioned the possibility of "a generation of peace."[6]

Although Churchill's leading motive was probably to preempt any political credit that might be claimed by Eisenhower, it is likely that a genuine apprehension about a possible nuclear war also played a part. The European allies were enthusiastic about his proposal, but the United States was predictably cool. Dulles, in particular, favored a tougher approach to the Soviet challenge. He was, however, overoptimistic in his estimate of success, arguing that "[if] we keep our pressures on, psychological and otherwise, we may either force a collapse of the Kremlin regime or else transform the Soviet orbit from a union of satellites dedicated to aggression into a coalition for defense only."[7]

It is now known that in October 1952, the American Psychological Strategy Board (PSB) had adopted the proposals put forward in a secret report commissioned two years earlier by the State Department.[8]

The guidelines envisaged psychological, political, and economic harassment of the GDR, as well as "controlled preparation for more active resistance." An important element in the campaign was the Radio in the American Sector (RIAS), based in West Berlin, which had built up a large audience of East German listeners. Anticipating the riots of June 17, 1953, the RIAS certainly contributed to the scale of the demonstrations.

In a secret SED analysis of the rising,[9] on July 20, 1953, the party blamed the disturbances on American agencies:

Supported by their existing spy centres in the GDR and by those groups of agents smuggled in during the uprising, and under cover of the dissatisfaction among the population resulting from the mistakes of party and regime, they temporarily managed to rope in broad segments of workers and employees, in particular in Berlin and Central Germany, for their criminal goals.[10]

Wrangling between Churchill and Eisenhower continued, as well as arguments within the U.S. administration over the best way to handle the opportunities created by the Berlin riots. On July 1, 1953, the Psychological Strategy Board hit on the idea of a major food program for the hungry East Germans. It was argued that free distribution of food would be seen as a humanitarian plan to relieve hunger, while offering no long-term improvement of the economic crisis. On the psychological side, it would keep the Soviet regime on the defensive and worsen relations between the SED regime and the population.

The RIAS gave considerable coverage of the new plan, thus creating a prodigious demand for the U.S. food packages. On the first day alone, 103,743 packages were distributed, and by the third day the daily figure had reached 200,000. By August 15, 865,000 East Germans had come to West Berlin to pick up these free rations.

SED archival documents reveal that the U.S. food program exacerbated tensions within the GDR and prevented the ruling party from achieving genuinely good relations with the people.[11] Initially, the SED evidently thought a hostile propaganda campaign was the best way to fight the U.S. initiative. The Party leaders were particularly dismayed to find that those seeking the food packages included a sizable number of Party members, and they responded by suspending the sale of train tickets to Berlin. But the hungry East Germans found other ways to cross the border and consume the food that was offered.

In desperation, the SED sent a delegation to Moscow, and the Soviets responded with competitive food deliveries; these, however, were too highly priced to compete with the free food packages from the Americans. The popular mayor of Berlin, Ernst Reuter, likened the food program to "an artillery attack."[12]

The British and French, however, were critical of the food program, fearing that it might stir the Soviets and their East German satellite to cut off Berlin's communications with the West.[13] Even Mayor Reuter began to doubt the value of the food program and claimed, on dubious grounds, that it brought no benefit to the old, the infirm, and the unemployed.[14]

The State Department also became critical of the program. As for Ulbricht, whose demotion the Americans and their allies would have welcomed, the unexpected outcome of the food program was to consolidate his position, presumably because the Kremlin would not wish it to be thought that its success had provoked his downfall.

On August 20, 1953, a high-level SED delegation was welcomed in Moscow, where the Soviets granted the GDR substantial economic aid and elevated the respective diplomatic legations to embassy level. Even before the visit, Ulbricht had launched a series of repressive measures, including thousands of arrests and summary trials and executions.

The flight of refugees from the Communist regime continued, averaging nearly 28,000 a month in the mid-1950s. The West had shown itself incapable of bringing down the East German regime, and the regime itself of stanching the flood of citizens fleeing to the West. Among them, inevitably, were a substantial number of undercover agents of STASI, East Germany's secret agency.

Eight years later, Khrushchev would decide that the human drain could not be allowed to continue, and would take drastic action.

CHAPTER SEVENTEEN

THE GHETTO WALL

1961

✦

T HE "DRASTIC ACTION" mentioned at the end of the preceding
chapter was the closing of the boundary between East and West
Berlin in August 1961. This was a major event in the Cold War, but it
was also a battle in the context of the Soviet Empire. According to a
West German official Yellow Book issued in September 1961, more than
2,500,000 East German citizens had fled the Communist regime installed by their Soviet conquerors. Among them were 3,371 doctors,
1,329 dentists, 700 dispensing chemists, and 132 judges and prosecu-
tors. Among the more distinguished refugees were Judge Horst Hetzar
of the East German Supreme Court, Rudolf Hoehn, director of the East
German Meteorological Institute in Potsdam, and Fritz Freytag, joint
designer of the East German "152" jet airliner. The brain drain was
considerable.

In retrospect, it is strange that the neo-imperialists in Moscow allowed the mass escape to go on for so long. Khrushchev and his Kremlin
colleagues may have thought for some years that a decision to stop the
westward flow could turn into a *casus belli*. However, the West had
shown itself incapable of bringing down the East German regime or, if
not incapable, then unwilling to risk war for that purpose. Moreover, the
flow westward had provided a minor but not unimportant benefit: a relatively easy way of sending undercover agents of the STASI, the East Ger-

man secret intelligence agency, into West Germany.* It could also be argued that the flight of opponents of the regime would reduce the numbers of hostile citizens in East Germany. Neither of these advantages, however, could be regarded as permanently valid.

THE COMMUNIST REGIME in East Germany—the German Democratic Republic or GDR—was in a dual sense part of the Soviet Empire: a satellite that lacked even the nominal sovereignty enjoyed by, say, Poland or Czechoslovakia. The subservience of the GDR to the USSR is clearly illustrated by the correspondence between the East German Communist leader, Walter Ulbricht, and his Soviet counterpart, Nikita Khrushchev, now available to Western scholars through the Woodrow Wilson Center in Washington, D.C.[1]

On November 30, 1960, for example, in a meeting with Khrushchev, Ulbricht spelled out a long list of complaints. One involved the shortage of goods in East Berlin. At that time, about 50,000 East Berlin workers were employed in West Berlin, attracted by the higher salaries on offer. Teachers and doctors were among them. Moreover, even if pay packets were raised in East Berlin, workers would spend their money in West Berlin because East Berlin did not offer the goods they wanted. Khrushchev's reply was unhelpful: "You will not encroach on our gold. . . . Don't thrust your hand in our pockets." (For further details, see Appendix F: Document 1.)

Ulbricht's meeting with Khrushchev went on to deal with the complex question of a peace treaty involving the two Germanies and the Western Allies, in the new situation created by the advent to power of President John F. Kennedy in the United States. The Soviet prime minister, A. N. Kosygin, and Foreign Minister A. A. Gromyko, joined in the debate, which ended inconclusively.

Ulbricht returned to this theme in a long letter to Khrushchev on January 18, 1961. He argued that it would be out of the question for West Berlin to be given recognition as belonging to West Germany. He called

---

*After the demolition of the Berlin Wall in 1989, the West German Security Service (BfV) estimated the network of East German agents in the Federal Republic at between 3,000 and 5,000, ranging from office cleaners to ministers. See Foreword by the late Sir James Goldsmith to Brian Crozier, *The KGB Lawsuits* (London: Claridge Press, 1995).

for special consultation on the West Berlin question in April 1961, not only between the GDR and the USSR but also with the Political Consultative Council of the member states of the Warsaw Pact.

Ulbricht's letter went on to raise economic matters, with emphasis on the fast-growing development of West Germany. The only way out of this situation, as Ulbricht saw it, lay in reducing East Germany's debts to the "capitalist countries," and in general in building close economic ties with the Soviet Union and "the socialist countries . . . to make our economy independent from the disruptive actions of the West German imperialistic and militaristic circles." The East German leader went on to blame East Germany's economic problems on its greater share of "the crimes and devastation of Hitler's Germany." (For extracts from Ulbricht's letter, see Appendix F: Document 2.)

Khrushchev's reply, dated January 30, though brief, was conciliatory. He concurred with Ulbricht on the need for a "broadening of economic cooperation between the GDR and the USSR." His main emphasis, however, was on the need to initiate "businesslike discussions" with America's new president, Kennedy. (For extracts from Khrushchev's letter, see Appendix F: Document 3.)

Some months later (on May 19) the Soviet ambassador to the GDR, M. Pervukhin, reporting to Foreign Minister Gromyko, mentioned that his diplomatic colleagues from Czechoslovakia and Poland had expressed concern that the Western Powers and West Germany might blockade the GDR if a peace treaty with East Germany was signed (unilaterally) with the USSR.

A fortnight later, President Kennedy left the White House for visits to General Charles de Gaulle in Paris, Khrushchev in Vienna, and Prime Minister Harold Macmillan in London. The relevant event was of course the meeting with Khrushchev that took place on June 3 and 4. For Kennedy, it was an eye-opening encounter with the reality of the Soviet challenge to the West and to the United States in particular.

The clash began at the first meeting, at which Kennedy had expressed the hope that the confrontation between two great nations, with different social systems, could be contained. This bland opening move sparked a tirade from Khrushchev about the indispensable need for U.S. recognition of the reality of Communism. When Kennedy replied that the problem was not that the democracies were trying to eliminate Communism in areas under its control, but the other way around—the Communists were trying to eliminate free systems in areas associated with the West—a further tirade from Khrushchev followed.

In their closing session, Kennedy declared that he recognized that the Soviet leader would make whatever decision he wanted to make about the German Democratic Republic, but he hoped that Khrushchev would not present him with a crisis over a question "so deeply involving the American national interest as Berlin."[2]

Khrushchev took this remark as a bellicose challenge, declaring that the United States wanted to humiliate the Soviet Union. Should the president insist on occupation rights after a treaty, and if East German borders were violated, war would follow.

THE CRISIS WAS now in full swing. In a televised broadcast on June 15, Khrushchev declared that in the event of a peace treaty between the USSR and the German Democratic Republic, the Western Powers would have to negotiate directly with the East German authorities on the question of access to West Berlin by road, water, and air. President Kennedy's reply to the Soviet leader's challenge came at a press conference on July 6. He referred to "the Soviet announcement that they intend to change unilaterally the existing arrangements in Berlin," and went on:

> The "crisis" over Berlin is Soviet-manufactured. . . . The Soviets . . . say that their unilateral action in signing a "peace treaty" with East Germany would bring an end to Allied rights to be in West Berlin and to have free access to that city.
>
> It is clear that such unilateral action cannot affect these rights, which stem from the surrender of Nazi Germany. Such action would be a repudiation by the Soviets of multilateral commitments to which they solemnly subscribed. . . . If the Soviets thus withdraw from their obligations, it is clearly a matter for the other three Allies to decide how they will exercise their rights and meet their responsibilities.
>
> Recent statements by leaders of [the East German] regime make it very plain that the kind of "free city" they have in mind is one in which the rights of the citizens of West Berlin are gradually but relentlessly extinguished. . . . No one can fail to appreciate the gravity of this threat.[3]

Two days later, Khrushchev announced that the Soviet government had decided to suspend its "unilateral reduction of armed forces" and "to increase defence expenditure in the current year by 3,144 million roubles [£1,257 million]." He attributed this decision to the U.S. president's request for additional military appropriations in a special Congressional Message, and to the "considerable growth of military expenditures in Britain, France, and other NATO countries."[4]

Reacting immediately to Khrushchev's announcement, President Kennedy ordered an urgent review of U.S. military capability. On July 17, American, British, and French Notes emphatically rejecting any unilateral Soviet attempt to alter the status quo in Berlin were presented in Moscow. The American Note was considerably longer than the British and French ones, and spelled out thirty-three points in response to the challenging document presented to Kennedy during his meeting with Khrushchev in Vienna on June 3 and 4.[5]

On August 3, similar but not identical replies from Khrushchev were presented to the United States, Britain, and France. In all three, the Soviet leader made several allegations of West German "militarism" and "revanchism." He declared his readiness to conclude a separate treaty with the German Democratic Republic if the Western Powers refused to join the Soviet Union in a peace treaty with both the German governments.

Despite these hostile exchanges, Khrushchev's decision to block access to West Berlin from the eastern side came as a shock to the Western Allies. On Saturday, August 12, 1961, 1,573 East Germans crossed the dividing line between East and West Berlin, registering as refugees at the Marienfelde reception center. They were the last to be allowed to leave the East without let or hindrance. It was the height of summer, and the West Berliners were relaxing and enjoying themselves. The only thing that might have spoiled their enjoyment was a rumor that barbed wire was being stretched across the imposing Brandenburg Gate separating East and West. The closure of the boundary took place at 2:30 A.M. on August 13, 1961.[6]

Two days later, work began on the Berlin Wall—a brick and concrete version of the Iron Curtain. It was a major project that took nearly two years to complete. The finished wall was twenty-eight miles long and nine feet high, topped with barbed wire. Those who dared to attempt to climb over it could be fired at by East German guards armed with machine guns.

By 1970, sixty-four aspirant refugees had been killed by East German border guards, although a few lucky or ingenious ones had survived.[7]

At midnight on August 12, Erich Honecker, in the name of Walter Ulbricht, announced the impending closure of the sector border. Trains were halted, and twenty Soviet divisions were placed on full alert. Although the number of guards at crossing points was increased, thirteen of the points were kept open, so that West Berliners visiting East Berlin could get home without being held up.

A communiqué issued in East Berlin announced that the Warsaw Pact member countries had instructed Ulbricht to take whatever measures were necessary to establish order on the border between East and West Germany. It complained of subversive activities that were "inflicting damage in the Communist camp."

The Social Democrat mayor of West Berlin, Willy Brandt, returning from West Germany at 8:30 A.M. on Sunday, was driven to the Brandenburg Gate, where he saw manned machine guns and tanks with massed troops in close formation. He called for a show of military strength on the Western side.

In Washington, the reactions were bewildered. Messages from Berlin made it clear that no Soviet forces had been sighted, and that there had been no attempt to interfere with the movement of Allied forces either in Berlin or on the Autobahn from West Germany. The U.S. secretary of state, Dean Rusk, who arrived at his office at about 10 A.M. on Sunday, was in receipt of conflicting advice from the State Department and the White House. The presidential advisers tended to be relieved that the flow of refugees was being stopped. The diplomats were displeased but were advising "Wait and see" rather than a display of Allied force.[8]

Years later, in an unpublished interview in August 1969, Rusk would argue that any Allied attempt to interfere with the erection of barriers in Berlin would have brought war. By and large, it is fair to say that the mood in Washington was one of appeasement, based on the unspoken premise that Berlin and the banning of East–West refugees were not sufficient cause for a retaliatory reaction.[9]

In this kind of situation, the ultimate decision falls to the president, as head of state and commander in chief. President Jack Kennedy, however, was in a relaxed holiday mood. Some hours before news of the crisis would have reached him, he had taken his family with him to the Kennedy

compound at Hyannis Port, a township on Cape Cod in southeastern
Massachusetts. His plan for the afternoon was to go sailing on his yacht,
the *Marlin,* away from the telephone and the radio. He had listened to the
news, but had not been stirred by it. At 11:30 A.M., however, Dean Rusk
telephoned him. Kennedy listened carefully and wanted to know if any Soviet troops had been sighted and whether the movement of Allied troops
had been hindered in any way. Rusk's reply to both questions was No.
There were no signs of an uprising in East Berlin on the lines of the great
crisis of 1953.

In his holiday mood, the president said, "Go to the ball game as you
had planned. I am going sailing." As Eleanor Lansing Dulles put it, "As
one looks back to that lazy warm holiday weekend, it seems that neither
diplomats nor politicians had their vacation disturbed. Kennedy and
Rusk deliberately pursued the leisurely plans they had made in advance.
No high level meeting was called. No action was initiated. It was summer
rest and relaxation as usual."[10]

ONE MAN COULD not share the relaxed indifference of the leader of
the Western Alliance: Chancellor Konrad Adenauer. The chancellor had a
remarkable record of successful leadership. He had steered West Germany
from the humiliation of total defeat and the rubble of destruction to the
industrious prosperity of the present.

Back in Bonn on Friday, August 10, from a holiday in Italy, Adenauer
was immediately confronted by the Berlin crisis. He also ran into a frustration inherent in the special status of Berlin as spelled out in the "reserve clause" of the Statement of Principles for Berlin on May 14, 1949,
and reaffirmed in a later draft dated May 5, 1955, which stipulated that
Allied authorities would exercise powers in the field of "relations of
Berlin with the authorities abroad." He had told his advisers that he
thought he ought to go to Berlin immediately, but was strongly advised
against going by his Minister for All-German Affairs, Ernst Lemmer, who
thought that the chancellor's presence there would produce undesirable
results: an explosion of patriotic fervor in East Germany leading to, at the
least, a local war, and possibly a global one. Moreover, if the Allies failed
to take action to meet the chancellor's wishes, there could be an explosion
of anti-Western feeling.

In the event, strong protest Notes were delivered in Moscow on August 17 by the United States, British, and French governments. On August 18, the West German Bundestag held an emergency meeting, marked by strong speeches from Adenauer and Brandt. Next day, the U.S. vice president, Lyndon Johnson, started a two-day visit to Berlin. With him were Charles Bohlen, a prominent Soviet specialist, and General Lucius Clay, who had been the American commander in chief in Germany at the time of the Berlin blockade in 1948.

At last, in the eyes of the populace, America was "doing something." A crowd estimated at half a million flooded into the streets to welcome the vice president. Johnson delivered an eloquent speech to a joint session of the West Berlin Senate and House of Representatives. He had words of enthusiastic praise for West Germany's achievement, which he contrasted with the "terrible and tragic failure" of the Communist regime in East Germany.

The words were welcomed, but next day—August 20—they were backed by action: 1,500 American troops and twenty vehicles arrived as reinforcements to the U.S. garrison in West Berlin. On August 23, a Soviet Note called on the United States, the United Kingdom, and France to put a stop to the use of the air corridors linking West Germany with West Berlin by "revanchists, extremists, saboteurs and spies." Three days later, the three Western Powers issued "a solemn warning" that any interference with free access to the city would have "the most serious consequences," for which the Soviet government would "bear full responsibility." The war of words, at any rate, was "hotting up."

On August 31, the Soviet government announced that it had decided to resume nuclear test explosions. It was later revealed that ten such explosions in the atmosphere had been carried out between September 1 and 7.

Regardless of nuclear test explosions, Khrushchev had achieved an imperial victory for the Soviet Union by ordering the building of the Berlin Wall. Before that, the drain of the population, and not least of some of its ablest and most qualified citizens, had threatened the survival of the German Democratic Republic—in economic terms the most important of the Soviet Union's imperial acquisitions. This was the true significance of the crisis of August 1961.

Nearly two years later, on June 26, 1963, President Kennedy paid an eight-hour visit to West Berlin. At the Brandenburg Gate, with Mayor Willy Brandt at his side, he gazed at the Berlin Wall, which the East German authorities had covered with huge red flags and propaganda placards. The sight of the Wall "shocked and appalled the President" (in the words of his biographer, Arthur M. Schlesinger, Jr.).[11] Later, he was made a freeman of the city and from the balcony of the town hall addressed a vast crowd estimated at well over a million: "three-fifths of the population of West Berlin, streaming into the streets, clapping, waving, crying, cheering."[12] His concluding lines were, "All free men, wherever they may live, are citizens of Berlin, and, therefore, as a free man, I take pride in the words: '*Ich bin ein Berliner.*'" [13]

Delirious applause followed his words; although it is said that there were also ripples of unanticipated laughter, his speechwriter having apparently been unaware that *Berliner* means not only a citizen of Berlin but a sausage much loved by Berliners.[14]

In 1970 and 1971, protracted negotiations on the status of Berlin took place between the powers concerned: the USSR, the United States, the United Kingdom, and the French Republic. The outcome, on September 3, 1971, was a Quadripartite Agreement, under which the Soviet Union guaranteed freedom of transit between West Germany and Berlin, while the three Western Powers conceded that the Western Sectors of Berlin "continue not to be a constituent part of the Federal Republic of Germany and not to be governed by it."

It is fair to say that in return for a (not unimportant) guarantee of access, the Western Allies conceded victory to the imperial power in Moscow.[15]

ON NOVEMBER 10, 1989, nearly thirty years after the crisis of 1961, the Berlin Wall was deliberately breached by the East German government on orders from Mikhail Gorbachev's ruling team in Moscow. The Soviet system was collapsing, and its East European satellites were falling. Those who had forecast a nuclear war and the end of civilization had been proved wrong.

CHAPTER EIGHTEEN

UNREST IN POLAND

1956–1957

———✠———

LIKE HO CHI MINH, the Polish leader Wladyslaw Gomulka was a
patriot as well as a Communist. Ideologically, the two are not necessarily incompatible. The patriotic Communist sees Communism as the best possible solution for his country's problems, but because he is a patriot he wants
to do things his own way, not necessarily the way the Soviet Union dictates.

Unlike many other European Communists, among them his rival Boleslaw Bierut, who spent the wartime years in Russia, Gomulka remained in
Poland. Twice in power, he was twice disgraced, each time for his opposition
to Moscow's methods. This did not mean that he was "soft" on those of his
countrymen who opposed him: he was as ruthless as "good" Communists always were. But he did not welcome orders from the Soviet Big Brothers.

During and immediately after World War II, two provisional "governments" competed for acceptance and legitimacy in Poland. One was in
exile, in London, where the aspirant prime minister, Stanislaw Mikolajczyk, was the leader of the Peasant Party; the other, initially known as the
(pro-Communist) Polish Committee of National Liberation, was based in
Lublin, under Soviet protection. Gomulka, who had led the left-wing Polish underground resistance and had been secretary general of the Workers' (Communist) Party, moved to Lublin in July 1944. A month later,
General Tadeo Bor-Komorowski and his (anti-Communist) Home Army
began an ill-fated uprising against the Nazis; Gomulka, on Stalin's orders,
stayed put as the Wehrmacht crushed the patriotic rebels.

In December 1945, the Workers' Party held its first congress in Warsaw, and Gomulka was reelected secretary general of the Central Committee and a member of the Politburo.

What kind of man was Wladyslaw Gomulka? Physically frail, and of a personality usually described as colorless, he was modest in demeanor; but his ruthless political character belied appearances.[1] At Yalta, the Big Three had agreed that Poland should come within the Soviet sphere of influence. In response, an apparently grateful Stalin had made what seemed to be a concession but was not, when he agreed that Mikolajczyk and some of his London colleagues should join the new Polish Government of National Unity, formally set up in Warsaw on June 28, 1945. The new premier was the Socialist leader, Eduard Osubka-Morawski; his deputy was Mikolajczyk.

The real power, however, was in the hands of Gomulka and his Workers' Party. Although the new government was recognized by the Western Allies, it soon became clear that its policy was in line with Soviet goals. On January 6, 1946, a new program of land reform and nationalization of all enterprises employing more than fifty workers was announced. Fearing for their future or their lives, many displaced Poles—most of whom had fought the war with the Western Allies—refused to be repatriated.

On June 30, a referendum approved the government's program, including a proposal for a single-house parliament. Gomulka's main strategic goals, however, were the crushing of Mikolajczik and his Peasant Party, and the absorption of the politically compatible elements of the Socialist Party. The first of these goals brought out the ruthless element in Gomulka's psychology. Individual members of the Peasant Party were beaten up and others cowed into inaction. As the campaign progressed, there were mass arrests, and Mikolajczyk was falsely accused of collusion with anti-Communist elements. When the first general election was held on January 19, 1947, the official outcome was 394 seats to the governing block, and only 28 for the Peasant Party. The British and American governments accused Gomulka's government of violating the Yalta provisions for free and honest elections.* Denied a share of the government, Mikolajczyk went into exile in London, never to return.

---

*The charge of electoral fraud is described as almost certain by Neal Ascherson in *The Polish August: What Has Happened in Poland* (London: Penguin, 1981), pp. 46–47. Any uncertainty must surely be waived in view of two facts: The Catholic Church had instructed

Gomulka went on to pursue his other main goal of absorbing the compatible elements of the Socialist Party while excluding the rest. By December 1948, the uncooperative "rightist" elements among the Socialists had been purged under Communist pressure, and on December 15, the two parties merged to form the Polish United Workers' Party, under Communist control.

When the government's program was implemented, as approved in the 1946 referendum, the wholesale nationalization of industry took place, but not the collectivization of the land. In fact, the largest landowners were already in exile, and the land in what was still an overwhelmingly rural population had mostly been redistributed into private hands.

Ruthless though Gomulka had been, he opposed Soviet policy on two vital matters: collectivization of the land and (in September 1947) the creation of the Cominform (see Chapter 6). The two issues were linked in that the Soviet pressure for collectivization of agriculture was expressed at the inaugural meeting of the Cominform. As Neal Ascherson puts it, "Gomulka went to this meeting with heavy misgivings."[2] Rightly, he feared that the Cominform would be yet another tool in Stalin's hands to enforce obedience on participating parties, especially the Polish one. Moreover, for years he and his party colleagues had reassured the Polish peasantry that they would be allowed to keep their land. Gomulka's criticism of the Soviet line was too much for Stalin, who ordered Gomulka to be charged with "Nationalist deviation." In September 1948, he was replaced by Bierut as secretary general of what was still the Workers' Party, and three months later, when the Party absorbed the Socialists, he was dropped from the Politburo. In January 1949, he lost his government posts, and in November, he was even stripped of his Party membership. In July 1951, he was jailed. Not easily intimidated, he refused to admit any guilt and impressed those who saw him by his calm dignity.

Not long after Gomulka's arrest, several trials of churchmen, on invented charges, took place. Among them was Cardinal Stefan Wyszynski, the Primate of Poland, who was confined in a monastery.

Gomulka was not released until the end of 1954, more than a year after Stalin's death. In February 1956, Nikita Khrushchev, who had

---

its faithful to vote against Communism; and the membership of the Peasant Party stood at 600,000 in 1946, against only 235,000 for the Workers' Party.

emerged as the victor in the post-Stalin power struggle, denounced a broad but selective list of Stalin's crimes in a speech to the Twentieth Congress of the ruling Communist Party. The speech was intended to be secret but was leaked to the CIA. The following month Gomulka's rival, Bierut, died (of natural causes), and although the new Party secretary, Eduard Ochab, repeated the charge of "Nationalist deviation," he admitted that Gomulka should not have been arrested.

In June, the workers of Poznan rioted in protest against social and economic conditions. The rioters, led by rail workers, marched shoulder to shoulder, shouting "Higher wages" and "Cheaper bread." Estimates of the dead varied between thirty-eight and more than 100. They included several Communist officials caught in the line of police fire. On hearing that a child was among those killed, the rioters fell into a rage and temporarily seized control of the town hall and secret police headquarters.

The riots were only one sign of agitation against the tyranny exercised to placate Stalin, which still prevailed more than three years after his death. The leaders of the Poznan riots were brought to trial, but in the face of a wave of anti-Russian feeling, the trials were abruptly halted on October 10. A few days later, several Communist leaders urged the removal of Soviet officers from the Polish Army.

The most specific among the leaders was Gomulka, who had spent most of his time during the summer meeting members of the Party's Central Committee and of the Politburo, arguing the case for Polish control of affairs. He wanted Soviet officers to be removed, not only from the armed forces, but from the security apparatus. In particular, he called for the removal of Marshal Konstantin Rokossovsky from the Politburo.

This hit a raw Soviet nerve. Rokossovsky, of Polish origin, was a full-fledged Bolshevik. He had joined the Red Army in 1918 and the Bolshevik Party the following year. During Stalin's vicious purge of the military after the fall of Marshal Mikhail Tukhachevsky (see Chapter 5), he was arrested, tortured, and jailed.[3] Freed on the eve of World War II, he became one of the Red Army's most successful senior officers and was chosen by Stalin to command the victory parade on May 24, 1945. After the war, Stalin sent him to Poland, where his official titles were Defense Minister and Deputy Prime Minister. In reality, if not in title, he was in effect Stalin's viceroy in the Soviet Union's major Slav satellite. In the eyes of

Gomulka and those who thought as he did, Rokossovsky was the living symbol of Soviet colonialism, and had to go.

The Soviet ambassador in Warsaw, Panteleimon Ponomarenko, called in the Polish Party leader, Ochab, on October 18 to tell him that Moscow was alarmed by the escalating anti-Soviet demonstrations in Poland. The CPSU Politburo, he said, would be sending a delegation to Warsaw the following day to discuss the situation.

Ochab, duly alarmed, called an emergency meeting of his own Central Committee and invited Ponomarenko to join in. The timing was awkward, as Ponomarenko knew, for on October 19, the Polish Party was to hold its Eighth Plenum. The prevailing view was that the Russians should defer their visit until the second or third day of the Plenum. Rokossovsky dissented, and said he thought it would be better if the Soviet visitors came before the Plenum opened. Not surprisingly, Ponomarenko agreed, and the appropriate message went out to Moscow.

By then, in any case, the situation had already gone too far in the eyes of Khrushchev and the other leaders of the world Communist movement in Moscow. In Stalin's day, the crisis would never have been allowed to reach this stage. Gomulka would doubtless have been shot instead of released from prison; and the Red Army would have moved in, as indeed would soon happen in Hungary. Khrushchev was no Stalin, although he had saved his own career in the Ukraine before and after the war as an uncritical executant of Stalin's ruthless orders. He was in a typically truculent mood when, at 7 A.M. on October 19, he and his closest colleagues landed at Warsaw airport. The other passengers were Lazar Kaganovich (the anti-Semitic Jewish member of the Politburo), the Armenian Anastas Mikoyan, Marshal Georgy Zhukov (Defense Minister), Marshal Ivan Konev (Commander of the Warsaw Pact Forces), Vyacheslav Molotov (Foreign Minister) and General Aleksei Antonov (Chief of Staff of the Warsaw Pact). In his memoirs, Khrushchev recalls Ponomarenko's report that "the tensions which had been building up had boiled over. . . . The situation was such [that] we had to be ready to resort to arms. . . . The Polish leadership . . . recommended that we not come. Their reluctance to meet with us heightened our concern even more. So we decided to go there in a large delegation." In other words, the time had come to bring the tiresome Poles to order.[4]

Detailed accounts of the talks that followed are now available from Polish sources, together with one from Ambassador Ponomarenko to Khrushchev.* The Soviet delegation had been met at the airport by, among others, Gomulka, Ochab, and Central Committee Member Josef Cyrankiewicz, plus the controversial Soviet-Polish Marshal Rokossovsky. (In advance of the arrival of the Soviet visitors, Rokossovsky** had ordered the Polish troops under his command to take positions near Warsaw. Troops on the Polish and Soviet sides of the border exchanged fire.) At 10 A.M., about three hours after the landing, the Plenum met as planned at the Belvedere Palace.

In the official report of the proceedings, Gomulka (referred to under his wartime pseudonym "Comrade Wieslaw") is quoted as complaining in strong terms about Khrushchev's behavior at the airport, when he had condemned "the treacherous activity of Comrade Ochab" in such a loud tone that "everyone at the airport, even the chauffeurs, heard it." Later, at the palace, Khrushchev had continued in the same vein. The man Khrushchev had attacked, Ochab, complained that it had been very painful to hear Comrade Khrushchev, adding, "I did not deserve such treatment." (For a fuller account, see Appendix G: Document 1.)

It became clear after the first day that, on reflection, Khrushchev and his colleagues came to agree that Gomulka was not hostile to the Soviet Union. Khrushchev's impression was that the demonstrations in Warsaw were basically in favor of a new leadership headed by Gomulka, although they also had a dangerously anti-Soviet character.[5]

In the event, the crisis was resolved when the Polish ruling party invited Gomulka to resume his leadership, replacing Ochab as first secretary. The Soviet-Polish talks, which had begun at the airport in such inauspicious circumstances, were resumed at 11 A.M. in the Belvedere Palace. The Polish participants were now led by Gomulka, and included fourteen members of the Politburo. The turning point came with an earnest speech by Gomulka stressing that Poland needed friendship with

---

*Woodrow Wilson International Center, Cold War International History Project, *Bulletin* 5 (Spring 1995).

**Bulletin* 5 does not mention Rokossovsky as among those who met the Soviet delegation at the airport. It is clear, however, from the official report of the Politburo meeting on October 19, 20, and 21, 1956 (Protocol: No. 129) that he was indeed present, perhaps by invitation from Ambassador Ponomarenko.

the Soviet Union more than the Soviets needed Poland. In his memoirs, Khrushchev quotes Gomulka as adding, "Without the Soviet Union we cannot maintain our borders with the West."[6]

Gomulka, however, insisted on excluding Rokossovsky from the Politburo, and in the end Khrushchev agreed that he should return to the Soviet Union. The Belvedere Palace talks ended at 3 A.M. on October 20. On October 24, Gomulka announced the return within two days of Soviet troops based in Poland. The withdrawal began the next day, but Soviet forces who had entered Poland from East Germany some days earlier stayed on.

On October 28, Rokossovsky returned, reluctantly, to the Soviet Union, where an investigation uncovered a plot by him to stage a military coup against Gomulka. Nevertheless, he retained his new post of Deputy Defense Minister until 1962.

On October 29, Cardinal Wyszynski was released from the monastery in which he had been held for five years. Next day, Gomulka's government felt bold enough to present the Soviet government with a bill for 15 percent of the German reparations payments to the Soviet Union.*

Three further events consolidated this protracted round of Gomulka's rehabilitation. On December 17, 1956, the role of Soviet troops in Poland was limited under a Polish-Soviet agreement. On January 20, 1957, a National Front, headed by Gomulka, was victorious in national elections; and on February 27, Parliament approved the new government of Josef Cyrankiewicz, Gomulka's choice as premier.**

Having won the complex power struggle, Gomulka would nevertheless be forced out of power for the second time in the crisis of December 1970.

---

*I know of no evidence that the Soviets accepted the bill.—BC

**Gomulka repaid Khrushchev with support in two further crises of the Communist world. As Jan Librach records, on an official visit to Budapest on May 10, 1958, Gomulka praised the Soviet crushing of the Hungarian uprising (see Chapter 19) as "correct and indispensable" (Jan Librach, *The Rise of the Soviet Empire*, Westport, Conn.: Praeger, 1964 and London: Pall Mall, 1965, p. 149). And during the Soviet-Chinese rift, he sided explicitly with Moscow, without any apparent effort to use the crisis to wrest greater freedom of action from Moscow, much as the Stalinist regime in Romania did.

CHAPTER NINETEEN

UPRISING IN HUNGARY

1956–1957

‒‒‒►●◄‒‒‒

I N TERMS OF international power, 1956 was a year of outstanding
turbulence. Three crises came to a head almost simultaneously: in
Poland, Hungary, and Suez. The Hungarian crisis reached an explosion
point on October 23, 1956, before the Polish unrest had fully died down.
That day Britain's foreign secretary, Selwyn Lloyd, flew to Sèvres in
France with his permanent under-secretary Patrick Dean, to coordinate
plans for an Anglo-French military intervention in the clash between Israel and Egypt. The Suez crisis, though not of direct relevance to this
chapter, does have an indirect bearing on it in two senses: otherwise engaged, neither Britain nor France could intervene in the Hungarian crisis,
even if either had been tempted to do so. Meanwhile, the United States
was deeply irritated by the failure of the British and French to consult
Washington over Suez, and found itself applying pressure not against the
Soviet Union but against Britain and France—particularly the former.

During the Suez crisis, the Soviet premier, Marshal Nikolai Bulganin,
issued several public and secret warnings to the British government,
headed by Sir Anthony Eden, that the Soviet Union was prepared to un-
leash a nuclear rocket attack on Britain if it persisted with its plan to invade Egypt. From the Soviet standpoint, this initiative served the useful
purpose of temporarily presenting a favorable image at the time when the
Hungarian revolution was being crushed. In fact, the British decision to
pull out was due entirely to a threat from President Dwight Eisenhower

to deny U.S. financial aid to Britain, which had vastly overspent its projected budget for the Suez expedition.

The Hungarian crisis had been building up over three years, with the usual clashes between Stalinists and patriots. The almost farcical failure of Béla Kun's revolution in 1919 had made a deep impact in the consciousness of Lenin's Bolsheviks. While the 1956 crisis was brewing, the prevailing attitude of Nikita Khrushchev's Politburo was that at whatever cost, revolution could not be allowed to fail a second time in Hungary.[1]

Complete victory was won by the Communists (who styled themselves the Hungarian Workers' Party, or HWP) in the general election of May 15, 1949. (See Chapter 10.) The elimination of anti-Communist forces was not, in itself, sufficient to satisfy Stalin. Another step had to follow: the elimination of those suspected of, or simply charged with, Nationalist unwillingness to take Moscow's orders. The execution of the Communist László Rajk in 1949 for "treason" and "Titoism" was only the start. On February 21, 1953, thirty Jewish Communists were purged, and on July 4, Prime Minister Mátyás Rákosi was forced to resign, ostensibly as a concession to the farmers and consumers. He was replaced by Imre Nagy. Two years later, on April 14, 1955, it was Nagy's turn for disgrace, when he was forced out of office on a charge of right-wing deviationism. His successor was the little known Andras Hegedüs.

As in many ruling Communist parties, personality clashes were rife, though almost always expressed in doctrinal terms. Rebellion in the ruling HWP grew rapidly in the spring and early summer of 1956. Rákosi, by now the Party boss, was bold enough to risk his career and possibly his life on March 29, when he announced that László Rajk had been posthumously rehabilitated and cleared of the charges of treason and Titoism that had led to his execution seven years earlier.

In that crucial year, the Soviet ambassador to Hungary was Yuri Andropov, who later would become the long-serving head of the KGB and later still the Party boss. In a telegram to Mikhail Suslov (the chief party ideologist) and Vyacheslav Molotov, the foreign minister, on April 29, Andropov reported at length on the worsening situation in the country, based on information provided by Rákosi and Prime Minister Hegedüs. On May 3, the Presidium of the Soviet Central Committee (which replaced the Politburo in 1952) met to consider Andropov's report. All the top leaders were present, including Bulganin and Voroshilov, Malenkov and Mikoyan, Khrushchev and Ponomarev. The report was classified as "STRICTLY SECRET" and carried the order "MAKING COPIES IS FORBIDDEN." (See Appendix H: Document 1.)

The report started on an optimistic note, with praise for the Hungarian Workers' Party's "strengthening of discipline." But bad news followed, which in effect demolished the initial note of optimism. There had been a show of "demagogy and provocation," and "right opportunists and hostile elements" had spread the idea that the HWP leadership, as it stood, could not implement in Hungary the decisions of the CPSU's Twentieth Congress. (See Chapter 20.)

Politically, the most interesting passages in Andropov's report concerned a decision of the Hungarian party to bring János Kádár into the Politburo. Rákosi and Hegedüs had criticized Kádár as "unstable," and Andropov's advice was to express Soviet misgivings to members of the HWP's leadership. Specifically, Andropov mentioned Kádár as among those who took the "provocative decision" to dissolve the Hungarian Communist Party during the war.

Rákosi's turn for disgrace came on July 18, when he was replaced as first secretary of the ruling Workers' Party by Ernö Gerö, a first deputy premier. Andropov reported at length on the situation before and after Rákosi's removal: first in a record of an animated conversation between Mikoyan and Rákosi, Hegedüs, and Gerö; and later in a report on a meeting of the HWP's Politburo at which Mikoyan was present.

As in Poland and elsewhere, the unrest in Hungary was stimulated by university students and other young intellectuals who had set up the Petöfi Circle, named after the lyrical poet Sandor Petöfi, hero of a patriotic revolution in 1848–1849.* Between July and October, the situation worsened, and on October 21, the students threatened to strike—not, in normal times, a threat to a government—if their demands for freedom were not met. In the tense anti-Soviet atmosphere of that time, however, the student threat sparked full-scale national rebellion.

On October 22 and 23, the students were joined by workers and even soldiers in massive demonstrations, not only in Budapest, but in Debreszen, Miskole, Szeged, Györ, and other cities. In the capital, representa-

---

*For a sample of the Petöfi Circle's prose, see Jonathan Steele, *Eastern Europe Since Stalin* (England: David & Charles, 1974), pp. 56–58.

tives of the high schools as well as the universities adopted a 22-point resolution calling, inter alia, for Nagy to head the Party as well as the government, the removal of Stalinists, the punishment of those guilty of past
errors, absolute equality in Soviet-Hungarian relations, the withdrawal of
Soviet forces, an end to the compulsory teaching of Russian in the schools,
and for reduced time in the teaching of Marxism-Leninism. Police opened
fire on the students, and heavy fighting broke out during the night of October 23–24. The police fire in effect turned the demonstration into a revolution. Led by General Pál Maleter, the defense minister, the Hungarian
Army joined the demonstrators, opening military depots and munitions
factories and handing out weapons and ammunition.

Dawn on October 24 brought an announcement: Nagy had taken
over from Hegedüs as premier. Drastic news items followed: A state of
emergency was proclaimed, along with censorship, a curfew, and the severing of all rail and air communications with the outside world. Gerö,
the new Party boss, then took the fatal, turning-point decision, invoking
the Warsaw Pact and appealing to the Soviet forces to restore order.
Meanwhile, local councils were springing up spontaneously all over the
country, and peasants reoccupied the lands from which they had been
expelled. It looked at this point as though the spontaneous revolution
had succeeded, even though by then Soviet tanks had opened fire on the
rioters.[2] The Soviet occupying forces were not the only target of the
rebels: another was the hated Hungarian security police, the AVH, which
was regarded, rightly, as an uncritical servant of the occupiers. To
demonstrate their strength of feeling, the rioters had pulled down the
Red Star from the Parliament buildings and hoisted the Hungarian flag
in its stead.

On October 25, the rioters achieved one of their political objectives
when the Stalinist Ernö Gerö was forced to step down as head of the ruling Party. His successor, judged to be acceptable in the heat of the hour,
was János Kádár, later to emerge as Moscow's man, despite the earlier
criticisms of him by Andropov. That evening, reports from neighboring
Poland described how thousands of young people were demonstrating in
the streets of Warsaw in support of the Hungarians.

By the evening of October 26, after three days of violence, some
3,000 Hungarians had been killed. In their nationalist frenzy, the rioters
attacked the Soviet tanks with their bare hands. Eyewitnesses reported

that at this stage, the state of Budapest recalled the devastation that reigned after the Red Army had ended its prolonged assault in 1945. In Madach Square, all the windows of the Astoria Hotel had been smashed. Rioters had cut the tram cables and dragged the trams away to serve as barricades.

In a broadcast that evening, Imre Nagy promised to start negotiations for "the withdrawal of all Soviet forces stationed in Hungary at present." First, though, he made it clear that the armed revolt would have to be suppressed. This was not quite what the rebels were seeking.[3]

Nagy, the "Titoist," had to measure his words carefully to avoid losing control on both fronts: the Hungarian people and the Soviet occupiers. "Some of the workers," as he put it, had joined the rebels. For this, he blamed "serious mistakes committed by the Hungarian government in the past." He promised "democratization" without delay. To his personal disadvantage, in career terms, he went on to promise that the political system, based on the predominance of the Communist (United Workers') Party and the elimination of opposition parties, would have to be reformed. He promised that reform would permit representation of "all democratic forces on the broadest basis."

A broadcast followed, calling on Budapest citizens to "go home and stay there." But the "citizens" were in no mood to obey. The sacking of Gerö encouraged them to seek further concessions. By October 27, the rioting had spread throughout Hungary. The ruling party promised to work for the withdrawal of Soviet forces as soon as the rioting stopped. As a further concession to the rebels, Nagy invited leaders of the Smallholders' Party (by now illegal) to join his cabinet.

That same night—October 27—in a telegram to the Central Committee, Mikoyan and Suslov reported that Imre Nagy had been found unconscious in his office. He had just had a heart attack, and the Hungarian doctor on duty had been startled. Suslov, however, happened to have some heart drops (validol), which brought Nagy round. Conscious again, Nagy thanked Suslov profusely. (See Appendix H: Document 2.) The Soviet comrades, however, were about to rid themselves of Nagy, conscious or otherwise.

Now came the master stroke. On October 30, the Soviet forces pulled out of Budapest. Scenting victory, Nagy made another radio speech in which he promised his countrymen free elections and a prompt end to the one-party dictatorship.

That day, unbeknownst to Nagy, Mikoyan and Suslov sent a joint report to the Presidium on the worsening situation and requested that Marshal Ivan Konev, commander of the Soviet ground forces and of the Warsaw Pact forces, be sent to Hungary urgently. (See Appendix H: Document 3.)

Next day, a famous Hungarian prelate came back into the headlines. Cardinal Josef Mindszenty had been jailed in 1949 for opposing the Communist nationalization of Catholic schools. Now, seven years later, rebel tank forces stormed the prison where he had been held and freed him. A cheering crowd accompanied him to the Episcopal palace. His first action was to celebrate Mass. As eyewitnesses described it, he was clearly tired, but "his large bright eyes had lost none of their intensity. A slight trembling of his hands was the only sign of the ordeals he had suffered and of the emotion he was trying to master."[4]*

Andropov now carried his deception a stroke further. On November 1, he called on Nagy and solemnly assured him that the Soviets were ready to negotiate the withdrawal of their forces.[5]

That night, Andropov summoned János Kádár to the embassy to discuss a plan to install a Soviet-protected regime.** Unaware of these machinations and in the belief that he had won, Nagy on November 2 denounced the Warsaw Pact of 1955 and appealed to the UN to deal with the Hungarian crisis. Indeed, a few days earlier (on October 28), the UN had already voted to discuss the Hungarian problem.

On the night of October 3, Andropov pulled off a further, and this time decisive, deception. He hosted a banquet for General Maleter and other ministers. By prearrangement, the meal was interrupted when the

---

*As the situation worsened, Cardinal Mindszenty sought asylum in the U.S. legation, where he stayed for the next fifteen years. In September 1971, he accepted Pope Paul VI's offer of hospitality and stayed at the Vatican until October, when he moved to Venice.

**Of the required working-class background in Communist politics, Kádár had been trained as a skilled mechanic. When he joined the Communist Party in 1932, it was illegal, and he was arrested more than once. His last arrest was in April 1944. By that time he had been a member of the Central Committee for two years; he joined the Politburo in 1945. Although he was appointed Minister of the Interior after World War II, he clashed with the Stalinist party leadership in 1950, was expelled and jailed where, reportedly, he was tortured on the orders of his former colleagues. Rehabilitated, he joined Imre Nagy's government during the 1956 revolution, which he secretly opposed. In sum, although anti-Stalinist, he was staunchly pro-Moscow, to the detriment of his anti-Moscow fellow Party members.

KGB chairman, Ivan Serov, and an armed contingent burst in and arrested Maleter and his compatriots.

Nagy's denouncement of the Warsaw Pact was a case of "famous last words." There had been ominous reports that five new Soviet divisions were on their way to Hungary from East Germany. On November 4, the reports were confirmed when the enlarged Red Army forces crossed the frontier. That day Moscow radio interrupted its programs to report that Kádár had set up a rival Hungarian government at Szolnok, headed by himself and clearly under Soviet protection. Three days later, Kádár returned to Budapest from Szolnok and, with Soviet backing, ousted Nagy and took over from him. In distant New York, the UN General Assembly adopted a resolution condemning the Soviet assault on Hungary and calling for an inquiry.

This was a verdict that the Soviet leadership could not allow to pass unchallenged. As on many other occasions, the Soviet channel for favorable propaganda was the World Peace Council (WPC). On November 7, the Soviet Presidium instructed the Soviet representatives to oppose any document for publication by the WPC "which might be viewed as interference in the internal affairs of Hungary." The Presidium also instructed the Soviet Committee for the Defense of Peace to "state that the counter-revolutionary revolt of reactionary forces in Hungary . . . led to an orgy of the most brutal terror against the progressive forces of the country [and], constituted a threat to the cause of peace and security in Europe."

It would be hard to quote a better example of what George Orwell called "Newspeak" and the French Sovietologist Françoise Thom termed *la langue de bois* ("the wooden tongue"). There was a follow-up in the form of appeals to prominent French leaders of the peace movement (including the physician and member of the French Communist Party Frédáric Joliot-Curie, and the journalist, politician, and former resistance fighter Emmanuel d'Astier de la Vigerie) to observe "the correct interpretation of the events in Hungary." (See Appendix H: Document 4.)

ONE OF KÁDÁR'S first concerns as Hungary's new and pro-Soviet leader was to speak out in justification of the second Soviet intervention, much as Gerö had done for the first. Once more, the dreaded AVH were out in strength "escorting Russian soldiers and picking out former insurgents for arrest."[6]

Belatedly realizing that he had been tricked, Nagy had taken refuge in the nearest "Titoist" shelter: the Yugoslav embassy. Perhaps anticipating the utility of an approach to Tito, the Soviet Presidium, in an "IMMEDI-ATE TOP SECRET" telegram had ordered the Soviet ambassador in Belgrade to arrange an "incognito" meeting of Khrushchev and Malenkov with the Yugoslav leader. (See Appendix H: Document 5.)

A follow-up came in the form of written guarantees by Kádár that Nagy and his colleagues who had also sought refuge under Yugoslav diplomatic protection could now go home safely, without fear of reprisals. Trusting his word, they boarded a coach that was to take them to their homes on the evening of November 22. A group of Soviet officers stopped the bus, seized the passengers, and delivered them to the Soviet military.

Victory for the Soviet side had already come on November 14 when the invading forces crushed the last rebel stronghold on Csepel Island.

In large numbers, Hungarian workers had fled to neighboring Austria and beyond. Now, those who had stayed behind called a general strike, and on December 12 the UN General Assembly passed a resolution condemning the Soviet repression in Hungary, calling for the withdrawal of Soviet forces and urging the restoration of Hungary's independence. As with so many UN resolutions, this one was ignored.

In charge of the Soviet role in the repression of any counter-revolutionary moves from the Hungarians was the then head of the KGB, Ivan Serov. In a report to the Central Committee, passed on to Khrushchev on November 27, 1956, he made these points:

- In most Hungarian industrial towns 60 percent or more of the workers had returned after fleeing to the country or idling in the towns.
- A delegation had been sent to talk to Nagy and ask him to confirm the "voluntary nature" of his departure from Hungary*, and press for an assurance that he had no intention of returning to political activity.
- The U.S. embassy was "beginning to find the presence of Cardinal Mindszenty a burden." The Hungarian government had declined to give the Cardinal "the opportunity to leave the country," and the Pope had refused to help. The KGB had sent an agent to see Mindszenty and

---

*Nagy had left the Yugoslav embassy, but was then deported to Romania. He was forcibly brought back to Budapest, tried, and executed.

offer to take him out of the country illegally. Should he agree, "it is intended to detain him after he leaves the Mission."

- As many as 700 people a day were still attempting to flee to Austria.
- Documents had been provided for Kádár to propose an overhaul of intelligence, counterintelligence, the police, and the frontier guards.
- To these ends, the KGB had proposed to provide "our Hungarian friends" with twenty-seven KGB advisers. (See Appendix H: Document 6.)

ON FEBRUARY 10, 1957, the Kádár government again made Russian a compulsory school subject, reverted to piecework payment instead of salaries for workers, and repudiated a promise of religious education made by the Nagy government.

On March 28, Khrushchev summoned Kádár to Moscow, where he signed agreements providing for Soviet economic aid and the continued presence of Soviet forces in Hungary. The delayed fate of the rebellious Hungarian leaders came on June 17, 1958, when Imre Nagy and Pál Maleter were executed after a secret trial.

AUSTRIAN ADDENDUM

HISTORICALLY, AUSTRIA HAD been the dominant section of the Austro-Hungarian Empire. From 1938 to 1945, however, Austria (Hitler's original home) was part of the Nazi Reich. When the Allies occupied it on April 28, 1945, it was given special treatment denied to Germany in that it was treated not as a defeated enemy but as a "liberated" country: a tacit recognition of the fact that it had been annexed by Hitler in the *Anschluss* of 1938. Nevertheless, it was occupied, as Germany was, by the four victorious Allies: the Soviet Union, the United States, Britain, and France. Specifically, the country was divided into four occupation zones, as was its capital Vienna. January 7, 1946, however, the occupying powers officially recognized the Austrian Republic within its pre-*Anschluss* frontiers.

Thereafter, the Western Allies treated Austria with leniency, but not the USSR, which requisitioned livestock and industrial equipment and insisted on major reparations from former German assets. This seriously slowed down the country's economic recovery. Indeed, the behavior of the Soviet occupying power stimulated a good deal of muted speculation as to whether

Stalin might be entertaining the possibility of turning its occupied area into another version of the German Democratic Republic. As it happened, the provisional Austrian government proclaimed in April 1948 was styled— ominously, to some Western ears—the "Democratic Republic of Austria." However, on October 9, 1949, the first general election since 1930 gave the People's Party (successor to the prewar Christian Socialists) a majority over the combined Socialists and Communists. Moreover, the strength of the Communists was negligible, and the Socialists were their enemies.

As late as February 6, 1953, a conference of Allied deputy foreign ministers on an Austrian Peace Treaty was deadlocked. However, on March 5, almost exactly a month later, Stalin died; almost immediately Moscow's attitude toward Austria softened.

On June 8, 1953, the Soviet Union lifted its control restrictions along the dividing line between the Soviet and Western zones. On July 30, the So- viets announced that from August 5 they would pay their own occupation costs, as the United States had been doing for the past six years. Although Moscow rejected an invitation from the Western Allies for a London meet- ing to discuss a full peace treaty with Austria, better news lay ahead.

On April 11, 1955, the Austrian chancellor, Julius Raab (who had headed a People's Party-Socialist coalition government for the previous two years) ar- rived in Moscow to discuss Soviet terms for a peace treaty. The follow-up was a conference of the four foreign ministers in Vienna, which culminated on May 15 in a state treaty calling for the withdrawal of all occupation forces from Austria by the end of the year. On July 27, 1955, the Allies held their last meet- ing in Vienna, and Austria formally regained its sovereignty, thus avoiding the partial satellization that for some years had seemed to threaten it.

As Jan Librach rightly observes, however, "Military and political con- siderations did not prevent the Soviet government from selling its consent to the Austrian Treaty for hard cash."[7] The Potsdam summit had prom- ised that Austria was to pay no reparations, but Moscow got around this pledge by selling back to Austria "property rights and interests held or claimed as German assets." Equipment or property "held or claimed as war booty" was similarly treated. Under Article 22 of the state treaty, the Soviet Union received a thirty-year concession to oil fields equivalent to "60 percent of the extraction of oil in Austria for 1947." There were fur- ther similar concessions. As Librach observes, "The Austrian government was prepared to pay heavily for the speedy departure of Soviet troops."

CHAPTER TWENTY

THE SINO-SOVIET
RIFT BEGINS

1955–1962

ONCE JOSEPH STALIN was dead, the Sino-Soviet rift was probably inevitable. Although Mao Tse-tung had praised Stalin in worshipful terms after the signing of the Soviet-Chinese Treaty of February 1950, after the Soviet dictator was gone he poured forth his resentful feelings. The reasons were innate to Mao, but they were exacerbated by specific events, both before and after Stalin's death.

First, the innate reasons. The primary one was undoubtedly Mao's Chinese pride. He saw himself as a new emperor of an ancient country, one with a far longer history than upstart Russia. He was ready to bow to Marxism as a theory and to Lenin as the leader of the world's first Communist revolution. Equally, he was ready to bow to Stalin as Lenin's successor and to the Soviet State as the first of its kind.

Beyond that, Mao was deeply resentful of Stalin's indifference during the long years of China's civil war and of his good relations with Chiang Kai-shek. Though well aware of his debt to Stalin for his intervention against Japan in the Pacific war and his transfer of seized Japanese weaponry to the Chinese People's Liberation Army, he resented Stalin's refusal to meet the costs of China's intervention in the Korean war. When Nikita Khrushchev emerged as Stalin's successor, Mao viewed him, too, as an upstart. From then on he insisted on equality of relations. Henceforth, there were two "equal" Communist great powers. Mao refused to bow to the occupant of the Kremlin.

The key specific events that influenced Mao were the Bandung conference of 1955; Khrushchev's secret speech of February 1956; Khrushchev's aid programs to other countries; his policy of improving relations with the United States; his refusal to help China acquire nuclear weapons; and Khrushchev's neutral stance in the Sino-Indian border clashes of 1959–1962.

SOVIET UNION EXCLUDED

THE BANDUNG CONFERENCE of Asian and African States was inspired and hosted by Indonesia's President Achmad Sukarno. Twenty-five nations sent delegations, and observers came from other places, including Cyprus, Israel, and South Africa (a group of African National Congress members). Despite its gigantic Asian lands, the USSR was not invited. By common consent, the man who dominated the conference was Mao's foreign minister, Chou En-lai.*

Since the idea of the conference did not originate in China, Moscow had no cause to blame Mao for its exclusion, but Khrushchev and his colleagues undoubtedly felt snubbed. Through the Soviet-controlled World Peace Council, an Indian emissary, purporting to be neutral but in reality acting for Moscow, persuaded President Gamal Abdel Nassar of Egypt (who had attended the Bandung gathering) to sponsor a "people's conference" in Cairo at the end of 1957. From it emerged a new front organization, the Afro-Asian People's Solidarity Organization (AAPSO).[1]

STALIN'S EXCESSES

NIKITA KHRUSHCHEV'S SECRET speech, which detailed some of Stalin's excesses, before the Twentieth Congress of the Soviet Communist Party (CPSU) was a turning point in the history of the USSR and of world Communism. The date was February 25, 1956, and, although the speech and the occasion were supposed to be secret, leaks soon occurred through the speeches of foreign Communist leaders who had been present. On March 27, the Polish Communist newspaper *Trybuna Ludu* carried a

---

*The spelling was changed to Zhou Enlai after his death in January 1976.

lengthy summary by Jerzy Morawski, one of the secretaries of the United Workers' Party. The official Polish translation came into the hands of the American CIA and was issued by the State Department on June 4, thence finding its way into many Western newspapers. It was a very long speech, running to 26,000 words.[2]

In it, Khrushchev disclosed that torture had been extensively used to extract "confessions"; thousands of innocent persons had been executed at Stalin's instigation; Stalin had been responsible for the ruthless and un-justified mass deportation of ethnic minorities during World War II. For good measure, Khrushchev bitterly attacked Stalin's "megalomania" and "self-glorification" (the "cult of personality"). Deriding Stalin's military capacities and wartime leadership, he added that Stalin had ignored re-peated warnings from Winston Churchill and others that the Germans were about to attack the Soviet Union.

A few weeks after Khrushchev's secret speech, Mao had a lengthy meeting with the Soviet ambassador, Pavel Yudin, on March 31, 1956.[3] According to Yudin, Mao was highly critical of Stalin. (For selected ex-tracts see Appendix I: Document 1.)

Also of interest are Chou En-lai's "observations on the Soviet Union," in an oral report to Mao and the Central Committee on January 24, 1957.[4] The foreign minister criticized the despatch of Soviet troops to Warsaw the previous October as "clearly interference in the internal affairs of a brotherly party by armed forces, but not an action to suppress counter-revolutionaries." But the Soviet party leaders denied that their in-tervention was a mistake. Chou complained that they kept avoiding any real discussion of Stalin's mistakes.

Chou went on to complain that the three top Soviet leaders (Khru-shchev, Bulganin, and Mikoyan) were unwilling to discuss criticisms of Stalin. They also demonstrated weakness in considering and discussing strategic and long-term issues. Despite all this, "Sino-Soviet relations are far better now than in Stalin's era."

In a further meeting with ambassador Yudin on July 22, 1958, Mao, who was evidently on relaxed terms with him, used heavy irony and, at one point, scatological language.[5]

As this conversation is a sequel to one that took place the day before, of which no record had been released when these lines were written, there is a one-dimensional air about it. Mao starts off by saying that "after you left yesterday, I could not fall asleep, nor did I have dinner. Today I invite you over to talk a bit more so that you can be [my] doctor: [after talking with you] I might be able to eat and sleep this afternoon." (See Appendix I: Document 2.)

Mao went on in the same vein, at one point describing relations between the Chinese and Russian parties as "between father and son or between cats and mice." He went on: "When did the Soviets begin to trust us Chinese? At the time when [we] entered the Korean War." Once again, he put the main responsibility for this state of affairs on Stalin. Recalling once again the way he was treated on his first visit to Moscow, he referred to a meeting with I. V. Kovalev, through N. T. Fedorenko as interpreter: "I got so angry that I once pounded on the table. I only had three tasks here [in Moscow], I said to them: the first was to eat, the second was to sleep, and the third was to shit."

He was particularly indignant at the behavior of a Soviet adviser in the Chinese military academy who would only allow the Chinese trainees to discuss Soviet military involvements. There could be no mention of China's battles. "For God's sake, we fought wars for twenty-four years; we fought in Korea for three years!"

ON THE ECONOMIC front, Mao had good reasons to be disappointed in Moscow's attitude. One reason was the Soviet failure to live up to promises (as Mao interpreted Stalin's words) to meet the costs of China's intervention in the Korean War. As Eric Chou put it, "He [Mao] was, therefore, shocked to find out, after the Korean truce, that China had to repay the Soviet Union an enormous sum for the military expenditure in Korea. Although he was 'too angry for words'" at a top level meeting, according to an eyewitness, he decided that the Russians should have every penny they asked for."[6]

Mao's understandable resentment was exacerbated by the obsolete or substandard industrial equipment and machines supplied by the Soviets to "help" China's industrialization program.

A FURTHER CAUSE for resentment surfaced in the aftermath of the Polish and Hungarian crises in October 1956 (see Chapters 16 and 17).

Mao's response to the Polish unrest was to support the "patriotic" Communist Wladyslav Gomulka and to urge the Soviet Union to avoid military intervention; and Khrushchev did indeed opt for a peaceful settlement with Gomulka.[7] (See also Appendix I: Documents 3 and 4.)

In the graver Hungarian crisis, Chinese senior officials, who had gone to Moscow on October 30 for emergency consultations with their Soviet colleagues, at first took the same line as they had over Poland. This may have been a factor in the initial Soviet decision to withdraw their armed forces.* However, when Khrushchev reversed his decision and sent the Soviet forces back to crush the uprising, Mao instantly sided with Moscow, especially when on November 1 Imre Nagy announced that Hungary was pulling out of the Warsaw Pact. As Mark Kramer puts it, China "became the most vocal supporter of the invasion, and even publicly welcomed the execution of Imre Nagy in June 1958."[8]

What Mao clearly had not allowed for was the economic consequences of the Polish and Hungarian crises. Whereas in the past few years, the Soviet Union had plundered the East European satellites, Mao now felt compelled, in the interest of stability, to plough back the Soviet Union's arbitrary profits. The well-known Sovietologist Edward Crankshaw estimated the "plough-back" at "something like a billion dollars."[9] As Crankshaw observed, China was hit very hard by this diversion of funds that could have been used to aid the Chinese economy.

As if to rub salt into China's wounded vanity, between 1971 and 1980 the Soviet Union signed treaties of "Friendship and Cooperation" with a number of Third World countries (Egypt, India, Iraq, Somalia, Angola, Ethiopia, Vietnam, and Afghanistan; see Chapter 28). By then, in any case, relations between the two major Communist powers had reached a low point.

No Nuclear Arms

OF ALL THE developments that contributed to sparking the Sino-Soviet rift, by far the most important was Moscow's flat refusal either to provide

---

*This is one interpretation of the situation. Another, to which I incline, is that the withdrawal was merely a deception. (See Chapter 18.)—BC

China with nuclear weapons and means of delivery, or to give the Chinese the technological know-how to build their own; or even to use their apparent superiority in this field to intimidate the United States (until the Cuba crisis of 1962, by which time the rift was an established fact).

On October 4, 1957, Moscow launched its first spacecraft. Mao and his regime were exultant. At last the "Socialist camp" had demonstrated its strategic, as well as its ideological, superiority over the American-led "imperialists." The time had come for the Soviet Union to impose its strategic aims on the United States and NATO. Khrushchev and his team were no less exultant, but were far more cautious in confrontational terms.

Ideological differences between China and the Soviet Union duly surfaced at the conference of twelve Communist parties in Moscow in November 1957, timed to coincide with the fortieth anniversary of Lenin's Bolshevik Revolution. Nevertheless, the Chinese had no difficulty in signing the final declaration.

The full significance of the developing rift can be understood only in the context of the hubris that overtook Mao Tse-tung in the mid-1950s. In 1957, he had launched a policy known as "the Hundred Flowers," during a speech he had made early in the year but released in an edited version that was published in June. In it, he appeared to be authorizing freedom of speech, but when many "intellectuals" took advantage of it to criticize the regime, it became clear that Mao's real objective was to trap dissidents into revealing their true thoughts. A mass persecution duly followed.[10]

By the following year Mao's megalomania may be said to have taken a "Great Leap Forward," to borrow the name of the policy that he launched in February 1958. The idea was to mobilize the entire population to industrialize the whole vast country in one frenetic movement. Steel, the symbol of advanced industrial success, was to be made in the backyards of the peasants. To meet the ambitious production targets, the Communist Party falsified the statistics on a massive scale. Along with the Great Leap Forward, in March came another demented idea: the merging of the entire peasant population into agricultural communes. Privacy was banned and peasant families were thus deprived of family reunions: their only consolation for, and escape from, lives of scarcity.[11]

As could have been predicted, these experiments ended in utter disaster. The backyard "steel" turned out to be mere iron, largely consisting of melted saucepans, and the diversion of peasant labor to fake metal industry, plus the upheaval of the communes, caused a disastrous famine, the existence of which was strenuously denied by Chinese propaganda but confirmed by a huge flow of refugees to Hong Kong.

The relevance of Mao's failed internal policies to this account of the Sino-Soviet rift was highlighted in July 1959, when the Party's Central Committee met in the summer resort of Lushan. Mao, full of bombast, was armed with the falsified statistics of the Great Leap Forward. Unexpectedly, he ran into a strong barrage of criticism from his defense minister, Marshal Peng Teh-huai. Although Peng was careful to speak words of praise as well as sarcastically outspoken criticism, the latter prevailed; he compounded his "offense" by spelling out his criticisms in a letter to Mao. Most notably, he dared to mention the fact that Mao's claims of success rested on false statistics. Mao called for a full discussion of Peng's letter, then ordered the Central Committee to sack him as defense minister. Although Peng was not executed, he was exiled with his wife to a remote village in Szechuan province and replaced by the more compliant Marshal Lin Piao.

It became known that Marshal Peng, during an extensive tour of the Soviet Union and Eastern Europe in the spring of 1959, had briefed Khrushchev about his views of Mao's initiatives. It was clear that Peng's real aim was the removal of Mao from the leadership of the Chinese Communist Party. At a meeting of Communist parties in Bucharest in June 1960, Khrushchev protested to the Chinese about Peng's removal, arguing that his only offense was that he had taken the Soviet Party into his confidence.[12] The Russians further manifested their displeasure in a

---

*One of the most important Soviet defectors, Anatoly Golitsyn, argued in his book *New Lies for Old* (1984) that the Sino-Soviet rift was a KGB disinformation exercise designed to fool the West. He persuaded the CIA's head of counterintelligence, James Jesus Angleton, that this unlikely thesis was indeed true, with unfortunate consequences for the CIA. The contrary view was expounded by a senior member of Britain's MI-6 (or Secret Intelligence Service: SIS), who covered and analyzed the Marshal Peng episode, under the name of David A. Charles in the *China Quarterly*, No. 8, 1961. This Anglo-American divergence of interpretation led to regrettable disunity at a key moment in the Cold War, as described in my autobiography, *Free Agent* (1993), pp. 44–45. Although personally I find the Golitsyn view completely unconvincing, it has to be said that Golitsyn's forecast of forthcoming events in Chapter 25 of his book was uncannily accurate. Writing before the ascension of Mikhail Gorbachev, he foresaw, among other things, the return of Dubček in Czechoslovakia, the freeing of Sakharov (the dissident scientist), and the demolition of the Berlin Wall.—BC

more damaging and fundamental way by removing all their technicians and advisers who had been stationed in China for years.*

This was "it": the rift had become a tangible reality. Against Mao's known wishes, Khrushchev went to the United States in September 1959, where he made speeches, friends, and enemies. Among the "friends" was President Eisenhower, with whom he spent three days in the isolated Presidential Lodge at Camp David in the hills of Maryland, culminating in an amicable joint communiqué. Back in Moscow, he praised Eisenhower as a wise, statesmanlike figure who could be trusted to keep the Pentagon warmongers under control.

On September 29, only twenty-four hours after his return from the United States, Khrushchev flew to Peking, where he faced a chilly, indeed hostile, reception. The Chinese leaders blasted American imperialism, while he praised peaceful coexistence. Unusually, there was no communiqué at the end of the Soviet leader's visit.

THE CHINA-INDIA CRISIS

THE CHILLINESS AND hostility arose not only from Khrushchev's praise of Eisenhower but perhaps even more from Chinese fury at the neutral stance adopted by Moscow when Chinese forces crossed the border with India in August 1959—a few weeks before Khrushchev's visit. In a lengthy statement on September 9, the Soviet government confirmed that it maintained friendly relations with both countries and called for a restoration of "the spirit of traditional friendship between the peoples of China and India."[13]

This was not at all the form of words the Chinese expected from the Communist superpower. *Neutrality* translated as "hostility."

Despite the blatant breach with the USSR, the Chinese attended the conference of eighty-one Communist parties in Moscow at the end of 1960. To nobody's surprise, Mao Tse-tung did not come. The principal Chinese spokesman was Teng Hsiao-p'ing, who attacked the Soviet stance in world affairs in the stylized ideological vocabulary that was difficult for outsiders to comprehend but was intelligible to the other participants. Apart from tiny Albania, by now heavily Maoist, all the responding speeches sided with Moscow. For the last time in the international Communist movement, the final declaration was signed by the Chinese as well as the Soviets. The key passage, for ideologically untrained Western leaders and commentators, was the following: "Peaceful co-existence of countries with different social systems does not mean conciliation of the socialist and bourgeois ideologies. On the contrary, it means *intensification of the struggle* of the working class, of all Communist parties, for the triumph of socialist ideas. But ideological and political disputes between states must not be settled through war." (Italics added.)

In plainer words, the Cold War would be intensified. Although the Chinese did sign the Final Declaration, one of the differences between their party and the CPSU was that Khrushchev was determined to avoid a nuclear war, whereas Mao favored brinkmanship, on the ground that the Socialist camp was now stronger than the "imperialist" one. In the Cuba crisis of 1962 (see Chapter 21), Khrushchev would demonstrate that he, too, was capable of brinkmanship, but was ready to withdraw when challenged.

PHASE V

THE PERIPHERAL
EMPIRE
1953–1990

CHAPTER TWENTY-ONE

THE RISE OF FIDEL CASTRO

1953–1962

B EFORE THE EMERGENCE of Fidel Castro as a leader in Cuba in
1959–1960, a tacit but reassuring "theory of contiguity" had prevailed in Western strategic circles. In other words, Western strategists
had assumed that the Soviet Empire would only expand if military contingents were available on the spot or in a neighboring country. And indeed, new Communist satellites had been added through occupation (as
in East Germany), conquest (as in Poland), or intimidating proximity (as
in Czechoslavakia in 1948). The Soviet takeover of Cuba, an island close
to the United States but thousands of miles from the USSR, marked the
start of what I have called "the peripheral empire."

A new and relatively bloodless technique had been executed successfully: a Communist, or potential Communist, seized power in the
satellite country; the KGB established a surrogate secret intelligence
service; economic dependence forced obedience to Moscow. Once a peripheral satellite was established, it might try to go its own way, but this
the imperial power would not tolerate. The dissident satellite would be
taught a lesson and brought to heel. There would be other examples of
dissident peripheral satellites—among them Somalia, Ethiopia, South
Yemen, and two mini-states—Grenada and the Seychelles.

FAILURE IN GUATEMALA

CUBA WAS NOT the first example of a Communist attempt to seize power by proxy in Latin America: it was the first *successful* attempt. Moreover, there were failed attempts in Africa as well. A Latin American failure had taken place earlier, in 1951, in the Central American state of Guatemala. At that time, Guatemala was a typical "banana republic," virtually a colony of the powerful United Fruit Company (UFC), a privately owned concern founded in 1899 to grow bananas in Central America and northern South America for the export market. Ten years earlier, on the morrow of the Japanese assault on the American fleet in Pearl Harbor in December 1941, Guatemala had declared war on Japan, "thus expressing the solidarity of the Guatemalan government and people with the United States." "Banana republics" were in effect satellites of the United States, and Guatemala was not alone in declaring war on Japan; Cuba, El Salvador, Honduras, Nicaragua, and Costa Rica did as well. This readiness to support America was doubtless beneficial to the banana republics, but unlikely to strike terror in Japanese breasts.

Nine years later, in November 1950, events in Guatemala would take an unexpected turn when an Army officer of Swiss origin, Colonel Jacobo Arbenz Guzmén, was elected president. He soon waged, in effect, a war against the United Fruit Company. In June 1952, the Guatemalan Congress passed a Communist-supported land reform bill, which President Arbenz signed on June 17. On February 25, 1953, the Guatemalan Agrarian Department informed the UFC that the government planned to expropriate 225,000 of the company's 300,000-acre holdings.

Although this threat was seen in Washington as a political challenge that should not be ignored, American reaction was not immediate. As late as October 14, the U.S. assistant secretary of state, John Cabot, declared that Guatemala could not expect any U.S. help or cooperation, since it was "openly playing the Communist game." A further lull followed. On January 29, 1954, the Arbenz government issued a warning that Nicaragua, with the "tacit assent" of the United States and support from several Latin American states, was planning a land, sea, and air invasion of Guatemala. On March 17, the State Department reported a major shipment of

"Communist-made" arms to Guatemala and expressed "grave concern" over the strong Communist movement that was developing there.*

What happened next amounted to a long-distance confrontation between the American Central Intelligence Agency (CIA) and the MGB, *Ministertsvo Gosudarstvennoy Bezopasnosti* (Ministry for State Security), immediate predecessor of the Soviet KGB. The CIA's (very willing) instrument was a former colleague of President Arbenz, Colonel Carlos Castillo-Armas, then in exile in Honduras. The CIA provided Castillo-Armas with a well-armed though tiny force of 150 soldiers, plus a small air force of P-47 Thunderbolts commanded by a CIA-appointed fighter pilot, Jerry Fred DeLarm.[1] On June 18, 1954, the P-47s bombed the Guatemalan port of San José on the Pacific coast.

The next target was Guatemala City: a leaflet drop, followed by a bombing and strafing raid. More U.S. planes were needed, and the CIA provided them through a gift of $150,000 to the government of Nicaragua. There was tough and uncompromising support from the American ambassador to Guatemala, John E. Peurifoy, and CIA clandestine radio operators spread false messages to create confusion.

The raids broke the Guatemalan president's nerve, and on June 27, Arbenz announced his resignation.

CASTRO'S RISE TO POWER

THE PREVAILING OFFICIAL wisdom in the West after the Communist fiasco in Guatemala was that it demonstrated the limitations of Soviet power and ingenuity. Any further attempts to introduce Communism in the Western hemisphere seemed doomed to failure. Fidel Castro's early attempts to do so, in 1953 and 1956, appeared to confirm this theory.

During this period—1952–1959—Cuba was ruled by a corrupt and self-serving dictator, Fulgencio Batista, who had seized power on March 10, 1952. Fidel Castro Ruz, the son of a Spanish migrant from Galicia, had the

---

*The Guatemalan Communist movement was set up in the early 1920s under the name of *Unificación Obrera Socialista*. In 1924, it changed its name to *Partido Comunista de Guatemala* and joined the Comintern. There was a further name change in 1952, when it became known as the *Partido Guatemalteco del Trabajo*, or PGT. (See the Hoover Institution's *Yearbook on International Communist Affairs*, 1966 edition.)

necessary blend of fanaticism, romanticism, and outsized ego to mount a challenge to Batista. Castro was impressive physically and was a natural and mesmerizing orator.

His first attempt to seize power took place on July 26, 1953, and was quixotic. At dawn that day, Fidel Castro and his small band of followers, armed and uniformed and crammed into thirteen cars, set out to seize Batista's military headquarters at the Moncada barracks in Santiago de Cuba. The amateur rebels were surrounded, and seventy-five of them were killed. The survivors were captured, and Castro was sentenced to fifteen years' imprisonment. He later turned the fiasco into a symbol: henceforth his movement was known as *el 26 de julio*.

Castro served only two years of his sentence, which was commuted in 1955 under an amnesty. He went into exile in Mexico, where he raised $20,000—mainly from ex-President Carlos Prío Socarrés—to buy a 62-foot yacht from an anonymous American. He gathered some eighty followers, who were trained, along with their leader, in the techniques and tactics of guerrilla war by a Republican exile from the Spanish Civil War, Colonel Alberto Bayo.

The yacht, named *Granma*, later gave its inoffensive title to the newspaper of Castro's *Movimiento del 26 de julio*. On November 26, 1956, Castro and his eighty guerrillas set forth from Tuxman on the Gulf of Mexico. They were armed and trained, but their leader had neglected the one indispensable ingredient for a successful revolution: secrecy. Six days later they landed on the southern shore of Oriente province and ran into Batista's alerted 1st Regiment. All but twelve of the rebels were killed. As fate decreed, the survivors included Fidel, his brother Raúl, and a young Argentino later idolized by the world's revolutionary students: Ernesto "Che" Guevara. It took the survivors twenty days, concealed in the marshes, to tramp their way to a natural stronghold in the Sierra Maestra mountains.[2]

In his mountain base, Fidel Castro built up his tiny band of rebels into an effective force. Belatedly, Batista realized what was happening and grasped that he had underestimated Castro. On May 30, 1957, Batista launched a major offensive against the rebels, who by then were under the direct command of Fidel's brother Raúl. Fourteen battalions totaling 10,000 men were deployed in an operation optimistically styled *Fín de Fidel* ("End of Fidel"), with artillery, air, and naval support. Despite their numerical and material inferiority, the rebels held firm. The Cuban Army's offensive lasted seventy-six days, but ended in collapse.[3]

On March 17, 1958, Fidel Castro issued a manifesto calling for "total war" against the Batista regime, to start on April 1. On the last day of the year, his forces captured Santa Clara, capital of Las Vilas province. By then, Batista's nerve had collapsed. On New Year's Day 1959, the Cuban president resigned and fled into exile. That same day Castro's forces took Santiago, and on January 3 they entered Havana. The rebels had won.

THEIR VICTORY WAS clearly a major event, but its full significance was not easy to analyze at the time. The key question was whether Castro's victory had turned Cuba into the Soviet Union's first remote-control satellite. The most confusing factor was that throughout the struggle the Cuban Communist Party had supported (or appeared to support) the Batista regime. Also supportive of Batista was the Communist-controlled trade union organization, the *Central de Trabajadores de Cuba,* whose leader Eusebio Mujal's staunch loyalty to the dictator arose from a debt of gratitude over Batista's backing in an earlier dispute with a rival labor leader. In August 1957, and again in April 1958, Castro had tried, but failed, to call an anti-Batista strike. Mujal's opposition had guaranteed the failures.

Another confusing factor was a declaration by Castro on April 17, 1959, while on an informal visit to Washington, that his regime was not Communist. The word he chose to describe his revolution was *humanistic.* In the light of later revelations, it is fair to assume that he made this disclaimer by agreement with his Soviet contacts. This was probably a piece of deliberate disinformation.

It had long been known that Fidel's younger brother Raúl was a Communist, as was Che Guevara. Although Fidel's Communist allegiance had been concealed for understandable reasons—to mislead public opinion in the West—links had been forged before they became publicly known. Founded in 1925, the *Partido Comunista de Cuba* changed its name in 1944 to *Partido Socialista Popular* (PSP). In June 1958, one of the senior PSP leaders, Carlos Rafael Rodríguez, visited Castro in his Sierra Maestra headquarters,[4] and in July 1959, Ramiro Valdés, chief of G-2 Rebel Army Intelligence, who was known Raúl's Number 2, visited

Mexico "for the sole purpose of making contact with the Soviet ambassador, Vladimir Bazikin, and other Soviet officials."[5]

More significant of Fidel Castro's real allegiance was the Stalinist-type show trial of the Rebel Army Major, Huber Matos Benítez, who resigned in a personal letter to Castro on October 19, 1959, on the ground that the revolution was heading toward Communism. Sentenced to twenty years' incarceration, he was severely tortured and held for the full term of his sentence.*

It would be fair to describe the contacts mentioned above as "feelers," but before long there were open signs of a developing close relationship between the new Cuban regime and the Soviet Union. On February 13, 1960, the Soviet first deputy premier, Anastas Mikoyan, signed an agreement in Havana for the purchase of 5 million tons of sugar, and for a Soviet credit of $100 million. Ten days later, Castro threatened to seize all U.S.-owned property and business interests in Cuba to meet "economic aggression" by the United States. In fact, hostility from the U.S. government *followed* the nationalization by Castro's regime of hundreds of millions of dollars of American-owned property. On July 6, President Dwight D. Eisenhower struck back by cutting America's quota of sugar imports from Cuba by 95 percent. Three days later, Soviet Premier Nikita Khrushchev threatened an attack by Soviet rockets if the United States intervened militarily in Cuba. At this stage, Khrushchev's response seemed disproportionate, but Cuban-American relations continued to deteriorate.

Not long afterward, in March 1960, Khrushchev started bribing Castro both nationally and personally. This began with an offer, in substance, of a blank check to enable Castro to buy weapons and whatever else he might need from Czechoslovakia, subject to reimbursement from Moscow. Then came an unstated personal honorarium for Castro, together with payments for specific items, such as $385 from the USSR for an article written by Castro and published in Moscow. In February 1961, he was given $8,000 for a collection of his speeches. Castro is reported to have exclaimed, "If everything I say is published, I will become a millionaire."[6]

---

*For the full texts of Huber Matos's letter to Castro, and description of the tortures inflicted on him, see Brian Crozier, *The KGB Lawsuits* (London: Claridge Press,1995), Appendices III and IV.

Meanwhile, Cuban relations with the United States had indeed deteriorated further. On January 3, 1961, after Castro had demanded that the U.S. embassy in Havana be reduced from 300 to eleven persons, the United States severed diplomatic relations. The newly elected president, John F. Kennedy, retaliated with a "secret" invasion of Cuba by 1,600 Cuban exiles who established a beachhead near the Bay of Pigs but were driven out with heavy losses.

Months later, on December 2, 1961, Castro publicly declared himself a Marxist-Leninist and announced the formation of a united party dedicated to bring Communism to Cuba. The true satellization of Cuba, however, took the form of a secret KGB operation conducted by a man known as Aleksandr Alexeyev (whose real name was Aleksandr Shitov), who arrived in Havana in 1959 ostensibly as a correspondent of the Soviet news agency, TASS. His "cover" assignment was to gather material for a feature on Fidel Castro and the Cuban revolution. His real purpose, as a KGB officer, was to prepare a Top Secret report for the KGB on the potential creation of a secret intelligence service on the Soviet model. In 1962, at Castro's request, Alexeyev was appointed Soviet ambassador to Havana, a post he filled until 1967.

The outcome of the Alexeyev mission was the creation in mid-1961 of the *Dirección General de Inteligencia,* or DGI.* With one important exception, the DGI closely followed the KGB model. There was a Legal Centers Department, consisting of accredited diplomatic or trade representatives reporting directly to the DGI. In parallel, there was an Illegal Centers Department, consisting of secret agents of all nationalities. The

---

*A detailed account of the satellization process, by Brian Crozier, was first published by the Institute for the Study of Conflict in April 1973, as *Conflict Studies 35,* under the title "Soviet Pressures in the Caribbean: The Satellisation of Cuba." It was reprinted as a chapter of a symposium, edited by Robert Moss, published in book form by the ISC under the title *The Stability of the Caribbean.* In 1987, a high-ranking defector from the Cuban intelligence service, the DGI, on a visit to my London office, asked me where I had obtained the details given in the *Conflict Study.* My reply was evasive, but in fact the text was based on a CIA report made available to me by British intelligence (MI-6). Benemelis quotes the *Conflict Study* twice in the opening chapter of his own memoirs: Juan F. Benemelis, *Castro, Subversión y Terrorismo en África* (Madrid, undated). See also Crozier, *Free Agent* (London: Harper-Collins, 1993), p. 287. Surprisingly, Szulc does not mention Alexeyev's KGB identity or the purpose of his mission in his biography of Castro; nor does he mention the names or the revelations of Cuba's two most important diplomatic defectors, Orlando Castro Hidalgo and Geraldo Jesús Peraza Amechazurra, who defected in 1969 and 1971 respectively.—BC

exception was the National Liberation Department, which Fidel Castro had insisted upon as an instrument for his expressed ambition to sponsor or encourage revolutionary uprisings in various countries, not only in Latin America but in Africa as well.

THE CUBAN MISSILE CRISIS

THE GREAT CUBAN Missile Crisis of October 1962 put considerable strain upon Soviet-Cuban relations. In August 1962, the CIA had reported to President Kennedy that the Soviet force on Cuban soil had built up to about 5,000 soldiers and was still growing. Heavy construction equipment and electronic devices were being unloaded daily. The initial agency analysis seemed to point to purely defensive measures: it would not be surprising, in the light of the Bay of Pigs landing, if the Soviet Union should decide to offer its small ally additional protection.

This reassuring though provisional diagnosis was soon judged mistaken, however, when the United States stepped up its U-2 reconnaissance flights high in Cuba's air space. In early September, they reported that Soviet merchant vessels carrying forty-two nuclear missiles had left the Black Sea. It soon emerged that the missiles were bound for the Caribbean.

Conclusive evidence came on October 14 with a U-2 flight that reported that a Soviet missile had been placed on the ground at San Cristobal, along with a launching pad and storage for further missiles. Challenged by American diplomats, their Soviet colleagues denied that any such threatening actions were taking place.

Kennedy knew better, and on October 22 he announced a U.S. air and naval "quarantine" to prevent any further arms shipments to Cuba. Khrushchev reacted to Kennedy's challenge with alternate blustering and conciliation. The president knew that he could afford to stand firm, mainly because of the sensationally detailed intelligence brought to the CIA by the Soviet double agent Oleg Penkovsky, which proved that contrary to earlier perceptions, the United States enjoyed absolute nuclear superiority over the USSR.[7]

On October 28, Kennedy and Khrushchev agreed that the Soviet Union would remove all its missiles from Cuba in return for an end to the U.S. quarantine and a U.S. promise not to invade Cuba. It was learned later that the U.S. victory, although real, was less complete than had originally appeared. Kennedy had given a formal agreement to make no further efforts to bring down the Castro regime, which, paradoxically, cleared the way for the Soviet Union, some years later, to bring Cuba under its complete control. Moreover, Khrushchev extracted an agreement from Kennedy to remove U.S. missiles in Turkey that were pointed at Soviet targets—in effect a betrayal of America's NATO allies.[8]

The Kennedy-Khrushchev agreement enraged Fidel Castro. The Cubans learned of it from a Moscow broadcast that morning. To make matters worse, from Castro's viewpoint, he had in the early hours of October 27 sent a message to Khrushchev that (presumably because of the time zones) had been received in the Kremlin very late that day. In his message, Castro had predicted (quite erroneously, as it happened) that U.S. military strikes, and quite possibly an invasion, were likely to take place within the next twenty-four to seventy-two hours (that is, in view of the time difference, conceivably ten or twelve hours after Khrushchev received the message). "We were profoundly incensed," Castro would say in a 1968 speech.

Presumably with the object of conciliating the outraged Cuban leader, Khrushchev sent Anastas Mikoyan of the Soviet Party Presidium to Havana on November 3, 1962. He stayed until November 12. Not surprisingly, Khrushchev gave precedence to Mikoyan's long experience over any personal consideration for his colleague: Mikoyan's wife of forty years, Ashken Tumanian, was dying in a Moscow hospital when he boarded the plane at Moscow airport. News of her death reached him while he was having his first, and most emotive, exchange with Castro on November 3.

On November 3, the only other person present at the meeting between Castro and Mikoyan was Ambassador Alexeyev, who interpreted. Mikoyan presented the Kennedy-Khrushchev deal as a Soviet-Cuban victory, not a surrender to U.S. demands, since the deal relieved Cuba from a possible nuclear attack. He came back, time and again, to this and similar arguments, at a third meeting on the afternoon of November 5. At least temporarily, Mikoyan's patience paid off, for that afternoon a grudging Castro expressed gratitude and an emotional declaration of "unshakable" respect and "complete trust" in the Soviet Union.

The trust and respect were short-lived, however, and Castro's temper was aroused once more, only minutes later, when Mikoyan tried to convince him to accept a United Nations inspection of the dismantling of the nuclear missile sites on the ground that this would deepen the sympathy of U Thant, the Burmese secretary-general of the UN, and remove any pretext for a continued U.S. blockade. Castro was not prepared to "buy" this argument, since it was clear that this was yet another arrangement Khrushchev had made without consulting him. "A unilateral inspection," he told Mikoyan, "would affect monstrously the moral spirit of our people."

Similar spirited clashes followed until Mikoyan, evidently tiring of Castro's rejection of his emollient arguments, reminded Castro that the Cubans were getting weapons and goods free of charge. The Soviets had also covered the Cuban balance of payments ($100 million) "in order to foil the Kennedy plan, designed to detonate Cuba from within."

The meeting of November 4 was attended by five other Cubans besides Fidel Castro, including President Osvaldo Dorticós, Raúl Castro, and Che Guevara. Fidel expressed indignant surprise that Cuba had not been informed, before the event, of the agreement between Khrushchev and Kennedy under which the American president agreed to withdraw U.S. missiles from Turkey. In reply, Mikoyan played down the deal: "I see now that the Cubans were regarding this demand as if it was some sort of exchange. There are USA bases not only in Turkey, but also in England and other European countries. But nowadays these bases do not have decisive importance insofar as the long-range strategic missiles, aimed at Europe, can quickly destroy them."

There was yet another meeting between Mikoyan and the Cuban leaders on November 5, which included a long exchange between Che Guevara, who was outspokenly critical of the Soviet role in the missiles crisis, and the Soviet visitor:

> Our stake in Cuba is huge in both a material and moral [sense], and also in a military regard. Think about it, are we really helping you out of [our] overabundance? Do we have something extra? We don't have enough for ourselves. No, we want to preserve the base of socialism in Latin America, but the camp of socialism still has not grown into its full capability to come to your assistance. We give you ships, weapons, people, fruits and vegetables.[9]

Mission accomplished, Mikoyan winged his way back to Moscow.

*   *   *

IT IS NOW known, through secret documents released in Havana as well as in Moscow, that although Castro had been informed in advance of the Soviet plan to station nuclear missiles on Cuban soil, known as Operation Anadyr, Khrushchev simply bypassed the Cuban leader during the actual crisis. Always known for his interminable pronouncements, Fidel Castro delivered a twelve-hour speech on January 25 and 26, 1968, before the ruling party's Central Committee. The speech was secret at the time, but key passages were released early in 1995.[10]

Castro disclosed (or claimed) that a Soviet delegation headed by the Uzbek Party chief, Sharif Rashidov, had come to Havana in May 1962 and proposed the installation of ballistic missiles in Cuba: "We saw it as a means of strengthening the socialist community . . . and if we were proposing that the entire socialist community be prepared to go to war to defend any socialist country, then we had no right to raise any questions about something that could represent a potential danger."

At the time of the Rashidov visit, Castro and his party were convinced that the United States would shortly invade Cuba. There were three grounds for this belief. One was that it made no sense, in Cuban eyes, to suppose that President Kennedy and his administration would not retaliate against the Bay of Pigs fiasco. Another was the January 1962 suspension of Cuba's membership in the Organization of American States (OAS) for violation of human rights and promotion of subversion in Latin America. A third, and more serious, reason for alarm was the development of "Operation Mongoose": a U.S. covert action, approved by Kennedy at the end of November 1961, at the time the largest CIA operation ever undertaken. The United States trained thousands of Cuban exiles who, on a mounting scale, conducted acts of sabotage in Cuba. Factories were being destroyed, fields set alight, and sugar exports contaminated. Although the DGI did not have access to CIA documents on Operation Mongoose, it had successfully infiltrated the exile groups and captured some of the saboteurs.

Castro had appealed to the Soviets to make a public announcement about the installation of nuclear missiles, as a deterrent to an American invasion. Keeping the operation secret, he argued in his 1968 speech, required

the resort to lies which in effect meant to waive a basic right and a principle. . . . Cuba is a sovereign, independent country, and has the right to own the weapons that it deems necessary, and the USSR to send them there, in the same light as the United States has felt that it has the right to make agreements with dozens of countries, without the Soviet Union ever considering that it had the right to intercede. From the very outset it was a capitulation, an erosion of our sovereignty.

As early as 1959, before the creation of the DGI, Cuban-organized expeditions had been sent to invade the Dominican Republic, Haiti, Nicaragua, and Panama. No Cuban fifth columns existed in these countries, and all the attempts flopped. These doomed attempts were proof of Che Guevara's influence upon Castro, for "the Che," as he was called, nursed the self-deluding fantasy that the mere fact of launching insurgencies would create *focos* or revolutionary centers. In other words, the launching of a revolution would spark it into life.

The Soviets had no time for such romantic delusions, but Castro, though disappointed at the Cuban-sponsored failures, chose to return to the charge on the symbolic date of July 26, 1963 (the tenth anniversary of Castro's movement). A Peruvian Trotskyist, Hugo Blanco, had already heeded an earlier appeal from Castro by launching a terrorist campaign with Cuban support in November 1962. Not long after, Blanco was arrested with most of his followers. In Colombia, the Cubans decided to support a band led by Pedro Antonio Marín, better known as *Tiro Fijo* ("Dead Shot") in recognition of his several hundred murders. In northeast Brazil, the Cubans helped Francisco Julião's Peasant Leagues. In Venezuela, the pro-Cuban *Movimiento de la Izquierda Revolucionaria* (Movement of the Revolutionary Left) joined the Venezuelan Communist Party to set up a militant arm under the name of *Fuerzas Armadas de Liberación Nacional* (FALN, or Armed Forces of National Liberation). The FALN launched terrorist campaigns in Caracas and in the countryside. In November 1963, three tons of arms were discovered in a remote spot on Venezuela's Paraguana Peninsula. A Cuban-sponsored attempt to sabotage the Venezuelan presidential elections in December failed, however, and full-scale violence did not resume until late in 1965.

In April 1965, Dominican revolutionaries trained in Cuba and Czechoslovakia came within an ace of seizing control of an initially democratic movement for the return of ex-President Juan Bosch. The attempt was broken by President Lyndon Johnson's decision to send in the Marines.

Although the Soviets disapproved, on doctrinal and practical grounds, of Fidel Castro's attempts to export revolution, they hesitated to oppose him too visibly. They played along with him, partly because they were aware of his appeal to revolutionary youth in many countries, and partly because they were being attacked in China for "revisionism" and for having abandoned revolution. They therefore allowed some limited lip-support from Moscow-line Communist parties (notably in Venezuela and the Dominican Republic), providing modest cash backing and inexpensive propaganda aid, such as broadcasts from Moscow's Radio Peace and Progress in the Quechua language calling on the Andean Indians to revolt and restore the Inca Empire.

AS FOR FIDEL CASTRO, he went on, in 1963, to a triumphal visit to the Soviet Union, and five years later to a confrontation that reduced his regime to a full satellite of Moscow.

CHAPTER TWENTY-TWO

THE TAMING OF FIDEL

1963–1972

———

A NATURAL SEQUEL TO Anastas Mikoyan's visit to Havana in
November 1962 was Fidel Castro's own first visit to the Soviet
Union in April 1963. His hosts fed his already giant ego by enabling him
to address enthusiastic crowds in mass rallies, including the May Day parade in front of the Kremlin. Mistakenly, they thought that by conferring
the highest honors on him they would secure his loyalty. Castro was given
the Order of Lenin with a gold star and was made a Hero of the Soviet
Union. Such honors merely fed his personal view that he had become the
world's leading Marxist revolutionary. There was, however, one important byproduct of his visit from the Soviet standpoint: the arrival in
Moscow of Cuban DGI officers for further training by the KGB.[1]

Meanwhile, Castro's ego continued to soar. In January 1966 (clearly
with Soviet approval), he convened a "tri-continental" conference in Havana, the outcome of which was the creation of the Afro-Asian-Latin
American People's Solidarity Organization (AALAPSO). From the Soviet
viewpoint, this was a useful broadening of the earlier Afro-Asian People's
Solidarity Organization (AAPSO) that had been set up in Cairo in 1957 by
President Gamal Abdel Nassar of Egypt, at Moscow's request. From Castro's standpoint, it was a further boost to his image as great international
revolutionary leader. He further irritated the Kremlin by claiming that the
key to national liberation was in Havana, not Moscow. Cuba, he claimed,
was moving toward Communism faster than was the Soviet Union.

At this stage of the game, the clear winner seemed to be Cuba's *Líder Máximo,* as he was increasingly known. In the face of KGB and general Soviet disapproval, Castro continued with his adventurous attempts to stir revolution in Latin America. The main incident in 1967 was the pathetic failure of Che Guevara's attempt to start a revolution in Bolivia. *El Che* had gone there as an ultimate test of his conviction that to start a revolution all you had to do was . . . start a revolution.

In May 1967, Guevara issued a call to Latin Americans to "create two, three, numerous Vietnams": a call of mass appeal to students worldwide, but meaningless in practical terms. By then he had disappeared— nobody seemed to know where he was. It turned out that Che had gone to the Bolivian Andes with a small band of revolutionary optimists. None of them spoke Quechua, the language of the apathetic Indian peasants they had hoped to lead into revolt. Revolutionary oratory in Spanish was lost on the locals. More to the point, perhaps, the Bolivian Communists, under Moscow's orders, declined to help Che's project. The Bolivian security forces soon captured and killed Guevara, who then acquired an even larger heroic image in the eyes of the New Left (but not in the minds of Moscow's international Communist movement). Guevara's posthumous diary revealed that he had had an acrimonious dispute with the Bolivian Communist leader, Mario Monje, over the leadership of any insurrection. Monje went to Moscow to report to the real leaders of world Communism. Another diary entry commented on the hostility of the Bolivian Communist Party toward Guevara's revolutionary mission.

Already in late June 1967, a savage attack on the Cuban ideology had come out in *Pravda,* the Soviet party's daily organ, to coincide with a brief visit to Havana of Soviet Premier Aleksei Kosygin from June 27 to 29. And in October of that year, a projected visit to Moscow by Cuba's President Osvaldo Dorticós had been canceled. And now, after the fiasco of Che Guevara's Bolivian venture, the Soviet ruling party's patience was nearly exhausted. They gave appropriate orders to the newly renamed Communist Party of Cuba, or rather to its pro-Moscow faction led by Aníbal Escalante.

In early 1962, Moscow had tried to arrange for Escalante to replace Castro as Cuba's Communist leader. In an impassioned televised speech on March 26, 1962, Castro denounced Escalante for arrogance and sectarianism. Escalante and his followers, he said (not untruthfully), had crept under their beds during the struggle against Fulgencio Batista, whereas he, Fidel, had come down from the Sierra Maestra and defeated Batista's army. Shortly afterward, Castro expelled Escalante from Cuba, who took refuge in Prague with Soviet approval. He stayed there until late 1967.

Under Soviet orders, Escalante then came back to Havana, where he attempted to replace Castro's followers by his own within the ruling party. Thereupon, in January 1968, Fidel summoned the Party's Central Committee, denounced what he called Escalante's "micro-faction," and had him jailed for fifteen years. Thirty-four other members of the pro-Soviet micro-faction received lesser terms, mostly for twelve years.

This was one step too far for the Kremlin. Stronger measures were needed to bring the tiresome junior *Líder* to heel. The measures were not publicized by either side at the time, but became known through the revelations of a young but important Cuban defector. Orlando Castro Hidalgo was thirty-one years old and was serving in the Cuban embassy in Paris when he sought asylum in the American embassy in Luxembourg in March 1969. The details were revealed in his book, *Spy for Fidel* (1971).

The Soviets threatened to cut off all economic aid to Cuba unless Castro stopped criticizing the Soviet Union and attempting to launch insurgencies without consulting Moscow. At first Castro took no notice, apparently believing that the Soviet leaders must be bluffing, as it could not possibly be in their interests to cause the Cuban economy to collapse. Leonid Brezhnev, who had taken over from Nikita Khrushchev in 1964, soon showed that the time for bluffing was over. He ordered the Soviet fleet to blockade Cuba. The flow of oil slowed to a trickle, and all Soviet supplies of industrial materials were halted for some weeks.

Fidel's brother Raúl, whom Moscow would have preferred as leader of the Cuban Party, diverted one-third of supplies of military fuel to civilian uses. Even then there was not enough fuel to keep Cuba's sugar mills, light industries, and vehicles moving. A number of factories had to be closed, and the workers were sent to the sugarcane fields.[2]

Nor was the pressure applied only by the Soviet Union, for Moscow mobilized the Latin American parties as well as the East Europeans, especially the Czechs, who also threatened to cut off their aid to Cuba. An extreme, and indeed ironical, indication of East European disapproval was Czechoslovakia's sale of $570,000 worth of arms to Uruguay in February

1968 to help the government counter the non-Communist urban insurgency of the so-called *Tupamaros,* named after the Peruvian Inca resistance leader Tupac Amaru, who was burned at the stake by the Spaniards in 1782.

In March 1968, the Yugoslav paper *Borba* carried a Mexico City dispatch reporting that all the Latin American Communist parties "accuse Cuba of embracing Che Guevara's senseless thesis on the alleged advantage of the 'man with the rifle' over the mature revolutionary work of an organized workers' party."

Such criticisms or attacks were mere words, which Fidel would normally have chosen to ignore. But he could not ignore the starving of the Cuban economy. There was no public renunciation of his policies, but his resistance to Soviet demands suddenly collapsed, signaling panic. A new economic agreement was negotiated, providing for some $350 million worth of oil, raw materials, and agricultural machinery annually. Most of the Soviet specialists had been withdrawn during the crisis. Now some 5,000 were on their way to the island to work in agriculture, mining, fishing, and atomic energy, as well as in the military and intelligence services. Nickel production was to be expanded, and the Soviets were to build an experimental nuclear power plant. As part of the new deal, the Soviets began to re-equip the Cuban armed forces with advanced weapons, including surface-to-air guided missiles.

Not long after the Soviet blockade, Fidel Castro was to give a spectacular demonstration of his new subservience to Moscow's authority. The Prague Spring drew to its brutal end when the Warsaw Pact armies, minus the Romanians, marched into Czechoslovakia on August 21, 1968. In Havana, Cuban and Czech sympathizers with the rebellious regime of Alexander Dubček—an anti-Soviet Communist who had been elected first secretary of the ruling party on January 3 that year— marched through the streets, carrying banners calling on the Russians to go home. On August 23, two days after the invasion, Castro broke his silence. Against popular expectations, he denounced the Czech leaders for "moving towards a counter-revolutionary situation, towards capitalism and into the arms of imperialism." He accused them of "camaraderie with pro-Yankee spies" and "the agents of West Germany and all that fascist and reactionary rabble." He went on to endorse the newly announced "Brezhnev Doctrine" claiming the Soviet Union's right to intervene in any Socialist country that moved "in the direction of the restoration of the capitalist system."

This was the act of public obeisance the Kremlin had aimed for. The young Castroite revolutionaries in such countries as France, Italy, West Germany, and Britain felt let down, while the Soviet leaders could gloat.

Although Castro had publicly bowed to Moscow's leadership, it took two more years for the Soviet Union to complete its satellization of Cuba. In July 1969, a flotilla of Soviet warships visited Cuba, and in November, the Soviet Politburo sent the defense minister, Marshal Andrei Grechko, to Havana. His mission was to oversee the building of a base for Soviet submarines at Cienfuegos, which in time became a major base for a Soviet naval role in the Atlantic.

The main Soviet target, however, remained the DGI. It was not enough that Aleksandr Alexeyev had, in effect, created it: the real problem was to control it, and this meant removing the man who ran it, Manuel Piñeiro Losada. Known as *Barba Roja* because of his red beard, Piñeiro was fiercely loyal to Fidel, an unconditional supporter of Castro's delusions of international grandeur.

In the autumn of 1969, Piñeiro (clearly with Castro's approval) visited North Korea to seek help for the DGI. By this time, Kim Il Sung's hard-line regime was training foreign revolutionaries in the techniques and tactics of terrorism and guerrilla war. The message to Moscow was clear: Despite Castro's speech backing the Soviet intervention in Czechoslovakia, *el Barbudo* ("the Bearded One," another of the Cuban leader's sobriquets) still intended to spark his own brand of Third World revolutions.

Although at this point Piñeiro was still in charge of the DGI, the Soviets had been relentlessly pursuing their takeover from within. Every year since 1964, sixty Cuban intelligence officers had been through a ten-month training in two Soviet intelligence schools near Moscow. Half of the trainees were from Military Intelligence and were given their training in the KGB's School of Military Counterintelligence near the Moscow underground station of Otroviskaya. The other half came from the DGI itself and were trained at another KGB school in a wide-ranging curriculum including Intelligence and Counterintelligence, Criminal Investigation, Military Tactics, and Russian Language. The course in intelligence covered the structure and work of the CIA and of the FBI, plus the major departments of the American administration, especially the State Department, and of

West European governments, with special reference to Britain, France, and Germany. The counterintelligence course dealt with the recruitment and handling of agents, agent penetration techniques, the organization of agent networks, and the handling of possible lawsuits.

The consensus in Western intelligence services was that, of the annual intake of sixty Cuban recruits, an average of five agreed to work primarily for the KGB. Undoubtedly, some of those so recruited reported to their Cuban superiors on their return to Havana, but the fear that others would report anti-Soviet words and deeds back to Moscow acted as a deterrent within the DGI.

As part of their strategic plan, the Soviets invited their favorite Castro brother to Moscow in April and May 1970. They strongly urged Raúl to recommend to Fidel that the Cuban Army be cut by 80,000 men and that the Soviet money thus saved should be transferred to the DGI. They also recommended that 130 to 140 additional DGI officers be sent overseas to replace Foreign Ministry personnel in embassy posts. On his return, Raúl transmitted these recommendations as *orders* and got his way (and the Soviets) in the face of fierce resistance from the Cuban ministers of the interior (nominally in charge of the DGI) and foreign relations.

On Raúl's return, the relentless Soviet pressure on Fidel Castro bore fruit: he fired Piñeiro as head of the DGI and replaced him with a Soviet nominee, José Méndez Cominches. For good measure, the Soviet Politburo sent their own man, General Vitaly Petrovich Semënov (sometimes known as Viktor Simënov) to exercise overall control over the DGI from an office next door. The takeover was thus complete.

To soften the blow to Fidel's pride, the Soviets decided to remain unobtrusive within the DGI. Major policy guidelines, decided by the Central Committee of the Soviet Communist Party, were simply passed on to Raúl via the Central Committee of the Cuban Party (PCC). As chief of the Security Commission of the PCC, Raúl had authority over all Cuban intelligence activities. This device saved the face of Cuban officials by making it appear that policy directives came from the Cuban Party.

Although Fidel Castro had sacked his closest adviser, he did give Piñero another job. Under Soviet pressure the former *Liberación Nacional* section of the DGI was abolished, but Castro immediately created a new and autonomous *Dirección de Liberación Nacional* (DLN) with Piñeiro Losada as its chief and the anti-Soviet ex-officers of the DGI as its personnel. However, there was a snag to this face-saving maneuver. Henceforth, all Soviet funding for Cuban intelligence was channeled through the purged DGI. No Soviet money was available for the DLN, which had to be financed by the small sector of the Cuban economy not directly subsidized by Moscow.

In July 1972, Cuba joined the Council for Mutual Economic Assistance (better known as Comecon); and on January 3, 1973, Fidel Castro announced five new credit agreements with the Soviet Union, totaling $350 million. The deal placed special emphasis on nickel and sugar, which was interpreted to mean that Cuba had been picked as the main supplier of these commodities to other Comecon countries. By early 1973, there were Soviet officers in all units of the Cuban Army. Although Fidel retained overall authority in military as well as political matters, he now chose, in many sensitive areas, not to exercise it, leaving it to Raúl to make most appointments in the leading ministries. In addition, Raúl controlled the internal security organization, the *Dirección de la Seguridad del Estado* (DSE).

An interesting inside comment on what had happened in Havana came from another Cuban defector, Gerardo Peraza. During his testimony before a subcommittee of the U.S. Senate in 1982, when asked why he had left the service of the Cuban government he replied, "The fundamental facts are these. First, there was a law which was promulgated in the intelligence service of Cuba making it mandatory to belong to the Communist Party. And second, the intelligence service of Cuba was transferred directly to the services of the Soviet intelligence service."[3]

Peraza went on to give a detailed account of the Soviet takeover.

THE ULTIMATE TEST of satellization comes when the imperial power pressurizes the satellite to involve itself in military activities. This ultimate test confirmed the satellization of Cuba on two major occasions. The first was the giant military airlift to Africa in 1978; the second was the strategic final stage of the satellization of Nicaragua the following year.

CHAPTER TWENTY-THREE

AFRICAN VENTURES

1954–1964

⟶·⟵

A T THE START of the 1950s, Africa had the least Communist Party subversive machinery of the five major continents. Communist parties in Africa were few, and those that did exist were mostly small and ineffectual. This applied notably to the Algerian Party, which had about 750 members; to the Moroccan, with 400 card-carriers; and to Nigeria's, whose membership was unknown. Broadly speaking, they were mere branches of the larger Communist parties of the colonial powers: Britain, France, and Portugal. The only relatively substantial parties were those of South Africa (SACP), a multiracial party, banned in 1950 but influential largely through its alliance with the African National Congress (ANC), and of Sudan, with a probable membership of between 5,000 and 10,000. A tiny party emerged in Lesotho in 1961, in effect as a branch of the SACP.

Moscow's peripheral activities in the immediate postwar period were mainly directed at South and East Asia and, to a lesser degree, at Latin America. In 1954, however, a major imperial plan for "black" Africa began to unfold with the publication in Moscow of a symposium entitled *The Peoples of Africa,* the first serious attempt to study Africa and interpret it in Marxist-Leninist terms.[1]

Because Russia had virtually no firsthand experience of Africa, this work was compiled almost entirely from foreign sources. March 1957 marked a turning point, when the Gold Coast, a British colony, became the first black African country to be granted independence and changed its name to Ghana. That month, Moscow radio announced the forthcoming publication of no fewer than fifty-five books on "the struggle of the peoples of Africa against colonialism and for their rights."

Over the next seven years, Moscow's African studies—the inevitable ideological preparation for action—were dominated by one name: Professor Ivan Izomovich Potekhin. Until his early death in 1964, at age sixty-one, Potekhin had both the necessary qualifications for the task: erudition in his chosen field, and unconditional ideological loyalty. He had been a member of the ruling party for ten years when he entered the Leningrad Institute of Oriental Studies in 1930. His special field was "the peoples and problems of Africa," with special reference to the Swahili language and the Bantu people who spoke it. In 1932, he organized a department of African studies—the first of its kind in this "Oriental" Institute. The thesis that brought him his doctorate of "Historical Sciences" in 1955 was entitled "The Formation of a National Society among the Bantus."

In a sense, Potekhin was squaring an ethnic circle in the interests of Marxist-Leninist orthodoxy: an essential exercise in Soviet academia. Essential, but exceptionally difficult for African society, where "classes" in the Marxist sense did not exist except in a rudimentary sense. In most African countries, the "proletariat" scarcely existed. Africa was a society of tribes and tribal subdivisions. Of this, Potekhin was surely well aware. It was therefore necessary to "fit" African society into the universal pattern of class struggle, leading inevitably to revolution and a Communist society.

His tentative first contribution to the revolutionary cause was an article in *Kommunist*, the theoretical organ of the CPSU, in June 1957. Three years later came Potekhin's definitive African statement, in a booklet entitled *Africa Looks to the Future*. His main thesis was simple: Africa had a vocation for Socialism. The simple statement begged a question: Which Socialism? The author cited various African versions, the better to demolish them. His examples included President Léopold Senghor of Francophone Senegal and his intellectual compatriot, Jacques Janvier, who opted for the Yugoslav model; Kwame Nkrumah of Ghana and Julius Nyerere of Tanganyika; and Gamal Abdel Nasser of Egypt. Having chided his list of distinguished Africans, he told his readers, firmly, that the Marxist variety of Socialism was the only suitable one for Africa, as it was for the rest of the world.

Potekhin argued that the reason the advocates of "African Socialism" were wrong was that they wanted to build Socialism on the peasantry.

While conceding that "class formation" was still incomplete in Africa, he noted that millions of Africans already worked for hire, constituting a nascent proletariat. Indeed, they were being organized into trade unions. Thus, Potekhin concluded, Africa could not be an exception to Marxist-Leninist theory. He went on to argue that the mere achievement of "independence" did not, of itself, mean the end of colonialism. The last vestiges of colonialism had to be removed through the establishment of independent economies, with Communist economic assistance and the issuing of national currencies. Moreover, the artificial linguistic divisions between English, French, and Portuguese-speaking African nations must go, to be replaced by the African national languages.*

In the years that followed Potekhin's ideological guidance, the Soviets made two disastrous attempts to influence events in the former Belgian Congo (later Zaïre). The KGB brought Ghana under its control, then lost it. Their proxies in the Sudan seized power and lost it. The Soviet Union's Cuban satellite did its best to export revolution to several African states, but their best was not good enough. Then came the seizure of power by proxy in the ex-Portuguese colonies of Angola and Mozambique and the protracted wars that followed; the successful teleguided coups in Somalia and Ethiopia, culminating in a war won by the Ethiopians; and the biggest airlift in history, by Soviet planes carrying Cuban forces to African destinations.

THE CONGO

THE BRITISH AND French, in their different ways, brought progress to their African colonies, but the same cannot be said of the Belgians in the Congo and its troubled neighbors, Ruanda and Burundi. The Congo, immense and rich in natural resources, was simply exploited, and so little thought had been given to the option of independence that the decision to pull out was the unplanned consequence, on January 4 and 5, 1959, of severe anti-European rioting in the capital, Leopoldville, in which seventy-one

---

*The flaws in these arguments must have been evident to the Africans whom Potekhin was addressing, in particular the replacement of two or three "colonial" languages by a multiplicity of tribal tongues, most of which did not, at that time, exist in written form; and the creation of a Communist-assisted national currency. The only example of the latter was the Francophone Guinea, whose East German-printed banknotes were internationally worthless.—BC

people were killed. On January 13, the Belgian government announced a program for "the evolution of independent rule." The following day Patrice Lumumba, a left-wing politician, accepted the plan. Elections followed in December 1959, and on June 30, 1960, Lumumba emerged as premier, with Joseph Kasavubu as president. So little Belgian effort had gone into education that when independence came, after its very short gestation, the ex-Congo had only seventeen graduates.

A period of strife and chaos followed. A right-winger, Moïse Tshombe, seized power in Katanga province, and Lumumba appealed to the UN to send a force to the Congo to restore order. Led personally by the UN's secretary-general, Dag Hammarskjöld, the force replaced Belgian troops in Katanga.

Erratic but spellbinding, Lumumba had a plentiful supply of Communist friends. The Belgian Communist Party, firmly responsive to Moscow's commands, had provided the new government with "technical advisers." The new Congolese army, the Belgian-trained *Force Publique*, mutinied. In the resulting breakdown of law and order, the classic conditions for a Leninist revolution appeared to be taking shape.

Seizing its opportunity, the Soviet Union launched a massive airlift of arms and trained agents to the Congo, and put aircraft and lorries at Lumumba's disposal. When the UN force arrived, the Russians represented their airlift as a contribution to the force while publicly vilifying the UN intervention. In no time, the Soviet and Czech embassies swelled inordinately. On September 5, the London *Times* reported that the two embassies between them now had at least 200 diplomats and "technicians," not counting medical teams. The Soviet ambassador, Mikhael Yakovlev, had built up a close personal relationship with Lumumba.

The logical climax must have seemed nigh. Instead, the whole enterprise ended in fiasco. On September 5, Kasavubu "dismissed" Lumumba, who responded by calling a special session of his cabinet next day and dismissing Kasavubu. On September 14, Colonel Joseph Mobutu, commander of the fledgling Congolese army, announced a military takeover and gave the Communist embassies a forty-hour ultimatum: out or face the consequences. The forty hours were well, though destructively, employed with bonfires of incriminating documents on the grounds of the two embassies. On September 17, the entire staffs of both left Leopoldville by air.

Mobutu later explained that the Russians had set up a spy ring and were operating a secret radio transmitter. They had been infiltrating Katanga and sabotaging mining and other installations in the Congo's richest province. In despair, Lumumba called on Mobutu at his Army camp, pleading with him to change his mind. Whether or not under compulsion, he left his briefcase with Mobutu, who later used the contents to harsh effect. Although some of the documents turned out to be forgeries, two genuine ones made the headlines. One was a letter signed by Lumumba and addressed to the Soviet Union, requesting troops, planes, lorries, and other supplies. The other was a letter from the Chinese Premier Chou En-lai, offering Lumumba's government £1 million.[2]

On November 25, 1960, Lumumba was captured by Mobutu's troops and detained. In mid-February 1961, he was reported to have been killed by "hostile tribesmen."[*] In death, more than in life, Lumumba became a lasting Soviet icon, when the Patrice Lumumba People's Friendship University was launched in Moscow as a training ground for Third World terrorists, the most notorious of whom was Ilich Ramírez Sánchez of Venezuela, better known as "Carlos the Jackal."

The death of Lumumba did not, however, mark the end of the Soviet and satellite intervention in Zaïre. Though expelled from Kinshasa (Leopoldville), they came back via Stanleyville (later renamed Kisangani) where Lumumba's right-hand man, Antoine Gizenga, had proclaimed himself prime minister. In August that year, they were back in Leopoldville, where a widely recognized government had been set up under Cyrille Adoula, with Gizenga as his deputy. Initially, in this second incarnation, the Leopoldville embassy was manned by diplomats only, at least declared as such. But the arms and "advisers" were being sent to Stanleyville, and, as confidence returned, the embassy staff started to grow again. "Having it both ways" did not work out, however, and in November 1963, for the second time in three years, the entire staff of the Leopoldville embassy, by then nearly a hundred strong, were expelled.

Nevertheless, the arms traffic continued, and on January 17, 1964, Adoula called a press conference to announce that a consignment of

---

[*]In contrast, Mobutu was still in power thirty-six years later, when these lines were written. He has since died.

Soviet and Czech arms had been delivered from Algeria and Egypt in
Soviet-built AN 12 transport aircraft.

Terrorist Training Course

THE CZECHS WERE not the only East European satellite involved with
Soviet subversion in Africa. The Bulgarians, who were even closer to the
imperial power, also played an active role. Details of a training course in
subversive violence at a special camp in Bulgaria reached Western intelligence in 1963. Some 200 Africans attended the course, including seventy-
six Kenyans and fifteen Cameroonians. The trainees were taught how to
throw bombs or deposit them in suitably vulnerable places, and how to
use small arms. The Cameroonians in particular were lured to Bulgaria by
promises of "scholarships," but learned that the offer was for military,
not academic, training. Of the fifteen trainees, six were arrested on government orders upon their return to Cameroon.

East Germany, too, offered training courses for guerrillas; and so did
distant Cuba, where Africans from Zanzibar and Kenya, South Africa
and Rhodesia, Mali and Ghana were taught the techniques of political violence at Cuba's main revolutionary training camp at Minas del Frío on
the slopes of the Sierra Maestra, where Fidel Castro had built up his own
revolutionary forces.

Ghana

GHANA WAS THE first African ex-colony to *invite* a Soviet subversive
presence. The Ghanaian leader, Kwame Nkrumah, had survived an assassination attempt in August 1962 and felt isolated and in need of friends.
He turned to the Soviets for help. This was a rare opportunity and one
not to be missed. The KGB offered to set up a special force of presidential
bodyguards and to organize a countersubversive network to guard Ghana
against hostile neighbors. Thereupon hundreds of KGB personnel landed
in Ghana, along with Czechs, East Germans, Poles, and Cubans. Presumably, Nkrumah must have turned to China as well, for the Chinese also
sent intelligence officers and instructors, along with North Koreans.

According to the American authority John Barron, the KGB officer in
charge of operations in the Ghanaian capital, Accra, was Robert Issa-

kovich Akhmerov, whose mother had been secretary to Lavrenti Beria, Stalin's secret police chief, and whose father was a KGB colonel. Akhmerov's deputy, Nikolai Ivanovich Gladky, had been Khrushchev's personal bodyguard. Two East German STASI officers, Jürgen Rogalla and Rolf Stollmeyer, were part of the KGB team.[3]

Nkrumah the autocrat was less popular than he had assumed, and his whole autocratic edifice came tumbling down in February 1966, while he was on his way to China for a state visit. Anti-Communist insurgents attacked the presidential headquarters in Flagstaff House on February 24. The ensuing battle lasted ten hours, and when the victorious insurgents stormed in, they seized eleven KGB officers and summarily executed them. Neither the anti-Nkrumah National Liberation Council that had seized power, nor the Soviet authorities in Moscow, publicly alluded to the executions. Each side evidently had its reasons for silence.

Not long after the coup, however, the new regime issued a White Paper on the secret files of the deposed regime that stated that "the discoveries made by the government of Ghana revealed that the danger to Africa was one hundred times more serious than anyone outside a small circle had revealed." The clear message was that the Soviet Union had intended, with Nkrumah's approval, to use Ghana as the subversive base for the ultimate subjugation of the whole continent.

MOSCOW'S PORTUGUESE CARD

Angola

In 1955, Portuguese Communists set up a clandestine Communist Party in Angola, the most advanced of Portugal's three African colonies. (The others were Mozambique and Guinea-Bissau). A year or so later, a cover organization emerged, known as the MPLA.* Of all the Western Communist parties, the most consistently loyal (that is, obedient) to Moscow was the Portuguese, which supported the Soviet position in the most controversial of international crises, such as the aggression against Finland in 1939 and the crushing of the Hungarian revolution in 1956. It is fair to assume that the decision to launch a rebellion against Portuguese rule in

---

Movimento Popular para a Libertação de Angola: Popular Movement for the Liberation of Angola

1959 was taken in Moscow and implemented by the Portuguese Communist Party.

For the next two years the MPLA simply vanished in Angola, although it was very active abroad in disseminating anti-Portuguese propaganda.[4] By 1961, the MPLA was ready for action, and the protracted Angolan civil war began, between the pro-Communist MPLA and the anti-Communist UNITA.* However, it was not until 1973 that details of the Soviet Union's active role in this war and the later one in Mozambique became known to Western intelligence services. It was learned that, since 1967, systematic courses in revolutionary techniques had been on offer to carefully selected members of foreign Communist parties, in Moscow, Odessa, Tashkent, Baku, and Simferopol. In Moscow in particular, the courses were run by the Lenin Institute, also known as the Institute of Social Sciences, the Institute of Social Studies, and the International School of Marxism-Leninism. (The terms were interchangeable and all referred to the same organization, closely controlled by the Central Committee of the CPSU.)[5] Non-Communist trainees, however, were handled by the Patrice Lumumba People's Friendship University.

After two years of guerrilla war, the MPLA came under the long-lasting control of Agostinho Neto, a hard-line left-wing socialist, who replaced a mild mulatto intellectual, Mario de Andrade. Thereafter, aid, equipment, and advisers were made available to the MPLA from East Germany and (non-Communist) Algeria as well as from the Soviet Union.[6]

Mozambique

The Soviet-supported insurgency in Mozambique began in 1961, led by a parallel organization to the MPLA known as FRELIMO.** FRELIMO was headed by Eduardo de Mondlane, an able intellectual who had been educated in South Africa, Portugal, and the United States. Initially based in Dar-es-Salaam, Tanganyika (which was renamed Tanzania in 1964 after merging with the islands of Zanzibar and Pemba), FRELIMO was given a training base at Nashingwea, with the personal support of the Tanganyikan president, Julius Nyerere. When Mondlane was assassinated

---

*União Nacional para a Independencia Total de Angole: National Union for the Total Independence of Angola

**Frente de Libertação de Moçambico: Liberation Front of Mozambique

at Dar-es-Salaam in February 1969, he was succeeded by Samora Machel, a hard-line Communist trained in Algeria and the USSR.

Guinea-Bissau

In comparison with the large territories of Angola and Mozambique (respectively, 480,000 square miles, population 6 million; and 300,000 square miles, population 8 million), Guinea-Bissau was tiny: 14,000 square miles, population 550,000. The necessary revolutionary organization called itself the PAIGC,* and was led by a highly intelligent agronomist, Amílcar Cabral, a Communist who launched his revolt in 1956 with a series of politically motivated strikes, quickly suppressed by the Portuguese authorities. Taking refuge in the mainland Francophone Republic of Guinea, Cabral sent his followers for training to China, the USSR, and Cuba, as well as to Guinea and non-Communist Senegal and Ghana. He launched his guerrilla campaign in July 1961.

Guerrilla leadership is a high-risk occupation. As had happened to Mondlane, Cabral was assassinated in January 1973. The Portuguese resistance to the PAIGC was initially tough and successful and yielded the seizure of a considerable haul of advanced weaponry, including Kalashnikov automatic rifles, PPSH Soviet machine guns, Cuban bazookas, Chinese recoil cannons, 82 mm Russian medium mortars, heavy Degtyarev machine guns, Breda machine guns and even U.S. Thompson sub–machine guns.[7]

THE COUP IN PORTUGAL

FOR THIRTY YEARS, Dr. Antonio de Oliveira Salazar ruled Portugal with a firm hand. The regime he had established under his 1933 constitution owed a lot to Mussolini's corporatist concept of the state. There was an elected Assembly with seats reserved for trade unions and employers, but there were no political parties. As Hugh Kay, a long-time authority on Portugal, has argued, Salazar's regime was more monarchical and paternalist than tyrannical, but no opposition was permitted.[8] Censorship and a pervasive Security Service saw to this.

Partido Africano da Independencia de Guinée Cabo Verde: African Party for the Independence of Guinea and Cape Verde

At whatever cost, Salazar was determined to hold on to Portugal's African colonies. Under his rule, Portugal's budget was invariably balanced, but the country was poor, and by the time Salazar died in 1970, having been incapacitated by a stroke during the last two years of his life, the African wars were absorbing 42 percent of the national income. His successor, Dr. Marcello Caetano, though able and intelligent, lacked Salazar's authority. In effect, he undermined his own position by introducing a new constitution in 1971, which envisaged self-determination for the overseas "provinces," as they were euphemistically known.

The regime was overthrown in a military coup on April 25, 1974. Exceptionally for a military intervention in a Western country, the Armed Forces Movement (AFM), as it called itself, had a Communist dimension. For nearly two and a half years, the Portuguese Communist Party (PCP) had operated its own terrorist organization: the *Ação Revolucionaria Armada* (ARA). Given the total loyalty of the PCP to the Moscow line, it may be assumed that in its acts of terrorism, it was acting under instructions from the International Department of the Soviet Central Committee. However, in May 1973, the ARA switched to nonviolent "political action," although it remained an illegal organization.

The PCP is believed to have had advance knowledge of the forthcoming military coup. The first meeting of the Armed Forces Movement, held on Sunday, September 9, 1973, at an isolated farm on Monte do Sobral, near Evora, was reported to have been hosted by a PCP member.[9] Among the fifty military men who attended, all in civilian clothes, was Colonel Vasco Gonçalves, who later became prime minister.

An event of more than symbolic significance took place in Moscow on February 22, 1974, when the ever-loyal veteran leader of the PCP, Alvaro Cunhal, was presented with the Order of the October Revolution by the Soviet Party leader, Leonid Brezhnev, in the presence of the two men most closely involved with international subversion: M. A. Suslov, the party's top ideologist, and Boris Ponomarev, who headed the International Department. In a celebratory speech, Suslov recalled statements by Cunhal that "permanent and indestructible solidarity with the Soviet Union and the CPSU are the unconditional duty of Communists and working people of all countries."[10] Back in Lisbon, by invitation of the AFM, Cunhal accepted a government post as minister without portfolio, thus providing the International Department in Moscow with its own man in the post-Salazar administration.

Diplomatic relations between Portugal and the Soviet Union were established in June 1974, and the standard KGB presence followed, headed by S. F. Kuznetsov, under diplomatic cover as Counsellor.

A period of internal confusion followed in Portugal, and on March 11, 1975, the nominal leader of the AFM, General Antonio de Spínola, who had assumed his country's presidency, attempted a further coup. He had resigned as president on September 30, 1974, and his anti-Left coup failed. He went into exile in Brazil after escaping to Spain.

It became known that the Soviet Union had been sending large sums of money to the PCP. Britain's then-prime minister, Harold Wilson, publicly endorsed a report that some £4 million a month was being transferred from Moscow.[11]

Considerable sums were also reaching the MPLA in Angola: an estimated £55 million between November 1974 and October 1975. The cost of training MPLA forces totaled about £730,000 for 1975 alone. In addition, on Moscow's orders, some 15,000 Cuban troops had been sent to Angola. The political reward came on November 11, 1975, when Portugal recognized Angola's independence, with the MPLA in occupation of the capital, Luanda.

The independence of Mozambique had already been recognized on January 25, with FRELIMO in occupation of the capital Lourenço Marques. Thus, on paper at least, Moscow could chalk up its first two victories in Africa. In both countries, however, the Communist victories were under challenge from anti-Communist insurgents: in Angola from the anti-Communist movement (UNITA), commanded by the Chinese-trained Jonas Savimbi; and in Mozambique, although FRELIMO reigned, its authority would be challenged in later years by RENAMO *(Resistencia Nacional Moçambicana)*, led by Afonso Dhlakama. In Guinea-Bissau, the situation was more ambiguous.

CHAPTER TWENTY-FOUR

THE RIVAL SUNS

1960–1972

T HERE CANNOT BE two suns in the sky," an ancient Chinese proverb says. If the sky means the world, this proverb helps to explain why Mao Tse-tung's subservience to Stalin was short-lived. It also throws light on the intense rivalry between the two giants of the Communist world—the Soviet Union and China—the early stages of which were dealt with in Chapter 20 on the Sino-Soviet rift. This rivalry expressed itself in a phenomenon I call "competitive subversion."

Early in 1964, Mao sent his loyal lieutenant, Premier Chou En-lai, on a seven-week tour of Africa, at the end of which Chou declared, "Revolutionary prospects are excellent throughout Africa." Once more, we are in the hazy world of ideological semantics. What did Chou mean by *revolutionary prospects?* In the context of the Bandung Conference of 1955, which China dominated and to which the Soviet Union was not invited, "revolutionary prospects" meant not only that the colonized peoples of Africa should overthrow the Western colonial powers, but that, in so doing, they should adopt the Chinese model of "liberation," not the Soviet one. Ideally, they should do this in one move, from the Western to the Chinese model. If, however, circumstances had forced them to adopt the Soviet model, they should discard it in favor of the Chinese. If anything, the Chinese model was even more totalist and tyrannical than the Soviet. Mao herded farm workers into "communes," suppressing even the marginal freedom that was available to families in the Soviet Union. He would go on (in his "Great Proletarian Cultural Revolution") to incite his youthful "Red Guards" to destroy the artistic inheritance of China's impressive past, on a scale vaster than even Stalin's tyranny.

So fiercely motivated were the Chinese Communists in the early years of the "struggle for Africa" that they went so far as to argue that there was a special affinity between the Chinese and the Africans in that both were "colored," whereas the Soviets were white. Thus, on March 12, 1962, during the Afro-Asian Writers' conference in Cairo, the following passage appeared in the Kenya newspaper *Daily Nation:* "In private lobbying the Chinese are adopting an openly racist line. These Europeans, they say, are all the same whether they are French, Americans, Russians or Poles; we non-whites must get together. One Chinese delegate even went so far as to talk about the 'importance of us blacks sticking together.'"

The same argument was developed more crudely and explicitly by Chinese delegates to the Afro-Asian People's Solidarity conference at Moshi, Tanganyika, in February 1963. The Chinese selected the Cuban crisis of the previous October as proof that the Russians would "let down" the colored peoples, and the "agreement on co-existence between Khrushchev and Kennedy" as a clear indication that the Russians, as whites, would support the Americans.[1]

When words turned into action, the Chinese were apparently at an advantage compared to the Russians. Mao's theory of revolutionary war (via guerrilla war) had proved itself and appeared to be suitable for an underdeveloped country; the Soviet view of revolution, however, even when adapted to African needs as Professor Potekhin perceived them, was hampered by the almost total absence of Communist parties, the Leninist instruments of total change.

In the event, for all the Maoist rhetoric, the Chinese were even less successful than the Soviets in Africa. Their first target appears to have been the West African territory of Cameroon. In 1960, the Chinese recruited nine Cameroonians for a ten-week training course at a military academy outside Peking. The training included the making of explosives, grenades, and mines. Six of the students, in effect graduates in Maoist guerrilla tactics, were sent home with a revolutionary agenda, which included the demolition of telephone installations, bridges, and railways.

Their orders were clear: to make contact with the ALNK *(Armée de Libération Nationale du Kamerun).* The move ended in fiasco, with the arrest of all six men. Undeterred, the Chinese continued to support the ALNK, although in September 1964 China sent a trade and goodwill mission to Cameroon, while the ALNK continued to kill peasants who were misguided enough not to join them voluntarily.

The main Chinese center for revolutionary activity, however, was in Dar-es-Salaam, capital of Tanzania. The large Chinese embassy there offered generous funds and training facilities for African "freedom fighters" from various countries.

The following month, May 1964, a young Chinese interpreter named Tung Chi-ping walked out of the Chinese embassy in Burundi's capital, Bujumbura, and was granted asylum in the U.S. embassy. He made a long statement, later released by the State Department in Washington. In it, he quoted a saying that he attributed to Mao Tse-tung: "Burundi is the way to the Congo, and when the Congo falls the whole of Africa will follow."

Whether the Chinese leader really used these words is unclear, but the theory attributed to him remained untested. Indeed, on January 29, 1965, Burundi broke off relations with China, installed a military police cordon around the embassy, and expelled the staff. Among those expelled were a large, though unstated, number of "domestic servants." The Burundi authorities had laid down that no more than eight nationals of any country could be accredited as diplomats. The Chinese embassy agreed, and tried to get round this inconvenient order by converting twelve of their diplomats into "domestic servants." In fact, as it turned out, the Chinese needed their large "diplomatic" staff to train, arm, and fund rebels from neighboring Congo (later Zaïre). Similar "help" was given to men from neighboring Rwanda.

A Chinese "journalist" named Kao Liang, ostensibly representing the New China News Agency but in fact a troubleshooter for the Chinese Foreign Ministry, had been playing a key subversive role, offering presents to well-placed Burundians or free trips to China, and always ready to expound on China's mission to help the peoples of Africa.

One of the main recipients of Chinese favors was the prime minister, Albin Nyamoya, who had been appointed in April 1964. The Mwami (King) of Burundi, Mwambutsa IV, had been watching events with a sour eye and sacked Nyamoya at the beginning of 1965. In his place, on January 11 the Mwami reappointed an ex-premier, Pierre Ngendandumwe. It was a short-lived premiership, however: four days later he was shot in the back on leaving the maternity hospital where his wife had presented him with a son and heir.

A very similar sequence of events had been going on in Congo-Brazzaville, formerly under French rule, which faces the former Belgian Congo on the opposite bank of the eponymous river. In August 1963, the right-wing dictator of Congo-Brazzaville, Abbé Fulbert Youlou, was unseated by the "progressive" Massemba-Débat. The new dictator was rewarded on October 1, by attending the fifteenth anniversary of the Chinese People's Republic in Peking.

In Brazzaville, as in Burundi, the Chinese embassy, opened in February 1964, grew rapidly and soon harbored twenty "diplomats," actively providing loans, technical assistance, and flattery. Meanwhile, in the neighboring ex-Belgian Congo, Chinese intervention had also been growing. Chinese-supported rebels launched an armed rebellion against the Congolese central government in Kwilu province. One of the rebel leaders, Pierre Mulele, had been a minister in the government of the murdered Patrice Lumumba. More interestingly, he had spent two years in China "graduating" in subversion and guerrilla techniques. Some two hundred of his followers were also trained in China. The Chinese provided money, arms, and instruction manuals, and—not least—a 75-kilowatt radio transmitter.

Despite Chou En-lai's optimism, this Chinese-supported rebellion petered out.[2]

OTHER MAOIST REVOLUTIONS

- Portuguese Guinea and Angola. In August 1963, a group of guerrillas from the PAIGC of Guinea and Cape Verde took part in a guerrilla course in China (see Chapter 23). A group from the pro-Communist MPLA in Angola underwent the same course.
- Kenya. On September 5, 1964, Nairobi's *East African Standard* reported that eighteen Kenyans were taking part in a guerrilla warfare course at China's Wuhan Military Academy. In December 1964, the first batch of Luo tribe saboteurs and guerrillas returned from China.

- Niger. In October 1964 an attempted uprising against President Diori was crushed. The president declared that the ringleaders had been trained in China.

It would be fair to say that whatever the aptness of Chinese methods of revolutionary guerrilla warfare, Peking's attempts to convert them into real power failed completely—though mainly, it would seem, because they were on far too small a scale to have any hope of success.

On February 2, 1965, President Diori of Niger and President Yaméogo of Upper Volta jointly condemned China's attempt to force "ideology, weapons, money and subversion" upon Africa. A few days later, the more authoritative voice of President Houphouët-Boigny of the Ivory Coast, a father figure to Francophone Africans, had this to say:

> The dangers threatening Africa today are those from communist China. . . . To reach their goal more rapidly, they have set up training camps for our African patriots from which communist subversion is organised to gnaw at our continent bit by bit. They have trained groups to be used to fight brothers and sisters in opposing camps. This is new to Africa and it is a tragedy that causes us anxiety.

In a desultory way, Chinese subversion continued from time to time without success. On January 24, 1972, for instance, a military court in Bujumbura, the capital of the former Belgian colony, Burundi, sentenced nine "Maoists" to death. They had been arrested in July 1971. Clearly, Chou En-lai's public optimism after his African tour turned out to have been excessive.

Although Sino-Soviet competitive subversion continued, not only in Africa, but also in Southeast Asia and Latin America, in the final analysis the Chinese were inadequately equipped to compete with the Soviets. This remained true even though, in many countries including West European ones, mini-parties ideologically committed to the Chinese model made their ineffectual appearance.

CHAPTER TWENTY-FIVE

VIETNAM II BEGINS

1958–1962

———————

I T IS HARD to put a date on the outbreak of the Second Vietnam
War. On June 14, 1954, an anti-Communist Catholic, Ngo Dinh
Diem, had been appointed prime minister of South Vietnam by the ex-
Emperor Bao Dai, who was still chief of state. The international negotia-
tions in Geneva to settle the First Indochina War were still in progress (see
Chapter 12), and ended on July 21 with the partition of Vietnam into two
roughly equal halves: the North to Ho Chi Minh's victorious Communists
and the South to the precarious but determined Diem.

Diem had spent some years in voluntary exile in the United States. Not
long after his return to Vietnam, he faced no fewer than three armed rebellions. Two were from religious sects: the Caodaists, an eclectic church; and
the Hoa Hao, a primitive Buddhist group. The third set of rebels, known as
the Binh Xuyen, were gangsters who had started off as river pirates but went
on to control the brothels and the gambling casino in Cholon, the Chinese
district of Saigon. In January 1955, Diem had closed down the casino, and
the Binh Xuyen gang went into action. From his exile in Paris, Bao Dai ful-
minated, for the Binh Xuyen had supported him in various ways.*

—————————————

*Shortly after the Binh Xuyen crisis, I had my second, and last, talk with Bao Dai in a Paris
hotel. I asked why he supported the Binh Xuyen gang. His reply was, "They have never
squeezed the people." We were talking in French, but he introduced a word in "Franglais":
"Ils n'ont jamais *squeezé* le peuple."—BC

Meanwhile, Diem had rejected ultimatums from the two religious sects and a cease-fire was signed on March 29. On April 28, Diem declared all-out war against the Binh Xuyen, and Cholon became an urban battlefield. Bao Dai formally withdrew Diem's authority over the South Vietnamese Army, but Diem ignored the order. After five days of heavy fighting, the Binh Xuyen forces were driven out of Saigon.

On May 5, a political congress summoned by Diem called for the ousting of Bao Dai. Three days later he rejected a French proposal that Bao Dai should return under a reorganized form of government. On May 20, the French gave in to Diem's demand that they move their remaining forces to the northern frontier to guard against a Communist invasion.

The political crisis came to a head on October 18, when Diem refused to bow to an order from Bao Dai dismissing him. On October 23, 1955, Diem called a referendum, which brought him an overwhelming vote of support. Three days later Ngo Dinh Diem proclaimed a Republic with himself as president.

Meanwhile, Ho Chi Minh had negotiated a deal with the Chinese Communists, under which they agreed to provide his government with $338 million of economic aid. It remains unclear, however, whether the Chinese ever honored this generous pledge.

If the Second Vietnam War is dated from the time of the American military intervention in support of South Vietnam, the starting point was President Lyndon Johnson's decision to commit American forces to the defense of South Vietnam in February 1965. For the preceding decade, however, a U.S. military mission was stationed in Saigon to advise the South Vietnamese government.

The real war, however, was between North and South Vietnam. Although no precise date can be put to it, the fighting began in late 1957.* Technically it was a civil war in that the same people, speaking the same language and with the same culture and history, lived on both sides of the artificial dividing line agreed to at the 1954 Geneva conference. In reality,

---

*As far as I am aware, the first printed reference to the resumption of fighting by the Communist guerrillas in South Vietnam was in the *Economist*'s then "Confidential" weekly bulletin, *Foreign Report*, of which I had been the editor since late 1954, in the issue dated January 30, 1958. The item, from the bulletin's Saigon correspondent, reported that unrest was being fomented in My Tho province, fifty miles south of Saigon, with propaganda support from subversive Communist agents who virtually controlled the local administration.

however, it was an international war between the Communist world and the West.

Most of the regular Vietminh Army troops had been evacuated to the north after Geneva. They soon infiltrated the Caodai and Hoa Hao bands and started a ruthless and highly effective campaign of murder and terrorism. Their targets were the local officials responsible to Saigon. As for the "ordinary" peasants, they were coerced into joining the Vietcong (Vietnamese Communist) gangs. Once in, there was no easy way out. The cleverest touch was that the Vietcong forbade them to pay Saigon's taxes. Instead, they paid considerably lower "taxes" to the Vietcong. As for rent to absentee landlords, this was past history. The Vietcong were continuously on the move but always left local agents behind. Anybody disobeying Communist orders was promptly executed.[1]

By the time the outside world realized what had been happening, the Vietnamese Communists had pulled off a masterly piece of disinformation. At a secret meeting, the Vietcong set up a front organization under the name of National Front for the Liberation of South Vietnam (NFLSV). Until the war ended with the departure of American ground forces in 1973 and the takeover of South Vietnam by the North in 1975, the antiwar media in the West uncritically swallowed the fiction that the NFLSV was an autonomous organization, independent of the Communist North. When victory came, the Front simply vanished.*

The decision to set up the NFLSV had been made at a critically important National Congress of the Lao Dong party in Hanoi in September 1960. A resolution was passed, which included this passage: "To ensure the complete success of the revolutionary struggle in South Vietnam, our people there must strive to establish a united bloc of workers, peasants and soldiers and to bring into being a broad national united front directed against the US-Diem clique and based on the worker-peasant alliance."

---

*At intervals, Hanoi reported the formation of no fewer than fourteen parties and organizations in South Vietnam. On April 16, 1962, Hanoi radio described Nguyen Van Hieu as secretary-general of the NFLSV, of the Radical Socialist Party, and of the South Vietnam Committee for the Defense of World Peace. In August of that year, he turned up in Budapest as vice president of the Association of Patriotic and Democratic Journalists. Evidently a busy man.

In January 1962 a new Communist party, calling itself the People's Revolutionary Party, was launched in South Vietnam. Its manifesto acknowledged its origins in (Ho Chi Minh's) Communist Party of Indochina and the Lao Dong. Its authority over the NFLSV was enshrined in an item that appeared in the Lao Dong's newspaper, *Nhan Dan,* on April 4, 1962: "The Vietnamese Revolutionary People's Party volunteers to act as the assault soldier in the front line of this struggle."[2]

In May 1962, the International Control Commission (ICC, set up at the Geneva conference), in an unprecedented burst of frankness, published its view that "there is evidence to show that the PAVN [North Vietnam's People's Army] has allowed the Zone in the North to be used for inciting, encouraging and supporting hostile activities in the Zone in the South, aimed at the overthrow of the Administration in the South."

The frankness was apparently due to the worsening of relations between India and China at the time, which made the Indian members of the ICC ready to publish a report that they would previously have vetoed so as not to offend the Chinese Communists. The Polish members brought out a dissenting minority report of their own.

From the start, relations between President Ngo Dinh Diem and the American representatives in Saigon were strained. Diem was not a loner. He was the senior member of a powerful family that included his younger brother Ngo Dinh Nhu, who was in charge of security and intelligence; his wife Mme. Nhu, who was influential in her own right; Monsignor Ngo Dinh Thuc, a Catholic bishop; and the youngest brother, Ngo Dinh Luyen, who became Diem's ambassador to London. A stubborn man, Diem was inflexibly resistant to change.

In the early months of Diem's presidency, the French in effect plotted to remove him and if possible replace him with someone more malleable. Although they did not succeed, they did persuade President Dwight Eisenhower's special envoy, General J. Lawton Collins, that Diem was a "hopeless proposition." Lawton did not need much persuasion, as he soon found he could not make any impression on Diem. On the other hand, Diem got along well with Colonel Edward Lansdale, the American specialist on counter-revolutionary operations who had helped President Rámon Magsaysay of the Philippines to defeat the Huk.[3] (See Chapter 13.)

Unfortunately, Lansdale was recalled to Washington at the end of 1956. Thereafter, the U.S. advisers, whether military or diplomatic, saw the war in conventional terms, whereas the enemy methods were subversive and secretive. After Diem's forces had decisively defeated the Binh Xuyen, the mood in Washington changed in his favor. It was recognized that stubbornness was not his only characteristic and that he had more honorable ones, including the rare one of incorruptibility. His brother Nhu, however, had virtually no American supporters. His security apparatus seemed to devote its prime activities to spying on South Vietnamese officials and politicians, "digging for dirt," as some of his American critics put it.

The British specialist on countersubversion operations, Sir Robert Thompson, who had learned the art in the last years of the Malayan "Emergency" (see Chapter 13) had been sent to Vietnam in 1961 at the head of an advisory mission. There he remained until 1965. After initial resistance, he had converted Nhu to his plan for "strategic hamlets": an adaptation of the "New Villages" that had yielded results in Malaya. The plan made some initial headway but ran into opposition from the American military advisers who were more concerned with streamlining and improving the South Vietnamese Army.

In the end, the consensus among the American advisers was that Diem, despite his good qualities, had to be removed. A complex plot by anti-Diem higher officers followed, with covert American approval, and on the night of November 1–2, 1963, three weeks before the very public murder of American President John F. Kennedy, both Diem and his brother Nhu were assassinated. The leader of the plot, General Duong Van Minh, took over. On January 30, 1964, however, he was himself removed by General Nguyen Khanh, who proclaimed himself chief of state. A series of further coups d'état followed.

The war escalated in August 1964 after two North Vietnamese naval attacks on U.S. warships on August 2 and 4, 1964. U.S. planes retaliated with air raids on North Vietnamese oil and naval installations. On August 5, President Lyndon Johnson obtained almost unanimous Congressional approval (with only two dissenters) for the "Tonkin Gulf Resolution," which authorized him to "take all necessary measures to repel any armed attack against forces of the United States and to prevent further aggression."

Until then, the Second Vietnam War could still have passed for a civil war, despite the Communist regime of the attacking North. After the Cuban missiles confrontation with the United States in October 1962, the

Soviet Union, still led by Nikita Khrushchev, seemed to have lost the drive for world dominion inherent in the Communist ideology.

In Ghana and the former Belgian Congo, the Soviet Union had been frustrated and humiliated. In Burma, too, in November 1963 General Ne Win had ordered the arrest of hundreds of local Communists. Moreover, in the border dispute between India and China, Khrushchev had sided with the Indians, to the wrath of the Chinese, who were on strong ground in accusing him of revisionism.

For that matter, why had Khrushchev, in April 1964, bestowed two of the Soviet Union's most prestigious medals on the victorious Algerian leader, Ben Bella: the Order of Hero of the Soviet Union and the Order of Lenin? Why, again, had he made President Gamal Abdel Nasser of Egypt a Hero of the Soviet Union on a visit to Cairo to inaugurate the Soviet-built Aswan dam? What worried his colleagues was that the Communist Party was banned in both Algeria and Egypt.[4]

These lapses might have been forgiven as mere eccentricities, but Khrushchev's self-chosen passive role on the international scene could not. The time had come for a change of leader.

CHAPTER TWENTY-SIX

POSTWAR THIRD WORLD SETBACKS

1958–1974

———⫸●⫷———

THE HISTORY OF the Soviet Empire as discussed so far has been overwhelmingly a record of imperial successes, marked by the ruthless crushing of rebellions, as in Hungary; the demonstration of superior strength, as occurred in the subversive competition with Red China; and the relative feebleness of Western response, as demonstrated with the Berlin Wall. One should not ignore the many failures and setbacks of the Soviet Union's attempts to increase its Empire, but one should be aware that the reverses were tactical, not strategic. Attempted pro-Soviet coups or uprisings were defeated, and in some countries the creation of satellites was frustrated; the imperial drive may have been thwarted, but no territories that had already been incorporated into the Empire were lost. The first *strategic* reversal would come with the U.S. occupation of Grenada in 1983 (see Chapter 38).

Another detail is relevant. Although most of the world's Communist parties were responsive to Moscow's orders, there were exceptions. Some parties probably acted of their own volition in the hope or expectation that the CPSU would back them, and, if necessary, rescue them. There were also "rogue" parties, which were not necessarily Moscow-controlled. Finally, as we saw in Chapter 21, Fidel Castro's governing party initially considered itself autonomous until Moscow brought the Cuban *Líder máximo* to heel.

Following are some disparate examples of Moscow-backed extremist groups or parties that failed in their imperialist endeavors.

THE ARAB MIDDLE EAST

THE ARAB MIDDLE EAST, and specifically Iraq, was never a major area of Communist activity or influence. The small Communist Party of Iraq, founded in 1934, was based in Eastern Europe during most of its history, under the name "Committee for the Defense of the Iraqi People Abroad." However, it played a minor role in the aftermath of a violent coup on July 14, 1958.

For thirteen postwar years (1945–1958) the Party had been banned, and most of its members were interned under the pro-British regime of the leading Iraqi politician, Nuri as-Said, a defender of his country's monarchy and an architect of the Baghdad Pact for mutual defense and cooperation between Iraq and Turkey, which Britain and Pakistan joined in February 1955.

The 1958 coup was led by an anti-Western Islamic Sunni fanatic named General Abdul Karim al-Kassem. The interned Communists were released just before the coup, presumably under orders from Kassem, whose first act was to order the assassination of the twenty-three-year-old King Faisal and proclaim a Republic. Nuri as-Said attempted to escape disguised as a woman, with his face veiled. He was unmasked, dragged through the streets, and killed.

The released Communists rejoined the pro-Communist civilian militia, the "Popular Resistance Forces," and took part in the mob violence that followed, including the sacking of the British embassy (for which Kassem later apologized). The Soviet leader, Nikita Khrushchev, cut short a visit to East Berlin a day early and returned to Moscow. There was speculation that the KGB had been tipped off about the impending coup in Iraq, while Britain's MI-6 and America's CIA were unaware that the coup was about to occur.[1]

We cannot assume that Kassem was pro-Communist—merely that he intended to use the Party for his own tactical ends. Indeed, although Kassem did not outlaw the Party, he restricted its activities. The violent Kassem was himself removed and killed in February 1963 in a coup d'état.

The new revolutionaries rounded up the Communists, and the government announced its intention "to crush absolutely the Communist Party."

LATIN AMERICA

IN 1963, THE Venezuelan Communist Party had launched a terrorist campaign against President Rómulo Betancourt, who had been elected at the end of 1958. On February 13, 1963, nine Party members hijacked a Venezuelan merchant vessel in the Caribbean, in an effort to demonstrate that the Betancourt government was incapable of stopping them. Five days later the hijackers docked in Brazil, where they were granted asylum. The Communist terrorist campaign continued in Venezuela, aided by incursions from Cuban-trained guerrillas and urban guerrillas. During the presidency of Raúl Leoni, elected at the end of 1963, the terrorists were gradually defeated, as the new leader's program of industrial, agrarian, and other improvements brought relative economic and social prosperity to the country.

IN NEIGHBORING BRAZIL, the Communist Party had been outlawed in May 1947. It remained active in clandestine maneuvers. The advent to power of a leftist politician, João Goulart, in September 1961, sparked revolutionary tensions. In February and March 1964, Goulart introduced reforms that were deemed unacceptable by the military: distributing of federal lands to landless peasants, doubling the minimum wage scale, and expropriating land next to federal highways. A few weeks later, he was ousted by a military coup. The new president, General Humberto Castelo Branco, launched an anti-Communist purge.

In July 1967, however, Castelo Branco died in a plane crash. He was succeeded by Costa e Silva, whose authoritarian methods were no less repressive. Left-wing terrorism continued to grow over the next few years, reaching a climax in 1970. There were two main terrorist groups (or urban guerrillas, as they preferred to style themselves): *Ação Libertadora Nacional* (ALN) and *Vanguardia Popular Revolucionaria* (VPR). Chronologically, the ALN came first, in 1969, and professed a Cuban-style ideology that, however, soon became more eclectic. The VPR started action the following year with a series of kidnappings. Despite such successes, the two terrorist groups were less successful than the forces of order. The ALN leader, Carlos Marighella, made a contribution to revolutionary literature; his *Mini-Manual of the Urban Guerrilla* became a cult text among rebellious European students as well as Latinos. Born in 1911 in Salvador, capital of the Brazilian Atlantic coast state of Bahia, he was of mixed blood: Italian on his father's side, black slave on his mother's.

Exceptionally for a guerrilla leader, he was well into middle age when the ALN made headlines in 1969. Marighella had spent most of his political career in the Brazilian Communist Party (*Partido Comunista Brazileiro,* or PCB), and was on the Executive Committee until he was expelled from the Party in October 1967 for advocating "armed struggle" and attacking the PCB at a meeting of the Latin American Solidarity Organization (OLAS), which had been "banned" by the Party.[2]

Trapped by a police ambush, he was shot in November 1969, on his fifty-eighth birthday. His successor, Joaquim Cãmara Ferreira, died of a heart attack the following year; and the VPR leader, Carlos Lamarca, was killed by security forces at Pintada, in the state of Bahia.[3]

ALTHOUGH THERE WAS no evidence of Soviet involvement in the Brazilian outbreak, there was irrefutable evidence to that end in a parallel outbreak in Mexico. In line with Lenin's example, a Communist action group calling itself the *Movimiento de Acción Revolucionaria* (MAR) robbed a bank in the center of Mexico City in February 1971, killing a watchman. The police arrested a student who confessed his guilt, and twenty other arrests followed. The picture that emerged was interesting. The MAR had consisted of only sixty men and women, all of whom had been trained at Moscow's Patrice Lumumba People's Friendship University, having gone there with scholarships from the Institute for Mexican-Soviet Cultural Exchanges. Their "cultural" subjects were Communist ideology, sabotage, guerrilla warfare, and terrorism. From Moscow, they had been taken to North Korea for military training. They had come back to Mexico via Moscow four or five years earlier, biding their time, then going into action.

On March 18, the Mexican government declared five members of the Soviet embassy *non gratae* and recalled its ambassador in Moscow, Carlos Zapata Vela, for the standard "consultations." The expelled Soviet diplomats included the chargé d'affaires, Dimitri Diakonov, who left for

Cuba on March 22. For him, the experience was not new: he had been expelled from Argentina in 1959. Had there been diplomatic relations between Mexico and North Korea, there would doubtless have been further expulsions: this time, of North Korean diplomats.

IN THE 1970s, Uruguay became one of the major targets of left-wing terrorism. On the surface, this deeply social democratic country, widely known as the Switzerland of Latin America, peaceful and long committed to a welfare system, should have been spared the traumas of urban guerrilla war. However, budgetary overspending had caused high inflation (136 percent by 1967) and widespread labor unrest. In the early 1960s, several terrorist groups sprang into action, of which by far the most important was the *Movimiento de Liberación Nacional* (MLN), better known as the *Tupamaros*, who began clandestine operations in 1962. By 1971, they could claim to be the most successful urban guerrilla movement in Latin America. They used the kidnapping of prominent people as a demonstration of power and as an effective publicity ploy. Among those affected were the Brazilian consul, Aloysio Dias Gomide, kidnapped in July 1970 and released in February 1971 on payment of a ransom of more than a quarter million dollars; and the British ambassador, Geoffrey Jackson, kidnapped in January 1971 and released in September (apparently without payment).[4]

Who was behind the Tupamaros? The official answer: The Soviet Union, East Germany, and Cuba. For ethnic and linguistic reasons, Cuba played a major role in the Tupamaros' attempt to destroy Uruguayan society from within; and, as in a number of other countries, Che Guevara became an icon of revolutionary struggle. The maximum period of guerrilla activity, however, was from 1970 to 1972 (Guevara died in 1967; see Chapter 22).

In June 1973, President Juan María Bordaberry dissolved the congress, and on July 27, 1974, the military were given control of the major state enterprises, including the central bank. From that moment Uruguay was, in effect, under military rule. The highly disciplined and professional Uruguayan Army ruthlessly crushed the revolutionaries to such a degree that it attracted a good deal of criticism from international human rights groups. By 1975, some 2,000 Tupamaros were serving sentences of indefinite duration in maximum security prisons. Uruguay did return to democracy, but not until 1985, eleven years after the military had taken over.

*   *   *

AN EXAMPLE OF special interest is the Dominican Republic, or more precisely, what happened there in the spring of 1963. The bare facts made little sense. The special interest lay in the facts that went unreported.

Like most Latin American countries at that time, the Dominican Republic had not been a model of democracy. On February 27, 1963, however, the country's first constitutionally elected president since 1924 took office. Juan Bosch Gaviño had been elected two months earlier but did not hold office for long: on September 25, 1963, he was overthrown in a bloodless military coup. In response, the United States broke off diplomatic relations and suspended economic aid.

The ruling junta did not last long, either: on April 24, 1965, it was overthrown in a coup by anti-Bosch elements in the Army led by General Elías Wessin. In the ensuing fighting between rival factions, the former junta regained power. American lives were believed to be at risk, and, on April 27 and 28, U.S. Marines landed in the Republic. The Organization of American States (OAS) arranged a truce, but fighting went on, and more U.S. troops were landed, this time with contingents from Brazil, Paraguay, Honduras, and Costa Rica.

The U.S. military intervention was widely criticized, not least by American liberals.[5] The important facts, however, had gone unreported. On April 26, the "legalist" rebels supporting Bosch appeared to have won and had proclaimed a provisional president, Molina Urena. At this stage, a few hundred armed civilians appeared from nowhere on the streets of Santo Domingo, killing and burning. General Wessin's forces went into action, and on April 27 the U.S. Navy began evacuating American (and British) citizens from the Dominican Republic. By then some of the Americans had been lined up against a wall and threatened with death.

By April 28 the legalists were collapsing, and "President" Molina took refuge in the Colombian embassy. It was at this point that President Johnson gave the order for the Marines to fight the rebels, instead of merely evacuating the U.S. and U.K. citizens.

President Bosch, who had taken refuge in the U.S.-owned Caribbean island of Puerto Rico, bided his time and did not feel safe to return home until September 25, 1965.

But who, then, were those mysterious armed civilians who appeared from nowhere to ravage the streets of Santo Domingo? Secretary of State

Dean Rusk lifted a corner of the veil when he told the House Foreign Affairs Committee that some of the armed civilians had been trained in Cuba and Czechoslovakia. This was true, but not enough of the truth to soothe the critics of the U.S. intervention.

In fact, during the previous several months, an unknown number of Dominican Communists of various hues had been trained in sabotage, terrorism, and guerrilla warfare and smuggled back into the Republic. Some belonged to the Moscow-line Communist Party that called itself the *Partido Socialista Popular Dominicano*. Others were members of two Cuban-trained groups: the *Movimiento Popular Dominicano* and the *Movimiento 14 de Junio*. Clearly, this was a plot by Moscow and aided by Havana to take control of a promising local crisis. If President Johnson had not intervened, the United States would have faced the double threat of two Caribbean dependencies of the Soviet Union, instead of only Cuba. In sum, the Soviet Union had suffered another tactical reverse.

CANADA

QUITE THE STRANGEST of the many outbreaks of urban terrorism in the 1970s occurred in Canada. On October 5, 1970, the senior British trade commissioner in Montreal, James Richard Cross, was kidnapped; five days later, so was the Quebec minister of labor and immigration, Pierre Laporte. In both cases, the kidnappers were members of an extremist separatist organization that called itself the *Front de Libération du Québec* (FLQ). In the Cross case, the FLQ demanded £208,000 in gold bars, and the release of "a certain number of political prisoners." The terrorists were less specific in the Laporte kidnapping, but in both cases they threatened to kill the victims.

The oddest aspect of these linked cases was the fact that the FLQ, for all its views on the "liberation of Quebec," was led by George Schoeters, a Belgian immigrant, while his second in command was a Hungarian immigrant, François Schirm. On October 17, Laporte was "executed." Cross was luckier: he was freed, unhurt, on December 3. In addition to the two kidnappings, which attracted international attention, the FLQ had set off bombs in various places.

Who was behind the FLQ? The available clues pointed in the direction of the Soviet Union, Cuba, and Palestinian extremists. In 1968, for instance, two leading members of the FLQ's political vanguard, the FLP *(Front de Libération Populaire)* had attended a conference sponsored by the Canadian Peace Congress, a Soviet-backed front organization. This in itself was not conclusive, since the object of such fronts is to involve (and ultimately, of course, to control) "anti-capitalist" or anti-Western activists not necessarily working to Moscow's orders. However, links with Cuba were proven. The kidnappers of James Cross were in fact given asylum in Havana,[6] while the murderers of Laporte were jailed for life in March and May 1971.

There were also claims by two members of the FLQ, at that time in a guerrilla camp in Jordan, that they had joined the Moscow-supported Popular Front for the Liberation of Palestine (PFLP), the most extreme of the Palestinian terrorist organizations. Further evidence of Moscow's involvement in subversion in Canada would come to light later.[7]

INDONESIA

A DEFEAT ON a far larger scale happened in Indonesia in 1965, the same year as the relatively minor Dominican crisis. In 1948, the two International Department's attempts to seize power, involving Musso and Tan Malaka, resulted in fiasco (see Chapter 13). By 1965, however, the very able Party leader, Dipa Nusantara Aidit, had built up a membership of some 3 million for his *Partai Komunis Indonesia* (PKI) and felt the call of destiny. The time had come, he thought, to overthrow the charismatic but irresponsible President Achmed Sukarno.

The regime established under President Sukarno styled itself "guided democracy," with Sukarno himself as the guide. He had coined a portmanteau word—*Nasakom*—to summarize the basis of his state: it was composed of the first syllables of Indonesian words meaning "nationalism," "religious forces," and "Communism." Lively, irrepressible, and a hypnotic orator, Sukarno had a taste for costly architectural follies and preferred demagogic speeches to responsible attempts to deal with his country's problems. Among these were a backward agriculture, an unbalanced budget and foreign trade, and the heavy overpopulation of Java compared to Sumatra, Indonesia's largest island.[8]

By mid-1965, Sukarno was suffering from advanced kidney failure, and the specialist sent at his request by Communist China had passed the word to the PKI that the president would soon die. The news spurred Aidit to rapid action. On the evening of September 30, Sukarno collapsed while addressing a meeting in Jakarta Stadium. Aidit, who was in the audience, thought the time had come, and slipped away. He did not know, therefore, that Sukarno had returned to the rostrum and resumed his speech. Meanwhile the rumor that the president had died spread like wildfire.

The commander of the presidential guard, Lieutenant-Colonel Untung, was a secret ally of the PKI. On Aidit's instructions, he ordered his troops to leave the palace grounds, kidnap the leading eight generals, and take them to Halim air base, fifteen miles from Jakarta's town center. Six of the eight generals were kidnapped, and were murdered after ghastly tortures. The other two generals escaped. One was General Abdul Haris Nasution; the other Major-General Mohamed Suharto, a man of cool nerve, caution, and natural political skill.

For President Sukarno, this was the beginning of the end. By stages, he surrendered power to Suharto, who maintained power until 1998, more than thirty years later. Following Aidit's mistimed attempted coup, the mass membership of the PKI fell victim to one of the worst massacres of a bloody century: 300,000 to 500,000 people were butchered between October 1965 and February 1966.[9] Among the first to go was Aidit. The biggest Communist party outside the Soviet empire had been utterly crushed.

In general, the 1960s were a bad time for Lenin's Comintern; the botched PKI coup rates as a major setback. The situation appeared to have changed for the better by 1971, when in October a major analytical article by the head of the International Department, Boris Ponomarev, was published in *Kommunist,* the theoretical journal of the CPSU. The cumbrous title struck a chord in the hearts and minds of the faithful: "Topical Problems in the Theory of the World Revolutionary Process." He returned to the theme in June 1974 in the *World Marxist Review,* in an article that appeared in Prague in several languages. This time the title was "The World Situation and the Revolutionary Process."

In the 1971 article Ponomarev criticized the so-called New Left for its lack of ideological consistency and its "adventuristic elements, including Maoists and Trotskyists," but found them potentially useful because of their "overall anti-imperialist direction."

Despite the reverses described in this chapter, events had, on the whole, been encouraging for the CPSU's International Department (the successor to the Comintern from May 1943). In Chile, the Allende government, which included the Communist Party, was doing well, as were, at that time, the Tupamaros of Uruguay. In Peru, a new military regime had shown itself capable of revolutionary ideas.

By 1974, when Ponomarev's second article appeared, some of the earlier hopes had been dashed. The Allende government had been overthrown in Chile, and the Tupamaros had been crushed. Ponomarev attributed these setbacks to the failure of the revolutionaries to apply Lenin's original teachings. They had failed to consolidate their gains or prepare to meet the challenge of a military coup.

More successes were on the way, however. The collapse of the Soviet Empire was still a long way ahead.

CHAPTER TWENTY-SEVEN

1968: THE PRAGUE SPRING
AND BEYOND

———>●<———

I T HAPPENED IN a men's lavatory in a Bratislava hotel, just before 7 P.M. on August 3, 1968, during a break in a multilateral Communist conference. The KGB station chief in that town had arranged for a member of the Soviet Politburo, Pyotr Shelest, to be there at that time. Waiting for him was Vasil Bilak, a hard-liner and the leader of the Slovak Communist Party. When the two men had identified themselves and shaken hands, Bilak presented Shelest with an envelope. It contained an urgent letter addressed to the Soviet leader Leonid Brezhnev, first secretary of the ruling party, who was taking part in the conference.

Shelest opened the envelope, read the letter, and thanked his Slovak colleague profusely. He went immediately to Brezhnev's suite and handed him the letter. Brezhnev instructed Shelest to convey his deep gratitude to Bilak and his colleagues, although he chose not to reply to the letter.

The text of this letter was sealed in the Soviet archives in a folder marked "NEVER TO BE OPENED." There it remained until July 1992, when Boris Yeltsin, by then Russia's president, sent it to Czechoslovakia's first post-Communist president, Vaclav Havel, who read it out on July 16. The letter appealed to the Soviet Union to intervene "to preserve socialism in the Czechoslovak Socialist Republic." To save time and give Brezhnev immediate access to the letter, which was drafted in Czech, the five signatories (of whom Bilak was one) had translated it into Russian.

The key passages follow:

Esteemed Leonid Ilich,

. . . The press, radio and television, which are effectively in the hands of right-wing forces, have influenced popular opinion to such an extent that elements hostile to the Party have begun to take part in the political life of our country. . . . These elements are fomenting a wave of nationalism and chauvinism, and are provoking an anti-Communist and anti-Soviet psychosis.

. . . The very existence of socialism in our country is under threat.

At present, all political instruments and the instruments of state power are paralyzed to a considerable degree. The right-wing forces have created conditions suitable for a counter-revolutionary coup.

. . . We are appealing to you, Soviet Communists . . . with a request for you to lend support and assistance with all the means at your disposal. Only with your assistance can the Czechoslovak Socialist Republic be extricated from the imminent danger of counter-revolution.

. . . We request that you treat our statement with the utmost secrecy, and for that reason we are writing to you, personally, in Russian.

Alois Indra Drahomir Kolder Antonin Kapek
Oldrich Svestka Vasil Bilak[1]

In the absence of a reply from Brezhnev, the signatories wrote a second letter to Brezhnev on August 19, 1968, but by then the Soviet leader had decided to rally the Warsaw Pact countries (minus Romania) to invade rebellious Czechoslovakia. The combined forces crossed the border on August 20.

HOW DID THE crisis begin? The story is well known, but the facts have to be restated if, decades later, the nature of the crisis is to be fully understood.

Having seized power in the bloodless coup of 1948, the Communist Party of Czechoslovakia, or CPC *(Komunistick·Strana Ceskoslovenska)* built up the highest ratio of members to the total population of any ruling Communist Party—in 1967, 1,700,000 out of a total population of 14,305,000[2]—and the number continued to grow. The buildup was necessary, from Moscow's viewpoint, because the urge for freedom and democracy was stronger in Czechoslovakia than in the other Soviet satellites. The intelligentsia was more outspokenly critical than elsewhere in

Eastern Europe. The economy was heading for bankruptcy, and the Party introduced a "New Economic Model" in 1966, but failed to implement it. In June 1967, the Union of Czechoslovak Writers held its Fourth Congress, at which the Communist regime was denounced outspokenly, with special emphasis on the repressive measures taken by the CPC.

The previous month, the Party's Central Committee had held a particularly fraught meeting, at which President Antonin Novotny, who was also first secretary of the Party, resisted calls for the separation of his two offices, and was harshly criticized by the Slovak contingent for neglecting their half of the Republic and treating it in an "insulting" manner. Novotny appealed to Brezhnev for support, but the Soviet leader ignored the appeal.

At the end of October, rebellious Czech and Slovaki students took to the streets. Several hundred of them had been left in darkness or candlelight following power cuts in a new hostel of the Charles University. The marching students, carrying torches or candles, shouted, "Give us light!" The security police attacked the demonstrators with tear gas and truncheons. Many of the students were taken to the hospital.

After the winter break, the Central Committee reconvened on January 3, 1968, and voted overwhelmingly to replace Novotny with the first secretary of the Communist Party of Slovakia, Alexander Dubček. What followed was a resolution best described as an ideological oxymoron: a call for freedom of expression and internal Party democracy, while at the same time reaffirming loyalty to Marxism-Leninism.

The Party resolutions and the speeches that followed Dubček's promotion illustrated either the new leader's apparent incapacity to see the contradictions for what they were, or his hopeful awareness that only by reaffirming his faith in the basic ideology could he hope to retain Moscow's support.

His first public address was made in Prague on February 1, before the National Congress of Agricultural Cooperatives. The key passage was, "Much will be achieved to begin with if . . . past obstacles to progress are removed and creative efforts set in motion . . . so that every honest citizen believing in socialism and the unity of this country feels that he is being useful and counts for something."

A marked exercise of freedom of expression followed, notably in the press, and two Party stalwarts whom Novotny had relegated to obscure posts—Gustav Husak and Josef Smrkovsky—began to speak their minds. There were pressing demands from trade union leaders for the removal of the many Party bureaucrats who had been appointed to superfluous posts in factories.

An unpredictable event had sparked this demand by the trade unions for personnel changes: the defection at the end of February 1968 of General Jan Sejna, chairman of the Party's Main Committee in the National Defense Ministry. Having disappeared, Sejna was charged with illegally appropriating alfalfa seeds valued at 300,000 crowns. The trade union daily *Préce* of March 6 had this to say:

> The Sejna case shows the moral failure of a certain group of bureaucrats who are using dogmatic phrases to fend off the application of democratic selection, because they have cogent reasons to fear it. These reasons have nothing to do with ideas. This is the case also of the man who placed such confidence in Sejna. How he impressed on us all the need for watchfulness and class vigilance. And under the candlestick—such darkness. Will he realise what he must do now?[3]

The "man who placed such confidence in Sejna" was of course President Antonin Novotny. The special significance of Sejna's defection (which eventually took him to the United States) was perhaps difficult for the Western public to grasp. Those who took refuge in the West fell into two incompatible categories: dissenters and defectors. The dissenters were those who had never accepted the totalist system and who had spoken out against it. Some of them had served time in the gulag. The best-known Russian dissident of them all—Aleksandr Solzhenitsyn—is an example. Defectors were career Party men who had served the system but feared a purge or dreaded the possible consequences of liberalization for their own careers. Sejna was a defector, indeed the highest ranking defector ever, at the time.

At the next Party plenum on March 22, Antonin Novotny was forced to resign as president of the republic and from his remaining party functions as a member of the Presidium and Secretariat. His post on the Presidium was taken by Josef Smrkovsky and on the Secretariat by Cestmir Cisar. The Party's choice as candidate for the presidency of the republic was Ludvik Svoboda—an appeasing gesture toward Moscow, to which he was uncritically loyal.

By then, the wave of freedom seemed unstoppable. One of the most significant factors was a fast-growing movement for the rehabilitation of political prisoners. In February, the Union of Anti-Fascist Fighters put pressure on the Party leadership for speedy action to rehabilitate nearly 40,000 ex-servicemen and resistance fighters who had fought in Spain, Yugoslavia, or the West and suffered discrimination later. On March 31, 1968, some 3,000 victims of political trials, all of them non-Communists, set up a "Club for the Rehabilitation of Political Prisoners." More embarrassing still to the authorities was a call for the rehabilitation of former Party stalwarts who had been tried and, in many cases, executed during the Stalinist trials of the 1950s. The most famous of them was Rudolf Slansky, the former CPC secretary-general, executed in 1953 on groundless charges of "Titoist-Zionist imperialist conspiracy." (See Chapter 9.)

During this period, a mass of articles in support of rehabilitation of the unjustly condemned appeared in the press. At least four senior Party members who had played condemnatory roles during the purges committed suicide.

Another raw point was censorship. In response to protests from journalists, the Party Presidium abolished preventive censorship on March 4. Eleven days later, the party officials of the Central Publishing Administration passed a resolution calling for the abolition of "preventive censorship." This was an unheard of case in the Communist Empire: the censors calling for an end to censorship. The climax came on April 9, with the publication of the new "Action Program" in the party's newspaper, *Rudé Právo,* calling for democratization. Specifically, the program called for:

- Protection by the judiciary of the constitutional rights of citizens;
- Freedom of speech, press, and assembly to be guaranteed by law;
- Full equality for national minorities and restoration of rights to citizens whose rights had been violated in the past;
- Freedom to travel abroad and to emigrate.

In a gesture toward orthodox Marxism-Leninism, however, the Action Program rejected the creation of opposition parties, while also rejecting any restriction of the rights and freedoms of non-Communists.

From Moscow and some (though not all) of the Communist capitals, these developments were followed with sour disapproval. On March 23, the ruling parties of the Soviet Union and five of its satellites (including Czechoslovakia itself) met in Dresden. The other four satellites were Bulgaria, East Germany, Hungary, and Poland. The communiqué expressed confidence "that the proletariat and all working people of Czechoslovakia under the leadership of the Communist Party of Czechoslovakia, would ensure the further progress of socialist construction in the country." Translated from "Newspeak," this was a barely disguised order to Dubček and his Party to fall in line or face the consequences.

On April 26, the ruling party of (relatively) dissident Romania issued a resolution strongly critical of the Dresden meeting, noting that the participants had discussed "questions of direct concern to Comecon and the Warsaw Treaty, of both of which Romania has been a foundation member," but complaining that the Romanian party had not been invited to Dresden.

By then the Party was caught in a trap of its own making. It had yielded to dissident views, thus jeopardizing the careers of its members.

Dubček and his new prime minister, Oldrich Cernik, with Smrkovsky (president of the National Assembly) and Bilak (first secretary of the Slovaki Party) were summoned to Moscow on May 4. The communiqué repeated the recent Newspeak warning, calling for "friendship and all-round co-operation between the CPSU and the CPC *on the basis of the principles of Marxism-Leninism and working class internationalism, to extend contacts at all levels, and to strive for stronger unity and cohesion of the countries of the Socialist Community and the world Communist movement"* (italics added). In other words: "Do as we say, or face the consequences."

A show of strength followed on May 17, when a Soviet military delegation came to Prague (at the invitation of the Czechoslovak Party), led by Marshal Andrei Grechko, the defense minister, and accompanied, among others, by General Aleksei Lepishev, chief of the Central Political Department of the Soviet Army and Navy (whose former "opposite number" had been General Sejna). The inevitable communiqué mentioned "concrete steps" to strengthen cooperation between the Soviet and Czechoslovak armies within the framework of the Warsaw Pact.

The Soviet prime minister, Aleksei Kosygin, also turned up in Prague, ostensibly for health reasons but also, doubtless, to add a political dimension to the military pressure.

By this time Dubček had clearly lost control over the events that he had allowed to happen. The Party's Central Committee convened a plenum on May 29 to deal with pressures "from the Right." For the first time Dubček asserted that the major danger to "democratization" came from the Right. He referred to the "intensification of anti-Communist tendencies," which, he said, were "endangering above all the peaceful socialist evolution and process of social regeneration." But he also mentioned danger from the Left, in that any revival of sectarianism "would do great harm to the Party."

At the end of June, a "2,000-word Manifesto" was drafted by a well-known dissident writer, Ludvik Vaculik, and signed by seventy prominent intellectuals. It urged the rapid removal of Party hard-liners from their public functions and urged that if this was not done, the people should resort to "public criticism, resolutions, strikes and boycotts."

The Czech branch of the KGB's SMERSH* denounced the Manifesto as "a fabrication of bankrupt exiles, branded as wartime Gestapo and [other] agents living in London under protection of US and British Intelligence."[4]

Events were gathering speed. In June and July, Warsaw Pact forces conducted "military maneuvers" on the territories of Czechoslovakia, East Germany, Poland, and the Soviet Union. Although the maneuvers ended officially on July 12, the Soviet forces remained on Czech soil under various pretexts, such as "abnormal traffic conditions." Two days later, the ruling parties of the USSR, Poland, Hungary, Bulgaria, and East Germany met in Warsaw. The Czech Party had been invited, but had declined the invitation on the ground that any further meeting should take place on Czechoslovak soil. This time, the Warsaw meeting expressed "deep anxiety" about developments in their absent neighbor.

To meet Czech objections, however, the entire Soviet Politburo met with the entire Czech Presidium from July 29 to August 1 at the small town of Ciern nad Tisou on the Czech side of the border with the Soviet Union. On August 4, government and Party leaders of Czechoslovakia and the five countries that met earlier at the Warsaw meeting gathered in

---

*SMERSH, short for *Smert Shpionam* or "Death to Spies": the KGB's mechanism for assassinating citizens regarded as traitors, wherever they might be.

Bratislava. It was on this occasion that Bilak and other hard-liners delivered their letter to Brezhnev.

In this rapidly worsening situation, moral support came unexpectedly from two other Communist countries, neither of which, at the time, took orders from Moscow: Yugoslavia, which had opted for neutrality outside the Soviet bloc, and Romania, which belonged to the Warsaw Pact but had declined to join in the anti-Czech pressure campaign imposed by the Soviet Union. In both countries, the press had supported the Czechoslovak stance, and their two leaders visited Prague in succession. Marshal Tito of Yugoslavia arrived on August 9 and left the next day; Nicolae Ceauşescu of Romania was there from August 15 to 17. Each of them was given a rapturous popular reception. Ceauşescu's support was the more remarkable, in that his regime was a good deal more repressive than Tito's. He carried his defiance of Moscow to the length of signing, with Svoboda, a Treaty of Friendship, Cooperation, and Mutual Assistance, optimistically scheduled to last twenty years.

The two state visits may have strengthened Dubček's will to resist pressures from the Soviet Union and the more obedient Warsaw Pact countries, but the situation was already out of hand. Scarcely had Ceauşescu returned to Bucharest than Moscow resumed its pressure, most appositely by organizing large-scale military maneuvers along the targeted borders.

The invasion started on the night of August 21, when a powerful Soviet force, with contingents from four other Warsaw Pact countries—Poland, Hungary, East Germany, and Bulgaria—crossed the frontier.

Initially, the consensus among Western correspondents on the scene was that the invading force totaled between 250,000 and 300,000 soldiers. By the end of August, the total had soared to around 600,000. In a broadcast at 1 A.M. on August 21, Prague Radio stressed that the troops had "crossed the frontiers of the Czechoslovak Socialist Republic": the word *invasion* was not used. The broadcast stressed, however, that "this happened without the knowledge of the president of the Republic, the chairman of the National Assembly, the premier or the first secretary of the Czechoslovak Communist Party Central Committee." It went on to appeal to all citizens "to maintain calm and not to offer resistance"; no command to defend the country had been issued.

One of the first acts of the KGB contingent among the invaders was to instruct its Czech counterpart, the StB, to arrest Dubček and several others, including Smrkovsky, chairman of the National Assembly, and Cernik, the prime minister. All of them were handcuffed, treated roughly, and bundled into an armored troop carrier. Next stop: Moscow. Once there, the Czech leaders were pressured into agreeing to accept a form of words proposed by the Soviet invaders. Svoboda, who had not been arrested, was also taken to Moscow. Officially, the talks began on August 24, but it is now known that on the previous day Svoboda joined the three top Soviet leaders, known at that time as the "troika"—the Party chief, Brezhnev, Prime Minister Kosygin, and the chairman of the Presidium, Nikolai Podgorny—where he was treated to a "no nonsense" presentation of Soviet views of the situation. After opening remarks by Brezhnev, the Czech leaders listened to a long speech in Slovak by vice premier and Slovak Party secretary, Gustav Husak. Brezhnev then turned on Husak and charged him, along with Dubček, with having "created a situation that covers the Communist Party of Czechoslovakia with shame." (For further details, see Appendix J: Document 1.)

When the decisive meeting began, with Dubček, Cernik, and the others having been brought to Moscow under duress, their "hosts" included Brezhnev, Kosygin, M. A. Suslov (the Party's leading ideologist) and Boris Ponomarev (who was in charge of the International Department).

Any uninstructed reader of the long communiqué that followed on August 27 might have concluded that whatever problems were considered had been resolved. It referred to "free and comradely discussion," attributed the said problems to "activization of imperialism's machinations against the socialist countries" and the Soviet side's "understanding and support of the Czechoslovak Communist Party." The sting came in the third of thirteen paragraphs, which noted the intention of the Party to implement decisions "with a view to improving the methods of guiding society, developing socialist democracy and strengthening the socialist system on the basis of Marxism-Leninism," in plain language, to obey Moscow's orders and stop liberalizing the system. It referred to the military occupation as "the temporary entry of troops of the five socialist countries into Czechoslovakian territory."

There had indeed been no "resistance" in the sense of an armed action to repulse the invaders. But the volume and ingenuity of passive resistance were impressive. In the words of Josef Josten, a well-known dissident who settled in London,

A mushroom growth of slogans immediately sprang up everywhere, in all shapes and sizes, on walls, in windows, on and around trams and monuments, or were carried as banners and placards. Chalked and painted slogans on walls and pavements added to the urgency and unanimity of the message. In Czech and Slovak, they exhorted and warned the population; in Russian, German, Polish, Hungarian and Bulgarian they confronted the uninvited guests with the unpalatable truth—that they were unwanted and illegal invaders.[5]

At night the invading soldiers tore the slogans down; by dawn a new crop was in place. Regardless of President Svoboda's views, his name was much used, since it meant "freedom." The crux of the messages was simply: "Russians go home!"

For once, the Soviet masters of propaganda were being outmaneuvered. The official line, as conveyed by Soviet embassies around the free world and in the United Nations, was that the five national armies had crossed the border in response to appeals from the Czech government and from citizens alarmed by the progress of the counter-revolutionaries. In a calm and factual style, the Institute of the Czechoslovak Academy of Science issued a *Black Book* recording what had happened and the fact that the authorities had had no advance notice of the invasion. In a further broadcast, at 6:45 A.M. on that fateful morning while the invaders were pouring in, Prague Radio called on the people "to remain calm and meet the occupation with passive resistance." By then, of course, passive resistance was in full swing.

Unlike the brutal Soviet crushing of the Hungarian revolution twelve years earlier, which took only four months, the Czechoslovak crisis dragged on for nearly two years. Reactions to the Moscow talks came at three mutually incompatible levels. At the top level, Svoboda and Dubček, back from Moscow, broadcast statements that were on the whole conciliatory toward their Soviet masters, the president's more so than the Party leader's. During his broadcast, Dubček broke down in tears several times. He ended with an appeal to all "to remain united, calm and above all prudent."

A rumor that proved well founded spread through Prague, that the Soviet leaders had insisted on the restoration of censorship in all the media, even though the Moscow communiqué had not mentioned it. The people were less interested in conciliatory words than in hard facts. The important thing was that their own leaders had failed to get the foreign forces out. Thousands of people marched from the central Wenceslaus Square to the National Assembly building, chanting, "We want the whole truth," and "We don't want to live on our knees." This was the second of the incompatible levels.

The third, surprisingly, was the National Assembly, which reacted on an unexpected note of indignation, at odds with the ruling party. Mincing no words, the Assembly passed a resolution condemning the occupation of the country by the Warsaw Pact countries as illegal. It called on the government to fix definite dates for the departure of foreign troops.

No such thing happened. Instead, further talks were held in Moscow between the Soviet and Czechoslovak leaders on October 3–4 and again on October 14–15. On the same day as the second round (October 14), the KGB's chairman, Yuri Andropov, provided his Polish and East German colleagues with a "Top Secret" report on "the activities of the counter-revolutionary underground in the CSSR (the Czechoslovak People's Republic), prepared on the basis of intelligence materials." The core of the "intelligence materials" consisted of a detailed analysis of the activities of a "Second Center" in Prague which provided material for secret anti-Communist "mass propaganda" aimed at "liquidating the political power of the ruling Communist Party." (See Appendix J: Document 2.)

The outcome of the bilateral talks was a Soviet-Czechoslovak Treaty, signed in Prague on October 16 by the two premiers, Kosygin and Cernik, and ratified in Moscow on October 18 by the Soviet Supreme Presidium and on the same day by the Czechoslovak National Assembly. The text consisted of fifteen Articles, the first and last of which referred to the Soviet military presence in Czechoslovakia as "temporary." Article 1 justified this presence as necessary "to ensure the security of the countries of the Socialist community against the increasing revanchist (seeking revenge) strivings of the West German militarist forces."

On paper, the treaty enshrined the imposition of Soviet authority on the Czechoslovak satellite and the Czechoslovak admission of political defeat. In reality, however, the Soviet imperialists had not yet won the political war. On November 11, 1968, the Soviet Party's Central Committee drafted a "Secret" report that was entrusted to the Soviet ambassador in Prague, Stepan V. Chervonenko, and the first deputy foreign minister,

Vasily Kuznetsov, to be presented to Dubček. The report expressed Moscow's displeasure at a new draft Resolution of the Czechoslovak Party in the following words: "On the whole, the perusal of the document has provoked very serious concern and anxiety regarding the implementation of the Moscow Agreement and the further course of the normalization of the situation in Czechoslovakia and of the development of relations between our Parties and countries." (For the full text of the Soviet document, see Appendix J: Document 3.)

Meanwhile, discontent and indignation still raged at the popular level. Printers refused to print the ultra-conformist paper *Tribuna*. Young intellectuals brought out a *Prague Manifesto* calling for the restoration of their country's sovereignty. A group of students decided that words were not enough and decided on a policy of suicide and self-sacrifice.[6]

What the students meant by "self-sacrifice" was demonstrated when the student group drew lots to pick "Torch Number 1." The sacrificial winner was Jan Palach, who, on January 16, 1969, drenched his clothes with petrol in Wenceslaus Square, struck a match, and died in a hospital three days later from his burns. Half a million mourners from all over the country assembled in Wenceslaus Square to attend his funeral. Thirteen other "Torches" ended their lives by self-immolation.

Two months later, on March 28, a sporting victory was turned to political advantage when the Czechoslovak team twice defeated the Soviet one in the world ice hockey championship in Stockholm. Cheering their champions, crowds gathered in Prague and other cities, shouting and displaying slogans. One of them compared the Stockholm victory with the failure of Soviet troops to defeat the Chinese in a clash on the Ussuri River bordering the two Communist giants. A phony provocation followed, when a small group of demonstrators threw paving stones at the offices of the Soviet state airline, Aeroflot, shattering the windows and causing further extensive damage. It later emerged that the incident had been organized by KGB agents in the Czech Ministry of the Interior. Some of the men had been brought in from other regional offices of the ministry, to avoid identification by resistance loyalists. On KGB orders, the ministry had removed Aeroflot files some days earlier.[7]

In Moscow three days later, on March 31, *Pravda* attacked Dubček for negligence over the wrecking of the Aeroflot offices. That same day the Soviet defense minister, Marshal Andrei Grechko, arrived unannounced at

Milovice, headquarters of the Soviet military in Czechoslovakia. A Note was issued, stipulating that:

1. Order will be restored . . . with the utmost severity. Preventive censorship will be introduced.
2. If the regime cannot restore order, other States of the Warsaw Pact will be asked to help liquidate the counter-revolution.

Emerging from his self-imposed low profile, Marshal Grechko went to Prague, where he confronted Svoboda, Dubček, and Prime Minister Cernik and demanded an immediate change of leadership. On April 17, Dubček was forced to resign. His place was taken by his fellow-Slovak, Gustav Husak.

Still the resistance continued. Driven underground, it prepared a mass celebration of the anniversary of the invasion on August 21, to be known as "The Day of Shame." Although there had been thousands of preventive arrests, a large crowd assembled and marched, chanting slogans. In Brno, the Moravian capital, popular indignation led to violent clashes, and an unpublished number of demonstrators were killed or wounded.

WHY THE INVASION?

THE QUESTION IS worth asking, and the answers that emerge are complex, although the dominant reason was purely imperial. Brezhnev spelled it out in November 1968, when he addressed the Fifth Congress of the Polish Communist Party. In logical terms, it was a squaring of the circle. On the one hand, as reported in *Pravda* of November 13, he reaffirmed respect for sovereignty; on the other, he claimed the right, on behalf of the Soviet Union, to intervene in a Socialist country where "Socialism" was deemed to be threatened. He defended his view in the following terms: "Socialist States stand for strict respect for the sovereignty of all countries. We are resolutely opposed to interference in the affairs of any States, to violation of their sovereignty."

He went on, however:

When internal and external supporters hostile to socialism attempt to turn the development of any socialist country in the direction of the restoration of the capitalist system, when a threat arises to the cause of socialism in that country, a threat to the security of the socialist commonwealth as a whole—it already becomes not only a problem for the people of that country but also a general problem, the concern of all socialist countries.

In such circumstances, Brezhnev went on, armed intervention was justified.[8] The Soviet leader's declaration became known in the West as the "Brezhnev Doctrine." It was an affirmation of pure Leninist orthodoxy. Since Leninism had called for the spreading of "Socialism," meaning Communism, to all countries without exception, it followed logically that once a country had been incorporated into "the Socialist commonwealth" there was no way it could opt out of it, and any attempt by the Western Powers, singly or in their NATO alliance, to intervene would be a *casus belli*.

At the time, most Western commentators misinterpreted the signals, whether through idealism or through ignorance or by deliberately ignoring the ideological dimension. What Dubček had done, or allowed to happen, was regarded in Moscow as far more dangerous and unpardonable than anything done by Tito or Ceauşescu in their respective countries. True, Tito had opted for neutrality, and Ceauşescu had refused to join his fellow members of the Warsaw Pact in invading Czechoslovakia—another member of the Pact. But both leaders had rigorously maintained their ruling parties' absolute monopoly of power. Thus "Socialism," in the Leninist sense, had not been under threat in either country.

Dubček, on the other hand, while professing his loyalty to the Warsaw Pact, had conferred on the Czechoslovak people liberal reforms that threatened "Socialism." Tito and Ceauşescu had avoided the cardinal sin of which Dubček was flagrantly guilty.

THIS ASSESSMENT OF the situation was reinforced by specific considerations of internal security and military requirements.

We have mentioned the KGB's role in the staged incident of the Aeroflot offices; a decade earlier, the KGB and its de facto StB subordinates had been involved in a plot to enable the hard-liner Novotny to stay in power by purging the Army of higher officers who opposed him.[9]

Between January and August 1968, the hundreds (or possibly thousands) of KGB agents in the Czechoslovak Army, police, and security services, tried (without much success) to discredit and weaken the post-Novotny reform movement. By March 1968, the Soviet agents were increasingly worried over the gradual but quickening removal of Stalinists from Party posts in Czechoslovakia.

In that fatal spring, the head of the StB, Josef Houska, was sent to Moscow several times to keep his Soviet hosts up to date on the alarming events in Prague. When summer came, he was made an honorary KGB colonel. However, this was a short-lived victory for him and for the KGB, for he was soon sent on leave and replaced.

Another KGB ploy was a program to monitor all telephone conversations in the Czech Ministry of the Interior. The KGB also infiltrated several newly formed non-Communist clubs and circulated forged documents that implicated them in nonexistent plots with Western intelligence services. Another KGB operation was to "find" NATO weapons, which the Soviet agents had themselves planted, in Western Bohemia.

Thus, these and other KGB operations in Czechoslovakia during the Prague Spring played an important role in strengthening the Soviet view that an invasion was necessary. There was also a parallel pressure on the military side. Whereas there were large-scale Soviet military deployments in other Warsaw Pact countries—East Germany, Poland, and Hungary—there was none in Czechoslovakia. Under Czechoslavakia's President Klement Gottwald and party leader Novotny in Prague, Soviet requests to station forces in Czechoslovakia had been rejected many times in the 1950s and 1960s.[10]

Indeed, the Soviet Union and Czechoslovakia had signed two agreements (in August 1961 and February 1962) entitling the Soviet Union to send nuclear weapons to Czechoslovakia in an emergency. Suitable sites were to be built jointly, with all costs charged to the Czechoslovaks. The facilities were to have been completed in 1967 but ran behind schedule, and reformist opposition grew rapidly when the Prague Spring got underway.

Important though these considerations of security and strategy were, they carried less weight in the end than the overriding political and ideological factors that led to the invasion and its natural sequel, the Brezhnev Doctrine.

CHAPTER TWENTY-EIGHT

AFRICAN CLIENT-STATES

1971–1977

~~~◆~~~

As WE HAVE been using the term, a "satellite" of the Soviet Union was, in practice, a colony. Though formally independent (and therefore entitled to a sovereign seat at the United Nations), the satellite's freedom of action was ultimately subject to Moscow's authority. This applied to the East European countries with the exception of Albania; and, after the Soviet-U.S. confrontation during the Missile Crisis of 1962, to Cuba. In 1971, seven years into the reign of Leonid Brezhnev, successor to Nikita Khrushchev, the Soviet leadership introduced a new method for the creation of a client-state, or in some cases the acceptance of satellite status: the signing of a friendship treaty.

What is a client-state? It is a country that is heavily dependent on the major power, economically, militarily, and/or culturally. This dependence, freely accepted at the start, inhibits independent action while leaving ultimate sovereignty intact. A satellite is punished should it attempt to go its own way, as happened in Hungary (and almost happened to Poland) in 1956, and of course Czechoslovakia was invaded in 1968 and Cuba was blockaded that year. (See Phase IV, Chapters 17 and 18; and Phase V, Chapter 22.) In mid-1972, however, Egypt's Anwar Al-Sadat demonstrated the reality of his country's sovereignty after some fourteen months as a client-state.

The first uses of the friendship treaty were with Egypt and India, where the chosen title was a twenty-year "Treaty of Peace, Friendship, and Cooperation" signed and ratified in August 1971. The Indian prime minister, Indira Gandhi, insisted on including a Soviet pledge to respect her country's policy of non-alignment (Article 4). Although India's relations with the Soviet Union remained friendly, it cannot be said that India ever came near to "graduating" from client-state to satellite.

EGYPT

THE EGYPTIAN TREATY, which came first chronologically, is of greater interest. In the last years of President Gamal Abdel Nasser, Egypt had been in the fullest sense a client-state and apparently destined, before long, to evolve into a satellite.* By the time Nasser died on September 28, 1970, there were thousands of Soviet "advisers" in Egypt, in the armed forces as well as in government, and at all levels. In addition, Soviet warplanes (including 30 MiG-25s) under direct Soviet command had been installed on the apparently valid pretext of improving Egypt's defenses against its main enemy: Israel. This potentially sinister further rapprochement was the outcome of a secret trip to Moscow by Nasser's successor, President Sadat, on March 1, 1971. Back in Cairo after two days of talks, Sadat announced on March 7 that he would not renew the cease-fire with Israel. Only weeks earlier, in a speech on February 4, he had proposed an unconditional thirty-day extension of the cease-fire and outlined a peace settlement, the main elements of which would be an Israeli withdrawal from the east bank of the Suez Canal, to be followed by the clearing and reopening of the Canal.[1]

Although the Israelis rejected Sadat's proposals, they had done so in a relatively conciliatory tone, and there had been agreement on both sides that the United States should act as broker. In Washington, President Richard Nixon had wasted no time in proposing that his secretary of state, William Rogers, should go to Cairo to discuss the situation with President Sadat.

From Sadat's viewpoint, the way was now clear to play one superpower against the other, which he did with considerable skill. In a speech

*There was a certain irony in Nasser's increasing dependence on Soviet support, in that (as the late Miles Copeland, a founder-member of the CIA, revealed in his memoirs), the Egyptian leader had been specifically picked by the Agency as a potentially useful ally of the United States. See Copeland, *The Game Player: Confessions of the CIA's Original Political Operative* (London, 1978, Chapters 16 and 19).

on May 1, he announced that he had decided to "give one more chance to the United States." On May 4, Rogers met with the Egyptian president. Although nothing concrete emerged, the meeting was cordial and encouraged pro-Sadat sentiments in Washington, even though the prevailing wisdom was that Sadat was unlikely to survive politically. The "wisdom" could hardly have been more mistaken. Next day, he summoned the Soviet ambassador, Vinogradov, and told him that he had decided to dismiss his Number 2, Vice President Ali Sabry, who was also the secretary of the ruling Arab Socialist Union.

From Vinogradov's point of view this was bad news, for Sabry had long made it clear that he was pro-Soviet. Sadat went so far as to tease Vinogradov by stressing that he did not want the Western press to say that he had removed Moscow's Number 1 man in Egypt. While the audience was still in progress, a Decree from Sadat was published recording the fact that Ali Sabry had been "relieved of his duties." Thereupon, Sabry was placed under house arrest.

Over the next fortnight, Sadat went on to arrest a number of other pro-Soviet high functionaries. He had evidently been planning this for some time, since he had already made a list of loyal Party men not noted for pro-Soviet sympathies to fill the vacancies he had just created. His coup d'état—for this was what the arrests amounted to—was complete by May 14.

By this time, the Kremlin was thoroughly alarmed, and on May 25 Moscow sent to Cairo a high-powered delegation headed by Nikolai Podgorny, president of the Supreme Soviet. An important member of the Soviet team was Boris Ponomarev, who for many years had headed the International Department—the successor to Lenin's Comintern—of the ruling CPSU. (See Chapter 6.)

At this point the Soviets produced their diplomatic secret weapon: the friendship treaty. After hearing Podgorny promise that the military supplies already pledged would arrive over the next four days, Sadat signed the proffered pact, the full title of which was the "Treaty of Friendship and Cooperation." As treaties go, it was a singularly noncommittal document, although certain of its clauses could be interpreted as sanctioning unilateral action on the Soviet side. Article 1 stipulated that "the friendship that unites the two partners shall never be broken." Article 2 provided for "the necessary conditions for the preservation and continued development of the social and economic gains of the two peoples." Article 5 bore the mark of the Soviet drafters by affirming that "the friendship that unites the two partners shall work to enlarge and deepen their cooperation in all domains." Article 7 went a step further, by affirming that "the two partners, starting from the great importance which they accord to the coordination of their activities in the international field, shall hold regular consultations at all levels on important questions." Articles 9 and 10 barred both signatories from entering any alliance or taking any action at variance with the Treaty.[2]

A few weeks later, on July 19, came an unforeseen crisis in Egypt's southern neighbor, Sudan, where a group of Army officers in league with the local Communist Party overthrew the government of the president, Major-General Gaafar al-Nimeiry. The new rulers immediately summoned a number of Sudanese Communist politicians who had taken refuge in Britain. The coup, however, was short-lived. On July 22, the Libyan leader, Colonel Muammar Ghadaffi, ordered the plane carrying the exiles to land at Tripoli, where he had two of them arrested. That afternoon, the coup leaders were overthrown, and Nimeiry was freed from his detention in the modest gardener's house of the presidential palace. Back in power, Nimeiry had the coup leaders and many of their followers shot or hanged. These included two of the top Communist leaders, Abdul Mahgoub (the general secretary) and Abdullah (the trade union leader), neither of whom (according to the French foreign correspondent Thierry Desjardins) had been involved in the coup.

In a sense, Nimeiry had asked for trouble earlier in the year when he banned the Sudanese Communist Party—the largest in Africa, with an estimated membership of about 5,000. Although he had stressed that the ban would in no way affect Sudan's close relations with the Soviet Union, there was alarm in Moscow, and the CPSU had sent a delegation to Khartoum in March to settle the differences between the government and the local Party. Nimeiry, who had declared on February 12 that he would destroy the Party, ignored Moscow's intervention. Nevertheless, at a parade on May 25, the Sudanese Army displayed for the first time Sam-2 missiles provided by the Soviet Union. This could be interpreted either as a gesture of conciliation or as an act of defiance.

The aftermath of the brief July crisis was more significant than the coup itself. In three important Arab capitals—Khartoum, Cairo, and

Tripoli—the official line was that a Communist coup had been defeated. According to Thierry Desjardins, the coup was not, in the true sense, a Communist one, in that it was in no way "teleguided" from Moscow.[3]

Whatever the truth of this interpretation, it suited the Egyptian, Libyan, and Syrian leaders to present it as such and, in clear violation of the friendship treaty, Sadat declared that "the USSR wanted to interfere in the affairs of the Arab world and outflank Egypt by attacking its traditional hinterland and the sources of the Nile." On July 23 he went even further by declaring that "those who want to ignore the United States are ostriches" and "war or peace, everything depends on the United States." Surprisingly, there was no reaction from Moscow.

The Soviet leaders were punishing Sadat in their own way by withholding the deliveries of arms they had promised Egypt. This denial was exposing Sadat to public criticism and even, on occasion, to hostile street demonstrations. Meanwhile, however, he was preparing a coup of his own. On July 14, 1972, he sent Prime Minister Aziz Sedki to Moscow. To Brezhnev's astonishment, Sadat announced that since the USSR had not sent the promised arms, Egypt had decided to dispense with the services of the Soviet military experts stationed in Egypt (who by then, totaled at least 18,000). He suggested, however, that to avoid unnecessary rejoicing in the "imperialist" camp, there should be a joint Soviet-Egyptian communiqué declaring in substance that since the Soviet experts had completed their allocated tasks, it had been jointly decided to repatriate them.

As there was no immediate Soviet response, Sadat summoned the Soviet ambassador on July 15, and told him that in view of Moscow's uncooperative attitude, he had decided to expel all the Soviet advisers, starting on July 18. Perhaps surprisingly, the Soviet government publicly accepted Sadat's decision. The "friendship" side of the treaty had proved short-lived.

SOMALIA

IN SUM, THE second experiment in friendship treaties had proved a fiasco. The Soviet leadership, however, clearly felt that the merits of the ploy had not been entirely discredited. Indeed, they had another target in mind: Somalia. As with most African countries, Somalia had only recently emerged from the colonial era. Until 1960 it consisted of the British Somaliland Protectorate and of the UN Trust Territory administered by

Italy, the former colonial power. In July 1960, the independent Somali Democratic Republic was created.

Culturally, the new nation was homogeneous in its customs and its spoken language; indeed, at the time it had no written language and literate Somalis used Koranic Arabic as their means of communication. Whatever their motives, the Soviets deserve credit for providing them with a written language of their own following the teachings of the late Professor Ivan Izomovich Potekhin. (See Chapter 23.) Indeed, Russian scholars supervised the writing of the first history of Somalia, in the new written language.* The real aim, of course, was imperial as well as cultural—or culture in service of the Soviet Empire.

Although Communist atheism was a retarding factor in Muslim Somalia, the Soviets rapidly established and developed a presence in this relatively primitive land, where the population of fewer than 3 million had been mostly illiterate in the Arabic script that had prevailed until the advent of the Soviet scholars. A further complicating factor was the administrative division of the country into six more or less autonomous clans. But the per capita income of "at most $60 a year" (as estimated by the World Bank) was a positive factor in Soviet eyes.

Within eighteen months of Somalia's independence in mid-1960, the Soviet Union had established a presence in Mogadishu, the capital, and in other places.[4] As in Egypt and elsewhere, the Soviets benefited from Western reluctance to provide armaments to a new state. Their interests were served when, in October 1969, a group of military officers ousted the weak central government. The emerging strong man, General Siad Barre, though not a Marxist-Leninist in a full ideological sense, inevitably came under heavy Soviet influence. Although inclined, at times of his own choosing, to defy his Soviet "benefactors," he was broadly pliant to their pressures.

At the time of Siad Barre's coup, the Russians had not yet tried out the friendship treaty ploy. In February 1972, the Soviet defense minister, Marshal Andrei A. Grechko, visited Somalia and raised the question of a friendship treaty. Initially, Siad Barre resisted the pressure, but the Soviets began to pour arms into the country and agreed to improve existing

---

*For some months in 1964, I contributed talks to the Somali service of the BBC, written on request in a very basic English to facilitate immediate interpretation into spoken Somali by the broadcasters.—BC

airport and harbor facilities. There was an immediate political dividend, as these deliveries, plus a minor economic aid program, boosted the military dictatorship against civilian politicians.

The determining event happened in the year of Grechko's visit but went unreported. There was a precedent for it in the KGB's molding of Fidel Castro's secret intelligence service. Since 1969, with Soviet assistance, Siad Barre had established a wide-ranging Somali National Security Service (NSS). "Security" included indoctrination. There were fourteen regional and sixteen district commissioners, nearly all of them personally chosen either by Siad or by men he had selected. Many of them were officers in the Army, and a few in the police.

In 1972, KGB chief Yuri Andropov made an unpublicized visit to Somalia to make sure the NSS was on the right lines. The man Siad had appointed to head both the NSS and Army intelligence was his son-in-law, Colonel Ahmed Suleiman Adbulle, who already enjoyed Andropov's support. Not long after Andropov's visit, Suleiman went to Moscow to study KGB methods and operations. At that time, the Kremlin regarded him as a natural successor to his father-in-law.

By then there were a dozen KGB officers in Mogadishu, operating from the NSS headquarters in the former Somali parliament building (which in Mussolini's time had been the Fascist headquarters). Revolutionary courts tried and sentenced political offenders. As in Cuba, the KGB officers had access to all Somali reports and investigations with full freedom to comment and advise. They had equal access to the separate secret services under the Army, the police, and the presidency's political office. Moreover, Somali diplomatic missions abroad had been assigned to collect intelligence for the KGB and GRU, with Somalia's diplomatic pouches and Somalia Airlines aircraft at their disposal.

At the same time, a system of political indoctrination and "thought control" had been set up fit to rival that in George Orwell's *1984*. It extended into schools and mass media. On Soviet advice, Siad had launched a people's militia called the *Gulwadayasha* ("Victory Pioneers"): an elite group of young vigilantes who reported on political dissidents, drummed up support for government programs, and kept ordinary citizens on the chosen path. Many, though not all, of the vigilantes had been trained in the Soviet Union. The Soviet advisers were clearly working toward an essential element that the Somali Republic still lacked: an all-pervasive vanguard Party.

Also on Soviet advice, Siad had established National Guidance Centers controlled by officers specially trained in the USSR in politically conscious "public relations." There were tempting benefits as well as coercive measures (including jail for citizens failing to "volunteer" for work). Scarce consumer and household goods were among the rewards.

Media control was centralized in Mogadishu and covered not only the press but films and local theater. By the time the "friendship mission" came to Somalia, in mid-1974, 90 percent of the minority with higher education had attended Soviet schools, and hundreds more were being coached in ideology under Russian instructors. In July that year a new indoctrination program was launched to bring the nomads—about two-thirds of the population—into line. In the hundreds, well-indoctrinated student teachers were sent into the countryside to preach and recruit the largely indifferent nomads—when they could be found.

Despite the profusion of military hardware, including advanced MiG-21 aircraft and SA-2 surface-to-air missiles, Siad had resisted Grechko's suggestion that a friendship treaty would be a natural sequel to the friendly relationship already established. One reason was the local Islamic opposition to special links with an avowedly atheistic regime. Indeed, in protest against the increasing Soviet influence, King Fahd of Saudi Arabia withdrew his ambassador to Somalia in the spring of 1974 and with him the prospect of Arab oil money. Moscow, however, reacted immediately. By then, close relations had been built up with another oil-rich country, Iraq, and the Iraqis offered to build a small oil refinery (capacity: 500,000 tons a year) in Somalia. The Soviets, on their side, were financing Somali imports of crude oil.

As in similar situations elsewhere, the Russians arranged for the arrival of special delegations from Cuba and East Germany; and in the light of Somalia's historic link with Italy, from the Italian Communist Party. These delegations, together with Soviet "friendship" groups, settled in various Somali towns to strengthen links with Moscow. The goal was reached in June, when Siad agreed to receive President Podgorny the following month.

Podgorny's delegation included V. A. Ustinov, head of the African Department of the Foreign Ministry, and V. N. Sofinsky, head of the Foreign Ministry's Press Department. The Somalis had named a modest street in Mogadishu "Vladimir Ilich Lenin," and President Podgorny declared the street name "deeply symbolic."

The Treaty of Friendship and Cooperation was duly signed on July 11, 1974, by President Podgorny and Siad Barre. It provided for close cooperation in all spheres: industry, farming, and livestock raising, natural resources, power engineering, science, art, literature, health, the press and radio, cinema, television, tourism, sport, the training of cadres and of military personnel. Article 1 called for strengthening of relations "on the basis of the principles of respect for sovereignty, territorial integrity, non-interference in each other's internal affairs, and equality." The inclusion of "equality" between two such monumentally unequal partners must surely qualify as one of the most striking political oxymorons of our age.

By the time of Podgorny's "friendly" visit, some 3,600 Soviet personnel (including families) were stationed in Somalia. The figure would grow to around 7,000. Before the Soviet connection, the Somali armed forces numbered no more than 4,000 ill-trained men, with a tiny navy and no air force. Shortly after the Podgorny visit, it would reach 17,000, with a volume and quality of equipment exceeding that of neighboring Ethiopia, with its 40,000 under arms.

With the signature of the friendship treaty, the satellization of Somalia appeared complete. Three years later, however, the carefully built edifice collapsed when the Soviet imperialists were faced with a choice between Somalia and its neighbor and historic enemy, Ethiopia, at the start of a regional war. For valid geopolitical reasons, the Soviet Union sided with Ethiopia, and Somalia retaliated by imitating Sadat's example and expelling its 7,000 Soviet advisers.

CHAPTER TWENTY-NINE

THE SECOND INDOCHINA WAR

1958–1975

M OSCOW'S DECISION TO commit itself to the Communist side in the Second Indochina War came six years after the war had begun, in November 1964. This tardiness is less surprising than it may sound. During the early 1960s, Khrushchev's main imperial preoccupation had been Cuba, culminating in the Missile Crisis of October 1962. For the first (and in retrospect the only) time, the two superpowers had come dangerously close to a nuclear war: the ultimate crisis that the Cold War was supposed to avoid. (See Chapter 21.)

After this, Khrushchev's foreign policy sank into inertia. (See Chapter 25.) Within the Party Presidium (as the Politburo now called itself) dissatisfaction with Khrushchev's leadership mounted.* The last straw was a persistent rumor that Khrushchev was planning to reshuffle the Presidium and the Secretariat at the next plenum of the Central Committee in November 1964.¹ Those under threat decided to act. In October 1964, exactly two years after the Cuban Missile Crisis, they ousted Khrushchev.

The Stalin era was over, and the coup was bloodless. Khrushchev was not executed: he was merely exiled—alive but an "unperson." There would

---

*The change of name took place at the Nineteenth Party Congress in 1952, when the membership of the all-powerful body was raised from eleven to nineteen. At the twenty-third Congress in 1966, the Presidium was changed back to the Politburo. For further details, see John J. Dziak, *Chekisty: A History of the KGB* (Lexington, MA: D.C. Heath 1988).

be no more mention of him in the media, and his many outsized portraits were removed from public buildings.

The new leader was Leonid Brezhnev, a long-serving *apparatchik*, as officials of the ruling party were known. Unlike Khrushchev, with his porcine face, Brezhnev was ruggedly handsome, smooth and well-mannered. He was unlikely to take off a shoe and bang it on a UN conference table, as Khrushchev had done. He was not the mastermind behind the coup, however, as he was absent from Moscow in the crucial week before it happened. That role was played by M. A. Suslov, the ultimate Party ideologist. It was Suslov who reeled off the "charges" against Khrushchev on October 14 in the Central Committee, while the deposed leader sat fuming. Suslov was not himself a candidate for supreme office: he was content to wield real power from behind the scenes. The Committee then accepted Khrushchev's (nonexistent) resignation on grounds of "advanced age and deterioration . . . of health." As a biographer of Brezhnev put it, "The only thing wrong with his [Khrushchev's] health at that moment was that his blood was boiling."[2]

Among the posts Brezhnev had occupied was that of president of the Supreme Presidium (in effect, president of the Soviet Union, in which capacity he traveled widely and met a number of heads of state). That post, however, was largely ceremonial; now he was the party's all-powerful first secretary (later general secretary). Although Mikhail Gorbachev would later blame him for the Soviet Union's "era of stagnation,"[3] Brezhnev would preside over the greatest and longest imperial expansion since Stalin.

The turning point in the great expansion came within weeks of the coup, in November 1964, when the National Front for the Liberation of South Vietnam (NFLSV) was invited to open an office in Moscow. Already, the NFLSV had offices in Peking, Pyongyang, Jakarta, Cairo, Havana, and East Berlin. The invitation passed almost unnoticed, but it was of great importance in that it indicated a Soviet readiness not only to continue to support North Vietnam but to increase the scale of its support. On November 26, the new premier, Aleksei Kosygin, announced, "We have been unanimous about the measures to be taken in order to strengthen the defense potential of North Vietnam."

The new and explicit Soviet commitment to Hanoi was indeed an event of high significance. It meant that the Soviets would no longer allow Mao Tse-tung's Communist Party to dominate Southeast Asia. The Sino-Soviet split was now at its height. During its passive phase, Chinese agents had cut out the pro-Moscow leadership in Burma and the Philippines, having already established Peking's primacy over the Malayan and Thai Communist parties. More important than these, however, was Ho Chi Minh's Lao Dong Dang (Workers' Party), which, until Khrushchev's removal, came increasingly under Chinese influence.

Having welcomed the NFLSV in Moscow, Kosygin led a high-powered delegation to Hanoi in early February 1965. On February 7, without consultation or prior warning, the Soviets' Vietnamese hosts faced them with a deliberately planned crisis by ordering the Vietcong guerrillas to attack an American airfield and barracks at Pleiku in the central highlands. It was a damaging success, with seventy Americans killed or wounded and seventeen helicopters destroyed, along with three transport planes. That afternoon U.S. and South Vietnamese planes attacked North Vietnamese targets.

Taken by surprise, the Soviet visitors did not hide their embarrassment and anger. On their side, the Vietnamese were elated. The Soviet visitors had been dropping hints about the need for peace talks, but Ho Chi Minh and his followers, including the great General Vo Nguyen Giap (see Chapter 12), were interested in victory, not peace. The attack on the Americans was designed to force the Soviet Union into their war. For a long time the North Vietnamese had listened to the dismissive phrase often reiterated by their Chinese supporters, describing the Americans as "paper tigers." There is reason to believe that the North Vietnamese, tacitly or otherwise, had discounted any significant reaction from the Americans.

They were wrong about the Americans and disappointed by the immediate Soviet reaction. Kosygin and his team left Hanoi without any further commitment to the North Vietnamese. Back in Moscow, they went ahead with preparations for an international Communist conference, which took place on March 1, 1965. One party boycotted it: the Lao Dong. Nevertheless, although Kosygin and his team had left Hanoi in a huff, a bonus for Ho and his followers came before long. Within months of Kosygin's visit, North Vietnam was receiving aircraft (including supersonic interceptor fighters), rockets, surface-to-air missiles, and quick-firing, self-tracking anti-aircraft guns.[4]

By then President Lyndon Johnson had made to Hanoi peace overtures that had been ignored. In June 1965, contrary to Soviet as well as

North Vietnamese expectations, the president decided to authorize the use of American combat troops in Vietnam. This was the start of the escalating international war that followed the relatively low-level fighting in the villages of South Vietnam.

The Soviets had little to be displeased about. As in the Korean War, they were not, and had no intention of being, directly involved in the coming hostilities. There was virtually no risk in shipping military supplies to Hanoi; another war by proxy suited their imperial designs.

In the escalating conflict that followed, a new and technological factor played a major, though unexpected, psychological role. For the first time in history, a major war was covered on the private television screens of the one superpower involved as a combatant. Inevitably, it was a one-sided coverage: any horrors on the U.S. side were seen in U.S. homes; but not the often worse horrors on the Vietcong side. The notorious My Lai incident, in which a U.S. lieutenant massacred several hundred villagers in 1968, was intensively covered; there was no corresponding coverage of Vietcong terrorism in the villages, which included the bayoneting of pregnant women. As Sir Robert Thompson put it, "The [Vietnam] war was lost on the television screens of the United States."[5] The First Indochina War coverage had not been so burdened, because it took place before the universal presence of TV screens in Western homes.

It was President Johnson's misfortune that his decision to commit American forces to this complex struggle (a civil war that had turned into an international ideological confrontation in which one of the superpowers merely armed and advised a distant satellite) soon coincided with the outbreak of student unrest not only in the United States but in other Western countries. The cause was just, in Cold War terms, but the political climate was wrong.

The Second Indochina War would demoralize one American President—Lyndon Johnson—and add considerably to the unpopularity of his successor, Richard Nixon.

One of the most psychologically devastating episodes of the war was the so-called Têt offensive: the first major operation launched by North Vietnam after the Soviet commitment of 1964–1965. The Têt is a Buddhist religious festival in Vietnam. The Communists chose this holiday pause in everyday life, on January 30, 1968, to attack one-quarter of the district capitals, thirty-six of the forty-four provincial capitals, and five of Vietnam's six largest towns. In the ancient imperial city of Hué they stormed the citadel and held it for twenty-six days, during which they massacred thousands of inhabitants (an event later recorded for history, but never seen on American TV screens). Their final round was an attack on the American embassy in Saigon, where they were routed by Marine guards and Army military police.

By military standards the offensive was a failure, but to view it this way is to miss the point. The American commander in Vietnam, General William Westmoreland, reported to President Johnson that by the end of February the American forces had killed about 45,000 of the 64,000 North Vietnamese and Vietcong southerners involved in the offensive. That was the military toll; but the psychological toll on the American side was measureless. The message reaching the American public through the media was that their country was involved in an apparently endless conflict that they could win only by invading the North, which would invite Soviet and, possibly, Chinese intervention.

Demoralized, President Johnson decided not to seek a second term in office. In terms of international understanding and strategic insight, his successor, Richard Nixon, was in a higher league, although he carried a controversial burden of unpopularity from the era of "McCarthyism."* One of his first decisions, on taking office in January 1969, was to appoint Henry Kissinger as his principal adviser on international security affairs. Both men realized that the United States was in a "no win" situation in Vietnam and faced increasing public disenchantment, and even hostility to the idea that America should continue its intervention.

Nixon's awareness that victory was unlikely did not mean that he was contemplating a military pull-out, leaving the South Vietnamese people to their fate. He allowed himself to think that an escalating use of force might, or would, compel the Communist side to agree to an honorable peace. In the early months of his presidency he sent several secret messages, which were ignored, to the North Vietnamese leadership.[6]

---

*The methods used by the late Senator Joseph McCarthy in the postwar decade to unmask alleged Soviet spies made him widely unpopular. However, most of those he accused were proved later to have been, indeed, working for the Soviet side. Many of the charges were confirmed by the "Venona Documents," consisting of wartime secret cables intercepted by American cryptographers and released in 1996 by the U.S. National Security Agency (NSA).—BC

Instead, in February 1969, just weeks after his arrival in the White House, the North Vietnamese launched a new major offensive.

The attack broke new ground in that it came not from North Vietnam but from Cambodia, where the North Vietnamese Army had built up joint bases with the Vietcong from the south. Faced with this new and unforeseen threat, President Nixon took a bold but vulnerable decision: to bomb the Communist bases in Cambodia, but to do so in secret, because of the possible political consequences at home—not least because he would be exposed to charges that he was attacking a neutral country. He had calculated that, on the other hand, a possible dividend would be a weakening of Vietnamese Communist resolve. In this, he was mistaken. As his British biographer, Jonathan Aitken, put it, "He genuinely believed that he would be seeing 'light at the end of the tunnel' within a year—and that a peace settlement would be reached in time for the congressional elections in 1970."[7]

Nixon wrote later that the bombing was not publicly announced because of "our concern that if it were, Sihanouk [king of Cambodia] would be forced to object to it." In the event, King Sihanouk did not object; in July 1969 Sihanouk invited Nixon to visit Cambodia.[8]

So determined was the president at this stage to keep the bombing secret that the U.S. Air Force was ordered not to mention it even in its own records.[9] As if to balance the bombing of the North Vietnamese bases, Nixon decided to withdraw 25,000 U.S. troops from South Vietnam and to send a personal and conciliatory letter to Ho Chi Minh proposing a phased withdrawal of North Vietnamese as well as U.S. troops from South Vietnam, free elections under international supervision, and a cessation of hostilities. A secret meeting in Paris between Henry Kissinger and a North Vietnamese representative named Mai Van Bo followed, at which the latter stuck to the demonstrably false assertion that there were no North Vietnamese forces in South Vietnam. A cold and uncompromising reply from Ho reached Nixon.

Not long afterward, on September 3, 1969, Ho Chi Minh died at age seventy-nine. Thus, the longtime leader of the protracted struggle for the "liberation" of his country was the one major player who was not going to be present at any forthcoming North Vietnamese celebration of victory. By then, however, he could hardly have doubted that victory was on the way.

In October of that difficult year, the unpredictable Sihanouk sanctioned the invasion of his own country by 40,000 North Vietnamese troops, as far as central Cambodia. In March the following year, however, he asked them to withdraw. There was no response, and Sihanouk took refuge in Peking. He was on a visit to Moscow on March 18, 1970, when the Cambodian parliament voted unanimously to depose him, in protest against his attempted balancing act between the Vietnamese Communists and the United States. The new Cambodian leader, General Lon Nol, was outspokenly anti-Communist.

The Cambodians were in no mood to condone the Vietnamese invasion. Indeed, a mob in Phnom Penh sacked the North Vietnamese and Vietcong embassies. On March 25, the North Vietnamese and the Lao Dong promised to withdraw their forces. An empty promise: the North Vietnamese aggression simply went on, undeterred either by the U.S. policy of aid to Cambodia or by the sacking of their embassies. Throughout April 1970, they continued to build up their Cambodian bases, in effect turning eastern Cambodia into one giant base with which to outflank the South Vietnamese and endanger the lives of U.S. servicemen.

By then, some 115,000 U.S. troops had been sent home, and on April 20, Nixon announced the withdrawal of a further 150,000 troops: a move that flummoxed his critics but alarmed the military, although he had been careful to say that the further reduction was on condition that the war should be "Vietnamized"—in other words, that South Vietnam should be given the means to continue the war on its own. At the end of the month, he announced his decision to attack the North Vietnamese base areas in Cambodia. His aim was limited: a stay of two months and a depth of twenty-one miles. Yet, despite this restraint, he was immediately and widely attacked by antiwar and anti-Nixon groups and in the media. As he wrote later, "To contend, as many still do, that the United States and the South Vietnamese 'invaded Cambodia'—in the sense of an aggressive act—is as absurd as it would be to charge that Eisenhower was committing aggression against France when he ordered the Normandy landings."[10]

The full force of the Soviet-controlled international propaganda machine was about to hit the Nixon administration. Mass demonstrations, collectively labeled "the Vietnam Moratorium" were part of the plan, and the

North Vietnamese premier, Pham Van Dong, publicly called on "U.S. progressive people" to join the struggle against "U.S. aggression." Although originally planned for October 1970, the "moratorium" was postponed until August 1971. Millions took part in it, and in a number of university campuses the demonstrations became violent.

On balance, the U.S. intervention in Cambodia was a success. Between them, the U.S. and South Vietnamese forces captured enough Communist weapons and ammunition to equip seventy-four North Vietnamese battalions and enough enemy food supplies to sustain them for four months.[11]

Although the talks with the North Vietnamese were resumed from time to time, there seemed little hope that they would yield results. Indeed, in spring 1972 they launched the third of their major offensives. By then, three years after Ho's death, General Giap had become the dominant figure in the North Vietnamese hierarchy, as he had been at the time of his victory over the French at Dien Bien Phu in 1954. The leading ideologue, Truong Chinh, was committed to the Chinese concept of "revolutionary war" as preached and practiced by his idol, Mao. Revolutionary war did not exclude a "final offensive" as the culmination of a struggle against a demoralized enemy, but despite the signs of a weakening of American resolve, it could hardly be argued that a North Vietnamese victory would result in a final defeat of the U.S. forces, and of the South Vietnamese regime.

Nor did it. But although the third major North Vietnamese offensive collapsed after several months, it undoubtedly strengthened the American resolve to pull out of the war.[12] Clearly, victory for the American side and their South Vietnamese protégés could have been achieved only by a U.S. invasion of North Vietnam, which neither American public opinion nor President Nixon could even have contemplated: a negative strongly emphasized by the Soviet propaganda and disinformation machine, especially the World Peace Council and its adherents in the West.

There was only one way in which Nixon could hit back: from the air. For despite the continuing flow of Soviet material aid, the North Vietnamese could not compete with the Americans in this domain. In a special operation in May 1972, the harbor of Haiphong was mined, along with several lesser ports. In December, the U.S. Air Force bombed Hanoi as well as Haiphong in the first precision bombing raids of modern warfare. By then, Richard Nixon had been reelected for a second term as president, easily defeating the liberal Senator George McGovern.

On January 18, 1973, two days before the swearing in, it was jointly announced in Washington and Hanoi that the Paris talks would resume on January 23. The previous day had brought the news of President Johnson's death, upon which his successor wrote, "I think that Lyndon Johnson died of a broken heart, physically and emotionally. He was an enormously able and proud man. He desperately wanted, and expected, to be a great President. . . . He might have been a great peacetime President but the combination of war abroad and at home proved too much for him."[13]

On January 23, as expected, Henry Kissinger and Le Duc Tho signed the peace agreement that brought U. S. intervention in the Second Indochina War to an end. In October that year, both men were awarded the Nobel Peace Prize.*

Announcing the agreement in a broadcast on the evening of January 23, Nixon claimed that "all the conditions that I laid down . . . have been met." An internationally supervised cease-fire would begin on the evening of Saturday, January 27. Within sixty days, all U.S. prisoners-of-war were to be released, and during the same period all U.S. forces would be withdrawn from Vietnam. Nixon added, "The people of South Vietnam have been guaranteed the right to determine their own future without outside interference." The U.S. government would continue to recognize the Republic of Vietnam under President Thieu as the sole legitimate government of South Vietnam.

All these conditions, and a large number of minor ones, had indeed been agreed upon by both sides, but only on paper. And this was the realm of power politics. The North Vietnamese had no intention of honoring their side of the peace agreement; and the Americans were no longer in a position to force them to do so.

At a press conference in Paris on January 24, Le Duc Tho (rightly) claimed the agreement as a victory for North Vietnam and maintained

---

*The award was to be shared by Henry Kissinger and Le Duc Tho but met with much international criticism, mainly on the ground that the Paris talks had failed to bring peace in Indochina. Le Duc Tho refused the prize because of alleged "violations" of the Paris agreement by the United States and South Vietnam. Kissinger accepted his share and donated it to a scholarship fund for children of U.S. servicemen killed in Indochina.

(again rightly) that the bombing of North Vietnam had failed to achieve its purpose.

REVOLUTIONARY WAR, AS conceived by Mao Tse-tung, his Vietnamese disciple Truong Chinh ("Long March"), and General Giap, was a war for the hearts and minds of a people, rather than for territory as such, although the long-term goal, of course, is populated territory.

The Paris Agreements of January 1973 marked the defeat of the American intervention in the Second Indochina War. Henceforth, South Vietnam was on its own, whereas North Vietnam continued to enjoy an almost unlimited flow of advanced Soviet arms and equipment. Inevitably, there would be a fourth major Communist offensive: the "final" one beloved of the Maoist theorists of revolutionary war.

The end came on April 30, 1975, when Giap's Army entered Saigon after overrunning the central provinces of Vietnam and defeating the South Vietnamese Army at Xuan Loc: the decisive battle of this longest war of the twentieth century. It had lasted nearly seventeen years.

THE SOVIET-SPONSORED VICTORY in Indochina was a major Leninist victory: a further triumph in Lenin's original aim of spreading Communism to all countries of the world without exception. In the non-Leninist sense, it was certainly an imperial victory, but a less complete one than, for instance, Cuba. Without Soviet backing, the Vietnamese Communists would not necessarily have achieved control over South Vietnam, and the two Vietnams might have continued to face each other indefinitely, as did North and South Korea. Moscow did not need to bring Hanoi to heel as it had done to Havana. Communism was already so deeply anchored in the mentality of the triumphant leaders of North Vietnam that intervention from Moscow was not necessary.

In geopolitical terms, however, Indochina was ill-placed to be considered a dependency of the Soviet Union. The presence of the Chinese People's Republic on its northern doorstep saw to that. The united Vietnam that emerged in 1975 retained control of Laos, but in Cambodia that year, a particularly evil and murderous brand of Communism, sponsored not by Moscow but by Peking, took over.

The name of the new tyrant was Pol Pot.

CHAPTER THIRTY

LIBYA, THE MAVERICK 'ALLY'

1969–1988

———————

COLONEL MUAMMAR GHADDAFI was only twenty-eight years old when he overthrew the senile King Idriss of Libya in 1969. Seven years later, he concluded the biggest arms deal in history with the Soviet Union, which made Libya another of Moscow's client-states. Despite the protracted ensuing pressures from the Soviet side of the deal, however, Ghaddafi's regime never graduated—or descended—to full satellite status, for two simple reasons. The first was Ghaddafi's character: politically and ideologically, he was a maverick, totally unpredictable and uncontrollable. The second was the vast oil wealth of his desert country: with a population estimated at no more than 3 million (a quarter of them nomads), and an army of between 22,000 and 30,000, Libya's oil production had reached 3,318,000 barrels a day by 1970—one of the highest totals in the world. Because of the oil price increases of 1973, Libya's gold and currency reserves rose dramatically even though the country's total production was reduced. By 1980 they would reach more than $13 billion.[1]

Initially Ghaddafi set up an Islamic Republic and was generally considered to be anti-Communist. On becoming aware that the Soviet Union's backing for terrorist groups coincided with his own aims, he changed his ideological views, or at least his public expression of them. Sadat's expulsion from Egypt of 18,000 Soviet advisers in 1971 in effect created a Soviet market for Ghaddafi's activities, specifically for his financial backing of many terrorist groups. Ghaddafi's "clients" included some right-wing groups not approved by Moscow, such as the pro-Arab Italian fascist *Avanguardia Nazionale,* which he felt deserved his support. One of their posters, for instance, stated, "We are with you, heroic Arab-Palestinian People, and not with the Dirty, Fat Jews!" Many of the terrorist groups supported by Ghaddafi, however, already enjoyed Moscow's support and were therefore in line with the Soviet Union's imperial drive. These included the Sandinistas in Nicaragua, the Irish Republican Army (IRA) Provisionals in Northern Ireland, Uruguay's Tupamaros, and Argentina's Montoneros. The most notorious of the individual terrorists supported by both Libya and the Soviet Union was "Carlos," also known as "The Jackal." Trained partly in Cuba, Carlos had attended a lengthy course at the Patrice Lumumba University in Moscow. After his most spectacular exploit (the kidnapping of eleven leaders of the oil-producing states in Vienna in December 1975), he was given asylum in Libya, plus a $2 million reward by Ghaddafi.

The Carlos incident was of course a tactical example of unity with Moscow. Strategically, the Libyan leader had imperial ambitions of his own that remained largely unfulfilled, and was interested in good relations with Moscow only because the Soviet Union had shown itself ready to feed those ambitions.

The great Libyan-Soviet arms deal was signed in Libya's capital, Tripoli, by Ghaddafi and the Soviet premier, Aleksei Kosygin, on May 23, 1976. Initial Western estimates of the total value of Libya's purchases were too low: the figure given in the media was a mere $400 million. On May 28, however, President Anwar Sadat of Egypt revealed in an interview with the *Los Angeles Times* that the global figure was $12 billion.* By late 1976, Soviet military advisory groups were on duty at the three main Libyan ports: Tobruk, Tripoli, and Benghazi. Within a year the Soviet advisory presence, including laborers as well as technicians, had grown to

---

*When I was received by President Sadat at his Cairo residence on November 10, 1980, he said, "Some years ago, when I estimated the value of his [Ghaddafi's] arms deal with Russia at $12 billion, my estimate was scorned in London and Washington, but I have been proved right. The point was that there was a down payment of $800 million, so it was fairly easy to work out the total." Although Sadat did not reveal his source, it was clear to me that Egypt's highly efficient secret intelligence service had served him well. (See Crozier, *Free Agent,* p. 162.) In an earlier study, "The Surrogate Forces of the Soviet Union" (*Conflict Studies* 92, February 1978, p. 4), I attributed a higher total ($13 billion) to Sadat.—BC

some 12,000. The training programs included operational techniques for T-55 and T-62 tanks, and MiG-23 fighter planes. After the deal, 700 Libyan military joined a smaller contingent already being trained in various Soviet centers.[2]

The $12 billion deal worked out to $4,000 for every man, woman, and child in Libya, and $400,000 each for Libya's Army.[3]

GHADDAFI'S IMPERIAL DESIGNS were his own, but to the extent that they clashed with the Soviet Union's own designs, they explain why Brezhnev and his colleagues decided on the massive arms deal of 1976. Apart from the utility value of Ghaddafi's support for international terrorism, their strategic aim was clearly to make Libya, as far as possible, dependent on Soviet military support.

Ghaddafi's dream of empire encompassed the Sahara, stretching from the western shore of Morocco on the Atlantic to Egypt on the Red Sea. His original role model had been Egyptian President Gamal Abdel Nasser, who never tired of repeating his concept of "one Arab nation, from the Atlantic Ocean to the Persian Gulf." Like Nasser, Ghaddafi had charisma, but the national differences were striking. Nasser's assets included Egypt's large and sophisticated middle class and an effective apparatus for intelligence, propaganda, and subversion. Ghaddafi could not match such educational and administrative assets, but Libya's oil wealth gave him a degree of economic independence that Egypt could not match. Specifically, Ghaddafi's Saharan vision stretched from the formerly Spanish western Sahara, through the Algerian Sahara south of Laghuat, the Tunisian Sahara, the northern regions of Mali, Niger, Chad, and Nigeria, Sudan, and (possibly) southern Egypt.

Realistically, there was never the slightest chance of his fulfilling a plan of such ambitious dimensions. The fact that the Libyan leader was known to think in such terms, however, was in itself an interesting indication of his personality. Sadat was wont to denounce him as "a mental case" and, on one occasion, as "a vicious criminal, one hundred per cent sick and possessed of a demon."[4] Sudan's President Gaafar al-Nimeiry had his own variation on this theme: "a split personality—both evil."

Whatever the description, it was clear that Ghaddafi combined a dangerous Islamic fanaticism and a form of megalomania, which were continually fed by the repeated successes of the terrorist groups he had been supporting.*

Regardless of Ghaddafi's ambitions, his plans served Soviet interests to the extent that they were anti-Western, and specifically anti-French in Francophone Africa. Meanwhile, the Soviet Union now enjoyed a major potential base on Libyan soil should they ever wish to use their own weaponry on a scale that would be impossible for Ghaddafi's forces alone.

The Soviet Union's own plans for Africa were in any case complementary to Ghaddafi's. During the previous few years, the Soviets had gradually extended their influence on the African continent. Despite reverses in Egypt and Somalia (see Chapter 28), Soviet influence was strong in Guinea, Benin, and Mali, and had grown in Nigeria and Ghana despite earlier setbacks. In East Africa, Ethiopia had become a Marxist-Leninist satellite, despite continuing resistance in Eritrea (see Chapter 32); Chad was under continuing subversive pressure.

Whenever possible, the Soviets tried to steer Libya in a more coherent direction and in a manner that would serve imperial interests. An interesting example was the conclusion of two parallel treaties, both of which involved Syria. These were the Syrian-Libyan unification declaration of September 10, 1980, and the Soviet-Syrian Treaty of Friendship and Co-operation of October 8. The significant point is that the two agreements were being negotiated at the same time.

Both countries had become client-states of the Soviet Union, although neither would reach satellite status. Both pacts were specifically anti-American. Article 10 of the Syrian-Libyan declaration asserted total opposition to the Camp David agreements (sponsored by President Jimmy Carter and involving the historic rapprochement between Israel and Egypt) as representing American imperialism and Zionism, and to their agent, Sadat.

Article 13 affirmed that the new Libyan-Syrian state was part of the world liberation movement and was allied with the forces of Socialism (that

---

*From this point forward, I will be drawing, at times heavily, from a "Restricted" monthly bulletin, initially entitled *Transnational Security,* later changed to *Notes and Analysis.* Edited by the author, the bulletin's readers included President Ronald Reagan and Prime Minister Margaret Thatcher, as well as the heads of American and British Intelligence. See Crozier, *Agent,* pp. 187 et seq. The issues used for this chapter are March 1980; May, July, September, and November 1981; March and May 1982; and May 1984. Copies of the bulletin are available only through the Hoover Institution, Stanford, California.—BC

is, with the Soviet bloc). As Ghaddafi put it, the pact was designed to prevent U.S. penetration in the "Arab fatherland." His relevant words were,

> They have occupied bases in Egypt, in Syria, in Somalia, in Oman.
> The Arab nation is on the way to losing its independence. We have
> therefore decided to arrest the advance of the Americans who have
> been setting up bridgeheads in several Arab countries. We must
> oblige the Americans, by force, to quit the Arab fatherland. We must
> act before the Americans establish themselves. Our choice is between
> death and the defeat of the American enemy.

Although this kind of rhetoric came naturally to Ghaddafi and
would not have required assistance from a Soviet speechwriter, the
words chosen were undoubtedly in line with Soviet objectives.* Following the Libyan-Syrian pact, Libya subsequently gave Syria $1 billion to
purchase Soviet arms, plus $600 million in economic aid. In return, the
Syrian leader, Hafez Assad, let it be known that he would support
Ghaddafi as head of a united state on condition that he (Assad) were
prime minister and chairman of a proposed Central Revolutionary
Council. However, nothing came of the Libyan-Syrian agreement to
merge into a single state.

AN UNSUCCESSFUL ATTEMPT by Colonel Ghaddafi to bring the Francophone Republic of Chad under Libyan control provided a good example of the inadequacy of the military force at his disposal and of the
apparent impossibility of Soviet attempts to bring him under Moscow's
control. In common with many other African countries, Chad had gained
independence from France in 1960. A confused civil war broke out in the
mid-1960s, mainly between the predominantly Muslim Arab guerrillas in
the north and the mainly black Christian and animist forces in the south.

On June 26, 1979, Ghaddafi invaded northern Chad with a force of
2,500 men, with support from French-built Mirage fighter-bombers.

---

*The same observation applied equally to the wording of the Soviet-Syrian Treaty. Although
Article 4 declared the Soviet Union's respect for "the policy of non-alignment pursued by the
Syrian-Arab Republic," Article 10 called for continued cooperation in the military sphere.
The treaty thus came closer to being a military alliance than the other friendship treaties, in
particular than the Soviet-Iraqi Treaty of 1972.

Fierce fighting followed, but by the end of July most of the Libyan invaders had been repulsed. In November, however, another 1,000-strong Libyan force crossed the border, this time with the approval of rebel leader Goukouni Oueddei, after a meeting with Colonel Ghaddafi in northern Chad.

From neighboring Senegal, President Léopold Senghor (Christian leader of a predominantly Muslim country) stated that Libya had trained an armed force of 5,000 men to foment unrest, not only in Chad, but also in Mali, Niger, and Senegal, with the aim of creating an Islamic "Republic of the Sahara" under Libyan control. This was indeed a concise restatement of Ghaddafi's known ambition.

The fact that Chad was Ghaddafi's first objective made sense not only because the existing unrest made it a tempting target, but also because the Libyan leader had made no secret of his ambition to acquire nuclear weapons—and Chad's natural resources included uranium.

AT HIS OWN insistence, Ghaddafi visited the USSR from April 27 to 29, 1981. The Soviet government indiscreetly let it be known, after the event, that they would have preferred to postpone the visit, presumably because they did not want to be seen as supporters of his expansionist policies. A Radio Moscow commentary in Arabic on April 24 simply defined the objects of Ghaddafi's visit as the consolidation of Soviet-Libyan political, economic, scientific, and cultural relations and the promotion of the Libyan revolution. Indeed, the Soviet Union intended "to assist by all means the revolutionary and independent development of this young Arab country in the interest of the Libyan people and of the anti-imperialist Arab national liberation struggle."

In Libya, the controlled press said the visit would further the aim of the "Steadfastness Front" formed a year earlier by Libya, Algeria, South Yemen, Syria, and the Palestine Liberation Organization (PLO) to oppose the Camp David agreements between Israel and Egypt.

The Soviet leader, Leonid Brezhnev, greeted Ghaddafi at the airport, and accompanied him there on his departure. The two leaders had two restricted meetings. Significantly, the Libyan delegation included the commander of the Libyan Armed Forces and the secretary of the Atomic Energy Agency, as well as Ghaddafi's foreign secretary and his chief economic adviser.

There was, not unexpectedly, give-and-take in the final communiqué. Ghaddafi endorsed the Soviet occupation of Afghanistan, and Brezhnev described the Libyan invasion of Chad as an effort "to normalize the situation" in that country. There were, however, significant differences in presentation. *Pravda* deleted certain passages from Ghaddafi's speech, including his request for a "decisive posture" of support for Arabs and for the Steadfastness Front, along with his request to the USSR to "guarantee the end of any sort of outside interference in Afghanistan." The deleted passages appeared in the version of the speech issued by the Libyan People's Bureau (Ghaddafi-speak for "embassy") in Moscow.

Brezhnev and his colleagues are said to have listened in stony silence to Ghaddafi's impassioned presentation of his proselytizing Islamic ambitions. For the record, Ghaddafi declined to give the Soviets permission to set up bases in Libya. This may have looked good on paper, but the Soviet side already had bases, in a practical sense, since they were known to have complete control over their massive stocks of arms in Libya, which by that time already included some 2,000 tanks and 200 combat aircraft.

Moreover, the Soviets were well aware that they could meet any emergency in Libya within a few hours by despatching troops in Antonov transport aircraft. By then, French sources (usually well informed on North African affairs through their Maghreb contacts, the intelligence and security services in the former French North African colonies: Morocco, Tunisia and Algiers) estimated that there were some 5,500 Soviet advisers in Libya, plus several hundred East Germans and several thousand Cubans; American estimates were substantially lower. In addition, under an economic protocol signed in Moscow, the Soviets had agreed to participate in the work of Libya's Center for Atomic Research, which, indeed, the Soviets had built.

Meanwhile, the flow of anecdotal evidence of Ghaddafi's irrational behavior seemed unstoppable. At a summit conference on May 22, 1981, at N'djamena, capital of Chad, he joined the presidents of Sierra Leone, Nigeria, and Chad and astonished his "colleagues" by calling on the Organization for African Unity (OAU) to refund the expenses he had incurred to bring peace back to Chad and claimed the Nobel Peace Prize for the same "service." He then provoked the displeasure of his host, President Goukouni Weddeye, by refusing to withdraw Libyan troops from Chad, thus reneging on a promise he had given previously in Tripoli.

By this time, Soviet representatives abroad, especially in Paris, were not hiding their increasing concern over Ghaddafi's "freelance adventurism," which threatened to destabilize the whole of northwest Africa, specifically Morocco, Algeria, Mauritania, and Senegal, plus Mali, where Soviet influence had been growing considerably. In March 1982, less than a year later, Ghaddafi had confided to personal friends that he feared a KGB assassination attempt. Although there was no independent evidence that any such operation was being considered, it cannot be ruled out that the KGB itself may have started the rumor.

At this time, the unpredictable colonel made two disastrous visits, to Algeria and to Tunisia. As he had not informed either government of his arrival, nobody was there to meet him when he arrived at Algiers and Tunis. He irritated the Algerian government by dropping in on students without prior notice. He went on to propose merger pacts to both governments. Each reacted coldly.

Despite his irrational and exhibitionist behavior, and the U.S. air raids on Libya, notably after the Lockerbie disaster of 1988, Ghaddafi proved himself to be a survivor. He even survived the USSR itself, despite his failure to fulfill his own, relatively modest, imperial ambitions.

CHAPTER THIRTY-ONE

THIRD TIME LUCKY
IN AFGHANISTAN

1978–1980

I N RETROSPECT, THE invasion of Afghanistan must rank as the worst blunder made by the Soviets in their drive to expand their empire. The protracted war that followed the invasion turned out to be unwinnable. Surprisingly, we now know, from the available Soviet archives, that in the spring of 1979 the unanimous view in the Politburo was that on no account should an invasion take place. What is not known, at the time these lines were written, was just why this sensible appraisal was reversed.

Between April 1978 and December 1979, the subversive apparatus of the Soviet Union had intervened twice in Afghanistan in attempts to ensure that a regime responsive to Soviet aims was firmly installed in Kabul. As always, the long-term Leninist principles had been applied. In 1965, an Afghan equivalent of a Communist Party had been created, calling itself the People's Democratic Party of Afghanistan, or PDPA. By 1978, some 400 Afghan military officers were being trained in Moscow

There were, however, certain weaknesses in the Soviet-trained power apparatus. For instance, back in 1967, the PDPA had split into two factions, called *Parcham* ("Banner") and *Khalq* ("Masses"). The split was due to personal rivalries, not ideological differences, although the Khalq spread the unfounded rumor that the Parcham was pro-Chinese.[1] The Khalq's leader was Nur Mohammed Taraki; the Parcham's, Babrak Karmal.

The political situation was tense in 1978. Five years earlier, in July 1973, the King of Afghanistan, Zahir Shah, had been overthrown in a military coup led by Mohammed Daud, who proclaimed himself president. Initially, Daud was pro-Moscow, but the Shah of neighboring Iran put pressure on him to get rid of PDPA members of his government in return for a loan that would cover the cost of a highway linking Iran with Pakistan via Afghanistan. His positive response was immediate, but his attempt to break the rising threat of the PDPA would prove to be his own downfall.

In November 1977, one of Daud's ministers had been murdered in retaliation for Daud's arrest of local Communists, an event that caused Daud to intensify his anti-Communist purge. In February 1978, he jailed all leaders of the PDPA, and on April 17 one of the leaders of the Parcham faction, Akhbar Khybar, was assassinated. His funeral that same day brought pro-Communist demonstrators onto the streets of Kabul. In retaliation, Daud ordered further arrests of PDPA members.

Under threat of summary execution from Daud, the PDPA sent an emissary to the Soviet ambassador to tell him that they were planning a coup of their own. Moscow's response was noncommittal, but by then most of the Afghan Army officers had been trained (and indoctrinated) in Moscow. One of them, Colonel Abdul Khadir, had been involved on Daud's side in the 1973 coup. Daud, however, had no time for Khadir's radical ideas, and he was one of a number of young officers who were marginalized by Daud. The latter's crackdown on the Communists was the signal for action that Colonel Khadir had been awaiting. On April 27, 1978, tanks and planes were deployed, and the presidential palace was stormed. President Daud and his family were shot.

According to the KGB defector Vladimir Kuzichkin (see note 1), the KGB had been instructed after the April 1978 coup to recruit Parcham members, initially to investigate their alleged pro-Beijing activities; they were to leave relations with the Khalq to the International Department of the Soviet Central Committee. The Parcham penetration soon showed that there were in fact no pro-Chinese elements, and the Parcham leaders were recruited by the KGB.

According to Kuzichkin, the KGB played no part in the coup, although he indicates that they did have a role in the choice of a political leader to take over from the late Daud. The Politburo instructed the KGB to produce a report on the Khalq and Parcham factions of the PDPA, and in particular on the relative merits of Taraki and Karmal as leaders of the emerging Communist regime. The report picked Karmal as "the more reasonable and disciplined of the two, . . . pro-Soviet and [ready] to listen to advice." In contrast, Taraki was seen as "stubborn, intolerant, irascible and shallow." Despite this verdict, the KGB's view was overruled by the ideological chief, M. A. Suslov, who opted for Taraki.

One of Khadir's first actions was to release all three of the PDPA's top figures: Taraki himself, and his Khalq deputy, Hafizullah Amin, along with Babrak Karmal of the Parcham faction. As Suslov had advised, the Army appointed Taraki as president and prime minister. The outcome was a new ruling body: the Military Revolutionary Council, which named Khadir as defense minister and Amin as deputy prime minister. The constitution was abolished, and the country was renamed the Democratic Republic of Afghanistan.

September brought rumors of a counter-coup and, as happened so many times in Communist history, the Afghan revolution began to devour its own children. The most prominent of them was Khadir himself, by then promoted to brigadier general, who was tried for treason and found guilty. It may be presumed that he was executed, as no further references to him can be found.

Babrak Karmal was sent to Prague as ambassador. As for Hafizullah Amin, he initiated a purge of the Parcham faction, most of whom were jailed or executed. The logical climax of Taraki's victory came on December 5, 1978, with the signature of a standard treaty of friendship between the Soviet Union and Afghanistan.

The treaty, seen in Moscow as yet another victory in the protracted process of world revolution, failed to consolidate the Communist takeover of Afghanistan. At the time of the coup, there had been 1,500 Soviet advisers in Afghanistan. By early 1979, the number had grown to at least 5,000 and possibly to as many as 7,000.[2]

Far from consolidating the Communist victory, this increase stimulated Islamic and tribal resistance to the new regime. Ignoring relatively moderate advice from the Soviet side, Taraki confiscated Mosque lands, set up Stalin-type collective farms, and started a major campaign against Islam: a risky move in a devoutly Muslim country. Around that time, an anti-Communist National Liberation Front was formed. Clashes followed between the Army and the tribal rebels in the Khunar, Laghan, and Pakria regions near the Pakistan border. In Khunar in particular, hundreds of soldiers died; the casualties included an unknown number of Soviet officers. In mid-March, a violent rebellion broke out in the city of Herat. Some Army units defected to the rebel tribes. According to Soviet Politburo records, Taraki and his deputy, Hafizullah Amin, made desperate calls to Moscow appealing for Soviet military forces to suppress the revolt.[3]

In response, on March 17, on receiving news of the grave situation in Herat, the Soviet Politburo convened an urgent meeting: "About the Exacerbation of the Situation in the Democratic Republic of Afghanistan and Our Possible Moves." Among those present were Prime Minister Alexei Kosygin, the foreign minister, Andrei Gromyko, and the head of the KGB, Yuri Andropov.

The passages available from the Soviet archives included the following:

> GROMYKO: We have to discuss what we will do if the situation gets worse. Today, the situation in Afghanistan for now is unclear to many of us. Only one thing is clear—we cannot surrender Afghanistan to the enemy. We have to think how to achieve this. Maybe we won't have to introduce troops.
>
> KOSYGIN: All of us agree—we must not surrender Afghanistan. From this point, we have to work out first of all a political document, to use all political means in order to help the Afghan leadership to strengthen itself, to provide the support which we've already planned, and to leave as a last resort the use of force. . . .

The deliberations continued on March 18, and if anything, the consensus against military intervention was even stronger than on the previous day. (See Appendix K: Document 1.)

The gist of these exchanges was presumably made available to Taraki, for, on March 20, 1979, he flew to Moscow with one dominant issue on his agenda: his government's request for Soviet military intervention. He was received that day by Kosygin, Gromyko, and two other Politburo members: Boris Ponomarev and Dmitry Ustinov. He went on to a further meeting with the Party's secretary-general, Leonid Brezhnev.

Kosygin tactfully explained why the Soviet leaders had decided against intervening with military force.

We must not allow the situation to seem as if you were not able to deal with your own problems and invited foreign troops to assist you. I would like to use the example of Vietnam. The Vietnamese are bravely defending by themselves their homeland against aggressive encroachments. We believe that there are enough forces in your country to stand up to counter-revolutionary raids. . . . During our telephone conversation with you we spoke of the need to begin already to create new military groups, keeping in mind that a certain amount of time will be needed for their training and preparation. . . .

Let's take the example of Herat. It seemed that all would fall apart, that the enemy would quickly entrench itself there, that the city would become a center of counter-revolution. But when you really took charge of the matter, you were able to seize the situation. . . .

Kosygin went on to promise "assistance with all available means—to ship weapons, ammunition, send people who can be useful to you in managing military and domestic matters, . . . specialists to train your military personnel to use the most modern types of weapons and military machinery."

Taraki shifted the conversation to a specific request for armored helicopters, to which Ustinov responded with a promise of six MI-24 helicopters in June and July, and a further six in the fourth quarter of the year. When Taraki asked if they could send pilots as well, Kosygin intervened to say that they could send maintenance specialists, but not pilots. Again, he cited Vietnam as an example of a country that had never asked for pilots. When Taraki suggested that they could ask for Vietnamese or Cuban pilots, Kosygin pointed out that the Soviets were training 400 Afghan officers: "Choose the people you need, and we will expedite their training."

The dialogue became more tense as Taraki asked for increased shipments of free wheat, pleading poverty, poor harvests due to land confiscations, and the abrogation of promised deals by Turkey and Pakistan. Kosygin countered by pointing out that since Kabul was "ready to pay for Pakistani wheat, you must have money." He suggested that Kabul should give the money to Moscow, which could then buy American wheat and transfer it to Afghanistan.

Taraki came up with a request of a different kind—that Moscow should build a 1,000-kilowatt radio station to "allow us to broadcast

propaganda throughout the world." This was a clear opening to Ponomarev, the International Department head: "We are taking energetic
measures to spread propaganda about the success of the DRA [Democra-
tic Republic of Afghanistan]." He offered to send "specialists in propaganda," and Kosygin changed the subject.

Taraki thereupon tried, yet again, to bring up the question of foreign
pilots (and tank operators). Ustinov agreed that there would be a need for
"additional military specialists," and Kosygin, by now clearly irritated,
said, "I cannot understand why the question of pilots and tank operators
keeps coming up. This is a completely unexpected question for us. . . .
The question of sending people who would sit in your tanks and shoot at
your people—this is a very pointed political question."

After a more conciliatory exchange between Taraki and Ustinov,
Kosygin came back with critical comments:

> We think it important that within your country you should work to
> widen the social support of your regime, draw people over to your
> side, ensure that nothing will alienate the people from the govern-
> ment. And finally, I would like to express my ideas on the impor-
> tance of a very careful and cautious approach toward your staff.
> One should take care of one's staff and have an individual approach
> towards it. Have a thorough and good understanding with each per-
> son before hanging any labels on them.

By then, Taraki was clearly crestfallen, and Kosygin reassured him
that, in the event of an invasion of Afghanistan, "then it will be a completely different situation." Taraki mentioned that China was persistently
pushing the Pakistanis against them, and Kosygin said they had already
warned the leaders of Pakistan and Iran against any such threats.

The Afghan visitor was then ushered into Brezhnev's Kremlin office,
where he listened, in effect, to a repetition of the arguments already used
by Kosygin, notably of the criticisms of the Afghan regime for not doing
enough to secure popular support.

At the time of the April 1978 coup and after, Moscow had been pres-
suring Taraki to broaden his government into a coalition with representatives of the various Afghan tribes and of the Muslim priesthood.
Summoned to Moscow in September 1979, he was virtually ordered to

act on this advice. On his return to Kabul, he decided as a first step to remove Hafizullah Amin as deputy prime minister. Taraki called a meeting of the government, but he had overlooked Amin's ambition to take over from him. When Taraki entered the presidential palace, several shots were fired at him. In the ensuing battle between his presidential guard and Amin's personal followers, Taraki and most members of his cabinet were killed.

The new dictator, Amin, soon proved even more recalcitrant to Soviet advice than Taraki had been. The Politburo finally decided to try to get rid of him and bring to power the man the KGB had recommended in the first place: Babrak Karmal.

The problem was, How best to get rid of Amin? According to Kuzichkin, the job was given to the Eighth Department of "S" Directorate of the KGB's First Chief Directorate.[4]

Their first move was to infiltrate into the presidential palace one of their trained illegals with a brief to poison Amin; Lieutenant-Colonel Mikhail Talybov was taken on as a cook. He failed, because Amin— cautious and suspicious—invariably mixed drinks and ate mouthfuls from several dishes in a row.

Meanwhile, the KGB learned that Amin had a counter-plan of his own. He was proposing to negotiate an understanding with the tribal rebels, then publicly announce that he was going to demand the withdrawal of all Soviet advisers from Afghanistan—just as President Anwar Sadat of Egypt had done, successfully, in 1972 (see Chapter 28). He would then appeal to the UN for help, and the Soviet Union would not dare to use force.

Alarmed by these reports, the Politburo decided to act as fast as possible. The KGB's plan was to send in a commando group to raid the palace, seize Amin, and replace his government with one Moscow could recognize and with which it would reach a settlement. The Party and the military proposed what the French would call *les grands moyens:* occupy Afghanistan, liquidate Amin, defeat the rebels, then withdraw. The KGB's plan might have worked, but the Politburo chose the other one, which would result a decade later in chaos and humiliation.

THERE ARE UNFORTUNATE gaps in the available Soviet archives covering this crucial period. It is logical to assume that the decision to invade Afghanistan was taken at a meeting of the Politburo on December 12,

1979, for this meeting is referred to in a (perhaps deliberately) obscure note, marked "Top Secret" of a top level gathering at "a dacha" (unidentified) on December 26. The participants were Brezhnev, Ustinov, Gromyko, Konstantin Chernenko, and Andropov. Three of them (Ustinov, Gromyko, and Andropov) reported on "the course of the implementation" of the Central Committee's Resolution No. P176/125 of December 12, 1979. The second paragraph read: "Comrade L. I. Brezhnev expressed a number of wishes, at the same time approving the plan of action sketched out by [his] comrades for the immediate future."

There was no specific mention of Afghanistan, and our translator noted that "this document is written in wooden, unclear, and ungrammatical Russian, (intentionally?) making the meaning difficult to grasp." A fair comment might be that deliberate obscurity and the omission of two key words (*Afghanistan* and *invasion*) gave an extra twist to "Top Secret."

FOR SOME MONTHS, Soviet forces had been building up along the Soviet-Afghan border. Most of them were Tadjiks or Uzbekis in Afghan uniforms. On December 28, 1979, the Soviet forces crossed the border. The KGB's plan had been incorporated into the Party's and military's proposal, and Soviet military aircraft landed at Kabul airport. The commando unit that alighted was a mixed one: KGB volunteers from the First Chief Directorate, and a Spetsnaz unit from the military intelligence GRU. The assault units forced their way into the palace grounds and into the palace itself, where they clashed with Amin's highly trained special guard. After fierce fighting, they killed off the guard, trapped Amin in his room, and riddled him with bullets. The fake cook Talybov took refuge under the stairs before emerging, speaking a torrent of Russian to protect him from his armed compatriots.

Babrak Karmal had been summoned to Moscow from Prague, and was then flown to Kabul after the fighting was over. On December 27, 1979, the day before the invasion, he had broadcast a speech from Moscow, claiming that as president he would free political prisoners, respect the Islamic faith, and allow free political parties and a free press.

That day, December 27, the Politburo met and Top Secret minutes were issued, to which an appendix on "the provision of Propaganda coverage . . . in respect of Afghanistan" was added. (See Appendix K: Document 2.)

On December 28, Kabul radio, by now under Soviet control, announced that Karmal would be head of state, prime minister, and chairman of the Revolutionary Council, as well as secretary-general of the PDPA and commander in chief of the armed forces.

That same day, American President Jimmy Carter used the hot line to appeal to President Brezhnev to withdraw the Soviet forces from Afghan soil. In a Top Secret reply on December 29, starting "Respected Mr. President," Brezhnev dismissed as "completely impossible" Carter's assessment of the situation (see Appendix K: Document 3). He also categorically rejected the U.S. president's assertion that the Soviet Union had undertaken to overthrow the government of Afghanistan. He went on:

> In your message you reproach us for not having consulted with the government of the USA on Afghan affairs before moving our military forces into Afghanistan. Well, it is permissible to ask you whether you consulted with us before beginning the massive concentration of naval forces in waters adjoining Iran . . . and in many other cases as well about which at the very least you should have informed us?

On December 30, *Pravda,* the Soviet Communist Party organ, claimed that the Soviet forces who had crossed the Afghan border were "a limited military contingent" to be "fully recalled" as soon as its mission was completed. The adjective *limited* was true, but only for the day of the announcement. Western estimates were closer to the truth: By early January, 1980, some 50,000 troops and 1,000 tanks had crossed the border. By the end of January, the manpower figure had risen to 85,000.

Verbal international reactions were strong, the keynote being that the Soviet Union had violated international law by invading a sovereign country. The Soviet response was to maintain that the Afghan government had invited Moscow, under the Friendship Treaty of December 1978, to send troops in the face of provocation from Afghanistan's external enemies.

What had caused the Soviet leaders to change their minds about Kabul's appeal for military support? In the absence of further relevant Soviet archives, the answer can only be speculative. One reason had to be the spectacle of an apparently appeasement-minded U.S. president—Jimmy Carter—who, demonstrably, had gone out of his way to respond passively to any signs of Soviet expansionism, most notably on May 22, 1978, at Notre Dame University, in a speech that included the following passage:

> Being confident of our own future, we are now free of that inordi-
> nate fear of communism which once led us to embrace any dictator
> who joined us in that fear. . . . We hope to persuade the Soviet Union
> that one country cannot impose its system of society upon another,
> either through direct military intervention or through the use of a
> client State's military forces, as was the case with Cuban intervention
> in Angola.*

There can be little doubt that the first of these sentences was interpreted in Moscow almost as an invitation to push ahead with expansionist policies, relieved of any fear of a U.S. response. The large-scale Soviet
airlift of Cuban troops to various destinations in 1978 without any serious response from the United States had already convinced the Soviet
leadership that there was virtually no limit to the current immunity from
a significant American response to whatever actions they took, so long as
Carter occupied the White House.

In Carter's eyes, however, the Soviet invasion of Afghanistan evidently
rated as a step too far on the Soviet side. Indeed he confided that he had
learned more about the true nature of the Soviet regime that day than in
his previous years in office. It was indeed the general view within NATO
that the Soviet Union had irremediably damaged the process of détente.
The United States now deferred consideration of the Senate ratification of
the Strategic Arms Limitation Treaty (SALT) signed in Vienna in June
1979. It also announced an embargo on grain deliveries to the Soviet
Union, along with a ban on the sale of phosphates and other fertilizers.
The president called for a boycott, or preferably a cancellation, of the
Olympic Games that had been scheduled to take place in Moscow in June.

These measures may have sounded strong, but they were soon shown
to be ineffectual. The grain embargo, for instance, while it advertised a
change of mood in Washington, was merely an inconvenience to the

---

*It has been alleged that the President's reference to an "inordinate fear of communism"
was included in this speech on the suggestion of the late Armand Hammer, the pro-Soviet
tycoon.

USSR, which simply shifted its grain purchases to Argentina. As for the Olympic Games, they went forward as planned despite the American call for a boycott.

On April 25, 1980, while the war in Afghanistan was raging, the international prestige of the United States plummeted to its lowest point. The new and markedly anti–U.S. Islamic fundamentalist regime in Iran had seized as hostages some 60 diplomats and staff from the American embassy in Tehran. The United States mounted a complex operation to free them, which ended in fiasco when an American helicopter collided with a tanker aircraft in a sandstorm in Iran's northern desert.

Meanwhile, the war the Soviet Union could not win went on.

CHAPTER THIRTY-TWO

THE ETHIOPIAN SATELLITE

1974–1989

———>●<———

T HE IMPERIAL REGIME of Ethiopia was overthrown in a military coup on February 28, 1974, in the wake of a devastating famine. Emperor Haile Selassie was arrested the following September. The oldest and largest state in Africa, with a history of sovereignty dating back to the fourth century A.D. and a population exceeding 22 million, Ethiopia was also one of the poorest and most backward African countries. Colonized by Italy under Benito Mussolini in 1935, it was restored to sovereignty after World War II, enabling the exiled emperor to return to his throne.

By June 28, 1974, the new military rulers had set up the Provisional Military Administrative Council (PMAC), soon known as the *Derg:* the Amharic word for "committee." The Derg was, in effect, a substitute for an elected parliament, consisting of three nominees for every unit of the Army and police, which totaled forty.[1]

A deceptive period of apparent calm followed the coup, but rivalries and controversial moves were bubbling beneath the surface. These came to a head in 1976 with the launching of the Ethiopian Communist Party (ECP) in August that year, together with a Marxist rival Ethiopian People's Revolutionary Party (EPRP). Initially, neither enjoyed Moscow's support.

The leading members of the Derg were Major Mengistu Haile Mariam, Major Atnafu Abate, and their superior military officer, Brigadier Teferi Banti. Mengistu had been initially biding his time, and had tried to disarm any rival claims from the two other members of the ruling triumvirate, by proposing Teferi Banti as head of state and Atnafu Abate as first vice president of the Derg. The underlying crisis came to a head on February 3, 1977, when Teferi Banti was reported to have been "executed." In fact, he and a number of his personal supporters had died in hand-to-hand fighting in the Grand Palace of the capital, Addis Ababa. Mengistu emerged with total power as Head of State, Supreme Commander of the Armed Forces and Chairman of the Standing Committee of the Derg. The next day, Mengistu's victory was publicly welcomed by Fidel Castro. Public support soon followed from the Soviet Union.

Atnafu Abate's turn came on November 12, 1977, when he was executed on Mengistu's order. By the time Mengistu completed his first year as Ethiopia's absolute dictator in February 1978, only 60 of the original 120 members of the Derg were still alive. More relevant to the subject of this book, it soon became clear that Mengistu's guiding ideology was Marxism-Leninism, and he was welcomed by Moscow as a willing satellite leader. What remained unclear, however, was the origin of that guidance. Unconfirmed reports circulated to the effect that he had completed his military training in the Soviet Union, but the reports remained unsubstantiated. It is tempting to assume that he was at some stage recruited as a Soviet agent, but no concrete details were available when these lines were written.*

The Derg, or PMAC, became and remained Mengistu's instrument for political change. On December 20, 1974, the PMAC announced a new guiding philosophy with a patriotic sounding name: Ethiopian Socialism, with five guiding principles—equality, self-reliance, the dignity of labor, the supremacy of the common good, and the indivisibility of Ethiopian unity.[2]

Not long after, seven banks and fourteen insurance companies were nationalized. Labor unions in the nine main industries came under a new

---

*In the 1960s, Mengistu was twice sent to the United States for further training: on the first occasion to a base in Alabama, and on the second to the Aberdeen Proving Grounds near Washington, D.C. He is said to have encountered racial discrimination (due, possibly, to his skin being darker than the average Ethiopian's), which may well have contributed to his markedly anti-American mindset. The question of whether he was recruited by the KGB at that time has been posed, but without substantiating evidence. See David A. Korn, *Ethiopia, the United States and the Soviet Union* (London and Sydney, 1986); and Paul B. Henze, *The Horn of Africa from War to Peace* (New York, 1991). However, in 1978–1979, more than 10,000 Ethiopian students were trained in Soviet military schools (Central Archive of Soviet Defense Ministry, 201-2416, Vol. 1112, p. 18; quoted in Sarin and Dvoretsky, *Alien Wars,* Novato, CA, 1996, p. 131).

controlling body, the All-Ethiopia Trade Union. On February 3, 1975, all land was nationalized, as were seventy-eight companies. In 1976, Mengistu launched a National Democratic Revolution Program, which he described as the party of the proletariat. As he put it, "Unless the party of the proletariat is formed, the revolution cannot have lasting guarantees. Building the socialist ideology is the right direction for the long march for the victory of socialism, to which there is no alternative."[3]

Predictably, the regime then called for a "Red Terror" to eliminate the White Terror allegedly practiced by it opponents. The announcement to this end, by the official *Voice of Revolutionary Ethiopia*, went on: "The broad masses will not be disturbed by the White Terror. Vigilant People, by keeping to their plans, will beat White Terror with Red Terror, and will finally be victorious."

Systematic state terror followed, more often than not carried out by individuals at the bidding of the regime. In the autumn and winter of 1977–1978, Cuban and East German commissars were brought in to improve the application of the policy of terror.[4] Between December 1977 and March 1978, some 10,000 arrests were made, mostly of young people, and about 1,500 were executed, often after torture.[5] Colin Legum, a British journalist specializing in African affairs for the London *Observer*, wrote, "There are, today, perhaps a hundred times the number of political prisoners than in the worst period of the late Emperor Haile Selassie's rule."[6]

The special relationship between Moscow and Addis Ababa was consecrated in the now-ritual friendship treaty, signed in Moscow on November 20, 1978.

In foreign and domestic affairs, the Mengistu regime faced two long-standing hereditary problems: expansionism from neighboring Somalia, and ethnic secessionism in the province of Eritrea. Somalia's clash with Ethiopia created an unprecedented problem for the Soviet empire builders: the need to make a choice between two mutually hostile satellites. Chronologically, Somalia came first; ideologically, the two were coequals. In the early stages of the rift, Cuba's leader, Fidel Castro, evidently with Moscow's approval, attempted to bring the two sides together. In a literal sense he succeeded, in that he called on Somalia's Siad Barre and Mengistu and persuaded both to meet in Aden, in his presence, and attempt to settle their differences. The meetings took place in late March 1977. In his own account of this initiative, in a statement to the East German leader Erich

Honecker in East Berlin on April 3, Castro made it clear that he had formed a considerably more favorable opinion of Mengistu than of Barre:

> Siad Barre . . . bared his claws. He told me that if Mengistu was a real revolutionary he should do as Lenin, and withdraw from his territory. I asked him whether he felt that there had been no real revolution in Ethiopia and that Mengistu was not a real leftist leader. He told me that there had been no revolution in Ethiopia.
>
> Barre is very convinced of himself. His socialist rhetoric is unbearable. He is the greatest socialist; he cannot say ten words without mentioning socialism.
>
> I spoke up. I explained that Siad Barre did not believe that there had been a real revolution in Ethiopia, that the events of 3 February had totally answered this question and that Mengistu was a revolutionary leader. . . . I declared that we could not possibly agree with Siad Barre's position.[7]

In the event, Soviet policy was guided simply by traditional power politics. It was made clear from the start that Moscow sided with Ethiopia, the weightier of the two in area and population.

In Mogadishu, Siad Barre's government announced on November 13, 1977, that all Soviet military and civilian advisers stationed in Somalia would have to leave the country within a week because of the Soviet Union's "collaboration with Ethiopia in preparation for an invasion of Somalia." The 1974 friendship treaty was abrogated, and all military facilities granted to the Soviet Union were withdrawn. Moreover, the staff of the Soviet embassy was to be reduced.

Two days later an official statement in Moscow blamed Somalia's unilateral abrogation of the friendship treaty entirely on the Soviet refusal to support Somalia's "territorial claims against a neighboring State" and "to facilitate the stirring up of fratricidal war in the Horn of Africa." The time for courtesies had passed: the Somali government was awarded two epithets, "chauvinistic and expansionist." Between November 15 and 30, some 7,500 Soviet citizens, including 2,000 civilian and military advisers, left Somalia, most of them by air and some by sea. All correspondents of the Soviet Tass and Novosti press agencies were also expelled. "Sensitive" military equipment was loaded onto three Soviet ships off the Somalian coast.

Two other Soviet satellites were caught in the dispute: Cuba and South Yemen. We have already noted Fidel Castro's failed attempt to mediate the situation. At the time of the rift, only forty-four Cubans had been living in Somalia; on November 15, they left for Aden. All major Western powers, including the United States under President Jimmy Carter, opted for neutrality in Somalia's clash with Ethiopia and the Soviet Union. One major power, however, chose to approve Somalia's stance: the Chinese People's Republic—providing yet another example of the Sino-Soviet rift.

Somalia's misguided aggressiveness was duly punished. By March 14, 1978, all Somali forces had withdrawn from the Mogaden region of Ethiopia, where the main fighting had taken place. Almost immediately, Mengistu's forces, with Soviet and Cuban assistance, opened an offensive against the Eritrean secessionist forces. Ideologically, there was a certain irony in the Ethiopian-Eritrean clash in that two of the three Eritrean secessionist movements were Marxist-Leninist. The non-Marxist one was the Eritrean Liberation Front-Popular Liberation Forces (WLF-PLF), supported by Saudi Arabia; the Marxist-Leninist ones—the Eritrean People's Liberation Front (EPLF) and the Eritrean Liberation Front-Revolutionary Council (ELF-RC)—enjoyed at least verbal support from the Communist countries. However, the Ethiopian forces benefited considerably from the major military supplies already provided by the Soviet Union and Cuba for their defensive war against the Somali invaders.

During the first seven months of 1978, the Soviet Union had carried out the biggest airlift on record, amounting to 5,000 flights, at a daily rate of nearly twenty-four flights. The figures break down as follows:

- 10,000 Cubans from Angola to Ethiopia, initially for the counter-offensive against Somalia, and later for use against the Eritrean separatists;
- 15,000 Cubans, brought directly from Cuba to Ethiopia;
- 10,000 Cubans, from Cuba to Angola, to keep the Cuban forces there up to strength;
- 10,000 "experts" and specialists of various kinds from the USSR, East Germany, Czechoslovakia, Hungary, and the PDRY (Popular Democratic Republic of Yemen). Those from the last named country were mainly East German security personnel.[8]

In October 1980, Mengistu led an Ethiopian delegation to Moscow where he had a tête-à-tête with Leonid Brezhnev. On October 31, the Soviet leader reported to the Politburo (see Appendix L: Document 1), stressing his approval of his Ethiopian visitor in these words:

> I have formed the impression that from one meeting to the next Mengistu is growing as an organizer and political leader. His statements provide evidence of a mature, well considered approach to the solution of the problems facing Ethiopia. All his deeds also speak in his favor. . . .
>
> However, the situation in the country remains difficult. Mengistu and [his] comrades-in-arms are having to try to solve the tasks of a national democratic revolution, which are complex enough anyway, in conditions of extreme economic and cultural backwardness and endless armed interventions from outside.

IN RETROSPECT, IT became clear that despite the volume of Soviet and Cuban assistance, the Mengistu regime had failed to defeat the Eritrean rebels, but the presence of the multinational "advisers"—especially those from East Germany—did help to consolidate the regime on Marxist-Leninist lines.

Exceptionally, in view of the events outlined, Mengistu's regime did not have a fully fledged Communist Party until 1984. Nor was it so named. As Paul B. Henze, a leading authority on Ethiopia, put it, "The Workers' Party of Ethiopia (WPE), brought into being in 1984 after a five-year preparatory period, was the world's last 'Marxist-Leninist Vanguard Party.'"[9]

Nor was the Ethiopian state itself renamed accordingly until September 12, 1987, when the "People's Democratic Republic of Ethiopia" was proclaimed (in Henze's words) "in lavish ceremonies . . . in the presence of veteran East European satraps of Moscow, such as Erich Honecker [East Germany] and Todor Zhivkov [Bulgaria] . . . [as] the last example of this anachronistic governmental system to come onto the world scene."

In mid-1985 a high-ranking Ethiopian defector brought with him to the United Kingdom previously unpublished details of the Mengistu security apparatus.[10] Having crushed the right-wing faction within the

Derg in 1976–1977, Mengistu created the Ministry of State and Public Security (MSPS). In addition to his other dictatorial functions (mentioned earlier), Mengistu was *de facto* head of the MSPS, whose *de jure* head was a close friend, Colonel Tesfaye Woldeselassie. The two men had both graduated from the same military academy in Genet (Hollota), southwest of Addis Ababa.

In Emperor Haile Selassie's time, Israeli specialists had organized Ethiopia's whole secret service system. With the help of the East German intelligence organization, the *Hauptverwaltung Ausklärung* (HVA), and with the tacit approval of the KGB, Mengistu restructured the MSPS into two departments to deal with internal and external intelligence. The HVA soon provided the Ethiopian service with modern intelligence equipment, including a radio communications network. Under the new regime, defense absorbed about one-third of the annual Ethiopian state budget, which totaled around $1.6 billion. The MSPS was the second largest spender, although the defector was unable to obtain the top secret exact figure.

The external intelligence department normally ran two of its employees in all Ethiopian embassies abroad under diplomatic cover and with first secretary rank. One was in charge of the codes and the other of the communications equipment. In practice, the MSPS "diplomats" enjoyed higher privileges than genuine diplomats, including the ambassadors. Their numerous "perks" included a yearly return to Addis Ababa, ostensibly for "reorientation." They invariably returned to their posts with the latest equipment.

Other targets were the capitals of neighboring countries, especially Nairobi, Khartoum, Djibouti, and Cairo. In 1984, Sudan had expelled three Ethiopian "diplomats" for the standard "activities incompatible with their status."

Another major task was the coordination of activities with the KGB and the HVA, especially in London, Bonn, Rome, and Washington. Indeed, such cooperation was specifically spelled out in the Ethiopian-East German protocol covering relations between the MSPS and the HVA.

In Ethiopia itself, the major targets of the intelligence wing of the MSPS were the various rebel fronts, which, by the mid-1980s, numbered six, in the following order of importance:

1. The Eritrean People's Liberation Front (EPLF). By 1985, the EPLF had emerged as the most important of the Eritrean movements and controlled most of the Sahel province bordering the Sudan. In comparison, the Saudi-backed Eritrean Unified National Council (EUNC) did not carry much weight.

2. The Tegray People's Liberation Front (TPLF). In control of the countryside in the Tegray province bordering Eritrea, and most towns, except Makale, the provincial capital, and Axum, the second-largest town. Axum, the center of orthodox Christianity, and the Axumite kingdom, were the core from which the nation-state of Ethiopia emerged as a sovereign country.

3. The Ethiopian Peoples' Democratic Movement (EPDM). The Marxist-sounding title was deceptive. It absorbed the remnants of the Ethiopian People's Revolutionary Party (EPRP) who escaped the "Red" and "White" terrors of 1975–1976. The EPDM controlled the Wag and Lasta areas in the Wollo region.

4. The Oromo Liberation Front (OLF) stepped up its activities between 1983 and 1985 and operated from three focal points. The eastern wing was based in the mountains of Hararghe and coordinated its activities with the Western Somalia Liberation Front (see following). The southeast wing operated in the Bale and Arsi areas, as well as in Borana in Sidamo province on the Kenyan border. Its strongest sector, however, was Wollega province on the Sudanese border. According to the Ethiopian defector, the Olomo Liberation Front was probably potentially the greatest threat to the Mengistu regime, as the Oromo represented about 20 percent of the Ethiopian population, way ahead of the other hundred or so linguistic groups.

5. The Western Somalia Liberation Front, or WSLF, was conducting sabotage and hit-and-run operations in the Ogaden, but its activities had been restricted by Derg air raids.

6. The Afar Liberation Front (ALF). The Afars, living in the eastern Wollo bordering on Djibouti, were united in wanting regional autonomy, but were at odds politically. The ALF was anti-Mengistu, but there was a rival, left-wing group known as the Afar National Liberation Front, which cooperated with the regime when it suited them.

Although the regime would probably not have lasted long without Soviet support, it has to be pointed out that the aid given was costly, especially for a poverty-stricken country. By mid-1985, Soviet arms deliveries had cost Ethiopia £3.5 billion, with interest at 2 percent over ten years. Under a secret protocol to the arms agreement, Ethiopia could buy spare parts only from the Soviet Union. Repayments of the loan were in hard currency, a requirement that had forced the Derg to step up coffee exports at the expense of diversifying its crops.

Ethiopia had also signed an agreement allowing for Soviet exploration for oil in the Ogaden. There were also hostile popular murmurs about Soviet aid to victims of the severe famine that prevailed in the early 1980s, consisting mainly of 10,000 tons of rice, which most Ethiopians do not normally eat.

The internal intelligence department of Ethiopia's revamped security system was responsible for numerous killings and "disappearances" after the revolution. Apart from the main center in Addis Ababa, there were fourteen regional offices, including Asmara, Makali, and Gondar in the north, and Dire Dawa and Harar in the east. Town dwellers were kept in order by the so-called Kebeles: community associations created by the Derg. Peasants were controlled through the All-Ethiopian Peasant Association and the trade unions through the All-Ethiopian Trade Union Organization. There was also a centrally controlled Revolutionary Ethiopian Youth Association, while all professional associations were similarly penetrated. Like the KGB's Third Chief Directorate, the Derg controlled its armed forces through "political commissars" in charge of Marxist-Leninist indoctrination programs in which the history of the Soviet Red Army was a compulsory theme. The East German HVA was actively involved in the MSPS training programs, and in 1982 more than two hundred MSPS trainees were sent to North Korea for special training in sabotage activities.

By that time, Mengistu's regime could accurately be described as a fully controlled satellite of the Soviet Empire, unlike Somalia, which had only reached the middle stage of satellization by the time Siad Barre decided to abrogate his country's Friendship Treaty with the USSR. By late 1989, despite the advice and assistance from the Soviet Union and East Germany, the survival of the Mengistu regime had become problematical. On September 19, the Politburo held a special session to consider appeals from Mengistu to the Soviet head of state, Mikhail Gorbachev, and a report on the situation presented the previous day by Eduard Shevardnadze, Aleksandr Yakovlev, Dmitri Yazov, and Vladimir Kryuchkov. The four reported a serious worsening of the military situation in the face of attacks from the EPFL. It was agreed that General V. I. Varennikov should be sent to Ethiopia to discuss "the question of withdrawing of all Soviet military experts from the areas of operational activities in the north of Ethiopia." Meanwhile, however, ammunition to the value of 18 million rubles would be sent, if necessary by air.

It was agreed that a special message to Mengistu from Gorbachev should be sent forthwith. The message, though emollient in tone, was negative in practical terms, as shown by the following extracts:

> I should like to confirm that the Soviet Union was and remains a loyal and sincere friend of the Ethiopian revolution. We are very concerned about its fate. . . . Of course, we are not going to abandon Ethiopia at this difficult moment for her. You can be assured of our support.

> We are confident that the wisdom and patience of which you, comrade Mengistu, speak . . . and the fortitude which the Ethiopian leadership has exhibited on more than one occasion when defending the supreme interests of the Motherland will help [you] to get the better of the current difficult period and go forth to the stage of peace, to which the Ethiopian people is so looking forward. (For the full text of the report to the Politburo and of Gorbachev's message to Mengistu, see Appendix L: Document 2.)

We have no record of Mengistu's response to Gorbachev, but he may well have thought that with friends like that, who needed enemies? Less than two years later, in May 1991, Mengistu was overthrown and fled the country. (See Chapter 49.)

CHAPTER THIRTY-THREE

ARAB UPHEAVALS

1961–1975

———⊳●⊲———

Between 1962 and the late 1970s, the Persian Gulf was the scene of what might be termed "serial upheavals"—assassinations, civil wars, coups d'état—in most of which the Soviet Union was involved, both for imperial reasons and at times for the more old-fashioned motives of power politics. The two labels overlap but are not identical. The imperial motive was simply the addition of another state to those already controlled by Moscow; power politics included concerns such as access to oil and hard currency and the need for land-based facilities in the Indian Ocean area.

By the mid-1970s, the Soviet Union was lagging behind the industrial West in oil consumption. Moscow's chosen preference was to rely on fuels, especially oil, that were directly under Soviet control. To raise oil consumption would require sufficient foreign currency to import oil, whereas exporting oil was one sure way of earning foreign currency: a vicious circle.

Another aspect of Soviet power politics in this region was the aim of acquiring two land bases in the Gulf region. One would be Somalia (see Chapter 28); the other, at least one of two geographically useful Arab countries: Yemen or Oman.[1]

Both in traditional power politics and in Communist-style expansionism, the Soviet Union faced problems and obstacles peculiar to the Persian Gulf region; the principal ones were Islam and Arab nationalism. Faced with parallel obstacles in the 1920s and 1930s, Stalin had solved them in his ruthless Leninist fashion, by imposing Communist rule in such countries as Kazakhstan or Turkmenistan, and in effect outlawing Islam. Stalin's heirs—Nikita Khrushchev, Leonid Brezhnev, and Yuri Andropov—carried on in the same atheistic vein.

Moreover, although Communist parties did exist in the Arab world, most of them were feeble: at best barely tolerated, more often suppressed. Nationalist rivalries and religious differences competed with Soviet imperialist ambitions: Syria, for instance, had designs on its weaker Arab neighbors, Jordan and Lebanon. The stronger neighbors, Iraq and Iran, whose populations respectively practiced the Sunni and Shi'ite versions of Islam, were mutually antagonistic. Egypt and Saudi Arabia had rival designs on Yemen. A distracting problem, or set of problems, was posed by the non-Arab, postwar state of Israel, whose Palestinian population was supported by the Arab states, whereas its controlling Jewish population enjoyed considerable political and financial support from the United States.

Nor does this brief survey cover the spectrum of regional problems that tended to exclude any support for Soviet aspirations. There was a natural antagonism between the feudal monarchies, of which the most important was Saudi Arabia, and the post-monarchic republics such as Egypt, which had overthrown its last crowned head, King Farouk, in 1952. Yet another obstacle, which turned out to be short-lived, was the union of Egypt and Syria in 1958 under the name "United Arab Republic." The "Union," however, lasted only three years.[2]

YEMEN

YEMEN, WHICH WOULD later be divided into North and South, had been one country, not two, and a monarchy before a civil war broke out in 1962. On September 27, 1962, the reigning Imam Mohammed Badr was overthrown by a republican group in the Army. The coup triggered the civil war, as the royalists tried to oust the newcomers. After five years of fighting, peace of a kind came, not by mutual agreement so much as by stages over several months at the end of 1967 and into January 1968. The main political outcome was the splitting of Yemen into two roughly equal halves, each of them a republic. North Yemen called itself the Yemen Arab Republic (YAR) and confirmed its new status under a constitution announced in Sana'a, the capital, on December 28, 1970.

Under British colonial rule for 129 years, South Yemen was better known as Aden, an important staging port on the exit from the Suez Canal and the Red Sea. With its largely desert hinterland, the area was officially styled "the Federation of South Arabia." The federation officially achieved independence on November 30, 1967, a few hours after the departure of the last British forces. For the previous four years— since December 10, 1963—the Moscow-line National Liberation Front (NLF) had waged a terrorist campaign in South Arabia in which fifty-three British troops were killed and 235 wounded.

The federation's new name was the People's Republic of South Yemen. The word *People* made its ideological leanings clear. As if to confirm that South Yemen had become a Soviet satellite, the word *Democratic* was added to the title, which on November 30, 1970, would become the People's Democratic Republic of Yemen, or PDRY.

During the civil war between North and South Yemen, the northerners had been supported by the kingdom of Saudi Arabia, and the southerners by Egypt, still at that time under President Gamal Abdel Nasser. In an agreement signed in Khartoum by President Nasser and King Faisal on August 31, 1967, the United Arab Republic (Egypt) agreed to withdraw its forces from South Yemen, while Saudi Arabia would cease to support North Yemen. As if no agreement had been reached, President Abdullah al-Sallal of South Yemen was overthrown in a military coup on November 5, 1967, while he was in Moscow to attend the celebration of the fiftieth anniversary of the Soviet Revolution. He took refuge in Iraq (where he was awarded a retirement pension).

Fighting resumed on another front: between Saudi Arabia and the PDRY. Between October 1970 and June 1971, political exiles from the PDRY had crossed the Saudi border. There were various incursions, all unsuccessful. In one raid in particular, between February 28 and March 3, 1971, some 500 guerrillas had crossed the border, only to lose 175 killed and fifty captured.

Despite these setbacks, the PDRY regime stuck to its Leninist principles, and indeed hardened. The hostility between the two Yemens worsened, not least because of the increasing flow of political exiles and nonpolitical refugees seeking relative peace in the Yemen Arab Republic. Soviet involvement continued but took a further ideological turn when a special Soviet-Cuban delegation visited Aden in April 1978 to advise on the formation of a Communist Party. The name chosen was the Yemen Socialist Party.[3]

Two bizarre assassinations followed. On June 24, the YAR President, Lieutenant-Colonel Ahmed al-Ghashmi, age thirty-eight, was blown up by a booby-trapped briefcase presented to him by an envoy of the PDRY president, Salem Rubaya Ali. Two days later it was the turn of the PDRY president, who was murdered in a military coup. It emerged that he had been negotiating secretly with the United States, which of course conflicted with the Moscow line. He was replaced by Moscow's choice, Fattah Ismail, secretary-general of the PDRY's National Front.[4]

By July 1978, the two Yemens were again locked in a relatively minor border war. Although both sides were threatening full-scale invasion, the influence of the Saudis on one side and of the Soviets on the other kept the fighting at a low level.

OMAN

ARMED UNREST SURFACED not only between North and South Yemen but also in the Dhofar province of southern Oman, adjacent to the PDRY. Incursions into Oman had been going on since 1963, mainly from PFLOAG (the Popular Front for the Liberation of Oman and the Arab Gulf). In the early days, the PFLOAG had been a Nationalist movement, but it was taken over by Marxist-Leninists in 1968.

With support from the British SAS (Special Air Service), the Sultan of Oman late in 1971 launched a major assault, dubbed Operation Jaguar, against the PFLOAG. Jordanian and Iranian support was also provided. The Communist side emerged from this clash severely weakened by the surrender (or defection) of three political commissars and six others from the "Ho Chi Minh" and "Lenin" units, on November 22 at Mirbat.[5]

Since 1971 the Soviets had supplied the PFLOAG with food, training, and revolutionary literature as well as weapons, including 300 Kalashnikov rifles and 200 Seminov machine guns. It soon became clear that the Chinese specialists in guerrilla war were proving more useful to the PFLOAG than the Soviet ones. Chinese ideology, Maoist methods, and Soviet weapons . . .

The Chinese advisers had lived and worked at the PFLOAG base of Hauf on the PDRY/Oman border, but in early 1973 they withdrew to

Aden, perhaps for linguistic reasons, since they now left the instruction to native Dhofaris trained in China and Iraq.

Soviet journalists visiting the training camps and indoctrination courses at Daug were disturbed at the prevalence of Chinese methods. The Soviet advisers took note and decided to bolster the Soviet side by importing some 150 Cubans—a presence acknowledged in a PDRY official statement on May 23.[6] In an interview with *Le Monde* the previous day, the PFLOAG spokesman Mohammed Abdullah declared, "The Chinese provide us with arms, ammunition and provisions, but they have never expressed a desire to fight in our place and there is no enforcement on our part."

As the fighting continued, it emerged that the PFLOAG, probably in 1975, had changed its initials to PFLO: the Popular Front for the Liberation of Oman. In addition to predictable support from the PDRY, the PFLO was not short of Communist patrons: the Soviet Union, Cuba, and the German Democratic Republic. Despite this local and foreign support, defections from the PFLO increased steadily. In 1974 they had run at about one a day: higher than the rate of recruitment. Over three years, nearly 1,000 had dropped out.

In areas cleared by the Omani forces, a reward system had encouraged PFLO defections. One outcome was a tribal police force known as the *firqats,* which consisted of surrendered enemy personnel and tribal irregulars. Despite such successes, the Omanis found themselves up against a new unit, trained in Lebanon by the most extreme of the Palestinian terrorist groups: the PFLP, or Popular Front for the Liberation of Palestine.[7]

Despite continued support from the Soviet Union, Cuba, and East Germany, the PFLO was decisively defeated by the Omani forces in December 1975. Its command structure had been destroyed, and its forces in the field had been reduced to isolated guerrillas. PFLO fugitives who crossed the border into the PDRY were told that Aden could no longer supply them with money, arms, or sanctuary. Indeed the Soviet Union had long been aware that this particular exercise in subversion had proved a failure. PFLO refugees were told that money, in modest quantities, could be given to PFLO terrorists, but only on condition that they agreed to join POLISARIO (People's Front for the Liberation of Saguiat el Hamra and Río de Oro), an Algerian-supported movement disputing Morocco's and Mauritania's control of the Western Sahara.[8]

*   *   *

BY NOW, AND despite the poor military performance of the PDRY, the Soviet Union had secured the base it wanted. The totals of Communist advisers had grown impressively: 1,500 Soviets, 700 Cubans, and 116 East Germans. Indeed, the base was a triple one: Aden, Mukalla, and the island of Socotra. Their respective allotted tasks were intelligence, communications, and paramilitary training.

The Soviets were building themselves an air base to handle sixty jet fighters, and a naval base in the Bay of Turbah. They had also taken over Mikalla's port and airport. In other words, the military failure of their latest satellite had not prevented the fulfillment of their strategic goals.

CHAPTER THIRTY-FOUR

REDS AGAINST REDS

1976–1979

THEY WERE ROUNDED up systematically, first in the capital, Phnom Penh, then in smaller towns, and forced to walk into the countryside. There were special targets: civil servants, teachers, students, businessmen, and technicians. Once well away from their houses or flats, or desks or work tools, they were forced to dig the trenches that soon became their own graves. Their "crime" was simple and involuntary. They represented *the past*: an interesting, varied, at times glorious past, preserved by the awe-inspiring ruins of the twelfth-century capital, Angkor Wat. At that time, the Khmer god-kings were creating a vast empire, stretching over Vietnam and Thailand, and much of the Malay peninsula. The Khmer era of glory was short-lived, however. By the fifteenth century, the Thais and the Vietnamese, each on their own, had driven the Khmers out of their respective territories, reducing Cambodia to a small area around its modern capital, Phnom Penh. In 1863, France turned Cambodia into a French protectorate. After a brief period of Japanese rule during World War II, the French came back in 1946, but not for long: they pulled out in 1954.

Cambodia's hereditary monarch, King Norodom Sihanouk, had come to the throne in 1941, at age eighteen. Politically astute, the young king went through many guises. Having won a referendum in 1955, approving his political program, he abdicated in favor of his father, King Suramarit, whom he served as prime minister. When the king died, in

April 1960, Prince Sihanouk (as he was now known) proclaimed himself head of state. He managed initially to keep Cambodia out of the Second Vietnam War but broke off diplomatic relations with the United States in 1965, when the war spread to Cambodia. While in Moscow on March 18, 1970, he was ousted by a military coup in Phnom Penh. He went on to Beijing and formed a royal government in exile, but the new right-wing government under General Lon Nol renamed his country the Khmer Republic. The Communist *Khmer Rouge* ("Red Khmer") move-ment promptly announced its support for Prince Sihanouk. Four years later they ousted the right-wingers and started their sweeping massacre of their compatriots.

The Khmer Rouge simply wanted to destroy the past to make it disappear, so that a new Communist society could be built. The edu-cated few were seen as the ultimate enemy, because they were the heirs of past waves or static periods of relative peace. The new society, to be built on the peasantry, would be unique, even in the Communist world, owing nothing to Mao Zedong* or Ho Chi Minh, and still less to Stalin.

And yet, the great Khmer massacres would not spare even the peas-ants. Communist death squads moved systematically into village after vil-lage, breaking up all families and dividing them up into groups of ten unrelated people, of whom nine formed three arbitrary cells of three people each plus one supervisor. Each member of each cell was responsi-ble for the behavior of the other two, with death the penalty for failure, as decided by the supervisor.

The ranking officers of the defeated Cambodian Army were killed indiscriminately, and when they were gone the conscripted privates were next.

How many people were killed in Cambodia in 1975 and 1976? It is impossible to give an accurate figure, and estimates vary widely from 100,000 to between 2 and 3 million.[1] The diplomatic consensus was that about 20 percent of the total population had been killed. But what was the population? There was no systematic head count to use as a guide.

---

*Henceforth, we shall use the modernized pinyin system of transliteration for such names as Mao Tse-tung (Mao Zedong) and Peking (Beijing).—BC

Estimates varied between 6 and 7 million, yielding a total of somewhere between 1.2 million and 1.4 million.*

IF ANY OF the higher estimates is accepted, the massacre was proportionately the worst of the century, surpassing even those of the Soviet Union, Nazi Germany, and the Chinese People's Republic. The instigator of it was the Khmer Communist leader known as Pol Pot. Like many East Asian Communist leaders, including Deng Xiaoping and Chou En-lai of China and Ho Chi Minh of Vietnam, Pol Pot developed his ideas of Communism while studying in Paris and other French cities.[2]

Years after Pol Pot gained his evil world renown, it became known that his real name was Sar Salogh. According to the register of births kept by the French colonial administration, he was born into a prosperous farming family in the village of Prek Sbauv, ninety-five miles north of Phnom Penh. In August 1949, he was awarded a government scholarship for studies in Paris, where he spent three years. Although widely reported to have chosen radio electricity as his subject, there are no traces of this choice in the records. Two names headed his short list of major influences upon his thinking: one was Jean-Jacques Rousseau; the other was Stalin. He seems to have placed Robespierre's *Terreur* of the French Revolution of 1789 and Stalin's own terror as coequals in his panoply of role models. Certainly his "Center S-21," where prisoners chosen at random were tortured and executed, owed more to Stalin's NKVD and gulags than to Robespierre's public executions. After the collapse of the Khmer Rouge regime, a rich paraphernalia of torture was found in the cells of the Center S-21, along with many corpses that had not been disposed of.[3]

Although the Pol Pot massacres are only indirectly related to the central theme of this history, they cannot be considered in isolation. They were followed by two important though minor wars, each of which

---

*Details of the massacre were provided to the author by the CIA. I offered an article to the London *Times,* which declined to publish it. It was used, however, in the *Illustrated London News* of October 1976. As far as I am aware, this was the first published account to appear in the world's press. Jean Lacouture, the well-known French journalist from *Le Monde* and a left-wing specialist on Indochina, was in Phnom Penh shortly after the massacre, but apparently decided to ignore it and praised the Khmer Rouge as "Marxists of high quality." Three years later he confessed that he was wrong, first in a short book, *Survive le peuple cambodgien (May the Cambodian People Survive),* and later in a frank and humble interview in the center-right news magazine *Valeurs Actuelles* (November 13, 1978).—BC

involved Communist Vietnam. The first was Vietnam's invasion of Kam-puchea (as Cambodia was now known) at the end of 1978; the second was a Chinese incursion into Vietnam's frontier territory in early 1979. During these clashes Kampuchea emerged clearly as a vassal of China, while Vietnam was supported by the Soviet Union.

The Mekong valley in South Vietnam, and indeed the whole of the southern province known as Cochinchina, had long been contested terri-tory. Annexed by the Vietnamese from the Khmer Empire in the eighteenth century, it continued to harbor a large minority of ethnic Khmers. When the French conquered the peninsula of Indochina in the late nineteenth century, the new colonial power transferred four more Khmer areas to Vietnam, thus deepening Khmer resentment of Vietnamese ascendancy.

Between 1930 and 1951, Cambodian-Vietnamese relations were fur-ther complicated by Communist rivalries. When Ho Chi Minh founded his "Communist Party of Indochina," he was registering his view of a Marx-ist-Leninist future in which the Vietnamese would play the dominant role, with the Cambodian and Laotian members bowing to Vietnamese leader-ship. Ho was always ready to compromise, however, if the situation de-manded it. Thus, in 1941, with the colonial power—France—defeated at home, and Japan merely a bellicose Asian presence on the horizon, the Party decided that the peoples of Indochina could either form a federation or simply become independent states. At this early stage, Ho chose to dis-guise the Communist nature of his political organizations. So he created the League for the Independence of Vietnam (better known as the Viet-minh), the Khmer Patriotic Front, and the Lao Patriotic Front.

Ten years later, in February 1951, with Japan defeated and the French still resisting the Communist challenge, Ho decided on further title changes. His original Communist Party of Indochina became the Vietnam Workers' Party, with two ethnic equivalents: the Cambodian People's Revolutionary Party, and a Lao version of the same. The Cambodian one was soon known, for short, as the Khmer Vietminh, while a rival party, strictly Khmer and specifically Communist, broke away, operating in the shadows. The leader of the Communist Party of Kampuchea (CPK, its real but unpublicized name) was a hitherto unknown man named Sar Sa-logh. By the time Salogh emerged from the shadows, he was using the pseudonym Pol Pot. (Indeed his real name was not known until after the overthrow of the Khmer Rouge in 1979.)

Among the differences between Pol Pot's CPK and Ho's Vietminh was a particularly important one: Pol Pot wanted to oust Prince Sihanouk, while Ho had supported the monarch, just as in 1945 he had given the ex-Emperor Bao Dai the short-lived title of "Supreme Adviser" (see Chapter 12). Sihanouk, in line with his mercurial temperament, is said to have coined the name *Khmer Rouge,* which was henceforth used in the world's media in preference to "Communist Party of Kampuchea."

IN THE EARLY stages of the second Vietnam War, the Vietnamese Communists (by then known as the Vietcong) had used Cambodia's eastern provinces as a base for their forays into South Vietnam, with Sihanouk's approval. Although the Vietcong provided much support for the Khmer Rouge, friction between them had developed by the time of the signing of the Paris Peace Settlement in 1973, and the Vietnamese cut their support for them. From then on there were increasing clashes between the two camps.

In a near-total news blackout, the Khmer Rouge seized power in April 1975, at about the same time as the Vietnamese Communists fought their way to power in Saigon. Two months later, Pol Pot led a CPK delegation to Hanoi. The Cambodians claimed that the purpose of the visit had been to settle the border question but that the Vietnamese had avoided the issue. The Vietnamese had a different version: that the Cambodians had suggested a bilateral friendship treaty but had not proposed immediate talks on the frontier question.

A year later, in April 1976, both sides agreed to meet in June to discuss a possible treaty. Discussions followed, but no treaty. The tension increased dangerously, and on December 21, 1977, a Cambodian statement claimed that over the previous two years Vietnam had "carried out criminal activities in an attempt to stage a coup d'état to smash Democratic Cambodia through a handful of traitorous forces which were Vietnam's agents." In fact the situation along the border had been sharply deteriorating since March 1977.

As the clashes continued, the search for allies within the Communist world progressed. In May, Cambodia recalled its attaché in Moscow, thus in effect severing diplomatic relations. In late September and early October, Pol Pot led a delegation to Beijing and Pyongyang, returning with strong declarations of support from China and North Korea. The chairman of China's Communist Party and prime minister, Hua Guofeng, presided over a banquet for their Cambodian visitors and declared that China and Cambodia "always stand together with the other third world countries and peoples in the struggle against imperialism and hegemonism"—a Party-jargon reference to the United States and the Soviet Union. He went on to denounce the "aggressive and expansionist" superpowers. In a relatively moderate reply, Pol Pot made it clear that Cambodia stood by China in the Sino-Soviet dispute. As the conflict developed, Soviet support for Vietnam was affirmed, with additional support from Cuba, Mongolia, and the Marxist-Leninist governments of Angola and Mozambique, while Yugoslavia and Romania remained neutral.

Meanwhile, the Vietnamese Communists were losing patience with their ideological neighbors. On December 25, 1978, 100,000 troops of Hanoi's regular Army invaded Cambodia. Less than a fortnight later, on January 7, 1979, the invaders occupied Phnom Penh. Shortly before the invasion, anti–Pol Pot Cambodians had set up the "Cambodian National United Front for National Salvation," which in turn announced a "People's Revolutionary Council"—in effect a provisional government headed by Heung Samrin, which was immediately recognized by the Soviet Union and its satellites. On their side, Pol Pot's Khmer Rouge reverted to guerrilla war, inflicting heavy casualties on the invading Vietnamese.

The new Cambodian government was immediately recognized by Vietnam and Laos (not surprisingly) and by the Soviet Union, Poland, Hungary, Bulgaria, East Germany, and Czechoslovakia, and within days by Afghanistan, Mongolia, Ethiopia, and Cuba.

What followed was a curious descent into international bathos. One of the most murderous regimes in contemporary history had been ousted by a neighboring Communist regime that, in relative terms, had a strong claim to be seen as a liberating force. The United Nations Security Council, with full support from the United States, chose to condemn the invading liberators.

The way the U.S. State Department spokesman put it on January 3 was that although "the United States takes great exception to the human rights record" of the Cambodian government, "as a matter of principle, we do not feel that unilateral intervention against that regime by a third power is justified." A week later the Cambodian Revolutionary Council

announced "the complete abolition of the dictatorial, fascist and genocidal regime of the reactionary Pol Pot-Ieng Sary clique, and the founding
of the People's Republic of Kampuchea."

On January 7, 1979, the Soviet Union's Tass news agency denounced
Pol Pot's government as "a reactionary dictatorial clique" and added, "All
progressive humanity salutes the nation which has risen in the struggle for
national salvation." A suitably opposite view was expressed a week later
by the Chinese government, which asserted that "the Vietnamese aggressors" had been "aided and abetted by Soviet social-imperialism." Thus,
ironically, the Chinese People's Republic sided with the United States, its
former main enemy until President Nixon's visit in 1972.

The adaptable Prince Sihanouk revealed that the (notoriously hostile)
Pol Pot had sent for him on January 5 and asked him to represent Cambodia at the UN; he had immediately accepted. He added that his reason
for accepting was that he regarded Pol Pot as "our legal leader of Democratic Kampuchea, which was created by the people in the resistance
against American imperialism and the Lon Nol regime."

When the UN Security Council met in New York on January 11,
Prince Sihanouk asked for a resolution demanding the withdrawal of the
Vietnamese forces from Cambodia and the cessation of all international
aid to Vietnam. He refrained, however, from calling for a formal condemnation of Vietnam.

The Security Council allowed Ha Van Lau, Vietnam's representative
at the UN but not a member of the council, to have his say. He denounced Pol Pot's brutal regime, which had transformed the country
into a "living hell" of massacres, forced labor, famine, and human
degradation.

For the Soviet Union, Oleg Troyanovsky accused the Pol Pot regime
of committing "open genocide" in the construction of a Maoist society.
For the United States, Andrew Young said that although the Pol Pot
regime had committed "some of the worst violations of human rights in
history," the essential fact was that one country's troops were occupying
another's territory and should be withdrawn immediately.

On January 15 a resolution drafted by seven non-aligned countries,
all non-members of the Security Council, was submitted. It appealed for
a cease-fire and called for the withdrawal of all foreign forces in Cambodia. When the vote was taken, the United Kingdom, the United States,

and France voted with China. Against were the Soviet Union and Czechoslovakia. As the USSR was a permanent member of the Security Council, its negative vote had the force of a veto.

On February 16, 1979, the Vietnamese premier, Pham Van Dong, visited Phnom Penh. On February 18, a twenty-five-year Treaty of Peace, Friendship, and Cooperation was signed on behalf of Vietnam and the new regime it had installed in Cambodia. Thus Cambodia became a satellite of a Soviet satellite. (The same would happen a few months later to Nicaragua, with Cuba in Vietnam's role—see Chapter 36.) At almost exactly the same moment, at dawn on February 17, a Chinese force estimated at 70,000 to 80,000, with tanks and artillery and with reserves of perhaps 120,000, invaded Vietnam at twenty-six points along the 450-mile border. An official statement in Beijing claimed that the Chinese had been driven beyond forbearance by Vietnamese border attacks—thirty of them. It went on to declare that "we do not want a single inch of Vietnamese territory, but neither will we tolerate wanton incursions into Chinese territory."

It was generally assumed that the main reason for China's attack (or counterattack if one accepts the Chinese presentation of events) was to relieve Vietnam's pressure on the Khmer Rouge forces in Cambodia. On the Vietnamese side, some 50,000 well-trained regular troops with the same number of local militia went into action.

The attackers were apparently taken by surprise at the performance of the defending force and halted their advance, having reached points only six miles into Vietnamese territory. They halted the offensive and called in reinforcements totaling a further 400,000 men, of whom some 100,000 joined the attackers.

The Soviet Union seized the opportunity to turn the propaganda tables on the Chinese People's Republic in a statement on February 18 accusing the invaders of exposing "the real essence of Beijing's hegemonistic policy in Southeast Asia." The Chinese leadership, the statement went on, was attempting to "plunge the world into war."

A U.S. State Department spokesman quoted President Jimmy Carter as making it clear to China's paramount leader, Deng Xiaoping, on a visit to Washington on January 29, that "the United States opposed any further military action in the region." This anodyne statement was in effect contradicted by the president himself on February 20, when he declared that the invasion would not damage the normalization of Sino-American relations, which was "already an accomplished fact."

On March 5, Vietnam issued a decree proclaiming general mobilization, ordering all men aged 18 to 45 and all women from 18 to 35 to join the militia, guerrilla, and self-defense forces, and all workers and students to devote two hours a day to military training or guard duty. That same day, Beijing made it clear that it had not crossed the border to stay forever. The government announced that the Chinese troops, having "attained the goals set for them," were withdrawing to Chinese territory. There was a relatively mild sting in the tail: "The Chinese side reserves the right to strike back again in self-defense" in the event of a recurrence of Vietnamese "armed provocation and incursions." The statement called for negotiations to bring the matter to an end.

Desultory clashes followed, nevertheless. After all, Sino-Vietnamese differences had a long history, going back for centuries before the emergence of rival Communist states.

CHAPTER THIRTY-FIVE

TROUBLE IN PARADISE

1977–1987

SEYCHELLES

WHEN THE TELEPHONE rang at 3:45 A.M., President James Mancham of the Seychelles was fast asleep in his suite in London's famous Savoy Hotel, with his own guest beside him, "sleeping prettily." Reaching out from his deep sleep, he spoke to a friend of his calling from Paris, the Saudi tycoon Adnan Khashoggi, who was the bearer of bad tidings: There had been a coup in Mancham's island country, and he had been overthrown by his own prime minister, France-Albert René.[1]

The timing could not have been worse from Mancham's viewpoint, or better from René's. Mancham was in London at the invitation of Her Majesty's government, in his capacity as president of the new Republic of Seychelles, to take part in Queen Elizabeth's twenty-fifth Jubilee celebrations. It was June 5, 1977, and Mancham was due to address the Commonwealth Heads of Government conference in two days' time.

Three nights earlier, the overthrown president and his self-proclaimed successor had dined together and discussed plans to celebrate the first anniversary of the new republic. Next day René had come to the airport and, all smiles, had wished Mancham bon voyage. Now, in London after the devastating news, Mancham thought of Judas Iscariot. . . .

* * *

WITH ITS POPULATION of only 62,000—the size of one of the smaller London suburbs—Seychelles consists of ninety-two islets in the Indian Ocean just south of the equator. Mancham was not the only one to think of it as a paradise: so did many jet-setting tourists. White sands glowed in the tropical sun, and the palm trees swayed in the Indian Ocean breeze. With René's coup, the new republic was about to become a candidate for ultimate absorption into the Soviet Union's peripheral empire.

At the time of René's coup, the islands had no Army, but René mustered a sixty-man armed "task force" including some members of the police force. The "task force" was soon supplemented by some two hundred "militant workers," and the combined force seized the police armory in the capital Victoria (on the main island of Mahé), at a cost of six civilian lives. The time was 2 A.M. on June 5. In addition, a key role was later known to have been played by imported Tanzanian troops, who had been brought in only hours before the coup and stayed on afterward.

René soon revealed himself to be a good student of Communist methods, including disinformation. An unsigned statement was issued by the (unnamed) leaders of the action, described as a "coup d'état" by "the people of Seychelles with the entire cooperation of the police force." A twenty-four-hour curfew was imposed, and violators of the curfew were liable to be shot on sight. Mr. Mancham was described as a "dictator" who had "adopted a style of life which involves lavish spending" and had not spent more than three weeks in the country since independence in 1972. Replying to these charges, Mancham claimed that his extensive travels had been spent on negotiations for foreign aid.

The most impressive morsels of disinformation followed. René claimed that he had had no advance knowledge of the coup but had accepted an invitation from the coup leaders to take over the presidency. He went on to say that his government would introduce a "non-Marxist form of Socialism" and would continue the Mancham government's commitment to non-alignment.

In a broadcast at 4 P.M. on the same day (June 5), Albert René claimed that the reason he had agreed to form a new government was that Mancham had tried "to create a situation whereby he would be president for ever" by postponing elections, against his advice. Moreover, René went on, the Seychelles would have found themselves "slaves of the capitalists and of foreign countries."

A few days later, on June 9, Moscow had its say, in the form of a TASS commentary attacking a report in that day's "right-wing London newspaper, the *Daily Express,*" to the effect that what had happened in the Seychelles was the result of "Moscow intrigues to get war bases in the Indian Ocean." Nothing of the kind, said the Tass commentator Sergey Kulik. "The USSR does not call for the liquidation of war bases belonging to the imperialist powers in order to replace them with its own. . . . The lies of the *Daily Express* show up the plans of the imperialist powers, who hide behind allegations that there is a Soviet menace and try to justify their own military preparations in the Indian Ocean."[2]

THE SEYCHELLES CONNECTION with the British Crown had lasted 153 years. There had been three consecutive general elections under universal adult suffrage. Close relations with Britain were cemented with an official visit by the queen and her consort Prince Philip on March 20, 1972. James Mancham had won a landslide majority for his Seychelles Democratic Party. Whether through good will or naïvete, Mancham had invited Albert René to join him in a coalition government, even though René's Seychelles People's United Party (SDUP) had been involved in terrorism, apparently to undermine the public's will to maintain the British connection. Under James Callaghan's Labor government in Britain, however, the Seychellois were pressured into accepting "independence."

Having seized power, René lost no time in denouncing the Westminster-model constitution that had been approved by the British Parliament and agreed upon by René as well as Mancham in 1974 at the London Independence Constitutional Conference.

FRANCE-ALBERT RENÉ'S early life and career bore a curious though probably fortuitous resemblance to that of a more important dictator of a considerably bigger country: Josef Dzhugashvili, better known as Stalin.[3] Of "poor white" parents, René attended a seminary in Switzerland to become a Catholic priest, after completing his secondary education in the Seychelles. As Stalin had done decades earlier, he abandoned his religious studies and went to London to study law. While in London René attended meetings organized by the British Communist Party and took part in Communist-inspired street demonstrations in the early 1960s. During academic recesses he made several visits to the Soviet Union.

On April 30, 1978, the Seychellois Ministry of Internal Affairs announced that a plot to overthrow the new regime had been uncovered. The police were said to have discovered several arms caches, and a vessel was reported to have been ready to leave Mombasa, Kenya, with mercenaries on board. Had the "plot" not been uncovered, the timing at least would have made sense, as President René was on a visit to China and North Korea and would therefore not be blamed for the "plot."

On May 2, it was announced that twenty-one people had been arrested on a charge of treason, for allegedly conspiring to inspire an armed invasion of the Seychelles. American citizens employed at the U.S. tracking station in the Seychelles had been expelled for alleged involvement in the aborted coup.

The previous day René had been received in Beijing by Chairman Hua Kuo-feng, who declared that the Chinese People's Republic was "squarely behind Seychelles's just proposal for turning the Indian Ocean into a zone of peace." Next day, agreements on economic and technical cooperation were signed between giant China and tiny Seychelles. René went on to Pyongyang, where he told the long-established dictator, Kim Il Sung, that he had come to North Korea to learn from the experience of North Korea's Communists. A further agreement on trade and air services followed.

By the end of 1979, some eighty Seychellois, including officials, businessmen, and an unnamed journalist, had been imprisoned under the draconian legislation that included curfews and censorship. In October 1979, René had spread an unverified rumor of a plot to overthrow him. The closest reality to a plot appeared to have been a protest by 3,000 schoolchildren against a plan to send some of them to a distant island in the Seychelles for military training and political indoctrination.[4] Following the alleged crisis, a penalty of two years in jail was introduced for making public jokes about René or reading clandestine news sheets.

René's public commitment to the non-alignment movement was no more genuine than Fidel Castro's, as he showed in September 1979, when he attended the Sixth Conference of Heads of State of the Non-Aligned Movement in Havana. There he proclaimed his pride in associating with Socialist Cuba, and in a long private talk with Castro was reported to have told his host that seventeen years earlier, during the Cuban Missile Crisis, he had been among the thousands who had marched through the streets of London chanting, "Kennedy, *No!* Castro, *Si!* Cuba, *Si!*"

He went on: "Today, seventeen years later, I am proud to state here in free and Socialist Cuba: 'Imperialism, *No!* Castro, *Si!* Cuba, *Si!*'" For good measure he "condemned" the refusal of the United States to grant self-determination and independence to the people of Puerto Rico, declared his solidarity with the struggle of the people in the "fascist regimes" in Latin America, Africa, and Asia; and hailed "with pride" the success of the peoples of Iran, Nicaragua, Uganda, Kampuchea, and Grenada.[5]

On his return to Mahé, René's regime established closer ties with Cuba. In 1980 his foreign minister, Jacques Hodoul, paid several visits to Havana. Hodoul's successor, Maxim Ferrari, a fervent Marxist, attended the next Congress of the Cuban Communist Party. The defense minister, Berlouis, made several unpublicized visits to Cuba bearing personal messages to Castro from René.

An undisclosed number of young people were sent from the Seychelles to Cuba for "training." On their return they organized the Seychelles National Youth Movement. Their sixteenth birthdays were a turning point. On reaching it, each of the Cuban-trained youngsters, known as "the Young Pioneers," was required to join René's People's Progressive Front, the sole party permitted in the Seychelles.[6]

It would be a mistake, however, to conclude that the Seychelles had been turned into another "satellite of a satellite," in advance of the Nicaragua model (see next chapter). Understandably, however, the Cubans were particularly useful to the Soviets because they merged easily with the multiracial native population. At the time of René's coup in 1977, there was no Soviet presence in Victoria. Two years later, the Soviet diplomatic presence was the most numerous: more than fifty, including military advisers and KGB personnel. A new block of nineteen flats had been built to accommodate them, on land purchased by the Soviet mission.

THE ISLAND REPUBLIC was again temporarily in the news in November 1981, when a farcically inept attempted coup by some forty mercenaries led by an Irishman, Colonel Michael Hoare (aptly known as "Mad Mike"), was thwarted at the Mahé airport. A customs officer had noticed an AK-47 rifle protruding from a suitcase carried by one of Hoare's team, who were traveling disguised as rugby players and other sportsmen. The mercenaries seized the airport's control tower and forced an Air India Boeing 727 to fly them to Durban, where passengers and crew were released. Seven of the mercenaries were arrested in the Seychelles and brought to trial; the rest were tried in South Africa. Sentences of death and jail were passed in both countries.*

An official White Paper issued by the René government declared, convincingly, that the coup had been planned on South African territory, "with advice and logistical support from the Pretoria regime." On June 3, 1980, sixteen months before the attempt, Mike Hoare had gone to the Seychelles with a forged Irish passport in the name "Boarel": "The letter H had been replaced by the letter B and the letter L had been added to the end of his name."[7]

WITHIN TWENTY-FOUR HOURS of the failed coup, a Soviet guided missile cruiser of the Kana class and a guided missile frigate of the Krivak-2 class, together with a destroyer, anchored at the port of Victoria, in a gesture of support for René's regime, for which the president publicly thanked the Soviet Union. There were similar acts of maritime support at other times of tension, in August 1982 and March 1983.

The little republic voted in support of the Soviet Union in all UN General Assembly votes between 1977 and 1983. On one key occasion, on November 20, 1980, the Seychelles voted in support of the Soviet Union against motions calling for the removal of all foreign troops from Afghanistan.

Apart from doctrinal links, the Seychelles were of clear strategic value to the Soviet Union because of their geographical position on the Persian Gulf oil supertanker route between the Gulf and the Cape of Good Hope. They were specifically valuable for electronic surveillance of the important U.S. naval base on the mini-island of Diego García, 500 miles to the southeast. By late 1984, East Germans, North Koreans, and Libyans had joined the Soviets and Cubans on the islands. The East Germans had set up three radar units to monitor Diego García; a North Korean contingent of sixty soldiers had bolstered René's 120-strong Tanzanian bodyguard;

---

*A member of Colonel Hoare's team, Colonel Jerry Puren, ascribed the failure of the attempted coup "squarely" to Hoare, for two reasons: He should have dropped off arms on the island beforehand, so that his men could "go through customs clean"; and he could even have brought the island under control by pressing home the attack *after* the arms had been uncovered. See Jerry Puren as told to Brian Pottinger in *Mercenary Commander* (South Africa: Galago, 1986, p. 379).

while the Libyans, recently expelled from another Indian Ocean island, Mauritius, were handling weapons deliveries for the Soviet bloc.[8]

On April 17, 1983, President René, in a message of congratulations to Konstantin Chernenko, the new general secretary of the ruling CPSU, expressed his wish for close collaboration between the Seychelles and the USSR and declared that the two countries had common goals.

MORE THAN FOUR years later, on November 8, 1987, the London *Sunday Times,* quoting U.S. intelligence sources, claimed that Soviet troops had secretly established a military base in the Seychelles. Some fifty Soviet naval infantry had landed there in October 1986 from the *Ivan Rogov,* a Soviet amphibious landing ship. The landings followed yet another attempted coup against René the previous month, in which the president's defense minister was sacked and several senior army officers were arrested.

Two years earlier, on November 29, 1985, Gérard C. Hoarau, leader of the anti-René Seychellois National Movement, was assassinated in London, where he had sought refuge. The unknown assassin was never found.* It is not fanciful to assume that René's security staff had suspected, rightly or wrongly, that Hoarau might have been plotting a coup against his island country's left-wing regime.

IN DECEMBER 1991, as the USSR was collapsing, legislation legalizing opposition parties was adopted in the Seychelles. The reins of power, however, remained in President René's hands. Multiparty elections on July 23, 1993, brought René himself and his Seychelles People's Progressive Front a landslide victory.

Although no evidence had emerged at the time of writing that the Soviet Union had actually sponsored or guided France-Albert René's 1977 coup, the later Soviet involvement in the Seychelles justifies its

---

*Hoarau had been a regular visitor to my Regent Street office, and had much impressed me by his intelligence and integrity. As Jerry Puren put it, "The youthful Seychellois had just returned from an early morning visit to his doctor. As he approached his door in London's Edgware district a swarthy man moved from the shadows. . . . He drew a pistol from under his coat and pumped four shots at point blank range into Hoarau. . . . The assassin disappeared—clearly a professional who had carried out a contract killing. . . . The Hoarau family remained convinced the murder had been commissioned by a wealthy Italian businessman, Mafia connected and a close friend of René's, either with René's knowledge or on his instructions." (Pottinger, *Mercenary Commander,* pp. 379–90.)

inclusion here. It could be argued that René's ideological commitment to Marxism-Leninism and his admiration of Fidel Castro amounted to an application to join the peripheral empire, soon granted by Cuba and later by the Soviet Union.

ANOTHER TROUBLED MINI-STATE

THE MOSCOW LINK is more clearly visible in the parallel case of São Tomé e Príncipe.

São Tomé e Príncipe

Yet another mini-state had been, in effect, added to Moscow's peripheral empire when the former Portuguese island colonies of São Tomé and Príncipe (population 80,000) became independent on July 12, 1975. The single party in power was the MLSTP *(Movimento para a Libertação de São Tomé e Príncipe)* founded in exile in 1972, with headquarters in Libreville in the former French colony of Gabon on the west coast of Africa. After the collapse of the Marcello Caetano dictatorship in Portugal in April 1974, a pro-MLSTP Civic Association had been formed in the islands to mobilize the population, discreetly, in support of independence.

The Portuguese government was not opposed to independence, and in November 1974 it set up a provisional government with MLSTP ministers to guide the islands to independence. An ideological conflict followed between a left-wing faction led by Pinto da Costa and a conservative one under Carlos da Graça. Pinto won and da Graça took refuge in Gabon. Another conservative, Miguel Trovoada, also lost out and was driven into exile.

By its own definition, the winning faction of the MSLTP was a "revolutionary front of democratic, anti-colonialist and anti-imperialist forces."[9] According to a well-informed source, the alleged plot by da Graça was phony: a device to enable the MSLTP government (in which he served as health minister) to appeal to Moscow for assistance. It was on Soviet orders that the Angolan forces numbering between 1,000 and 1,500 were sent in, under Soviet and Cuban officers. Once there they stayed on, identifying the two islands as an Angolan (and therefore Soviet) protectorate.[10]

The da Graça government was in fact entirely Communist. Da Graça himself had completed his studies at Pankow, in East Germany. His two closest collaborators took their orders from Moscow. They were Daniel Dayo, whose portfolios combined defense and the interior (a dictatorial combination), and Alda Espírito Santo, minister of information (another pillar of any Leninist government). Espírito Santo, in particular, had been a member of the Portuguese Communist Party, and was arrested in Lisbon as a student, for clandestine activities. In fact, she became the leading agent for the Bolshevization of the new mini-republic.

In classic (Hungarian) style, relatively moderate politicians were gradually evicted, by "salami tactics" (see Chapter 10). One minister, Lionel d'Alva, was sent to East Berlin for "re-education." Another, José Frede, was jailed.

The Stalinist elimination of relative moderates, and indeed the whole takeover of the islands, was clearly facilitated by the "Reds" in the Portuguese Armed Forces Movement, which overthrew the post-Salazar regime in Portugal, and by the consequently enhanced influence of the Portuguese Communist Party in 1975–1976. Another favorable condition for the island coup was of course the MPLA's seizure of the central government of Angola in November 1975. (See Chapter 23.)

CHAPTER THIRTY-SIX

The Chilean Crisis

and Beyond

1970–1982

⸺⸺◆⸺⸺

ON NOVEMBER 3, 1970, the Chilean Socialist leader Salvador Allende was inaugurated as president. In the presidential elections held two months earlier, his Socialist-Communist coalition had won only 36.3 percent of the popular vote, but his closest rival, the former president, Jorge Allesandri of the Nationalist Party, had carried even fewer votes—34 percent. Power was conferred on Allende by a joint session of the congress, by a decisive vote of 153 to 35.

During the next three years, Allende transformed his country, in effect, into a satellite of Cuba, and hence into an incipient addition to the Soviet Empire. By the end of 1972, the membership of the Chilean Communist Party, led by Luis Corvalán, had increased from 150,000 to 200,000. In numbers, it was probably the largest Communist Party in Latin America, including Cuba's.[1] In ideological terms, however, it was less revolutionary than the extreme left faction of the Socialists led by Senator Carlos Altamirano, and still less than the Miristas, so-called from the initials in Spanish: MIR, for *Movimiento de la Izquierda Revolucionaria,* or Movement of the Revolutionary Left.[2]

As their share of the division of spoils after the 1970 election, the Communists were allotted the Ministries of Labor and Finance, while the Ministry of Economics went to Pedro Vuslovic, who worked closely with the Party's Central Committee, although he styled himself an "independent Marxist."

The Communist strategy for Chile, known as "the Santiago model," was aimed at driving the private sector out of business, mainly by reviving a dormant 1933 law that provided for the appointment of an official administrator—styled an *interventor*—to oversee businesses shown to be running at a loss. Workers were encouraged to seize factories after locking the management out. Any such business was declared to be "in recess," whereupon an interventor would be appointed. The new circumstances made this easy, since the Communists controlled not only the Ministry of Labor but about 80 percent of organized labor through the key trade union organization, the *Central Única de Trabajadores*. Simultaneously, President Allende encouraged large-scale seizures of land by militant peasants. Dispossessed farmers organized a resistance movement. The outcome was a confrontational situation that pointed the way to a probable civil war.

Another effective technique was exercised through the finance ministry, which would order firms to grant instant wage increases that were equivalent to the previous year's inflationary rise in the cost-of-living index. By the time Allende was overthrown in September 1973, the yearly rate of inflation had reached 1,000 per cent: a sign of a collapsed economy.

By then, Chile could be truthfully described as a Marxist state in ideological and economic terms. If that had been all, Chile would not necessarily have threatened its neighbors. From a strategic viewpoint, however, it had been turned into a major base for Soviet and Cuban subversive operations, including terrorism, throughout Latin America. In diplomatic terms, the center was the Cuban embassy in Santiago, which expanded rapidly when a new brand of "diplomats" moved in: they belonged either to the Soviet-controlled General Directorate of Intelligence (DGI) or to Fidel Castro's nominally independent Directorate of National Liberation (DLN). Indeed, the DLN consisted of anti-Soviet personnel who had been transferred from the DGI when the Soviets completed their satellization of Cuba.

Soon the Soviet KGB was recruiting Mirista members for training courses in terrorism. In other camps, North Korean specialists were training young members of Allende's Socialist Party, following a visit to the

North Korean capital, Pyongyang, by Senator Altamirano, who had flown there from Havana in a presidential plane provided by the North Korean dictator Kim Il Sung.

Strange as it might seem to outside observers, the Allende presidency *encouraged* a breakdown of law and order by forbidding the security services to use force, dissolving the riot police (known as the *Grupo Móvil*), and releasing the Mirista terrorists who had been jailed under the previous government. To prevent the Miristas from threatening his personal power, Allende went on to transform those he had released into a palace guard to protect the president: himself.

THE ANTI-ALLENDE STRIKE

FROM ITS HEADQUARTERS at Langley, Virginia, on the outskirts of Washington, the CIA did more than merely watch these developments and report on them for the White House. It was also working to bring down the increasingly threatening Allende regime. To this end, one of its main contacts in Santiago organized a massive strike of trucks through the National Confederation of Truck Owners. About 45,000 trucks were immobilized beginning on July 26, 1973. In effect, most of the country's food and fuel distribution ground to a halt. In a broadcast on August 13, President Allende declared that the country was "on the brink of civil war."

On August 20, the defense minister, General Carlos Prats, who was also commander in chief of the Army, resigned after attending a meeting of the Army generals and officers of the Santiago garrison. The meeting had been chaired by Generals Augusto Pinochet and Guillermo Pickering. Allende thereupon appointed General Pinochet as the new commander in chief of the Army. In retrospect it could be said that in so doing Allende was signing his own death warrant.

On September 11, 1973, the armed forces seized power and appointed General Pinochet as Chile's president. A few minutes after 2 P.M. that afternoon, Allende was found dead. In his hand was a machine gun that had been presented to him by Fidel Castro, who declared that Chile's Socialist president had been assassinated. However, on September 17, Allende's widow confirmed that he had committed suicide.

PINOCHET'S SEVENTEEN YEARS

THE LONG REIGN of General Pinochet had begun. It would last seventeen years. One of the most important of its considerable achievements was the privatization of the economy, following the model of the "Chicago school" made famous by Professor Milton Friedman. The outcome was the reduction of inflation from the 1,000 percent it had been under Allende to between 5 and 6 percent. During Pinochet's first years in power, he presided over a ruthless suppression of the revolutionaries who had ruined their country while they were turning it into a base for Communist revolution.

In April 1990, the first post-Pinochet civilian government, under President Patricio Aylwin, appointed a Truth and Reconciliation Commission, chaired by Raúl Rettig, a former Supreme Court judge, to investigate human rights abuses during Pinochet's rule. On March 4, 1991, President Aylwin released the Rettig Report (as it was then known), which documented the death of 2,279 people, including 1,068 who died under torture or were executed, and 957 disappeared prisoners, presumed dead. The latter were known in both Chile and Argentina as *los desaparecidos*. A modified version of the facts claimed that these figures included the fallen on both sides.[3] Around 1,000 had died during the first four months of military rule, when Chile was in effect a combat zone.

In a plebiscite on October 5, 1988, a majority of nearly 55 percent voted against Pinochet's remaining in office after the expiration of his term in 1990. On November 25, 1988, he promised to hand over power to a democratically elected successor and to "depart quietly." He kept his word and resigned when Patricio Aylwin, leader of the Coalition for Democracy, won the presidential elections on December 14, 1989; but he stayed on as commander in chief of the armed forces. In March 1998, he retired as commander in chief and became a designated (that is, unelected) member of the Senate.

NICARAGUA: CASTRO'S SATELLITE

ON JULY 19, 1979, armed units of the *Frente Sandinista de Liberación Nacional* (FSLN, or the Sandinista National Liberation Front) entered

Managua, capital of the Central American republic of Nicaragua. The Sandinistas were manipulated by Fidel Castro's regime, to the ultimate benefit of the Soviet Union.[4] Nicaragua thus became the first lasting example of the "satellite of a satellite."

Two days earlier, on July 17, 1979, President Anastasio Somoza Debayle had resigned and left the country. The departing president was the third in a family dictatorship that had begun in 1936 with the advent to power of his father, Anastasio Somoza García. When the original Somoza was assassinated in 1956, his elder son, Luis Somoza Debayle, took over after a brief interlude. A fatal heart attack removed him in 1967, and his younger brother Anastasio stepped in. Luis had constitutional views of his own, but the younger Anastasio was simply a dictator after his father's model, ruling with an iron hand through the ruthless National Guard.[5] In September 1980, Sandinista agents assassinated the third Somoza in Paraguay, where he had taken refuge after his resignation.

Both regionally and internationally, the dominant public reaction at the time was that the Sandinistas deserved credit and gratitude for ridding their country of a nasty dictatorship. This was true, and deserves to be said. Nevertheless, unsavory though the Somoza dictatorship was, it did not threaten the outside world, whereas the Soviet-Cuban dictatorship that replaced it did.

MOSCOW'S CUBAN STRATEGY

MORE THAN A year after the Sandinista victory, however, the CIA provided President Jimmy Carter with detailed intelligence showing that the final offensive had been planned in minute detail by the Cuban general staff. In overall charge was the Cuban general Zenen Casals, whose previous battle experience had included a spell in Angola. The Cubans had planned to use the Sandinista model for revolutionary risings in Guatemala, El Salvador, and other countries of Central America.*

---

*The evidence was contained in a detailed CIA report dated May 2, 1980, and classified "SECRET: NO FORN DIS" (meaning "No foreign distribution"), which reached me through a senior general in the Pentagon. I passed the document to my then-associate Robert Moss, who used it in his column in the *Daily Telegraph,* London, on August 6, 1980. Significantly, President Jimmy Carter, who was in office at the time, had clearly decided not to make the evidence public.—BC

Moreover, as early as August 1979, a few days after the Sandinista victory, five Soviet generals and vice generals arrived in Managua to advise the Sandinista chief of staff, Joaquín Cuadra. Thereafter, training was in fact carried out in Havana at the Mateos Academy. Although the Soviets supervised it, they were not actually involved in the training. That task was handled by Cuban instructors, with help from Chilean and other Communists.[6]

Until the ousting of Somoza, the Soviet Union did not have diplomatic relations with Nicaragua, but on July 21, 1979, just two days after the Sandinista takeover, the Soviets let it be known that the time for such links had come, although the first Soviet embassy personnel did not arrive until January 1980.[7] Relations between Moscow and Managua were sealed in a more significant manner in March 1980, when the Sandinistas made their first formal (though unpublicized) visit to the Kremlin.[8] Their delegation included the ministers of defense, the interior, and planning, covering the key areas of military cooperation, security, and economic readjustment on the Communist model. Agreements on these issues were signed, plus scientific and cultural pacts. Most important, close links were established between the two ruling parties: the CPSU and the FSLN.

Under the military agreement, the Soviets would provide $125 million between 1980 and 1982 to cover the services of 250 Soviet technical and military personnel, plus fifty T-54/55 tanks, anti-aircraft guns, missiles, and transport aircraft. Appropriately, in view of the key role Cuba had played in the Nicaraguan revolution, Fidel Castro flew to Managua in July 1980 to join the Sandinistas in celebrating the first anniversary of their victory. He went on to a secret gathering of intelligence and security officers in Monimbó.* Among those present was Manuel Piñeiro Losada, Castro's ex-head of the DGI, who had been shunted sideways, at Soviet insistence, to preside over the *Departamento de los Américas* (DA) and aspirant revolutionaries from Mexico, Guatemala, and El Salvador.

*   *   *

---

*As G.W. Sand aptly points out (*Soviet Aims in Central America,* p. 105), having testified on "Terrorism: The Role of Moscow and Its Subcontractors" in *Hearings Before the Subcommittee on Security and Terrorism* of the U.S. Congress, Senate Committee on the Judiciary (97th Congress, 1st session, June 1981). Robert Moss, with Arnaud de Borchgrave, used *Monimbó* as the title of their joint novel (New York: Simon & Schuster, 1983).

LIKE THE TUPAMAROS of Uruguay, the Nicaraguan revolutionaries
had used a hero's name as the name of their movement. Their chosen hero
and icon was General Augusto C. Sandino, who, in the late 1920s and
early 1930s, had led an uprising against the United States' occupation of
Nicaragua. Sandino was neither a Leninist nor a member of Nicaragua's
Communist Party, nor even an "anti-imperialist" in the Communist sense.
He was simply a Nicaraguan patriot who had formed a guerrilla fighting
force, consisting mainly of peasants in his country's northeastern mountains, that he called the Army for the Defense of National Sovereignty.

His goal was precise: the expulsion of the U.S. Marines who had intervened on Nicaraguan soil as early as 1909 and had come back several
times, notably in 1927. Volunteers from other Latin American countries
had joined Sandino's guerrillas, for the United States—in their eyes, and
even objectively—was still wont to intervene on their territories, following the example of the late President Theodore Roosevelt, who had seized
the Panama Canal Zone in 1903.

Eluding capture both by the U.S. Marines and Somoza's thuggish National Guard, Sandino continued to lead his guerrillas until the Marines
pulled out in 1933. Thereupon, he made his peace with the Nicaraguan
government. But not with some members of the National Guard, who resented the government's leniency toward the rebel general and assassinated him the following year. This, of course, gave his heroic image an
additional aura of martyrdom.

The founder of the Nicaraguan Communist Party, Augustín Farabundo Martí, had joined Sandino's staff as his private secretary on instructions from Moscow, which was praising the general as one of their
own. Sandino saw through the maneuver and fired Farabundo Martí in
1930, with the struggle still in progress. Thereupon, the Comintern denounced Sandino's "betrayal."

Farabundo's own life was ended by execution. Before facing the firing
squad, he expressed his Red-tinted disillusion with Sandino, who, he said,
"had raised only the flag of independence, of emancipation, while my aim
was social revolt."[9]

INITIALLY, IN THE early 1960s, Communists had dominated the Sandinista movement, but in the 1970s, the FSLN would evolve into three

ideologically divided groups: a Maoist-Guevarist one known as the *Guerra Popular Prolongada* (GPP), which advocated a peasant war of attrition; a Marxist-Leninist one, *Tendencia Proletaria* (TP, or Proletarian Tendency); and *Los Terceristas* (advocates of a Third Way), the largest of the three, which was (or claimed to be) initially non-Marxist in that it included a wide range of more democratically minded rebels.

The FSLN was founded in 1961 by Carlos Fonseca Amador, who was quick to see that whatever the ideological rift between Sandino and the Marxist-Leninists, the inspirational image of the great patriot of the 1920s was more likely than that of Lenin—or still less, Stalin—to rally guerrilla volunteers. Initially, however, the movement called itself simply the National Liberation Front (FLN; the Sandinista initial was added later). Another founder-member, Sergio Ramírez, revived interest in Sandino's writings by editing an anthology under the title of *El Pensamiento Vivo de Sandino (The Living Thought of Sandino).*[10] Fonseca and another cofounder, Tomás Borge, immersed themselves in Marxist texts while living in Guatemala during the short-lived dictatorship of the leftist President Jácobo Arbenz (see Chapter 21) in the early 1950s. They went on to organize a Communist group among university students in the Nicaraguan city of Granada.[11]

Fonseca later attended the Sixth World Youth Festival in Moscow in 1957, and stayed on in the Soviet Union for four months, while in Managua his ideological partner Borge was jailed. Later, Borge and two other early converts, the brothers Humberto and Daniel Ortega, received military training in Cuba.

Two key events deserve attention. One was a natural disaster, the other a spectacular guerrilla operation. By coincidence, both happened at Christmas time: the first in 1972, the second on December 27, 1974. In the earthquake of 1972, 10,000 lives were lost, with Managua reduced to ruins and a humanitarian shambles. Relief funds poured in, notably from the UN, but were shamelessly misappropriated by Somoza and his clique of supporters. More than any earlier phase, this "earthquake corruption" alienated the population, to the benefit of the Sandinistas.

In a brilliantly successful coup in December 1974, the rebels seized thirty hostages—all government functionaries—at a diplomatic party in the American embassy. Earlier that year, the Sandinistas had been out of the news; now, they made the biggest headlines.

In exchange for the hostages, they obtained the release of the FSLN prisoners, including Daniel Ortega, plus a $1 million ransom and the chance to broadcast their revolutionary message to the wider Nicaraguan public.

In response, Somoza imposed martial law in 1975–1976 and launched a ruthless repression that brought death to Fonseca and jail to Borge. The Sandinista response was victory for the Terceristas, who, by then, were the most Leninist of the Sandinista groups. They took control of the FSLN's Directorate, under a new platform, mainly drafted by Humberto Ortega.

There was one more Sandinista "spectacular." On August 22, 1978, a group of only twenty-five Sandinistas seized the National Palace in Managua, taking 2,000 hostages, before releasing them on receipt of $500,000 as ransom money, plus the freeing of all FSLN prisoners including Borge, and a further helping of access to the media.

The palace coup had been planned by Edén Pastora, better known to the populace as "*Comandante Cero*" (Major Zero: a reference to Carlos Fonseca's essay, "Nicaragua Zero Hour"). In the first Sandinista government, under the new president, Daniel Ortega, Pastora was vice minister of the interior, responsible for overseeing the Sandinista People's Militias. He was never a true Communist, however, and he would resign without fuss or publicity in June 1981, vanish, and turn up in San José, Costa Rica, on April 15, 1982.[12]

Thus, when the Sandinista rebellion gained momentum in early 1979, it had apparently solid claims to be a broad national insurgency. By then, with Cuban, and to a lesser degree, Soviet support, the FSLN's membership had grown from about 500 to more than 5,000 and the Somoza regime's unpopularity had been rising fast.

It became clear soon after the Sandinista victory in 1979 that Nicaragua had been turned into a regional base for Communist guerrilla or terrorist groups in neighboring countries, notably Guatemala and El Salvador. The Sandinistas' forces were enlarged and reorganized, and within a year, had expanded into three sections: the main *Ejército Sandinista del Pueblo* (Sandinista People's Army), the militia, and the reserve battalions headed by Cuban advisers. The People's Army was equipped with new Soviet AK assault rifles, the older weapons having been passed to the militia and the reserve battalions.

GUATEMALA AND EL SALVADOR

UNLIKE NICARAGUA, THE Soviet-directed pressures exerted through Cuba and Nicaragua on both Guatemala and El Salvador failed to bring either country into the Soviet peripheral empire. In Guatemala, this failure was due in part to the repressive excesses of the retired General Efraén Réos Montt, who had been handed power by a junta of younger officers who carried out a military coup on March 23, 1982. Montt, a fundamentalist Protestant convert in a Catholic country, was denounced by Pope John Paul II during the Pope's visit to Guatemala in 1984. However, his offer to negotiate with the leftist guerrillas was turned down.[13]

On the rebel side, the most active group was *Ejército Guerrillero de los Pobres* (EGT, or Guerrilla Army of the Poor). Other rebel groups included: the *Fuerzas Armadas Revolucionarias* (FAR, or Armed Revolutionary Forces), the armed organ of the Communist Party (*Partido Guatemalteco del Trabajo* or PGT: Guatemalan Labor Party), which had been banned in 1954 after the overthrow of the leftist President Jácobo Arbenz and on a smaller scale, the *Fuerzas Armadas Rebeldes* (also FAR, or Rebel Armed Forces: a confusing identity of acronyms).[14]

IN EL SALVADOR in the early 1980s there was a multiplicity of guerrilla or terrorist bands: at least thirteen could be listed. Five of them were controlled under an umbrella organization that called itself the *Frente Farabundo Martí de Liberación Nacional* (named after the Communist peasant leader who lost his life in an attempted coup in El Salvador in 1932; usually simplified to FMLN). The FMLN, in turn, controlled five political groups under another umbrella: the *Coordinadoria Revolucionaria de las Masas,* or CRM (Revolutionary Coordinate of the Masses). In all these groups, the leader was secretary-general of the Communist Party, Shafik Jorge Handal, of Palestinian origin.[15]

CENTRAL AND SOUTH AMERICA

IN 1983, GUERRILLA organizations from Colombia, Venezuela, Ecuador, Peru, El Salvador, and Guatemala combined their forces for operations in Central and South America. It seemed clear, from the ideological approach of the individual organizations, that Cuba's Moscow-controlled DGI was behind the combined effort.

The first sign of a unified guerrilla force came on September 17, 1983, when a Venezuelan Army outpost named Cutufi, near the Colombian border, was raided by 100 guerrillas. One soldier was killed and the rest of the army unit disarmed.

The Soviet Union stayed publicly aloof during this phase of militancy. A visit to Moscow by Daniel Ortega in June 1983, reportedly in search of further supplies of arms from the USSR, ended without a Soviet response other than a general statement of support by the then-general secretary, Konstantin Chernenko. True, Soviet Bloc arms deliveries to Nicaragua since the revolution had already been considerable.

A U.S. State Department assessment in June 1984 declared that the number of tanks and armored personnel carriers possessed by the Sandinista forces had doubled during the first half of the year by means of two large deliveries by Bulgarian vessels. These deliveries brought the total of Soviet arms in Nicaragua to 100 Soviet T-54 and T-55 tanks and 120 other armored vehicles. In addition, Soviet supplies were reported to have included twenty Pt-76 light amphibious tanks, more than fifty 52-mm and 122-mm howitzers, twenty-four multiple rocket launchers, around 120 anti-aircraft guns, and about 700 SAM-7 ground-to-air missiles. Large numbers of military transport vehicles had also been supplied (1,000 from East Germany alone since 1980), and the Soviet Union had also delivered at least six heavy ferries, potentially a major contribution to the mobility of Nicaragua's armored forces. Indeed, and although the primary purpose of these arms may well have been defensive, their arrival had caused a potentially disturbing change in the regional balance of power.

CHAPTER THIRTY-SEVEN

THE POLISH TURNING POINT

1980–1982

The idea that small events may have large consequences is not new, but the Polish crisis that began in 1980 does provide a dramatic example of it. In July and August 1980, a rise of 60 percent in the price of popular cuts of meat as a result of new government measures to overhaul retail distribution intensified labor unrest, and this in turn led to the formation of a rebel trade union group that attracted a mass membership. Faced with the resulting crisis of political authority, the Soviet Union contemplated military intervention, either directly or by East Germany, but lost the nerve it had shown in previous satellite crises in 1956 and 1968. Instead it put in charge in Poland a military dictator who, under Soviet pressure, proclaimed martial law. It was a loss of nerve that would foreshadow the great imperial collapse of 1989–1991.

At stake was the authority of the ruling Polish United Workers' Party (PUWP); in the 1956 crisis the threat of a Soviet military intervention was enough to bring the PUWP to heel under the Moscow-line leader Wladyslav Gomulka (see Chapter 18). In the crisis of the 1980s, the imperial power (still under the weakening Leonid Brezhnev) would undermine the Brezhnev Doctrine of readiness to intervene in force if any "Socialist" government's authority was challenged.

Although the labor strikes were stimulated by higher prices and low wages, they soon became political in character. Calls for the independence of trade unions from Party control were the new element, which was

intolerable to the absolutist PUWP. Moreover, the strikers were also calling for a free uncensored press, for the release of jailed dissidents, and for
the strengthening of the Roman Catholic Church, which had been increasingly loud in its criticism of the ruling party's security policies.

In previous industrial crises in Poland, in 1970 and 1976, demonstrations had become violent. Not this time: the striking workers were impressively self-disciplined. Stoppages nearly paralyzed Gdansk and Szeczin
(better known as Danzig and Stettin), both of which had militant pasts.
But the paralysis spread to the relatively peaceful coal, copper, and sulfur
mining areas in and around the southwestern area of Silesia. At the height
of the 1980 summer, the Party secretary Edward Gierek, the most powerful man in Poland, felt obliged to resign. He was succeeded on September 6 by the head of Polish Secret Intelligence, Stanislaw Kania. The prime
minister, Edward Babiuch, also resigned in September after a troubled
reign of only seven months: he had taken over from Piotr Jaroszewicz in
February. The new premier was Jozef Pinkowski—who would prove to be
an ineffectual choice.

For the first time, the wider world became aware of a name that had
briefly been in the headlines in 1970: Lech Walesa. In the earlier demonstrations he had lost his job as an electrician in the Gdansk shipyards. On
January 25, 1980, he was voted a member of a workers' committee that
was set up to agitate for the reinstatement of twenty-five workers, himself
among them. A small, stockily built man with a big mustache, Walesa was
a fervent Catholic, as indeed were many of his fellow Poles. In an interview with a well-known Italian journalist, Oriana Fallaci, he made a sar-
donic comparison between Communist propaganda and Catholic faith:

> If you choose the example of what we Poles have in our pockets and
> in our shops, then . . . communism has done very little for us. But if
> you choose the example of what is in our souls, I answer that com-
> munism has done very much for us.
>
> In fact our souls contain exactly the opposite of what they
> wanted. They wanted us not to believe in God, and our churches are
> full. They wanted us to be materialistic and incapable of sacrifice.
> They wanted us to be afraid of the tanks, of the guns, and instead we
> don't fear them at all.[1]

At a meeting on May 7 and 8, Roman Catholic bishops condemned "the recent intensification of repressive measures" by the Polish authorities.

It was at the height of the labor troubles, in July and August 1980, that meat prices soared by 60 percent as a result of new government measures to overhaul retail distribution. A new wave of strikes followed, at the Usus tractor factory near Warsaw, at the Polmo car components factory at Tczew (south of Gdansk), and at a paint and chemical plant at Wloclawek (northwest of Warsaw). A television statement by Party Secretary Gierek on July 9, promising raises for the lowest paid workers but ruling out any more widespread increases on economic grounds, was seen as a provocation, and the strikes continued to spread.

In September, many new and independent trade unions were formed and were soon vocal. On September 17, Lech Walesa presided over a national conference of the new unions, which took the name "National Committee of Solidarity" (*Solidarnosc* in Polish). On October 3, Solidarity called a one-hour token strike to protest the failure of the authorities to implement agreed-upon wage increases.

A few days earlier, an ominous article had appeared in Moscow's *Pravda,* the organ of the ruling CPSU. Not surprisingly, the article appealed to the highest ideological authority of all: Lenin, it said, had insisted on Communist Party control of all trade unions. The implication was clear: The Polish authorities had departed from Lenin's teaching by tolerating the new and independent unions that had sprung up in Poland.

Pravda then carried a more explicitly threatening editorial underlining Poland's defense and political links with the other Warsaw Pact countries. The article was picked up in full by the Czechoslovak and East German Party newspapers *Rude Pravo* and *Neues Deutschland.*

Clearly the Polish crisis was drifting into the international domain, threatening by implication a military intervention by the Soviet Union and its satellite comembers of the Warsaw Pact. There was no reaction from NATO as such, but *sotto voce* semi-warnings started coming from the United States. The State Department let it be known that it was monitoring "very closely" all military activities in the Soviet and East German areas near the Polish frontiers. On September 11, a State Department spokesman declared that Soviet officials had been told, twice, that "restraint was necessary by all outside parties." Ten days later, President

Jimmy Carter addressed a conference of the (U.S.) Polish National Alliance and declared that the United States expected other countries to allow Poland to solve its own problems without intervention.

The Soviet Union was not going to yield before mild White House "warnings" from a weak American president who, as the Democratic candidate, was unlikely to win the impending U.S. presidential election. Indeed the November poll brought a landslide victory to the Republican candidate, Ronald Reagan.

A few days earlier, on October 31, 1980, Brezhnev had reported to the Politburo on a visit to Moscow by Kania, the new first secretary of the Polish United Workers' Party, and Pinkowski, the new prime minister. It was already clear that events in Poland were taking a turn for the worse, and he complained of "indecisiveness" on the part of the two Polish leaders. (See Appendix M: Document 1.)

As an element in the imperial collapse, the Polish turning point would be only marginally less important than the foredoomed invasion of Afghanistan (see Chapter 40). The "Restricted" newsletter *Transnational Security,* dated December 1980–January 1981 (of which this author was the editor and publisher), offered these comments:

The true significance of the Polish events lies in these points:

- The emergence of an independent trade union organization, if tolerated and allowed to function over a long term, would constitute an inadmissible challenge to the Leninist basis of all Soviet-controlled States, including the USSR itself. It would (and may yet be) *the beginning of the end of the Soviet empire.*

- Lech Walesa's Solidarity organisation must therefore be sabotaged by legalistic and security police harassment, regardless of any agreements reached with the Polish party bureaucracy. This job has been entrusted to Kania as the new party boss, and the reason for his appointment to succeed Gierek in his previous post as head of the Polish secret intelligence organisation.

- If Kania fails, the Soviets will have no option but to intervene militarily, as they did in Hungary in 1956, in Czechoslovakia in 1968 and in Afghanistan at the end of 1979.

In the final event, the Soviet Union refrained from a military intervention. In February 1981, the Polish defense minister, General Wojciech Jaruzelski, replaced the inadequate Jozef Pinkowski as prime minister. Jaruzelski had been, in the full Communist sense, a *political* general. He had risen to the key position of head of the Central Political Department of the armed forces. In other words, he was Moscow's man in Warsaw, for the Polish contingents of the Warsaw Pact were of course based in Warsaw itself, under the command of the Soviet Marshal Victor H. Kulikov.

In March, shortly after Jaruzelski's appointment, secret intelligence reached the London headquarters of the private sector operational agency known as "The 61" to the effect that during the night of March 28–29 a state of emergency would be proclaimed in Poland, and units of the East German *Volksarmee* would cross the border.[2] This vital intelligence was immediately passed on to the White House, 10 Downing Street in London, the Elysée Palace in Paris, and the Vatican (the latter because of the crucial role of the Polish-born Pope John Paul II).

Although there is no evidence of American plans to intervene militarily, should the Soviet Union or any of the Warsaw Pact forces actually invade Poland, President Reagan records in his memoirs that he warned Brezhnev several times that any Soviet military intervention "would be resisted by us through every diplomatic means at our disposal"; there would be no further nuclear arms agreements or better trade relations; and he was to expect "the harshest possible economic sanctions from the United States if they launched an invasion."[3]

From reports reaching The 61, the decisive moment of the Polish crisis came that month (March 1981), when both Prime Minister Jaruzelski and the Party's first secretary Kania had been genuinely exploring with Lech Walesa the possibility of settling Poland's labor problems by common consent. There followed the beating of Solidarity members by the police at Bydgoszcz (Bromberg) on March 19: an event clearly designed to provoke the workers into reckless reactions to discredit both Kania and Jaruzelski. There are grounds for reports that neither Kania nor Jaruzelski was briefed in advance on the police violence at Bydgoszcz; this supports the probability that the action was an independent provocation organized by the KGB.

There was strong evidence that high officials of the secret services were involved, with the support of "foreign friends" who took advantage of the absence from a meeting of the Politburo of both Jaruzelski and Kania. Jaruzelski was on an inspection tour of the Warsaw Pact military maneuvers, while Kania was in Hungary for a meeting with his opposite number János Kádár. Moreover, at that time talks were in progress between Walesa and one of Jaruzelski's new vice premiers, Mieczyslaw Rakowski, editor of the weekly journal *Polityka* and a Party member. The talks soon broke down after angry exchanges between the two men. While Walesa was doing his best to damp down attempts to stir up the trade union delegates (clearly penetrated by hostile agents), the Politburo was taken aback by unexpected remonstrations from the Party's rank and file against the "infamous events" at Bydgoszcz. At this troubled time, the Roman Catholic primate of Poland, Cardinal Stefan Wyszinski, was allowed on March 20 to make a radio broadcast in which he warned the authorities not to tolerate "irresponsible actions by the security forces," but went on to stress the need for moderation on all sides. Later that day he had talks with Jaruzelski.*

In Moscow, however, a decision had been made to extend the Warsaw Pact exercise known as Soyuz 81 and launch the final phase ("Counter blow/Destroy the enemy"). In the early hours of that same day—March 20, 1981—KGB units at regimental strength were assigned to the maneuvers; and KGB General Bogdanov, with his staff, left Moscow for East Berlin and then to Prague and Warsaw.

Some days later the East German Politburo took formal cognizance of the "faulty assessment" of the East German intelligence service on the state of mind of the Polish armed forces and military police. A formal rebuke to the head of the MfS (*Ministerium für Staatssicherheit,* or Ministry for State Security), General Erich Mielke, was upheld by the Politburo.

Shortly afterward, on March 30, 1981, Ronald Reagan was shot and seriously wounded in a flawed attempt on his life. As soon as he was out of the hospital, on April 11, he sent chilly letters to Brezhnev, who, however, refused to abandon the "Brezhnev Doctrine," enshrining in his eyes the right of the Soviet Union to intervene militarily in any "Socialist" country that was under threat (although he did not actually use the term "Brezhnev doctrine").

---

*Cardinal Wyszinski died shortly afterward, of cancer, on May 28, 1981. He was seventy-nine.

Two days earlier the Soviet Politburo had held an important meeting, the main point of which was a depressingly detailed report on the Polish crisis by Yuri Andropov, head of the KGB. With the defense minister Dmitri Ustinov, he had held a secret meeting with the top Polish leaders, Jaruzelski and the Party's first secretary Stanislaw Kania. In the interests of secrecy the four men had met in a railway carriage near Brest. The meeting had begun at 9 P.M. and went on until 3 A.M. The two Poles had seemed "very tense," and "it was obvious that they were near the end of their tether." The two Soviet participants told them they should have proclaimed martial law long ago. Kania had painted a dismal picture of the situation, and it was clear to their visitors that he and Jaruzelski were at odds. Ustinov confirmed Andropov's impressions and added that they had tried hard to dispel Polish objections to martial law. (For the full text of the Andropov and Ustinov reports, see Appendix M: Document 2.)

At about the same time as the attempt on President Reagan's life, The 61 was receiving startling and important reports from the controversial anti-Soviet Russian nationalist organization, the NTS (*Narodno-Trudovoy Soyuz Rossiyshikh Solidaristov,* or Popular Labor Alliance of Russian Solidarists), based in Frankfurt.* In its issue of May 1981, the bulletin *Transnational Security* returned to the earlier theme in these words: "There is little disposition in Western establishments to consider contingency planning for the greatest contingency of all: *the collapse of the Soviet system.*"

The NTS reports listed the following points:

- A steady decline of the Soviet economy, through mismanagement and prohibitive military expenditure;
- Unacknowledged food rationing spreading rapidly;
- Increasing ethnic tensions;
- Fast-growing Russian religious and patriotic revival;

---

*The NTS was regarded as suspect by British Intelligence (SIS or MI-6), partly because of the role played by the Soviet General Andrei Vlasov, an NTS man, captured by the Nazis in 1942, who later commanded units of former Russian prisoners of war. Handed over to Stalin by the Americans, he was executed. However, Vlasov was anti-Soviet, not pro-Nazi. There was a further element when anti-Soviet operations involving the British traitor Harold Philby went wrong. The SIS blamed the NTS, and the NTS blamed Philby. In a speech on the fiftieth anniversary of the Soviet secret police on December 22, 1967, Yuri Andropov named the NTS as "enemy number one."—BC

- Mounting human, political, and economic cost of the war in Afghanistan;
- Example of Polish workers potentially a powerful stimulus for labor unrest;
- Consumer dissatisfaction feeds increasing anxiety over the future of the USSR;
- Widespread fear of war with China;
- Foreign travel, the most valued privilege of the ruling Nomenklatura, becoming drastically reduced;
- The hesitancy and apparent helplessness of the West in the face of continued Soviet aggression. Examples of Western passivity quoted: the uprising of Berlin workers in 1953; over Hungary, Czechoslovakia, and Afghanistan; inaction or inadequate response over surrogate takeovers of Vietnam, Laos, Cambodia, Angola, Ethiopia, Cuba, and others parts of Latin America.

Of particular relevance in 1980 and 1981 was the cynically frank attitude of Soviet delegates to various conferences in the West, especially in Germany in informal talks with interpreters, most of whom were members of the NTS. The points stressed in such talks were the shortcomings of the system, the unchallenged power of the KGB, and the prevailing confidence that the West, whether at government or business level, would always be ready to help the Soviet Union to survive. In a word: appeasement.[4]

On September 10, 1981, the Soviet Politburo had a further debate on the Polish crisis. Brezhnev, who chaired the session, referred to an "Appeal to the Peoples of Eastern Europe" adopted by Solidarity, which he described as "a dangerous and provocative document." He suggested that the collectives of major Soviet enterprises, such as the Kirov factory in Leningrad, should issue letters to rebuff "these demagogues." (See Appendix M: Document 3.)

A week later Brezhnev reported to the Politburo on the reactions of East European leaders (Erich Honecker of East Germany, János Kádár of Hungary, Todor Zhivkov of Bulgaria, and Gustav Husák of Czechoslovakia) on the Politburo's view that Kania was "exhibiting inadmissible liberalism." (See Appendix M: Document 4.)

Not surprisingly, all agreed with the Soviet view, and in October 1981, in the wake of mass Solidarity rallies, Kania was removed as

Party secretary, and his job was taken over by General Jaruzelski, who briefly retained his post as prime minister. In Moscow, Andropov scored a remarkable disinformation success when Western correspondents were told that Jaruzelski was a kind of Polish *caudillo* (a military dictator on the model of General Francisco Franco of Spain) who had to take over because the Party had lost control. A number of the correspondents fell for this absurd ploy, which was still being peddled years after the event.[5]

The view that the so-called coup was a Soviet deception was later confirmed by Oleg Gordievsky in these words: "The KGB's candidate to lead the coup was General Wojciech Jaruzelski."[6]

Interesting insights on the great Polish crisis are in David Pryce-Jones's book, *The War That Never Was,* in part from a long conversation he had with Jaruzelski some years later.[7] In 1980 and 1981, the general had been summoned three times to the Soviet Union. He had been given an ultimatum: Either the internal situation had to be brought under control by the beginning of 1982 or they would cut off supplies of oil, gas and other raw materials.

The wave of strikes continued in Poland. By October, the membership of Solidarity had grown to the spectacular total of 9,500,000. The organization held two national rallies, both in Gdansk: one from September 5 to 10 and the second from September 26 to October 7. Meanwhile, there had been a considerable buildup in the number of Polish-speaking KGB officers not only to the Warsaw *Rezidentsiya* but also to the Soviet consulates in Gdansk, Cracow, Poznan, and Szeczin.[8] At the end of 1981, it became known that mass arrests of Solidarity members had been made from lists compiled under KGB direction.

On October 29, the Soviet Politburo heard a report from their colleague K. V. Rusakov about his journey to East Germany, Czechoslovakia, Hungary, and Bulgaria, to sound out, once again, their respective views on the best course to adopt regarding the Polish crisis. (See Appendix M: Document 5.)

At a further meeting of the Politburo on November 21, Brezhnev revealed that he had instructed the Soviet ambassador in Warsaw (Averkii Aristov) to visit Jaruzelski and "convey to him [an] oral communication from Comrade L. I. Brezhnev." The communication was in fact on paper but met the "oral" qualification when Aristov read it out to Jaruzelski.

Although by that time the Soviet leaders were deeply disappointed in Jaruzelski, the message was couched in polite and even friendly terms. Responding to a proposal from the Polish leader that he should visit Moscow with a Party and state delegation, Brezhnev agreed and suggested that the visit should take place on December 14–15 "if, of course, this is convenient to you." (See Appendix M: Document 6.)

The tone of the "oral" message remained friendly and courteous even though Brezhnev went on to suggest tougher attitudes and measures. How deep Soviet dissatisfaction was is evident not only from the documents quoted earlier but also from a verbatim account of a special session of the Soviet Politburo on December 10. Moreover, whatever Jaruzelski may have hoped, and the West have feared, the Soviet leaders had firmly decided against any direct military intervention in Poland.

The Politburo had sent a senior Party man, Nikolai Baybakov, and Marshal Victor Kulikov, commander in chief of the Warsaw Pact forces, to the Polish capital to discuss the situation with Jaruzelski. The special session had been called, in part, to listen to Baybakov's report on the crisis. After dealing with Polish expectations of economic assistance (including 30,000 tons of meat), he went on to say that Jaruzelski was "highly distressed" while the Party organizations had "collapsed and are not functioning." (See Appendix M: Document 7.)

Nor was this the only criticism of Jaruzelski during this meeting. K. V. Rusakov quoted Jaruzelski as referring to a speech by Kulikov in which he had "supposedly" said that the armed forces of the USSR and allied states would be forthcoming; whereas in fact Kulikov had simply repeated some words of Brezhnev to the effect that "we would not leave the Polish People's Republic in the lurch." In the final event, the Jaruzelski government did proclaim martial law (as ordered by the Soviet leadership) on the night of December 12–13, after Solidarity had called for a national referendum challenging the authority of the government. On the following night the armed forces arrested Walesa and nearly all coleaders of Solidarity. A new "Military Council for National Salvation" banned all political activity by the trade unions.

The already tense situation worsened, and Western intelligence agencies carried fresh reports of Soviet invasion plans. On December 13, a Sunday, the Polish military government closed all borders, halted communications with the outside world, arrested the leaders of Solidarity, and imposed martial law. As President Reagan put it, "The crackdown fell short of the military intervention we had warned against, but our intelligence experts established that the entire exercise had been ordered from and orchestrated by Moscow."[9]

At the White House press conference on December 23, President Reagan revealed that the proclamation of martial law had been *drafted and printed in Moscow* as long ago as the previous September.[10] He went on to order a (temporary) halt in American shipments of grain to Poland and to impose restrictions on Polish shipping in U.S. waters. He also banned exports of computers to the Soviet Union.

The relative firmness of the U.S. response (which, however, stopped short of any threat of military intervention) was not matched on the European side of the Alliance. In an interview on BBC Radio 4 on December 21, 1981, the British Foreign Secretary Lord Carrington played down the Soviet role and said that there was no hurry for action. In Paris, President François Mitterrand's government issued strong statements but took no action. His minister for external relations, Claude Cheysson, took a strong line in public, but France went on to sign a twenty-five-year contract for the purchase of 8 billion cubic meters of Soviet gas a year. In Germany, the Social Democrat chancellor Helmut Schmidt chose the moment of Poland's agony to go to East Berlin to meet the Communist leader Erich Honecker. On December 27, the appeasement-minded West German foreign minister Hans-Dietrich Genscher publicly opposed American sanctions and declared that neither the West nor the East should intervene. "The East," in fact, was actively intervening.

In early January 1982, the British prime minister Margaret Thatcher complained of a report from the Joint Intelligence Committee concluding that there was no hard evidence of Soviet involvement in the Polish crisis. A further report was issued within forty-eight hours emphasizing the reality of Soviet intervention.[11]

Doubtless as a result of the pressure from Mrs. Thatcher, Lord Carrington changed his line, and on January 19, 1982, addressing the House of Lords, he declared that there was no doubt about the extent to which Russia was "directly and indirectly involved in Poland's military clampdown." He called for strong and concerted economic measures against the USSR. Schmidt and Genscher also reversed their previous exoneration of the Soviet Union.

Because of the worsening situation, Jaruzelski was unable to visit Moscow on December 14–15, 1981, as Brezhnev had suggested. Nor indeed was he able to join other Warsaw Pact leaders on December 18 for the celebration of Brezhnev's birthday. He did go to Moscow, but not until March 1–2, 1982, by which time the Polish leader had restored a semblance of order by adopting Moscow's tough-line proposals. At a dinner in honor of the Polish delegation, Brezhnev voiced his approval in these words:

> We received with full understanding the news of the national decision taken by our Polish friends to defend the people's power and cool passions, and to pull the country out of a protracted and excruciating crisis. These were timely measures. Had the Communists given way to counter-revolution, had they wavered under the furious attacks by the enemies of socialism, the destiny of Poland and the stability of Europe and even of the world at large would have been at risk.

The repression went on for several more years. As David Pryce-Jones put it, "In his determination to keep Poland subjected to the Soviet Union, Jaruzelski slipped across the tenuous line dividing collaboration from outright betrayal. Thirteen thousand army officers were purged from the party. Dissolved and banned, Solidarity could no longer operate."[12]

For nearly a year, Walesa was detained at a remote hunting lodge in eastern Poland. He was released on November 12, 1982, and allowed to return to Gdansk. But the political persecution continued. By March 1982, 6,905 people had been interned; 732,042 cases had been heard by summary procedures; of these 196,595 involved violations of martial law. As with other cases of state repression in the Communist world, the leaders were not necessarily spared. Among those interned at the end of 1982 was Edward Gierek, the former first secretary of the ruling PUWP, for "abuse of power" while in office.

One particularly sordid case of (semi-official) repression was the brutal murder of Father Jerzy Popieluszko, a Catholic activist for Solidarity noted for his outspoken vocal attacks on the regime. Kidnapped on October 19, 1984, his body was found in a reservoir on the river Vistula. He had been bound, beaten, and strangled. His funeral mass at the church of

St. Stanislaw Kostka in Wroclaw attracted a crowd of around 50,000. To be fair to the Jaruzelski regime, the murder appears not to have been officially ordered. Four members of the security services were tried for it and were sentenced on February 7, 1985, to between fourteen and twenty-five years in jail. Unauthorized repression, even by state employees, was clearly not approved.

CHAPTER THIRTY-EIGHT

GRENADA: THE FIRST
STRATEGIC DEFEAT

1983

———————

IT HAPPENED ON October 25, 1983, when a U.S. force of 1,900 men
landed on the small Caribbean island of Grenada. Fifteen hundred of
them were members of the 82nd Airborne Division and four hundred
were Marines. With the Americans came a 500-strong contingent of police and troops from neighboring Caribbean islands: Jamaica and Barbados, Dominica and Antigua, St. Lucia, St. Vincent, and the Grenadines. A
further contingent of 300 troops from the same islands landed on
Grenada shortly afterward. Two of the smaller islands—Montserrat and
St. Kitts-Nevis—had opted out of the operation, which the Americans
had called "Urgent Fury."

Four days before the landing, the U.S. naval task force, which was on
its way to Lebanon, had been diverted to the Caribbean. It included the
aircraft carrier *Independence* and the assault ship *Guam*. The invasion was
not a walkover. The U.S. forces ran into determined resistance from the
1,500-strong Grenadian "People's Revolutionary Army" and from exactly
784 Cubans, forty of whom were military advisers, the rest construction
workers who had been building an airport for military purposes.

Fighting in the capital St. George's ended on October 27, but went on
elsewhere for a few more days. The stated pretext of the U.S. landing was
to rescue 603 American medical students. This was indeed one of the reasons for the landing, but the real reason was spelled out by President
Ronald Reagan, who said on October 29 that Grenada, far from being an

"island paradise," was in fact "a Soviet-Cuban colony being readied for use as a major military bastion to export terror." He added, "We arrived just in time."

In strategic terms, however, the real significance of the successful operation far exceeded its scale and the stated objectives: *For the first time since the Bolshevik revolution, a Communist government in a sovereign state had been removed by an outside power's military force.* To point this out is not to claim that until then Soviet expansionism had never suffered any reverses, but the earlier ones had been tactical, not strategic. After World War II, Stalin had ordered the Iranian Tudeh ("Masses") Party to set up the "Autonomous Republic of Azerbaijan" under the protection of the Red Army. In January 1946, however, under public pressure from President Truman of the United States, he had withdrawn his forces. (See Chapter 7.)

Another example occurred in Austria when Stalin's successors, Nikolai Bulganin and Nikita Khrushchev, decided in May 1955 to withdraw their forces from Austria (see Chapter 19). They had reached this decision without pressure from the West, partly as a prelude to their decision to set up the military alliance known as the Warsaw Pact, designed to counter NATO.

The loss of Grenada demonstrated for the first time that the spread of Soviet-style Communism to all countries of the world, as envisaged by Lenin (and indeed enshrined in the 1977 Soviet Constitution), was not after all fatally inevitable.

THE STORY BEGAN as late as March 11, 1979, when the Grenada United Labor Party (GULP) government of Sir Eric Gairey was overthrown in an almost bloodless coup by Maurice Bishop, whose instrument for power was his party: the New Jewel Movement. Until then, Grenada, a mere twenty-one miles long and twelve miles wide, was just one among the island mini-states of the Caribbean and a member of the (British) Commonwealth. Most of its 108,000 inhabitants were black; there was a small number of Indians and whites. Bishop was a bearded black lawyer, thirty-six years old, when he seized power. He lost no time in setting up a seven-member cabinet and proclaiming the People's Revolutionary Government (PRG) with himself as premier.[1]

Was Bishop a Communist? Not in a formal sense, but his New Jewel Movement, founded in 1972, became indistinguishable from a Communist

Party from the moment he seized power seven years later. His deputy prime minister Bernard Coard appears to have been at least as committed as he was to seeking formal links with the Soviet Union and Cuba.

At the end of August 1979, Grenada was officially admitted to the Non-Aligned Movement (which had been formally launched at the Bandung conference in 1955). In October and November, a total of more than fifty arrests were made on charges of plotting two coups. (Neither coup materialized.) Supporters of Sir Eric Gairey were blamed for the plotting, and on November 3 "great amounts" of arms and ammunition were seized from the plotters. In the aftermath of the October plot, the *Torchlight,* a conservative newspaper, was closed down by the Bishop government.

The next installment of the suppression of the former regime came in December 1979, when eight members of the Gairey government's former police, labeled the "mongoose gang," were sentenced to terms of twelve to sixteen years on charges of attempted murder. Although thirty-five detainees were released over the next few months, three more arrests were made on May 1, 1980, in the suppression of an alleged plot by members of the government's own People's Revolutionary Army (PRA) to seize a military camp and stage a coup. Fifteen other members of the PRA were suspended. All were described as "ultra-leftists" who were aiming to set up "an unworkable Socialist state," which implied either that Maurice Bishop's PRG was less leftist than had been thought or that they merely belonged to a rival clique. Allegations were made that the plotters were involved in drug running and had links with North American crime syndicates.

In Moscow that same month, a treaty was signed with the Soviet Union giving landing rights for long-range reconnaissance aircraft at the new airport recently built at Point Salines. The signatory was not Maurice Bishop but his deputy and incipient rival Bernard Coard. Satellization had begun.

As a former colony and member of the Commonwealth, Grenada still had a governor-general, as indeed had more imposing Commonwealth states such as Australia. In June 1980, the holder of that exalted office, Sir Paul Scoon, narrowly escaped assassination when a time bomb exploded at a reception in his residence. Was the bomb intended for him? More likely targets were Maurice Bishop and possibly the Cuban ambassador, both of whom were present. Bishop described the bombing as "a monstrous crime committed by imperialists." The unspoken question was, "Which imperialists?" The old colonialists? Or those American "new imperialists"? On New Year's Day 1981, at a conference of Commonwealth foreign ministers, Bishop vented his wrathful suspicions, accusing the United States of trying to overthrow his government and citing what he alleged was a three-stage plot by the CIA.

Talk of a plot, real or imaginary, is a useful prelude to anti-democratic measures, and on June 19 that year the remaining independent newspaper, the *Grenadian Voice,* mimeographed for reasons of economy and discretion, was closed down. Next day a new law was announced, banning the launching of any new newspaper in Grenada pending a new "media policy" to cater to the needs of a "revolutionary society." By this time the revolutionary island was down to one newspaper, the *Free West Indian,* and it was state-owned.

Perhaps Bishop and his PRG had good reasons other than paranoia for concern about counter-revolutionaries. On July 11, still in 1981, four members of a so-called Gang of 26 were arrested in connection with an alleged "CIA plot to overthrow the government."

On August 20, Bishop followed up by sending a message to the then-secretary-general at the UN, Kurt Waldheim, accusing the Reagan administration of planning to invade Grenada. The allegation was naturally denied in Washington. UN and NATO naval exercises in the Caribbean followed, and on August 26 Bishop claimed that these were obviously a "practice run" for an invasion of Grenada. Events would show that he was not altogether wrong, although he would not be around to witness the vindication of his charges.

This sequence of events and words was causing concern in the Old Country (Britain) as well as in the West's one superpower (the United States). On a visit to the Caribbean in January 1982, Britain's minister of state for foreign and Commonwealth affairs, Richard Luce, expressed his government's concern (that is, Prime Minister Margaret Thatcher's) over the "considerable number of political prisoners in Grenada," and the hope that the PRG would "vigorously pursue its stated objective of holding elections and introducing a new Constitution."

But Bishop had other things on his mind.

A few weeks after Luce's expression of concern, at a meeting in Barbados on February 6, 1982, with five East Caribbean leaders, President Reagan accused Grenada of having joined with the Soviet Union, Nicaragua, and Cuba in promoting Marxism in the region.

At approximately this point, the relatively minor crisis brewing in and around Grenada was overshadowed by the major one that burst on the international scene with Argentina's invasion of the British-held Falkland Islands in the distant South Atlantic, and Britain's decision to oust the invaders. When the members of the Caribbean Community (CARICOM) met in April 1982, all but one of the countries present supported the British. The exception was Grenada. On June 14, 1982, Argentina surrendered.

In Moscow between July 26 and 28, 1982, Bishop signed wide-ranging economic and political agreements, including a binding interparty agreement with the ruling CPSU. Within the PRG, however, trouble was brewing for Maurice Bishop. A crisis of leadership common to all Communist regimes followed, differing only in scale from the Kremlin crisis of 1964 that broke Khrushchev's authority. At a Central Committee plenary meeting of the New Jewel Movement in October, Bishop was verbally attacked and his deputy and emerging rival, Bernard Coard, resigned.

A year later, on October 14, 1983, Bishop was ousted and arrested in a coup led jointly by Coard and "General of the Army" Hudson Austin.[2] Three days later Austin (whose "Army" totaled 1,500 troops) announced the expulsion of Maurice Bishop from the ruling party's Central Committee for having "disgraced the Party and the revolution." Several ministers were also arrested. The wording alone would have shown that in Grenada Moscow had a collective disciple. In another word, a satellite.

As in other Communist countries, the new regime did not enjoy genuinely widespread support. On October 19, a crowd of about 3,000 marched on the Army barracks to free the jailed ministers. In the clashes that followed, some 200 demonstrators were killed. When the carnage ended, an Army statement declared that Bishop and an unstated number of ministers had died during an exchange of fire, but strong rumors claimed the dead had been executed by firing squad. Maurice Bishop's body was never found.[3]

Army bulletins issued to the troops claimed that Bishop "and other people of the bourgeois and upper bourgeois strata" had been distributing arms to "the masses," had stripped several women at the Army's headquarters in Fort Rupert, and were planning to murder all officers and party members.[4]

Interestingly, the overthrow of the Bishop government was welcomed by the Soviet Union, but unambiguously condemned by Fidel Castro in a broadcast on October 25 in which he declared, "No doctrine, no principle or position held up as revolutionary, and no internal division justifies atrocious proceedings like the physical elimination of Bishop. . . ."

Castro went on to declare that the guilty parties should "punished in an exemplary way."[5]

The crisis raged on. On October 20, General Austin, with himself in the chair, had set up a Revolutionary Military Council. Next day the Organization of East Caribbean States (OECS) called an emergency session to discuss the Grenadian crisis. "Appropriate" but undefined action would be taken. CARICOM held an emergency meeting at which Jamaica and Dominica announced a breaking of diplomatic relations with Grenada and the suspension of Grenada's membership.

ONE OF THE side benefits of the short-lived American occupation of Grenada was that the occupying force uncovered a vast collection of official archives, the importance of which far transcended the small size of the island or the number of its inhabitants. In kind though obviously not in quantity, they were comparable to the secret archives of the German Wilhelmstrasse or foreign ministry that were discovered by the Allied forces at the end of World War II.

In all but name Grenada had become a Communist country with a murderous clique in power. This sequence of events contributes to an understanding of President Reagan's decision to intervene. It may be assumed that the CIA, through its own agents and probably Britain's, would have provided the president with unpublicized details of the depth and extent of the island regime's links with the Communist world, which of course were made available to the wider world when the secret documents were found and published. The most important ones were these:

1. **"TOP SECRET" Agreement with the USSR, July 27, 1980**
   - Free delivery to Grenada via a Cuban port of "special and civil equipment" valued at 10 million rubles;
   - Training of Grenadian servicemen in the USSR and by Soviet specialists in Grenada;
   - All expenses covered by the Soviet Union except accommodation, medical services, and transport, to be borne by Grenada.

2. **Agreement with Bulgaria (Undated)**
   - PREAMBLE. Friendly relations between the Bulgarian Communist Party (BCP) and the New Jewel Movement and between the two countries "in the interest of the unity and cohesion of all progressive and anti-imperialist forces in the world in the struggle against imperialism, for peace, democracy and social progress . . .";
   - Exchanges of delegations;
   - BCP to grant NJM ten allowances for training ten cadres in Bulgaria;
   - Further promotion of "more intensive cooperation between the public and mass organizations" of both countries.

3. **Note from Czechoslovakian to Grenadian Embassies in Havana (Undated)**
   - (As REQUESTED BY BERNARD COARD ON VISIT TO PRAGUE IN JUNE 1980) CZECHOSLOVAKIA TO PROVIDE, FREE OF CHARGE:
     - 3,000 automatic rifles (7.62 mm, type 52-57);
     - 30 boxes of spare parts for automatic rifles, as above;
     - 1 million cartridges;
     - 50 bazookas P27;
     - 5 boxes of spare parts for P27;
     - 5,000 projectiles for P27.

4. **Agreement with East Germany, June 10, 1982**
   - PREAMBLE. Deepening friendly relations between New Jewel Movement and Socialist Unity Party of (East) Germany "in the spirit of anti-imperialist solidarity and proletarian internationalism";
   - Socialist Unity Party to assist NJM in training of cadres and for "the acquisition of a knowledge of scientific socialism";
   - Details of exchanges of delegations.

5. **Request to USSR for Military Assistance, July 7, 1982**
   - Request made by "People's Revolutionary Armed Forces of Grenada" calling specifically over a three-year period (1983–1985) for:
     - Further consolidation of one Permanent Infantry battalion, five Reservist Infantry battalions, and support units;
     - The creation of two more regular Infantry battalions and four more reservist battalions.

6. **NJM-CPSU Agreement, July 27, 1982**
   - Called for commitment to common goals of peace, national liberation, and the struggle against imperialism, neocolonialism, and racialism, training cooperation, development of interstate and mass organizations.

7. **Agreement with North Korea, April 14, 1984**
   - Called for free military assistance from North Korea to a total of US$12 million.

8. **Letter from Maurice Bishop to Daniel Ortega in Nicaragua, July 17, 1981**
   - The letter started, "My dear Daniel, Warmest fraternal and Revolutionary greetings"; and ended, "Long live the unbreakable bonds of friendship between the people of Grenada and Nicaragua! Forward ever, backward never! A warm embrace, Maurice."

9. **Letter from "General of the Army" Austin to Yuri Andropov, February 17, 1982**
   - Austin extended "our deepest sympathy to your Party and people on the passing away of Comrade Suslov [the top Soviet ideologist], a true Bolshevik and hero of revolutionary people worldwide."
   - He went on to "formally request" a "basic course in counterintelligence" for one year to "three comrades"; and a "basic course in intelligence" for one year for "one comrade."

The above summaries by no means cover the full range of the documents seized by the Americans. They are, however, more than sufficient to confirm the view that Grenada had become an integral part of the Soviet peripheral empire. President John F. Kennedy had failed to rid the first Soviet satellite in the Western hemisphere, Cuba, of its regime, although he did stand up to the threat posed by the presence of Soviet nuclear weapons on the island. In comparison, Grenada was a relatively easy target, and President Reagan had rightly decided to tackle the threat on a scale sufficient to remove it.

This view, however, was far from unanimously supported by the West European members of NATO. The most surprising opposition (to this) came from Britain's Conservative Prime Minister, Mrs. Margaret Thatcher, when she told the House of Commons on October 25—the day the invasion began—that the government had "communicated to the United States their very considerable doubts . . . about initiating action and [had] asked them to weigh carefully several points before taking any irrevocable decision to act." Five days later she declared that "if you are going to pronounce a new law that wherever communism reigns against the will of the people . . . the United States shall enter, then we are going to have really terrible wars in the world."*

On October 26, the day after the U.S. landing, Ms. Eugenia Charles, Prime Minister of Dominica and Chair of the Organization of East Caribbean States, told the UN Security Council that Britain's governor-general Sir Paul Scoon had appealed for help on October 21. Despite this revelation, the Security Council passed a resolution deeply deploring the invasion as "a flagrant violation of international law." Britain abstained; the regrettable fact, however, was that Britain's government had in effect sided with the West's enemy against Britain's closest ally.

Not surprisingly, on October 27 the Commonwealth general secretary Shridath Ramphal called for the withdrawal of the U.S. forces and their replacement by a peace-keeping force from Commonwealth member countries.

On November 1, India's Prime Minister Indira Gandhi wrote a personal letter to Fidel Castro, strongly condemning the American intervention and calling for pressure to secure "the immediate withdrawal of the invading force."[6]

On November 3, a week after the Communist resistance had collapsed on Grenada, the United States answered Mrs. Thatcher's charges through the U.S. permanent representative at the UN, Mrs. Jeane Kirkpatrick, who observed that Mrs. Thatcher had "misunderstood the whole basis of our action." She added, acerbically, "We cannot give our allies a veto power over our national security."

---

*The real reasons for Mrs. Thatcher's opposition to the U.S. intervention in Grenada appear to have been: (1) the fact that President Reagan had not adequately consulted her before taking action, and (2) that she anticipated embarrassment at the forthcoming Commonwealth summit in New Delhi, which she would attend. The author discussed the Grenada crisis with the prime minister at her country residence, Chequers, on October 29, 1983, two days after the collapse of resistance to the U.S. force. See *Free Agent,* pp. 262–65.—BC

Two days earlier the U.S. House of Representatives had called for the removal of all troops within sixty days under the provisions of the 1973 War Powers Act. And on November 9, Sir Paul Scoon announced the appointment of a nine-member interim executive body for Grenada, one of whose primary aims would be to prepare for general elections to enable the Grenadian people to choose their own government.

Later that month the United States announced that the Agency for International Development had allocated $15 million in economic aid to Grenada. A third of it would be allocated to revive the island's financial system, $4.5 million to rebuild roads, $2.5 million for health and social services, $2 million for the private agricultural sector, and $1 million to promote tourism and industry. On November 23, the United States announced that a further $15 million would be provided to assist training for a Caribbean police force.

By December 15, all U.S. combat troops had withdrawn, while 300 noncombat personnel would stay behind.

The crisis was over, and the Soviet Union had suffered its first strategic reversal.

CHAPTER THIRTY-NINE

THE INTERNATIONAL MACHINE AT WORK

1974–1989

⸻⸻◆⸻⸻

I N CHAPTER 4, we traced the history of Lenin's Comintern, which was designed to spread the revolutionary message of Marxism-Leninism throughout the world. "Dissolved" by Stalin in 1943 to reassure his Western allies, Lenin's expansionist machine reemerged after the war as the International Department (ID) of the Soviet Communist Party's Central Committee.* The man in charge of the ID was Boris Ponomarev, who had earlier served on the Comintern.

Officially, the International Department's main function was simply to coordinate relations between the Soviet Communist Party and other Communist parties throughout the world. In reality its activities were far wider: to transmit the Politburo's directives to the other parties, and to formulate Soviet subversive strategy on a world scale in cooperation with the KGB and the GRU (military intelligence). In effect, the ID determined Soviet foreign policy. It defined Soviet targets during the Cold War and ultimately controlled one of the most fundamental elements in Moscow's Cold War strategy, known as "Active Measures" (in Russian, *Aktivnyye Meropriyatiya*). What exactly are Active Measures? They include *dezinformatsiya* or disinformation—the deliberate spreading of falsehoods or distortions of events by "planting" stories in the media or by any other

---

*For a fuller account of the Comintern's revival as the International Department, see *This War Called Peace,* Chap. 2, "The Iron Curtain Falls."

means, including the widespread use of forgeries. Other techniques included:

- The use of "front" organizations, such as the World Peace Council, designed to trap the unwary into supporting Soviet policies; and
- The use of agents of influence. An agent of influence might or might not have been aware that he was being used by the KGB. Those who did not know the true position were termed "witting" in America and "conscious" in Britain. They might or might not be on the Soviet payroll. Even if they were in receipt of Soviet money, they were not necessarily breaking the law, for *it was not an offense to be a paid agent of a foreign power in any of the Western democracies.* An offense was committed only when an agent (paid or not) passed on a secret document.

In the U.S. however, it was (and remains) an offense to act for a foreign government if the agent has not registered as such. American law is remarkably impartial in this domain, and made no distinction between working for, say, the Republic of Andorra or the Principality of Monaco.*

The examples given in Chapter 4 illustrated the breadth of the Comintern-ID's activities from 1919 into the 1960s; not least was the vast burden of expenditure involved in maintaining Communist parties, large and small, throughout the non-Communist world. It could even be argued that this burden contributed in no small measure to the collapse of the Soviet system—surely the ultimate paradox of Lenin's mission to spread Communism to "all countries of the world without exception."

In a speech to the Twenty-Eighth Party Congress in Moscow in July 1990, the then-Soviet foreign minister Eduard Shevardnadze revealed that the cost of what he termed the "ideological confrontation with the West" over the past two decades totaled 700 *billion* rubles. It is fair to assume that "ideological confrontation" was a Party euphemism for propaganda, disinformation, and other Active Measures. At the admittedly artificial

---

*The above description of Active Measures is quoted verbatim, apart from changes of tense, from the author's book, *The Gorbachev Phenomenon* (London: Claridge, and Lexington, Mass.: D.C. 1990, pp. 81).

exchange rate of the ruble during that period, Shevardnadze's figure worked out at about US $56 billion a year (or £35 billion).[1] It must be pointed out that the individual figures mentioned in the memoranda run into millions, not billions, but this does not exclude much higher potential figures for Active Measures.

As in Chapter 4, the examples that follow are drawn from the collection of Soviet archives known as Fond 89 (see Appendix B: Document 1), made available to the author by the Hoover Institution on War, Revolution, and Peace. The examples range from 1974 to 1989.

Cyprus   A memorandum from the head of the KGB, Yuri Andropov, to the CPSU Central Committee on July 8, 1974, reported on secret deliveries of small arms and ammunition to the Progressive Party of the Working People of Cyprus.[2]

South Africa   In a resolution on July 19, 1974, the CPSU Central Committee agreed to a request from South Africa's African National Congress (ANC) for 100 Swaziland passports to be "manufactured" (that is, forged) by the KGB. The request had come in a letter dated June 6 from the chairman of the South African Communist Party (SACP), Josef Dadoo.[3]

Lebanon   The minutes of the CPSU Politburo meeting on October 10, 1975, approved instructions to the Soviet ambassadors in Beirut and Damascus concerning a request from Lebanon for a supply of weapons to be delivered via Syria.[4]

South Africa   Under a resolution of the CPSU's Central Committee Secretariat on April 4, 1977, Moscow agreed to a list of requests from the leadership of South Africa's African National Congress (ANC) to set up a training camp for 600 ANC guerrillas with arms, ammunition, food, and Soviet military instructors. The request was relayed by Zimbabwe (formerly Rhodesia).[5]

Salvador   On August 20, 1980, the CPSU's Central Committee approved a request from the Communist Party of Salvador for a delivery of Western-manufactured small arms from Hanoi to Havana. Arrangements were made through telegrams to the Soviet ambassadors in Vietnam and Cuba.[6]

United States In a letter to the CPSU, the general secretary of the American Communist Party (CPUSA), G. Hall, requested admission of his personal representative for special training by the KGB. On September 5, 1980, the CPSU passed a resolution granting this request.[7]

Paraguay At a meeting on February 13, 1987, the CP Central Committee Secretariat ordered the KGB to provide a member of the Paraguay Communist Party with travel documents and special training free of charge at the request of that Party. The object was to facilitate the member's clandestine return to Paraguay.[8]

Lebanon On February 9, 1987, the Secretariat had agreed to a request from the Progressive Socialist Party of Lebanon to provide special military training for thirty activists, free of charge, with all travel and living expenses covered.[9]

Madagascar On October 26, 1987, the Secretariat agreed to meet a request for the delivery of "special equipment" to the Madagascar Party of the Congress of Independence.[10]

Laos On December 23, 1987, the Central Committee's Secretariat agreed to a request from the Laos People's Democratic Republic for free arms, equipment, and medical supplies.[11]

Lebanon Three groups of Lebanon Communist Party activists were to be trained by the KGB in "methods of conspiracy" under a resolution passed by the Central Committee Secretariat on December 25, 1987.[12]

Angola The Soviet Politburo agreed on February 7, 1989, to supply armaments to Cuba to replace those left behind in Angola.[13]

DOLLARS FOR THE LEFT

IN A MEMORANDUM from the Politburo on December 30, 1985, Ponomarev was informed that the proposal from his International Department to contribute $17 million to Left-Wing Workers' Organizations in 1986 had been accepted. (See Appendix N: Documents 1–6 for full text.) Moreover, the USSR State Bank would be instructed to supply Ponomarev with US $17 million "for special purposes." The Politburo instructed Ponomarev to inform the main Communist parties in Eastern

Europe that their contributions to the International Fund for the Assistance of Left-Wing Workers' Organizations in 1986 would be

- Socialist Unity Party of Germany: $1,200,000
- Communist Party of Czechoslovakia: $850,000
- Hungarian Socialist Workers' Party: $750,000
- Bulgarian Communist Party: $550,000. (See Appendix N: Document 1.)

In 1986, Ponomarev was eighty-one years old, and Mikhail Gorbachev, who had come to supreme power in 1985, eased him into retirement. Gorbachev chose the then-Soviet ambassador to the United States, Anatoly Dobrynin, to succeed Ponomarev as head of the International Department. When Dobrynin retired in October 1988, he was succeeded by Valentin Falin, who had been ambassador to West Germany. Reporting on December 5, 1989, on assistance to friendly parties and organizations, Falin revealed that because of problems with hard currency over the past two years, the ruling parties of East Germany, Czechoslovakia, and Bulgaria had opted out of contributions to workers' organizations, leaving it to the USSR to pick up the burden. In 1987, the contributions from the three parties had come to US $2.3 million. In 1989, the CPSU's contribution had been made in hard currency rubles (known as *invaliutnyi* rubles). The sum amounted to 13.5 million hard rubles, valued at US $22,044,673 at the official rate of exchange.

On December 11, 1989, the Soviet Politburo agreed to Falin's request for $22 million "for special purposes," and the Board of the USSR State Bank was instructed to supply "Comrade Falin" with that amount. (See Appendix N: Document 2.)

A fair comment on this state of affairs would be that it reflected the loss of Soviet imperial authority after the destruction of the Berlin Wall and the Soviet withdrawal from Afghanistan (see Chapter 40).

And yet, as a minor but significant example shows, as late as July 1989, non-governing Communist parties continued to rely on Moscow for services that would enable them to carry out their own covert actions. The chairman of the Communist Party of Argentina, Amos Fava, appealed to the Central Committee of the CPSU on July 21 "to prepare fifteen passports and [the same number of] identity cards for men and for women," totaling forty-five forged documents in all. On behalf of the ID, Falin passed on Fava's appeal to the Central Committee, which voted in favor on September 15, as recorded in a Top Secret Special File. Among the voters were Gorbachev and his "mentor" Aleksander Yakovlev.* In anticipation of a favorable response, Falin had written a note to Fava two days earlier (also classified as Top Secret Special File), which had been passed on to the Soviet Central Committee's Secretariat and which included the following passage: "The requirement for the above-mentioned documents . . . is explained by the need to carry out illegal work in conditions where the special services are stepping up their activities, and also to render assistance to the Paraguayan Communist Party, which is operating in the underground." (See Appendix N: Document 3.)

Not all appeals for assistance from other Communist parties (or with countries considered friendly) were handled by the ID, as the following examples show:

Sudan In June 1988, the Sudanese Communist Party asked the CPSU to provide military training to twenty members of its Party and to cover all traveling expenses. The request was granted under a resolution of the Soviet Central Committee on June 24 with the agreement of the head of the GRU (Soviet Military Intelligence) V. M. Mikhaylov. (See Appendix N: Document 4.)

Iraq In December 1989, Iraq (still under Saddam Hussein's brutal dictatorship) asked Moscow to buy back Soviet aircraft previously delivered to that country, replace them by more up-to-date ones, or agree to their sale to third countries. Not surprisingly, the Politburo saw no point in buying the aircraft back but agreed that Iraq should pass them on to "socialist and friendly developing countries." (See Appendix N: Document 5.)

---

*For years, Yakovlev, an academic, had advocated *glasnost* as part of a more open Soviet society. For his pains, the then-Party leader Leonid Brezhnev had exiled him to Canada in 1973, as ambassador. There, ten years later, Gorbachev had met him on a visit to Ottawa. By the time Gorbachev had reached the top as general secretary, on March 12, 1985, he was a complete convert to Yakovlev's ideas. He recalled his mentor to Moscow, put him in the Politburo, and in 1988, he appointed Yakovlev as chairman of the Central Committee's Commission on International Policy.

People's Republic of Congo (better known as Congo-Brazzaville) On March 7, 1990, the Politburo considered a request from the President of the People's Republic of Congo (D. Sassu Ngesso) for "special equipment for the needs of the Command of the Forces of Public Security of Congo and for the training of Congolese specialists in the USSR." By that time the resources of the Soviet Union were under strain. The Soviet ambassador in Brazzaville was instructed to point this out to the president and to explain that it would be impossible to meet this request free of charge. However, "bearing in mind the friendly nature of Soviet-Congolese relations it would be possible to provide for delivery in 1990 five GAZ-53-12 lorries, five VAZ-2106 limousines, 16 Dnieper MT-16 motorcycles with sidecars, 30 standardized suitcases, 160 gas-masks, photographic, film and audio equipment and other equipment" to a total value of about 500,000 rubles. However, the Congolese would have to pay that sum, and the Soviet Union would charge for any training provided. (Appendix N: Document 6.)

THE INTERNATIONAL DEPARTMENT appears to have continued its activities until the end, that is, until the collapse of the Soviet system at the close of 1991, much as a mechanical toy continues to run until there is nobody to wind it up. The international front organizations went on similarly, but in a climate that had ceased to be favorable. An interesting example was that of the most important of all the fronts—the World Peace Council—whose last major conference outside the Soviet bloc ended in spectacular failure.

The date was September 1986. Presumably conscious of increasing Western skepticism, recent WPC conferences had been held in the protective environment of Iron Curtain capitals such as Prague or Sofia. The venue for this one was Denmark's capital Copenhagen. Not only the audience but even the organizing committee had been penetrated by members of the anti-Soviet organization known as "The 61." Shouts of laughter as well as of protest had greeted the deployment on the Western side of a banner which read, "Welcome to the KGB's peace conference." Delegates from imaginary peace groups were scattered in the audience.[14]

It would hardly be an exaggeration to see this propaganda fiasco as the death knell of the ID's web of international fronts. By then, in any case, the long-drawn Soviet campaign against NATO's response to the deployment in 1977 of the Soviet SS-20 medium-range missiles had failed. These triple-headed and highly accurate missiles would have been capable of destroying all of NATO's military targets in one surprise attack. Soviet propaganda efforts against a NATO response had been successful for several years. Although the NATO powers did decide in December 1979 to deploy its U.S. counter-weapons—Cruise and Pershing II—the actual deployment was to be deferred until the end of 1983, but even then only if by that time there had been no substantial progress in arms control talks between the two superpowers.[15] As it happened, deployment had in fact begun well before the Copenhagen conference.

THE END
LOOMS AHEAD

CHAPTER FORTY

DEFEAT IN AFGHANISTAN

1986–1989

───⫸⚫⫷───

IN FEBRUARY 1989, the last Soviet troops pulled out of Afghanistan. The war had lasted just over nine years—more than twice as long as Stalin's "great patriotic war" against Hitler—and had ended in defeat. On the Soviet side, the casualties had been relatively light: 15,000 Soviet troops killed and 37,000 wounded. On the Afghan side, the dead exceeded 1 million, including civilians as well as combatants. The population of Afghanistan had declined by six times as many as those shot, mined, or bombed to death, for some 5 million Afghans had taken refuge in neighboring Pakistan or Iran.

One could argue that this was the first Soviet war of aggression against a foreign land, if one accepts that Lenin's war of reconquest was merely aimed at restoring the Tsarist empire superseded by the Soviet system. Stalin's war against his erstwhile ally Hitler had started as a defensive war against invading forces, even though the resultant Soviet occupation of Eastern Europe had turned half a dozen "liberated" countries into satellites of the imperial conquerors.

In retrospect, the Soviet defeat in Afghanistan in 1989 may be seen as a decisive turning point of a long imperial expansion. The first strategic reversal had happened six years earlier, with the U.S. occupation of Grenada, but the Caribbean island was a relatively minor territorial loss. Afghanistan was a major one: 250,000 square miles, with a population of some 15 million—historically a buffer state between the Russian and

British Empires—possession of which would have facilitated further Soviet advances into Iran, Pakistan, and India. With this defeat, the myth of Soviet invincibility was shattered. The Leninist vision of an unstoppable spread of the Communist ideology to "all countries of the world without exception" could at last be seen as deeply flawed, for the Afghan resistance—an amalgam of Islamic fervor and patriotic commitment—had defeated the heavily armed bearers of an alien ideology.

This victory was of course not the first for Afghanistan. Twice in the nineteenth century, Afghan tribes had risen against British invaders; and twice the invaders had been driven out despite apparently decisive victories in pitched battles. In both cases, the final defeats had resulted not from military superiority but from the constant harassment of regular forces by the guerrillas of the tribal resisters. What had happened in the first Afghan war of 1838 to 1842 happened again in the second war of 1878 to 1880. In a brief third war, this time pitching Afghan invaders of imperial India against the British defenders for one month in 1919, the British won a decisive military victory only to concede the political victory to the Afghans. Under the peace treaty of August 8, 1919, Britain recognized the independence of Afghanistan. Further agreements signed on November 22, 1921, confirmed the fact, and Amanollah Khan, who had seized the throne from his younger brother Nasrullah, established diplomatic links with the wider world.

The Soviet defeat was remarkable because the patriotic rebels were fighting not only the heavily armed Soviet force, totaling 110,000, but also a Soviet-supplied regular Afghan Army, which was viewed by the guerrillas as puppets. The Soviet military force was a variable machine, reaching 80,000 at its largest but dwindling to 27,000 through desertions and casualties. The Soviet-installed dictator Babrak Karmal publicly admitted its weaknesses and tried to remedy its disastrous performance by rounding up young men and coercing them into military service while offering higher pay incentives to noncommissioned officers and lowering the conscription age from twenty-one to eighteen. According to one source, the number had "grown" to 50,000 in 1984, but the Soviet Politburo had been told in March 1983 that it had reached 140,000.[1]

The ruling People's Democratic Party of Afghanistan (PDPA) used characteristically Communist methods to impose its rule, but never fully succeeded. Such measures as abolishing dowries to brides and forcing women as well as men to attend rural literacy classes flew in the face of Islamic traditions, not least of the *purdah* tradition of isolating veiled women from male company other than husbands or brothers.

When Babrak Karmal took over from Hafizullah Amin (see Chapter 31), there was a rapid buildup of the police, but the key instrument for the imposition and spread of central power was the new secret security agency, KHAD (State Information Services), with a high level of funding from Moscow and intensive training of cadres by the KGB and the East German STASI. The Director of the KHAD, Major-General Mohammed Najibullah—usually known as "Najib," deleting the Islamic ending *(ullah)*—was an unconditional servant of Moscow. With remarkable speed, the KHAD was built up to a force of 30,000 that infiltrated the guerrillas, exacerbating individual or group rivalries and building up a wide network of paid informers.[2]

Broadly speaking, the combined efforts of the PDPA and its Soviet and East German advisers brought central control of three of the main cities: Kabul, Jalalabad, and Mazar-e-Sharif. But even by 1987 the ruling party had failed to gain control over two other provincial centers: Kandahar and Herat.

As early as March 1983, Soviet leaders were clearly worried about the mounting difficulties encountered by their invading Army, as released archival material of this period confirms. A key meeting of the CPSU's Politburo took place on March 10. The then-general secretary Yuri Andropov chaired the meeting; others present included Konstantin Chernenko (who would succeed him), Mikhail Gorbachev (who would succeed Chernenko), and Andrei Gromyko (still Foreign Minister).

Gromyko dwelt on the difficulties of the situation, especially the activities of rebel gangs, but went on to draw attention to the encouraging aspects, particularly the growth of the Afghan Army, which had reached 140,000. Andropov called for patience and understanding, reminding his colleagues of the fact that in its early years the Soviet Union had also faced the problem of banditry. All those present agreed that talks with Babrak Karmal were needed. A draft resolution of the USSR Council of Ministers (Cabinet) to provide additional economic assistance to the Afghan Republic was approved. (See Appendix O: Document 1.)

The predictable political crisis in Kabul followed three years later, in stages:

- **Stage 1:** In February 1986, Babrak Karmal attended the Twenty-Seventh Congress of the Communist Party of the Soviet Union (CPSU) but was unable to gain access to General Secretary Mikhail Gorbachev.
- **Stage 2:** The Soviet Politburo met on March 20. By then, Gorbachev had been in power for a year and chaired the meeting. He read out a pessimistic memorandum on Afghanistan, which said, among other things, "The situation is quite dramatic. B. Karmal is very much down in terms of health and in terms of psychological disposition. He [has begun] to pit leaders against each other."

    Reading out a cable, Victor Chebrikov (successor to Andropov as head of the KGB) intervened: "Karmal tells himself that he cannot cope with his functions."

    Gromyko proposed that Mikhail Sergeevich (Gorbachev) could be instructed "to speak with him."
- **Stage 3:** On March 31, Karmal flew to Moscow, ostensibly to have a private "medical checkup" for a rumored lung ailment. He stayed on until May 1, and it is not clear whether he was received by Gorbachev. During his stay, he missed the parade in Kabul on April 27 marking the eighth anniversary of the 1978 *Sowr* revolution (named after the relevant month of the Afghan calendar).
- **Stage 4:** In a letter to the PDPA plenum on May 4, Babrak Karmal asked to be relieved of his duties on grounds of "ill health," "international problems," and "an accurate assessment of my possibilities." He did not attend the meeting. At this stage, however, Karmal remained a member of the PDPA Politburo as well as president of the Revolutionary Council and chairman of the Revolutionary Council Presidium. By then, it had become clear that the Soviet leaders were not alone in disapproving of Karmal's performance; another critic was President Zia ul-Haq of Pakistan. Karmal's partial removal was interpreted as a signal to Pakistan that the Soviets wanted a negotiated settlement to the Afghan problem.
- **Stage 5:** On May 15, it became clear that Major-General Najib, head of the KHAD, had in effect though not in name taken over from Karmal. He announced a new collective leadership. Karmal, still in charge of the Revolutionary Council, would concentrate on running the organs of state; the chairman of the Council of Ministers (the

nominal prime minister) Soltan Ali Keshtmand would run economic policy and improve the work of individual ministries; while Najib himself would transform the PDPA into a party of "revolutionary actions."

- **Stage 6:** For Babrak Karmal, the end came on November 20, when the PDPA, in his absence, unanimously approved a request from him that he be relieved of all his remaining Party and state posts, although he would remain nominally a member of the Revolutionary Council.

A WEEK EARLIER, on November 13, 1986, a note of pessimism bordering on despair was detectable (through the fog of Newspeak) in a Top Secret account of a meeting of the Soviet Politburo. With Gorbachev as chair, those present included Gromyko, Chebrikov, Foreign Minister Eduard Shevardnadze, Boris Yeltsin, and the former Soviet ambassador to the United States, Anatoly Dobrynin, who had recently been appointed to the key job of head of the International Department, replacing the aged Ponomarev.

Gorbachev complained that Karmal was "walking like a *pretzel*"—a derogatory expression derived from a term for the weaving and unsteady gait of a drunkard. In pessimistic mode Gorbachev went on, "We have been fighting in Afghanistan for already six years. If the approach is not changed, we will continue to fight for another twenty or thirty years." Differences emerged over a proposal that Najib should be invited to come to Moscow (for the first time). Dobrynin commented, "Karmal must be removed. But we must remember that not a single member of the CC PDPA Politburo supports Najib." He went on, however, to agree that Najib must be invited to Moscow.

After further discussion, Gorbachev complained that the goal set in October 1985—to expedite the withdrawal of the Soviet forces while ensuring a friendly Afghanistan—had not been realized: "The strengthening of the military position of the Afghan government has not taken place. National consolidation has not been ensured mainly because comrade Karmal continued to hope to sit in Kabul under our assistance." He went on to call, again, for the withdrawal of 50 percent of the Soviet troops from Afghanistan in 1987 and the remaining 50 percent the following year. A resolution to this effect was passed. (See Appendix O: Document 2.)

* * *

IN SOME RESPECTS, Afghanistan was for the Soviets what Vietnam had been for the Americans, but there were important differences. One was public opinion about the war. A major factor in the U.S. defeat, it played virtually no part in the Soviet retreat, for there was no *glasnost,* no openness, during the first few years of the war: Gorbachev—the man who launched the policy of glasnost—did not come to supreme power until March 1985.

Another difference was the absence of a pro-Soviet subversive force among the Afghan peasantry. The KHAD had its agents in the villages, but there was no pro-Soviet equivalent of the Vietcong. Initially the enormous firepower of the invading Army favored massacres from the air, mainly by Soviet helicopter gunships. Then in the early months of 1980, the situation changed rapidly as one of the best Soviet defensive weapons—the surface-to-air Sam-7s—reached the guerrillas in vast numbers. The irony lay in the fact that these were *Soviet* weapons. The Sam-7 was particularly effective against slow-flying helicopters. Portable, shoulder-operated, and accurate up to five miles, it operated on a heat-seeking principle.

How and from where did the Sam-7s reach the Afghan guerrillas? Although the Islamic world was divided on this issue, Iraq and Iran owned Sam-7s in vast numbers and "solidarized" with the Afghans. Publicly, Libya, Syria, and Algeria supported the Soviet Union, but their sympathy for the Afghan resistance, although nominally secret, was visible to close observers.

The issue had been hotly debated in May 1980 at an Islamic Conference at Islamabad in Pakistan, where the Palestine Liberation Organization, heavily supported by Moscow, took a pro-Soviet stance. The Iranian participants, although vociferously anti-American, took the lead in rallying opinion behind the Afghan freedom fighters.

The exact role played by the CIA in the acquisition of Sam-7s was not made public, but it is fair to assume that they acquired vast numbers of them at the then-"going price" of US $18,000 each plus $3,500 per launcher. At that time Ethiopia was in the market for such purchases, which were also available in Tanzania. The main distribution point was Pakistan, conveniently close to Afghanistan, and also an Islamic country.

Six years later, in March 1986, the British prime minister Margaret Thatcher met with Abdul Haq, a faction leader in Hizb-i-Islami, one of the leading Mujaheddin (Holy War) groups. The Afghan authorities described the meeting as a "provocative act," and Mr. Haq as a "well-known professional terrorist and felon." At that time the Afghan government was still in the hands of the pro-Soviet Najib and Babrak Karmal. The outcome of Haq's meeting with Thatcher was repeated deliveries of Blowpipe anti-aircraft missiles (made in Belfast) to Haq's faction within the Mujaheddin.

The Belfast-made Blowpipes were not, however, the most effective anti-aircraft weapons available. From the fall of 1986, U.S.-made Stinger missiles started reaching the Mujaheddin guerrillas in considerable numbers. These deliveries achieved "kill ratios" of nearly 50 percent, resulting in a turning of the tide in the guerrillas' favor. In the ensuing year, the Soviet side was estimated to have lost 270 Soviet aircraft, at a cost of around $2.2 billion.[3]

Pakistan's role naturally attracted hostile attention from the Soviet side, while its 1,200-mile shared frontier with Afghanistan exposed it to incursions from the other side. In 1985 alone, according to one account, there were more than 200 Afghan or Soviet violations of Pakistan's air space or territory with artillery fire or air bombardment. By 1987, the number had increased to 600.[4] In Afghanistan itself, Soviet methods, both in offensive and defensive operations, were based on indiscriminate terror. On the offensive side, they included "deliberate destruction of villages, indiscriminate carpet bombing, execution of civilian hostages and use of booby-trapped toy bombs."[5] To these should be added airborne commando raids, night ambushes, and surprise attacks on guerrilla positions. Moreover, tens of millions of land mines—perhaps the most indiscriminate weapons of all—were planted on Afghan soil south of the Hindu Kush, creating an extensive no man's land.[6]

A year after taking over as general secretary of the CPSU, Gorbachev ordered a massive offensive into Paktia, which included the destruction of about twenty major Mujaheddin bases. A definitive Soviet victory, however, remained elusive despite their overwhelming military superiority.

ON NOVEMBER 29 and 30, 1987, a *Loya Jirga* (a nationwide traditional gathering of tribal leaders), described loosely as a "Grand National Assembly" met in Kabul, unanimously elected Najibullah as president, and adopted a new constitution. The Soviet-inspired name of the Afghan state—"Democratic Republic of Afghanistan"—was shortened by cutting out the word *Democratic*. The emerging state was defined as a non-aligned, Islamic nation. In his enthusiasm, Najibullah described the new constitution as one of "national reconciliation and democracy."

Since 1982, a kind of "peace process" had been in progress between Pakistan and Afghanistan. It came to fruition eventually, but not until April 14, 1988, with the signing in Geneva of agreements under which the two parties pledged non-interference in each other's internal affairs, along with provisions for the voluntary return of refugees. At the same time, the United States and the Soviet Union agreed to act as guarantors. A more significant outcome was a provision for the withdrawal of Soviet forces from Afghanistan.

The agreements were to be monitored by the United Nations and were signed by the Pakistani and Afghan foreign ministers, Zain Noorani and Abdol Wakil. Their counterparts from the two superpowers, U.S. Secretary of State George Shultz and Soviet Foreign Minister Eduard Shevardnadze, signed as guarantors on May 15, 1988.

From Moscow's standpoint, the Geneva accords provided a face-saving device to end the Soviet occupation of Afghanistan; and on August 14 Moscow Radio reported that the withdrawal of half the Soviet military personnel from Afghanistan had been completed, one day before the date agreed upon at Geneva.

Not surprisingly, there was a widespread international impression that the Geneva accords marked the end of the war. However, the Mujaheddin lost no time in emphasizing that as far as they were concerned, the accords did nothing of the kind. In the Pakistani city of Peshawar on April 9, a few days before the signing ceremony, Gulbuddin Hekmattyar, leader of one of the two Hizb-i-Islami factions and chairman of the seven-party Mujaheddin alliance, declared that the alliance would not be bound by the outcome of the Geneva accords. The war would continue, he added.

Again not surprisingly, President Najibullah greeted the Geneva settlement as "the happiest and most brilliant event" in Afghanistan's history. He spoke on April 15: the day of the signing in Geneva.

These idealistic words were not matched by reality. A series of battles had taken place around the town of Khost between November 1987 and January 1988 and again in late March 1988. The (London) *Times* of April 20 reported that intensive fighting had raged around Kabul during the previous week. A week later, heavy fighting erupted between government forces and rebel groups along the Afghan-Pakistani border. On April 27, a large lorry-bomb exploded in Pamira, a district of Kabul, killing seven and injuring twenty-nine.

A similar incident had taken place in an arms depot outside Islamabad four days before the signing of the Geneva accords, when a vast quantity of war material intended for the guerrillas was destroyed; 100 people died and 700 were injured.

In fact the civil war in Afghanistan went on after the departure of the Soviet forces, until the Mujaheddin could claim victory when the Najibullah regime collapsed on April 28, 1992. The protracted Soviet intervention had indeed ended in failure.* Two relevant Soviet documents of that period, made available some years later, while not explicitly presenting the withdrawal as a defeat, do make it clear that the Najibullah government was in a critical state. One of them, marked "Top Secret" and dated January 23, 1989, was a report on the Afghan situation presented the following day to the Politburo. The report draws attention to two critical dates: the beginning of February, when the last Soviet military units must leave Kabul, and February 15, when, under the Geneva accords, "the term of stay of our military contingent must end." The "Afghan comrades . . . point out that they cannot manage completely without our military assistance." (See Appendix O: Document 3.)

A much briefer "Top Secret" report, bearing six signatures, including those of Foreign Minister Shevardnadze and KGB Chairman Vladimir

---

*This was the view I expressed in "The Afghan Turning Point" in my column ("The Protracted Conflict") in *National Review* May 27, 1988, in these words: "In strategic and historical terms, Mikhail Gorbachev's decision to pull the Soviet forces out of their Afghan quagmire constitutes a major reverse for the October Revolution, comparable to the American decision to withdraw from Vietnam in 1973. In each case, the superpower involved tacitly conceded defeat." This view was not unanimously accepted at the time. Indeed Captain Kenneth L. Davison (whose otherwise excellent article I quote in note 6) writes, "The pullback of Soviet forces from Afghanistan cannot, at face value, be adjudged a defeat or even a policy reversal for the Soviet Union in the true meaning of that term. The Soviets invaded Afghanistan in 1979 for a variety of reasons, but hardly with the intent of maintaining a military occupation in perpetuity. Military force was deemed by Moscow not an end in itself, but the means to the end of Afghanistan's economic and political subjugation to the Soviet Union." True, but subjugation did not follow. Indeed, the Soviet system collapsed three years later.—BC.

Kryuchkov, was discussed by the Politburo on March 12. Requests from "comrade President Najibullah" for the urgent provision of weaponry were approved. The requests included transfers to the Afghan side of SU-22 and MiG-21 aircraft, plus R-17 missile launchers with warheads. (See Appendix O: Document 4.)

Another short report, dated May 12, was approved next day by the Politburo. It called for a speedup of arms deliveries to Afghanistan, "demonstrative redeployment of our aviation" at Soviet airports close to the Afghan border, and continuing diplomatic pressure on the United States, Pakistan, Iran, Saudi Arabia, and if possible on India and the non-aligned countries. (See Appendix O: Document 5.)

Clearly such ideas were calculated to reassure the Najibullah government that although the Soviet Union had decided to abandon him, they would continue to give the impression that they had not forgotten him. One cannot help wondering whether any, and if so how many, of the signatories of these two depressing reports realized that the end of the Soviet system and of its Empire was drawing near.

In a more substantial report dated August 11, Shevardnadze and Kryuchkov, back from a "working visit to Afghanistan," expressed alarm at the looming threat of Muslim fundamentalism, not only to Afghanistan but, more worrisome, to Uzbekistan and other Islamic Soviet republics. The report included this sentence: "In the event of a setback for [our] Afghan friends the most likely result is the coming to power in Afghanistan of the Islamic fundamentalists." (See Appendix O: Document 6.)

The quoted sentence was prophetic. Between September 25 and 26, 1996, the most extreme of the Islamic groups, the Taleban (Student Army), captured Kabul. One of its first acts was to order the execution of the former President Najibullah (who had restored the Islamic *ullah* to his name in an effort to placate the religious extremists). Taleban soldiers broke into the United Nations compound and abducted Najibullah. The former president was immediately shot, and his body, together with those of his brother and two close associates, was hung from a traffic kiosk near the presidential palace. International outrage followed, which the Taleban ignored, while it went on to impose a strict Islamic regime. One of its dominant points was the political and social demotion of women, who were forbidden to take part in politics or to show their unveiled faces in public.

CUBANS QUIT ANGOLA

IN THE WIDER reaches of the peripheral empire, two continents away, significant changes had also been taking place. On July 20, 1988, Cuba and South Africa had agreed on a timetable for the withdrawal of all foreign troops from Angola: a decision which the Communist government in the former Portuguese colony had endorsed. On July 26—a symbolic date in Castro's Cuba—Fidel had publicly committed himself to the withdrawal of all Cuban troops, and on August 22 a formal cease-fire was signed by the three countries involved: Angola, South Africa, and Cuba. Although the Cuban forces did pull out, this was not to be the end of the Angolan civil war.

CHAPTER FORTY-ONE

THE GLASNOST FACTOR

1985–1991

B Y THE TIME Mikhail Sergeevich Gorbachev took over the leadership of the ruling CPSU in March 1985, three of the turning points in the Soviet imperial expansion—Poland, Afghanistan, Grenada—had been reached and were doing their work. To these Gorbachev would add a fourth, called *glasnost* ("publicity" in Russian, but usually presented as "openness.")

An ultimately fatal error of judgment—the invasion of Afghanistan—had come at the end of 1979. The great Polish crisis started a year later, at the end of 1980, with the emergence of Lech Walesa's defiant trade union known as *Solidarnosc*. And the first strategic reversal—minor but significant—came from outside, with President Ronald Reagan's decision to occupy Grenada in October 1983. (See Chapters 37, 38, and 40.)

As a rising younger member of the Politburo, which he joined in 1980 at age forty-nine, Gorbachev had inherited the decision to invade Afghanistan, and was involved with the handling of the Polish crisis. The Grenada crisis had come as an unexpected blow from the leader of "the main enemy": the first of its kind, unanticipated and outside the parameters of central planning. For years the imperial power center in the Kremlin had been in the hands of ailing gerontocrats: Leonid Brezhnev, who died in 1982, followed by Yuri Andropov (former head of the KGB), who passed away in February 1984, and Konstantin Chernenko, who will probably go down in history as the most immobile of all Soviet leaders. When Chernenko died in March 1985, Gorbachev was only fifty-four.

Historically, Gorbachev was the first *homo sovieticus* to rule over Lenin's bequest. All the others, from Stalin to Chernenko, were born before 1917. Gorbachev's birth date was March 2, 1931; he was born at the height of Stalin's ruthless "collectivization" of the farms. Surprisingly, given his clever and sophisticated handling of international relations in later life, he was born into a peasant family in southern Russia. After the war he had worked as a driver for a machine tractor station at Stavropol in the northern Caucasus.

He presumably acquired his sophistication as a student in the Law Faculty of Moscow State University, the MGU. While there he also worked as an informer to the KGB through the Ministries of State Security (MGB) and Internal Affairs (MVD).[1]

His rapid promotion to the higher ranks of the Party followed his fortuitous meeting at a spa in the Caucasus with Andropov and M. A. Suslov, the then-top ideologist and Number 2 man in the ruling hierarchy.[2]

By the time Gorbachev took over as general secretary in 1985, the Soviet system was deep in crisis, with very high rates of alcoholism, drug addiction, and crime, life expectancy that ranked 32d in the world, very high infant mortality (30 per 1,000), a doubling of deaths from lung cancer in the twenty-year period of 1965–1985, and an intolerable level of public corruption.[3]

The implications of this situation in the home of Marxism-Leninism can be understood only in the context of the ideological underpinning of its system. Throughout Communism's history it had been publicly assumed that Communism was the highest stage of economic and social development. Any flaws could therefore be attributed only to individual human shortcomings. As Stalin's reign of terror illustrated, the logical remedy for any failures was the liquidation of the guilty, as decided at the highest level. By the time Gorbachev came to power, the practice of mass liquidations was over, although exile to the gulags still existed. Moreover, one of the innovations introduced by Gorbachev's mentor, Andropov, was the psychiatric torture of dissidents.

The key problem with the catastrophic failure of the system was that the doctrine of Leninist infallibility was no longer believed even by Party members, although daily reiteration of the credo was required in conversations as well as in public speeches.[4] To his credit, Gorbachev did not order mass executions, but his reaction to the visible decline of the system and to the cynicism of the Nomenklatura (the privileged class of Party members and officials) was not unorthodox: a culprit was needed, and his choice was Brezhnev, who was dead and therefore unable to defend himself.

Unlike most of his predecessors, Gorbachev took naturally to public relations. He was also well advised in this field, most notably by Brezhnev's critic Aleksander Yakovlev, who had been sent by Brezhnev to Ottawa as ambassador but whom Gorbachev lost no time in repatriating. The objectives were clear: to "restructure" *(perestroika)* the whole system and to introduce a measure of "openness" *(glasnost)* designed to attract economic support from the West. To launch his new ideas, Gorbachev undertook, even before he took office, a major international charm offensive. It was not of course the first of its kind: both Nikita Khrushchev and Brezhnev had set examples, although the former had destroyed his own efforts by boasting, in a casual but much-quoted remark during his 1957 American tour that "we will bury you," a lapse that Gorbachev was too skillful to allow.

His first exercise in international salesmanship took place three months or so before he actually took office as general secretary; his first target, in December 1984, was Margaret Thatcher, Britain's "Iron Lady" (so labeled by Moscow Radio after she had made an anti-Communist speech). After the dull meetings of the past, most notably with Brezhnev in his dotage, Gorbachev came as the proverbial breath of fresh air, and the prime minister in effect conferred a seal of approval upon her Soviet visitor when she declared publicly that he was "a man I could do business with."

Gorbachev's choice of slogans—*perestroika* and *glasnost*—call for critical analysis. It was widely but wrongly assumed in the West that his intent with *perestroika* was to overhaul the economic and industrial structure of the regime, whereas in reality the aim was to overhaul and improve the whole vast apparatus of propaganda and "Active Measures" (discussed in Chapter 39). As for *glasnost,* the Russian word means "publicity," but the favored meaning disseminated by the international propaganda apparatus was "openness."

As for industrial and economic restructuring, there was none. Instead, Gorbachev introduced a number of repressive measures against various forms of corruption and financial irregularities. His drive started on May 28, 1986 (just over a year after his assumption of supreme power), with a Law against Unearned Income. In short order, some 800,000 salesmen or shop managers were arrested or forced to resign.[5]

On June 10, a fortnight after the new law had gone into effect, the Moscow Soviet adopted a resolution requiring citizens fit for work to produce a "certificate of employment"—in effect a ban on living off the black market.[6]

More measures followed, all of them coercive, none of them reformist in a real sense, for any such measures would threaten "Socialism," which Gorbachev was not prepared to do. A drive was launched in favor of cooperatives, specifically of students, housewives, and pensioners not employed in the state sector; another was a doomed attempt to undermine the huge black economy. The most unpopular initiative of all was a major campaign against alcoholism, through price increases of up to 25 percent and production cuts of 32 percent for vodka and 68 percent for wine. The predictable outcome was a massive upsurge of home brewing, or a resort to alcohol substitutes such as hair lotions or eau de cologne. Deaths from alcohol dropped dramatically from 47,300 in 1984 to 20,800 in 1986; they were offset by 11,000 deaths from alcohol substitutes, plus 200,000 prosecutions for home brewing.[7]

Other coercive measures included the creation of a State Commission for Quality Control (which sounded refreshingly customer-oriented but resulted by March 1987 in 32,000 fines and 18,000 pending prosecutions for producing shoddy goods). The victims were indignant and fought back with complaints that with inferior raw materials and antiquated machinery that was state-provided, what else could be expected?[8] A new Law on Enterprise in 1987 made the Party responsible for each enterprise, while state orders for goods would continue to take precedence over private demand.

In July 1988, Leonid Albakin, Director of the Economics Institute of the Academy of Sciences, revealed at the Nineteenth All-Union Party conference that the Soviet Union's gross national product was now lower than during Brezhnev's Eleventh Five-Year Plan.

This depressing disclosure came a year after the publication of Gorbachev's first book, *Perestroika: New Thinking for Our Country and the*

World. This was his vehicle for putting across three major themes: Lenin was always right; Brezhnev's legacy* was the age of "stagnation"; and perestroika would cure the system of its ills and produce solutions of which Lenin would have approved. Gorbachev diagnosed the legacy of the Brezhnev era in these words:

> At some stage—this became particularly clear in the latter half of the seventies—something happened that was at first sight inexplicable. The country began to lose momentum. Economic failures became more frequent. Difficulties began to accumulate and deteriorate, and unresolved problems to multiply. Elements of what we call stagnation and other phenomena alien to socialism began to appear in the life of society. A kind of "braking mechanism" affecting social and economic development formed. And all this happened at a time when scientific and technological revolution opened up new prospects for economic and social progress.[9]

He went on to dwell on the paradox—widely noted in the West—of a system able to send space rockets to Venus but incapable of producing high-quality domestic appliances. How was it for that matter that the Soviet Union, the world's biggest producer of steel and fuel, could find itself short of both? He thought of an image to illustrate his argument: a huge turning flywheel of a powerful revolving machine with loose drive belts and a skidding transmission.

Not surprisingly, since he was searching for a scapegoat, he was somewhat unfair to (the unnamed) Brezhnev. Although everything he said about stagnation then and later was true enough, he drew no public attention either at home or abroad to the considerable imperial achievements of Brezhnev's sixteen years in power. These included the transformation of the Soviet Navy from a small old-fashioned force to a world-class fleet comparable in power and range to the U.S. Navy. He had given the Soviet Union parity with the United States in strategic weapons systems and in-

---

*Interestingly, he does not mention Brezhnev by name; he merely identifies the period ("in the latter half of the seventies") when Brezhnev was in power. Indeed, the only Soviet political figure mentioned is Lenin, to whom Gorbachev makes repeated references, invariably adulatory. In an evasive reference to Stalin's massacres (quoted later in this chapter), the leader himself is not mentioned. Apart from Lenin, the only politicians mentioned are Westerners: a curious interpretation of his own glasnost.—BC

deed superiority in some domains. He had enabled the Vietnamese Communist regime to defeat the United States, thus completing Ho Chi Minh's original plan to unite not only North with South Vietnam but all three countries of the former French Indochina empire (Vietnam, Laos, and Cambodia).

Also to Brezhnev's credit were the teleguided coups in South Vietnam, Ethiopia, and Grenada; he had presided over the biggest airlift in history, brought a pro-Soviet regime to power in Nicaragua, and approved the Soviet invasion of Afghanistan. Admittedly the last item in this list turned out to be a major error, but in imperial terms, Brezhnev's reign was far from being an age of stagnation, however great the corruption, the crime, and the declining standards of living and of public health.

Not once could Gorbachev bring himself to question the inherited Leninist doctrine, for everything—the ideal Socialist society of Marx's imagination and Lenin's vision—ultimately depended on it. Like his speeches, his written text is replete with worshipful references to Lenin. Once again, however, he falls considerably short of glasnost in the officially approved meaning of "openness" in the following passage: "Gravely ill, Lenin was deeply concerned for the future of socialism. He perceived the lurking dangers of the new system. We, too, must understand this concern."[10]

Clearly this can only be a subtle reference to the founder's New Economic Policy (NEP): his belated attempt at solving the problems created by Socialism through a reversion to capitalism. One has to assume that Gorbachev cannot quite bring himself to ask whether Lenin, had he lived to do so, might have gone so far as to keep the NEP, thereby shedding Marxism and the essential aim of the Revolution. Indeed it seems highly unlikely that Lenin would have done this, given his militant activism and his many revolutionary writings. So the closest Gorbachev comes to an unthinkable repudiation of doctrine is the vague reference to "the lurking dangers of the new system."

Another example of Gorbachev's evasion of glasnost occurs in a passage about Stalin's brutal collectivization of agriculture. Just as he does not mention Brezhnev when attacking him, nor identify Lenin's NEP directly, so he manages not to mention Stalin or the human cost of his program. He refers to "the extreme backwardness of agricultural production" because it was "small scale and fragmented" and goes on in these

amazingly un-glasnostian words: "If, finally, we try to make a correct assessment of the actual results of collectivisation, one simple conclusion is
inescapable: collectivisation was a great historic act, the most important
social change since 1917. Yes, it proceeded painfully, *not without serious
excesses and blunders* in methods and pace." (Italics added.)[11]

Not long after this negative dismissal of one of the major atrocities of
the twentieth century an official figure was issued in Moscow: The "excesses" Gorbachev had mentioned totaled *14 million* dead. As for the
total of Stalin's multiple genocides, *Nedelya*—a weekly supplement to the
government daily *Izvestiya*—gave the official figure of deaths caused by
Stalin's prolonged "great terror" as *50 million.*[12]

LET US TURN now to perestroika: What did it really mean—in practice
as distinct from propaganda? Once more we enter a paradox, for the only
restructuring Gorbachev ordered and accomplished was a complete overhaul of the huge propaganda apparatus, not least of the Active Measures
section of it. The concept of *Aktivnyye Meropriyatiya* is complex, consisting of *dezinformatsiya* or "disinformation," "front organizations," and
"agents of influence." Misinformation can be unplanned, and even fortuitous, but not *dis*information—the deliberate dissemination of falsehoods
or distortions of events by "planting" stories in Western media or by
making and distributing forgeries.

Lenin himself invented "front" organizations, which he saw as
"transmission belts" for the conveying of the ruling party's policies to the
"masses." The best known were the World Federation of Trades Unions
and the World Peace Council, especially the latter, which served to supply
and coordinate the various antinuclear pressure groups in the West, such
as the Campaign for Nuclear Disarmament in the United Kingdom. As
for "agents of influence," they could be either paid and were therefore
"conscious" of what they were required to do, or were "unconscious"
and therefore unpaid. Western journalists often have difficulty in understanding the concept of an "unconscious" agent. How, they ask, can an
agent be "unconscious," that is unaware of what he is doing? The answer
lies in the careful professional cultivation of various contacts, especially
among journalists and politicians who were susceptible to flattery and
lavish hospitality, or through simple naïvete could be persuaded to disseminate "facts" or arguments useful to the Soviet side.

The Active Measures apparatus was huge, and its guiding organ was the International Department (ID) of the Central Committee of the CPSU, the direct descendant of Lenin's Comintern. As mentioned in Chapter 39, Gorbachev pensioned off the longtime head of the ID, Boris Ponomarev, who had served under Lenin and was in his eighties, replacing him with Anatoly Dobrynin, the highly successful Soviet ambassador to the United States who was only sixty-six. He replaced the International Information Department—Brezhnev's creation—by merging its functions with those of the Central Committee's Propaganda Department under his friend and mentor Yakovlev. All the main branches of the ID were overhauled, including the foreign affairs weekly *New Times;* the State Committee for Television and Radio *(GOSTELERADIO);* the State Committee for Publishing Houses, Printing Plants, and the Book Trade *(GOSKOMIZDAT);* the *Novosti* Press Agency (a major supplement to the better known *Tass* Agency); and the All-Union Copyright Agency *(VAAP).* These were his first wave of true perestroika changes. He supplemented them in his major "coup" of September 30, 1988, when he created six new "commissions," of which three were to supervise the work of the existing branches of the Active Measures apparatus: an International Policies Commission under Yakovlev to oversee the work of the ID; the Ideological Commission to head the old Ideology Department; and the Legal Policy Commission under the former chairman of the KGB, Viktor Chebrikov, who had been succeeded by Vladimir Kryuchkov.[13]

This then was the reality of Mikhail Gorbachev's perestroika: a vastly overhauled disinformation apparatus designed not only to improve the raw material but to widen its dissemination.

GLASNOST, MORE THAN any other element in Gorbachev's apparatus of deception, was supposed to persuade the West that the system of lies that had permeated the Soviet regime from its earliest days was gone. If the policy of glasnost were taken seriously, one would recognize a direct contradiction of the reality of perestroika. It is hardly fanciful to see glasnost as the release of a "genie" from a bottle.

Much as Gorbachev talked about glasnost, he made very limited use of it himself. But he soon found that the "genie" he had released could not easily be pushed back into the figurative bottle. Examples of unprecedented freedom of speech—because of glasnost—came at the All-Union

Party Conference on June 28, 1988: a spectacular event attended by 5,000 delegates from all over the USSR. A number of delegates took glasnost seriously enough to express criticisms that would have been unheard of under previous Soviet governments. One worker from Nizhny Tagil was particularly outspoken: "The workers are asking bluntly: 'Where is the restructuring?' The situation concerning food supplies in the shops is as poor as it was before. Furthermore, sugar rationing has now been introduced. There was no meat before, and there is none now. And as for consumer goods, they seem to have vanished altogether."[14]

Lest any delegates present might allow themselves to hope that democracy in the Western sense was on the way, Gorbachev had this to say:

> As you know, we have on several occasions recently run up against attempts to use democratic rights for anti-democratic ends. Some people think that it is possible to solve any issue by this means, from the redrawing of borders to *the creation of opposition parties*. The CPSU considers that *such abuses of democratisation* run fundamentally counter to the tasks of restructuring and are contrary to the interests of the people. (Italics added.)[15]

He went on to call on those present to "support the purposeful work of the leadership of the KGB, the Ministry of Defense and the General Staff." The last two words were presumably a veiled reference to military intelligence (the GRU)—an appendage of the General Staff and (unlike the KGB) never to be mentioned in public.

Despite two major purges of the ruling party (covered in Chapters 42 and 43), the pressure for Western-style democracy continued to mount. Thus on October 24, 1989, the Supreme Soviet voted to eliminate the hundred seats reserved for the Communist Party in national and local elections.[16] Worse still, on December 7, 1989, the Lithuanian Supreme Soviet decided to delete Article 6, which guaranteed the Communist Party's leading role, from its own constitution (see Chapter 42). The delayed consequence followed on February 7, 1990, when a special plenum of the Soviet Central Committee, called by Gorbachev himself, made a decision widely hailed as "historic" to revise Article 6 of the Soviet Union's constitution.

Things would never be the same again.

CHAPTER FORTY-TWO

CRACKS IN THE EMPIRE

1986–1990

⟶➤●◄⟵

T
HE NATIONALITIES ISSUE (the many nations of the Soviet Union) was the most intractable problem facing Mikhail Gorbachev.[1] This was of course as true in Lenin's day as in Gorbachev's, and the founder of the Soviet Union had entrusted the job of dealing with it to Stalin, who solved it by making sure that Stalinist Communists ruled over all of them. In attempting to solve the problem of nationalities within the context of perestroika, Gorbachev could hardly resort to the total repression favored by Lenin and Stalin.

The Soviet Union comprised in fact more than 100 nationalities, many of them in Russia itself. From the beginning of the Union's existence, the separatist aspirations of ethnic entities had been pushed to one side, with power in the hands of local Communist parties, each in turn ultimately controlled by the Politburo of the Central Committee of the CPSU. Clearly, Gorbachev's limited and necessarily flawed attempt to democratize the electoral system (see Chapter 41) was bound to encourage centrifugal forces in the wider USSR. Each national Communist Party felt its hold on power to be jeopardized by Gorbachev's "reforms."

As early as December 1986, warning signals came from Alma-Ata, the capital of Kazakhstan. At that time the Kazakh Party's first secretary was a crony of Leonid Brezhnev's in the Politburo, Dinmukhamed Kunaev. Not surprisingly, given Gorbachev's demonization of Brezhnev, he forced Kunaev to resign on the pretense that, at seventy-three, the Kazakh wished to retire.[2] Gorbachev's choice of a replacement, however, was demonstrably crass. Had Gorbachev chosen a Kazakh candidate, the change would doubtless have passed peacefully, but he chose a Russian named Gennady Kolbin, whose only special qualification to fill the gap was that he spoke Kazakh. He was an experienced Party man, but his main experience had been in Georgia from 1975 to 1983. Inevitably Kolbin had been in "the good books" of the then-first secretary of the Georgian Party, Eduard Shevardnadze, now the Soviet foreign minister and a close associate of Mikhail Gorbachev's. Kolbin would have been an ideal choice for Georgia, but not for Kazakhstan.

The inevitable outcome in Alma-Ata was a wave of riots, which were contained by the use of water cannons and ended with an undisclosed number of deaths and injuries. In time Gorbachev recognized that his appointment had been "a mistake."[3]

But this was not to happen until June 1989, when Kolbin was moved to Moscow. Surprisingly, the retired Kunaev had recommended the appointment of a non-Kazakh to succeed him, for a personal reason: he was on bad terms with the strongest local contender for the succession, Nursultan Nazarbayev, at that time chairman of the Council of Ministers. After Kolbin's removal, Nazarbayev achieved his ambition, took over the leadership of the Kazakh Party, and became one of the leading figures in Soviet (and post-Soviet) politics.

Two years earlier, in July 1987, a demonstration of greater news value but less importance to Gorbachev's reform program had taken place in Moscow's Red Square. The demonstrators were Crimean Tatars. Expelled as World War II was ending, the older survivors and their offspring had a simple demand to make: repatriation. This time the police were gentle, and the demonstrators were not beaten up—wisely at a time when the free world's media would have sent words and images back for display or projection. A commission chaired by Andrei Gromyko yielded guarded support for the language and culture of the Tatars. The return to their homeland, to which the demonstrators aspired, would have to be small in scale and gradual in time.

Next on the list was the far more bitter and sanguinary dispute between the Armenians and Azeris in the enclave of Nagorno-Karabakh, surrounded by the territory of Azerbaijan. No fewer than eight out of ten dwellers of the enclave were Armenian, and the agitators understandably wanted to be transferred to the Armenian Republic. The dispute was religious as well as ethnic: the Armenians were Christians, the Azeris were Shi'ite Muslims. As such, the Azeris were fundamentalists and resistant to any claims of "infidels."

In February 1988, mass demonstrations took place in Yerevan, the Armenian capital, and ethnic clashes followed in various places. In one of them, the industrial center of Sumgait, Azerbaijan, twenty-six Armenians were killed, plus six Azeris. Many more Armenians were injured while their homes were wrecked and looted. Gorbachev sent Yegor Ligachev to Baku and Aleksandr Yakovlev to Yerevan to address the respective Central Committees. Since neither recommended any structural changes, the disputes went on and Gorbachev opted for direct rule over Nagorno-Karabakh.

The Soviet Politburo sent Arkady Volsky, a veteran of the Andropov and Chernenko eras, to Nagorno-Karabakh. He arrived in the enclave in July 1988 and stayed until November the following year. The reforms he initiated were real but insufficient to meet local aspirations: he made available Armenian textbooks, access to Armenian television, the teaching of Armenian history in the local schools, and opened a theater to produce plays in the Armenian language. These palliatives were insufficient to meet Nationalist aspirations, however, and in November 1989 the special committee he had appointed to rule over the enclave was dissolved, and Azerbaijan was allowed to reassert its authority over Nagorno-Karabakh.[4]

During the Volsky interlude, nature added a painful extra dimension to the troubles on December 8, 1988, when a catastrophic earthquake hit the Spitak region of the Republic, causing thousands of deaths. Gorbachev put in an appearance—a normal gesture by a political leader—but his visit coincided with the arrest of members of the "Karabakh Committee," a group of Armenian intellectuals pressing for the transfer to Armenia of authority over the enclave.

The bloody tensions resumed. In Baku in January 1990 some sixty Armenians were killed in a deliberate massacre. A roundup and killing of Azeris in Baku by Soviet troops followed, with a toll of eighty-three dead. On January 14, Yevgeny Primakov, at that time chairman of the Supreme Soviet, arrived in Baku urging tough action to restore order. Whether or not he was responsible for the killing of Azeris remained unclear.

By then even more serious troubles had broken out in Georgia. In March and April, thousands of citizens of the Abkhaz Autonomous

Republic demonstrated in favor of secession from the Georgian Republic. In Tbilisi, the Georgian capital, a counterdemonstration by some 100,000 Georgian activists followed. Some of them went on a hunger strike, while workers downed tools and trains were halted.

One of the most brutal episodes of this troubled period followed. Non-Georgian troops had been sent to Tbilisi to deal with the situation and to support the Georgian Interior Ministry contingent. Violent clashes followed, and at some point on the night of April 8–9 the Soviet troops who were being "bombarded" with stones retaliated with gas canisters. The gas they sprayed on the demonstrators was not relatively harmless tear gas but a highly toxic mix of chemicals causing paralysis of the nervous system. Nineteen or twenty demonstrators died, and 138 were kept in hospital. Later more and more cases were reported, reaching a total of at least 700 hospitalized.[5]

The responsibility for this lethal response has been hotly contested. Was Gorbachev or Shevardnadze in any way responsible? The evidence collected by Archie Brown (an Oxford University specialist on Soviet affairs) suggests that they were not. The worrisome element was the fact that the troops sent from Moscow had brought the deadly canisters with them. Moreover, the local hospitals had been warned to expect heavy casualties.[6]

Gorbachev and Shevardnadze had visited Cuba and, on their way home, London. They cut short their journey and flew back to Moscow, arriving late on April 7. They were met at the airport by a Politburo delegation that included the KGB chief Viktor Chebrikov, and Ligachev. They were briefed by Chebrikov. Shevardnadze records in his memoirs that Gorbachev had declared, "No matter what, the situation must be settled by political means."[7] It was of course in Shevardnadze's interest to present Gorbachev's reaction in these terms if only to avoid guilt by association, but further evidence points the finger to the Georgian Party boss Dzhumber Patiashvili.

Gorbachev instructed Shevardnadze to go on immediately to Tbilisi. Before doing so, Shevardnadze telephoned Patiashvili, who told him the situation was under control and there was no need to hurry to Tbilisi. Back from Havana and London and due in Berlin on April 10 for a gathering of Warsaw Pact foreign ministers, Shevardnadze presumably heard Patiashvili's words with relief. However, as worse news came in from Tbilisi, he canceled his trip to Berlin and went to his home capital on

April 9. By the time he arrived, the gas canister massacre was history. In his memoirs, Shevardnadze condemns the methods used as "absolutely unacceptable" and accuses those responsible of trying to conceal the use of chemical weapons.[8] A commission appointed by the Congress of People's Deputies of the USSR and presided over by Anatoly Sobchak (said to be a friend of Boris Yeltsin) exonerated both Gorbachev and Yeltsin from all blame. The commission established that Patiashvili, in the absence of Gorbachev and Shevardnadze, had appealed to Ligachev, the CPSU's chief ideologist, for Ministry of the Interior and regular Army troops to deal with the crisis. Ligachev responded favorably, then went on holiday on April 8.

Patiashvili's request was therefore dealt with by KGB chief Chebrikov, and the defense minister Dmitri Yazov (later one of the leaders of the August coup of 1991) decided to give command of the operation to General Igor Rodionov, a notorious hard-liner in command of the Transcaucasian military district. After the event Patiashvili was sacked, Chebrikov was "dropped from the Politburo and pensioned off" (in Archie Brown's words),[9] and General Rodionov was deprived of his Transcaucasian command but appointed head of the Military Academy of the General Staff of the Soviet Armed Forces.

At about the same time as the Georgian crisis, a similar one had broken out in Tashkent, capital of the Central Asian Republic of Uzbekistan. So rarely is Uzbekistan in the news that its crisis attracted little international attention. A large Nationalist rally in Tashkent was broken up by troops and tanks on April 10 and 11.

There were also ethnic riots in Yakutia, home to a Turkic-speaking people in northeastern Siberia, and also in the southern Turkic Republics of Tajikistan and Kazakhstan. To the west, near Romania, thousands had been demonstrating against the Russification of their small Republic of Moldavia.

TRAGIC AND DIFFICULT though the troubles had been in Kazakhstan, Nagorbo-Karabakh, Azerbaijan, and Georgia, they were less threatening to the unity of the USSR than the parallel crises that were developing in the Baltic Republics. A very specific constitutional challenge came from Lithuania on December 7, 1989. That day the Lithuanian Supreme Soviet voted to delete Article 6 from its constitution (like other Soviet republics' a carbon copy of the Soviet Union's). Article 6 had always been the key one, guaranteeing the ruling party's leading role.

A fortnight later at an extraordinary congress, the Lithuanian Communist Party took a bold and unprecedented step by declaring itself independent of the CPSU. On paper, the successive Soviet constitutions, including the fourth one known as "the Brezhnev Constitution" and promulgated in 1977, guaranteed the right of secession to its republics. But like so many provisions of the various constitutions, this one was a *trompe l'oeil,* valid only on paper and not to be invoked under unstated penalties, such as military occupation. By 1990, however, Lithuania had concluded that it could get away with it.

Gorbachev, by that time president of the fast-crumbling USSR, made a three-day trip in January 1990 to the Lithuanian capital Vilnius, where he tried to talk the Lithuanian party out of its decision. Tried, and failed. He returned to Moscow empty-handed. (See Chapter 43.)

EAST EUROPEAN CHALLENGES

THE CRISES IN the constituent republics would have been easier to deal with had they not coincided with an apparently irresistible wave of challenges to Communist rule in the East European satellites. The crucial year was 1989, when the Brezhnev Doctrine was tested to destruction in Poland and Hungary, in Czechoslovakia, and even in East Germany. Although Lech Walesa's independent trade union organization, Solidarity (see Chapter 37), had been broken up and apparently extinguished by the Soviet-backed military dictator General Wojciech Jaruzelski, it now stirred into life again. On April 5, 1989, a Round-Table Agreement gave Walesa a junior role in Jaruzelski's government. The "junior" character of the deal was short-lived, however, and on June 4 partial elections brought a landslide victory for Solidarity.

This was the first free though limited poll since Communism had been imposed by Stalin. Solidarity won 92 of the 100 seats in a newly constituted Senate and 160 of the 161 seats it had been allowed to contest in the Sejm (the Lower House). The test of the popular will was only partial, however, as the Party had reserved 65 uncontested seats for itself and its allies.[10]

There was a runoff poll on June 18, but relatively few voters deigned to turn up: they had already made their views clear. In September Jaruzelski realized that his "era" was over. On September 12, a non-Communist coalition took over, with Solidarity as the senior partner. The new prime minister was Tadeusz Mazowiecki, whose sad face mirrored the sad legacy he had inherited: runaway inflation plus a de facto Communist stranglehold on industry and local government.

Hungary came next. Tens of thousands of "ordinary" citizens filed past a huge black catafalque on which the coffins of Imre Nagy and other executed leaders of the 1956 uprising had been laid. The follow-up was more than symbolic: Nagy and the rest were officially "rehabilitated"—the Communist way of recognizing its own unadmitted crimes from the past.

On July 6, 1989, the man chosen by Nikita Khrushchev to restore and enforce Moscow's authority over Hungary—János Kádár—died: in hospital, not riddled with bullets. Over the years he had softened Communist rule, and his reward had been his ejection as Party boss in May 1988. The end was drawing near. In June, Kádár's successor Karoly Grosz was himself demoted when the normally all-powerful post he held—general secretary of the Party—was itself devalued. A new leader, Reszöe Nyers, made a brief appearance in history as chairman of the Party with a four-man Presidium. His high-sounding title was short-lived: on October 8 the Hungarian Socialist Workers' (Communist) Party voted itself out of existence, and a new era began.

The formal end of the Brezhnev Doctrine came on October 27, when the assembled foreign ministers of the Warsaw Pact proclaimed the right of each nation freely to "choose the roads of its social, political and economic development, *with no external interference*" (italics added). There was no formal renunciation of the Brezhnev Doctrine. Instead, a statement that went beyond a formal rejection was issued in Moscow on December 4, when the Soviet occupation of Czechoslovakia—the *raison d'être* of the doctrine—was officially condemned as "an interference in the internal affairs of sovereign Czechoslovakia."[11]

BREACH IN THE BERLIN WALL

BY THEN THE most dramatic incident in the collapse had occurred: the Berlin Wall, infamous symbol of Soviet repression, was breached on November 10, 1989. For the previous two months, the signs of East Germany's impending collapse had been multiplying. On September 11, neighboring Hungary, itself in the last throes of exit from the Communist regime, made a generous contribution to a similar end in the *Deutsche Demokratische Republik* (DDR) by lifting border controls for "visitors" from East Germany. Few if any were genuine visitors: the great majority were refugees whose simple aim was to cross Hungarian territory into Austria, and through Austria into West Germany. Many others had sought refuge in West Germany's embassies in Prague and Warsaw with the same aim in mind. As the exodus intensified, a wave of pro-democracy demonstrations spread throughout the DDR.

On October 7, Gorbachev visited East Germany, ostensibly to celebrate the fortieth anniversary of its founding. In hard reality Gorbachev contributed to the collapse of Communism in East Germany by calling for changes. He made it clear that he wanted a less hard-line team at the top, to be replaced by supporters of an East German variant of perestroika. In effect this was a briefly deferred kiss of death. On October 18, Erich Honecker resigned as Party boss after eleven years at the top. His last act as general secretary was to appoint a much younger man, Egon Krenz, born in 1937, as his successor. In a less perilous situation it is unlikely that Krenz would have been Honecker's choice, but he knew Gorbachev favored the young pretender, and even that Erich Mielke, the minister for state security, wanted Honecker out and Krenz in, as the least of available "evils."

In the words of the long-serving head of East German Intelligence, Marcus Wolf, "He was ill-equipped for the extremely arduous task he faced." A few days earlier Wolf, who had resigned his own key post in 1986, had approached Krenz, "the solid, unimaginative functionary everyone expected to succeed Honecker," and told him he "feared bloodshed if nervous internal security forces were deployed against demonstrators with a situation they knew only from their manuals."[12] The Politburo of the ruling Socialist Unity Party fell, and mass resignations from the dreaded security service (the *Staatssicherheitsdienst,* or SSD) followed.

On November 4, a vast crowd estimated at around a million was on the streets of East Berlin. A week later double that number flooded into West Berlin through breaches that had been made in the dividing Wall. This was a time for fervor but not for tidal political change: only about one percent of the vast crowd applied for West German citizenship.

In Bonn, the West German chancellor Helmut Kohl, like millions of Westerners, watched these stirring events on television. He had already decided that the time had come, unpredictably sooner than he or anybody else had thought possible, to reunify divided Germany. On November 9, he had flown to Warsaw for talks with the recently liberated Poles. He flew back to Bonn earlier than scheduled and reached Egon Krenz by telephone. Honecker's successor had not yet grasped the fateful truth, that the DDR was in its death throes. His words to Kohl were, "German reunification is not on the agenda."

These would soon be last words. The chancellor called an emergency cabinet meeting, then flew back to West Berlin, where he addressed a crowd before the Schöneberg city hall. It was still November 10; he described that day as "an historic day for Berlin and for Germany. . . . We are and will remain one nation, and we belong together. Step by step we must find the way to our common future."

In East Berlin another newcomer to the higher ranks, Hans Modrow, took over as chairman of the (still, just) ruling *Sozialistische Einheitspartei Deutschlands:* Socialist Unity Party of Germany (SED). For Krenz, events were moving much too fast for any residual complacency. On December 6, he resigned as chairman of the Council of State and of the National Defense Council.

A fortnight later, Kohl and Modrow met in Dresden and signed a joint treaty on "cooperation and good-neighborliness." The large crowd that had gathered were cheering Kohl, not Modrow. The two men met at the Brandenburg Gate on December 22 to celebrate its reopening, which symbolized the end of the Cold War's East-West divide.

Marcus Wolf records another event, painful for him personally: "On January 15, 1990, an angry crowd—including several well-prepared groups—stormed my old ministry and seized files, which were then handed over to Western secret services."[13]

Full and formal reunification came in three further installments. First was the signing on May 18 of a state treaty on "the creation of a monetary, economic and social union." The second stage was the signing in East Berlin on August 31 of a 900-page treaty of unification. The agreed-upon date for the accession of East Germany to the Federal Republic was October 3, 1990. The third and final stage was reached in Moscow on

September 12. This amounted to a formal end to the Cold War. Six foreign ministers signed a treaty on the final settlement on Germany: "The
Two"—the Federal Republic of Germany and the German Democratic
Republic—were joined by "The Four"—the Soviet Union, the United
States, France, and the United Kingdom. Under the terms of the treaty the
two Germanies announced "the renunciation of the production and possession of and power to use nuclear, biological and chemical weapons."
And the Soviet Union agreed to withdraw its forces from East Germany
by the end of 1994.

MASS DEMONSTRATIONS
IN PRAGUE AND ELSEWHERE

THE GREAT COLLAPSE had taken several months in Poland and Hungary; but it took only ten crowded days of mass demonstrations in
Czechoslovakia, in which a leading role was played by the dissident play-
wright and patriot Václav Havel, who had been jailed earlier in the year
of liberation. The climax came in Prague on December 10, 1989, when
President Gustav Husak swore in Czechoslovakia's first non-Communist
majority government since 1948. Husak had stood for Soviet repression
since 1968 but now stepped down. On December 28 and 29, two events,
each heavy with symbolism, occurred. One was the return to Prague of
Alexander Dubček, the Party boss who had stood up to the Soviets in
1968 and been sent into exile and oblivion as a gardener. The other was
the swearing in of Václav Havel as president.

By then, on November 10, the long-reigning Bulgarian Party boss,
Todor Zhivkov, had been ousted. A month later, coinciding with the
events in Prague, his successor Petar Mladenov had promised free elections and proposed to abandon the Communist Party's leading role under
a new constitution.

Romania's turn came in December. The corrupt and odious tyranny
of the ruling party's secretary-general and Romania's president, Nicolae
Ceausescu, in power since March 1965, ended in a short and bloody revolution. Even more, perhaps, than any other postwar Communist regime,
his protracted rule had been made possible only by the repressive secret
security apparatus known as the "Securitate." For years an uprising had
been waiting to happen. The missing element was a trigger, which came

on December 15, 1989, when a deportation order was served on a Protestant pastor named Father Laszlo Tokes, who had been brave enough to criticize the regime for its treatment of his fellow ethnic Hungarians. Next day several hundred people surrounded Father Tokes's home in Timisoara, near the western border with Hungary. Father Tokes appeared at a window displaying the marks of beatings by the Securitate, and the crowd, enraged at the sight, marched through the town center shouting slogans: "Down with Ceausescu!" and "Give us bread!"

The repression that followed was particularly brutal. The Securitate came in tanks or hovered above in helicopter gunships. When they opened fire, hundreds died. It was claimed later that the police had been backed by regular troops, but a rumor spread that some of the Securitate repressors had been wearing Army uniforms.

Judging the situation to be under control, Ceausescu had flown to Tehran on a three-day visit. Back on December 20, the president broadcast a speech declaring a state of emergency in Timisoara. He blamed the disturbances on "terrorists, fascists, imperialists, hooligans, [and, for good measure] foreign espionage services." Next day, again believing the situation to be under control, he addressed a large rally in central Bucharest. He offered a tiny palliative: across-the-board monthly wage rises of the Romanian equivalent of US $12—100 lei.

The occasion was seen on television by millions of Western viewers. It was worth seeing if only because, for the first time, aggressive hecklers continually interrupted the dictator. Nothing like this had happened since 1966, and the images showed his astonishment, soon turning to demoralization. Sections of the crowd broke away to stage antigovernment demonstrations in other quarters of the capital. Clashes also took place in Blasov, Cluj, Arad, and Sibiu.

Ceausescu proclaimed a national state of emergency. The first casualty that followed was the death of his defense minister Colonel-General Vasile Milea. The official version was that Milea had committed suicide, but it emerged that he had been shot dead by a presidential guardsman for refusing to use his troops to disperse the crowds.

A few hours later Ceausescu appeared on the balcony of the Communist Party's headquarters. His attempt to address the hostile crowd was soon halted by united shouts of "Death! Death!" The TV screens showed his bewilderment as he stopped even trying to make himself heard. He and his wife Elena, who if anything was even more hated than himself, fled from the roof by helicopter with their bodyguards as demonstrators broke into the building. The Army did not intervene.

The end had come. Nicolae and Elena Ceausescu were captured by troops that evening near Tirgoviste, fifty miles from Budapest. The fugitives had landed near an air base at Boteni, commandeered a car that broke down, found another and driven on, but not for long. They were soon arrested and placed under close guard in an armored car. The hated couple were arraigned before a hastily convened military tribunal on charges of genocide, corruption, and wrecking the national economy. They were both sentenced to death and executed by firing squad on the Western world's Christmas Day. The execution, as well as their bullet-ridden bodies, was seen on TV screens throughout the world. Not long afterward, reports circulated to the effect that the anti-Ceausescu demonstrations had been carefully planned by agents of the KGB.*

Unlike most of the other fallen satellites—Poland, Hungary, East Germany, and Czechoslovakia—the overthrow of Romania's Communist regime did not herald the advent of a Western-style democracy. Former Communists reorganized themselves under a new identity, calling themselves the "National Salvation Front," led by a longtime Communist, Ion Iliescu. In Bulgaria too the formal demise of Communism was delayed.

One other Communist country in Eastern Europe—small and backward Albania—would remain under Communist rule for some years. (See Epilogue 2.) Within the USSR itself, the collapse of the regime was still two years off, and the violence of repression had not ended.

---

*The KGB case is argued at considerable length in the last chapters of Michel Castex, *Un mensonge gros comme le siée: Roumanie, histoire d'une manipulation* (Paris, 1990). The fact that the Romanian Communist Party and the Securitate were clearly ready to take over in the wake of the execution of the Ceausescu couple is of course significant. Unfortunately, Castex, at the time the Agence France-Presse correspondent in Bucharest, spoils his case by frivolously telling it in the form of an imaginary dialogue between Sherlock Holmes and Dr. Watson.—BC

CHAPTER FORTY-THREE

MORE CRACKS
IN THE EMPIRE

1990

———⟶⊰⊱⟵———

T HE CHALLENGE TO Mikhail Gorbachev and to the Kremlin's in-
creasingly precarious hold on the Empire sharpened dramatically in
January 1990. The scene was Vilnius, capital of the Baltic Republic of
Lithuania.

THE LITHUANIAN CRISIS

ON DECEMBER 25, 1989, when President Nicolae Ceausescu of Romania was executed, the CPSU's Central Committee called a plenum to
discuss the declaration of independence made by the Lithuanian Communist Party (CPL). Gorbachev was in an uncompromising mood, and condemned the CPL's leader, Algirdas Brazauskas, for compromising with
Nationalist and separatist forces. He described as "illegitimate and invalid" the CPL's decision to delete Article 6, which guaranteed the Party's
leading role, from Lithuania's constitution. He linked the future of perestroika to any proposals for reforming the Soviet Union's federal structure. In other words, he was hinting that perestroika would work only if
the Soviet Union remained united.

Although the plenum was described as "stormy," the conclusions
reached were relatively bland. A further plenum was scheduled for January, but it was agreed that before it was convened Gorbachev himself
would visit Vilnius and assess the situation. First, however, a preliminary

visit should be made by Vadim Medvedev, a protégé of Gorbachev, who in September 1988 had appointed Medvedev head of a new Ideological Commission. That reshuffling amounted in effect to an internal Party coup. Yegor Ligachev, Gorbachev's main "conservative" (that is, anti-reformist) opponent, the Party's Number 2 man and successor to the late M. A. Suslov as the guardian of ideological purity, had been shunted sideways and downward to take over the Agriculture Commission. Thus in effect, though not on paper, Medvedev had taken over from Ligachev.[1]

On January 8, Medvedev arrived in Vilnius. He was not alone: with him were more than forty Central Committee members. The group attended meetings at factories and on collective farms to sound out the glasnost version of public opinion. It was a short visit, and Gorbachev followed on January 11.

By this time in Lithuania the sacred principle enshrined in the Soviet constitution's Article 6 had been breached. There were two rival Communist parties: the original CPL, now converted to secessionism, and the rival "Lithuanian Communist Party on the CPSU platform," a Moscow-line breakaway faction. Before leaving Moscow, Gorbachev had met with representatives of both parties, as well as with four leading members of the Lithuanian restructuring movement known as "Sajudis," who were chaired by a mild piano teacher named Vytautas Landsbergis. Such a meeting in itself would have been unthinkable under any of Gorbachev's predecessors. Indeed the Sajudis leaders would soon have been executed (in Stalin's day) or at best banished to the gulag.

On the afternoon of Gorbachev's arrival in Vilnius, Landsbergis had organized a mass rally, estimated at 300,000 people, in the capital's Cathedral Square. There were CPL leaders present as well as Sajudis separatists. All speakers called for Lithuania's unconditional independence.

Gorbachev began his visit with a walkabout in the center of Vilnius, during which he referred to Lithuania's relationship with the Soviet Union and commented, "Nothing will be decided without you. We shall decide everything together." He added, less reassuringly, that any republican contemplating independence should reflect "a thousand times."

His first formal engagement was a meeting with Lithuanian intellectuals at the Academy of Sciences. He refrained from denouncing Article 72 of the Brezhnev Constitution ("Each Union Republic shall retain the right freely to secede from the USSR"). Instead, he announced that a new law was being drafted to prepare a "mechanism for how a republic could leave the Soviet Union." This, he said, would include "the time frame for leaving, defense, communications and a whole series of questions." He declared himself "in favor of the principle of self-determination, stopping short of secession" in substance—a political oxymoron.

He went on to express the conviction that the way to political sovereignty of the constituent republics, economic independence, and cultural autonomy was a restructuring of the Soviet Union as a federation of sovereign states. In other words, "sovereignty" was not really on offer.

Next day a member of Gorbachev's entourage and of the Soviet Politburo, Yuri Maslyukov, said that the secession of a republic could only be settled by a referendum. The Lithuanians who had listened to Maslyukov were given to understand that he meant a referendum in *all* the republics of the USSR, not merely in the republic concerned.

That day—January 12—Landsbergis, the chairman of Sajudis, dismissed Gorbachev's proposals as "a cheap lie" designed to impress the Western media. Others hazarded the view that the proposed mechanism might actually make secession impossible.

On January 13, Gorbachev went on a tour of factories and farms, then addressed CPL activists. In impassioned terms he called on the Party to reconsider its break with the CPSU. Mission accomplished, Gorbachev returned to Moscow. Two days later the Lithuanian Supreme Soviet elected Algirdas Brazauskas as president of Lithuania (in formal terms, chairman of the Party Presidium). Although the days of unanimity were over, only four members voted against him, with nineteen abstentions; 228 had voted in his favor. That day the Lithuanian Supreme Soviet voted on the Soviet Law on Supervision of the Constitution passed by the Congress of People's Deputies the previous month. Overwhelmingly, the voters declared it invalid on Lithuanian territory. The following day, January 16, President Brazauskas declared that the aims of the CPL remained unchanged, whatever Gorbachev had said.

UNREST IN LATVIA AND ESTONIA

LITHUANIA WAS NOT alone among the three Baltic Republics in its defiance of Soviet authority and pressure. On January 11, the Latvian

Supreme Soviet had voted (by 225 to four with nineteen abstentions: almost a replica of the Lithuanian vote) to abolish Article 6 from its constitution.

Although the three republics did not necessarily act simultaneously, the rule seemed to be that if one of them took a decision and acted upon it, so did the others, in due course. On November 12, 1989, the Estonian Supreme Soviet had declared illegal the vote taken by the *Duma* of independent Estonia, in July 1940, to join the Soviet Union on the (valid) ground that the decision had been secured by Soviet military coercion. Now that Lithuania and Latvia had decided to secede, it was Estonia's turn to follow suit.

Under the Tartu Treaty of 1920, Soviet Russia had recognized Estonia's independence. On February 2, 1990, the seventieth anniversary of the treaty, a mass rally was held in Tallinn, the Estonian capital, including 3,000 deputies at all levels from rural soviets to the Supreme Soviet of the USSR. The deputies went on to adopt a declaration calling on the USSR Supreme Soviet to joint talks on "the restoration of Estonian state independence." The deputies representing Estonia's large Russian minority immediately countered with the formation of a committee to work toward a restructured Soviet federation to include a separate state for Estonia's Russians.

On February 23, the Estonian Supreme Soviet, in line with Lithuania and Latvia, abolished Article 6. So all three Baltic Republics had now given themselves the right to be ruled by non-Communist parties.

TURMOIL IN THE RULING PARTY

THE PRESSURES FROM the Baltic Republics, combined with disturbances elsewhere in the Soviet Empire, stirred unprecedented turmoil within the ruling CPSU. (It is fair to say that the crisis in Azerbaijan that followed Gorbachev's visit to Vilnius by a few days helped to deflect any repressive tendencies from Moscow toward the Baltic Republics.) On January 22, 1990, the Politburo had failed to endorse a new platform said to have been largely the work of Gorbachev's friend and mentor Aleksandr Yakovlev. In one sense the platform was politically suicidal, as it included provision for the Party to renounce its constitutionally guaranteed monopoly of power. The two men had called for a Party plenum to endorse the draft platform. The "conservatives" were fiercely opposed to any such development; the reformists were determined to get their way. The Party was thus facing a dual but related problem: the bid for national independence and the end of the Party's monopoly of power. The one meant the end of Lenin's recreated Tsarist Empire; the other the end of Communism, for it implied the emergence of a Western-style multiparty democracy.

Did Gorbachev and Yakovlev sincerely want either of these developments? Certainly they did not want the former; as for the latter, Gorbachev is less than frank in his memoirs. Glasnost emerges, yet again, as a device to convince the West that he really believed in Western-style democracy, including freedom of speech—an essential device for securing financial and economic aid from the "capitalist" systems Lenin had vowed to destroy.

As the Soviet leader put it, "We could not deny the right of nations to self-determination, even to the point of secession. It was provided for in our Constitution. Nevertheless, we had to do everything possible to show the people the catastrophic consequences of this step."[2]

On January 20–21, reformist Communists in more than a hundred Soviet cities met in a conference that called on the CPSU to drop "democratic centralism" (yet another immutable Leninist doctrine), leading to a multiparty democratic system. Various groups sprouted from the seeds of the conference; the one that attracted most notice was the Democratic Platform of the CPSU. On February 4, the groups organized the biggest unofficial demonstration ever seen in Moscow, estimated at 150,000 people. This was an instance of true glasnost, for it included a wide range of persuasions, from right-wing Russian monarchists and Nationalists to anarchists and separatists from outside Russia. Moscow Radio, one of the true glasnostian institutions, which had taken Gorbachev's slogan at face value, had announced the march in advance, and television crews brought it into people's homes with closeups showing the occasional placard calling for Gorbachev to step down and banners with slogans attacking the Communist monopoly of power. Although police drew the line at allowing the demonstrators to march onto Red Square, they were allowed to carry their varied messages into Manezh Square next to the Kremlin.

Ominous reports were coming in from distant places, including Tyumen in Western Siberia, Volgograd in Russia's European South, and Chernigov in the Ukraine. In all of them, hard-liners had been toppled.

Did all these signs of disturbance mean that Gorbachev was winning his battle with the "conservatives" or that he really was committing political suicide? On February 5, a plenum of the (still ruling) Party's Central Committee met to discuss the draft platform.

Gorbachev's opening speech had a tortured ring about it, but went further than ever before in the direction of ending the Party's monopoly of power. He called on the Party "drastically to restructure itself" (a reference to perestroika) by ridding itself of authoritarianism, bureaucratism, and ideological dogmatism. He let it be known that the Party was "rethinking the principle of democratic centralism": Lenin's teaching, revised.

He was cautious on multiparty democracy but moved a further step in that direction: "The extensive democratization currently under way in our society is being accompanied by mounting political pluralism. . . . This process may lead at a certain stage to the establishment of parties."

He also called for the abolition of the post of general secretary—his own post—and its replacement by that of Party chairman.* The all-powerful Politburo, too, would have to be replaced by a new body more closely in tune with the Soviet Union's federal structure, while the Central Committee would be reduced in size and become a permanent working body, rather than one to be called when the need arose.

The response demonstrated the turmoil that had been building up among the "conservatives." A number of those assembled spoke out against Gorbachev's plans, among them:

• Anatoly Kornienko, first secretary of the Ukrainian Communist Party's Committee, who declared that the Soviet Party platform had no ideological foundation and gave the impression that the Central Committee did not know which way to turn;

---

*The rumor that Gorbachev was stepping down as leader of the governing party caused nervous reactions in Washington, Bonn, Paris, and London and a dramatic fall in stock markets in New York, Tokyo, and London. There is reason to believe that it was circulated deliberately, with a view to provoking a pro-Gorbachev reaction in the West on the ground that only he could change the system on Western lines. When it started, he had been closeted with close advisers outside Moscow for more than a week when one of them leaked the "news," which was carried on the U.S. Cable News Network (CNN) on January 30, 1990. A full analysis appeared in the February 1990 issue of the London-based confidential newsletter *World Briefing.*

- Valentin Mesyats, first secretary of the Moscow *oblast* (province), who said that no force other than the CPSU was "capable of uniting the people";
- Vladimir Brovikov, the Soviet ambassador to Poland, who accused Gorbachev of being obsessed with democratization: "It is said that the people back perestroika. But what perestroika? The one that for the past five years had brought us into crisis, anarchy and economic decay?"; and
- Boris Gidaspov, first secretary to Leningrad city and *oblast,* went even further, exclaiming that "complete disorganization of the executive mechanism" was responsible for the country's growing destabilization.

To Western observers it would not have been surprising, after such outspoken criticisms of Mikhail Gorbachev, had the plenum gone on to vote him out of office. Instead, Party discipline won the day for the man who was under attack for destroying it. In the vote, a show of hands that followed the speeches, all those present with only two exceptions voted in favor of Gorbachev's draft platform. One of the exceptions merely abstained. The other voted against. His name was Boris Yeltsin.

During the plenum, there was a debate on the Lithuanian Communist Party's declaration of independence in December 1989. On this provocative action by a minor republic, the Central Committee was almost as tough as in the good old days. The declaration was labeled as having "no standing," and the Lithuanian Communists were urged to suspend their decision to break with CPSU until the matter was debated at the forthcoming Twenty-Eighth Party Congress, to be opened on July 1.

On February 24, less than three weeks after the Party plenum, the Lithuanian Supreme Soviet held elections that put control of the Party firmly in the hands of the Sajudis (now styling itself the nationalist "Popular Front for Perestroika"). On March 11, the reformed Party, defying the massively larger CPSU, unilaterally declared Lithuania independent. The day before, the Lithuanian Supreme Soviet held the second round of the first free multiparty elections ever held in the Soviet Union (to which Lithuania still belonged). The Communist Party of Lithuania won more seats (forty) than the rival parties, including the pro-CPSU Communist Party, which scored only five, but fewer than the candidates calling themselves "independents" (seventy). The other parties were the Social

Democrats (nine); the Greens (four); the Democrats (three); and the Christian Democrats (two). One other party also presented itself, under the name of "Humanism and Progress," but it did not win a single seat.

NICARAGUA'S SANDINISTAS IN TROUBLE

AT ALMOST EXACTLY the same time, in distant Nicaragua, the ruling Sandinista National Liberation Front (FSLN) lost its hold on power in free presidential and legislative elections on February 25, 1990. Most observers had expected the Sandinistas to win, and they might well have done so without the presence of an estimated 2,500 international observers. These included a United States team led by ex-President Jimmy Carter and representatives of international bodies: the United Nations, the Organization of American States (OAS), and the European Parliament.

The unexpected winner was the chosen candidate of the *Unión Nacional de Oposición* (UNO), Violeta Barrios de Chamorro, age sixty, widow of Pedro Joaquín Chamorro, who had been murdered in 1978, in a prelude to the Sandinista revolution that overthrew the long-reigning Somoza dictatorship the following year. Thus in the peripheral empire as well as in the nearby Stalinist one, Communism appeared to be collapsing.

CHANGES TO THE SOVIET CONSTITUTION

IN THE SOVIET UNION, meanwhile, the speed of events, as well as their significance, was increasing. On March 13, 1990, in a session of the Congress of People's Deputies, the Communist Party's guaranteed monopoly of political power was ended by a crucially important amendment of the Soviet constitution. The relevant Article 6 now read, "The Communist Party of the Soviet Union, other political parties, trade unions, youth and other social organizations and mass movements participate in the formulation of the policy of the Soviet state and in the administration of state and social affairs through their representatives elected to the soviets of people's deputies and in other ways."

uchkov (new head of the KGB), Vadim Bakatin, Eduard Shevard-
lze, the Arabist Yevgeny Primakov, and (closest of all to Gorbachev)
ksandr Yakovlev. The absence of Yegor Ligachev confirmed the fact
t he had been excluded from the higher reaches of power.

EW LAW ON SECESSION PASSES

IE STAGE WAS now set for a reversal of the previous hard-line oppo-
ion to independence for the constituent republics. In April, bowing to
e inevitable, Gorbachev carried through a Law on Secession, which, for
e first time, spelled out conditions to be fulfilled if any constituent re-
iblics wished to break away from the Union. A referendum would be
ld, yielding a positive vote by two-thirds of the electorate. Thereafter
ere would be a five-year transition period, at the end of which the
oviet legislature would be required to endorse the decision to secede.

Thus, in legal and constitutional terms, the totalist Russian- and
Communist-dominated home empire Gorbachev had inherited appeared
o have turned into a Western-style federation. This, however, was
merely one way of interpreting the measures taken. A more realistic in-
erpretation soon revealed itself: The new measures were held to justify
pressure on Lithuania to conform to Moscow's decrees or face the consequences. On March 15, President Gorbachev sent two messages to his
nominal counterpart Lithuanian President Vytautas Landsbergis. One
was the text of a resolution passed that day by the Soviet Congress of
People's Deputies calling on Lithuania to conform to the new restrictions
on any declaration of independence by a constituent republic of the
USSR. The other was a personal message to Landsbergis demanding,
within three days, a report of measures taken to conform to the conditions laid down in Moscow.

Landsbergis replied immediately, with words of defiance: a decision
made in a "foreign" country was not binding on Lithuania. The Soviet response was to begin a war of nerves, with helicopters and military transport planes circling over Vilnius and armored vehicle convoys driven at
regular intervals through the city. The Lithuanian Supreme Council had
already passed a resolution stating that Lithuanian conscripts in the Red
Army were no longer required to serve and could desert without incurring
criminal charges. On March 27, the commander of the Baltic Military

Another amendment had been proposed to the
should be no actual mention of the Party, but although
1,067 votes to 906, it narrowly failed to secure the nec
majority. However, Article 7, which had defined the offi
nizations affiliated to the CPSU, was amended to read as
litical parties, social organizations and mass movements,
the functions stipulated in their programs and rules, op
framework of the Constitution and Soviet law."

A parting shot came from Gorbachev, with the revela
law on setting up political parties was being drafted.

Also in that crowded session of March 13, the Cong
Deputies announced the creation of the post of presiden
Two days later, the congress elected Gorbachev to the ne
carried extensive executive powers. Why, it may be asked,
opt for a change of official role, from Party boss to preside
bling federation? Two years earlier, he had discussed the id
dency with his closest cronies.[3] At that time, he had preferr
all-powerful post of general secretary and had opted for the
of the Congress of People's Deputies as a kind of substitute
embracing title he now chose.

There had been considerable and protracted discussion
within Gorbachev's inner circle, centering around the choice o
Western model. Some of his advisers—especially the Armen
Shakhnazarov, a senior adviser to Gorbachev since 1987—
model of the French Fifth Republic, on the ground that a presi
premier who would make most of the lesser decisions would
time for the higher ones; whereas an American-style president
also head of the government, might be overwhelmed, particu
time of complex changes and political unrest. In the end, (
opted for a combination of the French and American presidenti
though marginally closer to the French since there would be a p
well as a president.[4]

Also elected, on March 15, was Anatoly Lukyanov as cha
the Supreme Soviet. Finally, on March 24–25, the sixteen membe
Presidential Council (in effect a Cabinet) were likewise voted in.
cluded a number of Gorbachev's closest friends or advisers:

District, Colonel-General Fyodor Kuzmin, seized a couple of dozen Lithuanian deserters. Two days later, however, the Soviet Defense Ministry offered an amnesty to other deserters on condition that they rejoin their units immediately. Meanwhile, the Soviet forces had seized the premises of the Lithuanian Communist Party.

On April 13, the Soviet Union issued a forty-eight-hour ultimatum to Lithuania. Not surprisingly the Lithuanian Sajudis ignored it, and on April 18 a near-total economic blockade began. Although self-sufficient in foodstuffs, Lithuania was heavily dependent on Soviet supplies of oil and gas. Within the next few days, crude oil supplies to Lithuania's main refinery at Mazeikiai were cut off, and gas supplies were reduced by more than 80 percent.

The Lithuanian assertion of sovereignty was soon imitated in the other two Baltic Republics: in Latvia on May 4 and in Estonia on May 8. Latvia's choice of means to an agreed-upon end was to restore its constitution of February 1922; and Estonia's, five key articles of its independent 1938 constitution. A few days later, on May 14, Gorbachev issued decrees outlawing both republics' declarations of independence for violating the USSR constitution and specifically the Soviet law of April 3, 1990, defining the procedures for any republic's secession from the USSR. He did not, however, issue an ultimatum to either republic. For coming first, Lithuania bore the brunt of Soviet reprisals.

On June 29, however, Lithuania's parliament voted to suspend for one hundred days its March 11 declaration of independence so that negotiations on the republic's future could be held with the Soviet authorities. The immediate Soviet response was to lift the economic blockade that had been in force since mid-April.

THE RISE OF YELTSIN

AT THIS STAGE Gorbachev's political rival began to play an increasingly important role. Boris Yeltsin's rise, over the next eighteen months, would coincide with Gorbachev's decline. As a candidate member (awaiting promotion as a full member) of the Politburo, he had drawn passing attention to himself in October 1987 when he was expelled after a critical speech during a plenum of the Party's Central Committee. A period of potential peril for Yeltsin followed. In his two books of memoirs, *Against the Grain* and *The View from the Kremlin*,[5] he paints vivid pictures of the callous political isolation inflicted on him by Gorbachev.

The two men could hardly have been more different. As noted earlier, despite his humble roots, Gorbachev was a smooth Party apparatchik, highly skilled in public relations.* In contrast, Yeltsin was a rough diamond who spoke as he thought without mincing words, often at the cost of wishing later that he had been more tactful. One such occasion was the October 1987 plenum of the Central Committee, at which he made a speech of such brutal frankness that "afterwards I often wondered whether . . . I really needed to have charged in as I did, guns blazing; to have caused the uproar which resulted in such a drastic change in my whole life."[6]

Thereupon, after the 1987 speech, Gorbachev attacked him venomously and Yeltsin was politically ostracized, even by Politburo members whom he had thought of as his friends. The strain on him was such that on November 9 that year, he was taken to the hospital with severe headaches and chest pains. Two days later, Gorbachev in person rang him at the hospital and instructed him to attend the forthcoming plenum of the Moscow city committee. Yeltsin replied that he could not come, as he was in bed and the doctors would not let him get up. However, Gorbachev would not take "No" for an answer:

> However much Gorbachev may have disliked me, to act like that was inhuman and immoral. . . . The obedient doctors, who only a few hours ago had not only forbidden me to get up and move about, but still less to go outside, started to pump me full of sedatives. My head was spinning, my legs were crumpling under me. I could hardly speak because my tongue wouldn't obey.[7]

At the Moscow plenum, Yeltsin's enemies, who now included his "friends," attacked him systematically while he was not only physically unable to reply but actually barred from doing so. He was duly expelled from the Politburo and henceforth politically ostracized, although in February 1988 he was given a well-paid job as first deputy chairman of Gosstroi, the state construction trust.

---

*As Richard Nixon put it, Gorbachev "was born with a master's degree in public relations" (quoted in a personal letter to me from Nixon, referring to a "secret," or at any rate discreet, speech he made to the editorial team of *Time* magazine in New York).—BC

Although Gorbachev had not sent Yeltsin into Siberian exile or to a distant gulag, his new job at the Gosstroi was a serious demotion.

> A feeling of dead silence and emptiness surrounded me. . . . Gorbachev appeared to be gracious, sparing and pitying me. But few people know what torture it is to sit in the dread silence of an office, in a complete vacuum, subconsciously waiting for something. . . . As I whiled away the long hours . . . I finally figured out my relations with Gorbachev. I saw both his strengths and weaknesses and felt the vibrations of trouble and peril emanating from him. I had never intended to fight with him personally; moreover, in many ways I had followed in his footsteps as he dismantled communism. But why hide it—the motivations for many of my actions were embedded in our conflict, which had arisen in earnest just prior to the central plenum in 1987 that had led to my being ousted from the Politburo.[8]

Gorbachev's vendetta against Yeltsin nevertheless continued, apparently orchestrated by the KGB. One occasion was Yeltsin's first visit to the United States at the invitation of several universities and friendly politicians. The visit had been planned for two weeks, but the Central Committee cut it to eight days. In a characteristic disinformation ploy, *Pravda* reproduced a hostile article in the Italian newspaper *La Repubblica* describing Yeltsin as permanently drunk; while *Vremya,* the main current affairs program, slowed down a video of Yeltsin delivering a speech, so that he appeared to be under the influence of drink and slurred of speech.[9]

There was even worse to come. After meeting some of his Sverdlovsk constituents he was being driven to a friend's dacha in the village of Uspenskoye outside Moscow. He dismissed his driver so that he could walk the last few hundred yards, when another car appeared behind him and he found himself in the river in nearly ice-cold water. With cramp in his legs, he swam to the bank, rested and went to the nearest police station, where his wife and daughter picked him up.[10]

YELTSIN BECOMES RUSSIA'S PRESIDENT

YELTSIN'S ISOLATION ENDED dramatically on May 29, 1990, when he was elected chairman of the Russian Supreme Soviet: in effect president of the Russian Federation. No fewer than thirteen candidates had presented themselves, and Yeltsin's success had come after several days of acrimonious debate. He had announced a fourteen-point political plan at the center of which was an assertion of Russia's sovereignty, with laws to take precedence over those of the Soviet Union and independence in foreign policy. He had also called for Russia to have a multiparty democracy.

As it happened, Mikhail Gorbachev arrived in Canada on the day of his rival's success, and was quoted as saying that he was "somewhat worried" by Yeltsin's victory. During the debate Gorbachev had accused Yeltsin of "seeking to separate Russia from Socialism," and by implication seeking the break-up of the Soviet Union.

Yeltsin was more conciliatory: on the same day, he said he hoped to build a partnership with Gorbachev, "not on confrontation but on a businesslike basis, on dialogue and talks."

GORBACHEV FACES
HOSTILE SLOGANS

ON MAY DAY 1990, that symbolic date of the massed international power of the workers of the world, an unofficial parade of some 40,000 opposition groups had followed the officially sponsored one in Moscow's Red Square. On the balcony of the Lenin Mausoleum, Gorbachev and his close associates, including Yakovlev, had seen and heard in anger the anti-regime and anti-Gorbachev slogans, printed and vocal. In their anger they left the balcony, and the demonstration continued for another hour.

Two days later, it was learned from a British source at NATO headquarters in Brussels that on February 25—an earlier day of hostile demonstrations at the height of the Lithuanian crisis—a 6,000-strong Red Army division had been mobilized on the outskirts of Moscow. The point of the unpublicized show of military force was to warn the Politburo that it should not ignore the views of the armed forces in ongoing disarmament negotiations with the United States.*

---

*The source was in fact Desmond Donnelly, Director of the Soviet Studies Research Center of Royal Military Academy at Sandhurst, who at the time was an adviser at NATO headquarters. For further details, see Brian Crozier, in *Désinformation-hebdo 163,* May 16, 1990, weekly bulletin of the Paris-based Institut d'Etudes de la Désinformation.

MORE CRACKS IN THE USSR

BEFORE LONG THE centrifugal forces unleashed by the Baltic Republics had spread to other components of the USSR. The first to proclaim its sovereignty was the biggest of all: Russia, under its new president, Boris Yeltsin. The fateful date was June 12, when, after an understandably heated debate, the new Congress of People's Deputies issued a fifteen-article declaration proclaiming the right of the Russian Federation to suspend USSR acts contravening Russia's sovereign rights. Moreover, it claimed the sole right of the Russian people to own, dispose of, and utilize Russia's natural wealth; and to form its own diplomatic links not only with other Soviet republics but with foreign countries as well. It was almost as though the events and decisions of March and April had not taken place.

Eight days later, on June 20, Uzbekistan did likewise, followed on June 23 by Moldavia. Sovereignty fever now seemed unstoppable. On August 4, the Armenian Supreme Soviet elected Levon Ter-Petrosyan as president, defeating the Armenian Communist Party's first secretary Vladimir Movsiyan. On June 22, Turkmenia proclaimed its sovereignty, followed three days later by Tajikistan.

These manifestations of sovereignty were not necessarily uniform, however. In Turkmenia and Azerbaijan, the ruling Communist parties won elections in September and October.

In unexpected ways, independence proved internally contagious. For example, the Russian population in the Dnestr Valley in eastern Moldavia, where it was in a majority, met on September 2 to proclaim secession from Moldavia and the creation of a Dnestr Soviet Republic. A similar move came from the less known Gagauz minority in August. The Moldavian Supreme Soviet empowered its new president, Mircha Snegur, to introduce direct presidential rule in regions bold enough to defy the Moldavian constitution. The situation erupted in violence in October, and on October 31 the new Gagauz Supreme Soviet convened to confirm its sovereignty. The same phenomenon manifested itself in Georgia on September 20, when the Supreme Soviet of the autonomous region *(oblast)* of South Ossetia proclaimed its independence: a move immediately denounced as unconstitutional by the Georgian Supreme Soviet Presidium.

*   *   *

MEANWHILE, DESPITE THE open split between Gorbachev and Yeltsin, the two leaders had agreed on August 1 to sponsor a draft for the transition of the Russian Federation and the wider USSR (to the extent that it still existed) to a market economy. For Gorbachev, though not for Yeltsin, this was a major step away from the Leninist orthodoxy that had dominated his thinking until then. As Yeltsin put it, "Everyone knows that Gorbachev had always been an advocate of socialism with a human face. That looks nice in theory. But in practice, the former General Secretary was so afraid of making the painful break with the past, was so steeped on our Soviet system that at first he was horrified by the very concepts of 'the market' and 'private property.'"[11]

On August 15, President Gorbachev issued a decree restoring Soviet citizenship to Aleksander Solzhenitsyn and other ideological exiles. Two days earlier, in an attempt to overturn history, he had passed another decree, restoring civil and socioeconomic rights to peasants who had suffered imprisonment and expropriation during Stalin's collectivization of agriculture and to all citizens persecuted for "political, social, ethnic, religious and other reasons." In his 1987 book, *Perestroika,* he had sidestepped these poignant issues. Now he declared that the victims of Stalinist repression must be rehabilitated for society's "moral regeneration."

The split between Yeltsin and Gorbachev appeared to be narrowing when the two men got together on November 11, 1990, to discuss a Union treaty designed to settle the contentious issue of incompatible claims between the Russian Federation and the USSR on the delineation of state power, the ownership of state property, and the disposal of natural resources. Events, however, were moving so fast that no real progress was made. On November 16, Gorbachev delivered an eighty-minute speech to the Supreme Soviet on the state of the nation. By common consent, it was one of his poorest oratorical performances; he took refuge in empty phrases such as exhortations to rival forces to unite behind perestroika and complaints about "destructive and separatist tendencies."

By then the USSR as a whole was caught in a somber crisis. In the last two months of 1990, food rationing was introduced in Leningrad and in scattered lesser areas of the vast country. An international airlift of emergency food aid was seen by many as a humiliating exposure of the faults of Soviet Socialism. Indeed, a quarter of the combine harvesters had broken down in the summer for lack of spare parts. Much of the potato and vegetable harvests were allowed to rot on the ground for lack of man-power. An announcement on November 1 that the grain harvest had broken records at 240 million tons was reduced to a realistic figure of about 140 million because 100 million tons had rotted either on the ground or in storage for lack of attention or transport.

On December 2, President Gorbachev removed the (relatively) liberal interior minister Vadim Bakatin. He gave no reason, but senior military and KGB officers had been criticizing Bakatin for his alleged failure to tackle a dramatic rise in crime. More relevant, he had been accused of proposing that limited contingents of Interior Ministry troops should be transferred to the control of certain republican governments. Ironically, his removal was being called for by the Soyuz group of conservative deputies who had backed him earlier in March of that year (1990) as a candidate for the presidency in opposition to Gorbachev.

Not only did Gorbachev sack Bakatin, but in his stead he appointed a known hard-liner, the Russian-born but ethnically Latvian Boris Pugo, a former KGB chief in Latvia (1980–1984). A further irony was unpredictable: Pugo would go on to join the anti-Gorbachev plotters of August 1991.

Two further verbal shocks followed. On December 11, the KGB chairman General Vladimir Kryuchkov (another Gorbachev appointee) delivered a hard-line, unscheduled, nationwide television statement. He claimed to be speaking at Gorbachev's request—a claim the president did not dispute. Antidemocratic forces, he claimed, were "rushing to seize power in a wave of anti-Communism"—an ideological oxymoron worthy of Stalin's day—and pledged that KGB troops would do their utmost to save the Soviet Union from collapse by continuing to "act as a barrier against those forces which seek to push the country towards chaos."

A few days later, on December 17, the Congress of People's Deputies met. In his opening speech Gorbachev appeared to reverse his earlier pledges of a less rigorous approach to contentious issues. Restoring order and discipline in the country, he declared, was the only way to overcome its current crisis. He called for a curb on "destructive actions by separatist and Nationalist forces" and described the role of the Army as "the vital bulwark of the country's state sovereignty." He went on to call for a referendum on the proposed draft Union treaty, which had been approved by the USSR Supreme Soviet on December 3.

His speech drew outspoken attacks from the Left and Right. The congress went on to approve his proposals, however, although delegations from all three of the Baltic Republics had made it clear that they would boycott the treaty, as did those from Moldavia, Georgia, and Armenia.

Another shock was on the way when Gorbachev's hitherto close friend and ally, the internationally popular foreign minister Eduard Shevardnadze mounted the podium on December 20 and announced his resignation. The reasons he gave were the ascendancy of reactionary forces and "the onset of dictatorship." He did not mince his words: "Comrade democrats, you have scattered. The reformers have gone to ground. . . . Dictatorship is coming, I state it with complete responsibility. No one knows what kind of dictatorship this will be. . . . I nevertheless believe that dictatorship will not succeed, that the future belongs to democracy and freedom."

Visibly angered by what he evidently saw as a friend's betrayal, Gorbachev dismissed Shevardnadze's prophecy of a dictatorship and declared that "to go now is unforgivable."

Over the years Shevardnadze had built up a reputation as a genuinely liberal reformer (surprisingly in view of his former role as the KGB chief in Georgia), and his departure was publicly deplored in the United States, France, and elsewhere. Despite his personal shock, Gorbachev later had a long talk with Shevardnadze and persuaded him to carry on as foreign minister for another month until the president's nominee as his successor, Aleksander Bessmertnykh, could take office.

DESPITE THIS PRIVATE reconciliation, the stage was now set for the bloody events that would follow.

CHAPTER FORTY-FOUR

COUP AND
COUNTER-COUP

1991

———⟫●⟪———

T HE FATEFUL YEAR 1991 began, as had 1990, with a crisis in
Lithuania. There the similarity ends: in January 1990, the Lithuanian
crisis had ended, although far from amicably, without violence; in January
1991, it erupted into brutality from the Soviet side, and settled nothing.

THE IMPATIENT LANDSBERGIS

THE NATIONALISTS, LED by President Vytautas Landsbergis, had
grown impatient over the delaying tactics of the Kremlin's diehard imperialists. "Talks about talks"—that favorite ploy of political masters unwilling to make concessions—had dragged on inordinately. The Lithuanians
had reasons for impatience. They had, after all, declared their country's
independence the previous March. On October 2, 1990, Landsbergis and
the then-Soviet premier, Nikolai Ryzhkov, had met in Moscow, then again
on October 10, when they had agreed that formal negotiations should
begin within weeks—although how many weeks remained unspecified.

Then came a blow on December 3, 1990, when the chairman of the
Soviet of Nationalities, Rafik Nishanov, announced that no such talks
could be held unless and until any of the aspirant republics had signed the
new Union Treaty. What next? Landsbergis's patience was under trial. A
week later he announced that the Soviet side had deferred a further round
of talks indefinitely.

No further word came from Moscow. By New Year's Day 1991, Landsbergis had run out of patience. On January 2, 1991, he announced that Lithuania's offer to suspend its independence declaration of March 1990 was being withdrawn. As he pointed out, more than six months had elapsed, and the Soviet side had failed to start negotiations on his country's future status.

That day a crackdown on neo-Stalinist lines followed, in the Latvian capital Riga as well as in Vilnius. In both capitals, units of a paramilitary police force known as OMON (or "Black Berets") went into action.* They seized Riga's main press building, which had been the headquarters of the pro-Moscow Latvian Communist Party. In Vilnius they occupied the Historical Institute and the former Communist Party's Central Committee building, which the newly formed Democratic Labor Party had wrested from the Communists.

On January 7, on orders from the Soviet Defense Ministry, paratroop divisions descended on all three of the Baltic Republics, as well as on Georgia, Moldavia, and Ukraine. In the Baltics, one of the immediate consequences of the troubles was sudden inflation, with price increases of between 200 and 300 percent. A pro-Soviet crowd of around 5,000, consisting mainly of Russians and Poles, used the price increases as a pretext for smashing windows and shouting antigovernment slogans. President Landsbergis appealed to his fellow Lithuanians to defend their parliament, and thousands responded by forming a ring around the building as parliamentary guards and police used water cannons to disperse the hostile crowds.

Next day, Lithuania's Prime Minister Kazimiera Prunskiene, unpopular for her apparent support of the Moscow line and for proposing the price increases, resigned. She took refuge in Switzerland and was succeeded by a more Nationalist candidate, Albertas Shiminas.

On January 10, President Gorbachev issued a message to the new Lithuanian Supreme Council (successor to the Supreme Soviet) blaming the disorders on flagrant violations of the Soviet constitution and of the constitution of Soviet Lithuania. In fact, the Lithuanian constitution had been scrapped by the Supreme Council when it declared independence.

---

*OMON had been set up by the USSR's Interior Ministry in 1987.

Gorbachev charged the Supreme Council with flouting citizens' political and social rights and using "slogans of democracy as a cover for a policy aimed at restoring a bourgeois system." This was no longer the voice of Gorbachev the reformer, of perestroika and glasnost. Instead it was a charge of ultimate ideological heresy in old-style Soviet parlance.

Next day the Soviet paratroopers began by staging several clearly provocative marches. They went on to seize the headquarters of the Lithuanian Defense Council, recently opened as the center for an independent Lithuanian Army. Their second target was the central newspaper printing works, where they shot a Lithuanian protester in the face. In the evening thousands of Lithuanians flooded into Vilnius to strengthen patriotic cordons around government buildings.

In the predawn darkness on January 13, the local Red Army garrison stormed the capital's television center. Soviet tanks ran over the local protesters, killing fourteen and injuring 230. The one soldier who died had been shot accidentally by his own side.

A few hours earlier, Gorbachev had reassured the Federation Council in Moscow that force would not be used. Next day he publicly denied that he had had advance knowledge of the attack. In the international outcry that followed, his protestation of innocence was widely rejected. Indeed the prevailing argument that "he must have known" not unnaturally carried weight.

To be fair to Gorbachev, his own explanation of events in his *Memoirs* also carried weight. He does indeed appear not to have had advance knowledge of the decision to resort to violence. As he puts it, "The mechanism that was triggered off during the night of 12–13 January has to this day not been clarified; neither have the people who gave the command been identified."[1]

He goes on to quote from a book by veterans of the "Alpha" unit entitled *Alpha—The Top Secret KGB Detachment,* according to which a joint KGB-military operation was being planned, apparently with the aim of launching what Gorbachev called "this reckless operation" to restore order under Soviet control before the arrival of a projected Federation Council delegation. On January 12, the council had met and recommended purely political measures to deal with the crisis.

Gorbachev telephoned Vladimir Kryuchkov immediately upon learning what had happened, but the KGB chief replied that neither he nor

Pugo had ordered the use of force. The order had been given locally, and he would look into it. He then rang the new defense minister, Marshal Dimitri Yazov, who told Kryuchkov that the order to use force had indeed been given locally. This seemed unlikely, Gorbachev added, but "at the time I trusted Yazov."

Not to Gorbachev's surprise, the political byproduct of the Vilnius brutality was negative. Apart from the Russian minorities in the Baltic Republics, "public opinion began to change throughout the [Soviet] Union. People asked themselves: 'Is it really worthwhile to keep the Balts by force and shed blood? If they really are so anxious to become independent, for God's sake, let them go.'"

As night follows day, bloody clashes in Latvia's capital Riga followed those in Vilnius. On January 13, the Central Committee of the Communist Party of Latvia had decided to back "demands of the workers' collectives" to dissolve the Supreme Soviet and all local soviets in the republic. The government would be required to quit, and new elections would follow.

On January 20, OMON launched an assault on the Latvian Interior Ministry. In the gun battle that followed between OMON and the local police, two police officers (both ethnic Russians) and a Latvian cameraman were killed.

That day in Moscow about 100,000 demonstrators marched in protest against the earlier killings in Lithuania, calling on Gorbachev, Yazov, and Pugo to resign. In a television statement two days later, Gorbachev declared himself "deeply upset" at the killings in Vilnius and Riga. The use of armed forces for the solution of political problems was "inadmissible." However, he went on to blame the crisis on the "unconstitutional acts" of the Baltic parliaments.

ALTHOUGH ESTONIA ESCAPED the repressive brutality of the other Baltic Republics, it was not entirely free of violence. On January 21, two bombs exploded at factories that were considered to be centers of ethnic Russian resistance to Latvian nationals. And three days later, the badly beaten bodies of two Swedish trade union officials were found in a gravel pit on the outskirts of Tallinn. Rumors circulated, blaming the murders on the KGB as a device to discredit the Estonian government as incapable of maintaining law and order.

By then Boris Yeltsin, in his capacity as president of the Russian Federation, had flown to Tallinn, where he signed a document on behalf of Russia that recognized the sovereignty of the three Baltic Republics, which he presented to their leaders. Thus the USSR had lost the battle for the Baltics.

THE SOVEREIGNTY BATTLE

IN THE WIDER USSR, the battle for and against sovereignty continued, gathering strength day by day. Both sides wanted sovereignty: the USSR to maintain its domination over all the republics from the center; the republics to assert their independence from Moscow. Increasingly, this was a battle between Gorbachev for the USSR, and Yeltsin against it, through his own authority in mother Russia.

An unpublicized directive issued by Defense Minister Yazov and Interior Minister Pugo on December 29, 1990, authorized joint Army and police patrols in the streets of cities and major towns throughout the Soviet Union, to fight violent crime, stop the desecration of monuments, and (above all) to police mass gatherings. The directive was leaked by the Russian-backed Interfax news agency, and thereupon confirmed officially on January 25, 1991, and publicly legitimized by a decree from President Gorbachev on January 29. With Yeltsin's authority, the Supreme Soviet of the Russian Federation made a formal complaint to the USSR Committee for Supervision of the Constitution. The Russian Federation had already complained that the joint patrols would constitute a violation of Russian sovereignty.

On February 19, Yeltsin denounced Gorbachev in a nationwide live television statement. After answering questions from two interviewers, Yeltsin suddenly picked up a prepared document and read from it:

> I warned in 1987 that Gorbachev has in his character an aspiration for absolute personal power. He has already done this and has brought his country to dictatorship, to presidential rule, as they call it. I distance myself from the position and the policy of the president and advocate his immediate resignation [and] the handing over of power to a collective body, the Federation Council.

It was soon clear that Boris Yeltsin could not automatically count on support, even within the Russian Federation. On February 20, *Pravda* condemned Yeltsin's "irresponsible appeal to confrontation." A resolution declaring that Yeltsin's statement violated the constitution was passed in the USSR Supreme Soviet by 292 votes to twenty-nine, with twenty-seven abstentions. Next day, Yeltsin's enemies within the Russian Federation's Supreme Soviet mustered the required one-fifth of deputies to convene an emergency session of the Federation's Congress of People's Deputies on March 28. One of the deputies was absent that day: President Boris Yeltsin.

Still less could Yeltsin count on support outside the USSR, as he discovered to his amazement and dismay when he decided to seek favorable publicity on a trip to Strasbourg to touch base with the European Parliament. He was still at that time a relative novice in the all-important matter of public relations. As Yeltsin puts it, "No ground work had been laid for this trip. We figured they were democrats and we were democrats. . . . But we were blasted in Strasbourg with a cold—I would even say icy—shower."[2]

He was described as a "demagogue" and an "irresponsible person." This was still at the height of the West's Gorbymania. The most widely reported snub came from Jean-Pierre Cot, chairman of the Socialist faction in the European Parliament, who reproached Yeltsin for presenting himself as in opposition to Gorbachev, "with whom, as he phrased it, 'we feel more reassured.'"

In his second book of memoirs, *The View from the Kremlin,* Yeltsin faithfully quotes the denigratory passages in *Le Monde,* the *Berliner Zeitung,* and the *New York Times,* all of which attacked him as the one man who stood in the way of Gorbachev's praiseworthy efforts to stabilize the international situation as well as that of the Soviet Union.

THE CLASH OF wills and votes went on, in diverse ways. On March 17, 1991, an "all-Union" referendum was held on the question of whether or not to preserve the USSR as "a federation of equal, sovereign republics, in which the human rights and the freedoms of all nationalities will be fully guaranteed." A cynical but realistic comment might be that the voters were being asked to "preserve" something that had never existed in the first place. The referendum had no legal force but was regarded as a test of public opinion. Six of the republics opted out of the poll: the three

Baltic Republics, plus Armenia, Georgia, and Moldavia, on the ground that to participate would be to recognize the Soviet Union's constitutional legitimacy, which they had renounced. Nevertheless, the boycotting republics went on to organize their own national referendums on an individual basis.

The turnout in Moscow, Leningrad, and other major cities was poor. In Moscow, for example, only 67 percent of voters voted, and barely 50 percent of these voted "Yes." On the whole, however, Gorbachev had reason to be pleased with the results, with high percentages (in the 90s) in favor in the nine republics that took part, although in Russia, with a turnout of 75.4 percent, only 52.8 voted "Yes."

In the referendums held individually in the "boycotting" republics, the vote in favor of independence was uniformly high (95 percent of participants, or more). In Armenia the "Yes" vote was 71.6 percent of a 72.1 percentage of voters: a phenomenal 99.3 of those participating.

Yeltsin had attacked the whole concept of a referendum, arguing that the individual republics should first establish genuine political and economic sovereignty and only then decide on whether to approve membership of the USSR. In a broadcast on Radio Russia on March 15 he argued that the real purpose of the referendum was to attract support for "the present leadership." Earlier, addressing a public rally on March 9, he had called on his fellow radicals to "declare war on the leadership of the country which has led us into a quagmire."

At this point tensions were high, but Gorbachev found a way of lowering them by inviting Yeltsin and the presidents of Azerbaijan, Belarus, Kazakhstan, Kirghizia, Tajikistan, Turkmenia, Ukraine, and Uzbekistan to a day of talks at Novoye-Ogaryovo, one of the Soviet President's dachas in a suburb of Moscow. Yeltsin describes "the small ceremonial conference room, where everything glittered with State splendour."[3] As he puts it, "First, Gorbachev would speak in his dilatory, circumspect, manner; then he would invite us to begin a discussion. In the end, I usually had to seize the initiative myself if a fundamental issue was involved and do all the arguing. That suited everyone fine."

So with two "poles, the Soviet Union and Russia," to choose from, it suited the other participants to listen to Gorbachev pleading the case for the first, and Yeltsin for the second. This seemed to suit Gorbachev, whose responsibility for global matters of defense and foreign policy was still his own, unchallenged, whereas Yeltsin could deal with the nationalities issue and be blamed for anything that went wrong.

In the end, Gorbachev secured the outcome he wanted: the signing by himself and all nine of the presidents of a joint declaration in support of a proposed new Union Treaty, to be drafted within the next three months. Within a further six months a new Union Constitution would be promulgated, followed by fresh elections to the Congress of People's Deputies.

The meeting had taken place at the height of a major economic crisis, involving inflationary price hikes and a wave of strikes, most notably with some 200,000 coal miners in voluntary idleness. On April 2, prices had risen by an average of 60 percent, with 300 percent rises in the prices of bread, rice, flour, and meat.

Both Yeltsin and Gorbachev had registered political victories, respectively before and after the dacha gathering. On April 5, Yeltsin's supporters had easily defeated no-confidence motions. During the preceding debate Yeltsin had delivered an outspokenly anti-Communist speech, labeling perestroika as "the last phase of the stagnation period."

On April 25, at a closed session of the CPSU's Central Committee, it was Gorbachev's turn, when he defeated an attempt to force his removal as general secretary of the party—the post he had resigned from in February 1990 but to which he had been reelected during the Twenty-Eighth Party Congress the following July. It was at this session of the congress that Yeltsin had solemnly resigned from the CPSU on July 12, tearing up his membership card and walking out. Now, on April 26, having weathered fierce attacks on his leadership—notably from the leader of the Russian Communist Party, Ivan Polozkov—Gorbachev offered to resign, but his offer was turned down by 382 members of the Central Committee, with thirteen in favor (that is, against him) and fourteen abstentions. Gorbachev's real power was diminishing daily, but his formal power was still supported.

The ensuing weeks brought further cracks in the Communist edifice of power. In Georgia's first-ever direct presidential election on May 26, the winner was a longtime dissident, Zviad Gamsakhurdia. His popular victory reaffirmed his election to the position the previous November by a big majority (232 to 5) in the Georgian Supreme Soviet.

On May 23, 1991, Moldavia's Supreme Soviet had adopted a resolution dropping both "Soviet" and "Socialist" from the republic's formal name, henceforth to be known simply as "the Moldavian Republic." Earlier that month, a less attractive organizational change had taken place in Russia after an exchange of views between President Yeltsin and General Kryuchkov, head of the KGB. On May 5, the two men had agreed to create a separate KGB for Russia as distinct from the USSR. The head of the new Russian KGB was Major-General Viktor Ivanenko.

THE AUGUST COUP

THE OUTSIDE WORLD was stunned when a group of Soviet hard-liners attempted to seize power and restore the Soviet Union they had known and loved and in which they had made their careers until Gorbachev came along and ruined everything. Much has been written about the August coup, but quite the most arresting sentences are the first two in Gorbachev's own short work *The August Coup: The Truth and the Lessons*[4]: "The possibility of a *coup d'état* with the use of force and rumours of the preparations being made for it had been circulating in Soviet society for many months. Consequently the coup did not come unexpectedly, like a bolt from the blue."

To the outside world, in contrast, the hard-liners' attempt to seize power from Gorbachev on the morning of August 19, 1991, did come as "a bolt from the blue." That morning tanks were on the streets of Moscow and other big cities, and it was announced that President Mikhail Gorbachev had in effect been deposed. The news came in a statement signed by three members of an ad hoc State Committee for the State of Emergency (SCSE): Gennady Yanayev, vice president of the Soviet Union (and thus Number 2 to Gorbachev), Prime Minister Valentin Pavlov, and Deputy Chairman of the Defense Council Oleg Baklanov. The statement, distributed by the official TASS news agency, said that in line with the constitution, presidential power had been transferred to Vice President Yanayev, "due to Mikhail Gorbachev's inability to perform his duties for health reasons."

A state of emergency had been introduced in various (though unspecified) areas of the USSR for six months "to overcome the profound crisis, political, ethnic and civil strife, chaos and anarchy that threaten the lives and security of the Soviet Union's citizens." The SCSE, whose members were listed in the statement, had been formed "to run the country and effectively exercise the state of emergency."

Apart from those named in the initial statement, the other members of the SCSE were Vladimir Kryuchkov, chairman of the KGB (who turned out to have been the prime instigator of the attempted coup); Marshal Dimitri Yazov, the defense minister; Boris Pugo, the interior minister; Vasily Starodubtsev, chairman of the Farmers' Union (consisting of heads of the state collective farms); Aleksandr Tisyakov, president of the Association of State Enterprises; Valery Boldin, chief of Gorbachev's staff; General Yury Plekhanov, the head of the KGB's Presidential Security; and Oleg Shenin, member of the CPSU Secretariat.

History offers many examples of bungled coups, and this one was a worthy accretion to the list. The actual crisis lasted only three days. Isolated in their dacha at Foros on the Crimean coast, Mikhail and his wife Raisa Maksimovna had no idea what was happening.

They had arrived for their holiday on August 4. In the true sense, however, it turned out to be a working holiday, at least for the president. In the very full account of the coup crisis that he gives in his *Memoirs,* he records various telephone conversations, notably with Boris Yeltsin on August 14, when they reached a kind of tacit agreement on concluding the long-drawn-out process of drafting the Union Treaty discussed at the Novo-Ogaryovo meeting by signing the agreed text.

The first Gorbachev knew about trouble came at about 5 P.M. on the afternoon of August 18, when the head of his presidential security guard told him that a group of officials had arrived unannounced at the dacha. Their names were Oleg Baklanov, Oleg Shenin, Valery Boldin, Valentin Varennikov, and Yury Plekhanov. Since Gorbachev had not invited them, he was taken by surprise, as indeed was the head of his security guard, who told his boss that the guards had let the visitors in because Plekhanov and Boldin, Gorbachev's head of security and chief of staff, were among them. Normally no visitors were admitted without the president's prior consent.

It was only then that Gorbachev had his first signal that all was not well: he tried to telephone Kryuchkov, the head of the KGB, and found that all five of his telephones were dead. He walked out to the verandah to tell Raisa what was happening. She was "shaken . . . but remained cool."

The guards told him that the visitors were "edgy." He then found that the uninvited guests had come up to the second floor without being asked. "Their general behavior was uncivil, almost as if they were the hosts." Their spokesman was Baklanov, deputy chairman of the defense council and member of the SCSE, who told him that an emergency committee had been set up. He declared that the country "was sliding into disaster," and in effect issued an ultimatum: sign the decree on declaring a state of emergency, or else. . . .

Baklanov named the members of the SCSE, mentioning Anatoly Lukyanov (an old friend of Gorbachev's from university days). He claimed that Yeltsin was under arrest, then immediately contradicted himself. (Yeltsin was to be arrested on his return from a visit to Alma-Ata.) Gorbachev goes on:

> I had promoted all these people—and now they were betraying me! I refused to sign any decree. If they were truly worried about the situation in the country, I told them, we should convene the USSR Supreme Soviet and the Congress of People's Deputies. "Let us discuss and decide. But let us act only within the framework of the Constitution and under the law. Anything else is unacceptable to me."[5]

Baklanov went on to express solicitude for Gorbachev's poor state of health, which he attributed to the stressful perestroika period. He quite understood, he said, that Gorbachev wouldn't wish to sign the decree, so perhaps he could authorize Yanayev to do so on his behalf. "Needless to say, I rejected this despicable proposal."

When Varennikov asked him why he didn't resign, Gorbachev called them criminals who would be "held accountable for their folly." End of conversation, but not of words from the president, who "lost his cool and swore at them, Russian-style."

When the crisis was over, Gorbachev was often asked why he did not detain the plotters, since he had armed guards who could have done the job. His explanation makes sense. He could indeed have had them arrested, but the leaders of the plot were still in Moscow, able to act and with the means to do so. Moreover, the group had thought of such an emergency and had brought their own guards with them, who were deployed, in double, around the dacha and down to the sea. The dacha was now totally isolated with no means of communication with the outside world.

Back in Moscow, the conspirators reported on the failure of their mission. Gorbachev continues:

> Their report sowed discord in the midst of the conspirators. Yanayev wavered and reached for the bottle. It seems that Pavlov also went on a drinking bout, feigning illness. Lukyanov wasted no time in preparing his fall-back positions. Marshal Yazov was pensive and later said: "What the hell possessed me, old fool, to get involved in this mess!" Voices were heard suggesting that it might be better to stop. But it was too late. They had gone too far to sound a retreat. Boldin told the others: "I know the President; he will never forgive such treatment." There was no other way for them but forward.[6]

Gorbachev goes on to quote extensively from his wife's diary of the next events. They tuned in to the BBC's World Service to find out what was happening. They learned that Boris Yeltsin had publicly denounced the plotters and called for resistance to their demands. Gorbachev showed himself to the outside world, so that the guards and the crew of ships at sea could see for themselves that he was in good health. The Gorbachev family had a video camera on which they recorded a speech by the president and made four separate tape recordings of his words, which they hid in different parts of the dacha. Through the guards they sent a message to Moscow asking for the telephones to be reconnected and for a plane to bring the "prisoners" back to Moscow.

On Wednesday, August 21, they listened to news of clashes in Moscow with resulting dead and wounded. That afternoon they were told that two Zils and a Volga had arrived, bringing Yazov, Kryuchkov, Baklanov, Vladimir Ivashko, Lukyanov and Plekhanov, asking to see Gorbachev. The president ordered them to be taken into custody, adding, "I refuse to see anyone unless government communications are restored." At 5:45 his wish was fulfilled: telephones were switched on again after seventy-three hours of isolation.

Gorbachev was calm. He rang Boris Yeltsin: "Mikhail Sergeevich, dear man, are you alive?" President and Barbara Bush sent their greetings to him, saying they had been praying for the Gorbachev family for the last three days.

The president still refused to see the waiting conspirators. Instead he received a loyal delegation that had just arrived: Aleksandr Rutskoi, Ivan

Silayev, Vadim Bakatin, Yevgeny Primakov, Nikolai Stolyarov, Svyatoslav Fedorov, plus deputies and the press. Suddenly Gorbachev became aware that he had won: the plotters had been defeated. Through the reconnected telephone, Gorbachev issued orders. Yazov was dismissed. Gorbachev spoke to Lukyanov and Ivashko in the presence of Bakatin and Primakov, and told them what he thought of them. He decided against meeting Kryuchkov and Yazov. From Kryuchkov, the chairman of the KGB, he received a handwritten note, telling him that "on the whole, I do feel very remorseful." It was a revealing confession from the head of the largest and most powerful security and espionage agency in the world.

At 2 A.M. on August 22, the Gorbachevs' plane landed at Vnukovo airfield. The world's television viewers saw the president, in holiday attire with an open-collared shirt, alight from the aircraft. Over the coming days, most of Gorbachev's time was spent catching up with events and accumulated work. Not long after his return, articles started appearing, alleging that he had been "in collusion" with the conspirators. The opening sentences of his account of the failed coup, quoted earlier in this chapter, do suggest that he was aware, possibly through a specific forewarning, that a coup was on the way. It is difficult to rule out the possibility that if the plot had succeeded he might have been persuaded to return as the president of a revived hard-line regime. But this is merely a hypothesis. It is clear beyond doubt that he was *not* involved in the plot itself, tempting though such speculation might be in a political environment with a long-established tradition of disinformation.

What soon became clear, however, is that his days as the president of a collapsing empire were numbered. The new man of the hour, much to the chagrin of Western leaders and the media, was Boris Yeltsin.

CHAPTER FORTY-FIVE

BIRTH OF THE CIS

1991

T HE FAILED AUGUST coup destroyed what was left of Gorbachev's image, first in the dying Soviet Union, and later in the reluctant eyes of Western leaders. In his defense, he did stand up to the coup leaders: an act of courage in a difficult and perilous situation, under house arrest and cut off from the outside world. On the other hand, he admitted that he had foreknowledge of a coup, but did nothing to forestall it. Moreover, he himself had appointed all the hard-line coup leaders.

Boris Yeltsin played a key role in the aftermath of the abortive coup. On the eve of it, on August 18, he was in Alma-Ata, the capital of Kazakhstan, where as president of the Russian Federation he had signed a bilateral agreement with the Kazakh president, Nursultan Nazarbayev. Reports of unrest were coming in as Yeltsin flew back to Moscow's Vnukovo airport, from which a car drove him and his family to their dacha at Arkhangelskoye. Yeltsin learned later that the plotters of the coup against Gorbachev, on proclaiming a state of emergency, had ordered that the plane on which Yeltsin had traveled "should be destroyed in the air at night." He remained uncertain whether this "order" was supposed to be obeyed, or was merely intended to contribute to the atmosphere of danger and tension. As Yeltsin put it, "As I review those days, I am persuaded once again that we were walking on the edge of a precipice."[1]

The plotters had organized an intimidating display of military force—including motorized rifle and tank divisions—through the streets of Moscow. With praiseworthy foresight, Yeltsin had visited General Pavel Grachev, commander of the model Tula Division before the coup, to ask him whether he could be relied upon to react in the event of a coup. Unhesitatingly, Grachev had said he could. On August 19, Yeltsin rang Grachev to remind him of their conversation. After a long silence, the general said he would send a security squad to protect Yeltsin.

Another Yeltsin initiative on that fateful day was to summon his Soviet and Russian political allies to his dacha, where they jointly drafted an appeal to the Russian people, declaring the coup "unlawful." Some hours later, clad in a heavy bulletproof vest, Yeltsin left Arkhangelskoye by car on his way to the Russian Parliament, known as the White House. From his office window, he saw a tank, just outside the building: "Suddenly, I felt a jolt inside. I had to be out there right away, standing with the people." He clambered on to the tank, pulled the text of his appeal out of his pocket, raised his voice to its maximum, and read it out to the swelling crowd. The scene was filmed and shown on the world's television screens.

Next, Yeltsin telephoned the KGB chief, Vladimir Kryuchkov:

As the driving force behind the putsch, the KGB did not want to bloody its hands. . . . It was very important for me to understand the mindset and train of thought of the KGB's chairman. A quiet old man with a steely gaze, Kryuchkov was the most dangerous of the conspirators.

Do you really not understand what you are doing? I asked him. People are throwing themselves under tanks; there may be countless casualties. No, said Kryuchkov, there won't be any casualties. First, this is a strictly non-violent operation: no ammunition will be used in order to impose order [*sic*]; and no military objectives have been set. All the agitation is coming from you, the Russian leadership. According to our reports, people are calm and life is normal.[2]

Yeltsin decided that Kryuchkov was being frank about his intentions. Later, he and his fellow-plotters would change their minds, but "by then it was too late." That evening Yeltsin, in his capacity as president of

Russia, appealed to the Muscovites not to obey the decrees of the "self-styled emergency committee."

Within days of Gorbachev's return to Moscow on August 22, it became clear not only that he had lost his authority but also that he was still living in the past. At a press conference later that day, he declared his continuing support for the now-discredited CPSU. His words were, "I shall fight to the end for the renewal of the party." A day earlier, somewhat late, the Party had stated its opposition to the coup.

The defining moment came on August 23, when Yeltsin summoned the Russian Supreme Soviet in Gorbachev's presence. The session was televised internationally, and the world audience saw Yeltsin interrupting Gorbachev, pointing his finger at the Soviet president, and obliging him to read out the record of the USSR cabinet meeting of August 19 when, with one exception, the entire cabinet endorsed the proclamation of a state of emergency. The exception was the relatively junior environment minister, Nikolai Vorontsov.

At that same dramatic session, on August 23, Yeltsin signed a decree, before Gorbachev's eyes, suspending all activities of the Russian Communist Party, "pending the investigation by juridical bodies of its involvement" in the coup. That day, Gorbachev agreed to Yeltsin's demands that he sign decrees endorsing the Russian government's measures during the coup, which thereby became constitutionally binding. A new decree, also approved that day, transferred all USSR enterprises and natural resources on Russian territory to the jurisdiction of the Russian Republic.

Yeltsin describes a telephone call he made at night pointing out to Gorbachev that he had been appointing as members of his cabinet men who had been involved in the coup, "either overtly or covertly." Gorbachev conceded the point, reluctantly. Next morning Yeltsin confronted him and in effect obliged him to rescind the appointments.

A paradoxical ambiguous situation seemed to emerge of its own accord. Gorbachev, the head of the country, was appointing as his immediate subordinates people who intended to overthrow him. The mechanism itself, the machinery of the coup, was being preserved untouched—the bureaucracies of the Union, where at all levels there were people prepared to impose a state of emergency.[3]

On August 24, Gorbachev announced his resignation as CPSU general secretary. Although he remained nominally president of the fast-dissolving USSR, he no longer enjoyed the substance of power.

The discrediting of Gorbachev created a vacuum of leadership that could only be filled by his rival Boris Yeltsin, the man who had publicly broken with the Communist Party during its Twenty-Eighth Congress. The Western leaders, having committed themselves to supporting Gorbachev, whom they saw as a great reformer, found it difficult to switch their support to Yeltsin, who was widely labeled a "maverick" by the Western media.

The person who found it most difficult to grasp the new situation was France's president, François Mitterrand. Widely known in his own country as *le Florentin* because of his alleged Machiavellian pragmatism, he revealed on television on Monday, August 19, 1991, that he had been in touch with Gennady Yanayev, at that time seen as the initiator of the coup, whom he described as "the new leader." The implication appeared to be that France could do business with Yanayev. For this apparent instant switch of loyalties, Mitterrand was widely attacked in the press and parliament.

Only two days later, Mitterrand was back on television, defensively acknowledging Yeltsin's role. Another switch came on Thursday, when the Elysée Palace flourished a message from Gorbachev thanking Mitterrand for convening a European summit.

From Germany, Chancellor Helmut Kohl assured the plotters of the coup that Germany would stick to its treaties. Until then, Kohl's line had been that he was Gorbachev's best friend in the West. He made no mention of Yeltsin. By Friday, August 23, Kohl and his habitually pro-Soviet foreign minister Hans-Dietrich Genscher were heaping praise on Yeltsin.[4]

The British prime minister, John Major, was more cautious than the French and German leaders. On Monday, August 19, he had condemned the coup. He recognized Gorbachev's contribution "over recent years," but stopped short of calling for his reinstatement. His predecessor, Margaret Thatcher, called on the Soviet people to take to the streets to support Yeltsin, but only so that Gorbachev could be brought back to power—a strangely illogical conclusion. Two days later Major began to praise Yeltsin.

* * *

NOT SURPRISINGLY, GIVEN the profound differences between Gorbachev and Yeltsin, and the way the former had treated the latter (see Chapter 43), Gorbachev's view of the dramatic events during and after the coup differed substantially.

In Gorbechev's own words, he discovered, for example, that some of those whose appointments he had confirmed on his return to Moscow "had been ready to run with the hares and hunt with the hounds." He therefore had to make staff changes. "It was disgraceful," he wrote, "that a majority in the Secretariat of the Central Committee and many regional Party bodies supported the Emergency Committee." Understandably, he objected to articles written in September asserting, "implicitly or explicitly," that he had been in collusion with the conspirators.

He particularly objected to Yeltsin's attempt to ban the Communist Party (later reversed by the Constitutional Court) during the session of the Supreme Soviet that both men had attended. "At that encounter, Yeltsin was gloating with sadistic pleasure." A more objective view would perhaps have been that Yeltsin was "getting his own back" after the way Gorbachev had treated him, most notably when Gorbachev had summoned him from his hospital bed to be expelled from the Politburo.

When one of those present at the Supreme Soviet had booed Gorbachev and declared "in a hysterical voice" that all Communists "must be swept out of the country with a broom," he had responded in a passage which the press ignored, but to which Gorbachev still adhered: "Even Stalin's sick brain did not breed such ideas. Do you really expel eighteen million Communists from the country—if you include their families, 50 to 70 million people? If you call yourselves democrats you have to act accordingly."[5]

To the end, Gorbachev stuck to his defense of the Party that he had led, claiming that the majority of members favored perestroika and disagreeing with "attempts to malign the whole history of the party, portraying its founder as a villain." In other words, to the end, he had stuck to the discredited view that the Communist system could be reformed.

IN THE AFTERMATH of the coup, two of its leaders committed suicide. One was Interior Minister Boris Pugo, on August 21; the other, three days later, was Marshal Sergei Akhromeyev, who had been Gorbachev's chief military adviser.

On August 22, a powerful symbolic gesture had taken place in Moscow, when a crowd toppled the giant statue of Feliz Dzerzhinsky, Lenin's appointee as first head of the Cheka, forerunner of the KGB, from its site in front of its headquarters in the infamous Lubyanka, the KGB's dreaded prison.

ETHNIC STIRRINGS IN THE REPUBLIC

MEANWHILE, ALL OVER the vast and now disunited Union, ethnic forces were taking over. The "constituent republics" were breaking away from the fading central power. The three Baltic Republics had lived through tense hours on August 19, when it looked as though the coup leadership would take over; but their leaders had declared the Emergency Committee illegal, although the Russian-speaking communities in all three of the Baltic States publicly supported it.

Kazakhstan and Ukraine (after Russia, the largest republics of the Union) had both denounced the Emergency Committee, whereas Azerbaijan had welcomed the takeover. Some of the other republics—Uzbekistan, Tajikistan, Belarus, Georgia, and Armenia—had neither welcomed the coup nor condemned it. However, the separatist Dniestr and Gagauz districts of Moldavia had welcomed it, as had the autonomous republic of Abkhazia and the autonomous region of South Ossetia in Georgia.

Anxiety had run high in the former Soviet satellite of Eastern Europe, and representatives of Poland, Hungary, and Czechoslovakia met in Warsaw on August 20 to discuss the impact of the coup. President Lech Walesa of Poland observed that it had proven the need for a continuing NATO presence in Europe. In Romania, the government expressed concern for "our brothers in the republic of Moldava" and issued a warning that "any nostalgia for Communist totalitarianism is nothing but the harmful consequence of a dangerous lapse of memory"—a curious comment from the post-Ceausescu government still dominated by former Communists.

From September 2 to 6, the Congress of People's Deputies met in Moscow, in its Fifth Extraordinary session, mainly to consider a joint Statement by the Presidents of Ten Republics: the Russian Federation (RSFSR), Ukraine, Belarus, Kazakhstan, Uzbekistan, Kirghizia, Tajikistan, Turkmenia, Armenia, and Azerbaijan. The three Baltic Republics, at last secure in their assertions of independence, declined to participate, as did Georgia and Moldavia.

The joint statement hailed the failure of the coup as having created "an historic opportunity to accelerate the radical transformations and renew the country." The signatories called for a treaty to create a "Union of Sovereign States." Should any of the republics of the former USSR wish to opt out of the Union, they could hold talks with the USSR to resolve matters arising from independence, such as the armed forces, a share of the national debt, and so forth.

The statement was approved by 1,669 votes to twenty-four, with forty-nine abstentions. Gorbachev himself, as president of the (dying) USSR, had chaired the session, in effect presiding over the forthcoming loss of his own job. The congress made two further decisions: to dissolve the Supreme Soviet, which had failed to condemn the attempted coup, and to set up a new State Council, which, in the words of the newly appointed foreign minister, Boris Pankin, "was a structure unique in the history of our State, combining both legislative and executive powers."[6]

Pankin's colorful descriptions of the assembled presidents of the newly independent former Soviet Socialist Republics owe more to his earlier career as a journalist than to his new (and short-lived) post as head of Soviet diplomacy. There was Leonid Kravchuk of Ukraine, whose "always upright head at once reminded me of characters in Gogol"; Ayaz Mutalibov of Azerbaijan as "a teenage street thug . . . who had lost touch with his bad companions but never quite shed his old habits." More worthy of descriptive attention was Saparmurad Niyazov of Turkmenistan, who sent an official mission to his native village to delve into his ethnic past when the value of his Communist credentials began to erode. "Naturally, concrete evidence of his high extraction" was soon found, so that "Niyazov could officially call himself Turkmenbashi, 'chief' or 'father' of the Turkmen people." Thereafter, his image was placed everywhere, even on banknotes, "something even Stalin had shrunk from." He won the presidential elections of 1992 with "a tolerable 98.3 percent of the vote."

So impressed was the Kirghiz leader Askar Akayev by Niyazov's example that he declared himself to be a direct descendant of a former ruler, Khan Shiban, and therefore the legitimate heir to the Kirghiz throne. The president of Uzbekistan, Islam Karimov, was also worthy of Pankin's attention. Recalling the mediaeval military feats of Tamerlane (Timur Leng, as modernized), the fourteenth-century Turkish conqueror, he had the giant statue of Karl Marx removed and replaced by a suitably imposing one, several meters high, of Tamerlane.

With Yeltsin on his right, Gorbachev chaired the early sessions of the State Council. They were rowdy and undisciplined, because Gorbachev had ceased to inspire the discipline that prevailed before the system started collapsing. Yeltsin and his followers, together with the newly anointed leaders of the self-assertive republics "tended to gloat over confusion that denoted such an obvious decline in Gorbachev's authority."[7]

By far the most important of the republics (after Russia itself) was Ukraine, with its 233,000-plus square miles and its population of more than 48 million. On August 31, on the eve of the Fifth Extraordinary Congress, Leonid Kuchma had banned all activities of the republic's formerly ruling Communist Party, on the ground that it had supported the coup. On September 20, the Ukrainian KGB was dissolved, but replaced by a security service under independent Ukrainian control. A fortnight earlier, on September 4, the Supreme Soviet of the Crimean Autonomous Republic, the peninsular extension of Ukraine, declared its independence, while recognizing its status as part of Ukraine.

Indeed, either before, during, or shortly after the meetings of the congress or of the State Council, all the remaining republics had proclaimed their independence.

MAJOR CHANGES IN the ex-Soviet KGB were initiated immediately after the collapse of the coup. On August 28, Gorbachev had placed the KGB under the authority of the Defense Ministry. With Kryuchkov under arrest as one of the coup leaders, Gorbachev had appointed Vadim Bakatin as the new head of the KGB. He was only in charge for a month, for on September 30 Gorbachev replaced him with Yevgeny Primakov, the distinguished Arabist who had maintained good relations with Saddam Hussein of Iraq during the Gulf War.

On October 29, the new State Council formally abolished the old KGB, to be replaced by separate units to deal with border security, intelligence, and counterintelligence. Of main concern to the outside world was the new Foreign Intelligence Service, or FIS. It soon became apparent that although the new service had virtually abandoned the "dirty tricks" (officially known as Active Measures) for which the KGB was notorious, there was no diminution in Russia's espionage activities, although there was some change of substance, in the sense that there was a considerable expansion of scientific and industrial spying.

THE END, FOR both the Soviet Union and for Mikhail Gorbachev's political career, came in December 1991. The leaders of the Slav Republics (Russia, Ukraine, and Belarus, Belorussia's new name)—Boris Yeltsin, Leonid Kravchuk, and Stanislav Shushkevich—had been meeting in a dacha at Belovezhskaya Pusha, near Minsk. They emerged on December 8 to announce, "The USSR, as a subject of international Law and a geopolitical reality, ceases to exist." It had been replaced by the Commonwealth of Independent States (CIS), membership of which would be open to all republics of the former Soviet Union, and indeed to any other state that shared its aims.

In a pathetically futile last attempt to maintain his deceased authority, Gorbachev described the Minsk declaration as an "illegal and dangerous" constitutional coup. President Nazarbayev of Kazakhstan attempted to save Gorbachev's face, if not his authority, when he attended a meeting with Gorbachev himself and Yeltsin (representing the Minsk group) on December 9. Although Nazarbayev said that Gorbachev was still needed as a central force, any such hope had vanished.

Three days later, Nazarbayev met with the leaders of the other Central Asian Republics—Kirghiztan (formerly Kirghizia), Tajikistan, and Turkmenistan (formerly Turkmenia)—and decided unanimously to join the CIS, on condition that they were given the status as cofounders (which, of course, they were).

A further meeting of the republican leaders was held on December 21 at Alma-Ata, capital of Kazakhstan. Also present were the leaders of Moldovia, Azerbaijan, and Armenia. Georgia, by then rent by a struggle for power between the dictatorial anti-Communist president, Zviad Gamsakhurdia, and his enemies, could only send observers. All participants signed the December 8 protocol on the formation of the CIS. The best-known leader of all, Gorbachev, decided not to attend. This decision spared him the embarrassment of a particular decision of the Alma-Ata participants: to abolish the post of president of the former Soviet Union. In a speech on December 25 (Christmas Day in the Western Christian countries but not in the territories of the Russian Orthodox Church),

Gorbachev resigned as president and as commander in chief of the armed forces. He and Yeltsin had met on December 23 to discuss transitional arrangements, and Gorbachev had handed over the nuclear codes to his rival and victor in the struggle for supreme power, Boris Yeltsin.

IN COMBINATION, THE December meetings marked the demise not only of the Soviet Union, but also of the Soviet Empire. It did not, however, mark the final collapse of Communism, the ideological cement that had extended the empire and held it together. The post-imperial situation is discussed in the chapters of the Epilogue.

EPILOGUE

———⟫•⟪———

THE RED
PHOENIX

CHAPTER FORTY-SIX

CHAOS AND REBIRTH

IN THE EX–USSR

———————

T HROUGHOUT THE HISTORY of the Soviet Empire, ideology was
the justifying instrument of Soviet imperialism and expansionism. It
was also the cement that kept imperial outposts within Soviet control.
Paradoxically, a variant of the original Leninist ideology provided the
"justification" for the continued existence of Communist parties (usually
organized under different names) after the collapse of the Soviet Union
and the discrediting of the ideology.

To illuminate this idea, one chapter—and one only—of a celebrated
fellow-traveling book of the 1930s—*Soviet Communism: A New Civilization* by Sidney and Beatrice Webb (1937)—deserves to be reread. (In the
original edition, the book's title ended with a question mark. In later editions, certainty having replaced doubt, the question mark was removed.)
The title of the important chapter was "The Vocation of Leadership." To
summarize its ideas in one sentence: Party members, whether men or
women, are supercitizens who have responsibilities greater than those of
ordinary citizens, to whom they must serve as examples.

The authors compare the role of the ruling party to that of religious
orders such as the Society of Jesus within the Church of Rome. The difference, of course, is that the doctrine to which Party members subscribe
is not Christianity but atheistic Marxism.

Shortly after the end of World War II, the celebrated British author
George Orwell, a repented ex-Socialist, in two of his key books (*Animal*

Farm and *1984*) pointed to the terror made possible by this "vocation" of Party members. In his "animal farm," some of the dwellers were "more equal than others."*

There was no significance to the title *1984* other than the inversion of 1948, the year of the book's publication. Certainly, some years before 1984, the "supercitizens" of the Soviet Union, by now known collectively as the "Nomenklatura," had lost any sincere faith in the ideology, but they continued enjoying the power and privileges conferred by Party membership, as described in fascinating detail by Michael Voslensky in his book—*Nomenklatura*—published in 1980. (See chapter 41, note 4.)

One last detail completes the picture. The late Professor Hugh Seton-Watson, a multilingual British authority on Eastern Europe, drafted the following passage in *European Security and the Soviet Problem:*

> The present rulers of the Soviet Union are heirs to the Tsars' domin-ions as well as to the State philosophy established by Lenin and consol-idated by Stalin. Their foreign policy is thus a hybrid of Great Russian imperialism and Marxist-Leninist ideology. *The ideology, shorn of its earlier idealism, has turned into a carapace of self-righteousness, which protects them from self-doubt.* (Italics added.)[1]

By merging these quotations or references one creates the following definition: The Communist Party, originally a vocation of leadership equiv-alent to a religious order but without the divine element, has transformed itself into a totalist organism corrupted by power but relieved of all remorse by a carapace of moral self-satisfaction.

The factitious protection, this moral self-satisfaction, this feeling of hav-ing been designated by the reigning power as its own instrument, appears to have protected the Communist parties from the worst consequences of the collapse of Communism in its original homeland—Russia—including that homeland. Another paradox: The arrogance of power seems to have sur-

---

*In his dying days, George Orwell compiled a list of 130 acquaintances whom he suspected of being Communists, crypto-Communists, or fellow-travelers, some of whom were Soviet agents of influence. In so doing, he was working for the Information Research Department (IRD) of the British Foreign Office, a semi-secret department established by Britain's post-war Labor government to counter the ever-mounting flow of hostile Soviet propaganda. (*Daily Telegraph,* London, June 22, 1998; extracted from *The Complete Works of George Orwell,* 20 vols., Ed. Peter Davison, London, 1998.)

vived the collapse of that very power. "Normal" parties (that is, democratic ones) would have been totally demoralized by the traumatic events of 1991, especially the (short-lived) decision of the Russian Parliament, under Boris Yeltsin's directive, to "outlaw" the hitherto ruling party. But the Communist parties were not "normal" parties. Their "vocation of leadership" survived their own collapse. In Russia, the "outlawing" of the Party was soon reversed by the Constitutional Court.

Outside Russia, the former ruling parties were soon reborn under different names and came back to power. In Russia, fragments of the Party emerged, to form by March 1994 no fewer than fifteen competing parties, each using the word *Communist*. Of these, the most important was the Communist Party of the Russian Federation (CPRF), launched in June 1990, and briefly banned along with the remnant of the original CPSU. Two of the others also carried weight: the Union of the Communist Party-CPSU and the Russian Communist Workers' Party.[2] Elsewhere in the ex-Soviet Union, most (though not all) of the old ruling Communist parties dropped the "C" word. All of the East European ex-satellites did.

ANOTHER VERY IMPORTANT aspect of the situation tends to be ignored by Western leaders and commentators: the de facto immunity of political criminals in the Communist world. The best way to grasp the problem is to compare the aftermath of World War II with that of the Cold War. The Allied victory in the former was total, and the Allies, having imposed an unconditional surrender upon the Nazi regime, were able to bring the Nazi leaders to trial at Nuremberg even though the three top leaders—Adolf Hitler, Hermann Goering, and Joseph Goebbels—opted for suicide.

No such demonstration of absolute victory was on offer at the end of the Cold War; I have pointed out elsewhere that the West did not, in a full sense, "win" the Cold War; *the Soviet side lost it*. It was not within the power of the NATO allies to bring Soviet or satellite political criminals to justice. There was at least one exception: Chancellor Helmut Kohl's West German government, having seized the opportunity created by the demolition of the Berlin Wall to impose control over Communist East Germany, was able to bring selected East German leaders to trial for such crimes as ordering the deaths of individual East German citizens who were attempting to flee to democratic West Germany. Most of the officials brought to trial were found innocent on the ground that they were merely obeying the orders of the regime which they served. However, East Germany's last Communist leader, Egon Krenz, was sentenced to 6½ years in jail on August 25, 1997. His plea that he was obeying orders from Moscow was rejected.

In Czechoslovakia (later the Czech Republic and Slovakia), an attempt to punish political criminals of the old regime petered out in a maze of political and judicial complications. One major exception was the summary execution of Nicolae Ceauşescu of Romania by the fellow-Communists who had overthrown him (see Chapter 42). Indeed, throughout the blood-stained history of the Soviet Empire, the executioners of Communists charged with crimes were always fellow-Communists who had come out on top in power struggles. The greatest criminal of all, Pol Pot of Cambodia, was spared the death penalty when he was brought to trial in July 1997 by his own Khmer Rouge, which was no longer in power. (See Chapter 48.) He died in his bed in April 1998.

Thus the three greatest Communist criminals of all—Joseph Stalin, Mao Zedong, and Pol Pot—all escaped the death penalties that they had inflicted on millions of their contemporaries. For that matter, the other mass murderer, Adolf Hitler, died by his own will in Berlin at the end of the war he had inflicted on the world. Hitler knew the shame of utter defeat, whereas two of the Communist trio were spared the shame of witnessing the downfall of the absolute regimes over which they had presided.

This history of untrammeled violence and cruelty was an ineradicable part of Communism's legacy to Boris Yeltsin, along with high infant mortality, one of Europe's lowest life expectancies, and empty shelves. Yeltsin had himself been a member of the ruling party until the late 1980s, when he had the clarity of vision to declare publicly that the promises of the system were "pie in the sky" and the courage to tear up his Party card while surrounded by his ex-comrades. Prophets of doom are themselves unpopular, not least when their visions of collapse turn into reality.

Yeltsin's legacy therefore also included the hatred of the hard-liners of the old Nomenklatura, who were thirsting for the wealth and power of recent times past. And of course there was the older legacy of Tsarist Russia, including the lingering resentment of the minor nationalities who were dominated by the imperial Russians. Since the collapse of the USSR, the larger nationalities of the component republics had gained the sovereignty to which they aspired. Within the Russian Federation itself, however, the autonomy of certain regions fell short of the independence for which they craved.

The nostalgia for lost power and privilege resulted in one of the two major crises that challenged Yeltsin: the hard-line rebellion of October 1993. The thirst for independence erupted in the disastrous war in Chechnya, with relatively minor outbreaks in Moldavia and Azerbaijan, neither of which was within Russia's sphere of authority.

The direct cause of the hard-line rebellion was Yeltsin's decision on September 21 to suspend the Russian Parliament; the underlying cause was the hostile, confrontational attitude of opposition deputies, which had brought Parliament as a whole to a frustrating immobility. Yeltsin may have reigned as the elected president, but whatever initiative he attempted was simply blocked by the hostile deputies, of whom the most determined were Ruslan Khasbulatov and Aleksander Rutskoi. Singly, each had an impressive résumé; together, they were a formidable pair.

A professor of law, Khasbulatov had been chairman (that is, speaker) of the Russian Parliament since October 1991. Major-General Rutskoi had been awarded the title of Hero of the Soviet Union for his distinguished service in Afghanistan. The Soviet Union had lost the Afghanistan war and no longer existed, but in the eyes of the populace Rutskoi was still a hero. Moreover, he had been vice president of the Russian Federation for the past two years—that is, President Yeltsin's Number 2.

In the second of his autobiographical volumes, Yeltsin describes in detail the agonizing days leading up to his decision to suspend Parliament.[3] He had made his decision in early September but had told nobody, not even his closest aides: "Russia simply could not go on with a parliament like this one." He knew well in advance that his decision to dissolve Parliament would be "like a match to a powder keg" and therefore would have to be kept secret until he was ready to announce it. This would take time, for he would need to consult his team to make sure the decree was properly drafted.

The first person to know would be Viktor Ilyushin, who had been Yeltsin's chief aide for the previous year. Yeltsin watched Ilyushin's face carefully as he spelled out his decision and what needed to be done before it could be made public. Clearly he had appointed the right man for the job—the perfect, unflappable civil servant: "As usual he was composed, as if he were being assigned to draft a decree about cattle fodder for the coming winter." In reply to Ilyushin's relevant questions and in the interests of secrecy, Yeltsin instructed him to tell only a few members of his team and to assign the drafting of different sections to different people so that nobody except the president himself and Ilyushin would be fully in the picture.

On September 12, Yeltsin summoned the chosen members of his cabinet, minus one, to a government dacha at Starugoryovo (a Moscow suburb) and broke the news. All of them supported him. Yeltsin told them that his proposed decree would be announced a week later, on September 19. The news was greeted with approval, although one of Yeltsin's favorites, the soft-spoken foreign minister Andrei Kozyrev, created a moment of tension when he said, "I have a serious comment. I am not in agreement with one fundamental point, Boris Nikolayevich." However, the tension eased with his next words: "Such a decree should have been passed long, long ago."

The absent cabinet member was Prime Minister Viktor Chernomyrdin, who was in the United States but due to return to Moscow the next day. A stolid, loyal, and unfanatical ex-apparatchik, Chernomyrdin, longtime boss of the state gas industry, Gazprom, signed the draft decree without hesitation.

Several dates for the announcement had been proposed: September 19, 24, 29. September 19 was rejected because it would echo the failed coup on August 19, 1991, and September 24 and 29 because each would have clashed with other events. In the end, Yeltsin opted for September 21 on learning that a leak from an unknown source had reached the two anti-Yeltsin rebels, Rutskoi and Khasbulatov, who had been building substantial stocks of weapons in the White House, the popular name for the Russian Parliament.[4]

Where had the leak come from? Yelstin speculated that the news must have been passed to two former ministers, recently sacked: Viktor Barannikov, the former security minister, and Andrei Dunayev, the former deputy interior minister. But events were now moving too fast, and what had been done could not be undone. Yeltsin's original plan had been to occupy Parliament in advance of his announcement. By now it was clear that Rutskoi and Khasbulatov and their followers would stay put.

His cabinet ordered the police to stand by, unarmed, near the presumed demonstrators, "pitting their rubber truncheons and shields against the rebels' machine-guns, Molotov cocktails, sawn-off shotguns and jack-knives." Yeltsin was deeply conscious of the legal paradox at the heart of his plan. His aim was to establish a true democracy and the rule of law through new elections. But he could see no way of achieving this other than by adopting antidemocratic measures and dispersing Parliament, whereas Parliament was going to defend the constitution in order to overthrow the legitimately elected president and return to arbitrary Soviet rule.

He would soon find out that, if anything, what happened was even worse than he had anticipated. On September 21, he issued his decree under the cumbersome title of "On stage-by-stage constitutional reform in the Russian Federation." All "legislative, administrative, and control functions" of Parliament were suspended. Elections to the Russian State's *duma* (the lower house) would be held on December 11 and 12, 1993, as part of a plan for a new bicameral legislature to be known as the Federal Assembly.

The other main provisions of the decree were

- Any attempt to obstruct the elections would be deemed "a criminal act."
- The Ministries of Defense, the Interior, and Security were empowered to "take all necessary measures to ensure the security of the state and society."

The decree also accused the Supreme Soviet of blocking the process of economic and constitutional reform and systematically usurping executive and judicial functions from other institutions.

That evening Yeltsin appeared on television claiming that the developing political stalemate would ultimately have led to "the disintegration of Russian statehood" with "catastrophic results." The legislature, he went on, had discredited itself, and the security of Russia and its peoples was "more important than formal obedience to contradictory norms" established by that legislature.

Aleksander Rutskoi, Yeltsin's hard-line vice president and rival, lost no time in denouncing the president's decree, claiming that it was unconstitutional. That evening the Constitutional Court called an emergency meeting, and concluded that Yeltsin's decree and his televised statement were "in violation of the constitution" and formed "the basis for impeaching the president."

Nor did the president's opponents stop at words. Rutskoi called an emergency meeting of the Congress of People's Deputies on September 23. The session ended on the morning of September 24 with a vote to impeach Yeltsin. The Congress also swore in Rutskoi as president in anticipation of Yeltsin's impeachment.

Yeltsin's other main enemy, Ruslan Khasbulatov, chairman of the Supreme Soviet (the electoral offshoot of the Congress of People's Deputies), joined Rutskoi in calls for industrial action against the decree.

As though nothing had changed in post-Communist Russia, Igor Kloshkov, leader of the Federation of Independent Trade Unions of Russia, denounced Yeltsin's restrictions on the Supreme Soviet as unconstitutional and threatened to call a general strike. In fact things *had* changed, and no strikes followed.

Abroad, messages of support for President Yeltsin came from President Bill Clinton of the United States, Chancellor Kohl of Germany, France's Foreign Minister Alain Juppé, and Britain's Foreign Office.

In the confused situation that followed Yeltsin's decree, Rutskoi dismissed several ministers who had been appointed by Yeltsin, and brought in his own supporters in their place. On September 22, however, Defense Minister Pavel Grachev, on a walkabout with Yeltsin, claimed that senior ministers were united behind him. That day, General Mikhail Kolesnikov said he would take orders only from Grachev and Yeltsin.

That same day, all Parliament telephone lines were cut. Two days later, the electricity supply was cut off and the water supply reduced. That evening demonstrators, many of them armed with light weapons that had been stored in the Parliament, gathered outside. Most of the demonstrators were middle-aged or old, like most of the citizens who were nostalgic for the Communist past.

On September 26, some ten thousand pro-Yeltsin demonstrators gathered in Moscow's streets; next day the White House was sealed off by around 2,000 troops in a pro-Yeltsin demonstration. By then Yeltsin had imposed state control over the media, and Rutskoi's demand for television time had been ignored.

The threatening situation came to a head on the evening of October 3, a Sunday. From Yeltsin's own emotional account in *The View from the Kremlin,* it is clear that, in fear of a full-scale civil war, he had been resisting all hints or calls within his own camp to make sure the police or military forces on his side should be armed, whereas the Rutskoi-Khasbulatov ones already were. The rebels seized the mayor's office and were trying to take over the state television headquarters in a verbal confrontation with the staff. Yeltsin and others gathered in a room at the Defense Ministry. There senior Army officers revealed that many of the soldiers were in the fields packing potatoes and had no inclination to involve themselves in the political clash. The Army was outside politics.

With strong support from Chernomyrdin, the issue was hotly debated. Defense Minister General Grachev "raised his hands and addressed me, slowly measuring out the words: 'Boris Nikolayevich, are you giving me sanction to use tanks in Moscow?'" Chernomyrdin told him he had been assigned to command the proposed operation. What else did he need? Evasively, Grachev made it clear that he needed a written order. Yeltsin went back to the Kremlin, where Ilyushin drafted the document for him. Yeltsin signed it and conveyed it to Grachev.

Having seized the mayor's office, two floors of the television center, and the ITAR-TASS news center, Rutskoi and Khasbulatov jumped to the conclusion that the Army and the KGB's special division Alpha were on their side, and that victory over Yeltsin and his reformers was assured. On the evening of October 3, Rutskoi went so far as to tell ITAR-TASS that "today we must take over the Kremlin."

Instead, the forces now mustered in support of Yeltsin took over the Parliament. Tanks had been used in an intensified attack from 7 A.M. till noon on October 4. Incendiary bombs had set the building on fire, and when the rebel leaders surrendered in the early evening, they emerged from a blackened White House. Rutskoi, Khasbulatov, and fourteen others were detained under guard at the high-security Lefortovo Prison. On October 15, they were charged with "organizing mass disorder" and faced a maximum jail sentence of fifteen years. No such sentence was passed, however. In February 1994, Rutskoi, Khasbulatov, and the other rebels were amnestied and released.

At the critical time, however, major Western statesmen supported Yeltsin. President Clinton blamed the Rutskoi-Khasbulatov forces and added that "Yeltsin [had] bent over backwards to avoid the use of force." Britain's Prime Minister John Major stated that Yeltsin "has our total and unequivocal support."

On October 16, Yeltsin decreed that on December 12, the day of the legislative elections, a referendum on his draft constitution would also be held. On October 7, Yeltsin had suspended the Constitutional Court for having "placed the country on the brink of civil war by its hasty actions and decisions." On October 27, he reintroduced trial by jury, which had been abolished in one of Lenin's first revolutionary measures in 1917. That day Yeltsin legalized the free sale and purchase of land—thus reversing a key principle of Communism that had been reaffirmed by the now-abolished Russian Congress of People's Deputies.

Did the post-Soviet regime succeed in preventing efforts to restore Communism? In early 1999, the short answer is "Yes," even though Yeltsin's choice for premier of Yevgeny Primakov—a former head of the KGB and an ally of the Iraqi dictator Saddam Hussein—discouraged ideological optimism.

The same was not true, however, of a number of the former constituent republics of the USSR, now listed as "independent states" within the post-Soviet Commonwealth of Independent States (CIS). The three Baltic Republics not only opted out of the USSR while it still existed but also declined to join the CIS; they are considered in Chapter 47. Their departure reduced the potential CIS from fifteen republics to twelve. Russia has been dealt with previously; the summaries that follow deal with the situation in the remaining eleven.

These fall into two broad categories: those that remained Communist or soon returned to Communist control; and those that opted out of Communism.

COMMUNIST REPUBLICS: NO CHANGE

Azerbaijan

In June 1992, Professor Abulfaz Elchibey, a longtime anti-Communist who had served time in prison for his outspoken views, was elected president. Almost exactly a year later, he was overthrown in a semi-military coup and replaced by Geidar Aliev, a notorious *mafioso* (denounced as such in *The*

Soviet Mafia, a well-researched book by the Soviet journalist Arkady Vaksberg, published in 1991). A protégé of Leonid Brezhnev, who had brought him into the Soviet Politburo, Aliev put his popularity to the test in October 1993 and won the presidential elections with a crushing majority.

Georgia

Much the same sequence of events occurred as in Azerbaijan. The anti-Communist Zviad Gamzakhurdia was elected president in May 1991. He turned out, however, to be of autocratic temperament and was overthrown the following January, when he vanished from the public scene. His body was found at the end of 1993. In September 1992, his rival, Gorbachev's world-renowned foreign minister Eduard Shevardnadze, had been elected president with a sweeping majority. A former high official of the KGB, Shevardnadze launched a new ruling party, the Union of Citizens of Georgia. Shevardnadze later survived two attempts to assassinate him: on August 29, 1995, when a large car bomb exploded as he was leaving Parliament; and in October 1996.

Kazakhstan

In September 1991, the Kazakh Communist Party changed its name to the "Socialist Party of Kazakhstan." In the legislative elections of March 25, 1990, the Communists had won a large majority of the seats, eighty-one of which (of a total of 360) were reserved for official organizations. On December 1, President Nursultan Nazarbayev swept the board as the sole candidate in new presidential elections, with 98.76 percent of the votes: just as in the "good" old days.

Tajikistan

In line with the other Soviet Republics, Tajikistan proclaimed its independence on August 25, 1990. In November 1991, a directly elected presidency was instituted. The leader of the Tajik Communist Party during the Brezhnev era, Rakhman Nabiyev, had seized power in September. Although he resigned and contested the elections, he was elected president with 58 percent of the vote in a turnout of nearly 85 percent of voters. The Communist Party, after a brief change of name as the Socialist Party, resumed its original name on January 20, 1992, and stayed in power.

Turkmenistan

A political and ideological carbon copy of Kazakhstan, Turkmenistan's former Communist Party, renamed the Turkman Democratic Party (TDP),
stayed in power, with the same man as leader: Saparmurad Niyazov. The
TDP won the elections of June 21, 1992, with a majority of 99.5 percent of
the votes.

Uzbekistan

Islam Karimov, leader of the Democratic People's Party (DPP: the new
name of the Communist Party) was elected president on December 29,
1991, with 85.9 percent of the votes cast.

NON-COMMUNIST REPUBLICS: CHANGES IN DEPTH

Armenia

Having proclaimed its independence on August 23, 1991 (before the dissolution of the USSR), the new Armenian government suspended the
Communist Party in September. In the presidential elections in October
1991, the victor was Levon Ter-Petrosian, leader of the National Pan-
Armenian Movement.

Belarus

The ruling Communist Party was suspended in August 1991 but allowed
to resume activities in February 1993. However, in the presidential elections of July 1994, the Communist candidate lost heavily, with only 4.6
percent of the vote. The new president, Aleksandr Lukashenka, running
as an independent, was elected with a relatively small percentage (44.8) of
the vote. Although not a Communist, he soon made it clear that he was
an authoritarian.

Kirgistan

President Askar Akayev, a former Communist, proclaimed his country's
independence at the end of August 1991, and (as in Armenia) before the
dissolution of the USSR. His Democratic Movement of Kirgistan adopted
a Nationalist and reformist program.

Moldavia

On August 27, 1991, the Republic of Moldavia declared its independence from the Soviet Union. In December that year a nationally elected presidency was introduced. Both the CPSU and the Moldavian Communist Party were banned, but the legislature continued to be dominated by the Left. Membership in the CIS was ratified in April 1994. However, on August 27, 1994, exactly three years after independence had been proclaimed, a new constitution was launched, defining Moldavia as a "presidential parliamentary republic" based on political pluralism and "the preservation, development and expression of ethnic and linguistic identity."

Ukraine

Next to Russia the most important of the former Soviet Republics, Ukraine banned the Communist Party in 1991, but (as in Russia) the ban was soon lifted. In two-round elections in April 1994, the Communists won eighty-six seats, which made them the largest group in a parliament of 450 members but a long way from an absolute majority. In July that year Leonid Kuchma, a reformed ex-Communist, was elected president on a policy of a modified Western-style economy.

With six republics in the "no change" list and five, including Ukraine, in the "changes in depth" one, the balance in favor and against Communist rule was remarkably even.

CHAPTER FORTY-SEVEN

RED NAME CHANGES

———◦———

IN SOME, THOUGH not all, of Stalin's East European satellites, Communist parties returned to power after a brief spell in the political wilderness. Unlike Russia, however, the parties changed their names. Although this trend was disquieting, democracy eventually worked its magic, notably in Poland. And there were encouraging exceptions to the pattern: in the Czech Republic and (for quite different reasons) in the former German Democratic Republic.

The pattern was similar in three of the satellites: Poland, Hungary, and Bulgaria. A slightly different pattern formed in Slovakia (which had split away from the former Czechoslovakia) and the Baltic Republic of Lithuania. (In the other two Baltic Republics—Estonia and Latvia—the Communists remained out of power.) There were four stages in this political mutation:

- Stage 1: The Communist Party renames itself.
- Stage 2: The restyled Party demonstrates its reformed character by accepting the outcome of free and fair elections, won by an anti-Communist party or coalition of parties.
- Stage 3: The winning party, lacking any experience of running a government, botches its opportunity, at a high cost in unpopularity.
- Stage 4: The restyled ex-Communist Party wins its way back to power.[1]

POLAND

Not surprisingly, the man who did more than anyone else to oust the Communist regime, the Solidarity trade union leader Lech Walesa, was elected president of Poland on December 9, 1990. Although he remained in power for nearly five years, he had to contend with a parliament (the *Sejm*) that initially was still dominated by the Communists, with a 65 percent guaranteed majority. In the 1993 general elections, the anti-Communist government of Hanna Suchocka was overthrown by a familiar coalition of Communists (now calling themselves the "Democratic Left Alliance") and the Peasant Party.

By then a charismatically handsome younger man, Aleksander Kwasniewski, had taken over the leadership of the ex-Communists. Wisely, in the light of recent history, he gave the premiership not to his own party but to the leader of the allied Peasant Party, Waldemar Pawlak. After repeated clashes between President Walesa and Premier Pawlak, the latter stood down on February 7, 1995. The left-wing coalition remained in power, but not for long. In a new general election on September 21, 1997, a new right-wing multiparty grouping calling itself the Solidarity Electoral Alliance swept into power with its allies, the pro-business Freedom Union.

Democratic practice had now established itself, and mainly Catholic Poland was treated to the spectacle of ex-Communist President Kwasniewski appointing an evangelical Protestant as prime minister on October 17.[2] The new leader was a hitherto obscure chemistry professor, Jerzy Buzek. However, Buzek had not wasted his time in obscurity, for he had helped to organize Solidarity's underground movement in Silesia at the height of the crisis, when, under intense pressure from Moscow, General Wojciech Jaruzelski had proclaimed martial law (see Chapter 37). Moreover, he had been acting as economic adviser to Marian Krzaklewski, who had taken over the Solidarity trade union and its political offshoot, now in power. And, to complete Buzek's political curriculum vitae, he was popular with the junior partner in the new coalition, the Freedom Union, whose leader, Leszek Balcerowicz, was appointed deputy prime minister and finance minister.

On November 14, Buzek's coalition government replaced the heads of Poland's three security and intelligence services: a symbolic farewell to the repressive past.

HUNGARY

THE HUNGARIANS HELD their first post-Communist elections for their parliament (the Országgyülés) in March and April 1990. On May 23, a three-party government was formed (excluding the Communists, who now called themselves the Hungarian Socialist Party). The leading party in the coalition was the conservative Hungarian Democratic Forum (HDF). On August 3, the parliament chose a new president of the republic: Arpad Göncz, leader of the liberal Alliance of Free Democrats.

At this stage the ousting of the Communists was, or appeared to be, an irreversible reality. The situation reversed itself, however, when the HDF was heavily defeated in further general elections in May 1994. The victors were the ex-Communists of the Socialist Party, led by the former foreign minister Gyula Horn. Backed by the liberal Alliance of Free Democrats, he took office on July 15.

BULGARIA

MUCH THE SAME happened as in Hungary. Until November 1990, Bulgaria had been a typical Soviet satellite, a "People's Republic," but it now renamed itself the Republic of Bulgaria, with a parliamentary government and a directly elected national president: Zhelyu Zhelev. A new constitution came into force on July 9, 1991, and throughout that year membership in the former Communist Party, now calling itself the Bulgarian Socialist Party (BSP), declined—to a new low of 50 percent. In the parliamentary elections of October 13, 1991, the anti-Communist Union of Democratic Forces (UDF) won 110 seats, narrowly ousting the Socialists, who had 106. Moreover, the UDF depended for its tiny majority on the ethnic Turkish Movement for Rights and Freedoms.

The new UDF government introduced bills to restitute properties confiscated by the Communists to their former owners and was awarded a stabilization fund of US $2 billion by the International Monetary Fund (IMF). In September 1992, Bulgaria's former Communist leader from 1954 to 1989, Todor Zhivkov, was jailed for seven years on charges of embezzling state funds and inciting racial hatred. The post-Communist phase, however, was marred by serious financial problems and, in 1991, a threefold increase in crime over the previous year.

In further elections on January 25–26, 1995, the Bulgarian Socialist Party returned to power, with their leader Zhan Videnov as prime minister. The vicious circle had been completed.

SLOVAKIA

ON NEW YEAR'S DAY, 1993, the second half of Czechoslovakia broke away from the first to form the Slovak Republic. Whereas the Czech Republic, under President Václav Havel, remained a Western-style democracy, Slovakia immediately came under the control of ex-Communists, and remained so.

From the first, the dominant personality was Vladimir Meciar, a former minister of the interior in Slovakia in the Communist era, who in that capacity had controlled the secret police. In June 1990, he had become prime minister of the Slovak half of the joint republic. At the time of Havel's "velvet revolution" in December 1989 (see Chapter 42), rumors spread to the effect that Meciar had delved into secret police files to intimidate his political rivals. Separatist unrest simmered in Slovakia, culminating in mass demonstrations in March 1991. Despite such unrest, the division of Czechoslovakia into two separate but equal states took place peacefully, on the "velvet" model exemplified by Havel.

A parliamentary consensus had emerged on a new president. The ruling party was Meciar's Movement for a Democratic Slovakia (HZDS), and on February 15, 1993, the Slovak Parliament, known as the National Council, picked Michal Kovak (also an HZDS man) as Slovakia's new president. A former banker, Kovak was seen as a reform-minded ex-Communist, and his views on independence did not coincide with the prime minister's. Kovac favored a confederal link between the Czech and Slovak Republics rather than the complete break envisaged by Meciar. The new president's first move, to affirm a non-party stance, was to resign from the ruling HZDS.

Meciar's assumption of power coincided with a crisis within his government that arose out of a clash between himself and Foreign Minister Milan Knazko, whom he saw as a challenger to his own authority. When Meciar called on Kovac to dismiss Knazko, the president referred the request to the Constitutional Court; Maciar threatened to resign if his request were turned down. Then, but only then, the president dismissed Knazko.

In Slovakia, as in other former Soviet satellites, the economic direction was away from the disastrous Marxist theories that had impaired living standards in all Communist countries. The political reality, however, was heavily marked by Meciar's Communist past. By February 1995, he had fired the police chief Stefan Lastovka and the intelligence chief Vladimir Mitro, as well as most top officers in both services. President Kovac had tried, but failed, to veto an amendment presented by the prime minister to have the right to appoint and dismiss the intelligence chief. By then it was widely believed that Meciar had already surrounded himself with police and intelligence informers of the Communist period.[3]

Two main issues dominated political concerns in Slovakia: membership of NATO and presidential elections by universal suffrage instead of a parliamentary vote. Clearly the first issue was one of foreign policy, while the second concerned domestic politics. As drafted by the Central Referendum Commission and announced on May 16, 1997, voters would be called upon to vote on four questions covering both issues:

1. Should Slovakia join NATO?
2. Should nuclear weapons be placed in Slovakia?
3. Should there be NATO bases in Slovakia?
4. Should a Slovak president be elected directly according to the constitutional draft bill (enclosed)?

Meciar objected—not illogically—to the inclusion of the fourth question in the referendum, whereas President Kovac insisted on it. Meciar won the argument, and the referendum was held on May 23–24. It was a fiasco. Kovac refused to cast his vote on a three-question ballot, and a large majority joined him in his boycott. The nationwide turnout was only 9.6 percent, and the Central Referendum Commission declared the referendum invalid.

In June 1997, Meciar called on the opposition to attend round-table talks on the future of Slovakia. All the main opposition parties boycotted the talks. Although Meciar had, negatively, won the day, he was increasingly unpopular; Slovakia had missed its chance to join NATO, in line with its former federal partner, the Czech Republic, Poland, and Hungary.

ROMANIA

The revolt of December 1989 in Romania rid the country of its corrupt and tyrannical dictator Nicolae Ceauşescu, but not of the ruling party. The beneficiaries of the coup were a group of Communists led by Ion Iliescu, who changed the party's name to the National Salvation Front (NSF). In May 1990, the NSF swept into power with an overwhelming majority, and Iliescu emerged as president of Romania.

Western observers had been fooled into believing that the elections had been free and fair, but they had not. For instance, the longtime Romanian patriot and exile Ion Ratiu, a leader of the National Peasants' Party,* was physically harassed, and the authorities cut off the power supply for a printing press he had bought and imported. His house was set on fire at the beginning of 1994, as was another dwelling into which he had moved with his wife. Not surprisingly, perhaps, the Party won only 4.29 percent of the vote, compared to the NSF's 85.07 percent.

It would be misleading, however, to assert that nothing had changed in Romania, although there was some point in rival claims that the NSF was in effect in power immediately after Ceauşescu's summary execution; indeed, some twenty parties had contended for power. Moreover, a new constitution, approved by referendum on December 8, 1991, provided for political pluralism, human rights, and a free market.

A key question was, Whatever happened to Ceauşescu's brutal and repressive secret police, the Securitate? On paper, the Securitate was disbanded after the revolt, and a new (secret) Romanian Intelligence Service (RIS) was launched on April 25, with Virgil Magureanu as its director. Officially the RIS was empowered to collect data on foreign espionage, terrorist groups, and political extremists. In practice it was widely rumored that many of the Securitate's former career personnel had been seamlessly absorbed into the new RIS, which led to rumors that things had not changed radically.

The National Salvation Front had two changes of name. In its first mutation it became the *Democratic* National Salvation Front (DNSF),

---

*Later renamed the National Peasant Party-Christian Democrat (*Partidul National Taranesc-Crestinsi Democrat,* or PNT-CD).

and in the second (on July 10, 1993) it restyled itself the Social Democracy Party of Romania (SDPR). The power monopoly of Iliescu's party ended when Iliescu himself was defeated in the second round of presidential elections in November 1996. The victor was Emilio Constantinescu with 54.41 percent of the vote to 45.50 for Iliescu. Constantinescu was a former geology lecturer: his party, the Democratic Convention of Romania (DCR), was committed to promises of speedy social, economic, and political reforms including anticorruption measures.

It could therefore be hoped that, allowing for the seven years' interregnum of Ion Iliescu, Romania was now set on a democratic course.

BALTIC REPUBLICS

Lithuania

All three of the Baltic Republics asserted their independence before the total collapse of the Soviet Union. Lithuania did so on March 11, 1990; Latvia on May 4, 1990; Estonia, although its Supreme Soviet had declared the republic to be "sovereign" as early as November 1989, declared full independence only after a referendum on March 3, 1991. The other Baltic Republics likewise, held referendums before *declaring* (as distinct from *asserting*) their independence.

Of the three, only Lithuania went through the four-stage sequence outlined earlier. Its assertion of independence had been challenged in January 1991 when Soviet troops stormed the television center in Vilnius, killing civilians. (See Chapter 43.) In the referendum that followed in February 1991, 90.47 of the votes cast favored independence. The hero of the hour was Vytautas Landsbergis, who had led a mass rally on the day of Gorbachev's arrival in Vilnius. In March he was elected president by the new 141-member Supreme Council.

For all his patriotism and his populist performance in an hour of need, the mild piano teacher was not a political leader and was outmaneuvered by the Communist chief Algirdas Brazauskas. As early as December 1989, the Lithuanian Communist Party proclaimed its independence from the Soviet ruling party. A year later it renamed itself the Lithuanian Democratic Labor Party (DLP). When Lithuania's first post-Soviet democratic general elections were held on 25 October, 1992, the DLP topped the poll, and Brazauskas began his reign as acting president. The "acting" appendage was discarded when he won the first direct presidential elections on February 14, 1993.

Latvia and Estonia

After a referendum in March 1991, Latvia reaffirmed its independence on August 21, 1991, and was admitted to the United Nations on September 17. The center-right Latvian Path won the elections of June 1993.

Estonia's referendum confirmed its own affirmation, and independence was proclaimed. The right-wing Pro-Patria Group won the elections of September 20, 1992, but the considerable Russian minority was denied the vote. The center-right coalition was, however, compelled to resign in a phone-tapping scandal in October 1995. A new center-right coalition was sworn in on November 3. There appeared to be no likelihood of a Communist revival.

ALBANIA

ALBANIA'S COMMUNIST LEADER Enver Hoxha had ruled with an iron hand from 1944 until his death in 1985. The ruling Albanian Communist Party was founded in November 1941 by two emissaries of the Yugoslav leader Josip Broz (Tito), on instructions from the Comintern. When Tito broke with Moscow in 1947, the Comintern ordered its Albanian wing to break with Yugoslavia and purge itself of its pro-Tito elements. Hoxha was happy to oblige, and various pro-Tito followers were executed as "Titoite revisionists." At the Party's First Congress in November 1948, it changed its name to the Albanian Party of Labor (PLA).[4]

Stalinist purges suited Hoxha, who resorted to them many times during his long reign. As a result Albania was never, in the full sense, a Soviet satellite: it was a backward, inward-looking closed society. Had Hoxha survived the collapse of the Soviet Union he might well have succeeded, unlike the leaders of neighboring countries, in maintaining a Communist dictatorship, as had happened in China, Vietnam, and in North Korea. However, Hoxha's successor, Ramiz Alia, after long years of subservience to him, evidently lacked the self-confidence to carry out a self-perpetuating act. As a leading specialist on Albania put it, "A reduced militancy in pronouncements and unusual degree of candour in alleviating 'errors' seem to characterize the Alia leadership style."[5]

In December 1990, mass protests by workers and students in the capital Tirana spread to other cities. The protesters knew what they wanted: an end to one-party rule, the institution of multiparty elections, and a free economy. Alia sent in troops to restore order, and 157 protesters were jailed for up to twenty years. Simultaneously, however, he fired five opponents of reform in the ruling party, and on December 11, independent political parties were allowed.

This "soft-hard" approach spelled the end of the Communist dictatorship. It came in two installments. In the first multiparty elections in March–April 1991, the ruling PLA won a large majority in the People's Assembly, but in further elections on March 22, 1992, the new Democratic Party (PDS) won a clear majority. On April 3, Ramiz Alia resigned, and three days later the PDS leader, Sali Berisha, was elected president.

Although the collapse of a Communist regime is a legitimate if negative cause for rejoicing, it cannot be said that the advent of democracy was an immediate success. The collapse of a string of so-called "pyramid" schemes (with promises of fast enrichment for gullible investors) in January 1997 caused runaway inflation and ruined many families. Violent demonstrations followed. The collapse of Communism had brought neither order nor prosperity.

CHAPTER FORTY-EIGHT

SEMI-SURVIVAL

IN ASIA

———➤●◄———

T HERE WAS AN important but largely overlooked contrast between
the methods chosen by Mikhail Gorbachev and by Deng Xiaoping
to ensure the survival of their respective Communist regimes. Where Gorbachev had opted for perestroika (restructuring of the economy) and glasnost (a limited but deeply damaging freedom of expression), the older and
wiser Deng had chosen the path of economic capitalism, with a continuing ban on free speech.[1] It was not the first time a Chinese leader had decided to deviate from the Moscow line. In his early career, Mao Zedong
had defied Lenin's teaching by opting for a revolution of the peasantry in
preference to the orthodox uprising of the urban proletariat.

During the Great Proletarian Cultural Revolution of the 1960s, Mao
had ordered the youthful Red Guards to drag Deng through the streets
with a donkey's bonnet on his head. True, in 1973 Mao ordered the Party
to rehabilitate his old comrade of the Long March, but three years later
denounced him as a "capitalist roader." Fortunately for China, this label
turned out to be accurate; and fortunately for Deng the "Great Helmsman" died on September 9, 1976, after several months of senility. Although in the years that followed Deng held no official position, he was
known as "the Paramount Leader"—a very Confucian label—and in fact
his word was law.

In the autumn of 1977, Deng embarked on his sensationally successful capitalist experiment; although, typical for a regime that still called

itself "Communist," the term "capitalist" was not used. Instead the approved label was "Socialism with Chinese characteristics." Deng began with a lecture tour of Guangdong province (the capital of which is Canton). In ideological terms, the theme he was preaching was heresy. In practical terms, it was a runaway success. The Chinese have always been natural traders and entrepreneurs. While mother China was stagnating under the Maoist regime, the Chinese diaspora was turning certain countries of South-East Asia into havens of prosperity: Singapore, Malaysia, Indonesia, but above all Taiwan (regarded on both sides of the ideological divide as a Chinese province) and Hong Kong (transferred to Chinese rule on July 1, 1997).

And now, with Deng at the helm, China itself started growing at a spectacular pace. In 1992, the economic growth was truly phenomenal: at 13 percent, it was way ahead of the United States, Japan, Germany, France, and the United Kingdom. Although the rate of growth slowed down in subsequent years, it remained very high, especially in certain areas designated as "special economic zones," of which the best known was Shendzhen, adjoining Hong Kong. With expansion came inflation, which in the first quarter of 1993 reached 35 percent in Shendzhen, although it was a mere 8 percent on average in the rest of China, according to Professor Li Yining of Beijing University.

Though scarcely noticed in the rest of the world, major ideological changes were in progress in Chinese higher education. In February 1992, Beijing University announced that henceforth Marxism and "scientific Socialism" would no longer be part of the curriculum. Instead the academics would teach property management, marketing, international relations, international commerce, the management of human resources, and fiscal policies. A new Chinese law on investments and stocks and shares would be based on similar laws in the United States, Japan, Singapore, Taiwan, and Hong Kong.

These changes would have been unthinkable in Mao's day. Indeed they were totally incompatible with the Maoist ideology that alone had been held to justify the absolute power of the regime. Deng's new policy of private capitalism under ultimate Party control amounted to a squaring of the ideological circle. In these new circumstances, could the regime survive?

My own view at the time was that it could not, but it did not follow that collapse would be instantaneous, or even rapid. China has a long history of dictatorial rule and no tradition of democracy. Moreover, Deng Xiaoping did not make Gorbachev's fatal error of freeing speech and information, even in the limited form of glasnost. The massacre of the "Democracy" demonstrators on Tienanmen Square in June 1989 was seen by millions on television screens the world over. It was Deng himself who gave the order to fire on the demonstrators, knowing full well that the massacre would give China a bad press after several years of an improving international image. He also knew that a tarnished image would not last forever in a world anxious to trade with China, even though the incident might delay any American conferral of the coveted "Most Favored Nation" label on the Chinese People's Republic. The Tienanmen massacre did indeed tarnish China's image and delay the MFN label (which was not bestowed until June 1995, and was initially subject to an annual reappraisal, to Beijing's displeasure).

Four years later, in October 1993, the Party introduced a new law forbidding the production or purchase of any apparatus permitting the reception of satellite television. The message was clear: The regime feared above all the free circulation of information.

Some months earlier, on April 1, President Jiang Zemin had delivered an important speech on the economy, but it was not released for publication by the official news agency Xinhua until June 1: two months of Party censorship of the Party leader's words. Why the delay? On the release date, June 1, 1993, the well-informed Hong Kong daily, the *South China Morning Post,* put its finger on the reason. The explanation was simply that Jiang's speech contained a coded anti-Deng message: "By saying that the cadres must interpret Deng's instructions in a comprehensive and correct manner, Jiang was revising them in reality."

Despite the persistence of censorship, it was loosened de facto, if only because of the exponential rise in violent crime and corruption as the new policy of semi-capitalism gathered momentum. As in post-Soviet Russia, rapes and murders multiplied. So too did executions, and soon the Chinese press was full, as the Western newspapers always are, of corresponding news items. In Hunan province alone, on December 4, 1993, 104 persons were executed for crimes of violence. Nor were these the only items reported. At the end of that year the president of China's Supreme Court, Ren Jianxin, announced that between January 1 and the end of November tribunals had heard 2.8 million charges of economic crime, of which 333,000 were confirmed.

During that year the health of the aging Paramount Leader was a constant theme of speculation: whispered in China, audible elsewhere. At eighty-eight, Deng was said to be in excellent health for his age, but in May 1993 he had spent time in hospital, reportedly with early signs of Alzheimer's and Parkinson's diseases. For two months, the hard-line prime minister Li Peng had disappeared from public view. He had not hesitated to carry out Deng's order to stop the Tienanmen demonstrators with lethal fire, but he was very critical of Deng's "capitalist" policies. At first he was reported to have a cold; later it was said to be a heart attack. Reports circulated to the effect that some way had to be found to prevent Li Peng from publicly criticizing the Paramount Leader.

At the end of this interesting year, on December 26, 1993, the centenary of the birth of Mao Zedong was celebrated in Beijing. Ten thousand party members, bureaucrats, and military officers gathered to hear a celebratory speech by the president of the republic, Party general secretary, and commander in chief of the armed forces: Jiang Zemin. Before he rose, the Party's official spokesmen had been circulating an agreed-upon but mathematically flawed verdict on Mao's legacy: 76 percent "good," 30 percent "bad." A considerable drop in reputed infallibility; but any verdict of, say, 50 percent "bad" would have seriously damaged the Party's standing.

Under a gigantic portrait of the Great Helmsman, Jiang stood and orated. He began with fulsome praise of Mao as a great leader, before mentioning that Mao had also committed certain "errors." He went on to say that the said errors had been "rectified" by Deng Xiaoping in person. Mao, he said, was the national hero of China's modern history; Deng, author of the theory of the Socialist market economy, was "the pillar of the spiritual vigor of the Chinese people." Jiang omitted any comment that Deng Xiaoping, in his sixteen years of unchallenged power, had destroyed Mao's economic heritage or mention that he owed his own career to the unraveling of Maoism during the 1980s.

The symbolism of the occasion was irreproachable. Alone among the seven members of the Politburo's permanent committee, Jiang was wearing a duplicate of Mao's gray tunic, drawing instant attention as a visual tribute to Mao's portrait.

Li Peng was in attendance but had presumably been told to watch his words. He merely introduced Jiang and, when the president had finished, delivered words of praise.

The man who had launched China's new economic policy, Deng Xiaoping, died on February 19, 1997. He was ninety-two. Six days of official mourning followed, and on the last day, February 25, President Jiang Zemin, frequently wiping tears away, delivered a forty-five-minute eulogy before 10,000 party members in Beijing's Great Hall of the People. One passage confirmed that Deng's squaring of the ideological circle would continue. Deng, he declared, was "a great Marxist," thereby brushing aside the fact that Deng's reforms directly contradicted the policies advocated by Karl Marx. He referred to "the bright prospects of the Socialist modernization" and pledged that Deng's reform policies would continue.

Deng's reforms had concentrated on agriculture and the creation of the Special Economic Zones that acted as a magnet for entrepreneurial ventures. In terms of overall economic growth, his policies had paid off spectacularly, but the growth was uneven and a major sector of stagnation was left untouched: some 370,000 state-owned enterprises (SOEs). At the Fifteenth Congress of the Chinese Communist Party in Beijing in mid-September 1997, Jiang declared that reform of the SOEs was essential to phase out "the shackles of irrational ownership systems on productive forces." He conceded that the "laying-off of workers" was an inevitable part of the reform process, but claimed that this would be good for "the long-term interest of the workers."

When China's national People's Congress met in mid-March 1998, Li Peng resigned as prime minister while remaining chairman of the congress. His successor, encouragingly, was Zhu Rongji, one of the main architects of China's economic takeoff. Like Deng Xiaoping, Zhu had suffered the penalties of "disgrace" imposed by the ultimate tyrant Mao Zedong. Labeled a "rightist" in 1957, he was sentence to four years of agricultural labor. Returning in 1962, his Party career looked promising until Mao's Great Proletarian Cultural Revolution. In 1970, he served a second period in the countryside, this time tending pigs and goats and cleaning the toilets of more fortunate Party dignitaries.[2] In the 1980s, Zhu Rongji served as mayor of Shanghai. An opponent of the Tienanmen massacre of 1989, he announced that the People's Army would not be turned against the people in "his" city. Although an engineer by training, he went on to demonstrate exceptional administrative and financial skills. He liberalized Shanghai's industry and in 1993 was appointed governor of the People's Bank of China. His promotion to prime minister gave him the power to steer China's economy further along the road to prosperity, though not necessarily toward political freedom.

IN ADDITION TO China, the Asian legacy of the Soviet Empire comprises five lesser regimes: Mongolia, North Korea, Vietnam, Laos, and Cambodia. Each of them deserves consideration.

MONGOLIA

BEGUN IN JULY 1921, the Mongolian People's Republic was the first external satellite of the Soviet Empire. In area it was one of the largest; in population one of the smallest: twice the size of Turkey, with only 2.3 million inhabitants (a mere 650,000 in 1921). After the collapse of the Soviet system, it asserted another exceptional claim: It was the first Asian satellite to adopt a new constitution renouncing Communism. The date of its proclamation was February 1992, a few weeks after the collapse in Russia. The People's Republic became the "State of Mongolia."

In line with its abandonment of Communism, the new constitution welcomed private property and introduced political pluralism. Admittedly the true picture is somewhat less encouraging than the new constitution suggests. The outgoing Communist Party changed its name to "Mongolian People's Revolutionary Party" (MPRP) and won seventy of the seventy-six seats in the first elections to the parliament, called the People's Great Hural, held on June 6, 1992.

In presidential elections, reportedly free and fair, in May 1997 the MPRP leader Natsagiyn Bagabandi won with 61 percent of the vote. Although Moscow-educated, Bagabandi declared, "There are no Communists in Mongolia. I believe in private enterprise. And, of course, I'm a democrat."[3] He pledged, however, to slow down the pace of reforms and to provide greater aid to the poor, the elderly, and the unemployed.

The Communists had won, but Communism had lost.

NORTH KOREA

THE LONG REIGN of Stalin's choice as North Korea's leader, Kim Il Sung, parallels that of Enver Hoxha in Albania, in character as well as in longevity. On October 14, 1945, in the uniform of the Soviet Red Army,

Kim returned to his country as a Stalin-designated national hero. He presided over the birth of the Korean People's Democratic Republic and remained in power until his death on July 8, 1994, at age eighty-two.

He created and ran probably the most hermetically sealed society on Earth. For example, the internal passport, without which North Korean citizens could not move from one place to another, included not only biographical notes of the carrier but those of his or her parents and grandparents. The cult of personality that permanently magnified his own personality surpassed even that of Mao Zedong or Fidel Castro.

In October 1992, two North Korean refugees arrived in Seoul, capital of the rival republic of South Korea, and revealed for the first time the ghastly conditions that prevailed in North Korea's gulag. They knew what they were talking about, for they had served time in one of them: Yodok. There were twelve such camps in all, with 200,000 political prisoners.[4]

One of the many "improvements" decreed by Kim Il Sung was the introduction of the (monarchical) hereditary principle. In all other Communist countries, the successor to a dead leader had been decided by the ruling party's Politburo. Not in North Korea, where Kim Il Sung had decreed that he would be succeeded by his son, Kim Jong Il. By common consent, outside as well as inside North Korea, Jong Il was not in his father's league. He was seen as a "spoiled brat," hooked on debauchery and fast driving regardless of deaths on the road. Kim Il Sung was known as the Great Leader; Kim Jong Il's label, the Beloved Leader, strained public acceptance, not least within the Army.

On April 15, 1993, the Great Leader's eighty-first birthday, the ruling party publicly revealed changes in North Korea's constitution, hacked out in secret. Gone were all references to Marxism-Leninism. Instead, the approved ideology was to be Juche, a curious mix of Nationalism, autarky, the primacy of the ruling party, and unattributed borrowings from Marxism-Leninism. There were even specific mentions of the Beloved Leader Kim Jong Il.

In effect, the succession issue had been shelved by the device of an official three-year mourning period, so that no serious consideration was given to the accession of Kim Jong Il to supreme authority until July 1997. No relevant announcement followed, however, in the ensuing months.

During that same period, increasingly disturbing reports of a major famine seeped out of North Korea. Refugees and defectors arriving in

South Korea confirmed the severity of the food shortages but—presumably for reasons of prestige—the Pyongyang regime resisted international efforts to send food for the starving. To admit the problem, even though it had been caused by a natural disaster—severe flooding that ruined the rice harvest—would amount to publicizing the failure of Juche: North Korea's version of Communism.

VIETNAM

THROUGHOUT ITS HISTORY, Vietnam has asserted its independence of the Greater Dragon to the North, and this is as true of Vietnam and China under Communism as it had been through the centuries of imperial rule in both countries. And yet, time and again, the Lesser Dragon of Vietnam followed examples set by China. Thus, Mao's massacre of landlords was matched by Ho Chi Minh, as was Mao's false promise of free speech during the Hundred Flowers period.

Ho died in 1969, six years before his regime's victory over the United States and South Vietnam. He therefore missed Deng Xiaoping's imminent launching of a new policy of private enterprise, disguised as "Socialism with Chinese characteristics." Inevitably Deng's successful program spread to the Lesser Dragon, but not immediately. In January 1994, Vietnam's ruling Communist Party met in Hanoi. As the meeting ended, on January 25, the Party's general secretary Do Muoi appealed to the whole membership for a struggle against corruption, waste, and bureaucracy. This was the negative side. The positive side was more important: The Party voted unanimously in favor of a market economy and a welcome to foreign investments. But as in China and no less unanimously, it rejected political pluralism. There was no question of sharing power with other parties.

Before the conference the deputy prime minister, Nguyen Khanh, had warned the Party's provincial chiefs that the country's "social vices" could no longer be tolerated. Officially, the number of prostitutes was given as 200,000, with drug addicts at 75,000.

In "Socialist" Vietnam, as anywhere else, the war against social vices could hardly be won overnight, and in early February 1996 the government launched a national drive against "social evils"—an interesting change of label. There were public burnings of illegal videotapes and pornographic materials.

When the National Assembly met, the following month, Vice Premier Phan Van Khai reported an increase of 9.5 percent in the gross domestic product in 1995, compared to the previous year's 8.8 percent. In Vietnam, as in China, private enterprise was delivering the goods. Compared with 1994, foreign investment had increased by a phenomenal 85.4 percent, and industrial output was up by 14 percent. Again as in China, the state sector (state-owned enterprise, or SOE) was ailing. In October 1997, Phan Van Khai declared that reforming the SOEs was the cornerstone of building a more competitive economy, although the 300 healthy SOEs would continue to receive state support. He suggested, however, that portions of such companies might be sold off to private investors including foreigners.[5]

Again in Vietnam as in China the men in power were old. General Secretary Do Muoi, reelected at the Eighth Party Congress in June 1996, was seventy-nine; President Le Duc Anh was seventy-five; and Prime Minister Vo Van Kiet a youngster of seventy-three. When the National Assembly met in September 1997, however, Le Duc Anh was replaced by Tran Duc Luong, and the reformist Phan Van Khai was promoted to prime minister. The guideline for the changes was health rather than age, and the oldest of the three, Do Muoi, stayed put. But not for long: he was replaced on December 29, 1997, by General Le Kha Pieu, whose reputation as a "conservative" hard-liner caused murmurings of apprehension among the reformers, who feared that he might object to Phan Van Khai's modernizing ideas.

Again as in China, corruption was rife. In January 1997, six people had been sentenced to death in Ho Chi Minh City (formerly Saigon). The most publicized trial was that of Pham Huy Phuoc, former head of the ruling party's import-export organ, found guilty of embezzling money provided through bank loans to buy a US $200,000 villa for his mistress and to settle his gambling debts. In May, in a trial in Hanoi, twenty-two defendants were tried and convicted of drug offenses.

And finally, once more as in China, freedom of speech was out of the question. For example the editor of the Hanoi-based newspaper *Doanh Nghiep,* Nguyen Hoang Linh, was arrested for publishing details of corrupt practices by customs officials.

LAOS

IN THE ERA of French colonialism, Laos was the idyllic backwater of Indochina. The Communist victory in the First Indochina War had given it nominal sovereignty, but with two of its provinces still under Communist rule. The Communist victory in the Second Indochina War ended with the withdrawal of the U.S. forces and the emergence of the whole of Laos as the "Lao People's Democratic Republic," as announced by the Communist victors in December 1975. A constitution was duly proclaimed, but not until August 1991. As everywhere else in the Communist world, there was only one "legal" party, which called itself the "Lao People's Revolutionary Party" (LPRP). The long-serving Party leader Prince Souphannouvong died in January 1995, aged eighty-six.

In March 1996, the LPRP held its Sixth Congress, in the presence of Wen Jiabao, an alternate member of the Chinese Communist Party's political bureau, and of the Vietnamese Party boss Do Muoi. The congress was dominated by representatives of the 37,000-strong Laotian Army under General Khamtay Siphandon. Of the various changes announced at the congress, the most significant was the removal of Khamphoui Keoboualapha, a leading economic reformist. One informed outside commentator reported that he "was felt to be pushing reforms, such as privatisation, too far."[6]

In general elections in December 1997, 99.37 percent of eligible voters (numbering 2.28 million people) cast their ballots in favor of the 159 candidates approved by the ruling LPRP's Lao Front for National Construction. Interestingly, the Front had allowed four "independent" businessmen to run for election, but only one of them made it to the ninety-nine-member National Assembly.

CAMBODIA

ON APRIL 15, 1998, the body of Pol Pot, the genocidal leader of Cambodia's Communist Khmer Rouge in the mid-1970s, was found by his wife in a hut in Thailand's southern jungle. He appeared to have died of a heart attack, according to the Thai medical team who inspected his corpse, although some commentators wondered whether his end might have been hastened with a poison administered by his erstwhile followers, who, on July 25, 1997, had brought him to trial by a "people's court" and sentenced him to lifelong "house arrest."

The charge brought against him was not, as might have been hoped, his guilt in ordering the mass killing of his compatriots (see Chapter 34), but the simpler one of murdering his former comrade-in-arms and defense minister, Son Sen. The news was reported in the August 7 issue of the *Far Eastern Economic Review* by a staff journalist, Nate Thayer, who had witnessed the trial. A video of the trial was later shown on Western television channels.

In October 1997, Nate Thayer interviewed Pol Pot in depth. By then the monster of the 1970s was suffering from the aftermath of a stroke, heart disease, and partial blindness. Of the many crimes attributed to him, he admitted only to ordering the death of Son Sen. That killing, along with fourteen family members, including grandchildren, had taken place on June 10, 1997. But Pol Pot did not own up to having ordered the death of the younger ones. As for the genocide all he had to say was, "I came to carry out the struggle, not to kill people."[7]

TWENTY YEARS AFTER Pol Pot's horrific rule, Cambodia had not recovered either unity or stability. The (relatively) beneficent occupation of Cambodia by the Vietnamese Army in 1978 had forced the Khmers Rouges to seek refuge in the Thai jungle across the border.

After thirteen years of guerrilla warfare and civil war, a peace accord put an end to the fighting. By then Pol Pot was reported to have settled in China under the regime's protection, and the leader of the Khmer Rouge negotiating team was Kieu Samphan. In July 1993, the provisional Cambodian administration was replaced by a royal government under Prince Norodom Sihanouk, home after a lengthy exile.

In August 1996, Ieng Sary, one of the Khmer Rouge leaders, defected to the royal government and was granted an amnesty by King Norodom. He had been deputy prime minister and foreign minister, although he had been sentenced to death in absentia by a people's revolutionary tribunal in August 1979. He claimed to have differed from Pol Pot from the start, and his claim was defended by Hun Sen, the second prime minister. Ieng Sary was, in fact, Pol Pot's brother-in-law. The *Far Eastern Economic Review* of September 26 refuted his claim that he differed from Pol Pot, asserting that in reality he was close to Pol Pot and had sent to their deaths some 800 Cambodians who had returned from abroad to serve in his ministry.

In February 1997, fighting broke out between Hun Sen's followers and forces loyal to the King's son, Prince Norodom Ranaridh. In May, however, Hun Sen and the prince made up and embraced before attending a cabinet meeting. It turned out later that the rift still existed. Indeed a month later fighting broke out between the two men's bodyguards. In July 1997, Hun Sen went on to stage a coup that ousted Ranaridh. Fighting between rival factions continued. The trial of Pol Pot followed.

IT WOULD BE comforting to report that by the time of Pol Pot's death in mid-April 1998 Cambodia had recovered, or at least was recovering, from the nightmare of his rule. But it had not, and was not. The Vietnamese-installed regime was less dementially evil than Pol Pot's, but only in degree. As one well informed observer put it,

> Not surprisingly, it perpetuates Pol Pot's legacy. Cambodia is still a communist country with a total fusion between the ruling party and the State apparatus, and a tight control of the population through a dense network of spies and militiamen. There is a culture of violence and impunity in which the people in power can perpetrate any crime. As in Pol Pot days, scores of critics, dissidents and opponents are eliminated by all means, including shootings and grenade attacks in broad daylight.[8]

In the spring of 1998, the nightmare of Asian Communism remained a living reality in Cambodia.

CHAPTER FORTY-NINE

CHAOTIC CHANGE

IN AND AROUND AFRICA

ETHIOPIA

DESPITE PROTRACTED EFFORTS both alone and in competition with China, the Soviet Union added to its peripheral empire only two genuine satellites in Africa: Somalia and Ethiopia. Moreover, when war broke out between the two in late 1977, Moscow was forced to choose between them, and naturally opted for the larger of the two—Ethiopia—thereby losing Somalia. (See Chapters 28 and 32.)

The Ethiopian dictator Mengistu Haile Meriam was what might be called a "convenience Communist." He appears to have decided to opt for Communism as probably the best device for seizing power, and for dependence on the USSR because it was clear that he could not hope for support from the other superpower, the democratic United States. His callous brutality may have consolidated his rule in the early stages, but certainly did not bring him any true popularity. When it became clear, by late 1990, that the Soviet Union was heading for disintegration, a coalition of disparate political groups calling itself the "Ethiopian People's Revolutionary Democratic Front" (EPRDF) emerged, and on May 27–28, 1991, overthrew the Mengistu regime.

By then Mengistu had understood what was happening and had fled the country a few days before the coup. Late on May 21, he had arrived in Harare, capital of Zimbabwe, and on May 23 was granted asylum there. Thus, the one surviving Soviet satellite in continental Africa had ceased to exist.

ANGOLA AND MOZAMBIQUE

THERE WERE, HOWEVER, two near-satellites in black Africa which never quite achieved full satellite status because of unfinished civil wars: Angola and Mozambique. Both had been Portuguese colonies. (See Chapter 23.)

Angola's anti-Communist uprising, led by Jonas Savimbi's UNITA *(União Nacional para a Independência Total de Angola),* had begun as an anticolonial struggle against Portuguese rule, as had Mozambique's RENAMO *(Resistência Nacional Moçambicana)* led by Afonso Dhlakama. Initially UNITA had been a guerrilla rival to the Communist-led and Soviet-trained MPLA *(Movimento Popular de Libertação de Angola),* as RENAMO had been to the Communist-led and Soviet-trained FRELIMO *(Frente de Libertação de Moçambique).*

In both countries the overthrow of Portugal's fascist regime in 1974 brought victory to the Communist-led guerrillas and transformed the anticolonial war waged by UNITA and RENAMO into an anti-Communist one. The Communist regimes that took over in both countries had no objection to satellite status, but in both the anti-Communist movements were too strong to be ignored. By 1988, the UNITA guerrillas controlled the southern half of Angola.* In Mozambique, too, RENAMO held considerable areas.

At this point a new and unexpected factor intervened, the full import of which was not immediately grasped in the West: the Soviet Union advised Fidel Castro that it could no longer subsidize the Cuban military presence in Angola nor even maintain its own military presence in Cuba. On December 13, 1988, the foreign ministers of Angola, Cuba, and South Africa signed an agreement at Brazzaville in the ex–French Congo. All

---

*The situation in Angola at that time sparked a wave of optimism among Western students of Communism. Thus in France one of the West's foremost specialists, Branko Lazitch, wrote in effect a celebratory booklet, *Angola 1974–1988: Un échec du communisme en Afrique,* the subtitle of which translates as "a failure of communism in Africa" (Paris, 1988). Also committed were Lazitch's junior co-author, Pierre Rigoulot, and the distinguished journalist and author Jean-François Revel, who wrote a substantial preface.

Cuban troops were to be withdrawn from Angola over the next twenty-seven months. At the time of the signing, some 50,000 Cuban troops were based there. South Africa and Angola agreed not to allow mutually hostile guerrillas to hold bases in their respective countries.

At UN headquarters in New York on December 22, the three foreign ministers, after talks mediated by the United States, signed statements incorporating their Brazzaville agreement.

The impending departure of the Cuban forces obliged the MPLA government to negotiate with Savimbi, whose UNITA movement was the real loser of the tripartite agreements of Brazzaville and UN headquarters. In the prolonged negotiations that followed, culminating in a pact in May 1991, Savimbi agreed to participate in countrywide elections. Whether unwittingly or in a spirit of unjustified optimism, UNITA did take part in the elections in September 1992, under supervision by international observers. Catastrophe: UNITA lost the elections and the civil war was resumed.

Much the same happened in Mozambique. In Rome in October 1992, President Joaquim Chissano and RENAMO's leader Dhlakama signed a peace agreement. Although fighting continued in a desultory fashion, the UN secretary-general, the Egyptian Boutros Boutros-Ghali, went to the Mozambican capital Maputo where, under his chairmanship, the rival leaders agreed on electoral arrangements. Polling took place in late October 1994, and as in Angola the anti-Communists lost out to the Communist FRELIMO, by 129 seats to 112. In the presidential elections, Chissano received 53.30 percent of the votes, to less than 34 percent for Dhlakama. Some 2,500 international monitors endorsed the elections as free and fair.

Unlike Savimbi, Dhlakama had lost his commitment to a continuing struggle, and peace came to Mozambique. In Angola on May 18, 1995, Savimbi announced that he recognized the victory of President José dos Santos. Nevertheless, he declined to surrender the extensive territory occupied by UNITA. The outcome was thus an unstable truce.

Nearly two years later, on April 11, 1997, UNITA joined the MPLA-PT (the last two initials standing for "Workers' Party") in a coalition government. It was, however, a coalition of unequals: of the thirty ministerial posts only four—Geology and Mines, Health, Trade, Hotels and Tourism—were allotted to UNITA, none of them in the top rank. Savimbi sulked on in his shifting jungle headquarters. On August 28, 1997, the UN Security

Council imposed further sanctions on UNITA, barring the admission of UNITA officials and their families in member-states and banning flights to and from UNITA areas. UNITA had claimed to have only 2,963 guerrillas left. "Not credible," said the UN, quoting the Angola Defense Ministry's estimate of some 35,000 in a "secret Army." In a desultory way, the civil war resumed.

SOUTH AFRICA

IT SEEMS APPOSITE to conclude this epilogue with a look at the curious and disquieting situation in South Africa. In general and with few exceptions, the West saluted the decision by President F. W. de Klerk in February 1990 to free the African National Congress (ANC) leader Nelson Mandela, after twenty-five years in prison. Simultaneously he abandoned the racist Afrikaner policy of apartheid, which enshrined white supremacy. Subsequently both men were awarded the Nobel Peace Prize.

Although de Klerk's radical change of policy was widely regarded as inevitable, the outcome was in many respects discouraging. Far from vanishing, violence increased dramatically, not only between whites and blacks, but between blacks and blacks, notably between the ANC and the Zulu Inkatha Freedom movement of Chief Gotsha Buthelezi. There was also a phenomenal and ever-increasing rise in criminal violence. One of the most worrisome aspects of the new situation was the role of the long-standing alliance between the ANC and the South African Communist Party (SACP).[1]

Founded in 1921, the SACP was one of the earliest creations of Lenin's Comintern. By then, however, the ANC had already been in existence for nine years. In his revolutionary youth, Nelson Mandela had been unaware of any incompatibility between the two parties. Was he a secret member of the Communist Party? Probably not, but he was demonstrably a Communist by conviction, for at his trial in 1963–1964 one of the main pieces of incriminating evidence produced by the prosecution was a long paper handwritten by Mandela under the title "How to Be a Good Communist."[2] This paper was clearly inspired by a book with the same title, published in 1939, by the one-time Chinese Communist Party ideologist Liu Shao-chi.

After the tragic Sharpeville massacre in 1960, when sixty-seven black South Africans were killed by the South African police, and the terrorist revenge attacks that followed, both the ANC and the SACP were banned. In their ensuing clandestineness the two parties formed an alliance that still endured at the time of Mandela's release. On its side, the Communist Party launched a terrorist organization known as "the Spear of the Nation" (*Umkhonto we Sizwe,* or the MK) with Mandela as president. In reality and certainly during Mandela's long years of imprisonment, the MK's strategist and leader was Joe Slovo, a white South African of Ukrainian origin, a longtime member of the Communist Party and reportedly in the service of the Soviet KGB. In 1985, Slovo became the first white member of the ANC's national executive committee. In Mandela's first speech after his release on February 11, 1985, he said, "The armed struggle goes on." He went on to confirm his past commitment in favor of nationalizing the mines, the banks, and industrial "monopolies." In fairness he soon renounced this commitment, not long after his exposure to current economic realities. Indeed, as de Klerk's new policy of democratization and racial equality was reaffirmed, Mandela's speeches became more moderate in tone.

Nevertheless, the existing alliance between the ANC and the Communist Party continued. It was another alliance of unequals: the ANC was a mass party; the CP had no more than 60,000 members and could count on a mere 1 percent of support in national opinion polls. The hard reality was that Mandela's first government, after the country's first free and nonracial elections in April 1994, included no fewer than sixteen Communist ministers in a total of twenty-six. The presence of Mandela's longtime supporter Fidel Castro, at the ceremony of Mandela's investiture as president of the South African Republic, was significant.

On the economic side, many promises of aid, notably from the United States, poured in, and foreign investments were plentiful. But the problems were many and deep: ethnic divisions, unemployment, poverty, violent crimes, internal divisions within the ANC and also within Chief Buthelezi's Inkatha Freedom Party. Increasingly, as time went on, Mandela's main interest was concentrated on the kudos and honors heaped upon him during his international travels, while inside South Africa the social, political, and economic problems steadily worsened.

SEYCHELLES

IN CHAPTER 35, we looked at the tragicomic case of the Seychelles, geographically a multi-island appendage of Africa, politically a mini-member of the (formerly British) Commonwealth. After general and presidential elections on March 23, 1998, France-Albert René, who had seized power in 1977, was still president, head of government, and commander in chief of the armed forces (totaling three hundred men in arms). Since the Soviet Union had ceased to exist, the Seychelles had ceased to be its mini-satellite. More significantly, René had ceased to be a Communist; although he had never belonged to a Communist Party, his doctrinal and oratorical commitment had been impressive.

Sir James Mancham, the man René had ousted in 1977, was back, unharmed. He had contested the 1998 presidential elections and lost to René by 36.72 percent of the vote to René's 59.50; his Democratic Party trailed René's by five seats to twenty-seven. René remained the virtual dictator, controlling business as well as politics, although on paper the ex-Communist ruler had turned his island mini-state into a democracy.

CHAPTER FIFTY

FIDEL ON HIS OWN

B ETWEEN 1988 AND 1990, Cuba dropped from one of Moscow's most financially favored satellites to a new status of economic solitude. In the earliest of those years, Fidel Castro's regime was at the receiving end of a Soviet annual bounty totaling between US $4 and $5 billion a year, including the costs of Cuba's expeditionary force in Angola. Cuba was not the only recipient of Soviet "aid": Nicaragua (Cuba's own satellite) was getting between US $600 and $800 million; Ethiopia and Mozambique about US $3 billion; Vietnam US $4–5 billion; and Afghanistan, between US $300 and $400 million a year, on a descending level as the Soviet Union pulled out of its disastrous military adventure.[1] (See Appendix P: Document 1.)

At that time, the global export revenues of the USSR amounted to a mere $30 billion a year—a quarter of the foreign earnings of General Motors. Mikhail Gorbachev and his team had decided to pull out of Afghanistan, and a similar decision about Angola followed soon after. Castro followed this news closely, though from afar. Essentially, ever since the early 1960s, his main source of revenue had been the annual bartering of the island's sugar crop in return for Soviet oil.

Between 1985 and 1987, he had purged his ruling party of all pro-Gorbachev elements. The purge started in the top ranks of the DGI (the secret intelligence service), the police, and the armed forces; some months later, it was extended to the State Council, the Central Committee, and the provincial secretariats.[2]

In 1987, Castro extended his purge to the media, collective farms, youth and women's organizations, and finally to the labor unions. Never had Fidel been so unpopular. In increasing numbers, young Cubans sought and obtained refuge in the United States. At the same time, and in defiance of his purge, agitation in favor of a Cuban equivalent of glasnost and perestroika grew. Castro was even criticized with allusive subtlety in the Party newspaper *Granma*. At the same time there was a considerable increase in the anti-Cuban broadcasts of Radio Martí and other anti-Communist stations, such as *La Voz del CID, Alfa-66, Radio Mambí, Radio Clarín,* and *La Cubanísima.*

During this troubled period, the Cuban *Líder*'s international image was increasingly tarnished by the regime's inability or refusal to settle international debts, its decision to boycott the Olympic games in South Korea, its role in international drug traffic, and its friendly relations with the sinister Medellin cartel in Colombia.

The "Ochoa affair" further tarnished Castro's image, both domestically and internationally. General Arnaldo Ochoa, a much-decorated veteran of the Angola war, holder of the "Hero of the Republic" medal, had just retired and had become the most popular Cuban personality, acclaimed in the streets wherever he was. This unofficial status was unacceptable to Castro, who resented plaudits that were not addressed to himself.

Although lacking any convincing evidence, Castro suspected Ochoa of plotting against him. To make matters worse, Fidel's brother Raúl, still Cuba's Defense Minister, was on very friendly terms with Ochoa and had nominated him for the key post of commander of the Western sector, which included the defense of Havana. A furious Fidel summoned Raúl for a fierce reprimand: Drop Ochoa, or else. . . . [3]

Taken aback, Raúl delivered a somewhat disjointed speech on June 14, 1989, complaining that General Ochoa, in a recent conversation with him, had criticized the *Líder Máximo*. Two days earlier, Ochoa had been arrested, with two close colleagues and four officers of the internal security service. Doubtless with the aim of diverting gossip about Fidel Castro's own dealings with the Colombian cartels, Ochoa was charged with accepting a bribe of US $400,000 for having arranged the delivery, through Cuba, of six tons of cocaine, on its way to the American market. For good measure, he was also charged with high treason and for activities damaging to the "moral and international prestige" of his country.

This was pure Stalinism, plus high tech. The trial was televised, for the "benefit" of the people, who saw and heard the hero of the Angola war accuse himself: "I despise myself. I have no reason to live. . . . I promise you that my last thought will be for Fidel and the Great Revolution he has given the people."

On July 13, 1989, Arnaldo Ochoa, with three of his "accomplices," was executed by firing squad.

AT THE END of 1990, Moscow informed Castro that he could no longer count on long-term Soviet economic aid. A new bilateral agreement was signed, but unlike previous ones it was valid for one year only instead of the usual five. Soviet subsidies were drastically reduced, and Soviet deliveries of oil would henceforth barely meet the needs of individual families, but not those of industry.

In September 1991, Gorbachev announced the withdrawal of the 11,000 Soviet troops stationed on Cuba. Times had changed. The Cuban Party's organ, *Granma,* denounced the new deal as a "unilateral" one that would give the United States the green light for its "program of aggression" against Cuba.

In October 1991, the Cuban Communist Party held its Fourth Congress, at Santiago de Cuba. Fidel Castro delivered his usual protracted speech (five hours), but, for the first time, it was neither broadcast nor televised. After the event a self-censored version of it was published, in which Castro complained that Soviet deliveries had fallen well short of the levels agreed in Moscow. At the end of the year, he would announce massive cuts in the hours allowed for television, air conditioning, street lighting, sporting events requiring special lighting after dark, and urban transport. Taxi services were restricted to transport to hospitals and cemeteries.

In July 1992, Castro made significant amendments to the 1976 constitution. All references to the Soviet Union were deleted. The ultimate aim of "building a Communist society" was retained, but the state monopoly of external trade was abolished, although the state would retain its right to control it and direct it. This was of course a minimal recognition of a new order, in which Cuba would cease to recognize itself as a satellite of an imperial power that no longer existed.

There were other economic consequences of the Soviet collapse. For the first time, Cuban sugar would have to be sold at the low prevailing market price, no longer at the preferential price on offer from Moscow in the good old days. Henceforth, Boris Yeltsin's Russia would take only 50,000 tons of sugar in exchange for petrol. Kazakhstan would take 200,000 tons, and Latvia 50,000. The net balance of unsold sugar was at least 1.5 million tons.

Whatever its nostalgic wishes, the regime had to find new customers, and in fact these were not lacking. In defiance of American pressures, more than 700 foreign companies took part in Havana's Trade Fair in November 1991, on the eve of the Soviet collapse. Many of them came from France, Germany, Italy, and Spain, but not from Britain, which respected U.S. wishes. Castro embarked on salesman travels. He was given a friendly reception in Mexico. Diplomatic ties were restored with Colombia, and Vice President Carlos Rafaël Rodríguez led a Cuban delegation to Beijing. And finally, under the pretext of an invitation by UNESCO, Fidel Castro was received with full presidential honors by President François Mitterrand of France and his determinedly left-wing wife. Little by little, it seemed, the regime was coming out of its isolation, despite an American decision to strengthen its commercial embargo.

During that whole difficult readjustment period, Cuba's military evacuation of Angola continued. The last contingent arrived back in Havana in May 1991. No longer would Fidel play the part of the Soviet "emperor's" servant.

All through the difficult transition period, and beyond, the Cuban Communist Party (PCC) remained the only legal party. For the first time, all 589 members of the National Assembly of People's Power were directly elected on February 24, 1993—which may have made the 589 feel good, or better, but all of them were Party members. The PCC monopoly was unbreached. That day, the new Assembly reelected Fidel Castro as president for a further five-year term, and his brother Raúl as vice president.

The U.S. trade embargo continued, even though, on November 2, 1995, the UN General Assembly condemned it, for the fourth consecutive year.

Soon Castro would make a charismatic but unexpected new "friend" when, in November 1996, he visited the Vatican. Pope John Paul II returned the compliment on January 21, 1998, when he landed at Havana for a four-day visit that attracted huge crowds. The fourth of his Catholic masses was attended by a prominent atheist named Fidel Castro. It would be fair to comment that the Pope enjoyed the opportunity to mingle with the Cuban crowds, while Castro enjoyed the apparent blessing of the Christian world's leading apostle. During the mass attended by Castro, John Paul II had denounced the U.S. embargo as "ethically unacceptable"; but he had also called for greater freedom in Cuba and urged the authorities to open up to the world.

There can be no doubt that the papal visit contributed to restoring some popular support to Castro's regime. On February 12 the release of 299 prisoners was announced. Of these, seventy-five, including an unspecified number of political detainees, were on a list of 302 compiled by the Vatican; the rest were freed for "humanitarian reasons."

NICARAGUA

TO THE SURPRISE and disappointment of Western left-wing intellectuals, Nicaragua's Cuban-backed Sandinistas were defeated in presidential elections on February 25, 1990 (see Chapters 36 and 43). The victor was Violeta Barrios de Chamorro, widow of an anti-Communist politician, Pedro Joaquín Chamorro, whose murder in 1978 had sparked off the Sandinistas' revolution. Her right-wing National Opposition Union (*Unión Nacional de Oposición,* or UNO), which consisted of fourteen political groups, attracted 54.7 percent of the vote. The Sandinistas' share of seats was thirty-nine to UNO's fifty-one.

With unemployment at 21.8 percent of the workforce and a balance of payments deficit of US $729 million, President Chamorro was not short of problems. Her path was made easier, however, on February 21, 1995, when General Humberto Ortega retired as commander in chief of the Army. In June 1995, the so-called Paris Club of Western creditor nations agreed to provide the anti-Sandinista government with US $1.5 billion in aid.

With the collapse of the imperial Soviet Union, it seemed unlikely that Castro's Cuba would restore Communism to Nicaragua.

CHAPTER FIFTY-ONE

REFLECTIONS:
THE EXORBITANT PRICE
OF LENIN'S UTOPIA

S OCIALISM IS AT the heart of the twentieth century's totalist experiments, whether in Lenin's Russia, Mussolini's Italy, or Hitler's Germany; in Mao Zedong's China, Castro's Cuba, or Kim Il Sung's North Korea. Wherever it has been tried it has failed: in Britain as in Sweden as in India. The degrees of failure vary in proportion to the intensity of its application.*

So do the degrees of pain and death. Benito Mussolini's corporatist version of Socialism, known as Fascism,** led to two relatively minor wars (in Ethiopia and Greece). Hitler's National Socialist (Nazi) model led to the massacre of the Jewish population, known as the Holocaust, and to the most destructive war in history. Lenin's version led to its imposition in many countries, to a futile war in Afghanistan and other wars by proxy, notably in Korea and Vietnam, and to the largest massacres, by far, in world history.

Lenin's Communist Party, brought to power by his "October Revolution," believed itself entitled, in the name of history, not only to perpetu-

---

*I have discussed these propositions in detail in *Socialism: Dream and Reality* (London, 1987), and in *The Minimum State: Beyond Party Politics* (London, 1979).—BC

**In 1926, the Italian Fascist dictator, Mussolini, created major corporations, embracing workers' trade unions or syndicates, professional bodies, industrial and agricultural employers. In July of that year, he set up the National Council of Corporations (in effect, his substitute for a parliament), under his personal chairmanship.

ate its power by terror, but to extend it to all other countries in the world. Today, some years after the collapse of the system he created in Russia, the human cost of Leninism and its foreign variants can be estimated, at least in acceptable approximations.

In November 1997 (on the eightieth anniversary of Lenin's "October Revolution"), a massive volume (846 pages) appeared in Paris under the title *Le Livre noir du Communisme: Crimes, terreur, répression* (Robert Laffont). Its six authors[1] presented meticulously researched studies of the crimes committed by ruling Communist parties in the USSR; in Eastern Europe; in China, North Korea, Vietnam, Laos, and Cambodia; in Cuba; in Ethiopia, Angola, and Mozambique; and in Afghanistan. Their collective numerical conclusions were as follows:

China: 65 million deaths;

Soviet Union: 20 million;

Cambodia: 2 million;

North Korea: 2 million;

Africa: 1.7 million;

Afghanistan, 1.5 million;

Vietnam: 1 million;

Eastern Europe: 1 million;

Latin America: 150,000.

The total of 94.35 million is then rounded off to "up to 100 million deaths," which the authors compare with a "mere" 25 million attributed to the Nazis (who, admittedly, were in power for only twelve years).

As Philip Vander Elst (a British specialist on Communism) pointed out in his review of the *Livre Noir*,[2] other researchers have calculated massively higher death tolls. One of them, Professor Kurganov, in a 1964 study quoted by Russia's best-known dissident Solzhenitsyn, calculated that in the Soviet Union alone some 66 million people had been slaughtered. Another researcher, Jean-Pierre Dujardin, in a study published by *Figaro Magazine* in November 1987, estimated the overall human cost of Communism at 143 million dead.

The powerful point made by the authors of the *Livre Noir* was that, like the Nazis, the Communists in power assumed the right to torture and/or kill any members of any social groups, regardless of guilt or innocence. The "crime" in Nazi Germany was to be a Jew; in the Soviet Union, to be "bourgeois," or merely a dissident. The unacknowledged guiding principle, in the Union of Soviet *Socialist* Republics as in the National *Socialist* Third Reich, was the dehumanization of the people.

The Nazi regime was of course totally—and rightly—discredited by the time of its total defeat and collapse in 1945. In contrast, Stalin's USSR, despite its temporary alliance with Nazi Germany, emerged from World War II as the West's "glorious ally." All the Western countries, in varying degrees, had legal Communist parties; in two of them—Italy and France—the Communist Party had a mass membership: roughly of 3 million and 2 million respectively. In Britain, with a small Communist Party (CPGB), the Communists gained an influence out of all proportion to their numbers, through their patient but effective penetration of the trade unions, which for many years, in effect virtually "owned" the Labor Party.

To illustrate the "respectability" of Britain's CPGB, it was considered "normal" for the British Broadcasting Corporation (better known as the BBC) to invite Communist trade unionists to appear on radio or television programs without being identified as Communists; it would have been in effect unthinkable to invite members of any Fascist group to do so, except to expose him or her to hostile vocal attacks. To say this is not to advocate a free platform for Fascists or Nazis, but to deplore the unconditional offer of a platform to members of a no less morally discredited group.

In France, the major Communist Party (PCF) was brought into President François Mitterrand's first government, in partnership with his own Socialist party.* Sixteen years later, in June 1997, President Jacques Chirac, leader of the (anti-Communist) *Rassemblement pour la République* (RPR), in a misguided decision, called an election that brought Lionel Jospin's Socialist Party to power, in coalition with the PCF.

---

*It is only fair to point out that Mitterrand, who regarded the PCF as a dangerous challenge to his authority, included the party in his first government with the object of discrediting it. His Machiavellian strategy paid off, and in 1984 the Communists, by now weakened and partially discredited, pulled out of his coalition. See Crozier, *Free Agent*, pp. 218–20.—BC

In Italy the Communist Party, for long years the largest in the Western world, split after the Soviet collapse. A hard-line section now called itself the *Rifondazione Communista* (Communist Refoundation), while a more reformist majority of the former members restyled themselves the *Partito Democratico de la Sinistra* (PDS, or Democratic Party of the Left). Neither party expressed remorse for its former association with the long-ruling CPSU. By an irony of history, the PDS came to power in October 1998 when President Oscar Luigi Scalfaro invited its leader, Massimo D'Alema, to form a new government. Through the long years of Communist autocracy in the Soviet Union, Italy's Communist Party had been the largest of its kind in Western Europe, but had never come to office. Now, after the collapse of Communism in its original home, a relatively modest successor to the Italian Communist Party had taken over.

In the United Kingdom, the small CPGB segmented, without public expressions of remorse for the Soviet past. A prominent life member, Professor Eric Hobsbawm, declared his continuing loyalty to the Party, and was awarded the Order of Merit by Tony Blair's ruling Labor Party.

Such random fact-finding makes depressing reading. In many countries, parties dedicated to the principles of Marxism-Leninism, and by unacknowledged association, to the sanguinary policies of the Communist parties formerly in power, survive, still committed to the doctrine that, wherever it has been applied, has led to tortures and massacres, collectively on the largest scale in history.

As long as the many Communist parties remain in existence, the hypothesis of an advent or return to power of parties committed to that doctrine cannot be ruled out. The Soviet Empire has collapsed. But the rise of another Communist empire cannot, in 1999, be ruled out.

• THE END •

APPENDIXES

APPENDIX A

DOCUMENTS FOR CHAPTER 5

—————⟫•⟪—————

DOCUMENT 1
*Speech by I.V. Stalin**

19 August 1939
to the Plenum of the
Politburo of the Central Committee
of the All-Union Communist Party****

THE QUESTION OF war or peace is entering a phase which for us is critical. If we conclude the Treaty of Mutual Assistance with France and Great Britain, Germany will renounce its claim to Poland and seek a *modus vivendi* with the Western powers. The war will be set aside, but subsequently events could take on a dangerous character for the USSR. If we accept Germany's offer for the conclusion of a non-aggression pact, she will naturally attack Poland and the entry of France and Great Britain into the war will become inevitable. Western Europe will be caught up in serious troubles and disorders. In these conditions, we shall have good chances to stay outside the conflict, and we may expect our entry into the war to be favorable for us.

The experience of the past twenty years demonstrates that in time of peace the Communist movement in Europe has no chance of being strong enough to seize power. The dictatorship of a Communist Party may be envisaged only as a result of a great war. We shall take our decision and this will be without any

---

*Text discovered by T.S. Bushchevoy in the special archives of the USSR (Depot Center of the Historical-Documentary collection of Ancient Special Archives of the USSR, F. 7, op.1.d. 1223). Unable to obtain a copy of the Russian original, I translated into English a French version provided by Prof. Françoise Thom (Sorbonne, Paris). I have no reason, however, to doubt the authenticity of the text.—BC

**V.KP(b): *Vsiérossiiskaya Kommunisticheskaya Partya Bol'chevikov.* The name of the Communist Party of the Soviet Union (KPSS) dated December 1952.

equivocation. We should accept the German proposal and politely send the Franco-British mission home. The first advantage that we would gain would be the seizure of Poland up to the gates of Warsaw, including Ukrainian Galicia.

Germany is reserving complete freedom of action for us in the Baltic States and will raise no objection to the return of Bessarabia to the USSR. They (the Germans) are ready to give us Romania, Bulgaria and Hungary as part of our sphere of influence. The Yugoslav question will remain open . . . at the same time we must take into consideration the consequences not only of a defeat but also of a victory of Germany. In the event of a German defeat, the Sovietization of Germany and the creation of a Communist government will follow inevitably. We should also not forget that a Sovietized Germany would be in great danger, in the event that this Sovietization should be seen as the consequence of a lightning defeat. Britain and France would still have suffi- cient forces to seize Berlin and to prevent the emergence of a Soviet Germany, and we would not have the means to come to the aid of our Berlin comrades.

Thus, our task consists in making sure that Germany should be involved in war as long as possible, so that England and France would be so exhausted that they would no longer be capable of presenting a threat to a Soviet Germany. We shall maintain a position of neutrality, while biding our time; the USSR will grant aid to present-day Germany to provide raw materials and general supplies. But it is self-evident that our aid in this direction should not exceed a level that might damage our own economy or weaken the offensive capacity of our army.

At the same time, we should carry out an active Communist propaganda, in particular in the Franco-British bloc—and above all in France. We should be prepared, in these countries, for the probability that the Party will be forced to give up its legal activities and to go into clandestinity. We are very conscious of the fact that this work will make many victims, but our French comrades will not hesitate. The collapse and demoralization of the Army and of defense in general will be part of the task. When this preparatory activity has been carried out, as it should be, the security of Soviet Germany will be assured, and this will be a step in favor of a Sovietization of France.

For these plans to be realized, it is indispensable to prolong the war as long as possible, and it is in this precise direction that we should guide all the forces with which we shall act in Western Europe and in the Balkans.

Let us now consider a second hypothesis, namely a German victory. Some people have presented the viewpoint according to which this eventuality would put us in grave danger. There is a tiny quantum of truth in this affir- mation, but it would be an error to think that this danger would be as close and as great as some people are presenting it. If Germany wins, she will emerge from the war too weakened to engage in a military conflict that would last at least ten years.

Germany's principal concern would be to supervise the defeated states of Britain and France. From another side, a victorious Germany will seize immense territories and will therefore be occupied for many years with their exploitation and with the installation of a German order. It is evident that Germany will be too occupied elsewhere to be able to turn against us. There is another thing that serves our security. In a defeated France, the PCF will be very powerful. The Communist revolution will happen inevitably and we shall then be able to exploit these circumstances to come to the rescue of France and make her our ally. Moreover, all the peoples who have fallen under the "protection" of a victorious Germany will also become our allies. We have before us a vast field of action to develop the world Revolution.

Comrades! It is in the interests of the USSR—the Fatherland of the Workers—that war should break out between the Reich and the Franco-British capitalist bloc. We must do everything so that the war should last as long as possible with the aim of weakening both sides. It is for these reasons that we must give priority to the approval of the conclusion of the pact proposed by Germany, and to work so that this war, which will be declared within a few days, shall last as long as possible. It is therefore necessary to strengthen the work of propaganda in the countries that will have entered the war, so that they shall be ready for the after-war period.

DOCUMENT 2
Letter to Stalin

5 March 1940
Hoover Archives
Top Secret
of 5.III-40
USSR
PEOPLE'S COMMISSARIAT
OF INTERNAL AFFAIRS
MARCH 1940
NO. 794/B
MOSCOW

[Four signatures——apparently those of I. Stalin, K. Voroshilov, V. Molotov, and A. Mikoyan—are written across the text on page 1 of this document. In the left-hand margin someone has written "comrade Kalinin—in favor [;] comrade Kaganovich in favor."]

CC A-UCP (b)

[All-Union communist Party (Bolsheviks)]

To Comrade STALIN

A large number of former officers of the Polish army, former employees of the Polish police and intelligence services, members of Polish nationalistic counterrevolutionary parties, participants in counterrevolutionary insurgent organizations which have [now] been broken up, deserters and others are presently being held in prisoner-of-war camps of the USSR NKVD [People's Commissariat of Internal Affairs] and in prisons in the western regions of Ukraine and Belorussia. All of these people are sworn enemies of Soviet power, brimming with hatred of the Soviet system.

The captured officers and policemen are trying to continue [their] counterrevolutionary work while they are in the camps and they are conducting anti-soviet agitation, and each of them is only waiting to be freed in order to have the chance to get actively involved in the struggle against soviet power.

A number of counterrevolutionary insurgent organizations have been uncovered by the organs of the NKVD in the western regions of Ukraine and Belorussia. In all these counterrevolutionary organizations the active leading role was played by former officers of the former Polish army and by former policemen and gendarmes.

Amongst the detained deserters and violators of the state frontier, a considerable number of persons have also been exposed as participants in counterrevolutionary espionage and insurgent organizations.

All in all (not counting private soldiers and non-commissioned officers), the prisoner-of-war camps are [currently] holding 14,736 former officers, civil servants, landowners, policemen, gendarmes, prison officers, *osadniki* [in Polish, *osadnicy*—settlers, ethnic Polish soldiers who, when they left the army, were given plots of land in Eastern Poland largely, it seems, to increase the percentage of ethnic Poles in an area with a large Belorussian and Ukrainian population—Trans.] and intelligence officers, over 97 percent of whom are Poles by nationality.

Of these there are:

Generals, colonels, and lieutenant-colonels	295
Majors and captains	2,080
First lieutenants, second lieutenants, and cornets	6,049

Police, frontier-guard, and gendarme officers and junior commanders	1,030
Rank and file policemen, gendarmes, prison officers, and intelligence officers	5,138
Officials, landowners, Roman Catholic priests, and *osadniki*	144

In all, 18,632 persons under arrest (10,685 of whom are Poles) are being held in prisons in the western regions of Ukraine and Belorussia, comprising:

former officers	1,207
former policemen, intelligence officers, and gendarmes	5,141
Spies and saboteurs	347
Former landowners, factory owners, and officials	465
Members of various counterrevolutionary and insurgent organizations and assorted counter-revolutionary elements	5,345
Deserters	6,127

In view of the fact that all of them are sworn and incorrigible enemies of Soviet power, the USSR NKVD considers it essential:

I. To submit to the USSR NKVD:

[Added in hand-writing in the margin:—*A matter for the USSR NKVD.*]

1) The cases of 14,700 people located in prisoner of war camps—former Polish officers, officials, landowners, policemen, intelligence officers, gendarmes, *osadniki* [soldiers], and prison officers

2) and also the cases of the 11,000 people arrested and located in prisons in the western regions of Ukraine and Belorussia—members of various counterrevolutionary espionage and subversive organizations, former landowners, factory owners, former Polish officers, civil servants and deserters—with the proposal that it [the USSR NKVD] examine [these cases] by special procedure, with the application of capital punishment by shooting.

II. The examination of the[se] cases is to be carried out without summoning those under arrest and without presentation of the accusation, without a [written] decision on the completion of the investigation and without a bill of indictment—in the following order:

a) for persons located in prisoner of war camps—on the basis of documents issued by the Directorate for the Affairs of Prisoners of War of the USSR NKVD,

b) for persons who are under arrest—on the basis of case documents presented by the UkSSR [Ukrainian] NKVD and the BSSR [Belorussian] NKVD.

III. Review of the cases and pronouncement of sentence to be entrusted to a *troika* [three-man team] consisting of comrades MERKULOV, KABULOV, and BASHTAKOV (head of the First Special Department of the USSR NKVD).

> [The first name—apparently that of Beriya—on the original typed list has been obliterated and the name of Kabulov written in by hand in second place.—Trans.]

PEOPLE'S COMMISSAR of INTERNAL AFFAIRS
of the UNION of the SSR
[signature] *L. Beriya*
(L. BERIYA)
[added by hand:]
Issue
Beriya
I 13/144
5. III-40.

DOCUMENT 3
Memo from Stalin

February 1959
Hoover Archives
To be returned within 24 hrs to the 2nd
Section of the Special Sector of the CC
(Resolution of the CC Politburo
of 5.V.27, Record No. 100, item 5)
STRICTLY CONFIDENTIAL
(From O. P.)
All-Union Communist Party (of Bolsheviks). CENTRAL COMMITTEE
No. P18/144.

To Comrade Shelepin
7 [?] February 1959.
Extract from Record No. 18 of the Session of the CC Politburo of 193.

Decision of 5. III. 40.
144.—Question to the USSR NKVD.
I. Proposal for the USSR NKVD:

1) Cases of the 14,700 people located in prisoner of war camps—former Polish officers, civil servants, landowners, policemen, intelligence officers, gendarmes, *osadniki* [soldiers], and prison officers,

2) and also the cases of the 11,000 people arrested and located in prisons in the western regions of Ukraine and Belorussia——members of various counterrevolutionary espionage and subversive organizations, former landowners, factory owners, former Polish officers, civil servants, and deserters——are to be reviewed in accordance with a special procedure, with the application to them of the supreme measure of punishment—shooting.

II. The review of the cases is to be carried out without summoning the arrested and without presentation of the accusation, without the decision on the completion of the investigation and without the bill of indictment—in the following order:

a) for persons located in prisoner of war camps—on the basis of documents issued by the Administration for the Affairs of Prisoners of War of the USSR NKVD

b) for persons who have been arrested—by case documents prepared by the UkrSSR NKVD and the BelSSR NKVD.

III. Review of the cases and pronouncement of sentence to be entrusted to a *troika* consisting of comrades Merkulov, Kabulov, and Vashtakov (the head of the First Special Department of the USSR NKVD).

SECRETARY OF THE CC I. STALIN.
[rubber stamp:] CC Communist Party of the Soviet Union
                [translation of last four lines of instructions in left-hand margin:]

COPYING OF THE aforesaid documents and writing out extracts from them are categorically forbidden.

A note and the date of familiarization are to be entered on each document personally by the comrade to whom the document is addressed, and signed by him personally.

Basis: Resolution of the Plenum of the Russian Communist Party (of Bolsheviks) CC of 19/VIII-24

DOCUMENT 4
Letter to Khrushchev, March 1959

6 March 1965

Hoover Archives

<u>Top secret</u>

[rubber stamp:]

to be returned

0680

9 MAR[CH] 1965

6th SECTOR

in the CPSU CC—General Department

TO COMRADE N. S. KHRUSHCHEV

Since 1940 the records and other materials pertaining to the imprisoned and interned officers, gendarmes, policemen, *osadniki* [soldiers], landowners and similar persons from the former bourgeois Poland who were shot in that same year have been kept in the Committee of State Security attached to the Council of Ministers of the USSR. In accordance with the decisions of the special *troika* of the USSR NKVD, in all <u>21,857</u> persons were shot. Of these, <u>4,421</u>—in the Katyn Forest (Smolensk region); <u>3,820</u>—in the Starobelsk camp near Kharkov; <u>6,311</u>—in the Ostashkovo camp (Kalinin region); and <u>7,305</u> were shot in other camps and prisons in Western Ukraine and Western Belorussia.

The whole operation to liquidate the aforesaid persons was carried out in accordance with the Resolution of the CPSU CC of 5 March 1940. All of them were condemned to the supreme measure of punishment on the basis of the records kept on them since 1939 as prisoners of war and internees.

From the moment of carrying out the above-mentioned operation, i.e., from 1940, no information on these cases has been provided to anybody, and all the case documents, totaling 21,857, have been held in sealed premises.

For the Soviet organs, none of these cases possesses either any operational interest or any historical value. It is unlikely that they can possess any real interest for our Polish friends. On the contrary, some kind of unforeseen fortuity might lead to a breach in the rules of security surrounding the implementation of this operation, with all the ensuing undesirable consequences for our state. This is all the more the case, because so far as the persons shot in the Katyn Forest are concerned there is an official version [of this event], confirmed by the investigation carried out on the initiative of the Soviet organs of power in 1944 by a Commission entitled "The Special commission to ascertain and investigate the shooting of Polish officers, prisoners of war, in the Katyn Forest by German-fascist aggressors."

According to the conclusions of this commission, all the Poles who were liquidated there are regarded as having been exterminated by the German invaders. The materials of the investigation at this time were widely covered in the Soviet and foreign press. The conclusions of the commission have taken firm root in international public opinion.

Proceeding from the above account, it would appear to be advisable to destroy all the records of the persons who were shot in 1940 during the previously mentioned operation.

In order to be able to deal with possible inquiries through the CPSU CC or Soviet government, one could leave the Records of the sessions of the USSR NKVD *troika* which condemned the aforementioned persons to be shot, and the documents on the implementation of the decisions of the troikas. In volume these documents are insignificant, and they could be kept in a special folder.

The draft of a resolution of the CPSU CC is attached.

Chairman of the Committee of State Security

attached to the USSR Council of Ministers

A. Shelepin

3 March 1959 [Shelepin's signature]

No. 632-sh

Draft

Top secret

Resolution of the Presidium of the CPSU CC

of _____ 1959

To permit the Committee of State Security attached to the USSR Council of Ministers to liquidate all the case materials relating to the operation carried out in accordance with the Resolution of the CPSU CC of 5 March 1940, apart from the Records of the sessions of the USSR NKVD *troika*.

[Shelepin's signature appears on the left-hand side at the foot of this page.]

DOCUMENT 5

Draft of Instructions to Soviet Ambassadors in London

15 April 1971
Hoover Archives
Proletarians of all countries, unite!
Communist Party of the Soviet Union. CENTRAL COMMITTEE
TOP SECRET
No. P1/35

To COMRADES BREZHNEV, Kosygin, Suslov, Andropov, Katushev,
    Ponomarev, Gromyko, Rusakov.
Extract from Record No. 1 of the Session of the CPSU CC Politburo
    of 15 April 1971

CONCERNING THE REPRESENTATION to the Ministry of Foreign Affairs of England in connection with the anti-Soviet campaign around the so-called "Katyn Affair."

To approve the draft of instructions to the Soviet ambassadors in London and Warsaw (attached).

SECRETARY of the CC
15/af
vd

[words in the left-hand margin:] To be returned not later than within a 7-day period to the CPSU CC (General Department, First Sector)

Re. item 35 of Record No. 1

Secret

LONDON—SOVIET AMBASSADOR

Copy: WARSAW—SOVIET AMBASSADOR

Call on the Ministry of Foreign Affairs of England and state the following:

"According to information available to the Embassy, the BBC television company has the intention of showing a film which it has prepared and which is hostile to the Soviet Union about the so-called "Katyn Affair." Timed to coincide with this is the publication in England of a libelous book on the Katyn tragedy.

The English side is well aware of the fact that the guilt of the Hitlerites for this crime was irrefutably proven by the authoritative Special Commission, which conducted an investigation at the site of this crime immediately after the expulsion of the German invaders from the Smolensk region. In 1945–46 the International War [Crimes] Tribunal in Nuremberg found the main German military criminals guilty of carrying out the policy of extermination of the Polish people and, in particular, of the shooting of Polish prisoners of war in the Katyn Forest.

In this connection astonishment and indignation cannot but be aroused by the striving of certain circles in England again to drag out into the light of day the insinuations of Goebbels's propaganda machine in order to blacken the Soviet Union, whose people, by the blood they shed, saved Europe from fascist enslavement.

The Embassy expects that the Foreign and Commonwealth Office will take the appropriate measures to prevent the dissemination in England of the above-mentioned libelous materials, calculated, in the intentions of their authors, to cause a worsening of relations between our countries."

You can leave the text of this Representation with [your] interlocutor.

Cable <u>re.</u> implementation.

(<u>Only for Warsaw:</u> Inform the Ministry of Foreign Affairs of the Polish People's Republic of the said instructions to the Soviet Ambassador in London.)

451-am

vd

<u>Circulated to members of the</u>
<u>CPSU CC Politburo for voting</u>

<u>Secret</u>
CPSU CC

IN ENGLAND FOR some time past there have been attempts to whip up an anti-Soviet propaganda campaign around the so-called "Katyn Affair." In particular, various sorts of "eye-witnesses' reminiscences" have been published in the press. The publication of a book entitled "Katyn—The Unprecedented Crime" is planned for 19 April this year. On the same day the BBC television company intends to show a "documentary" film which it has prepared.

The USSR Ministry of Foreign Affairs considers it advisable to instruct the Soviet Embassy in London to make a Representation to the Ministry of Foreign Affairs of England in connection with a campaign which is hostile to the Soviet Union.

It would be appropriate to inform our Polish friends, who are also considering the matter of making representations to the English, about our demarche.

The draft of the resolution is attached.

Submitted for consideration. [Added by hand:] *See extract P1/35*

A. Gromyko

12 April 1971

No. 585/GS

20—zm

13. IV. 71.

1—17

[added by hand:] *TsK* [= CC]—*14015*

DOCUMENT 6
Draft of Letter to Soviet Ambassador in London

7 September 1972

Hoover Archives

[probably rubber stamp:]

Records of the Politburo

No. 60 item 46

Circulated to members of the

CPSU CC Politburo for voting

Secret

CPSU CC

REACTIONARY CIRCLES IN England are again undertaking attempts for anti-Soviet purposes to stir up the so-called "Katyn Affair." To this end the campaign to collect funds for the construction of a "Memorial to the Victims of Katyn" in London is being made use of.

The USSR Ministry of Foreign Affairs would consider it advisable to draw the attention of the English government to this campaign, hostile to the Soviet Union, in England by making the appropriate oral representation to the English Embassy in Moscow.

Simultaneously to inform [our] Polish friends about our representation.

The draft of the resolution is attached.

[added by hand:] *see extract from P60/46*

Submitted for consideration.

V. Kuznetsov

7 September 1972

No. 1780/GS

20/zv

7. IX. 72

60-31 [added by hand:] *No. TsK* [= CC]—*29328*

Re. item 12 in Record No. 80

Secret

LONDON

SOVIET AMBASSADOR

Call on the Minister of Foreign Affairs [= Foreign Secretary] and, referring to [your] instructions, state the following.

The attention of the Government of Great Britain has already been drawn to the fact that attempts are afoot in England to whip up a campaign for purposes hostile to the Soviet Union around the inventions—long ago exposed— of the Goebbels propaganda machine concerning the so-called "Katyn Affair." In the representation made by the USSR Ministry of Foreign Affairs on 13 September 1972 to the Embassy of Great Britain in Moscow for transmission to the English government it was stressed that the notion, inspired by certain circles, of erecting a "memorial" in London to the victims of Katyn cannot but arouse legitimate indignation in the Soviet Union.

Judging, however, from materials published in the English press, this provocation with the "memorial" has by no means been discontinued. It is announced, in particular, that the authorities of the London borough of

Kensington-Chelsea have apparently given [their] consent for a "memorial" of this nature to be established on the territory of their borough near the church of St. Luke and have already approved the design. The character of the inscriptions which, according to reports, have been sanctioned on the aforesaid "memorial" is particularly outrageous. The historical facts about the true perpetrators of the Katyn tragedy are distorted in them [= the inscriptions] in the crudest manner and in essence replicate the odious inventions already put about by the Nazis during the Second World War in order to cover up the bloody atrocities of the Gestapo's executioners which are known to the entire world.

The position adopted in this matter by the English government is in clear contradiction to its assurances that it is striving to improve relations with the Soviet Union. It is expected in Moscow that the appropriate measures will be undertaken on the part of the English government to put an end to this campaign which is hostile to the Soviet Union and which has been unleashed around the construction in London of the so-called "memorial" to the victims of Katyn.

Cable <u>re.</u> implementation.

52-mm

DOCUMENT 7
Draft of Presentation to English Embassy in Moscow

8 September 1972

Hoover Archives

Proletarians of all countries, unite!

Communist Party of the Soviet Union. CENTRAL COMMITTEE

<u>TOP SECRET</u>

<u>No. P60/46</u>

TO COMRADES BREZHNEV, Kosygin, Suslov, Andropov,
    Ponomarev, Katushev, Gromyko, Smirtyukov.
Extract from Record No. 60 of the Session of the CPSU CC Politburo
    of 8 September 1972

Concerning the Representation to the English Embassy in Moscow in connection with the anti-Soviet campaign in England around the proposed construction in London of a "Memorial to the Victims of Katyn."

1. To approve the draft of the oral representation to the English Embassy in Moscow on this matter (attached).
2. To instruct the USSR Ministry of Foreign Affairs to inform [our] Polish friends of our representation to the English, and also to express an interest in their intentions in this connection.

SECRETARY of the CC

[added by hand:]

See P 80/12 of 2. II.

15/yav

if

[words in the left-hand margin:] To be returned not later than within a 7-day period to the CPSU CC (General Department, First Sector)

Re. item 46, Record No. 60

Text of oral statement

to English Embassy

in Moscow

IN ENGLAND FOR some time past attempts have again been undertaken, with aims hostile to the Soviet Union, to whip up the libelous invention of the Goebbels propaganda machine about the so-called "Katyn Affair." With this goal in mind, a campaign has been staged by certain reactionary circles to collect funds for the construction of a "Memorial to the Victims of Katyn" in London. According to data in the English press, the initiators of the campaign have already won the agreement of the local authorities to erect this "memorial-obelisk" in the London borough of Kensington-Chelsea.

As is well known to the English government, the responsibility of the Hitlerites for the crime which they committed in the Katyn Forest with respect to Polish prisoners of war was irrefutably proven by the authoritative Special Commission which investigated this crime at the site immediately after the expulsion of the German aggressors from the Smolensk region. This found its reflection also in the relevant materials of the international war [crimes] tribunal in Nuremberg, which deemed the main German military criminals guilty of executing a policy for the deliberate extermination of the Polish people in the years of the Second World War.

In the light of this, the above-mentioned anti-Soviet campaign around the notion of a "memorial" cannot but arouse justified feelings of profound indignation in the Soviet Union, whose peoples made enormous sacrifices for the sake of saving Europe from fascist enslavement.

The Ministry expresses the hope that the English government will take all appropriate measures on its part to oppose this provocative action, which can only cause damage to Soviet-English relations.

24—ma

pe

ob

DOCUMENT 8
Draft Resolution Regarding Katyn Affair

27 February 1973
Hoover Archives
[probably rubber stamp:]
Records of the Politburo
No. 80 item 12
Circulated to members of
the CPSU CC for voting

Secret
CPSU CC

IN ACCORDANCE WITH resolution of the CPSU CC No. P60/46 of 8. IX. 1972, the USSR Ministry of Foreign Affairs has made a representation to the English Embassy in Moscow in connection with attempts by certain circles in England to whip up, for anti-Soviet purposes, the so-called "Katyn Affair." However, according to a report from the Soviet Embassy in London, the hurly-burly around the erection of a "memorial to the victims of Katyn" is continuing. The design of a memorial of this sort has been approved, together with the inscription, which is hostilely libelous with regard to the USSR, ascribing to the Soviet Union responsibility for the destruction of 14,500 Polish prisoners of war in Katyn and in other places.

The USSR Ministry of Foreign Affairs would consider it advisable to make a representation to the English government through the Soviet ambassador in London in connection with the continuation of this campaign, which is hostile to the Soviet Union.

Inform [our] Polish friends of our demarche.

The draft of the resolution is attached.

[added by hand:] *See extract P80/12*

Submitted for consideration.

V. Kuznetsov

27 February 1973

No. 434/GS

20-zm

27. II. 73

79-66

DOCUMENT 9
Memo Regarding Katyn Affair

30 March 1976

Hoover Archives

Circulated to members of the

CPSU CC Politburo for voting

Secret

CPSU CC

THE IMPERIALIST CENTERS of ideological subversion, especially the major Western radio stations, have recently begun to return very frequently to the so-called "Katyn Affair" in the well-known Goebbels interpretation. Attempts to erect "memorials to the victims of Katyn" with anti-Soviet inscriptions are unceasing. (A brief memo is attached.) In connection with the ap-proaching 35th anniversary of the crime of the German fascists in the Katyn Forest (autumn 1976), this provocative anti-Soviet campaign may intensify.

Realizing the danger and harm of such propaganda, our Polish friends have approached us through the USSR Embassy in the Polish People's Republic with a proposal to hold Soviet-Polish consultations with the aim of drawing up possible joint countermeasures.

A Department of the CPSU CC, the USSR Ministry of Foreign Affairs and the Committee of State Security attached to the USSR Council of Ministers deem it advisable to regard the wishes of our Polish friends with favor, and also to undertake the appropriate steps on the Soviet side.

The draft of the Resolution is attached.

[added by hand:] *see re. P3/75*

Submitted for your consideration.

Yu. Andropov   V. Kuznetsov   K. Katushev

30 March 1976

No. 861/GS

[added by hand:] *TsK [=CC] 22796*

22-ke

31. III. 76.

3-31

Secret

"THE KATYN AFFAIR"

(Brief memo)

After the liberation of Smolensk and its environs from Hitlerite troops in September 1943, graves with the remains of Polish prisoners of war were discovered in the area of the Katyn Forest 15 kilometers from the town.

A Special Commission to ascertain and investigate the circumstances of the shooting of Polish prisoners of war in Katyn was established in accordance with a Decision of the Extraordinary State Commission for the Ascertainment and Investigation of the Atrocities of the German-Fascist Aggressors and their Accomplices. This Special Commission confirmed that, up to the time when the Hitlerites seized Smolensk, Polish prisoners of war, officers and men, who were billeted in three special purpose camps 25–45 kilometers to the west of Smolensk, were employed on road-building works in the western districts of the province. After the beginning of the Great Fatherland War, as a result of the new situation, it was impossible to evacuate the camps in good time, and about eleven thousand Polish prisoners of war were taken into captivity by the Germans, and later, in the autumn of 1941, they were shot in the Katyn Forest.

In the winter of 1942–43, when the overall military situation had changed markedly to the detriment of fascist Germany, the Hitlerites took steps to cover up their atrocities. They counted thereby on libeling the Soviet Union and worsening Soviet-Polish relations. In April–June 1943, with these aims in mind, the "International Medical Commission," set up by the Hitlerites and comprising representatives of the satellite countries, carried out an "investigation" of the circumstances of the shooting of the Polish prisoners of war in Katyn. The German Information Service then published a book on the results of the "activities" of this Commission under the title "Official Material on the Mass Murder in Katyn," in which the Hitlerite propaganda machine attributed its own crimes to the Soviet Union.

The conclusions of the Special Commission to ascertain and investigate the circumstances of the shooting of Polish prisoners of war in the Katyn Forest by the German-Fascist aggressors were reflected in the corresponding materials of the International War [Crimes] Tribunal in Nuremberg, which found the fascist ringleaders guilty of this crime.

At the place of the burial of the Polish prisoners of war a site was prepared on which a memorial has been erected with the inscription "Here lie buried Polish officers, prisoners of war, brutally tortured to death by the German-Fascist invaders in the autumn of 1941."

The grave and the memorial are accessible for visits by Soviet citizens. Polish delegations go there from time to time and lay wreaths. Visits to the memorial by foreign tourists have not been registered, inasmuch as this district around the Katyn Forest is not utilized by them for tourist purposes.

In spite of the fact that the aforementioned provocation by the Hitlerites has been exposed and incontrovertibly proven, reactionary circles in the West periodically launch an anti-Soviet campaign around the so-called "Katyn Affair."

For instance, a special commission of the U.S. Congress on matters relating to Katyn was set up in 1951; in 1952 the U.S. State Department sent the Soviet ambassador a letter from the chairman of this commission and a resolution expressing the desire to receive some sort of "proof" from the Soviet government regarding the murder of the Polish officers in the Katyn Forest.

On 29 February 1952 in a note to the government of the United States on this matter, the Soviet government qualified these actions as being in violation of the generally accepted norms of international relations and as offensive to the Soviet Union. It was stated in the note that bringing up the matter of the Hitlerites' crime at Katyn eight years after the conclusion of the official Commission "can only pursue the goal of libeling the Soviet Union and thereby rehabilitating the universally recognized Hitlerite criminals"; the above-mentioned report of January 1944 by the Special Commission was attached. These documents were published in *Pravda* and other Moscow newspapers on 3 March 1952.

In connection with the anti-Soviet hullabaloo unleashed around the sessions of this [American] Commission, the government of the Polish People's Republic published a statement in February 1952 resolutely condemning this provocative campaign.

For some time past the imperialist centers of ideological subversion have again been stirring up anti-Soviet propaganda around the so-called "Katyn Affair." In July 1972 the BBC radio station reported that the government of Great Britain supposedly has at its disposal some documents which allegedly provide evidence that "the guilt for the crime in the Katyn Forest rests not with fascist Germany but with the Soviet Union." In June 1975 a press conference was organized in the building of the English Parliament; the organizers appealed to the International Court in The Hague to "investigate this case." According to a report in the *Daily Telegraph* newspaper, "a document shedding new light on the fate of more than ten thousand Poles who, it is believed, were executed by the Russian secret police" has appeared in the West. The "Free Europe" radio station immediately picked up this provocative ballyhoo in its broadcasts to Poland. Catholic preachers, when they address Polish believers, not infrequently mention the "ten thousand best representatives (the elite) of Polish society who were wiped out despite being innocent" with anti-Soviet innuendoes. The Soviet Embassy in the Polish People's Republic reports that there are not a few people who are inclined to believe anti-Soviet fabrications of this nature.

Provocative actions like the November 1975 opening, on the initiative of reactionary Polish émigré circles, of a memorial to the "victims of Katyn" with anti-Soviet inscriptions on the territory of a private estate in Stockholm serve the aims of maintaining an anti-Soviet hullabaloo around the Katyn Affair. At the present time a campaign is being waged to erect a monument of the same sort in one of the cemeteries in London. These and similar facts are extensively utilized in inimical, anti-Soviet propaganda aimed at Poland.

All this alarms our Polish friends who, according to information from the Soviet ambassador, are thinking about steps to counteract the propaganda pressure from hostile centers and expressing views in favor of holding consultations with the Soviet party on this question.

22-yav,ma

ob

DOCUMENT 10

Extract of Report to CPSU Central Committee, April 1976

5 April 1976

Hoover Archives

Proletarians of all countries, unite!

Communist Party of the Soviet Union. CENTRAL COMMITTEE

TOP SECRET

[rubber stamp:]

DECLASSIFIED

No. P3/75

To the SMOLENSK Regional Committee of the CPSU;

 To Comrades Brezhnev, Kosygin, Andropov, Gromyko,

 Kirilenko, Ponomarev, Katushev, Smirtyukov.

Extract from Record No. 3 of the Session of the CPSU CC Politburo

 of 5 April 1976

On Measures to Counteract Western Propaganda on the So-called "Katyn Affair."

1. Give [our] consent to [our] Polish friends regarding consultations with the aim of discussing possible joint measures to counteract Western propaganda on the so-called "Katyn Affair," entrusting the holding of consultations to a Department of the CPSU CC and the USSR Ministry of Foreign Affairs.

   While doing this, proceed from the necessity for the close coordination of measures taken by the USSR and the Polish People's Republic to counteract and neutralize the anti-socialist and anti-Soviet actions and campaigns in the West connected with the "Katyn Affair."

   Regard declarations containing any sort of official statements on our part as inadvisable, in order not to provide grounds for hostile forces to take advantage of polemics on this issue for anti-Soviet purposes.

2. Instruct a Department of the CPSU CC and the USSR Ministry of Foreign Affairs to study the views expressed by [our] Polish friends in the course of the consultations, and in case of need to put forward the appropriate proposals to the CPSU CC.

[in the left-hand margin:] To be returned within a 7-day period to the CPSU CC (General Department, First Sector)

3. The USSR Ministry of Foreign Affairs, in close contact with diplomatic representatives of the Polish People's Republic, is to give a decisive rebuff to the provocative attempts to utilize the so-called "Katyn Affair" to inflict damage on Soviet-Polish friendship, guided in this purpose by the Resolution of the CPSU CC of 2 March 1973. (No. P80/12.)

4. Through unofficial channels the USSR KGB is to give persons in governmental circles of the relevant Western countries to understand that the new utilization of various kinds of anti-Soviet forgeries is regarded by the Soviet government as a specially contrived provocation aimed at the worsening of the international situation.

5. Instruct the Smolensk Regional Committee to take supplementary steps to ensure the maintenance of the memorial to the Polish officers and the territory around it in good order.

SECRETARY of the CC

DOCUMENT 11
Memo from Shevardnadze and Others

26 April 1988
Hoover Archives
Re. item VIII of Minutes No. 119
CC CPSU

ON MEASURES FOR the amelioration of the burial ground of Polish officers in Katyn (Smolensk region) and for the widening of access to it for citizens of the PPR [Polish People's Republic] and other countries

In accordance with the Resolution of the CC of the CPSU of 11 February 1988 (P103/XI), we submit our views on the amelioration of the burial ground of the Polish officers in Katyn (Smolensk region) and on the inauguration of wide-scale access to it for citizens of the PPR [Polish People's Republic] and other countries.

A group of officials on the staff of the CC of the CPSU and the USSR MID [MFA: Ministry of Foreign Affairs] went out to Katyn on 16–18 March 1988, in order to acquaint themselves with the place of the interment. [We] would deem it possible to agree with the top-priority measures proposed by the Smolensk Regional Committee of the CPSU for the amelioration of the burial ground of the Polish officers and the widening of access to it for citizens of the PPR [Polish People's Republic] and other countries.

At the same time, bearing in mind the repeatedly expressed wishes of W. Jaruzelski and other members of the Polish leadership (J. Baryla, M. Ozechowski, M. Rakowski, and others) for a memorial complex to be created on the site of the burial of the Polish officers in Katyn, [we] would deem it advisable to instruct the USSR Ministry of Culture to submit proposals on this matter and carry out consultations with the Polish Side in 1988 regarding its possible participation in the construction of the memorial.

It also appears to be justified to install, on the same site as the memorial to the Polish officers who perished [there], a monument in honor of the Soviet prisoners of war who participated in the work of exhumation and were then exterminated by the Hitlerites and buried on this same territory (about 500 people).

Additional work is required on the question of simplifying the procedures for visits to the monument in Katyn by relatives of the Polish officers who perished [there].

E. Shevardnadze   V. Chebrikov   A. Yakovlev   V. Medvedev
26 April 1988
No. 434/os
31-ag
ld

DOCUMENT 12
Extract from Politburo Session

5 May 1988
Hoover Archives
Proletarians of all countries, unite!
Communist Party of the Soviet Union. CENTRAL COMMITTEE
TOP SECRET
[printed sideways in the left-hand margin:]
To be returned not later than within a 3-month period to the CC of the CPSU (General Department, First Sector)
No. P119/VIII

To THE SMOLENSK Regional Committee of the CPSU;

To COMRADES GORBACHEV, Gromyko, Ryzhkov, Vorotnikov, Ligachev,
  Chebrikov, Shevardnadze, Yakovlev, Razumovsky, Yazov, Dobrynin,
  Lukyanov, Medvedev, Vlasov, Zakharov, Pavlov, Melentyev,
  Venediktov, Tereshkova, Voronov, Sklyarov, Smirtyukov.

Extract from Minutes No. 119 of the session of the CPSU CC Politburo
  on 5 May 1988

ON MEASURES FOR the amelioration of the burial ground of Polish officers in Katyn (Smolensk region) and for the widening of access [to it] for citizens of the PPR [Polish People's Republic] and other countries

1. Agree with the views set out in the memorandum of comrades E. A. Shev-
    ardnadze, V. M. Chebrikov, A. N. Yakovlev, and V. A. Medvedev of 26 April
    1988 (attached).

2. Instruct the USSR Ministry of Culture and the RSFSR Ministry of Cul-
    ture to submit proposals for the erection, during the period of the next
    Five-Year Plan, of a memorial complex to the Polish officers in Katyn,
    with the participation of the Polish Side (in the event of its agreement),
    and also of a monument in honor of the Soviet prisoners of war extermi-
    nated by the Hitlerites in Katyn.

3. By 1 July 1988, the USSR MVD [Ministry of Internal Affairs], the USSR MID
    [Ministry of Foreign Affairs], the USSR State Committee for Foreign Tourism,
    the Smolensk Regional Committee of the CPSU, the Executive Committee
    of the Union of Red Cross, and Red Crescent Societies of the USSR and
    the Union of Soviet Societies for Friendship and Cultural Relations with
    Foreign Countries are to submit proposals for simplifying the procedures
    for visits to the monument in Katyn by relatives of the Polish officers who
    perished [there].

4. The Smolensk Regional Committee of the CPSU is to work out measures
    for putting the territory of the forest reserve in order, agreeing them as
    necessary with the relevant organs of the USSR Ministry of Defense and
    the USSR KGB.

5. The Propaganda Department of the CC of the CPSU, a[nother] Depart-
    ment of the CC of the CPSU and the USSR MID [Ministry of Foreign Af-
    fairs] are to provide for propaganda coverage of the complex of measures
    carried out within the framework of this Resolution.

CC SECRETARY

[The notes added by hand are of minimal interest and importance.—Trans.]

31-ea

nb

DOCUMENT 13
Resolution Regarding Katyn

"22" April 1989

Hoover Archives

Secret

CC CPSU

22 Apr[il] 89 09287

TO BE RETURNED TO THE

GENERAL DEPARTMENT OF

THE CC OF THE CPSU

CC CPSU

ON THE QUESTION of Katyn

We are reporting in accordance with instructions (P 152/15 of 31 March 1989).

Perusal of the materials at our disposal concerning the death of some twelve thousand Polish officers who were interned in the Soviet Union in 1939 provides grounds for thinking that only some of them perished in Katyn. For the time being the fate of the remainder is unknown. Information in Polish and Western publications indicates that Polish officers perished in the districts of Bologoe (Kalinin region) and Dergachi (Kharkov region).

In order to clarify all the circumstances of what took place it appears to be essential to instruct the USSR Procuracy, together with the USSR KGB, to carry out a careful investigation.

Inasmuch as this has become a matter of quite extraordinary sensitivity in Poland and is being exploited to the detriment of Soviet-Polish relations, it would be advisable to arrange some publicity about the careful investigation being carried out by the competent Soviet organs shortly before the arrival of W. Jaruzelski in the USSR on a working visit (27–28 April 1989).

A draft of a Resolution of the CC of the CPSU is attached.

[signature]   A. Sukharev

[signature]	V. Kryuchkov
[signature]	I. Aboimov
[signature]	A. Pavlov
[signature]	V. Falin
[signature]	A. Kapto

"22" April 1989

No. 17-305

Top secret

Draft

RESOLUTION OF THE CC OF THE CPSU
On the question of Katyn

1. Agree with the views set out in the memorandum on this question.
2. The USSR Procuracy, together with the USSR KGB, are to carry out a careful investigation of the fact of the mass shooting of Polish officers in the district of Katyn (Smolensk region) and inform the CC of the CPSU of its results by 1 August 1989.
3. The Main Archival Administration attached to the USSR Council of Ministers, the USSR MVD [Ministry of Internal Affairs], the USSR Ministry of Defense and the USSR MID [Ministry of Foreign Affairs] are to provide assistance to the USSR Procuracy and the USSR KGB in the search for surviving documentary materials on this question.
4. The State Television and Radio [Company] of the USSR and the "Pravda" and "Izvestiya" newspapers are to publicize [materials on] the investigation being carried out by the competent Soviet organs into the circumstances of the death of the Polish officers.

CC SECRETARY

DOCUMENT 14
Letter to Gorbachev Regarding Katyn Affair

22 February 1990

Hoover Archives

[A message written by hand across the typewritten text of this page reads:]
To comrades Yakovlev, Shevardnadze, Primakov, Boldin. I ask you to report your views.

[Signature—presumably of Gorbachev. 23. II. 90]

[stamped:] 26 Feb 90 00361

6th sector

23 FEB 90 03900

TO BE RETURNED TO THE GENERAL

DEPARTMENT OF THE CC OF THE CPSU

Secret

ADDITIONAL INFORMATION

on the tragedy in Katyn

Respected Mikhail Sergeyevich [Gorbachev]!

Hitherto unknown materials of the Chief Directorate of the USSR NKVD [People's Commissariat of Internal Affairs] for the Affairs of Prisoners of War and Internees and the NKVD Directorate of Escort Troops, dating from 1939 and 1940 and relating to the so-called Katyn Affair, have been brought to light by a number of Soviet historians (Yu. N. Zorya, V. S. Parsadanova and N. S. Lebedeva) who were admitted to the stacks of the Special Archive and the Central State Archive of the Main Archival Administration attached to the USSR Council of Ministers, and also [to the stacks] of the Central State Archive of the October Revolution.

According to these materials, as of the beginning of January 1940 there were about 14,000 former Polish citizens from the ranks of army and naval officers, employees of the police and gendarmery, military and civilian officials, [secret] agents of one sort or another, and also [people] from the military chaplaincy, in the camps of the NKVD's Chief Directorate for the Affairs of Prisoners of War and Internees in Ostashkov in the Kalinin region, Kozelsk in the Smolensk region and Starobelsk in the Voroshilovgrad region.

None of these persons (NKVD Order No. 00117 of 1939) was to be freed and allowed to go home. The question of their fate was examined in several goes. There exist documents containing instructions from Beriya and Merkulov to speed up the investigation and to prepare materials on former employees of the [Polish] punitive organs and intelligence service for examination at the Special Conference of the USSR NKVD.

In April and May 1940 the inmates of all three camps were transported [and placed] at the disposal of various regional directorates of the NKVD. The lists [of names] were compiled in a centralized way [this may mean "in Moscow"—Trans.] with a continuous numbering system; each of them contained an average of a hundred people, and they [the lists] came out regularly, sometimes four or five a day. Every day reports were sent to Moscow about the dispatch [of the prisoners]. Directions were issued to leave agents-cum-informers and persons of operational interest out of the groups being transported. In contrast with the usual practice when prisoners were being moved from one location to another, the camp commanders were given an instruction to put an entry [about the prisoners' departure] only in the camp's card index on the cards of those who were leaving ("left on list No. . . . on such and such a date and month"), without sending the filing cards [on these prisoners] to the center [i.e., Moscow?—Trans.].

Shortly before the start of [this] action an instruction was issued on instituting control of [these prisoners'] mail and on confiscating all incoming and outgoing correspondence. It was forbidden to give answers of any sort to inquiries about the inmates of the[se] camps. All officials in the[se] camps were warned about "maintaining strict secrecy about the places of dispatch" of [this] contingent [of prisoners].

After the completion of the action all the "files" on the internees who had vacated the camps were "finalized, put in the proper order and consigned to the archives of the first special department of the NKVD." Directions were issued to originate "completely new files for the records and for the registration of the [type of labor camp] regime" of the new contingents [of prisoners] who were arriving at the[se] camps. Later the materials of the Kozelsk and Ostashkov camps were sent for storage to the Chief Directorate [of the NKVD], while the materials of the Starobelsk camp were destroyed. Persons who were being held in all three camps up to April–May 1940 did not figure in statistical reports after that date.

The Kozelsk and Starobelsk camp was [sic—Trans.] subsequently utilized for holding persons of Polish nationality who had been removed from the western regions of Ukraine, Belorussia, and the Baltics. Moreover, information about the previous contingent of these camps was carefully concealed from them. In August 1940 the buildings of the Ostashkov camp were transferred to the museum of local history.

In consequence, documents from the Soviet archives make it possible to trace the fate of the interned Polish officers who were held in the NKVD camps in Kozelsk, Starobelsk, and Ostashkov, even in the absence of [written] orders for them to be shot and buried. A selective comparison of the surnames on the lists [of people] to be dispatched from the Kozelsk camp and the identification lists compiled by the Germans during the process of exhumation in the spring of 1943 revealed that they tallied completely, which is evidence of the interrelationship between the events that occurred.

Materials for publication have been prepared by Soviet historians on the basis of new, documented facts. Some of these materials have already been approved by editorial boards and are already in the pipeline. Publication is planned for June–July.

The appearance of such publications would in a certain sense create a new situation. Our line that no materials revealing the true state of affairs with regard to the Katyn tragedy had been uncovered in the state archives of the USSR would no longer hold water. The materials brought to light by scholars—and there is no doubt that they have got entry to only some of the hiding-places—in conjunction with the data on which the Polish side bases its assessments, will hardly permit us to stick to [our] earlier versions any longer and avoid a final summing-up. Bearing in mind the forthcoming fiftieth anniversary of Katyn, it would be necessary one way or another to spell out our position.

The following scenario is apparently the one that entails the least costs:

Inform W. Jaruzelski that as a result of a careful inspection of the relevant archival depositories we have not found any direct evidence ([written] orders, instructions, etc.) making it possible to identify the precise time and specific perpetrators of the Katyn tragedy. At the same time indications have been discovered in the archival holdings of the NKVD's Chief Directorate for the Affairs of Prisoners of War and Internees, and also of the NKVD's Directorate of Escort Troops for 1940, that put in doubt the reliability of the "N. Burdenko Report." On the basis of the above-mentioned indications it is possible to draw the conclusion that the death of the Polish officers in the district of Katyn is the work of the NKVD and of Beriya and Merkulov personally.

The question arises as to when and in what form this conclusion is to be brought to the notice of the Polish and Soviet public. Here the advice of the President of the RP [Republic of Poland] is required, bearing in mind the need to put an end to this problem from the political point of view and at the same time to avoid an explosion of emotions.

I ask you to examine [this matter].

Yours,

[signature] *V. Falin*

22. 2. 90

[The last three lines are written by hand——Trans.]

APPENDIX B

DOCUMENTS FOR CHAPTER 6

———➤●◄———

DOCUMENT I
Memo to Stalin

17 January 1950
Hoover Archives
Fond 89
Finding aid 38
Document 22
Top Secret
No. P72/269

TO COMRADES: MOLOTOV, [V. V.] Kuznetsov (of the All-Union Council of
Trade Unions) and Grigor'ian
17 January 1950
Re: The Fund for Assistance to Leftist Workers' Organizations attached
to the All-Union Council of Trade Unions.
<u>Resolution of 17 January 1950</u>

1. Attached to the All-Union Council of Trade Unions there is to be estab-
    lished the Fund for Assistance to Leftist Workers' Organizations with the
    purpose of providing financial assistance to leftist parties and progressive
    workers' and social organizations abroad that are being repressed and
    persecuted.
2. Whenever financial assistance is provided to the organizations mentioned
    above, it has to be approved by the TsK VKP(b) by means of a resolution
    and handed out by the fund's board of directors.
3. Comrade K. S. Kuznetsova is to be appointed Chair of the Board of Di-

rectors of the Fund for Assistance to Leftist Workers' Organizations. The TsK Secretary

---

To: COMRADE STALIN

Enclosed you will find the draft resolution of the TsK VKP (b) regarding the establishment of the Fund for Assistance to Leftist Workers' Organizations, attached to the All-Union Council of Trade Unions.

[signed]

V. Kuznetsov

[signed]

V. Grigor'ian

17 [?] January, 1950

Copies to comrades: Malenkov, Molotov, Beriia, Mikoian, Kaganovich, Bulganin.

Re: The Fund for Assistance to Leftist Workers' Organizations, attached to the All-Union Council of Trade Unions

1. A Fund for Assistance to Leftist Workers' Organizations, attached to the All-Union Council of Trade Unions is to be established with the purpose of providing financial assistance to communist and progressive workers' parties and social organizations abroad.
2. Whenever financial assistance is provided to the organizations mentioned above, it is to be approved by the TsK VKP (b) by means of a resolution and handed out by the Fund's board of directors.
3. Comrade K. S. Kuznetsova is to be appointed Chair of the Board of Directors of the Fund for Assistance to Leftist Workers' Organizations.

DOCUMENT 2
Memo to Stalin Regarding Leftist Workers' Organizations

20 July 1950
Hoover Archives

Fond 89
Finding aid 38
Document 23
Top Secret
No. P76/122
To COMRADES: Molotov, Malenkov, and Grigor'ian
20 July 1950
Excerpts from the minutes No. 76 of the TsK VKP (b) [All-Union
   Communist Party (of Bolsheviks)] Politburo meeting on . . .
Re: The Establishment of the Fund for Assistance to Leftist Workers'
   Organizations.
Resolution of 19 July 1950

1.   The Fund for Assistance to Leftist Workers' Organizations is to be estab-
     lished in Bucharest, attached to the Romanian Council of Trade Unions,
     with the purpose of providing financial assistance to leftist parties and
     progressive workers' and social organizations abroad.
2.   The level of funding of the International Trade Union Fund for Assis-
     tance to Leftist Workers' Organizations is to be fixed at $2 million. The
     contributors will be the VKP (b) with $1 million or 50 percent and the
     Communist Party of China with $200,000 or 10 percent of the funding;
     the Socialist Unity Party of Germany, the Polish United Workers Party,
     the Communist Party of Czechoslovakia, the Romanian and Hungarian
     Workers' Parties will each contribute $160,000 or 8 percent.
3.   Whenever financial assistance is provided this is to be unanimously ap-
     proved by the Board of Directors of the International Fund for Assis-
     tance to Leftist Workers' Organizations. The members of the board are
     appointed each year in agreement with the communist parties mentioned
     in paragraph 2 of this resolution.
4.   For the year 1950 representatives of the VKP (b), the Workers' party of
     Romania and the Polish United Workers' party are to be appointed Di-
     rectors of the International Fund for Assistance to Leftist Workers' Orga-
     nizations.
5.   Comrade B. N. Ponomarev (of the TsK Commission for Foreign Policy) is
     to be sent to the leaders of the communist parties to discuss with them
     the procedures of establishing the Fund.

Top Secret

To: COMRADE STALIN

Attached is the draft resolution of the TsK VKP (b) regarding the establishment of the International Fund for Assistance to Leftist Workers' Organizations with the purpose of providing material and financial assistance to leftist parties and progressive social and Trade Union organizations.

Please review.

[signed]

(V. Grigor'ian)

Chairman of the TsK VKP (b) commission for Foreign Policy

24 June 1950

Copies to comrades: Malenkov, Molotov, Beriia, Mikoian, Kaganovich, Bulganin

---

Top Secret

Draft Resolution of the TsK VKP (b)

Re: The establishment of the International Trade Union Fund for Assistance to Leftist Workers' Organizations.

1. The International Trade Union Fund for Assistance to Leftist Workers' Organizations is to be established in Budapest, attached to the Hungarian Council of Trade Unions with the purpose of providing financial assistance to leftist parties and progressive social and Trade Union organizations abroad.

2. The level of funding of the International Trade Union Fund for Assistance to Leftist Workers' organizations is to be fixed at $2 million. The contributors are the VKP (b) with $1 million or 50 percent and the Communist Party of China with $200,000 or 10 percent of the funding; the Socialist Unity Party of Germany, the Polish United Workers Party, the Communist Party of Czechoslovakia, the Romanian and Hungarian Workers' Parties will each contribute $160,000 or 8 percent.

3. Whenever financial assistance is provided this is to be unanimously approved by the Board of Directors of the Fund for Assistance to Leftist Workers' Organizations. The members of the board are appointed each year in agreement with the communist parties mentioned in paragraph 2 of this resolution.

4. For the year 1950 representatives of the VKP (b) the Workers' party of Hun-

gary and the Polish United Workers' party are to be appointed directors of the International Fund for Assistance to Leftist Workers' Organizations.

5. Comrade B. N. Ponomarev (of the TsK Commission for Foreign Policy) is to be sent to the leaders of the communist parties to discuss with them the procedures of establishing the Fund.

Top Secret

To: Comrade Stalin

As requested [by the Politburo] (see the TsK VKP (b) resolution of 19 June 1950), comrade Ponomarev, Deputy Chairman of the Commission for Foreign Policy, was sent to discuss the establishment of the International Fund for Assistance to Leftist Workers' Organizations with the comrades Gheorgiu-Dej, Rákosi, Gottwald, Pieck and Bierut.

All the leaders of the communist and workers' parties, mentioned above, fully agreed with Ponomarev that the establishment of an International Fund for Assistance to Leftist Workers' Organizations is necessary and timely. They also approved of the organizational details, as proposed by the TsK VKP (b), i.e., the level of funding for the Fund, the amount to be contributed by each party, its being attached to the Romanian Council of Trade Unions, the formation of the Fund's board of directors, and the latter's duties.

In the course of his conversation with comrade Ponomarev, comrade Rákosi stated that the Workers' Party of Hungary had provided financial assistance to a number of communist parties in the past few years. In 1950 the French Communist Party received around $150,000.

The same issue came up in the conversation with comrade Bierut. He also pointed out that the United Workers' Party of Poland had been continually assisting the French Communist Party financially. In 1950 this party had received around $100,000.

Comrade Gottwald on behalf of the Communist Party of Czechoslovakia agreed to contribute to the Fund for Assistance to Communist Parties of Capitalist Countries. However, in the course of the conversation, he emphasized numerous times that the Communist Party of Czechoslovakia had already provided financial assistance to the French Communist Party in the amount of $100,000 this year. Moreover, he said that 50 communist workers from France and five–seven workers from England were on paid holiday in Czechoslovakia at this time, that Czechoslovakia supported an Italian Communist Party school [located in Czechoslovakia] and that 4,000 Greek children were permanently living in Czechoslovakia. Furthermore, as Gottwald put it, "Prague has become the bridge to Moscow," since on their way to or from Moscow a great number of delegations and individual workers of various communist parties were traveling through Prague. He pointed out that various international congresses and meetings were simultaneously taking place in Prague at the moment: the International Student Congress, the meeting of the Bureau of the Permanent Committee of the World Congress of the Defenders of Peace, a meeting of the jury of this Committee, etc. All these events put the Communist Party of Czechoslovakia to great expense. In the end comrade Gottwald announced that the Communist Party of Czechoslovakia, having paid its share of $160,000 to the International Fund for Assistance to Leftist Workers' Organizations, will not be able to provide further financial assistance to communist parties of other countries. Comrade Gottwald also made it clear through his questions and remarks that he believes Poland should be contributing more to the Fund than Czechoslovakia.

Overall, comrade Gottwald was less in favor of the idea of establishing an International Fund for Assistance to Leftist Workers' Organizations than the leaders of the other communist parties.

On 28 July of this year Mao Zedong was informed through comrade Ludin about the plan to establish an International Fund for Assistance to Leftist Workers' Organizations. At the same time the Communist Party of China has been offered the opportunity to participate. No answer has been received as yet.

[signed]

V. Grigor'ian

Chairman of the TsK VKP (b) Commission for Foreign Policy

16 August, 1950.

Copies to comrades: G. M. Malenkov and V. M. Molotov

DOCUMENT 3
Letter to Stalin from Chairman of the TsK VKP

20 January 1951

Hoover Archives

Fond 89

Finding aid 38
Document 24
Top Secret

To: COMRADE STALIN

In compliance with the TsK VKP (b) resolution about the International Trade Union Fund for Assistance to Leftist Workers' Organizations, attached to the Romanian Council of Trade Unions, assistance to communist parties has been provided through this Fund since the second half of 1950.

Thus, in accordance with the decision of the board of directors of the International Fund for Assistance to Leftist Workers' Organizations, attached to the Romanian Council of Trade Unions, the French Communist Party received $300,000 (in addition to the $300,000 paid to them earlier in 1950); the Italian Communist Party received $400,000, the Belgian Communist Party $50,000, the English $100,000 and the Finnish $374,000 (i.e., 200,000 Finnish markkas). The Socialist Party of Italy obtained $100,000, the Communist Party of the Free Territory of Trieste $40,000, the Communist Party of Norway $20,000, the Greek Communist Party $50,000, the Austrian Communist Party $100,000 and the communist parties of Syria and Lebanon each $25,000.

In this way the Fund has spent the entire $2 million at its disposal; there is now even a deficit of $59,000.

At present a number of communist parties (of Australia, Holland and others) are seeking the Fund's financial assistance in 1951.

The contributions to the Fund last year were as follows: the VKP (b) paid $1 million, China $200,000, the communist and workers' parties of Czechoslovakia, Hungary, Poland and Romania, and the Socialist Unity Party of Germany contributed $160,000 each.

It is expedient to come to an agreement with the leaders of the sister parties, mentioned above, about their 1951 contributions to the Fund and to inform them as to how the funds were spent in 1950.

According to the TsK resolution about the establishment of the Fund we also have to appoint new members to the Fund's board of directors for 1951.

A draft resolution is enclosed.

Please review.

[signed]

(V. Grigor'ian)

Chairman of the TsK VKP (b) commission for Foreign Policy

20 January 1951

Copies to comrades: Malenkov, Molotov, Beriia, Mikoian, Kaganovich, Bulganin, and Khrushchev.

DOCUMENT 4
Excerpt from Minutes of TsK VKP Politburo Meeting

February 1951

Hoover Archives

Top Secret

To COMRADES: Molotov, Grigor'ian, and V. V. Kuznetsov—paragraphs 1, 2, 3, and 4.

To: COMRADE ZVEREV——only the second sentence of paragraph 2.

February . . . 1951

Excerpts from the minutes No. 80 of the TsK VKP (b) [All-Union Communist Party (of Bolsheviks)] Politburo meeting on . . .

Re: The International Fund for Assistance to Leftist Workers' Organizations, attached to the Romanian Council of Trade Unions

Resolution of 8 February 1951

1. It is to be considered expedient to fix the level of funding for the International Trade Union Fund for Assistance to Leftist Workers' Organizations, attached to the Romanian Council of Trade Unions at $1.5 million for the year 1951.

2. The VKP (b) will contribute $750,000 to the International Trade Union Fund for Assistance to Leftist Workers' Organizations, attached to the Romanian Council of Trade Unions.

    The USSR Ministry of Finance (comrade Zverev) is to be directed to pay comrade V. G. Grigor'ian $750,000 for special purposes.

3. It is to be considered expedient that the Fund's Board of Directors inform the communist parties contributing to the Fund as to how its money was spent in 1950. Further, it is expedient to make arrangements with the communist parties concerning their annual contribution for 1951; the Communist Party of Czechoslovakia, the Romanian and Hungarian Workers' parties, the United Workers' Party of Poland and the Socialist Unity Party of Germany should each contribute $120,000, China's share should be $150,000.

Comrade V. V. Kuznetsov is directed to make these suggestions to the Fund's board of directors.

4. It is considered expedient to appoint representatives of the TsK VKP (b) and the Workers' Parties of Romania and Hungary directors of the Fund for 1951.

Comrade V. V. Kuznetsov is to be assigned to this position as representative of the VKP (b).

The TsK Secretary

DOCUMENT 5
Notes Regarding Funding to Communist Parties

7 January 1963
Hoover Archives
Fond 89
Finding aid 38
Document 25
Top Secret
P76/36

To: COMRADE PONOMAREV—the entire text.
To: COMRADE KOROVUSHKIN—part A), paragraph 2.
To: COMRADE SEMICHASTNYI—part B).
Excerpts from the minutes No. 76 of the TsK VKP (b) [All-Union Communist Party   (of Bolsheviks)] Politburo meeting on 7 January, 1963.
Concerning the International Department of the TsK KPSS.

A) Concerning the financial maintenance of the International Fund for Assistance to Leftist Workers' Organizations, attached to the Romanian Council of Trade Unions, for the year 1963.

1. The proposal of the International Department of the TsK KPSS about fixing the level of funding for the International Fund for Assistance to Leftist Workers' Organizations, attached to the Romanian Council of Trade Unions for the year 1963 at $14,650,000 is to be accepted. The KPSS's contribution to the fund will be $9,600,000.

2. The board of directors of the USSR State Bank (comrade Korovushkin) is to be charged with paying comrade B. N. Ponomarev $9,600,000 for special purposes.

3. The International Department of the TsK KPSS is to be directed to inform the leaders of the communist parties contributing to the Inter-national Fund as to the Fund's expenditures in 1962. Moreover, the International Department of the TsK KPSS will have to discuss the level of funding for 1963, designated at $14,650,000, with the contributing parties and the amount of money to be paid by each of them, designated as follows:

CP of China	$2,000,000
CP of Czechoslovakia	$500,000
United Workers' Party of Poland	$500,000
Romanian Workers' Party	$500,000
Hungarian Socialist Workers' Party	$500,000
CP of Bulgaria	$350,000
Socialist Unity Party of Germany	$200,000

B) Concerning the financial assistance to be provided to CPs and national democratic organizations in 1963.

1. In 1963 financial assistance will be provided to a number of CPs and national democratic organizations. They will receive as follows:

Italian CP	$5,000,000
CP of Venezuela	$500,000
CP of the United States	$500,000
CP of Algeria	$250,000
CP of Chile	$200,000
CP of Greece	$200,000
Italian Socialist Party	$190,000
Democratic Party of Iraq	
[Kurdish Dem. Party] (Bârzâni)	ID 60,000 Iraqi dinars
CP of Iraq	ID 60,000 Iraqi dinars
CP of Sweden	$70,000
CP of Canada	$62,000
Swiss Workers' Party	$60,000

Progressive Party of the Working People (Cyprus)	£20,000 pounds sterling
CP of Luxembourg	$50,000
Portugal	$50,000
Lebanese CP	$40,000
Syrian CP	$40,000
CP of Sudan	£12,000 pounds sterling
Popular Vanguard Party of Costa Rica	$30,000
People's Party of Unity (Haiti)	$20,000
CP of Honduras	$20,000
African Party of Independence (Senegal)	$20,000
Dominican People's Socialist Party	$20,000
All-People's Congress of Sierra Leone	$15,000
Indonesian newspaper *Bintang Timur*	$12,000
CP of Nicaragua	$12,000
CP of Turkey	$9,000
CP of Réunion	$8,000

2.   The KGB (comrade Semichastnyi), attached to the USSR Soviet of Ministers, is to be entrusted with the transfer of money.

Comrade Semichastnyi has to ensure that the parties, when receiving the funding, are told that financial assistance is being provided to them by the International Trade Union Fund for Assistance to Leftist Workers' Organizations, attached to the Romanian Council of Trade Unions.

The TsK Secretary

APPENDIX C

DOCUMENT FOR CHAPTER 7

DOCUMENT 1

Stalin's Plan to Assassinate Tito

CWIHP Bulletin 10 (March 1998)

The following excerpt is from a document discovered and published by Russian military historian Dmitri Volkogonov (1928–1995) in the Presidential Archive of the Russian Federation in Moscow, outlining various options to assassinate the Yugoslav leader Josip Broz Tito with the help of Iosif Romual'dovich Grigulevich—alias "Max"—a Soviet agent who had been involved earlier in operations to kill Trotsky and later became a historian and corresponding member of the USSR Academy of Sciences. The document, classified as top secret and prepared in the Ministry of State Security (MGB), was addressed personally to Stalin (in its only copy). While, according to Volkogonov, Stalin did not indicate his authorization of the operation on the document, it is likely that he approved of it since preliminary preparations began. Grigulevich, for example, had to write a "farewell letter" to his wife to cover up Soviet government involvement in case the assassination failed. Following Stalin's death in March 1953, however, the operation was terminated.

THE MGB USSR requests permission to prepare a terrorist act (*terakt*) against Tito, by the illegal agent "Max," Comrade I. R. Grigulevich, a Soviet citizen and member of the Communist Party of the Soviet Union since 1950 ([biographical] information attached).

"Max" was placed in Italy on a Costa Rican passport, where he was able to gain the confidence and enter the circles of South American diplomats as well as well-known Costa Rican political and trade figures visiting Italy.

Using these connections, "Max," on our orders, obtained an appointment as the special plenipotentiary of Costa Rica in Italy and Yugoslavia. In the course of his diplomatic duties, in the second half of 1952, he visited Yugoslavia twice. He was well received there, with entrée into circles close to Tito's clique; he was promised a personal audience with Tito. "Max's" present position offers us opportunities to carry out active measures (aktivnye deistviia) against Tito.

In early February of this year, we summoned "Max" to Vienna for a secret meeting. While discussing options, "Max" was asked how he thought he could be most useful, considering his position. "Max" proposed some kind of active measure against Tito personally.

In relation to this proposal, there was a discussion with him [Max] about how he imaged all of this and as a result, the following options for a terrorist act against Tito were presented.

1. To order "Max" to arrange a private audience with Tito, during which a soundless mechanism concealed in his clothes would release a dose of pulmonary plague bacteria that would guarantee death to Tito and all present. "Max" himself would not be informed of the substance's nature, but with the goal of saving "Max's" life, he would be given an anti-plague serum in advance.

2. In connection with Tito's expected visit to London, to send "Max" there to use his official position and good personal relations with the Yugoslav ambassador in England, [Vladimir] Velebit, to obtain an invitation to the expected Yugoslav embassy reception in Tito's honor.

   The terrorist act could be accomplished by shooting with a silent mechanism concealed as a personal item, while simultaneously releasing tear gas to create panic among the crowd, allowing "Max" to escape and cover up all traces.

3. To use one of the official receptions in Belgrade to which members of the diplomatic corps are invited. The terrorist act could be implemented in the same way as the second option, to be carried out by "Max," who as a diplomat, accredited by the Yugoslav government, would be invited to such a reception.

   In addition, to assign "Max" to work out an option whereby one of the Costa Rican representatives will give Tito some jewelry in a box, which when opened would release an instantaneously effective poisonous substance.

   We asked Max to once again think the operation over and to make suggestions on how he could realize, in the most efficient way, actions against Tito. Means of contact were established and it was agreed that further instructions would follow.

It seems appropriate to use "Max" to implement a terrorist act against Tito. "Max's" personal qualities and intelligence experience make him suitable for such an assignment. We ask for your approval.

[Published on 11 June 1993 in Izvestiia]

APPENDIX D

DOCUMENTS FOR CHAPTER 14

———————

DOCUMENT 1

Stalin's Conversations with Chinese Leaders

16 December 1949
CWIHP Bulletin 6–7 (95/96)

[Classification level blacked out: 'NOT SECRET' Stamped]

Record of Conversation between Comrade I. V. Stalin and Chairman of the Central People's Government of the People's Republic of China Mao Zedong on 16 December 1949

Comrade Mao Zedong: The most important question at the present time is the question of establishing peace. China needs a period of three–five years of peace, which would be used to bring the economy back to pre-war levels and to stabilize the country in general. Decisions on the most important questions in China hinge on the prospects for a peaceful future. With this is mind the CC CPC [Central Committee of the Communist Party of China] entrusted me to ascertain from you, comr[ade] Stalin, in what way and for how long will international peace be preserved.

Comrade Stalin: In China a war for peace, as it were, is taking place. The question of peace greatly preoccupies the Soviet Union as well, though we have already had peace for the past four years. With regards to China, there is no immediate threat at the present time: Japan has yet to stand up on its feet and is thus not ready for war; America, though it screams war, is actually afraid of war more than anything; Europe is afraid of war; in essence, there is no one to fight with China, not unless Kim Il Sung decides to invade China?

Peace will depend on our efforts. If we continue to be friendly, peace can last not only five–ten years, but twenty–twenty-five years and perhaps even longer.

Comrade Mao Zedong: Since <u>Liu Shaoqi's</u> return to China, CC CPC has been discussing the treaty of friendship, alliance, and mutual assistance between China and the USSR.

Comrade Stalin: This question we can discuss and decide. We must ascertain whether to declare the continuation of the current 1945 treaty of alliance and friendship between the USSR and China, to announce impending changes in the future, or to make these changes right now.

As you know, this treaty was concluded between the USSR and China as a result of the Yalta Agreement, which provided for the main points of the treaty (the question of the Kurile Islands, South Sakhalin, Port Arthur, etc.). That is, the given treaty was concluded, so to speak, with the consent of America and England. Keeping in mind this circumstance, we, within our inner circle, have decided not to modify any of the points of this treaty for now, since a change in even one point could give America and England the legal grounds to raise questions about modifying also the treaty's provisions concerning the Kurile Islands, South Sakhalin, etc. This is why we searched to find a way to modify the current treaty in effect while formally maintaining its provisions, in this case by formally maintaining the Soviet Union's right to station its troops at Port Arthur while, at the request of the Chinese government, actually withdrawing the Soviet Armed forces currently stationed there. Such an operation could be carried out upon China's request.

One could do the same with KChZhd [Chinese Changchun Railroad, which traverses Manchuria], that is, to effectively modify the corresponding points of the agreement while formally maintaining its provisions, upon China's request.

If, on the other hand, the Chinese comrades are not satisfied with this strategy, they can present their own proposals.

Comrade Mao Zedong: The present situation with regard to KChZhD and Port Arthur corresponds well with Chinese interests, as the Chinese forces are inadequate to effectively fight against imperialist aggression. In addition, KChZhD is a training school for the preparation of Chinese cadres in railroad and industry.

Comrade Stalin: The withdrawal of troops does not mean that Soviet Union refuses to assist China, if such assistance is needed. The fact is that we, as communists, are not altogether comfortable with stationing our forces on foreign soil, especially on the soil of a friendly nation. Given this situation anyone could say that if Soviet forces can be stationed on Chinese territory, then why could not the British, for example, station their forces in Hong Kong, or the Americans in Tokyo?

We would gain much in the arena of international relations if, with mutual agreement, the Soviet forces were to be withdrawn from Port Arthur. In addition, the withdrawal of Soviet forces would provide a serious boost to Chinese communists in their relations with the national bourgeoisie. Everyone would see that the communists have managed to achieve what [Nationalist Chinese leader] Jiang Jieshi [Chiang Kai-shek] could not. The Chinese communists must take the national bourgeoisie into consideration.

The treaty ensures the USSR's right to station its troops in Port Arthur. But the USSR is not obligated to exercise this right and can withdraw its troops upon Chinese request. However, if this is unsuitable, the troops in Port Arthur can remain there for two, five or ten years, whatever suits China best. Let them not misunderstand that we want to run away from China. We can stay there for twenty years even.

Comrade Mao Zedong: In discussing the treaty in China, we had not taken into account the American and English positions regarding the Yalta agreement. We must act in a way that is best for the common cause. This question merits further consideration. However, it is already becoming clear that the treaty should not be modified at the present time nor should one rush to withdraw troops from Port Arthur.

Should not Zhou Enlai visit Moscow in order to decide the treaty question?

Comrade Stalin: No, this question you must decide for yourselves. Zhou may be needed in regard to other matters.

Comrade Mao Zedong: We would like to decide on the question of Soviet credit to China, that is to draw up a credit agreement for 300,000,000 dollars between the governments of the USSR and China.

Comrade Stalin: This can be done. If you would like to formalize this agreement now, we can.

Comrade Mao Zedong: Yes, exactly now, as this would resonate well in China. At the same time it is necessary to resolve the question of trade, especially between the USSR and Xinjiang [Sinkiang], though at present we cannot present a specific trade operations plan for this region.

Comrade Stalin: We must know right now what kind of equipment China will need, especially now, since we do not have equipment in reserve and the request for industrial goods must be submitted ahead of time.

Comrade Mao Zedong: We are having difficulties in putting together a request for equipment, as the industrial picture is as yet unclear.

Comrade Stalin: It is desirable to expedite the preparation of this request, as requests for equipment are submitted to our industry at least a year in advance.

Comrade Mao Zedong: We would very much like to receive assistance from the USSR in creating air transportation routes.

Comrade Stalin: We are ready to render such assistance. Air routes can be established over Xinjiang and the MPR [Mongolian People's Republic]. We have specialists. We will give you assistance.

Comrade Mao Zedong: We would also like to receive your assistance in creating a naval force.

Comrade Stalin: Cadres for Chinese navy could be prepared at Port Arthur. You give us people, and we will give you ships. Trained cadres of the Chinese navy could then return to China on these ships.

Comrade Mao Zedong: Guomindang [Kuomintang] supporters have built a naval and air base on the island of Formosa [Taiwan]. Our lack of naval forces and aviation makes the occupation of the island by the People's Liberation Army [PLA] more difficult. With regard to this, some of our generals have been voicing opinions that we should request assistance from the Soviet Union, which could send volunteer pilots or secret military detachments to speed up the conquest of Formosa.

Comrade Stalin: Assistance has not been ruled out, though one ought to consider the form of such assistance. What is most important here is not to give Americans a pretext to intervene. With regard to headquarters staff and instructors, we can give them to you anytime. The rest we will have to think about.

Do you have any assault landing units?

Comrade Mao Zedong: We have one former Guomindang assault landing regiment unit, which came over to join our side.

Comrade Stalin: One could select a company of landing forces, train them in propaganda, send them over to Formosa, and through them organize an uprising on the isle.

Comrade Mao Zedong: Our troops have approached the borders of Burma and Indochina. As a result, the Americans and the British are alarmed, not knowing whether we will cross the border or whether our troops will halt their movement.

Comrade Stalin: One could create a rumor that you are preparing to cross the border and in this way frighten the imperialists a bit.

Comrade Mao Zedong: Several countries, especially Britain, are actively campaigning to recognize the People's Republic of China. However, we believe that we should not rush to be recognized. We must first bring about order to the country, strengthen our position, and then we can talk to foreign imperialists.

Comrade Stalin: That is a good policy. In addition, there is no need for you to create conflicts with the British and the Americans. If, for example, there will be a need to put pressure on the British, this can be done by resorting to a conflict between the Guangdong province and Hong Kong. And to resolve this conflict, Mao Zedong could come forward as the mediator. The main point is not to rush and to avoid conflicts.

Are there foreign banks operating in Shanghai?

Comrade Mao Zedong: Yes.

Comrade Stalin: And whom are they serving?

Comrade Mao Zedong: The Chinese national bourgeoisie and foreign enterprises, which so far we have not touched. As for the foreigners' sphere of influence, the British predominate in investments in the economic and commercial sectors, while the Americans lead in the sector of cultural-educational organizations.

Comrade Stalin: What is the situation regarding Japanese enterprises?

Comrade Mao Zedong: They have been nationalized.

Comrade Stalin: In whose hands is the customs agency?

Comrade Mao Zedong: In the hands of the government.

Comrade Stalin: It is important to focus attention on the customs agency as it is usually a good source of government revenue.

Comrade Mao Zedong: In the military and political sectors we have already achieved complete success; as for cultural and economic sectors, we have as yet not freed ourselves from foreign influence there.

Comrade Stalin: Do you have inspectors and agents overseeing foreign enterprises, banks, etc.?

Comrade Mao Zedong: Yes, we have. We are carrying out such work in the study and oversight of foreign enterprises (the kailan [?] mines, electric power plants and aqueducts in Shanghai, etc.).

Comrade Stalin: One should have government inspectors who must operate legally. The foreigners should also be taxed at higher levels than the Chinese.

Who owns the enterprises mining wolfram [tungsten], molybdenum, and petroleum?

Comrade Mao Zedong: The government.

Comrade Stalin: It is important to increase the mining of minerals and especially of petroleum. You could build an oil pipeline from western Lanzhou to Chengdu [?], and then transport fuel by ship.

Comrade Mao Zedong: So far we have not decided which districts of China we should strive to develop first—the coastal areas or those inland, since we were unsure of the prospects for peace.

Comrade Stalin: Petroleum, coal, and metal are always needed, regardless of whether there be war or not.

Can rubber-bearing trees be grown in southern China?

Comrade Mao Zedong: So far it has not been possible.

Comrade Stalin: Is there a meteorological service in China?

Comrade Mao Zedong: No, it has not been established yet.

Comrade Stalin: It should be established.

We would like to receive from you a list of your works, which could be translated into Russian.

Comrade Mao Zedong: I am currently reviewing my works, which were published in various local publishing houses and which contain a mass of errors and misrepresentations. I plan to complete this review by spring of 1950. However, I would like to receive help from Soviet comrades: first of all, to work on the texts with Russian translators and, secondly, to receive help in editing the Chinese original.

Comrade Stalin: This can be done. However, do you need your works edited?

Comrade Mao Zedong: Yes, and I ask you to select a comrade suitable for such a task, say, for example, someone from CC VKP/b/ [All-Union Communist Party of Bolsheviks].

Comrade Stalin: It can be arranged, if indeed there is such a need.

Also present at the meeting: comrs. Molotov, Malenkov, Bulganin, Bychinskii, [Soviet translator N. T.] Fedorenko and [Chinese translator] Shi Zhe/Karskii/.

Recorded by comr. Fedorenko.

[signature illegible 31/XII]

[Source: Archive of the President, Russian Federation (APRF), fond (f.) 45, opis (op.)1, delo (d.) 329, listy (ll.) 9–17; translation by Danny Rozas.]

Document 2

II. Conversation Between Stalin and Mao, Moscow

22 January 1950
CWIHP Bulletin 6–7 (1995/1996).

RECORD OF CONVERSATION BETWEEN COMRADE I. V. STALIN AND CHAIRMAN OF THE CENTRAL PEOPLE'S GOVERNMENT OF THE PEOPLE'S REPUBLIC OF CHINA MAO ZEDONG

22 January 1950

AFTER AN EXCHANGE of greetings and a short discussion of general topics, the following conversation took place.

Stalin: There are two groups of questions which must be discussed: the first group of questions concerns the existing agreements between the USSR and China; the second group of questions concerns the current events in Manchuria, Xinjiang, etc.

I think that it would be better to begin not with the current events, but rather with a discussion of the existing agreements. We believe that these agreements need to be changed, though earlier we had thought that they could be left intact. The existing agreements, including the treaty, should be changed because war against Japan figures at the very heart of the treaty. Since the war is over and Japan has been crushed, the situation has been altered, and now the treaty has become an anachronism.

I ask to hear your opinion regarding the treaty of friendship and alliance.

Mao Zedong: So far we have not worked out a concrete draft of the treaty, only a few outlines.

Stalin: We can exchange opinions, and then prepare an appropriate draft.

Mao Zedong: Judging from the current situation, we believe that we should strengthen our existing friendship using the help of treaties and agreements. This would resonate well both in China and in the international arena. Everything that guarantees the future prosperity of our countries must be stated in the treaty of alliance and friendship, including the necessity of avoiding a repetition of Japanese aggression. So long as we show interest in the prosperity of our countries, one cannot rule out the possibility that the imperialist countries will attempt to hinder us.

Stalin: True. Japan still has cadres remaining, and it will certainly lift itself up again, especially if Americans continue their current policy.

Mao Zedong: Two points that I made earlier are cardinal in changing our future treaty from the existing one. Previously, the Guomindang spoke of friendship in words only. Now the situation has changed, with all the conditions for real friendship and cooperation in place.

In addition, whereas before there was talk of cooperation in the war against Japan, now attention must turn to preventing Japanese aggression. The new treaty must include the question of political, economic, cultural and military cooperation. Of most importance will be the question of economic cooperation.

Stalin: Is it necessary to keep the provision, stated in article 3 of the current Treaty of Friendship: "This article shall remain in force up until that time when, by request of both High Participants in the Treaty, the United Nations is given the responsibility of preventing any future aggression on the part of Japan"?

Mao Zedong: I don't believe it is necessary to keep this provision.

Stalin: I don't believe that it is unnecessary. What provisions do we need to specify in the new treaty?

Mao Zedong: We believe that the new treaty should include a paragraph on consultation regarding international concerns. The addition of this paragraph would strengthen our position, since among the Chinese national bourgeoisie there are objections to the policy of rapprochement with the Soviet Union on questions of international concern.

Stalin: Good. When signing a treaty of friendship and cooperation, the inclusion of such a paragraph goes without saying.

Mao Zedong: That's right.

Stalin: To whom shall we entrust the preparation of the draft? I believe that we should entrust it to [Soviet Foreign Minister Andrei] Vyshinskii and [Chinese Foreign Minister] Zhou Enlai.

Mao Zedong: Agreed.

Stalin: Let us move over to the agreement on KChZhD. What proposals do you have on this question?

Mao Zedong: Perhaps we should accept as the guiding principle the idea of making practical changes concerning the KChZhD and the Port Arthur agreements, while legally continuing them in their present state?

Stalin: That is, you agree to declare the legal continuation of the current agreement, while, in effect, allowing appropriate changes to take place.

Mao Zedong: We must act so as to take into account the interests of both sides, China and the Soviet Union.

Stalin: True. We believe that the agreement concerning Port Arthur is not equitable.

Mao Zedong: But changing this agreement goes against the decisions of the Yalta Conference!

Stalin: True, it does—and to hell with it! Once we have taken up the position that the treaties must be changed, we must go all the way. It is true that for us this entails certain inconveniences, and we will have to struggle against the Americans. But we are already reconciled to that.

Mao Zedong: This question worries us only because it may have undesirable consequences for the USSR.

Stalin: As you know, we made the current agreement during the war with Japan. We did not know that Jiang Jieshi would be toppled. We acted under the premise that the presence of our troops in Port Arthur would be in the interests of Soviet Union and democracy in China.

Mao Zedong: The matter is clear.

Stalin: In that case, would you deem the following scenario acceptable: declare that the agreement on Port Arthur shall remain in force until a peace treaty with Japan is signed, after which the Russian troops would be withdrawn from Port Arthur. Or perhaps one could propose another scenario: declare that the current agreement shall remain in place, while in effect withdrawing troops from Port Arthur. We will accept whichever of these scenarios is more suitable. We agree with both scenarios.

Mao Zedong: This question would be thought through. We agree with the opinion of Comrade Stalin and believe that the agreement on Port Arthur must remain in force until a peace treaty is signed with Japan, after which the treaty shall become invalid and the Soviet soldiers will leave. However, we would like for Port Arthur to be a place for military collaboration, where we could train our military naval forces.

Stalin: The question of Dalny [Dairen; Dalian]. We have no intention of securing any Soviet rights in Dalny.

Mao Zedong: Will Dalny remain a free port?

Stalin: Since we are giving up our rights there, China must decide on its own the question of Dalny: will it remain a free port or not. During his time Roosevelt insisted that Dairen remain a free port.

Mao Zedong: So the preservation of the free port would be in the interests of America and Britain?

Stalin: Of course. It's a house with open gates.

Mao Zedong: We believe that Port Arthur could serve as a base for our military collaboration, while Dalny could serve as a base for Sino-Soviet economic collaboration. In Dalny there is a whole array of enterprises that we are in no position to exploit without Soviet assistance. We should develop a closer economic collaboration there.

Stalin: In other words, the agreement on Port Arthur will remain in force until a peace treaty is signed with Japan. After the signing of the peace treaty the existing agreement shall become invalid and the Russians shall withdraw their troops. Did I sum up your thoughts correctly?

Mao Zedong: Yes, basically so, and it is exactly this which we would like to set forth in the new treaty.

Stalin: Let us continue the discussion of the KChZhD question. Tell us, as an honest communist, what doubts do you have here?

Mao Zedong: The principal point is that the new treaty should note that joint exploitation and administration will continue in the future. However, in the case of administration, China should take the lead role here. Furthermore, it is necessary to examine the question of shortening the duration of the agreement and to determine the amount of investment by each side.

Molotov: The conditions governing the cooperation and joint administration of an enterprise by two interested countries usually provide for equal participation by both sides, as well as for alternation in the appointment of replacements for management positions. In the old agreement the administration of the railroad belonged to the Soviets; however, in the future we think it necessary to alternate in the creation of management functions. Let's say that such an alternation could take place every two to three years.

Zhou Enlai: Our comrades believe that the existing management of KChZhD and the office of the director ought to be abolished and a railroad administration commission be set up in their place, and that the offices of the commission chairman and of the director should be replaced by Chinese cadres. However, given Comrade Molotov's proposals, this question required more thought.

Stalin: If we are talking about joint administration, then it is important that the replacements for the managing position be alternated. That would be more logical. As for the duration of the agreement, we would not be against shortening it.

Zhou Enlai: Should we not change the ratio of capital investment by each side, by increasing the level of Chinese investment to 51 percent, instead of the current requirement for parity?

Molotov: This would go against the existing provision for parity.

Stalin: We do indeed have agreements with the Czechs and the Bulgarians which provide for parity and equal-footing for both sides. Since we already have joint administration, then we might as well have equal participation.

Mao Zedong: The question needs to be further examined, keeping in mind the interests of both sides.

Stalin: Let us discuss the credit agreement. We need to officially formalize that which has already been agreed to earlier. Do you have any observations to make?

Mao Zedong: Is the shipment of military arms considered a part of the monetary loan?

Stalin: This you can decide yourself: we can bill that toward the loan, or we can formalize it through trade agreements.

Mao Zedong: If the military shipments are billed towards the loan, then we will have little means left for industry. It appears that part of the military shipments will have to be billed towards the loan, while the other part will have to be paid with Chinese goods. Can't the period of delivery of industrial equipment and military arms be shortened from five to three–four years?

Stalin: We must examine our options. The matter rests in the requisition list for our industry. Nevertheless, we can move the date that the credit agreement goes into effect to 1 January 1950, since the shipments should begin just about now. If the agreement specified July 1949 as the time for the commencement of the loan, the international community would not be able to understand how an agreement could have been reached between the Soviet Union and China, which at the time did not even have its own government. It seems that you should hasten somewhat to present the requisition list for industrial equipment. It should be kept in mind that the sooner such a list is presented, the better for the matter at hand.

Mao Zedong: We believe that the conditions of the credit agreement are generally favorable to China. Under its terms we pay only 1 percent interest.

Stalin: Our credit agreements with people's democracies provide for 2 percent interest. We could, says comr. Stalin jokingly, increase this interest for you as well, if you would like. Of course, we acted under the premise that the Chinese economy was practically in ruin.

As is clear from the telegrams that we have received, the Chinese government intends to use its army in the reconstruction of its economy. That is very good. In our time we also made use of the army in our economic development and had very good results.

Mao Zedong: That's right. We are drawing on the experience of our Soviet comrades.

Stalin: You raised the question of China receiving a certain amount of grain for Xinjiang?

Mao Zedong: Wheat and textile.

Stalin: For this you need to come up with the necessary requests that include numbers.

Mao Zedong: Very well, we shall prepare these.

How shall we proceed with the trade agreement?

Stalin: What is your opinion? Up until now we have only had a trade agreement with Manchuria. We would like to know what sort of a situation we should look forward to in the future: will we be signing separate agreements with Xinjiang, Manchuria and other provinces, or a single agreement with the central government?

Mao Zedong: We would like to have a single, central agreement. But in time Xinjiang may have a separate agreement.

Stalin: Just Xinjiang; what about Manchuria?

Zhou Enlai: A separate agreement with Manchuria can be ruled out, since in the agreement with the central government China's obligations would in essence be fulfilled by shipments made from Manchuria.

Stalin: We would like the central government to sanction and take the responsibility for the agreements with Xinjiang or Manchuria.

Mao Zedong: The agreement with Xinjiang must be signed in the name of the central government.

Stalin: Right, since [a] provincial government might not take many things into account, whereas things are always clearer to the central government.

What other questions do you have?

Mao Zedong: At the present time the main question is economic cooperation—the reconstruction and developments of the Manchurian economy.

Stalin: I think that we will entrust the preparation of this question to comrs. Mikoyan, Vyshinskii, Zhou Enlai, and [CCP CC member and Vice Chairman of Finance and Economics Commission] Li Fuchun.

Any other questions?

Mao Zedong: I would like to note that the air regiment that you sent to China was very helpful. They transported ten thousand people. Let me thank you, Comrade Stalin, for the help and ask you to allow it to stay a little longer, so it could help transport provisions to [CCP CC member and commander of the PLA's Second Field Army] Liu Bocheng's troops, currently preparing for an attack on Tibet.

Stalin: It's good that you are preparing to attack. The Tibetans need to be subdued. As for the air regiment, we shall talk this over with the military personnel and give you an answer.

The meeting took two hours.

Present at the meeting were comrs. Molotov, Malenkov, Mikoyan, Vyshinskii, Roshchin, Fedorenko, and Mao Zedong, Zhou Enlai, Li Fuchun, [PRC Ambassador to the USSR] Wang Jiaziang, [CCP CC member] Chen Boda, and Shi Zhe/Karskii/.

[Source: APRF.f.45, op.1, d.329, 11.29–38; translation by Danny Rozas.]

DOCUMENT 3
Mao's Conversation with Yugoslavian Communist Union Delegation

September 1956
CWIHP 6–7 (95/96)

MINUTES, MAO'S CONVERSATION with Yugoslavian Communist Union Delegation, Beijing, September 1956

We welcome you to China. We are very pleased at your visit. We have been supported by you, as well as by other brotherly [Communist] parties. We are invariably supporting you as much as all the other brotherly parties. In today's world, the Marxist and Communist front remains united, whether in places where success [of Communist revolution] is achieved or not yet achieved. How-ever, there were times when we were not so united; there were times when we let you down. We listened to the opinions of the Information Bureau in the past; although we did not take part in the Bureau's [business], we found it difficult not to support it. In 1949 the Bureau condemned you as butchers and Hitler-style fascists, and we kept silent on the resolution [condemning you], although we published articles to criticize you in 1948. In retrospect, we should not have done that; we should have discussed [this issue] with you: if some of your viewpoints were incorrect, [we should have let] you conduct self-criticism, and there was no need to hurry [into the controversy] as [we] did. The same thing is true to us: should you disagree with us, you should do the same thing, that is, the adoption of a method of persuasion and consultation.

There was, however, another factor which prevented us from responding to you: the Soviet friends did not want us to form diplomatic relations with you. If so, was China an independent state? Of course, yes. If an independent state, why, then, did we follow their instructions? [My] comrades, when the Soviet Union requested us to follow their suit at that time, it was difficult for us to oppose it. It was because at that time some people claimed that there were two Titos in the world: one in Yugoslavia, the other in China, even if no one passed a resolution that Mao Zedong was Tito. I have once pointed out to the Soviet comrades that [they] suspected that I was a half-hearted Tito, but they refuse to recognize it. When did they remove the tag of half-hearted Tito from my head? The tag was removed after [China] decided to resist America [in Korea] and came to [North] Korea's aid and when [we] dealt the U.S. imperialists a blow.

. . . Only after the dissolution of the Comintern did we start to enjoy more freedom. We had already begun to criticize opportunism and the Wang Ming line, and unfolded the rectification movement. The rectification, in fact, was aimed at denouncing the mistakes that Stalin and the comintern had committed in directing the Chinese revolution; however, we did not openly mention a word about Stalin and the Comintern. Sometime in the near future, [we] may openly do so. There are two explanations of why we did not openly criticize [Stalin and the Comintern]: first, as we followed their instructions, we have to take some responsibility ourselves. Nobody compelled us to follow their instructions! Nobody forced us to be wrongfully deviated to right and left directions! There are two kinds of Chinese: one kind is a dogmatist who completely accepts Stalin's line; the other opposes dogmatism, thus refusing to obey [Stalin's] instructions. Second, we do not want to displease [the Soviets], to disrupt our relations with the Soviet Union. The Comintern has never made self-criticism on these mistakes nor has the Soviet Union ever mentioned these mistakes. We would have fallen out with them had we raised our criticism.

The fourth time was when [Moscow] regarded me as a half-hearted Tito or semi-Titoist.

. . . We had no objection that the Soviet Union functions as a center [of the world revolution] because it benefits the socialist movement. You may disagree [with us] on this point. You wholeheartedly support Khrushchev's campaign to criticize Stalin, but we cannot do the same because our people would dislike it. In the previous parades [in China], we held up portraits of Marx, Engels, Lenin, and Stalin, as well as those of a few Chinese [leaders]—Mao, Liu [Shaoqi], Zhou [Enlai], and Zhu [De]—and other brotherly parties' leaders. Now we adopt a measure of "overthrowing all": no one's portrait is handed out. For this year's "First of May" celebration, Ambassador Bobkoveshi already saw in Beijing that no one's portrait was held in parade. However, the portraits of five dead persons—Marx, Engels, Lenin and Stalin, and Sun [Yatsen]—and a not yet dead person—Mao Zedong—are still hanging [on the wall]. Let them hang on the wall! You Yugoslavians may comment that the Soviet Union no longer hangs Stalin's portrait, but the Chinese still do.

As of this date some people remain suspicious of whether our socialism can be successfully constructed and stick to the assertion that our Communist Party is a phony one. What can we do? These people eat and sleep every day and then propagate that the Chinese Communist Party is not really a communist party, and that China's socialist construction is bound to fail.

. . . We oppose great power politics in international relations. Although our industry is small, all things considered, we can be regarded as a big power. Hence some people [in China] begin to be cocky. We then warn them: "Lower your heads and act with your tails tucked between your legs." When I was little, my mother often taught me to behave "with tails tucked between legs." This is a correct teaching and now I often mention it to my comrades.

. . . We are sorry that we hurt you before, thus owing you a good deal. Killing must be compensated by life and debts must be paid in cash. We have criticized you before, but why do we still keep quiet? Before [Khrushchev's] criticism of Stalin, we were not in a position to be as explicit about some issues as we are now. In my previous conversations with [ambassador] Bobkoveshi, I could only say that as long as the Soviet Union did not criticize Stalin, we would be in no position to do so; as long as the Soviet Union did not restore [diplomatic] relations with Yugoslavia, we could not establish relations with you. Now these issues can be openly discussed. I talk to you about it because you are our comrades. However, we still cannot publish this in the newspapers, because the imperialists should not be allowed to know about it. We may openly talk about one or two mistakes of Stalin's in the future. Our situation is quite different from yours: Tito's autobiography mentions Stalin because you have already broken up with the Soviet Union.

Stalin advocated dialectical materialism, but sometimes he lacked materialism and, instead, practiced metaphysics; he wrote about historical materialism, but very often suffered from historical idealism. Some of his behavior, such as going to extremes, fostering personal myth, and embarrassing others, are by no means [forms] of materialism.

Before I met with Stalin, I did not have much good feeling about him. I disliked reading his works, and I have read only "On the Basis of Leninism," a long article criticizing Trotsky, and "Be Carried Away by Success," etc. I disliked even more his articles on the Chinese revolution. He was very different from Lenin: Lenin shared his heart with others and treated others as equals, whereas Stalin liked to stand above every one else and order others round. This style can be detected from his works. After I met with him, I became even more disgusted: I quarreled a lot with him in Moscow. Stalin was excitable by temperament. When he became agitated, he would spell out nasty things.

I have written altogether three pieces praising Stalin. The first was written in Yanan to celebrate his sixtieth birthday [21 December 1939—Ed.], and the third was an article requested by *Pravda* after his death [March 1953—Ed.]. I always dislike congratulating others as well as being congratulated by others. When I was in Moscow to celebrate his birthday, what else could I have done if I had chosen not to congratulate him? Could I have cursed him instead? After his death, the Soviet Union needed our support and we also wanted to support the Soviet Union. Consequently, I wrote that piece to praise his virtues and achievements. That piece was not for Stalin; it was for the Soviet Communist Party. As for the piece I did in Yanan, I had to ignore my personal feelings and treat him as the leader of a socialist country. Therefore, that piece was rather vigorous, whereas the other two came out of [political] need, not my heart nor my will. Human life is just as contradictory as this: your emotion tells you not to write these pieces, but your rationality compels you to do so.

Now that Moscow has criticized Stalin, we are free to talk about these issues. Today I tell you about the four mistakes committed by Stalin, but, in order to maintain relations with the Soviet Union, [we] cannot publish them in our newspapers. Since Khrushchev's report only mentioned the conflict over the sugar plant while discussing Stalin's mistakes concerning us, we feel it inappropriate to make them public. There are other issues involving conflicts and controversies.

Generally speaking, the Soviet Union is good. It is good because of four factors: Marxism-Leninism, the October Revolution, the main force [of the socialist camp], and industrialization. They have their negative side, and have made some mistakes. However, their achievements constitute the major part [of their past] while their shortcomings are of secondary significance. Now that the enemy is taking advantage of the criticism of Stalin to take the offensive on a world-wide scale, we ought to support the Soviet Union. They will certainly correct their mistakes. Khrushchev already corrected the mistake concerning Yugoslavia.

Some of our people are still unhappy with the criticism of Stalin. However, such criticism has positive effects because it destroys mythologies and opens [black] boxes. This entails liberation, indeed, a "war of liberation." With it, people are becoming so courageous that they will speak their minds, as well as be able to think about issues.

Liberty, equality, and fraternity are slogans of the bourgeoisie, but now we have to fight for them. Is [our relationship with Moscow] a father-and-son relationship or one between brothers? It was between father and son in the past; now it more or less resembles a brotherly relationship, but the shadow of the father-and-son relationship is not completely removed. This is understandable, because changes can never be completed in one day. With certain openness, people are now able to think freely and independently. Now there is, in a sense, the atmosphere of anti-feudalism: a father-and-son relationship is giving way to a brotherly relationship, and a patriarchal system is being toppled. During [Stalin's] time people's minds were so tightly controlled that even the feudalist control had been surpassed. While some enlightened feudal lords or emperors would accept criticism, [Stalin] would tolerate none. Yugoslavia might also have such a ruler [in your history] who might take it well even when people cursed him right in his face. The capitalist society has taken a step ahead of the feudalist society. The Republican and Democratic Parties in the United States are allowed to quarrel with each other.

Few people in China have ever openly criticized me. The [Chinese] people are tolerant of my shortcomings and mistakes. It is because we always want to serve the people and do good things for the people. Although we sometimes also suffer from bossism and bureaucracy, the people believe that we have done more good things than bad ones and, as a result, they praise us more than criticize us. Consequently, an idol is created: when some people criticize me, others would oppose them and accuse them of disrespecting the leader. Everyday I and other comrades of the central leadership receive some three hundred letters, some of which are critical of us. These letters, however, are either not signed or signed with a false name. The authors are not afraid that we would suppress them, but they are afraid that others around them would make them suffer.

APPENDIX E

DOCUMENTS FOR CHAPTER 15

All appendixes excerpted from CWIHP 5 (Spring 1995)

➤●◀

DOCUMENT 1

Stalin's Meeting with Kim Il Sung, Moscow

5 March 1949

NOTES OF THE conversation between Stalin and a governmental delegation from the Democratic People's Republic of Korea headed by Kim Il Sung. Present were A. Ia. Vyshinsky, T. F. Shtykov, Kim I. M. (Translator). On the Korean side: Pak Hon-yong, Hong Myong-hui, Chong Chuntaek, Chang Shi-u, Paek Nam Un, Kim Chong-ju, the Korean ambassador to the USSR Chu Yong-ha, Mun Il (Translator).

Kim Il Sung says that after the liberation of Korea by Soviet troops, the Soviet government and the Soviet Army rendered aid to Korea in the matter of economic development, in the matter of the development of Korea along the democratic path, and that the Korean government understands that without further economic and cultural aid from the Soviet Union it will be difficult for the DPRK to restore and develop its national economy and culture. The assistance of the Soviet is required for the further development of the Korean economy and culture.

Stalin asks what kind of aid.

Kim Il sung answers—economic and cultural.

Stalin asks what precisely is needed.

Kim Il Sung says that they have confirmed a two year plan for the restoration and development of the national economy. They need economic assistance to fulfill this plan and to strengthen the foundation of the economy. They need machines, equipment and spare parts for industry, communications, transport—and also for other branches of the national economy. They also need technical assistance: sending Soviet specialists to Korea, drafting plans for the construction of new objects (factories and plants), conducting geological exploratory work.

Stalin asks what kinds of objects?

Kim answers, e.g., irrigation structures [at] Anju, the construction of which they have now moved toward, but they do not have enough specialists, and also the restoration and completion of the Seisin metallurgical plant, repair of the Sufun hydroelectric plant and others.

Stalin asks if there is iron ore in Korea.

Kim answers that there is very much iron ore in Korea.

Stalin says that it is possible to render this assistance, and it is also possible to provide specialists.

Kim indicates that until now trade between the two countries has been conducted successfully, but in the future, for the fulfillment of the two year plan, they need to import from the Soviet Union equipment, steam engines, electric locomotives, spare parts and equipment for the textile industry. But exports from Korea will not cover the imports, therefore they need credit from the Soviet government.

Stalin says, "Fine," and asks in what amount they need credit.

Kim answers from 40 to 50 million American dollars.

DOCUMENT 2
Ciphered Telegram from Shtykov to Vyshinsky

3 September 1949

ON SEPTEMBER 3 the personal secretary of Kim Il Sung, Mun Il (a Soviet Korean) came to me and at the commission of Kim Il Sung reported that they had received reliable information that in the near future the southerners intend to seize the part of the Ongjin peninsula which is located to the north of the 38th parallel, and also to bombard the cement plant in the city of Kaisiu.

In connection with this, Mun Il said, Kim Il Sung asks permission to begin military operations against the south, with the goal of seizing the Ongjin peninsula and part of the territory of South Korea to the east of the Ongjin peninsula, approximately to Kaesong, so as to shorten the line of defense.

Kim Il Sung considers, Mun said, that if the international situation permits, they are ready to move further to the south. Kim Il Sung is convinced that they are in a position to seize South Korea in the course of two weeks, maximum two months.

I asked [Mun] to transmit to Kim Il Sung that this question is very large and serious, it is necessary to think it through carefully and that I therefore urgently recommend to Kim Il Sung not to be in a hurry and not to take [any measures] while there is no decision on this question.

Kim Il Sung will probably raise this question again soon.

It has been established that the [North] Koreans truly did seize an order to the commander of troops on the Ongjin peninsula to begin artillery fire on the cement plant in Kaisiu on 2 September at 8:00 and to destroy it. From the order it is clear that the southerners consider this plant to be military. The period indicated in the order has passed, but so far there has been no shelling. The northerners have taken the necessary measures in case of firing on the plant.

Regarding the intentions of the southerners to seize part of the Ongjin peninsula to the north of the 38th parallel, we have only indications [of this] from deserters from the south.

There have not been any serious incidents at the 38th parallel since 15 August. Small exchanges of fire have taken place, [there have been] instances of artillery firing on the territory of North Korea on the Ongjin peninsula, trespassing of the parallel. The southerners are carrying out defensive work at the 38th parallel at a faster tempo. I ask your order. Tunkin.

[Source: AVPRF, Fond 059a, Opis 5a, Delo 4, Papka 11, Listy 136–48]

DOCUMENT 3
*Ciphered Telegram from Gromyko to Tunkin at the
Soviet Embassy in Pyongyang*

11 September 1949

You MUST MEET with Kim Il Sung as soon as possible and try to illuminate from him the following additional questions:

1. How do they evaluate the South Korean army, [its] numbers, arms and fighting capacity?
2. The condition of the partisan movement in the south of Korea and what real help they think they will receive from the partisans.
3. How do the society and people regard the fact that northerners will be the first to begin an attack? What kind of real aid can be given by the population of the south to the army of the north?
4. Are there American troops in the south of Korea? What kind of measures, in the opinion of Kim Il Sung, can the Americans take in case of an attack by the northerners?
5. How do the northerners evaluate their possibilities, i.e., the condition of the army, its supplies and fighting capacity?
6. Give your evaluation of the situation and of how real and advisable is the proposal of our friends.

Clarifications are demanded in connection with the questions they raised in conversations on 12 August and 3 September, 1949.

Immediately telegraph the results of the conversation.

[Source: AVP RF, Fond 059a, Opis 5a, Delo 3, Papka 11, Listy 45]

DOCUMENT 4
Ciphered Telegram from Tunkin to Soviet Foreign Ministry
(in reply to telegram of September 11)

14 September 1949

[HE REPORTS THAT he had meetings with Kim Il Sung and Pak Hon-yong on 12 and 13 September about the questions raised in the telegram of 11 September and gives their response—K. W.]

1. [Information about South Korean army, providing many figures—K.W.]
2. [Information about partisan units in South Korea, numbering 1,500–2,000 men—K. W.] Kim thinks they should not count on substantial help from the partisans, but Pak Hon-yong has a different opinion. He thinks the help [from partisans] will be significant. At any rate, they hope that the partisans will help in actions against the communications of the enemy and

that they will occupy the main ports of South Korea, though they will not be able to do this at the beginning of the campaign, maybe later.

3. With regard to the question of how the population will regard the fact that the northerners will begin a civil war, Kim Il Sung oscillates. During the conversation on 12 September he definitely stated that if the northerners begin military actions, this will produce a negative impression in the people and that it is politically disadvantageous to them to begin it. In connection with this, he recollected that during the conversation between Mao Zedong and the Korean representative Kim Il in the spring of this year, Mao stated that in his opinion the northerners should not begin military action now, since in the first place, it is politically disadvantageous and in the second place, the Chinese friends are occupied at home and cannot give them serious help. The thinking of Kim Il Sung amounts to waiting until the conclusion of the main [military] operations in China.

In the conversation on 13 September, Kim Il Sung, under the clear influence of Ho Ka-i (a Soviet Korean, secretary of the Central Committee of the Labor Party, who participated in the second conversation in order to translate), declared that the people will welcome an armed attack by the northerners and that if they begin military actions they will not lose politically because of this. Later in the course of the conversation, Kim Il Sung stated that if a civil war is drawn out, then they will be in a politically disadvantageous position. And since under present conditions it is impossible to count on a rapid victory, he does not propose to begin a civil war, but only to secure the Ongjin peninsula and a portion of the territory of South Korea to the east of this peninsula, for example to Kaidzio.

They consider that in case of a civil war the population of South Korea will be sympathetic toward the northern army and will help it. In the case of successful military actions, they hope to organize a number of uprisings in South Korea.

4. According to official data, there are 500 American military advisers and instructors in South Korea. According to secret service information, which needs confirmation, there are 900 American military advisers and instructors and 1500 soldiers and security officers in South Korea. In case of a civil war in Korea, the Americans, in the opinion of Kim Il Sung and Pak Hong-yong, can: send Japanese and Chinese [soldiers] to the aid of the southerners, support [the South Koreans] from the sea and air with their

own means; American instructors will take immediate part in organizing military actions.

5. The North Korean army numbers 97,500 men (including the air force and coastal defense units). The army has 64 tanks, 59 armored cars, 75 airplanes. The police force in the north numbers 23,200 men. Kim considers that the northern army is superior to the southern army in its technical equipment (tanks, artillery, planes), its discipline, the training of the officers and troops, and also in its moral-political relations.

In the northern army there are a number of insufficiencies: insufficient number and weak preparation of pilots, insufficient number of ships, large caliber arms are unprepared for military operations, insufficient military supplies.

The proposal of Kim Il Sung amounts to the following: at the beginning to strike the South Korean army on the Ongjin peninsula, to destroy the two regiments located there, to occupy the territory of the peninsula and the territory to the east of it, for example to Kaidzio, and then to see what to do further. After this blow the South Korean army may become demoralized. In this case, move further to the south. If the South Korean army is not demoralized as a result of the Ongjin operation, to seal the borders seized, to shorten in that way the line of defense approximately by one third.

It is not possible to hurry with the operation on the Ongjin peninsula. [It is necessary] to wait until additional arms arrive from the Soviet Union. Meanwhile [we must consolidate the defenses on the remaining] portions of the 38th parallel.

Kim Il Sung admits the possibility of the Ongjin operation turning into a civil war, but he hopes that this does not happen, since the southerners, in his opinion, do not dare to attack other portions of the 38th parallel.

Our formulations.

The partial operation outlined by Kim Il Sung can and will probably turn into a civil war between north and south. There are more than a few supporters of civil war in the leading circles of both the north and the south. Therefore, in beginning this partial operation it is necessary to calculate that it might be the beginning of a civil war. Is it advisable to the north to begin a civil war now? We propose that this is not advisable.

The northern army is insufficiently strong to carry out successful and rapid operations against the south. Even taking into account the help which will be rendered to the northern army by the partisans and the population of South Korea, it is impossible to count on a rapid victory. Moreover, a drawn out civil war is disadvantageous for the north both militarily and politically. In the first place, a drawn out war gives the possibility to the Americans to render corresponding aid to Syngmann Rhee. After their lack of success in China, the Americans probably will intervene in Korean affairs more decisively than they did in China and , it goes without saying, apply all their strength to save Syngmann Rhee. Further, in case of a drawn out civil war, the military casualties, suffering and adversity may elicit in the population a negative mood toward the one who began the war.

Moreover, a drawn out war in Korea could be used by the Americans for purposes of agitation against the Soviet Union and for further inflaming war hysteria. Therefore, it is inadvisable that the north begin a civil war now. Given the present internal and external situation a decision about an attack on the south would be correct only in such case as the northerners could count on ending the war quickly; the preconditions for it are not there.

But if the indicated partial operation were crowned with success and did not lead to civil war, then in this case the northerners, while having won strategically, would lose politically in many regards. Such an operation would be used to accuse the northerners of trying to inflame a fratricidal war. It would also be used for the purpose of further increasing American and international interference in Korean affairs in the interests of the south.

We propose that under the indicated conditions, to begin the partial operation conceived by Kim Il Sung is inadvisable.

[Source: AVP RF, Fond 059a, Opis 5a, Delo 3, Papka 11, Listy 46–53.]

DOCUMENT 5
Politburo Decision to Confirm the Following Directive to the Soviet Ambassador in Korea

24 September 1949

Copies to Malenkov, Molotov, Gromyko, Shtykov, Beria, Mikoyan, Kaganovich, Bulganin.

COMMISSION COMRADE SHTYKOV to meet with Kim Il Sung and Pak Hon-yong and, strictly adhering to the text given below, to declare the following:

In connection with the questions raised by you in conversation with me on 12 August of this year, I received an order to transmit to you the opinion of Moscow on the questions touched on by you. Your proposal to begin an attack by the Korean Peoples' Army on the south calls forth the necessity of giving a precise evaluation of the military as well as the political sides of this question.

From the military side it is impossible to consider that the Peoples' Army is prepared for such an attack. If not prepared for in the necessary manner, the attack can turn into a prolonged military operation, which not only will not lead to the defeat of the enemy, but will also create significant political and economic difficulties for North Korea, which, finally, cannot be permitted. Since at present North Korea does not have the necessary superiority of military forces in comparison with South Korea, it is impossible to acknowledge that a military attack on the south is now completely prepared for and therefore from the military point of view it is not allowed.

From the political side, a military attack on the south by you is also not prepared for. We, of course, agree with you that the people are waiting for the unification of the country and in the south they, moreover, are waiting for liberation from the yoke of the reactionary regime. However, until now very little has been done to raise the broad masses of South Korea to an active struggle, to develop the partisan movement in all of South Korea, to create there liberated regions and to organize forces for a general uprising. Meanwhile, only in conditions of a people's uprising which has begun and is truly developing, which is undermining the foundations of the reactionary regime, could a military attack on the south play a decisive role in the overthrow of the South Korean reactionaries and provide the realization of the task of the unification of all Korea into a single democratic state. Since at present very little has been done to develop the partisan movement and prepare for a general uprising in South Korea, it is also impossible to acknowledge that from a political side an attack by you on the south has been prepared.

As concerns a partial operation to seize Ongjin peninsula and the region of Kaesong, as a result of which the borders of North Korea would be moved almost to Seoul itself, it is impossible to view this operation other than as the beginning of a war between North and South Korea, for which North Korea is not prepared either militarily or politically, as has been indicated above.

Moreover, it is necessary to consider that if military actions begin at the initiative of the north and acquire a prolonged character, then this can give to the Americans cause for any kind of interference in Korean affairs.

In view of all that has been stated, it is necessary to acknowledge that at present the tasks of the struggle for the unification of Korea demand a concentration of maximum effort: in the first place, to the development of the partisan movement, the creation of liberated regions and the preparation of a general armed uprising in South Korea in order to overthrow the reactionary regime and successfully resolve the task of unifying all Korea; and secondly to further strengthen in every way the Peoples' Army of Korea.

[Source: AVP RF, Fond 059a, Opis 5a, Delo 3, Papka 11, Listy 75–77]

DOCUMENT 6
Ciphered Telegram from Shtykov to Vyshinsky

19 January 1950

STRICTLY SECRET. I report about the frame of mind expressed by Kim Il Sung during a luncheon at the Ministry of Foreign Affairs of the DPRK. On 17 January the minister of foreign affairs of the DPRK Pak Hon-yong held a lunch attended by a small circle of persons, on the occasion of the departure of the Korean ambassador Yi Chu-Yon to the Chinese People's Republic. At the luncheon, from the Korean side were Kim Tu-bong, Kim Il Sung, Pak Hon-yong, deputy minister of foreign affairs Pak Chong-jo, Yi Chu-Yon. The trade representative of the PRC Vyn Shi Chzhen attended the luncheon. On our side in attendance were myself and the advisers of the embassy Ignatiev and Pelishenko. The luncheon took place in a friendly, warm atmosphere. Kim Il Sung, Pak Hon-yong and also the Chinese trade representative in their toasts expressed a feeling of love and gratitude toward Comrade Stalin for the liberation [of Korea from Japanese rule] and for the selfless assistance to both the Korean and Chinese people.

Kim Tu-bong shared his impressions of his trip to the USSR for the seventieth birthday of Comrade Stalin. In his account, he repeatedly underscored the great interest of the Soviet people in Korea and the numerous wishes for quick unification of the country.

During the luncheon, Kim Il Sung and the Chinese trade representative, who was sitting next to him, many times enthusiastically conversed with each other in Chinese. From individual phrases it was possible to understand that they were speaking about the victory in China and about the situation in Korea. After the luncheon, in the reception room Kim Il Sung gave advice and orders to his ambassador to China Yi Chu-Yon about his work in China, and moreover, while speaking in Korean, Kim several times said phrases in Russian about how Yi would act boldly in China, since Mao Zedong is his friend and will always help Korea.

Then, after Yi Chu-Yon left, Kim, addressing the advisers Ignatiev and Pelishenko in an excited manner, began to speak about how now, when China is completing its liberation, the liberation of the Korean people in the south of the country is next in line. In connection with this he said:

"The people of the southern portion of Korea trust me and rely on our armed might. Partisans will not decide the question. The people of the south know that we have a good army. Lately I do not sleep at night, thinking about how to resolve the question of the unification of the whole country. If the matter of the liberation of the people of the southern portion of Korea and the unification of the country is drawn out, then I can lose the trust of the people of Korea." Further, Kim stated that when he was in Moscow, Comrade Stalin said to him that it was not necessary to attack the south. In case of an attack on the north of the country by the army of Rhee Syngmann, then it is possible to go on the counteroffensive to the south of Korea. But since Rhee Syngmann is still not instigating an attack, it means that the liberation of the people of the southern part of the country and the unification of the country are being drawn out. He (Kim Il Sung) thinks that he needs again to visit Comrade Stalin and receive an order and permission for offensive action by the Peoples' Army for the purpose of the liberation of the people of Southern Korea. Further, Kim said that he himself cannot begin an attack, because he is a communist, a disciplined person and for him the order of Comrade Stalin is law. Then he stated that if it is now possible to meet with Comrade Stalin, then he will try to meet with Mao Zedong, after his return from Moscow. Kim underscored that Mao Zedong promised to render him assistance after the conclusion of the war in China. (Apparently Kim Il Sung has in mind the conversation of his representative Kim Il with Mao Zedong in June 1949, about which I reported by ciphered telegram.) Kim said that he also has other questions for Mao Zedong, in particular the question of the possibility of the creation of an eastern bureau of the Cominform. He further stated that on all these questions he will try to meet with Comrade Shtykov and to secure through him a meeting with Comrade Stalin.

The advisers of the embassy Ignatiev and Pelishenko, avoiding discussing these questions, tried to switch the discussion to a general theme, then Kim Il Sung came toward me, took me aside and began the following conversation: can he meet with Comrade Stalin and discuss the question of the position in the south and the question of aggressive actions against the army of Rhee Syngmann, that their people's army now is significantly stronger than the army of Rhee Syngmann. Here he stated that if it is impossible to meet with Comrade Stalin, then he wants to meet with Mao Zedong, since Mao after his visit to Moscow will have orders on all questions.

Then Kim Il Sung placed before me the question, why don't I allow him to attack the Ongjin peninsula, which the People's Army could take in three days, and with a general attack the People's Army could be in Seoul in several days.

I answered Kim that he has not raised the question of a meeting with Comrade Stalin and if he raises such a question, then it is possible that Comrade Stalin will receive him. On the question of an attack on the Ongjin peninsula, I answered him that it is impossible to do this. Then I tried to conclude the conversation on these questions and, alluding to a later time, proposed to go home. With that the conversation was concluded.

After the luncheon Kim Il Sung was in a mood of some intoxication. It was obvious that he began this conversation not accidentally, but had thought it out earlier, with the goal of laying out his frame of mind and elucidating our attitude to these questions.

In the process of this conversation Kim Il Sung repeatedly underscored his wish to get the advice of Comrade Stalin on the question of the situation in the south of Korea, since [Kim Il Sung] is constantly nurturing his idea about an attack.

[Source: AVP RF, Fond 059a, Opis 5a, Delo 3, Papka 11, Listy 87–91.]

DOCUMENT 7
Ciphered Telegram from Stalin to Shtykov

30 January 1950

1. I received your report. I understand the dissatisfaction of Comrade Kim Il Sung, but he must understand that such a large matter in regard to South Korea such as he wants to undertake needs large preparation. The

matter must be organized so that there would not be too great a risk. If he wants to discuss this matter with me, then I will always be ready to receive him and discuss with him. Transmit all this to Kim Il Sung and tell him that I am ready to help him in this matter.

2.   I have a request for Comrade Kim Il Sung. The Soviet Union is experiencing a great insufficiency in lead. We would like to receive from Korea a yearly minimum of 25,000 tons of lead. Korea would render us a great assistance if it could yearly send to the Soviet Union the indicated amount of lead. I hope that Kim Il Sung will not refuse us in this. It is possible that Kim Il Sung needs our technical assistance and some number of Soviet specialists. We are ready to render this assistance. Transmit this request of mine to comrade Kim Il Sung and ask him for me, to communicate to me his consideration on this matter.

[Source: AVP RF, Fond 059a, Opis 5a, Delo 3, Papka 11, Listy 92.]

DOCUMENT 8

Information About the Soviet Union's Involvement in the Korean War

August 1966

The first decisive evidence of the respective roles of North Korea (the Democratic People's Republic of Korea or DPRK), the Soviet Union, and China was made public in a "Top Secret" document released by the post-Soviet Russian government in 1993. The document itself was written in August 1966 by staff of the Soviet Foreign Ministry to provide background information for Soviet officials, who were at that time discussing possible Soviet military aid to North Vietnam in its war with the United States.

(As originally quoted in Wilson, *Working Paper No. 8* (November 1993), the document is described as "a highly classified internal history of the Korean War," but does not mention the actual classification nor the names of the top Soviet leaders who received copies. It is also quoted in Issue 3 of the *Bulletin,* which gives the classification as "Top Secret," the date of distribution (9 August 1966) and the names of the recipients.

Copies of the document were sent, among others, to the ruling Party's general secretary, Leonid Brezhnev; the Soviet premier, Aleksei Kosygin; and to the foreign minister, Andrei Gromyko. The key passages were these:

CALCULATING THAT THE United States would not enter a war over South Korea, Kim Il Sung persistently pressed for agreement from Stalin and Mao Tse-tung to reunify the country by military means. . . .

Stalin at first treated the persistent appeals of Kim Il Sung with reserve, noting that "such a large affair in relation to South Korea . . . needs much preparation," but he did not object in principle. The final agreement to support the plans of the Koreans was given by Stalin at the time of Kim Il Sung's visit to Moscow in March–April 1950. Following this, in May, Kim Il Sung visited Beijing and secured the support of Mao.

. . .

At Stalin's order, all requests of the North Koreans for delivery of arms and equipment for the formation of additional units of the KPA [Korean People's Army] were quickly met. The Chinese leadership sent to Korea a division formed from Koreans who had been serving in the Chinese army, and poised to send food aid and to transfer one army closer to Korea "in case the Japanese enter on the side of South Korea."

. . .

By the time of the attack [at 0400 25 June, 1950], the North Korean armed forces had significant superiority over the South Koreans. The correlation of forces between South and North Korea was as follows: in number of troops 1:2; number of guns 1:2; machine guns 1:7; sub-machine guns 1:13; tanks 1:6.5; planes 1:6.

> The document goes on to say that the North Korean plan envisaged
> completion of the campaign within twenty to twenty-seven days.

APPENDIX F

DOCUMENTS FOR CHAPTER 17

All Appendixes extracted from CWIHP Working Paper 5 (May 1993)

———————✦———————

DOCUMENT I
Meeting of Khrushchev and Ulbricht

30 November 1960
Extracts from Record of Meeting of Comrade N. S. Khrushchev with
Comrade W. Ulbricht, 30 November 1960.
Russian Ministry of Foreign Affairs Archives.
Fond 0742, Opis 6, Por 4, Papka 43.
Secret

WEST BERLIN HAS strengthened economically. This is seen in the fact
that about 50,000 workers from East Berlin are now still working in West
Berlin. Thus, a part of the qualified working force goes to work in West
Berlin, since there are higher salaries there. We still have not taken corresponding countermeasures. The situation with the intelligentsia is also not favorable. For example, teachers in the West earn 200–300 marks more than in the
East. Doctors also earn two times more there. In addition, by leaving for West
Germany they receive large one-time grants there. All of these circumstances
exert influence on the less politically conscious part of the intelligentsia. Why
don't we raise our salaries for this category of people? First of all, we don't
have the means. Second, even if we raised their salary, we could not satisfy
their purchasing power with the goods that we have, and they would buy
things with that money in West Berlin. But still, we will try to do this. In addition, a group of children from East Berlin study in schools in West Berlin. We
have a law against this, but we have not yet implemented it, since we didn't
want to provoke conflicts.

Comrade Khrushchev said that we must aim for a summit conference in

1961 to discuss the question of a peace treaty with Germany and also to try to find a resolution of the West Berlin problem. We must force Adenauer, who has fallen into a blind all[e?]y, to change his position. You know, Adenauer hasn't achieved anything. He promised that he would achieve reunification by arming West Germany, that with the help of the four powers he would succeed in absorbing the GDR, but none of this has happened. So, we must force Adenauer to accept peaceful coexistence. At the same time, this is our method of pressure on the SPD. Now [the SPD official] Herbert and [West Berlin Mayor and SPD candidate for chancellor in 1961 Willi] Brandt are more right-wing than Adenauer and speak out against a peace treaty and against a trade agreement with the GDR. If they persuade Adenauer to change his position, then Brandt also will be forced to maneuver.

Let us make up our mind that a certain amount of metal will be allotted for the GDR and our Gosplan [State Planning Commission] will not have the right to touch it. We have only 5 million tons of steel which are over and above the increase in production. We must give the GDR as much metal as it needs. We cannot be blind money-counters and every time construct our trade around whether to give or not to give them 1,000 tons more. Malenkov and Beria wanted to liquidate the GDR, but we fired one and shot the other and said that we supported a socialist Germany. We must create a special group in our Gosplan with [GDR Economics Minister Bruno] Leuschner, which will receive everything needed on his demand. There is no other way. The GDR must develop and maintain the increase in standard of living of its populace. Let us look at what you need in individual categories. We have a plan and everything produced above the plan no longer belongs to Gosplan. But you will not encroach on our gold. Why give you gold? If you need cocoa, coffee, rubber, then buy them in Ceylon or Indonesia. Build something there. But free us from this and don't thrust your hands into our pockets.

W. Ulbricht. But how will we pay then?

N. S. Khrushchev. You will pay the comrades as we do. We just sold Indonesia naval vessels on credit, but for rubber. Sell your goods to the new African countries, and for this they will give you cocoa and coffee. By old habit, you try to do everything through us. You should have learned how to walk on your own two feet, instead of leaning on us all the time.

I say all of this so that we have good prospects if we use our resources intelligently. Of course, we also have our own needs, but we must understand that the GDR's needs are also our needs. We can't permit it that they come to us in such a state that either they sink or we throw them a rope. Let's stop playing games about this question. You can't run an economy this way.

The second question is about the coordination of the economy. For example, the Germans want chemical products very much, but they have few raw materials for this. For chloride you need salt and electro-energy. The Germans don't have coal and not enough energy. In our country in Siberia, coal costs six rubles a ton. We also have this there and salt and electro-energy. Let's do this: We will make chloride and present it to you. We chatter a lot about coordination and economic ties, but we do little. The Germans try to grab something for themselves, and so do we. With this we only hurt ourselves. They will never be able to compete with us in chloride or brown coal. Let us create joint enterprises on our territory. It is true that when we proposed similar things to Poland or China, they were against it. But we aren't China; we are not afraid of giving the Germans a start. Let us do it such that there are your shares and our shares. We will divide the product; this is advantageous.

W. Ulbricht. Let us at first make some comments on the question of the peace treaty. What you have said satisfied us very much. If we have enough strength to conclude a peace treaty after the upcoming [Vienna, June 1961 Khrushchev-Kennedy] summit, but before [the 17 September] West German elections, then this would be a defeat for Adenauer.

N. S. Khrushchev. This would mean publicly carving up Adenauer and [SPD Chairman Erich] Olenhauer.

W. Ulbricht. The result would be that after the elections Adenauer would have to form a coalition with Brandt. This would be favorable to us, since we could isolate the right-wing leadership of the SPD. But in the event that Adenauer is dealt this political blow, Brandt will maneuver, since he won't want to share the defeat with Adenauer. Then a struggle will unfold in West Germany.

If we succeed in concluding a peace treaty, then we are in full agreement with this. If we don't succeed in concluding a peace treaty, and we return to propaganda for a peace treaty, then we will discredit our policy and we will be able to recover our prestige only after one to two years. We cannot act the same [way we did] in 1960.

N. S. Khrushchev. Now that Kennedy has come to power, we no longer have an interim agreement with them on this question, but we will not conclude a peace treaty. This means that if we do not do this, then our proposal will be rejected. They will say about us: they jabber, but they are afraid. We do not have a way out. It will be very good if we succeed in achieving a temporary agreement. But maybe they will not want a temporary agreement.

Then we will sign a peace treaty with the GDR, and they will end up moving towards aggression, toward the "cold war." They will not remove their forces from West Berlin if we do not make the corresponding agreement. But we will not bring in our forces so that they will remove theirs. We will work out with you a tactic of gradual ousting of the Western powers from West Berlin, but without war. For this we will use the levers in the hands of the GDR.

W. Ulbricht. Good. Now onto economic questions. Our domestic situation is not a pretty one now. In 1960 supplies for the population were worse than in 1959. But our political situation is strong.

N. S. Khrushchev. We understand this well. For the Chinese the moral factor seems to decide everything. But our people also make demands for butter and other things.

W. Ulbricht. Here is the issue that worries us: If we proceed from the negotiations that your representative conducted with us, there will be a reduction of our planned figures. According to the figures adopted by you, we would have had a yearly growth in production of 6–7 percent. But with this growth we can't exist, we can't increase salaries for teachers and other categories of people. To maintain a normal situation we need a yearly growth of no less than 10 percent. Otherwise we will not provide the necessities. If I cannot pay a worker in Berlin a higher salary, he will go to West Berlin. This is the situation. We must improve the position of doctors and the intelligentsia and some workers, since the situation in West Germany is improving faster. In 1961 they already will have implemented a forty-hour working week, they will raise salaries, and we can't even think about this. Discrepancies have grown up between us. We cannot achieve our goals with the help of just propaganda. We can pass a beautiful law about work, but if we don't give answers to concrete questions with this, people will ask us questions. We cannot permit the discrepancies between us and West Germany to keep growing. We must examine this in developing our plans. Thus, a yearly growth must be provided in the plan, even if 9 percent.

N. S. Khrushchev. What concrete requests do you have for us?

W. Ulbricht. Fulfilling the figures of our plan depends on supplies of your materials. We are now impeding socialist competition, since there aren't enough raw materials.

N. S. Khrushchev. We must discuss all these proposals concretely with Leuschner.

DOCUMENT 2
Letter from Ulbricht to Khrushchev

18 January 1961
SED Archives, Berlin. IfGA, ZPA, J IV 2/202/129

SINCE IN 1961 a temporary compromise at least must be reached between the Soviet Union and the Western powers on the peaceful resolution of the German problem and the West Berlin issue, <u>a campaign is necessary in the entire world on the necessity of eliminating the remnants of the war in Germany and especially the abnormal situation in West Berlin.</u>

We assume that <u>a relationship of peaceful coexistence between West Berlin and the GDR</u> will be established. The GDR has no intention of interfering in the internal affairs of West Berlin. On the other hand, it expects that the Western powers and the Bonn government will stop using West Berlin for warmongering and revanchist policy.

We propose that the GDR government appeal to all countries of the anti-Hitler coalition and make its stand on the issue of eliminating the remnants of the war, the drawing up of a peace treaty, and a peaceful resolution of the West Berlin issue.

The Moscow Declaration of Communist and Workers' Parties again came out in support of the transformation of West Berlin into a demilitarized free city as the best possible resolution of the West Berlin issue.

Since all of Berlin lies on GDR territory, state membership of West Berlin to West Germany cannot be recognized in any way and from now on must be eliminated from every statement.

Under the condition that in West Berlin, the West Berlin population decides for itself and that no foreign states, also not the Bonn government, have influence on its internal development, we are prepared to abstain from any interference in West Berlin and to guarantee ties West Berlin will have with other countries.

The GDR government is prepared to regulate by treaty with West Berlin all necessary issues which the West Berlin Senate wants to regulate.

If the West Berlin Senate makes proposals which designate a representative for economic issues in the free city of West Berlin for the regulation of economic issues for both the GDR government and the Bonn government, we could accept this.

<u>We propose the consultation of a party and governmental delegation of the USSR and GDR in April 1961 with the goal of raising the authority of the GDR in future negotiations.</u>

We propose that the oral agreement made in November in Moscow and the agreements to be reached in connection with the preparation of the trade treaty for 1961 and the economic plans for 1961 through 1965 be signed in the form of a joint declaration at the proposed consultations of the party and governmental delegations. It must be emphasized that in connection with the four power negotiations on the preparation of a peace treaty and the peaceful resolution of the West Berlin question, economic blackmail against the GDR will have no chance of success. The aid which the Soviet Union guaranteed the GDR must be reported publicly.

Until now, most of the Warsaw Pact states have considered the peaceful resolution of the German and West Berlin questions as a matter which only involves the Soviet Union and the GDR. Although they report in the press about these problems, they basically feel uninvolved in this matter. Thus, we propose that after the consultation of the USSR and GDR party and governmental delegations, a meeting of the Political Consultative Council of Warsaw Pact states take place.

What ideas do we have of a compromise that should be achieved before the West German Bundestag elections?

The statement of the Bonn government that it would carry out the struggle against the GDR mainly by economic means and through an intensification of the cold war forces us to execute a change in the design of our Seven-Year Plan. On the basis of the consultations in November, it is necessary to carry out special measures in 1961 and 1962 to make the GDR economy as much as possible independent from disruptive measures by West Germany. We ask your opinion on our view that the following things are the most important in the GDR in 1961:

1. Making the GDR economy independent to a significant degree from West Germany with regard to the supply of crucial materials.
2. Achieving a stabilization which enables continuous production in the factories.
3. Reducing debts to the capitalist countries so that we will not have a situation as in 1960 where the GDR was not capable of paying for a time. This means that it is necessary to increase the GDR's foreign trade with the Soviet Union and the socialist countries.

The main contents of the November consultations last year was to make joint commitments for a close tie of the GDR economy with the Soviet Union, so as to achieve stability in the GDR economy and to make our economy independent from the disruptive actions of the West Germans imperialistic and militaristic circles.

Thus, the task of the delegation under the direction of Comrade Bruno Leuschner, which will come to Moscow in the next days, is to agree on the basis of the November meeting how the merging of the GDR economy with the Soviet Union should occur in the next two years and how this should be expressed in the trade treaty.

We are aware that we cannot entirely fulfill the key economic goals in 1961. The Politburo views the situation in the following way. First the development of the GDR economy must be made stable and the greatest possible guarantees must be made against disturbances in the socialist construction of the GDR by the imperialist forces in West Germany. This is a basic condition for the successful resolution of our main economic goals.

At the consultations in Moscow, you drew it to our attention that even with a resumption of the trade treaty between West Germany and the GDR, we will only have a breathing space. After the trade treaty with West Germany is again in force, we intend to use this trade economically. With this, we take into account that the Bonn government, just when we decisively demand the elimination of the remnants of the war, will create difficulties for us with the denial of the supply of certain crucial materials through a selective embargo. Thus, we will strengthen the campaign to secure the GDR economy through our own production from the disruptive actions of West German militarists and to gradually bring about interconnection with the USSR economy.

The projected GDR economic plan for 1961 foresees an increase in industrial production of about 7 percent. The Seven-Year Plan foresaw more than 9 percent. Just by this growth in production with which we will remain even farther behind West Germany, we cannot even out the balance of payments of foreign trade for 1961. The delegation led by Comrade Leuschner must clarify the following issues with our Soviet friends:

1. How can we actually supply crucial materials (sheet steel, pipes, etc.) that we ourselves cannot produce and that we should not obtain from West Germany in the interest of gradually making ourselves independent?

2. Which metallurgical equipment can the Soviet Union supply to the GDR, or the supply of which metallurgical equipment through the GDR can the Soviet Union forego, so that the production of sheet materials and special steels can be increased in the GDR? This is additionally necessary, since the small amount of certain special steels will not be able to be obtained from the Soviet Union, in the future, since this is very complicated. In addition, the supply of construction machines was discussed, but was not exactly agreed upon. This question is important both for the building industry and for the reconstruction of the city center.

3. Although we have already reduced the increase in industrial production to 7 percent, we cannot equalize the balance of payments in foreign trade for 1961. We have a deficit in the balance of payments of about 1.35 million hard currency marks, of which more than 800 million hard currency marks are to the USSR and more than 500 million hard currency marks are to the capitalist countries. We are not in the position to pay for the promised imports from the USSR entirely with exports. Thus, we request crediting the account vis-à-vis the Soviet Union, which is about 170 million rubles (800 million hard currency marks), whereby this credit can be repaid beginning in 1966.

In the Politburo we have examined again in as serious and comprehensive a manner as possible all sides of this issue and related issues.

If it is not possible to give us this credit, then we cannot maintain the standard of living of the population at the level of 1960. We would enter into such a serious situation in supplies and production that we would be faced with serious crisis manifestations, since we would then have to reduce imports of steel, non-ferrous metal, textile raw materials and food, and in addition export goods, which are absolutely necessary for supplying the population and for making important investments.

It is unpleasant for us that every year we must direct such requests for help to the CPSU CC Presidium. We will justifiably ask: What are the causes for this, and how must things continue until 1965? We came to agreement on the most important control figures for 1966–1980, but the questions of the economic foundation in 1961–1965 for the fulfillment of these future tasks require more clarification and agreement.

In order to resolve the basic problems of the GDR and to catch up with West Germany, we must invest more in the GDR for several years and must bring about a close economic association, a merger with the USSR economy. There is no other way.

We are a state that was created without having and still does not have a raw material base and that carries out the competition between both systems with open borders.

A reason for the difficulties lies of course in the fact that we, as the workers' and peasants' state for all of Germany, must bear the weight that resulted from the crimes and devastation of Hitler's Germany. In addition, the production apparatus in the eastern part of Germany was more heavily destroyed than in West Germany. While in the first ten postwar years we paid reparations by the withdrawal of existing plants and from current production, West Germany made no compensation from current production, and instead, received in addition large credits from the United States to save the monopoly capital system and German militarism. We devoted many resources in the first ten years to bring the production on line in Wismut [an East German-Soviet joint industrial enterprise] and to sustain it. Of course, this was all necessary to reduce at least a portion of the destruction which the Soviet Union had suffered and to strengthen the Soviet Union as the center of the socialist camp. These circumstances, however, brought us enormous difficulties in the competition with West Germany. West Germany could make large investments and achieve an extraordinary modernization of the production apparatus at a very early point on the basis of the millions of aid from the United States. Until the pardoning of reparations in 1954, the per-capital investment in West Germany was double as high as in the GDR. In the years 1950–1959 taken together, the per-capita investment in West Germany reached 7,400DM, while the economic strength of the GDR enabled per capita investment of only 4,650DM. With this we had a strong investment capability only from 1956 on, i.e., we had a significantly later starting point for the modernization of our production capacity than West Germany. Corresponding to our total population, we needed to have 50 billion marks more invested in comparison with West Germany.

This is the main reason that we have remained so far behind West Germany in work productivity and standard of living. Due to this, a constant political pressure from West Germany could be exercised over us. The booming economy in West Germany, which is visible to every citizen of the GDR, is the main reason that in over ten years about two million people have left our Republic.

We thank you very much for your efforts and help.

With communist greetings,
the first secretary of the SED CC
W. Ulbricht

DOCUMENT 3
Letter from Khrushchev to Ulbricht

30 January 1961
SED Archives, IfGA, ZPA, J IV 2/202/129
German unofficial translation of letter from Khrushchev to Ulbricht, 30 January 1961.

DEAR COMRADE ULBRICHT!

The CPSU CC has discussed carefully your letter from 19 January 1961, and expresses its agreement with the considerations regarding the measures which should be carried out in connection with the elimination of the remains of the war and the normalization of the situation in West Berlin. In the exchange of opinions with you in November of last year in Moscow, we fixed our measures in this direction; we are undertaking at this time the steps, which you know about, through diplomatic channels.

We, of course, agree with you that the questions of the elimination of the remains of the war and the occupation regime in West Berlin must be resolved on the basis of a peace treaty with both German states, and if this cannot be achieved, on the basis of a peace treaty with the GDR. In such a case, it would be understandable to the people of the entire world, including also the German people, that the Soviet Union, the GDR and the other socialist countries are striving for the strengthening of peace and a peaceful resolution of the German question, since they are submitting the proposal on the conclusion of a peace treaty with Germany. The Soviet Union, the GDR and the other socialist countries are striving to preserve peace and to resolve peacefully the German question. Therefore it is desirable that the measures dealt with in your letter, which under certain circumstances will prove necessary, be coupled with the conclusion of a peace treaty. If we don't succeed in coming to an understanding with Kennedy, we will, as agreed, choose together with you the time for their implementation.

Of course, we share completely the view expressed by you about measures in the area of the economic stabilization of the GDR and the broadening of economic cooperation between the GDR and the USSR. Concrete proposals on this question will be discussed now together with the GDR delegation led by Comrade Leuschner. We have instructed our delegation to let themselves be guided in these negotiations by the principled agreement between us in November of last year.

We support your proposal about a meeting of a party and governmental delegation of the USSR and GDR and would be glad to welcome a GDR delegation for the discussion of questions of interest to both sides. The time of this meeting can be settled later. The results of our exchange of opinion could be summarized in a joint declaration. We are in agreement that during this meeting we will discuss your proposal about the convening of the Political Consultative Committee of the Warsaw Treaty for the discussion of the question of the conclusion of a peace treaty with Germany.

With communist greetings,

N. Khrushchev

January 30, 1961

APPENDIX G

DOCUMENT FOR CHAPTER 18

DOCUMENT I
Politburo Meeting, October 1956

CWIHP Bulletin 5 (Spring 95)
Protocol No. 129
Meeting of the Politburo on 19, 20, and 21 October 1956

THE POLITBURO AGREES to the following press communiqué:

On 19 October at 10:00 A.M., the proceedings of the Eighth Plenum began. After the meeting was opened by comrade Ochab, and the agenda accepted, comrades Wladyslaw Gomulka, Marian Spychalski, Zenon Kliszko, and Loga-Sowinski were added to the Central Committee so that they could take part in the discussions as fully fledged members.

Comrade Wieslaw [Wladyslaw Gomulka's wartime pseudonym] informed the Politburo about the meeting at the airport with the Soviet delegation:

Talks like this I have never held with party comrades. It was beyond comprehension. How can you take such a tone and, with such epitaphs, turn on people who in good faith turned to you? Khrushchev first greeted, above all, comrade Rokossowki and the generals; underlining—"These are people on whom I depend." Turning to us, he said [in Russian], "The treacherous activity of Comrade Ochab has become evident, this number won't pass here!" You needed a lot of patience not to react to such talk. The entire discussion was carried out in this loud tone, such that everyone at the airport, even the chauffeurs, heard it.

I proposed that we drive with them to Belvedere Palace and speak calmly. I told them that above all else we had to open the Plenum. They would not agree to this. At Belvedere Palace the talks had a similar tone. They told us that we actually spat in their faces because we did not agree to meet with the delegation before the Plenum. They are upset with us because the Politburo Commission proposed a new list of members to the Politburo without a number of comrades who are supporters of a Polish-Soviet union—names, comrades Rokossowski, [Zenon] Nowak, Mazur, Jozwiak. I explained to them that we don't have such tendencies. We do not want to break the alliance with the Soviet Union. It came to a clash. Comrade Khrushchev said [in Russian], "That number won't pass here. We are ready for active intervention."

[Here Gomulka quotes his own remarks to Khrushchev:] I understand that it is possible to talk in an aggressive tone, but if you talk with a revolver on the table you don't have an even-handed discussion. I cannot continue the discussions under these conditions. I am ill and I cannot fill such a function in my condition. We can listen to the complaints of the Soviet comrades, but if decisions are to be made under the threat of physical force, I am not up to it. My first step in Party work, which I am taking after a long break, must be interrupted.

I don't want to break off Polish-Soviet friendship. I believe what we propose will strengthen the friendship. Any other form of resolution to these affairs will only strengthen the anti-Soviet campaign. I would like for the comrades to voice their views on this matter: intervention or the conditions under which to continue the talks.

Comrade Zawadzki: Comrade Wieslaw's position is correct. We do not see our situation, including the personnel decision taken by the Politburo, as a menacing upheaval in the country leading to a break in Polish-Soviet relations. Yet the decision not to change the position of the Politburo has to be taken with certain cautions in order not to intensify the situation. I also propose, in connection with the situation in Warsaw, to issue an appeal, signed by the Politburo and comrade Wieslaw, to the Enterprise Council, to students, about the arrival of the Soviet delegation in the common interest of the state and nation.

Comrade Zambrowski: The situation in the country is tense. I am on the side of what was said by comrade Wieslaw. Do not make any changes in the Politburo's propositions. I am opposed to the issuing of an appeal. Let the Plenum decide.

Comrade Rokossowski: Comrade Wieslaw gave us an objective assessment, but you can see that there are reasons why the Soviet comrades talk like this and why comrade Khrushchev vehemently exploded. I am of the opinion that four comrades should go to the discussions and listen to the arguments of the Soviet comrades. More cold-bloodedness. It is unnecessary to aggravate the situation.

[Source: AAN, KC PZPR, paczka 12, teczka 46a, str. 66–68]

THE LONG-AWAITED Eighth Plenum began at 10 A.M. Ochab opened the gathering with a brief statement and added, "I shall limit myself in this introduction to a report on the latest decisions of the Politburo."

Ochab appealed to the Plenum for "responsibility and wisdom" and declared, "We are meeting here in a difficult political situation." He told the delegates, "I would also like to inform you, Comrades, that a delegation of the Presidium of the Central Committee of the CPSU, composed of Comrades Khrushchev, Kaganovich, Mikoyan, and Molotov, arrived in Warsaw this morning. The delegation wishes to conduct talks with our politburo." Ochab suggested that the Plenum accept Gomulka and his colleagues in the Central Committee and that the proceedings be delayed until 6 P.M.

The Plenum unanimously accepted Ochab's proposition. The old Politburo and Gomulka were also empowered to conduct talks with the CPSU delegation. The debate barely lasted half an hour before the Plenum was adjourned. The Polish delegation returned to the Belvedere Palace to meet again with the Soviets.

While the Eighth Plenum met to debate Gomulka's return to the Central Committee, Khrushchev held a meeting with his generals at the Soviet embassy. The CPSU First Secretary stated in his memoirs, "Marshal Konev and I held separate consultations with Comrade Rokossowski, who was more obedient to us, but had less authority than the other Polish leaders. He told us that anti-Soviet, nationalistic, and reactionary forces were growing in strength, and that if it were necessary to arrest the growth of these counter-revolutionary elements by force of arms, he was at our disposal; we could rely on him to do whatever was necessary to preserve Poland's socialist gains and to assure Poland's continuing fidelity and friendship. That was all very well and good, but as we began to analyze the problem in more details and calculate which Polish regiments we could count on to obey Rokossowski, the situation began to look somewhat bleak. Of course, our own armed strength far exceeded that of Poland, but we didn't want to resort to the use of our own troops."

After the first Soviet encounter with Gomulka, Khrushchev must have been reassured that the newly proposed PUWP First Secretary was not hostile to the Soviet Union. Khrushchev used the occasion to gauge Gomulka's views on variety of matters. As he later put it, "Our embassy informed us that a genuine revolt was on the verge of breaking out in Warsaw. For the most part these demonstrations were being organized in support of the new leadership headed by Gomulka, which we too were prepared to support, but the demonstrations also had a dangerously anti-Soviet character." The Soviet leader added that Gomulka held "a position which was most advantageous for us. Here was a man who had come to power on the crest of an anti-Soviet wave, yet who could now speak forcefully about the need to preserve Poland's friendly relations with the Soviet Union and the Soviet Communist Party."

Ochab confirmed that Khrushchev manifested a sympathetic attitude toward Gomulka: "Basically our Soviet friends wanted to make Gomulka First Secretary." He continued, "At one point Khrushchev said to [Gomulka], we bring you greetings. Presumably they thought Gomulka would put the country in order and was the one to stake their bets on. . . . But Gomulka . . . displayed considerable toughness of character during those difficult talks."

The turning point came when "Gomulka made an anxious but sincere declaration," as Khrushchev characterized it. The CPSU First Secretary added that Gomulka acknowledged, "Poland needs friendship with the Soviet Union more than the Soviet Union needs friendship with Poland. Can it be that we failed to understand our situation? Without the Soviet Union we cannot maintain our borders with the West. We are dealing with our internal problems, our relations with the Soviet Union will remain unchanged. We will still be friends and allies." According to Khrushchev, Gomulka "said all this with such intensity and such sincerity that I believed his words. . . . I said to our delegation, 'I think there is no reason not to believe comrade Gomulka.'" The Soviet leader added, "We believed him when he said he realized we faced a common enemy, Western imperialism . . . We took his words as a promissory note from a man whose good faith we believed in."

The next contentious point concerned Rokossowski's exclusion from the new Politburo. Gomulka continued to call for Rokossowski's return to the Soviet Union. The Soviets continued to press Gomulka on the Rokossowski issue, but the Poles would not budge. Khrushchev later argued, "The people of Warsaw had been prepared to defend themselves and resist Soviet troops entering the city. . . . A clash would have been good for no one but our enemies. It would be a fatal conflict, with grave consequences that would have been felt for many years to come." He added, "With Poland in particular, I always tried to be sympathetic of flare-ups of anti-Soviet sentiment. Sympathetic in the sense that you have to remember history and that czarist Russia was a party to Poland's being carved up among the Germans, the Austrians, and the Russians. That left its stamp on the Polish soul."

APPENDIX H

DOCUMENTS FOR CHAPTER 19

DOCUMENT I
Telegram from Andropov

3 May 1956
Hoover Archives
Proletarians of all countries, unite!
STRICTLY SECRET
Communist Party of the Soviet Union. CENTRAL COMMITTEE
No. P13/XXIII

TO COMRADES SUSLOV, MOLOTOV (Ministry of Foreign Affairs)
    Extract from Minutes No. 13 of the Session of the Presidium of the Central Committee on 3 May 1956

TELEGRAM OF COMRADE Andropov from Budapest of 29 April 1956
Nos. 316–319
    Instruct comrade Suslov to discuss with the USSR ambassador to Hungary, comrade Andropov, the matter set out in his telegram Nos. 316–319 of 29 April 1956, in line with the exchange of opinions which took place at the session of the CC Presidium.
    CC SECRETARY
[printed sideways in the left-hand margin:]
    To be returned no later than within a 7-day period to the First Sector of the General Department of the CC CPSU.
    Strictly secret
    Ciphertelegram

MAKING COPIES IS FORBIDDEN

Copy No. 1 MARKING-OUT
Copy No. 2 comrade Bulganin
Copy No. 3 comrade Voroshilov
Copy No. 4 comrade Kaganovich
Copy No. 5 comrade Kirichenko
Copy No. 6 comrade Malenkov
Copy No. 7 comrade Mikoyan
Copy No. 8 comrade Molotov
Copy No. 9 comrade Pervukhin
Copy No. 10 comrade Saburov
Copy No. 11 comrade Suslov
Copy No. 12 comrade Khrushchev
Copy No. 13 comrade Khrushchev [sic!]
Copy No. 14 comrade Brezhnev
Copy No. 15 comrade Zhukov
Copy No. 16 comrade Mukhitdinov
Copy No. 17 comrade Furtseva
Copy No. 18 comrade Shvernik
Copy No. 19 comrade Shepilov
Copy No. 20 comrade Aristov
Copy No. 21 comrade Belyayev
Copy No. 22 comrade Pospelov
Copy No. 23 comrade Gromyko
Copy No. 24 comrade Kuznetsov
Copy No. 25 comrade Semenov
Copy No. 26 comrade Fedorenko
Copy No. 27 comrade Ilichev
Copy No. 28 comrade Kozyrev
Copy No. 29 comrade Kostylev
Copy No. 30 comrade Tsarapkin
Copy No. 31 comrade Ponomarev
Copy No. 32 comrade Copy
Copy No. 33 comrade Department 10
Copy No. 34 comrade For filing
Copy No. 35–42   comrade . . . [blank]

FROM BUDAPEST No. 16595   16596 16597 16598

14 hours 00 minutes   30 IV 1956   copy No.

Special No. 316–319

[Printed sideways in the left-hand margin:]

The telegram is to be returned to the Tenth Department of the USSR Ministry of Foreign Affairs on the expiration of forty-eight hours from the moment of receipt.

<u>Comrades Rakosi and Hegedus, each of them separately, informed me that the Politburo had recently discussed some further measures to carry out the decisions of the Twentieth Congress of the CPSU on the conditions prevailing in Hungary.</u>

<u>The Politburo affirmed that a further improvement of the situation inside the Hungarian Workers' Party had recently come into being.</u> The measures taken by the Politburo to elucidate the decisions of the Twentieth Congress of the Party, and especially the question of the cult of personality, have produced their positive results and contributed to a strengthening of discipline in the Party. Labor discipline among the workers has risen significantly.

At the same time the Politburo considers that, as a result of demagogy and provocation, the right opportunists and hostile elements have succeeded in instilling in some of the workers the idea that the leadership of the HWP [Hungarian Workers' Party] as presently constituted cannot properly guarantee the implementation in Hungary of the decisions of the Twentieth Congress of the CPSU because of the fact that some of the old members of the Politburo are supposedly putting up some resistance to these decisions, whilst the young comrades cannot carry out this work as a consequence of their inexperience. The aforementioned idea is seriously hampering the authority of the Politburo in the eyes of the Party activists and of a certain number of the workers.

As a result of this, the Politburo regards it as one of its top priority tasks, by elucidating its policy line and also by carrying out a number of practical measures to dispel these incorrect ideas, and to prove by [its] deeds to the Party masses and all the working people that the Politburo will continue to spearhead the Party's expansion of bold criticism of shortcomings in its work and aim to achieve an improvement in the activities of all levels of the Party and state leadership, strengthening and developing internal Party democracy. It is envisaged that in the very near future comrade Rakosi will give a speech at a meeting of the Budapest Party activists at which he will provide a wide-ranging elucidation of these matters. <u>Speaking about his forthcoming speech,</u>

comrade Rakosi said that he intends to dwell particularly on the question of the rehabilitation of people who were incorrectly [not *unjustly*—Trans.] repressed by the organs of state security and at the same time stress that it is in the first instance the Hungarian leadership which bears the responsibility for the mistakes permitted in this area.

Comrade Rakosi said that it is essential to do this because hostile elements, taking advantage of some unfortunate speeches by individual Hungarian comrades, have been provocatively attempting of late to place all the responsibility for the distortions in punitive policies in Hungary on the CPSU and its leadership. It is also intended to utilize the discussion of the directives on drawing up the new five-year plan for a wide-ranging explanation of the policies of the HWP.

Together with the proposals for these measures, the question of replenishing the membership of the Politburo was discussed. After lengthy discussions a decision was taken to bring Revai and Kadar into the membership of the Politburo. Informing me of this, comrade Rakosi and especially comrade Hegedus voiced a multitude of reservations, which make it clear that they are far from confident that the aforesaid decision is correct. Thus, for example, concerning the candidature of comrade Revai, comrade Rakosi said that Revai seemed to him to be unacceptable both because he is a worker [*rabotnik*] of non-Hungarian nationality and because he is a sick, unbalanced person with a pronounced proclivity for demagogy. As for Kadar, comrade Rakosi mentioned, first of all, that over a period of many years he [Kadar] has shown himself to have an unstable personality. After being arrested during the Horthy period, he gave away his comrades in the underground to the secret police. During the war he was one of those who took the provocative decision to dissolve the Hungarian communist party. Apart from that, Kadar played a rather unsavory role in the Rajk trial, helping Farkas to manufacture false documents for the investigation.

Comrade Hegedus told me exactly the same about Revai and Kadar. He too noted the demagogic inclinations of Revai and the oppositionist frame of mind of Kadar. Comrade Hegedus said that he is very worried that the decision to bring Revai and Kadar into the Politburo might threaten its unity; moreover, disagreements might arise not only on matters of principle but—what is worst of all—as a result of personal relations. Comrade Hegedus let it be understood that his fears are shared by other comrades as well.

From the talks outlined above, the impression builds up that the Politburo of the CC of the HWP took the aforementioned decision against the wishes of a significant number of Politburo members and under a certain pressure from comrades such as Kovacs, who has recently been acquiring ever greater weight, and Gero. From the provisos which comrade Rakosi made in his report, one can conclude that if he does not object directly, then at the very least he has strong doubts about the advisability of the aforementioned decision. I told comrade Hegedus that I got the impression from his remarks that the Politburo had not shown much enthusiasm for the aforesaid replenishment of its membership. Comrade Hegedus confirmed my words. He said that comrade Gero, who proposed the candidature of Kadar, justified this only by reason of the fact that the plenum "would demand his [Kadar's] membership of the Politburo anyway, even against the will of the Politburo."

It appears to us that the words of comrade Hegedus about the dangers for the unity of the leadership that arise as a consequence of bringing Revai and particularly Kadar into the Politburo deserve the most serious attention. In this connection there is a certain interest to be attached to the fact that the candidature of Kadar was proposed in the Politburo in March 1955 by Imre Nagy, who regarded Kadar as a person capable of standing up against the influence of comrade Rakosi. There are grounds for thinking that the candidature of Kadar is now again being lavished with praise by the rightists for the very same reasons. Having taken the decision to bring Revai and especially Kadar into the Politburo, [our] Hungarian comrades, in our opinion, are making a serious concession to the rightists and to demagogic elements, calculating that thereby they will weaken criticism from those quarters.

Despite the fact that [our] friends are not requesting our advice on this matter, it would be advisable to talk this over with them, frankly expressing to them our misgivings in connection with the decision to bring Revai and especially Kadar into the membership of the Politburo. 29. IV. 56 ANDROPOV

34 copies. dd

Run off I. V. 23.00

Dispatched

Issued by Shebanov

Nikitin

correct:

DOCUMENT 2
Transmittal Report of Hungarian Politburo Session

27 October 1956
Hoover Archives
<u>Top Secret</u>
<u>Deliver immediately</u>
[at the foot of the page in handwriting:]
To the archive
28. XI. 56   V. Chernukha
CC CPSU

I.

WE PARTICIPATED FOR more than three hours today in a session of the [Hungarian] Politburo at which questions concerning the formation of a government and the current situation were discussed.

Members of the Politburo have introduced changes to the original list of members of the government with the aim of improving [its] political stability. Thus, for example, Apro—a member of the Directory and of the Military Commission, who has made a very good impression during the past few days—has been confirmed as deputy chairman of the Council of Ministers, and he will be *de facto* the first deputy, inasmuch as the other deputy chairmen are not members of the Party and are less strong.

Sziladi's candidature as minister of internal affairs has been turned down, as he is a politically unstable person, and Munnich has been confirmed as minister. In connection with this Janza Karoi, a communist, reliable, with a working-class background and a former deputy minister of the home front, has been confirmed as minister of defense.

The candidature of Laszlo Kardas as minister of culture has also been turned down for the same reasons. Lukacs has been confirmed as minister— [he is] a well-known philosopher who, despite having caused a good deal of muddle in philosophy, is more trustworthy, politically speaking, and wields authority amongst the intelligentsia.

In order to strengthen the representation of non-party people, Zoltan Tildy, a well-known public figure in Hungary, has been confirmed as minister without portfolio. Comrade Imre Nagy proposed not including Zoltan Tildy because he is on very bad terms with the minister of agriculture, Bela Kovacs. However, this was not accepted.

It is characteristic that proclamations have appeared in the city [Budapest] during the night declaring that Imre Nagy is a traitor and proposing Bela Kovacs as prime minister and also calling for demonstrations to be organized in his honor.

On the instructions of the CC, Imre Nagy telephoned Bela Kovacs, who lives outside the city [and asked whether] he would agree to join the government. He [Kovacs] answered in the affirmative and added that he was getting invitations to go to a public meeting but, even if he went, he would speak against the demonstrators in favor of the government.

The non-party specialist Ribiansky has been confirmed as minister of state farms.

It is characteristic that all these candidatures were approved unanimously and that the replacement of individual people [by others] did not meet with any resistance on the part of Imre Nagy.

In informal discussions with us, [our] Hungarian comrades stated that they regarded this government as suitable both politically and from the point of view of efficiency. This was particularly stressed by Imre Nagy.

The formation of the government was announced today on the radio at 12 o'clock, local time.

We have the impression that on the whole the government is reliable and, so far as public opinion is concerned, more authoritative.

II.

The report on the military situation was given by comrade Apro in confident tones. He reported incidentally that about three thousand wounded Hungarians had been taken to the hospital; 250 of them had died in the hospital. They do not know how many others have been killed and wounded.

In connection with the volatile situation in the provinces, comrade Kadar raised the question as to whether the number of Soviet troops could be increased.

We stated that we have reserves and however many troops were required, they would be provided. The members of the Politburo were very happy about that.

Apro proposed a number of measures regarding the organization of the continuing struggle in the city and the establishment of order in the city.

Apro reported that a significant surrender of weapons by the insurgents has begun; seven hundred rifles have been handed in.

Apro reported that the situation on the periphery has begun to stabilize, although comrades Kadar and Hegedus regarded this announcement with skepticism.

[Our] Hungarian comrades have started to arm the Party activists who, as a result of this, have begun to feel more confident. It has been decided to add armed members of the Party to the personnel of the city's police force. It has also been decided to appoint military censors to the radio and newspapers.

The ministers were instructed to guarantee the smooth functioning of ministries and enterprises.

III.

Comrade Kadar reported that a new candidate member of the Politburo, Losconczy, and a new CC secretary, Donat, who had spoken at a session of the CC yesterday in a faint-hearted manner and whom some CC members had called traitors to the working class, had stated their disagreement with the policies of the CC and offered their resignation.

While comrade Kadar was imparting this information, Imre Nagy was absent, as he was busy negotiating with the [newly] appointed ministers, and then, as a result of intense exhaustion, he had a heart attack (incidentally, after a break in the session we found Imre Nagy unconscious in [his] office, and the Hungarian doctor did not know what to do, whereas comrade Suslov happened to have some heart drops [*validol*], with the help of which we brought Nagy round, for which he later offered us his profuse thanks).

Bearing in mind that Losconczy and Donat are closely linked with Imre Nagy and that the latter, as we have already said, was absent at that stage from the session, the Politburo decided to postpone the passing of a final resolution about them and to transfer them for the time being to work out with the CC.

We agreed with Kadar and Imre Nagy to have a heart-to-heart off-the-record discussion [with them] in the evening.

A. MIKOYAN
M. SUSLOV
27 October 1956
Received over high-frequency
communications link
Transmitted by Chistov
Taken down by Pavlova Oblitsova.

DOCUMENT 3
Transmittal Report of Hungarian Political Situation

October 1956
Hoover Archives
CC CPSU

1. The political situation in the country and in Budapest is not improving, but rather worsening. This makes itself felt in the following: In the leading organs of the Party, there is a feeling of helplessness, and in the Party organizations, processes of disintegration are at work. Hooligan elements have become more impudent; they are taking over district Party committees and killing communists. The work of organizing Party vigilante squads is making slow progress. Factories are at a standstill. The people are staying at home. The railways aren't working, whereas hooligan student and other insurgent elements have changed their tactics and are displaying greater activity. Now they are rarely shooting, but taking control of the institutions. For example, last night the printing house and the editorial offices of the central Party newspaper were seized.

    A hundred-strong company of troops sent in by the new Minister of Internal Affairs came up against more than two hundred people and did not open fire, because of advice from the Central Committee not to shed blood. This was late at night; Imre Nagy at that time was sleeping in his flat, and they evidently did not want complications with Nagy, fearing that to open fire without his knowledge would bring about a weakening of the leadership.

    They [it is not clear who—Trans.] occupied the local telephone exchange. The radio station is working, but it is not reflecting the opinions of the CC since it is in effect in alien hands.

    The antirevolutionary newspaper has not come out because it contained counterrevolutionary articles, and the workers at the printing house refused to print.

2. A grouping of the enemy in the area around the Korlits Theater has been holding negotiations with Imre Nagy about the peaceful surrender of weapons. However, up until now no weapons have been surrendered, apart from a few hundred rifles. The insurgents declare that they will sur-

render [their] weapons [only] after the departure of Soviet troops from Budapest, while some of them even say after the departure of Soviet troops from Hungary. Consequently, the peaceful liquidation of this center of resistance is virtually out of the question. We shall attempt to liquidate it by using the armed forces of the Hungarians. Only there are serious apprehensions: the Hungarian army has been taking up a wait-and-see position. Our military advisers say that the attitude of Hungarian officers and generals to Soviet officers has been worse during the last few days; the trust that existed earlier has gone. It could come about that the Hungarian units sent in against the insurgents may join up with them, and then military operations will again have to be undertaken by the Soviet armed forces.

3. Yesterday night Andropov was called in on the instructions of Imre Nagy and asked whether it was true that new Soviet military units were continuing to come in to Hungary from the USSR, and if so, for what purpose. We did not negotiate [or: come to any understanding—Trans.] about this.

Our opinion on this matter: we suspect that this might be a turning point in the change of Hungary's policies in the Security Council.

We propose to declare today to Imre Nagy that up until today the troops have been coming in in accordance with the understanding, and that for the time being there is no intention of sending in any more troops, on the assumption that the government will be able to cope with the situation in Hungary.

We suggest that the Minister of Defense be given instructions to cease the dispatch of troops into Hungary, while continuing to concentrate them on Soviet territory.

For so long as the Hungarian troops adopt non-hostile positions, the [current] number of [Soviet] troops is sufficient. If the situation worsens further, it will then, of course, be necessary to review the entire matter as a whole.

We do not yet have a final point of view in [*sic*—Trans.] the situation, so dramatic is its deterioration. After the meetings today in the CC, at eleven o'-clock Moscow time, the situation will be clarified, and we shall report to you.

We consider that the immediate arrival in Hungary of comrade Konev is imperative.

A. MIKOYAN
M. SUSLOV

Received on the high-frequency
communications link
30. X. 1956
Taken down by Pavlova

DOCUMENT 4
Communications Regarding Events in Hungary

7 November 1956
Hoover Archives
To be returned no later than within a 7-day period to the First Sector of the
General Department of the CC of the CPSU
Proletarians of all countries, unite!
STRICTLY SECRET
Communist Party of the Soviet Union. CENTRAL COMMITTEE
No. P54/1

To COMRADES SUSLOV, SHEPILOV, PONOMAREV
    Extract from Minutes No. 54 of the Session of the Presidium of the CC
on 7 November 1956

QUESTION FROM A Department of the CC of the CPSU

1. Obligate the Soviet representatives of the World Peace Council not to
    give their agreement to the publication of any document in the name of
    the World Peace Council in which the activities of the Soviet troops in
    Hungary might be viewed as interference in the internal affairs of Hun-
    gary.
2. In the event that any prominent figures in the World Peace Council or any
    individual national movements insist on addressing the question of the
    events in Hungary, the Soviet Committee for the Defense of Peace is to
    publish a statement in the press in which [it is] to state that the counter-
    revolutionary revolt of reactionary forces in Hungary, which was directed
    against the vital interests of the Hungarian people and which led to an
    orgy of the most brutal terror against the progressive forces of the coun-
    try, constituted a threat to the cause of peace and security in Europe. Ex-

plain in this statement that Soviet peace campaigners fervently support the Hungarian revolutionary government of workers and peasants which, in accordance with the will of the Hungarian people, liquidated the counterrevolutionary conspiracy of the enemies of the peace and security of the peoples. The participation of Soviet troops in the establishment of order in the country at the request of the legitimate Hungarian government is seen by Soviet public opinion as a series of activities directed towards the maintenance of peace between peoples.

3. Via the Soviet ambassador to Paris send a telegram to [our] French friends with a request to explain to Joliot-Curie and other leaders of the peace movement the correct interpretation of the events in Hungary.

The text of the telegram to the Soviet ambassador to Paris is attached.

CC SECRETARY
4-nb
Re: item 1 of Minutes No. 54
PARIS
SOVIET AMBASSADOR

ACCORDING TO INFORMATION at the disposal of the Soviet Committee for the Defense of Peace, the World Peace Council is preparing a statement in which it is proposed to condemn in principle any act of intervention of whatever kind; this will apply both to the Egyptian and to the Hungarian events. In addition to that, individual figures in the peace movement in the West are demanding that the Soviet Committee for the Defense of Peace issue an assessment of the events in Hungary, in which to some extent it would condemn the participation of Soviet troops in the crushing of the revolt in Hungary.

In connection with this, convey urgently to [our] friends a request concerning the need to talk [this] over with Joliot-Curie in order to explain to the leaders of the peace movement that the counterrevolutionary revolt of reactionary forces in Hungary, which was launched against the vital interests of the Hungarian people and which led to an orgy of the most brutal terror against the progressive forces of the country, posed a serious threat to the cause of peace and security in Europe; that the Hungarian Revolutionary Government of Workers and Peasants, which, in accordance with the will of the Hungarian people, liquidated the counterrevolutionary conspiracy of the enemies of the peace and security of the peoples, cannot fail to gain the support of all progressive forces. The participation of Soviet troops in the establishment of order in the country at the request of the legitimate Hungarian government cannot be regarded as intervention and interference in the internal affairs of Hungary, but rather represents a series of activities directed towards the preservation of peace, order and security in Europe.

Inform [us] promptly of the results.

Copy

TO THE CENTRAL COMMITTEE OF THE CPSU

Some well-known figures in the peace movement, Bernal, d'Astier de la Vigerie and the British Peace Committee, have approached the Soviet Committee for the Defense of Peace with a proposal to issue a statement of its position on the matter of the events in Hungary.

In a telephone conversation with Erenburg, d'Astier stated that three peace movements (the British, the French and the Italian) wanted to put out a joint official statement on this question. However, after the conversation with Erenburg, they refrained from a public announcement of this sort for the time being.

According to information coming from d'Astier de la Vigerie, the draft of a statement of the Presidium of the World Peace Council (the chairman and vice chairmen of the Council) apropos the Egyptian, but also the Hungarian, events is in preparation. In the draft of the statement there is a proposal to condemn any form of intervention in principle, and this will relate both to the Egyptian and to the Hungarian events. The draft of the statement will be sent to the Soviet representatives in the World Peace Council for agreement.

In the opinion of comrade Erenburg, it will be impossible in present conditions to preserve the unity of the peace movement without some sort of concession on the Hungarian question. We regard this point of view as incorrect.

In connection with the foregoing, we would consider it essential:

1. To obligate the Soviet representatives of the World Peace Council not to give their agreement to the publication of any document in the name of the World Peace Council in which the activities of the Soviet troops in Hungary might be viewed as interference in the internal affairs of Hungary.
2. In the event that any prominent figures in the World Peace Council or the above-mentioned national movements insist on addressing the question of the events in Hungary, the Soviet Committee for the Defense of Peace should publish a statement in the press in which [it is] to state that the

counterrevolutionary revolt of reactionary forces in Hungary, which was directed against the vital interests of the Hungarian people and which led to an orgy of the most brutal terror against the progressive forces of the country, constituted a threat to the cause of peace and security in Europe. Explain in this statement that Soviet peace campaigners fervently support the Hungarian revolutionary government of workers and peasants which, in accordance with the will of the Hungarian people, liquidated the counterrevolutionary conspiracy of the enemies of the peace and security of the peoples. The participation of Soviet troops in the establishment of order in the country at the request of the legitimate Hungarian government is seen by Soviet public opinion as a series of activities directed towards the maintenance of peace between the peoples.

It would be advisable also to send a telegram, via the Soviet ambassador to Paris, to [our] French friends with a request to explain to Joliot-Curie and other leaders of the peace movement the correct interpretation of the events in Hungary.

At the same time it would, in our opinion, be desirable to instruct the ambassador of the USSR to Budapest, comrade Andropov, to ascertain the possibilities of setting up a link between the representatives of the peace movement in Hungary and the World Peace Council, so that they could help the Peace Council to adopt the correct position on the question of the events in Hungary. In addition to that, we consider it essential for Comrade Andropov promptly to collect and send on to Moscow facts about the atrocities and orgies of the counterrevolutionary terror in Hungary which could be utilized in our propaganda.

Drafts of the telegrams to the Soviet ambassadors to Paris and Budapest are attached.

Head of the Department of the CC CPSU
for Liaison with Foreign Communist Parties   B. Ponomarev
Deputy Head of the Department of the CC CPSU
for Liaison with Foreign Communist Parties   V. Tereshkin

November 1956
25-S-23-71
Copy
BUDAPEST
SOVIET AMBASSADOR

According to information at the disposal of the Soviet Committee for the Defense of Peace, a number of figures in the World Peace Council are insisting that in its statement the Peace Council condemns in principle any act of intervention of whatever kind; this will apply both to the Egyptian and to the Hungarian events. Such sentiments of these figures are based on a misunderstanding of the essence of the Hungarian events and on a lack of knowledge of the facts.

In connection with this, ascertain, together with [our] friends, the possibilities of setting up a link between the World Peace Council and those authoritative representatives of the peace movement in Hungary who might be able to help the Peace Council to adopt the correct position on the question of the events in Hungary, explaining to it [the Peace Council] what a threat to peace and tranquillity was presented by the revolt of counterrevolutionary forces in Hungary and why the participation of Soviet troops in the establishment of order in Hungary was not interference in its internal affairs, but corresponded to the interests of the Hungarian people. It is essential to bear in mind that the Bureau of the Peace Council will be convened on November 16–18, when the presence of Hungarian representatives would be highly desirable.

It is also essential promptly to collect the most striking examples of the atrocities and orgies of the counterrevolutionary terror in Hungary which could be utilized in our propaganda against [the forces of] reaction. Convey the materials to Moscow via TASS. It would be desirable for such materials to be distributed in all other countries as well.

Inform [us] promptly of the results.

30/X. 1956

Respected Nikita Sergeyevich,

I am taking the liberty of troubling you about a matter on the resolution of which the future of the peace movement greatly depends. The Italian socialists and Professor Bernal have contacted the secretariat with some urgent proposals on how the World Peace Council should react to the events in Hungary.

This morning I wrote the draft of a statement which might satisfy our "fellow travelers." However, instead of this, the secretariat has been given a draft which, without a doubt, will provoke the most serious objections from persons such as Bernal, D'Astier, and Lombardy and might cause the entire movement to collapse.

During the recent meeting in Paris, Korneychuk and I, basing our remarks on a conversation with you, pointed out that the movement ought to represent a political bloc making mutual concessions. Campaigners from Western countries insisted that nowadays the movement can not [simply] follow in the footsteps of Soviet diplomacy. Bearing this point in mind, I drew up a draft of a statement which is different from the Soviet point of view, but is not directed against us. What is at stake here is whether we will lose even those parties or groups which are [still] going along together with us.

I am attaching the text of the draft.

With respect

I. Erenburg

The World Peace Council expresses its profound regret that blood-drenched events have darkened the life of Hungary and [dampened] its confidence that the Hungarian peace campaigners will spare no efforts to protect the great principles of peace and friendship between all the peoples.

The tragic direction that the events in Hungary have taken is closely linked with international tension which still exists, in spite of the efforts of the peoples.

The World Peace Council expresses the firm hope that from now onwards the Hungarian people will be able to work in peace and develop its state institutions without the overt or covert interference of external forces in its life.

The World Peace Council calls on the peoples of the whole world to stand up for the sovereignty of the Hungarian People's Republic and not to permit the Hungarian events to be utilized for a new aggravation of the international situation for purposes contrary to peace.

DOCUMENT 5
Central Committee Extracts

31 October 1956

Hoover Archives

To be returned no later than within a 7-day period to the First Sector of the General Department of the CC of the CPSU

Proletarians of all countries, unite!

STRICTLY SECRET

Communist Party of the Soviet Union. CENTRAL COMMITTEE

No. P49/U1 [or VI]

Extract from Minutes No. 49 of the Session of the Presidium of the CC on
31 October 1956

ON THE SITUATION in Hungary.

1. In accordance with the exchange of opinions at the session of the Presidium of the CC of the CPSU, authorize comrades Khrushchev, Molotov
   and Malenkov to conduct negotiations with representatives of the CC of
   the Polish United Workers' Party.
2. Approve the text of the telegram to the Soviet ambassador to Belgrade
   for comrade Tito. (Attached.)
       In the event of a positive response, authorize comrades Khrushchev
   and Malenkov to conduct negotiations with comrade Tito.
3. Instruct comrade Zhukov to draft, taking account of the exchange of
   opinions at the session of the Presidium of the CC of the CPSU, the appropriate plan of measures connected with the events in Hungary and report to the CC of the CPSU.
4. Instruct comrades Shepilov, Brezhnev, Furtseva and Pospelov to prepare,
   basing themselves on the exchange of opinions which took place at the
   session of the Presidium of the CC, the necessary documents and submit
   them for the consideration of the CC of the CPSU.

CC SECRETARY
3-mz
Re: item U1 [VI] of Minutes No. 49
Top secret
IMMEDIATE TOP PRIORITY
SPECIAL
BELGRADE
SOVIET AMBASSADOR
    Visit comrade Tito immediately and convey the following:
    "In connection with the situation which has come about in Hungary, we
should like to have a meeting with you incognito on the evening of the first of
November or on the morning of the second of November. We agree to go for
this purpose to Belgrade or another center on Yugoslav or Soviet territory of
your choosing. Our delegation will arrive in the persons of comrades Khru-
shchev and Malenkov. We await a reply through comrade Firyubin.

N. KHRUSHCHEV."

If comrade Tito is away from Belgrade, convey the present text to comrades Kardelj or Rankovic for express transmission to him.

Inform on implementation.

15-lb

nn

DOCUMENT 6
Message to Khrushchev from CC CPSU

7 January 1957

Hoover Archives

[At the foot of the page in handwriting:]

To the archive

7. 1. 57 V. Chernukha

CC CPSU to comrade N. S. KHRUSHCHEV

I am reporting about the work carried out by the organs of state security in Hungary.

1. At the present time there are no reports of any sort of serious anti-state manifestations in the country. In the provinces, filtration of people detained earlier is being carried out by the organs of state security. Detainees on whom no data revealing their hostile activities are available have been freed from custody and registered; at the same time, some of them who are of operational interest have been placed under observation by our agents.

    As of 26 November the total number of arrested persons comes to 1,473; of those who have been arrested, 768 are being held in Uzhgorod, the remainder are in places of detention belonging to the local security organs of Hungary. The organs of state security are currently carrying out intelligence work to uncover hostile elements.

2. In the majority of industrial towns in Hungary the enterprises have got down to work. Sixty or more percent of the total number of workers are turning up for work at their enterprises. In a number of places, the absence of coal, raw materials and electric power is keeping attendance at

work down. The local organs of [political] power are taking steps to supply these enterprises.

In connection with the removal of Imre Nagy and his group, there have been individual demands from the workers' councils to "organize talks with Imre Nagy for the purpose of ascertaining that he had left for Romania of his own volition."

On 24 November the Budapest council sent representatives to the commandant of the city, comrade Grebennik, with a request "to send a delegation to Nagy and question him about the voluntary nature of his departure from Hungary and to ask whether he does not have any intention to return to political activity."

Clarifications have been given by the commandant, after which the question has not been raised again.

3. According to data at our disposal, the American embassy in Budapest is beginning to find the presence of Cardinal Mindszenty in its mission a burden. Having received a refusal from the Hungarian government to provide Mindszenty with the opportunity to leave the country, the Americans have appealed for help to the Pope of Rome, who has also refused to help in this matter.

We have sent an agent into the mission to Mindszenty with a proposal to take him out of the country illegally. If Mindszenty agrees to this, it is intended to detain him after he leaves the mission.

Today we received data from our agents to the effect that the personal documents of Mindszenty and all the papers of the Committee on the Affairs of the Catholic Church had been transferred by him for safekeeping to the vicar Imre Szabo. A search was carried out and the documents were removed; their translation has been organized.

4. The number of persons attempting to escape to Austria is still large (as many as seven hundred people a day). It is becoming clear from the interrogation of those detained that the basic reason for fleeing is hostile propaganda about the imminent punishment of persons who had been taking part in the uprising.

5. According to the intelligence data at our disposal, antigovernmental work is continuing amongst writers, journalists and leading members of the bourgeois parties in the city of Budapest. Meeting illegally with individual members of the workers' committees, they are inciting them to go on strike and organize acts of sabotage, promising them political and

moral support in this. We have arrested the most inimically inclined [such] persons.

6. In order to organize the work of the organs of state security of Hungary more effectively we have prepared the following documents for a report to comrade Kadar:

   a) the structure of intelligence, counterintelligence and other services both in the capital and in the provinces. This framework allows for a minimal number of employees in the open sector of the organs, with the remainder operating as secret members of their staff. This has been done in order to conceal the actual number of employees of the organs, since there is great hostility towards the people who work for the organs of state security;

   b) a proposal is also being submitted on the organization of the organs of the police [*politsiya*] and their consolidation. At the same time Petze, the head of the Chief Directorate of the Police, is being replaced by someone else, because he behaved suspiciously during the uprising, on a number of occasions supporting the insurgents and at the present time doing nothing. Compromising data on Petze were reported by comrade Munnich to comrade Kadar, who agreed with his [Petze's] removal;

   c) with the aim of improving the frontier guards' administration, strengthening the protection of the borders and reducing the number of cases where violations of the frontier go unpunished, we have also prepared a framework and establishment for the frontier guards;

   d) in order to provide help to our Hungarian friends with the organization of operational work, we are submitting a proposal for the establishment of a body of KGB advisers, twenty-seven in total, of whom eighteen would work with the [Hungarian] organs of state security, five with the police, and four on special technology.

Comrades Malenkov, Suslov, and Aristov have been informed.

I. SEROV

Received on the high-frequency
communications link
27. XI. 1956

APPENDIX I

DOCUMENTS FOR CHAPTER 20

All Appendixes excerpted from CWIHP Bulletin 6–7 (Winter 95/96)

———◆———

DOCUMENT 1

Mao's Conversation with Soviet Ambassador P. F. Yudin

31 March 1956
Top Secret
Copy No 1
From the Journal of P. F. Yudin
April 5, 1956
No 289
(Extracts)

. . . DURING A CONVERSATION about I. V. Stalin's mistakes, Mao Zedong noted that Stalin's line on the China question, though it had basically been correct, in certain periods he, Stalin, had made serious mistakes. In his speeches in 1926 Stalin had exaggerated the revolutionary capabilities of the Guomintang, had spoken about the Guomintang as the main revolutionary force in China. In 1926 Stalin had given the Chinese Communists an instruction about the orientation to the Guomintang, having viewed it as a united front of the revolutionary forces of China. Stalin said that it is necessary to depend on the Guomintang, to follow after that party; i.e., he spoke directly about the subordination of the communist Party of China to the Guomintang. This was a great mistake, which had held back the independent work of the Communist Party of China on the mobilization of the masses and on attracting them to the side of the Communist Party.

Through the comintern, Mao Zedong continued, Stalin, having become after the death of V. I. Lenin the de facto leader of the Comintern, gave to the CC CPC a great number of incorrect directives. These mistaken and incorrect directives resulted from the fact that Stalin did not take into account the opinion of the CPC. At that time Van Minh, being a Comintern worker, met frequently with Stalin and tendentiously had informed him about the situation in the CPC. Stalin, evidently, considered Van Minh the single exponent of the opinion of the CC CPC.

Van Minh and Li Lisan, who represented the CPC in the Comintern, tried to concentrate the whole leadership of the CPC in their own hands. They tried to present all the Communists who criticized the mistakes of Van Minh and Li Lisan as opportunists. Mao Zedong said, "They called me a right opportunist and a narrow empiricist." As an example of how the Comintern acted incorrectly in relation to the Communist Party of China, Mao Zedong introduced the following.

Under the pretext that the Third Plenum of the CC CPC, while considering the coup-plotting errors of Li Lisan, had not carried the successive criticism of these mistakes to its conclusion, and allegedly so as to correct the mistakes of the Third Plenum of the CC CPC, the Comintern after three to four months had sent to China two of its own workers—[Pavel] Mif and Van Minh—charged with the task of conducting the fourth Plenum of the CPC. Nonetheless, the decisions of the fourth Plenum of the CC CPC, made under the pressure of Mif and Van Minh, were in fact more ultra-leftist than Li Lisan's line. In them it was stated that it is necessary to move into the large cities, to take control of them, and not to conduct the struggle in rural regions. In the decisions of the fourth Plenum of the CC CPC there was permitted such, for example, a deviation, that in the Soviet regions of China which were blockaded by the Guomintang, even the petty trading bourgeoisie was liquidated and all kinds of international trade was stopped. As a result of this policy the Chinese Red Army, which in 1929 was comprised of 300,000 fighters, was reduced by 1934–35 to 25,000, and the territory which made up the Soviet regions of China was reduced by 99 percent. CPC organizations in the cities were routed by the Guomintang and the number of Communists was reduced from 300,000 to 26,000 people. The Soviet regions were totally isolated from the remaining part of the country and remained without any products, even without salt. All this caused serious discontent among the population of the Soviet regions.

". . . Over the course of the time I spent in Moscow," said Mao Zedong, "I felt that distrust of us even more strongly, and there I asked that a Marxist representative of the CC CPSU be sent to China in order to become acquainted with the true situation in China and to get to know the works of the Chinese theoreticians and simultaneously to examine the works of Mao Zedong— since these works in the Chinese edition were not reviewed by the author in advance, while the Soviet comrades, counter to the wish of the author, insisted on their publication."

Mao Zedong reminded me that upon my (Yudin's) arrival in China, he had persistently and specially recommended to me to complete a trip around the whole country. In relation to this I told Mao Zedong about a conversation which I had with Stalin, in the presence of several members of the Politburo, upon my return from the trip to China. Stalin at that time asked me whether the ruling Chinese comrades are Marxists. Having heard my affirming response, Stalin said, "That's good! We can be calm. They've grown up themselves, without our help."

Mao Zedong noted that in the very posing of this question Stalin's distrust of the Chinese communists was also made apparent.

"Important things which, evidently, to some extent strengthened Stalin's belief in the CPC, were your (Yudin's) report about the journey to China and the Korean War performance of the Chinese people's volunteers."

In such a way, said Mao Zedong, if we look historically at the development of the Chinese revolution and at Stalin's attitude to it, then it is possible to see that serious mistakes were made, which were especially widespread during the time of the Comintern's work. After 1945, during the period of the struggle with Jiang Jieshi, because of the overestimation of the forces of the Guomintang and the underestimation of the forces of the Chinese revolution, Stalin undertook attempts at pacification, at restraining the development of the revolutionary events. And even after the victory of the revolution, Stalin continued to express mistrust of the Chinese Communists. "Despite all that," said Mao Zedong, "we have stood firmly behind the revolutionary positions, for if we had permitted vacillations and indecisiveness, then, no doubt, long ago we would not have been among the living."

Then Mao Zedong moved on to a general evaluation of Stalin's role. He noted that Stalin, without a doubt, is a great Marxist, a good and honest revolutionary. However, in his great work in the course of a long period of time, he made a number of great and serious mistakes, the primary ones of which were listed in Khrushchev's speech. "These fundamental mistakes," said Mao Zedong, "could be summed up in seven points."

1. Unlawful repressions;
2. Mistakes made in the course of the war, moreover, in particular in the beginning, rather than in the concluding period of the war;
3. Mistakes which dealt a serious blow to the union of the working class and the peasantry. Mao Zedong observed that this group of mistakes, in particular, the incorrect policy in relation to the peasantry, was discussed during Comrade Khrushchev's conversation with [PRC military leader] ZhuDe in Moscow;
4. Mistakes in the nationality question connected to the unlawful resettlement of certain nationalities and others. However, "Overall," said Mao Zedong, "nationality policy was implemented correctly";
5. Rejection of the principles of collective leadership, conceit and surrounding himself with toadies;
6. Dictatorial methods and leadership style;
7. Serious mistakes in foreign policy (Yugoslavia, etc.).

. . . . I observed that the main reason for Stalin's mistakes was the cult of personality, bordering on deification.

Mao Zedong, having agreed with me, noted that Stalin's mistakes accumulated gradually, from small ones growing to huge ones. To crown all this, he did not acknowledge his own mistakes, although it is well known that it is characteristic of a person to make mistakes. Mao Zedong told how, reviewing Lenin's manuscripts, he had become convinced of the fact that even Lenin crossed out and rewrote some phrases or other in his own works. In conclusion to his characterization of Stalin, Mao Zedong once again stressed that Stalin had made mistakes not in everything, but on some certain issues.

Ambassador of the USSR to the PRC
P Yudin

DOCUMENT 2
Conversation Between Mao Zedong and Ambassador Yudin

22 July 1958

AFTER YOU LEFT yesterday, I could not fall asleep nor did I have dinner. Today I invite you over to talk a bit more so that you can be [my] doctor: [after talking with you], I might be able to eat and sleep this afternoon. You are fortunate to have little difficulty in eating and sleeping.

Let us return to the main subject and chat about the issues we discussed yesterday. We will only talk about these issues here in this room! There exists no crisis situation between you and me. Our relationship can be described as nine out of ten fingers of yours and ours are quite the same, with only one finger differing. I have repeated this point two or three times. You haven't forgotten, have you?

I've thought over and again of the issues that were discussed yesterday. It is likely that I might have misunderstood you, but it is also possible that I was right. We may work out a solution after discussion or debate. It appears that [we] will have to withdraw [our] navy's request for [obtaining] nuclear-powered submarines [from the Soviet Union]. Barely remembering this matter, I have acquired some information about it only after asking others. There are some warm-hearted people at our navy's headquarters, namely, the Soviet advisers. They asserted that, now that the Soviet nuclear submarines have been developed, we can obtain [them] simply by sending a cable [to Moscow].

Well, your navy's nuclear submarines are of a [top] secret advanced technology. The Chinese people are careless in handling things. If we are provided with them, we might put you to trouble.

The Soviet comrades have won victory for forty years and are thus rich in experience. It has only been eight years since our victory and we have little experience. You therefore raised the question of joint ownership and operation. The issue of ownership has long before been dealt with: Lenin proposed the system of rent and lease, which, however, was targeted at the capitalists.

China has some remnant capitalists, but the state is under the leadership of the Communist Party. You never trust the Chinese! You only trust the Russians! [To you] the Russians are the first-class [people] whereas the Chinese are among the inferior, who are dumb and careless. Therefore [you] came up with the joint ownership and operation proposition. Well, if [you] want joint ownership and operation, how about have them all—let us turn into joint ownership and operation our army, navy, air force, industry, agriculture, culture, education. Can we do this? Or, [you] may have all of China's more than ten thousand kilometers of coastline and let us only maintain a guerrilla force. With a few atomic bombs, you think you are in a position to control us through asking for the right of rent and lease. Other than this, what else [do you have] to justify [your request]?

Lüshun [Port Arthur] and Dalian [Darinse] were under your control before.

You departed from these places later. Why [were these places] under your control? It is because then China was under the Guomindang's rule. Why did you volunteer to leave? It is because the Communist Party had taken control of China.

Because of Stalin's pressure, the Northeast and Xinjiang became [a Soviet] sphere of influence, and four jointly owned and operated enterprises were established. Comrade Khrushchev later proposed to have these [settlements] eliminated, and we were grateful for that.

You [Russians] have never had faith in the Chinese people, and Stalin was among the worst. The Chinese [Communists] were regarded as Tito the Second; [the Chinese people] were considered as a backward nation. You [Russians] have often stated that the Europeans looked down upon the Russians. I believe that some Russians look down upon the Chinese people.

At the most critical juncture [of the Chinese revolution], Stalin did not allow us to carry out our revolution and opposed our carrying out the revolution. He made a huge mistake in this issue. So did [Grigory Y.] Zinoviev.

Neither were we pleased with [Anastas] Mikoyan. He flaunted his seniority and treated us as if [we were] his sons. He put on airs and looked very arrogant. He assumed the greatest airs when he first visited Xibaipo in 1949 and has been like that every time he came to China. Every time he came, he would urge me to visit Moscow. I asked him what for. He would then say that there was always something for you to do there. Nevertheless, only until later when Comrade Khrushchev proposed to hold a conference to work out a resolution [concerning the relationship among all the communist parties and socialist states] did I go [to Moscow].

It was our common duty to commemorate the fortieth anniversary of the October Revolution. Up to that time, as I often pointed out, there had existed no such thing as brotherly relations among all the parties because [your leaders] merely paid lip service and never meant it; as a result, the relations between [the brotherly] parties can be described as between father and son or between cats and mice. I have raised this issue in my private meetings with Khrushchev and other [Soviet] comrades. They all admitted that such a father-son relationship was not of European, but Asian style. Present were Bulganin, Mikoyan, and [M. A.] Suslov. Were you also at the meeting? From the Chinese side, I and Deng Xiaoping were present.

I was unhappy with Mikoyan's congratulation speech, which he delivered at our Eighth National Congress and I deliberately refused to attend that day's meeting as a protest. You did not know that many of our deputies were not happy with [Mikoyan's speech]. Acting as if he was the father, he regarded China as Russia's son.

China has her own revolutionary traditions, although China's revolution could not have succeeded without the October Revolution nor without Marxism-Leninism.

We must learn from the Soviet experiences. We will comply with the commonly accepted principles, especially the nine principles stated in the "Moscow Manifesto." We ought to learn from all the experiences whether they are correct or erroneous. The erroneous lessons included Stalin's metaphysics and dogmatism. He was not totally metaphysical because he had acquired some dialectics in thinking, but a large part of his [thoughts] focused on metaphysics. What you termed as the cult of personality was one [example of his metaphysics]. Stalin loved to assume the greatest airs.

Although we support the Soviet Union, we won't endorse its mistakes. As for [the differences over] the issue of peaceful evolution, we have never openly discussed [these differences] nor have we published [them] in the newspapers. Cautious as we have been, we choose to exchange different opinions internally. I had discussed them with you before I went to Moscow. While in Moscow, [we assigned] Deng Xiaoping to raise five [controversial] issues. We won't openly talk about them even in the future, because our doing so would hurt Comrade Khrushchev's [political position]. In order to help consolidate his [Khrushchev's] leadership, we decided not to talk about these [controversies], although it does not mean that the justice is not on our side.

With regard to inter-governmental relations, we remain united and unified up to this date, which even our adversaries have conceded. We are opposed to any [act] that is harmful to the Soviet Union. We have objected to all the major criticism that the revisionists and imperialists have massed against the Soviet Union. The Soviet Union has so far done the same thing [for us].

When did the Soviets begin to trust us Chinese? At the time when [we] entered the Korean War. From then on, the two countries got closer to one another [than before] and as a result, the 156 aid projects came about. When Stalin was alive, the [Soviet] aid consisted of 141 projects. Comrade Khrushchev later added a few more.

We have held no secrets from you. Because more than one thousand of your experts are working in our country, you are fully aware of the state of our military, political, economic, and cultural affairs. We trust your people, because you are from a socialist country, and you are sons and daughters of Lenin.

Problems have existed in our relations, but it was mainly Stalin's responsibility. [We] have had three grievances [against Stalin]. The first concerns the two Wang Ming lines. Wang Ming was Stalin's follower. The second was [Stalin's] discouragement of and opposition to our revolution. Even after the dissolution of the Third International, he still issued orders claiming that, if we did not strike a peace deal with Jiang Jieshi, China would risk a grave danger of national elimination. Well, for whatever reason, we are not eliminated. The third was during my first visit to Moscow during which Stalin, [V. M.] Molotov, and [Lavrenti] Beria personally attacked me.

Why did I ask Stalin to send a scholar [to China] to read my works? Was it because I so lacked confidence that I would even have to have you read my works? Or was it because I had nothing to do myself? Not a chance! [My real intention] was to get you over to China to see with your own eyes whether China was truly practicing Marxism or only half-hearted toward Marxism.

Upon your return [to Moscow] you spoke highly of us. Your first comment to Stalin was "the Chinese [comrades] are truly Marxists." Nevertheless, Stalin remained doubtful. Only when [we entered] the Korean War did he change his view [about us], and so did East European and other brotherly parties drop their doubts [about us].

It appears that there are reasons for us to be suspect: "First, you opposed Wang Ming; second, you simply insisted on carrying out your revolution regardless of [our] opposition; third, you looked so smart when you went all the way to Moscow desiring Stalin to sign an agreement so that [China] would regain authority over the [Manchurian] railroad." In Moscow it was [I. V.] Kovalev who took care of me with [N. T.] Fedorenko as my interpreter. I got so angry that I once pounded on the table. I only had three tasks here [in Moscow], I said to them, the first was to eat, the second was to sleep, and the third was to shit.

There was a [Soviet] adviser in [our] military academy who, in discussing war cases, would only allow [the Chinese trainees] to talk about those of the Soviet Union, not China's, would only allow them to talk about the ten offensives of the Soviet Army, not [ours] in the Korean War.

Please allow us to talk about these cases! [Can you imagine] he wouldn't even allow us to talk about [our own war experiences]! For God's sake, we fought wars for twenty-two years; we fought in Korea for three years! Let [me ask] the Central Military Commission to prepare some materials concerning [our war experiences] and give them to Comrade Yudin, of course, if he is interested.

DOCUMENT 3
Speech by Mao Zedong: "On Sino-American and Sino-Soviet Relations"

27 January 1957
WW 6–7 (95/96)

[Let me] TALK ABOUT U.S.-China relations. At this conference we have
circulated a copy of the letter from [Dwight D.] Eisenhower to Jiang Jieshi.
This letter, in my view, aims largely at dampening the enthusiasm of Jiang
Jieshi and, then, cheering him up a bit. The letter urges [Jiang] to keep calm,
not to be impetuous, that is, to resolve the problems through the United Nations, but not through a war. This is to pour cold water [on Jiang]. It is easy for
Jiang Jieshi to get excited. To cheer [Jiang] up is to continue the hard, uncompromising policy toward the [Chinese] Communist Party, and to hope that internal unrest would disable us. In his [Eisenhower's] calculation, internal unrest
has already occurred and it is hard for the Communist Party to suppress it.
Well, different people observe things differently!

I still believe that it is much better to establish diplomatic relations with
the United States several years later than sooner. This is in our favor. The Soviet Union did not form diplomatic relations with the United States until seventeen years after the October Revolution. The global economic crisis
erupted in 1929 and lasted until 1933. In that year Hitler came to power in
Germany, whereas Roosevelt took office in the United States. Only then was
the Soviet-American diplomatic relationship established. [As far as I can antici-
pate], it will probably wait until when we have completed the third Five-Year
Plan that we should consider forming diplomatic relations with the United
States. In other words, it will take eighteen or even more years [before we do so].
We are not anxious to enter the United Nations either. This is based on exactly the same reasoning as why we are not anxious to establish diplomatic
relations with the United States. The objective of this policy is to deprive the
U.S. of its political assets as much as possible, so that the U.S. will be placed
in an unreasonable and isolated position. It is therefore all right if [the U.S.]
blocks us from the United Nations and refuses to establish diplomatic relations with us. The longer you drag on [these issues], the more debts you will
owe us. The longer the issues linger there, the more unreasonable you will appear, and the more isolated you will become both domestically and in face of
international public opinion. I once told an American in Yanan that even if

you United States refused to recognize us for one hundred years, I simply did not believe that you United States could refuse to recognize us in the one hundred and first year. Sooner or later the U.S. will establish diplomatic relations with us. When the United States does so and when Americans finally come to visit China, they will feel deep regret. It is because by then, China will become completely different [from what it is now]: the house has been thoroughly swept and cleaned, "the four pests" have altogether been eliminated; and they can hardly find any of their "friends." Even if they spread some germs [in China], it will have no use at all.

Since the end of the Second World War, every capitalist country has suffered from instability, which has led to disturbance and disorder. Every country in the world is disturbed, and China is no exception. However, we are much less disturbed than they are.

[Let me] also talk about Sino-Soviet relations. In my view, wrangling [between us] will continue. [We shall] never pretend that the Communist parties will not wrangle. Is there a place in the world where wrangling does not exist? Marxism itself is a wrangling-ism, and is about contradiction and struggle. Contradictions are everywhere, and contradictions invariably lead to struggle. At present there exist some controversies between China and the Soviet Union. Their ways of thinking, behavior, and historical traditions differ from ours. Therefore, we must try to persuade them. Persuasion is what I have always advocated as a way to deal with our own comrades. Some may argue that since we are comrades, we must be of the same good quality, and why in the world is persuasion needed among comrades? Moreover, persuasion is often employed for building a common front and always targeted at the democratic figures, and why is it employed toward communist party members? This reasoning is wrong. Different opinions and views do exist, even within a communist party. Some have joined the party, but have not changed their mindset. Some old cadres do not share the same language with us. Therefore, [we] have to engage in heart-to-heart talks with them: sometimes individually, sometimes in groups. In one meeting after another, we will be able to persuade them.

As far as I can see, circumstances are beyond what persons, even those occupying high positions, can control. Under the pressure of circumstance, those in the Soviet Union who still want to practice big-power chauvinism will invariably encounter difficulties. To persuade them remains our current policy and requires us to engage in direct dialogue with them. The last time our delegation visited the Soviet Union, [we] openly talked about some [controversial] issues. I told Comrade Zhou Enlai over the phone that, as those people are blinded by lust for gain, the best way to deal with them is to give them a tongue-lashing. What is [their] asset? It involves nothing more than 50 million tons of steel, 400 million tons of coal, and 80 million tons of oil. How much does this count? It does not count for a thing. With this asset, however, their heads have gotten really big. How can they be communists [by being so cocky]? How can they be Marxists? Let me stress, even ten times or a hundred times bigger, these things do not count for a thing. They have achieved nothing but digging a few things out of the earth, turning them into steel, thereby manufacturing some airplanes and automobiles. This is nothing to be proud of! They, however, turn these [achievements] into huge burdens on their backs and hardly care about revolutionary principles. If this cannot be described as being blinded by lust for gain, what else could this be? Taking the office of the first secretary can also become a source for being blinded by lust for gain, making it easy for one to be out of one's mind. Whenever one is out of his mind, there must be a way to bring him back to his senses. This time Comrade [Zhou] Enlai no longer maintained a modest attitude but quarreled with them and, of course, they argued back. This is a correct attitude, because it is always better to make every [controversial] issue clear face to face. As much as they intend to influence us, we want to influence them too. However, we did not unveil everything this time, because we must save some magic weapons [in reserve]. Conflict will always exist. All we hope for at present is to avoid major clashes so as to seek common ground while reserving differences. Let these differences be dealt with in the future. Should they stick to the current path, one day, we will have to expose everything.

As for us, our external propaganda must not contain any exaggeration. In the future, we shall always remain cautious and modest and shall tightly tuck our tails between our legs. We still need to learn from the Soviet Union. However, we shall learn from them rather selectively: only accept the good stuff, while at the same time avoiding picking up the bad stuff. There is a way to deal with the bad stuff; that is, we shall not learn from it. As long as we are aware of their mistakes, [we] can avoid committing the same mistakes. We, however, must learn from anything that is useful to us and, at the same time, we must grasp useful things all over the world. One ought to seek knowledge in all parts of the world. It would be monotonous if one only sticks to one place to receive education.

DOCUMENT 4
Report. Zhou Enlai to Mao Zedong and the Central Leadership

24 January 1957

HAVING ALREADY SPOKEN considerably about the achievements of the Soviet Communist leadership in public, now let [me] illustrate again the major mistakes it has made:

(1) In my view, the mistakes of the Soviet Communist leadership arise from erroneous thinking. They often set the interests of the Soviet Communist Party ahead of their brotherly parties; they often set their own interests as the leaders ahead of those of the party. As a result, they often fail to overcome subjectivity, narrow-mindedness, and emotion when they think about and resolve problems; they often fail to link together the interests of the above-stated sides in an objective, far-sighted, and calm fashion. Although they may correct one mistake, they are not free of making others. Sometimes they admit that they made mistakes, but it does not mean that they fully come to grips with their mistakes for they merely take a perfunctory attitude toward these mistakes.

   For instance, the dispatch of their troops to Warsaw was clearly interference with the internal affairs of a brotherly party by armed forces, but not an action to suppress counterrevolutionaries. They admitted that they had committed a serious mistake, and they even stated in our meetings this time that no one should be allowed to interfere with other brotherly parties' internal affairs; but in the meantime, they denied that [their intervention in Poland] was a mistake.

   When we had a general assessment of Stalin, analyzing the ideological and social roots of his [mistakes], they kept avoiding any real discussion. Although they seemingly have changed [their view] in measuring Stalin's achievements and mistakes, to me, such an alteration was to meet their temporary needs, not the result of profound contemplation.

   We immediately sensed this shortly after our arrival in Moscow. At the dinner party hosted by Liu Xiao on the 17th [of January], Khrushchev again raised the Stalin issue, spelling out a good deal of inappropriate words; however, he made no self-criticism. We then pushed him by pointing out that, given the development of Stalin's authoritarianism, ossified way of thinking, and arrogant and conceited attitude over twenty years, how can those comrades, especially those [Soviet] Politburo members who had worked with Stalin decline to assume any responsibility? They then admitted that Stalin's errors came about gradually; had they not been afraid of getting killed, they could have at least done more to restrict the growth of Stalin's mistakes than to encourage him. However, in open talks, they refused to admit this.

Khrushchev and Bulganin claimed that as members of the third generation [of Soviet] leadership, they could not do anything to persuade Stalin or prevent his mistakes. During [my visit] this time, however, I stressed the ideological and social roots of Stalin's mistakes, pointing out that the other leaders had to assume some responsibility for the gradual development of Stalin's mistakes. I also expressed our Chinese Party's conviction that open self-criticism will do no harm to, but will enhance the Party's credibility and prestige. Before getting out of the car at the [Moscow] airport, Khrushchev explained to me that they could not conduct the same kind of self-criticism as we do; should they do so, their current leadership would be in trouble.

About the Poland question. It is crystal-clear that the Poland incident was a result of the historical antagonism between the Russian and Polish nations. Since the end of [the Second World] War, many [outstanding and potential] conflicts have yet to be appropriately resolved. The recent [Soviet] dispatch of troops to Warsaw caused an even worse impact [in Poland]. Under these circumstances, the Polish comrades have good reason not to accept the policy of "following the Soviet leadership." The Polish comrades, however, admitted that they had yet to build a whole-hearted trusting relationship with the Soviet Comrades. For that purpose, [Wladyslaw] Gomulka is trying his best to retrieve the losses and reorient the Polish-Soviet relations by resolutely suppressing any anti-Soviet acts [in Poland]. Regardless, however, the Soviet comrades remain unwilling to accept the criticism that [they] practiced big-power politics [in resolving the Polish crisis]. This kind of attitude does not help at all to convince the Polish comrades.

(2) About Sino-Soviet relations. Facing a [common] grave enemy, the Soviet comrades have ardent expectations about Sino-Soviet unity. However, in my opinion, the Soviet leaders have not been truly convinced by our argument nor have the differences between us disappeared completely. For instance, many leaders of the Soviet Communist Party toasted and praised

our article "Another Comment on Their Historical Lessons of the Proletarian Dictatorship." Their three top leaders (Khrushchev, Bulganin, and Mikoyan), however, have never mentioned a word of it. Moreover, when we discussed with them the part of the article concerning criticism of Stalin, they said that this was what made them displeased (or put them in a difficult position, I can't remember the exact words). . . . Therefore, I believe that some of the Soviet leaders have revealed a utilitarian attitude towards Sino-Soviet relations. Consequently, at the last day's meeting, I decided not to raise our requests concerning the abolition of the long-term supply and purchase contracts for the Five-Year Plan, the [Soviet] experts, and [Soviet] aid and [Sino-Soviet] collaboration on nuclear energy and missile development. About these issues I didn't say a word. It was not because there wasn't enough time to do so, but because [I wanted to] avoid impressing upon them that we were taking advantage of their precarious position by raising these issues. These issues can be raised later or simply dropped.

(3) In assessing the international situation, I am convinced that they spend more time and effort on coping with specific and isolated events than on evaluating and anticipating the situations thoroughly from different angles. They explicitly demonstrate weakness in considering and discussing strategic and long-term issues. As far as tactics are concerned, on the other hand, lacking clearly defined principles, they tend to be on such a loose ground in handling specific affairs that they will fail to reach satisfactorily the strategic goals through resolving each specific conflict. As a result, it is very likely that some worrisome events may occur in international affairs. For instance, this time they conceded to our conviction that in today's world there existed two camps and three forces (socialist, imperialist, and nationalist) and agreed to our analysis. But the communiqué drafted by them included only vague statements about the union among the Soviet Union, China and India, as well as [about] possible Sino-Soviet collaboration on the production of atomic and hydrogen bombs. We regarded these statements as swashbuckling, which is not good, and they were finally deleted from the communiqué. As a result, we did not use the Soviet draft. The published communiqué was largely based on our draft.

(4) In spite of all of the above, however, Sino-Soviet relations are far better now than during Stalin's era. First of all, facing the [common] grave enemy, both sides have realized and accepted the necessity of promoting Sino-Soviet unity and mutual support, which had been taken as the most

important principle. Second, now the Soviet Union and China can sit down to discuss issues equally. Even if they have different ideas on certain issues, they must consult with us. The articles by the Chinese Party are having some impact on the cadres and people in the Soviet Union, and even on some [Soviet] leaders. Third, the previous dull situation in which the brotherly parties and states could hardly discuss or argue with one another no longer exists. Now, different opinions can be freely exchanged so that unity and progress are thereby promoted. Fourth, the majority of the Soviet people love China and feel happy for the Chinese people's achievements and growth in strength. Their admiration and friendship with the Chinese people are being enhanced on a daily basis. However, while [Russian] arrogance and self-importance have not been completely eliminated, an atmosphere lacking discipline and order is spreading. This time the [Soviet leadership] gave us a splendid and grand reception which indicated its intention to build a good image in front of its own people and the peoples all over the world. Fifth, on the one hand, extremely conceited, blinded by lust for gain, lacking far-sightedness, and knowing little the ways of the world, some of their leaders have hardly improved themselves even with the several rebuffs they have met in the past year. On the other hand, however, they appear to lack confidence and suffer from inner fears and thus tend to employ the tactics of bluffing or threats in handling foreign affairs or relations with other brotherly parties. Although they did sometimes speak from the bottom of their hearts while talking with us, they nevertheless could not get down from their high horse. In short, it is absolutely inadvisable for us not to persuade them [to make changes]; it is, however, equally inadvisable for us to be impatient in changing them. Therefore, changes on their part can only be achieved through a well-planned, step-by-step, persistent, patient, long-term persuasion.

APPENDIX J

DOCUMENTS FOR CHAPTER 27

—————➤●◄—————

DOCUMENT I

Verbatim Report of Negotiations of Brezhnev and Others

23 August 1968

Hoover Archives

VERBATIM REPORT

OF THE NEGOTIATIONS OF COMRADES L. I. BREZHNEV,

A. N. KOSYGIN, and N. V. PODGORNY with COMRADE

L. SVOBODA

[and others—Trans.]

23 August 1968

[pp. 46–47]

BREZHNEV . . . WHAT CAN WE talk about right now? Ludvik Ivanovich [Svoboda] says that the atmosphere right now in the country [Czechoslovakia] is such that it would be desirable if Cernik returned to the leadership of the government. Second, if Dubček returned. Evidently, from the viewpoint of the atmosphere which is taking place [*sic*—Trans.] especially in Prague, it's obvious that this would help to calm the situation down somewhat. But we would like to ask you—all the members of the delegation—to say honestly [what you think]. Third, it's probably desirable for Smrkovsky to return to the leadership of the National Assembly. But to do it just like that, to put Dubček and Cernik [back] in place, to find them and put them [back] in place—we'll find them all right—but we can't do this in conditions when an illegal [PartM] unless Dubček and Smrkovsky recognize that this Congress was incompetent. It seemed to us that if [our Czechoslovak] comrades fulfilled the terms of our honest talks in Cierna and Tisou, we won't have any objections;

but we must have a guarantee. We had [one] once, but it turned out to be a worthless scrap of paper. We don't want to be some sort of [naive] youths for a second time. That's why it's necessary to have your joint opinion that this [Fourteenth, "underground" Party] Congress is without authority, whereas the CC [Central Committee], which has been working up until the present time, is empowered, and the Presidium, as it is presently constituted, is [also] valid. If Dubček agrees, that means he'll go [back], if they approve a decision that the Congress was held in breach [of the rules] and that the current Presidium and CC are [legally] competent. Maybe it'll be necessary to dismiss one or two people, because nobody can be a secretary of the CC if he's an anti-Leninist. So it will be possible to dismiss [someone] from being a CC secretary, but leave him in some other post, in other words there must be certain conditions. In these conditions, we would be able to continue constructive talks. And then it's impossible to solve large-scale problems in one hour. It's necessary to understand these problems and discuss them. If agreement is given by the socialist countries, we must have a guarantee that it will be the CC, and not this Congress, that will be in charge. There will be attacks on Dubček, of course, but it will be his job to get the better of these attacks.

Because if we don't find an approach of this sort, it will be impossible to avoid bloodshed; it'll be impossible to avoid people getting killed and wounded both by our side and by your side. If the rightists go on broadcasting these hysterics over underground [radio] stations, do they really think that the Soviet, Hungarian, German, and Bulgarian troops will simply pack up and leave? That's completely out of the question. And because it's out of the question, there could be such a clash that it will lead to war. We've got to overcome this danger, but on principles that are acceptable to you and to us and to all the socialist countries.

Am I speaking clearly, comrades? Can you understand me? Or is it difficult to catch my meaning?

[p. 63, end of a long speech in Slovak by G. Husak:]

. . . I again thank comrades Brezhnev and Kosygin for their willingness to talk over all these questions. I want to assure you that we are motivated by the greatest good will in the resolution of these matters.

PODGORNY. The main thing is how to resolve them.

BREZHNEV. We need to talk, to think, and within two hours to make up our minds on all the difficult questions. It's necessary to exchange views, display patience, and find ways forward.

HUSAK. A crowd of people gathered in front of the CC building yesterday, demanding to be told where comrades Dubček and Cernik are.

BREZHNEV. Why only Dubček and Cernik? There's a Central Committee in Slovakia and there's a secretary of this Committee, comrade Bilak. Why is there no mention made of him as well? No one can give us any explanation as to why he was not chosen to be the First Secretary of the CC of Slovakia, why Piller or Indra and a whole string of other comrades haven't been selected. Who can explain all this to us?

Why have people hung a poster on the house where Piller lives saying that he's an enemy of the people? What has <u>he</u> done that's bad? <u>He</u> hasn't made any statements from anti-socialist or anti-Soviet positions; he hasn't come out against friendship. Why has nobody said even a word in defense of a whole large group of people who have been leaders of the [Czechoslovak Communist] Party for many years? After all, none of us, no one from the socialist countries, neither Gomulka nor anyone else, has ever said or written anything either against Piller or against Svestka.

HUSAK. Why talk about that now?

BREZHNEV. It's wrong to smooth out the situation in a one-sided way and depict us as such great enemies of the Czech people. Let's not [get at] one another. Our talks are difficult enough [as it is].

[p. 72]

BREZHNEV. We would like to direct our main efforts to the search for constructive decisions. As it was you [Husak] who gave a speech like that and as you are sticking to that sort of position [not to postpone the Party Congress due to open on 26 August], I have to tell you bluntly that as a member of the leadership you also bear responsibility.

Aleksey Nikolayevich [Kosygin] is right [when he says] that Dubček, the entire presidium of the CC, you [apparently Husak—Trans.] have created a situation that covers the Communist Party of Czechoslovakia with shame. You have created such an atmosphere in the attitude to the Party, and as it's in the attitude to the Party, it's clear what this means.

I'll give you one fact. Why did you put up with such terrible propaganda against your Party for an entire seven months? Two months ago [your] television showed a program about prisons for a whole two hours. A prison is a prison: people are behind bars, there are doors, someone is a prisoner. For two hours the television shows people who have suffered and are sitting here in prison. For two hours they are assaulting the brains of the working class.

Then they ask who's to blame for this. The presenter answers, the Communist Party of Czechoslovakia. And that's it—end of program, no more words. Why didn't you take any measures against the person who compiled a program like that and leveled an accusation like that against every decent communist? Why didn't you say anything, why didn't you defend the Party?

PODGORNY. They were afraid they might be called conservatives.

BREZHNEV. And you, comrade Husak, read your newspapers! What you tolerated for seven months. Is there even one well-grounded article in your articles [*sic*] in defense of the Party? Why don't you want to answer for all this? After all, you are in the leadership. You can't get out of it simply by saying that the telephones aren't working properly these days. Of course, they aren't. The army went in and somebody cut them off.

Look, the army has gone through the whole of Czechoslovakia and no one has fired a single shot. Comrade Svoboda and the Presidium of the CC issued an instruction. But as soon as the troops got to Prague, what did they come to blows over and where was the blood spilt? For the radio station, the television, for the editorial offices—in other words the rightists foresaw this and they didn't want to surrender the means of propaganda, the means of [dispensing their] ideology. That's where the blood was shed. Why don't you want to talk about that frankly? Why did they [the incoming troops] march for 700 to 800 kilometers without a single shot and then people began to beat each other up for [control over] the channels for spreading ideology? That means that they need them. Be self-critical, pluck up your courage. We can't say that we are such great heroes. We were obliged to do it. If you're really a communist, a genuine Leninist, you're bound to welcome the fact that we went in. We went in to save you, whereas you blame us for doing this. Of course, every question can be turned this way and that.

[p. 77]

BREZHNEV. . . . And now you say that the telephones have been cut off. But you yourselves have a look. Do you really think that we gave ourselves the task of setting the hospital on fire? And after all somebody did set fire to the hospital. Do you believe that we could [deliberately] set a hospital on fire? It's true that we tried to take control of the radio station. There was such a task, so that the Central Committee could conduct its propaganda operations freely. People put up some resistance and set the radio station on fire, and now they dump [the responsibility for] this on us.

[pp. 82–83/85]

BREZHNEV. Comrade Bilak, according to reports, twelve of the authors of "Two Thousand Words" have been elected to the new Central Committee. One can imagine the atmosphere.

PODGORNY. No doubt even Hanzelka has been elected.

BREZHNEV. This Czech millionaire went on an exotic trip at the expense of the Czech people, at the expense of other countries and at the expense of our country, and made a packet. But money alone wasn't enough for him.

VERBATIM REPORT OF THE NEGOTIATIONS

of comrades L. I. Brezhnev, A. N. Kosygin, N. V. Podgorny
and G. I. Voronov with comrades Dubček and Cernik
23 VIII 1968

[p. 29]

BREZHNEV. In overcoming [your] difficulties, count on us and all the socialist countries.

KOSYGIN. Wielding the power that we've got, we and you together can cut the Devil down to size, and not just a mere Goldstucker.

DOCUMENT 2
*Message from Andropov Regarding Activities
of Counterrevolutionary Underground*

14 October 1968
Hoover Archives
Top Secret
TO BE RETURNED
3762
14 OCT 1968
2 sector
to the CC of the CPSU
General Department
[to the] CC CPSU
[State emblem]
USSR

COMMITTEE
OF STATE SECURITY

attached to the COUNCIL OF
MINISTERS OF THE USSR

---

13 October 1968
No. 2374-A
city of Moscow

IN CONNECTION WITH the request of [our] German and Polish friends to
be provided with information on Czechoslovakia, the Committee of State Security considers it desirable to send to the leadership of the organs of state security of the GDR and the PPR [Polish People's Republic] the enclosed report on
the activities of the counterrevolutionary underground in the CSSR, prepared
on the basis of intelligence materials.
Agreement requested.
ENCLOSURE: 59 sheets.
CHAIRMAN OF THE COMMITTEE OF STATE SECURITY
ANDROPOV
[signature]
[three indecipherable signatures below the word *agreed*]
[note signed by Andropov: *Comments taken into account*]
Top secret
On the activities of the counterrevolutionary underground in
Czechoslovakia
I. The activities of anti-socialist forces before the entry
of allied troops into the CSSR
[from the foot of p. 7 to the top of p. 11]

The activities of the reactionary forces in Czechoslovakia were made easier by the fact that within the CC [Central Committee] of the CPCS [Communist
Party of Czechoslovakia], aside from the Presidium of the CC of the CPCS, there
came together and operated a "Second Center," which directed the work of
the means of mass propaganda in the name of the Party and had at its disposal a number of important posts in the Party apparatus, the Ministry of Internal Affairs, the Ministry of Foreign Affairs and other ministries and
departments of the CSSR. The "Second Center" maintained contacts with a
variety of reactionary organizations and clubs, and coordinated their activities.
    The chief of the staff of the "Second Center" was KRIEGEL. Together
with him, SIK, CISAR, MLYNAR (MULLER), SLAVIK, PAVEL, KOLAR,

SIMON, GOLDSTUCKER, and PELIKAN were members of the leadership of this Center.

Activities of the "Second Center" were coordinated and carried out jointly, with the CZERNY-PROCHAZKA group; in all their essentials, their plans coincide and boil down to splitting the workers' movement in Czechoslovakia, liquidating the political power of the CPCS by "dissolving" it in organizations and parties that are members of the National Front, and restoring bourgeois democracy in the CSSR.

KRIEGEL, GOLDSTUCKER, and SIK have revealed themselves as being active proponents of Zionist influence in the CSSR. They set up links with Zionist centers abroad, in particular with WIESENTHAL, a representative of the "Joint" organization in Vienna.

The leaders of the "Second Center" met regularly to work out practical measures whose aim was to enable their supporters to capture key positions in the political, economic and cultural life of the CSSR. KRIEGEL was given the task of the overall leadership and coordination of the activities of the rightist elements in the CPCS. CISAR and GOLDSTUCKER were charged with directing the means of mass propaganda and the activities of the youth organizations and the creative and scientific intelligentsia; MLYNAR was engaged in developing the political ideas of the "Czechoslovak model of socialism"; SIK was entrusted with questions of economic policy. Contacts with the country's noncommunist parties were handled by SLAVIK and PELIKAN. Control over the activities of the "Club of the Non-Party Activists," "Club-231," and other anti-socialist organizations was carried out via MLYNAR and PAVEL. "Club-231" was utilized by the "Second Center" to send out information to the West about the situation in the CSSR, in particular to the "Free Europe" radio station in Munich.

KRIEGEL's supporters planned to nominate CISAR for the post of leader of the CC of the CPCS, and SIK for the post of Prime Minister.

According to the plan devised by the "Second Center," the most important task, if its goals were to be realized, was to take control over the organs of the MVD [Ministry of Internal Affairs]. On the instructions of the "Second Center," PAVEL, once he became the head of the MVD, immediately proceeded to purge the organs of state security of "persons who had compromised themselves" and to sanction a campaign of "public denunciations." By continually maneuvering and exerting pressure on honest employees, PAVEL and his supporters wrecked any measures intended to normalize the situation in the organs of state security. On his insistence, ZARUBA and DEMJAN, deputy ministers of internal affairs, were removed from their posts, as were the heads of directorates SPELINA, KOSNAR, BERAN, KOVAN, and BOKR, as well as a number of other senior employees who had been speaking out in favor of normalizing the situation in the Ministry of Internal Affairs. The "Second Center" was planning little by little to fire experienced employees from the Ministry of Internal Affairs and replace them with protégés of the "clubs" and other counterrevolutionary organizations.

Another aim of the "Second Center" was to carry out a "purge" of the army so as to be able to utilize it in its plans to seize power in the country.

The KRIEGEL-CISAR-SIK group was making efforts to disarm the people's militia on the pretext that there were supposedly no anti-socialist forces of any real significance in the country, and consequently there was no need to have armed detachments of workers. At the same time, KRIEGEL issued an instruction to his people to set up special committees at enterprises and in institutions that were to "take the situation under control."

The activities of the "Second Center" displayed particular energy in the period when district and regional Party conferences were being held in April and May this year, in connection with the elections of delegates to the Fourteenth Congress of the CPCS. In the course of these conferences they placed their major stake on getting Party members who had joined the CPCS after 1959–1960, predominantly representatives of the intelligentsia, to form a majority of the delegates elected to the Congress. In the main, they succeeded in achieving this goal.

In this period, there was an intensification of the campaign inspired in the press and on radio and television to compromise the healthy forces in the CPCS by suggesting that they were "closet conservatives" and to remove them from the posts they were occupying. As a result of this campaign, more than three hundred senior Party workers were released from their posts, and they still do not have any full-time employment. According to information at our disposal, SIK and CISAR were standing in the wings behind this campaign.

With the knowledge and support of the "Second Center," the anti-socialist forces succeeded in putting out their political program under the title of "Two Thousand Words."

With the aim of exerting pressure on the Presidium in a way that would be advantageous to the "Second Center," letters and resolutions from "collectives of workers and employees," which were later presented as demands of the broad masses of the population, were dispatched in an organized way to the CC of the CPCS, the government and the National Assembly.

During the period of the "Sumava" command and staff exercises and after the Warsaw meeting, the leaders of the "Second Center" directed their main efforts at stirring up a nationalistic psychosis in the country against the presence of Soviet troops on the territory of Czechoslovakia. Considerable use was made of the press and other means of mass propaganda to work on the population in an anti-Soviet spirit, on the pretext of defending the "sovereignty" and "independence" of the CSSR. During the meeting in Cierna, CISAR and others were behind the campaign to collect signatures under the "Appeal of Citizens to the Presidium of the CC of the CPCS."

In the period of preparations for the Fourteenth Extraordinary Congress of the CPCS, the atmosphere in Czechoslovakia became ever more incandescent.

The number of leaflets and graffiti attacking the CPCS and the Soviet Union increased in June and July of this year. In particular, leaflets distributed in the region of Southern Moravia stated, "Ban the activities of the CPCS as a fascist party. Declare Marxism and scientific socialism to be a folly, and MARX, ENGELS, and LENIN to be charlatans." Leaflets appeared in Gotwaldov in June with crude anti-Soviet statements and insults.

[p. 59]

HEAD OF THE FIRST CHIEF DIRECTORATE OF THE
COMMITTEE OF STATE SECURITY
attached to the COUNCIL OF MINISTERS OF THE USSR

[signature]

A. SAKHAROVSKY

DOCUMENT 3
Message to Kuznetsov and Chervonenko
from the Soviet Ambassador in Prague

11 November 1968
Hoover Archives
Re: item 79 of Minutes No. 107
[this refers to the session
of the CC CPSU Politburo
of 11 November 1968—Trans.]
Secret
PRAGUE
SOVIET AMBASSADOR

to Comrades KUZNETSOV and CHERVONENKO

Visit comrade Dubček and, referring to instructions in connection with the draft Resolution of the plenum of the CC of the Communist Party of Czechoslovakia (CPCS) conveyed via you on November 9, say the following:

1.   Our comrades have naturally not had the time to study the draft Resolution carefully and to examine individual, particular clauses and formulations, and it therefore seems possible to impart [our] opinion only on particularly important matters of principle.

   On the whole, the perusal of the document has provoked very serious concern and anxiety regarding the implementation of the Moscow Agreement and the further course of the normalization of the situation in Czechoslovakia and of the development of relations between our Parties and countries.

2.   It seems to us that the section of the Resolution where the tasks of the Party in the immediate future are spelled out is a development of the Action Program of the CPCS, and here it is possible to note certain positive features.

   However, certain clauses in this section cause us to have doubts. This relates in particular to the question of strengthening the leading role of the CPCS. More than a little is said about this, but the language is too imprecise. For instance, one gains the general impression that the National Front is being placed on a par with the Party. We think that the clauses in this section, if the wording of them is somewhat improved especially with regard to the leading role of the Party, could provide the Presidium of the CC of the CPCS in its practical work with the opportunity to carry out its business in accordance with the fundamental principles of Marxism-Leninism and the overall logical development of the construction of a socialist society, as applicable to the conditions of Czechoslovakia.

   We recall that before the convocation of the then forthcoming Fourteenth Congress you had it in mind to work on the Action Program of the CPCS in this direction. Proceeding from this, we do not regard the clauses in this section as final and consider, as you evidently do as well, that they will be subject to improvement at subsequent plenums.

3.   A preliminary perusal of the section on international policy did not give rise to any specific comments by our comrades.

4.   At the same time we are obliged to state that the conclusions and assess-

ments of the situation in the country and in the Party contained in the first three sections of the Resolution find themselves, in a number of their cardinal propositions, in fundamental opposition to the conclusions and assessments on which the CPSU and other fraternal Parties have based and are basing themselves.

Naturally it has been noted that attempts are being made in these sections to reflect certain positions which have been particularly stressed in CPSU documents and during the bilateral and multilateral meetings connected with the events in Czechoslovakia. In the draft, mention is made of the dangerous activities of anti-socialist forces, of individual failings in the work of the CC CPCS Presidium, of the responsibility of the media, and so on. But the attempts to give an objective account of the post-January period touch only on details and incidentals. And if we are to speak of the picture as a whole, of the overall tendency of the draft, we cannot but come to the conclusion that the assessments and conclusions proffered are at variance with historical truth, contradict the essence and the spirit of the Moscow Agreements and in effect ignore the point of view of the CPSU and other fraternal Parties.

This is a matter not of the form of the wording, not of individual phrases and formulae, but of the general fundamental trend of the assessments of the problems whose significance has gone far beyond the frontiers of Czechoslovakia.

Touching only on the most important questions, it is impossible not to take note:

a) Above all, of the question of the reasons for and the meaning of the entry of the allied troops onto the territory of the Czechoslovak Socialist Republic.

Our comrades would like to remind you that during the numerous meetings and talks stretching over the last few months, we never came out against the course which was sketched out at the January plenum of the CC of the CPCS. This was made plain both in Czierna and in Bratislava. Our attitude to the changes brought about by the January plenum is also spelled out unambiguously in the Minutes of the Moscow negotiations of 26 August.

At the same time, we have repeatedly and insistently drawn your attention to the fact that anti-socialist and counterrevolutionary forces outside the Party have got involved in the positive developments generated by the January plenum and that right-wing revisionist elements in the CPCS are also trying to take advantage of it in their own interests.

With a certain delay, as it seemed to us, you paid serious attention to this, and at the May plenum of the CC of the CPCS, you passed an appropriate resolution. In a fraternal way we expressed our satisfaction to you at this decision. However, in reality it was left hanging in the air.

Subsequent events demonstrated that right-wing and anti-socialist forces, when they do not meet with a rebuff, show no inclination to give ground. They almost completely took the press, radio and television into their own hands. Their activities were becoming ever more impertinent, while support for the counterrevolution on the part of foreign reactionary and imperialist circles was growing ever more outspoken. The notorious appeal, "Two Thousand Words," and a whole series of other counterrevolutionary statements are an eloquent confirmation of this.

More than once, we expressed to you our serious concern at the course of events, providing references to concrete facts. We and other fraternal Parties utilized all possible political means to convince you of the necessity to give a rebuff to the counterrevolution, but we saw that despite our efforts, the development of events was taking on an ever more dangerous turn, so far as the achievements of socialism were concerned, and that things were moving towards their forfeiture in Czechoslovakia and towards a worsening of the positions of the entire socialist commonwealth. That is why we resolved and were compelled to go to extreme lengths and send in troops to help the Czechoslovak people to stave off the threat to [their] socialist achievements.

This action was incorrectly evaluated in the essentially anti-Soviet statement of the Presidium of the CC of the CPCS of August 21 this year. However, in the Moscow Protocol of 23–26 August this year, which both our Parties regard as the foundation stone for the normalization of relations and the development of friendly relations, it was spelled out that the presence of troops in Czechoslovakia is linked to the threat to the socialist achievements of the Czechoslovak Socialist Republic and to the threat to the security of the countries of the socialist commonwealth. Meanwhile in the draft Resolution we again find the words:

"The entry of the armies of five of the states of the Warsaw Pact onto the territory of the Czechoslovak Socialist Republic was perceived by the overwhelming majority of the population—the working class, the peasants, the intelligentsia and the younger generation—in the Czech Lands and in Slovakia as detrimental to political development. In spite of all the contradictoriness in the attitudes of the various sections and groups of the population to post-January developments, not one single group of any significance or size regarded this action as a necessary means for the defense of socialism in Czechoslovakia. This idea was also expressed in the statement of the CC Presidium of 21 August 1968."

We consider that the reinstatement of this assessment, as well as the attempt to corroborate the well-known statement of the CC CPCS Presidium of 21 August with the help of the authority of the CC plenum, are at odds with the understanding that has been achieved and are out of line with the interests of solving the main task—the genuine normalization of the situation in the CPCS and the CSSR.

b) On the causes of the emergence of difficulties in the post-January developments.

We have gained the opinion that the draft Resolution of the CC of the CPCS does not provide a principled, Marxist-Leninist analysis of the causes of the emergence of serious difficulties in the development of the CSSR after the January plenum.

In no way do we intend to come forward as defenders of Novotny. However, we have already stated more than once that a one-sided assessment of the twenty-year period of activity of the CPCS, joining forces with an unscrupulous, right-wing revisionist critique of socialism, not only fails to correspond to reality, but does not even make it possible to look with wide-open eyes at many of the darker and negative tendencies of the post-January period and objectively plays into the hands of the anti-socialist forces.

In the document it says that the implementation of post-January policies was in essence also hampered by the "narrow-minded impatience" and "adventurism" of certain sections of society and, on the other hand, by the "ossification of thought" and "dogmatism" of some members of the Party. This sort of argumentation, in our opinion, makes it in reality even more difficult to identify the main source

of the crisis that has come into existence. It is our profound conviction that this source lay in the fact that has been discussed above—in
the dramatic revival of the activities of the right-wing, revisionist,
anti-socialist and counterrevolutionary forces, which did not receive
a fitting rebuff from the leadership of the CPCS and the CSSR.

c) It is impossible to agree either with the clause that, although it is not
spelled out openly but rather follows from the resolution by implication, has it that the Warsaw letter of five fraternal Parties, by churn-
ing up a wave of nationalism, supposedly strengthened the positions
of the right-wing forces and thereby worked against the stabilization
of socialism in the CSSR and played a negative role.

We object categorically to such an assessment. Even now we
consider that the letter of the five countries could have played an
enormous positive role if the fraternal appeal it contained had been
correctly interpreted and utilized by the leadership of the CPCS.

The patently obvious effort in one way or another to place the
blame for the situation that has come about in Czechoslovakia on
the CPSU and other fraternal Parties, which supposedly incorrectly
assessed the essence of the events that were taking place, can not, we
are convinced, be in the interests of a genuinely objective analysis of
the situation or in consequence of a genuine normalization of the
state of affairs and the strengthening of the positions of socialism.

d) On the struggle against the right-wing and left-wing danger.

The document lays stress on the fact that the difficulties in the
development of the CSSR were mainly caused by "dogmatic and sectarian forces," which present themselves as the "only consistent supporters of the alliance with the USSR." In various places in the
document, the danger from "dogmatic and sectarian forces" is put,
in the first place, in comparison with the danger from the right, and
in item three of section two, it is said that the activities of those
communists who represent these forces were "aimed at the return to
pre-January relationships, and today [are aimed at the return] to the relationships which existed long before January, with all the implications that follow from that." We have been observing of late, more
and more frequently, instances of using the term "dogmatic and sectarian forces" to mean those communists who have been and are
striving to put up some active resistance to right-wing, revisionist

and anti-socialist forces and consistently to uphold the socialist achievements of the Czechoslovak people.

More than once we have drawn your attention to this attitude, which is patently at odds with the Moscow Protocol. People in our country think that in the concrete situation of today, if one looks at the state of affairs from the point of view of the Moscow Agreement, you are not bending your efforts in the right direction. It is no secret that the right-wing forces have once more started to operate extremely actively and openly. This is especially visible in the press, where for the time being you have in the main kept on all the personnel who have been giving voice to anti-socialist views. (For example, you have supposedly closed down [the newspaper] "Literary Pages," but, as you know, the very same editorial staff is in effect putting out the very same, but even more "cunning," Pages.)

In these conditions, we consider that the formulation of the question in the Resolution, drawing a veil over and blurring the right-wing danger, cannot be of any benefit to our cause. In practice, it is making the stabilization of the situation more difficult, encouraging the right-wing forces in their efforts to hold on to their positions and striking against the communists, who are striving not by any means to restore the pre-January state of affairs, but to establish Leninist principles and norms in the Party.

We have some comments to make on other matters as well, but here, as we have already said, we have touched only on the most important of them, the ones most directly concerning matters of principle and, moreover, ones which have already been discussed repeatedly at our meetings. And if we are to speak frankly, the interpretation of these questions in the draft Resolution is presented from the viewpoint of the right wing.

In our opinion, the adoption of such an analysis of the situation in the Resolution of the plenum would mean a significant step backwards, the negative consequences of which are hard to overestimate. It would facilitate the consolidation of the positions of the right-wing opportunist and nationalist elements, impede the process of normalization on a Marxist-Leninist basis and once again complicate the relations between the CPCS and the CPSU and between the CPCS and other fraternal Parties. If this analysis were to obtain, even those positive features which are to be found in the Resolution would lose their meaning. These general comments on matters of principle relate to the entire Resolution as a whole.

A deep-seated conviction is being expressed in our country that the adoption of the Resolution without taking account of the views expressed [above] would be taken as evidence of the fact that the leadership of the CPCS considers that it is not bound by the agreements it has with the CPSU and other fraternal Parties and is ignoring the terms of the Moscow Protocol and the results of the negotiations in Moscow on the third and fourth of October this year.

If you are prepared to make the relevant changes on matters of principle to the draft Resolution, we would naturally welcome such a step. In the contrary event, it would in our opinion be advisable to limit oneself at this plenum to a brief Resolution approving the treaty on the terms for the temporary stationing of Soviet troops on the territory of the CSSR and the jointly agreed communique on the negotiations on 3–4 October this year, and again confirm the starting positions for the activity of the CPCS, on the basis of the Bratislava statement and the Moscow Protocol (23–26 August). In this context the plenum could instruct the Presidium of the CC of the CPCS to continue work on the drafting of a wide-ranging Resolution for the following session.

To comrades Kuznetsov and Chervonenko. In addition to comrade Dubček, acquaint comrades Svoboda, Cernik, Husak, Bilak, Indra, and Strougal with this communication. When doing this, it should be said to comrade Husak that we would like to take account of his views on the draft Resolution, but that we could not react in a different fashion than we have done to the text as received by us.

447-zv

pe, kf

APPENDIX K

DOCUMENTS FOR CHAPTER 31

———⟶◆⟵———

DOCUMENT 1
Politburo Meetings Regarding Afghanistan

17–20 March 1979
CWIHP Bulletin 4 (1994)
Politburo meeting
"About the Exacerbation of the Situation in the Democratic Republic of Afghanistan and Our Possible Moves."
17 March 1979
Alexei Kosygin; Andrei Gromyko; Yuri Andropov.

Gromyko: We have to discuss what we will do if the situation gets worse. Today, the situation in Afghanistan for now is unclear to many of us. Only one thing is clear—we cannot surrender Afghanistan to the enemy. We have to think how to achieve this. Maybe we won't have to introduce troops.

Kosygin: All of us agree—we must not surrender Afghanistan. From this point, we have to work out, first of all, a political document, to use all political means in order to help the Afghan leadership to strengthen itself, to provide the support which we've already planned, and to leave as a last resort the use of force. . . .

18 March 1979

Andropov: We know Lenin's teaching about a revolutionary situation. Whatever type of situation we are talking about in Afghanistan, it is not that type of situation. Therefore, I believe we can suppress a revolution only with the aid of our bayonets, but that is for us entirely inadmissible. We cannot take such a risk. . . .

Gromyko: I fully support Comrade Andropov's proposal to exclude a measure such as the introduction of our troops into Afghanistan. The

[Afghan] army there is unreliable. Thus our army, if it enters Afghanistan will be an aggressor. Against whom will it fight? Against the Afghan people first of all, and it will have to shoot at them. Comrade Andropov correctly noted that indeed the situation in Afghanistan is not ripe for a [socialist] revolution. And all that we have done in recent years with such effort in terms of a détente in international tensions, arms reductions and much more—all that would be thrown back. Of course, this will be a nice gift for China. All the non-aligned countries will be against us.

In a word, serious consequences are to be expected from such an action. There will be no longer any question of a meeting of Leonid Ilych [Brezhnev] with [U.S. President] Carter, and the visit of [French President Valéry] Giscard d'Estaing at the end of March will be placed in question. One must ask, and what would we gain? Afghanistan—with its present government, with a backward economy, with inconsequential weight in international affairs.

On the other side, we must keep in mind that from a legal point of view too, we would not be justified in sending troops. According to the UN Charter a country can ask for assistance, and we could send troops, in case it is subject to external aggression. Afghanistan has not been subject to any aggression. This is an internal affair, a revolutionary internal conflict, battle of one group of the population against another.

Kosygin: Maybe we should invite [Taraki] here and tell him that we will increase our assistance to you, but we cannot introduce troops, since they would be fighting not against the army, which in essence has gone over to the adversary or is just waiting it out, but against the people. There would be huge minuses for us. A whole bouquet of countries would quickly come out against us.

Gromyko: We would be throwing away everything which we achieved with such difficulty, particularly détente, the SALT-II negotiations, which would fly by the wayside; there would be no signing of an agreement (and however you look at it, that is for us the greatest political act) . . . and our relations with Western countries, particularly the FRG [Federal Republic of (West) Germany] would be spoiled.

And so, despite the difficult situation in Afghanistan, we cannot embark on such an act as the introduction of troops.

No. P499
Top Secret
Special File
20 March 1979

Meeting of Kosygin, Gromyko, Ustinov, Ponomarev, Taraki

We must not allow the situation to seem as if you were not able to deal with your own problems and invited foreign troops to assist you. I would like to use the example of Vietnam. The Vietnamese are bravely defending by themselves their homeland against aggressive encroachments. We believe that there are enough forces in your country to stand up to counterrevolutionary raids. . . . During our telephone conversation with you, we spoke of the need to begin already to create new military groups, keeping in mind that a certain amount of time will be needed for their training and preparation. . . .

Let's take the example of Herat. It seemed that all would fall apart, that the enemy would quickly entrench itself there, that the city would become a center of counterrevolution. But when you really took charge of the matter, you were able to seize the situation. . . .

Kosygin: We will give you assistance with all available means—ship weapons, ammunition, send people who can be useful to you in managing military and domestic matters . . . specialists to train your military personnel for use of the most modern types of weapons and military machinery.

Ustinov: We will give you six MI-24 helicopters in June and July, and a further six in the fourth quarter of the year. . . . We could send maintenance specialists . . . but not pilots.

Kosygin: We are training four hundred Afghan officers. Choose the people you need, and we will expedite their training.

Kosygin: Since Kabul was ready to pay for Pakistani wheat, you must have money. He suggested that Kabul should give the money to Moscow, which could then buy American wheat and transfer it to Afghanistan.

Taraki: requested that Moscow should build a 1,000-kilowatt radio station "which would allow us to broadcast propaganda throughout the world."

Ponomarev: We are taking energetic measures to spread propaganda about the success of the DRA [Democratic Republic of Afghanistan] . . . and will send specialists in propaganda.

Ustinov: A need will arise for additional military specialists.

Kosygin: I cannot understand why the question of pilots and tank operators keeps coming up. This is a completely unexpected question for us. . . .The question of sending people who would sit in your tanks and shoot at your people—this is a very pointed political question.

. . . We think it important that within your country you should work to widen the social support of your regime, draw people over to your side, insure that nothing will alienate the people from the government. And finally, I would like to express my ideas on the importance of a very careful and cautious approach toward your staff. One should take care of one's staff and have an individual approach towards it. Have a thorough and good understanding with each person, before hanging any labels on them.

Kosygin: If an armed invasion . . . takes place, then it will be a completely different situation.

Taraki: China is persistently pushing the Pakistanis against us.

Kosygin: We have already taken measures to guard it from aggression. . . . We have sent corresponding messages . . . to Pakistan and Iran.

DOCUMENT 2
Appendix to Politburo Minutes Regarding Propaganda in Afghanistan

27 December 1979

[Appendix 6 to item 151 of the top secret Minutes of the Session of the Politburo of the CC of the CPSU on December 27, 1979

Reference No. P 177/151.—Trans.] Hoover Archives

On the Provision of Propaganda Coverage of our Action in respect of Afghanistan

BE GUIDED BY the following in our propaganda activities when covering—in the press, on television and on radio—the action undertaken by the Soviet Union at the request of the leadership of the Democratic Republic of Afghanistan to assist in the repulsion of foreign aggression.

1. In all propaganda work, use as the basis the tenets contained in the appeal of the Afghan leadership to the Soviet Union, requesting military assistance, and the Communiqué issued by TASS [Telegraph Agency of the Soviet Union] on this matter.

2. Bring out as the main point [the idea] that the dispatch of limited Soviet military contingents to Afghanistan, carried out at the request of the Afghan leadership, serves one purpose—to render help and assistance to the people and government of Afghanistan in the struggle against external aggression. This Soviet action pursues no other ends.

3. Emphasize that as a result of acts of external aggression and the growing

interference from outside in internal Afghan affairs, a threat to the achievements of the April Revolution and the sovereignty and independence of the new Afghanistan had come into being. In these conditions, the Soviet Union, to which the leadership of the Democratic Republic of Afghanistan had repeatedly appealed over the last two years with a request for assistance in repelling aggression, responded positively to this request, guided in particular by the spirit and the letter of the Soviet-Afghan Treaty of Friendship, Good Neighborliness and Cooperation.

4. The request of the government of Afghanistan and the compliance with this request on the part of the Soviet Union are exclusively a matter for the two sovereign states—the Soviet Union and the Democratic Republic of Afghanistan, which themselves regulate their own mutual relations. They, like any [other] member-state of the UN, possess the right to individual or collective self-defense, as is stipulated in Article 51 of the UN Charter.

5. When covering the changes in the leadership of Afghanistan, emphasize that this is the internal affair of the Afghan people, using as the basis the declarations published by the Revolutionary Council of Afghanistan and the statements of the Chairman of the Revolutionary Council of Afghanistan, Karmal Babrak.

6. Give a firm and well-argued rebuff to any possible insinuations about any alleged Soviet interference in internal Afghan affairs. Emphasize that the USSR did not have and does not have anything at all to do with the changes in the leadership of Afghanistan. The task of the Soviet Union in connection with the events in and around Afghanistan boils down to the provision of help and assistance in protecting the sovereignty and independence of a friendly Afghanistan in the face of foreign aggression. As soon as this aggression comes to a halt and the threat to the sovereignty and independence of the Afghan state is over, the Soviet military contingents will be withdrawn immediately and completely from the territory of Afghanistan.

DOCUMENT 3
Politburo Minutes Containing Breshnev's Reply to President Carter

29 December 1979
Hoover Archives

Proletarians of all countries, unite!
Communist Party of the Soviet Union. CENTRAL COMMITTEE
TOP SECRET
No. P177/220 Hoover Archives

To COMRADES BREZHNEV, Kosygin, Andropov, Gromyko,
   Suslov, Ustinov, Ponomarev, Zamyatin
Extract from Minutes No. 177 of the Session of the Politburo of the CC of
the CPSU on 29 December 1979

ON THE ANSWER to the appeal of President Carter over the hot line re-
garding the problem of Afghanistan.
   Approve the draft of the answer of comrade L. I. Brezhnev on this matter
(attached).
   Send the answer over the Moscow–Washington hot line.
CC SECRETARY
16—ri
pe
[printed sideways in the left-hand margin:]
To be returned within the course of 7 days to the CC CPSU (General Department, First Sector)
Re: item 220 of minutes No. 177
Top secret
   Respected Mr. President,
   In reply to your message of 29 December, I consider it essential to state
the following.
   It is completely impossible to agree with your assessment of what is currently taking place in the Democratic Republic of Afghanistan. Through your
ambassador to Moscow, we have already provided the American side and you
personally with confidential clarifications, based on the facts, of what is actually taking place there and also of the reasons prompting us to respond positively to the request of the government of Afghanistan to send in a limited
number of Soviet military personnel.
   The attempt made in your message to cast doubt on the very fact of the
request of the government of Afghanistan for the dispatch of our troops to
that country looks strange. I am obliged to note that it is certainly not somebody's perception or nonperception of this fact, [his] agreement or non-

agreement with it, that determines the real state of affairs. And that [the real state of affairs] consists of the following.

Over the course of almost two years, the government of Afghanistan has repeatedly addressed a request on these lines to us. Incidentally, one of these requests was sent to us on 26 December this year. We, the Soviet Union, know this, and it is equally well known to the Afghan side which has been sending us requests of this sort.

I want to stress once again that the dispatch of limited Soviet forces to Afghanistan serves one purpose—to render aid and assistance in repelling acts of external aggression which have been taking place over a long period of time and have now assumed an even greater scale.

The assertion contained in your message to the effect that the Soviet Union undertook something to overthrow the government of Afghanistan is completely unacceptable and at odds with reality. I have to stress quite explicitly that the changes in the Afghan leadership have been carried out by the Afghans themselves and only by them. Ask the Afghan government about that.

What is said in your message about the fate of the families of the former Afghan leaders likewise fails to correspond to reality. The data at our disposal refute the information that you have received.

I have further to declare to you clearly that the Soviet military contingents have not undertaken any military action against the Afghan side, and we, of course, are not intending to undertake any.

In your message, you reproach us for not having consulted with the government of the United States on Afghan affairs before moving our military forces into Afghanistan. Well, is it permissible to ask you whether you consulted with us before beginning the massive concentration of naval forces in waters adjoining Iran and in the region of the Persian Gulf, and in many other cases as well, about which at the very least you should have informed us?

In connection with the content and spirit of your message, I consider it essential to explain yet again that the request of the government of Afghanistan and the compliance with this request on the part of the Soviet Union are exclusively the affair of the USSR and Afghanistan, which regulate their mutual relations themselves in accordance with their own agreement and naturally cannot admit any sort of outside interference in these mutual relationships. Like any state that is a member of the UN, they possess the right not only to individual but also to collective self-defense, as is provided for in Article 51 of the UN Charter, which the USSR and the United States themselves drew up. And this was approved by all the member states of the UN.

Needless to say, there are no grounds for your assertion that our actions in Afghanistan supposedly represent a threat to peace.

In the light of all this, the intemperance of the tone of some of the wording in your message is particularly striking. What could the reason for this be? Would it not have been better to weigh up the situation a little more calmly, bearing in mind the supreme interests of peace and, not least, the mutual relations between our two powers?

As for your "advice," we have already informed you more than once, and now I am repeating this again, that as soon as the causes of Afghanistan's request to the Soviet Union no longer obtain, we intend to withdraw the Soviet military contingents from the territory of Afghanistan completely.

And here now is our advice to you: The American side could make its contribution to the cessation of outside armed interventions into the territory of Afghanistan.

I do not consider that work on the creation of more stable and productive relations between the USSR and the United States could prove to have been in vain unless, of course, the American side itself wants this to be the case. We don't want this. I don't think this would be to the benefit of the United States of America themselves. It is our conviction that the way relations between the USSR and the United States turn out depends on the behavior of each of the parties. We consider that these relations should not be subjected to oscillations brought about by any sort of attendant factors or events.

Regardless of divergencies over a number of questions of world and European politics, as we all clearly realize, the Soviet Union is a supporter of the idea of conducting affairs in the spirit of those agreements and documents which have been adopted by our countries in the interests of peace, cooperation on the basis of equal rights, and international security.

L. BREZHNEV

29 December 1979.

19—gr, em

pe

APPENDIX L

DOCUMENTS FOR CHAPTER 32

DOCUMENT 1
Politburo Transcripts Regarding Results of Negotiations with Mengistu

31 October 1980
[AU: Source?]
<u>Top secret</u>
<u>Only copy</u>
<u>(Working transcript)</u>
SESSION OF THE POLITBURO OF THE CC OF THE CPSU

IN THE CHAIR: comrade L. I. BREZHNEV
PRESENT: comrades Yu. V. Andropov, M. S. Gorbachev, V. V. Grishin,
    A. A. Gromyko, A. P. Kirilenko, A. Ya. Pelshe, M. A. Suslov,
    N. A. Tikhonov, D. F. Ustinov, K. U. Chernenko, T. Ya. Kiselev,
    V. V. Kuznetsov, B. N. Ponomarev, M. S. Solomentsev,
    I. V. Kapitonov, V. I. Dolgikh, M. V. Zimyanin, K. V. Rusakov.

1.   <u>On the results of the negotiations with the chairman of the Provisional</u>
    <u>Military Administrative Council and chairman of the Commission for the</u>
    <u>Formation of the Workers' Party of Ethiopia, Mengistu Haile Mariam</u>

BREZHNEV. The negotiations with the Ethiopian delegation were undoubtedly useful.

I have formed the impression that from one meeting to the next, Mengistu is growing as an organizer and political leader. His statements provide
evidence of a mature, well considered approach to the solution of the problems facing Ethiopia. And his deeds also speak in his favor. The position of

the revolutionary forces in Ethiopia has strengthened, and the political course of the leadership enjoys support.

However, the situation in the country remains difficult. Mengistu and [his] comrades-in-arms are having to try to solve the tasks of a national-democratic revolution, which are complex enough anyway, in conditions of extreme economic and cultural backwardness and endless armed interventions from outside.

The transcripts of the negotiations have been distributed, and [my] comrades have evidently taken cognizance of them.

I shall dwell only on the tête-à-tête with Mengistu, which was of a confidential nature. During it we also discussed such sensitive questions for the Ethiopians as their relations with Somalia and the national question in Ethiopia itself.

DOCUMENT 2
Extract Including Gorbachev's Response to Mengistu

18–19 September 1989
Hoover Archives
Communist Party of the Soviet Union. CENTRAL COMMITTEE
TOP SECRET
SPECIAL FILE
[Printed sideways in the left-hand margin:]

FOR INFORMATION
A comrade who receives top secret documents of the CC of the CPSU may neither pass them on to, nor acquaint with them, any person whatsoever without the express permission to do so of the CC.

Making copies of the said documents or writing out excerpts from them is categorically forbidden.

After acquainting himself with the document, the comrade to whom it is addressed places his personal signature and the date on the document.
No. P165/30
To Comrades Gorbachev, Ryzhkov, Shevardnadze, Yakovlev, Yazov, Baklanov, I. Belousov, Katushev, Kryuchkov, Belyakov, Falin, Shkabardnya.

Extract from Minutes No. 165 of the Session of the Politburo of the CC of the CPSU on 19 September 1989

ON OUR MOVES in connection with the appeals of Mengistu Haile Mariam

1. Agree with the views and proposals set out in the memorandum of comrades E. A. Shevardnadze, A. N. Yakovlev, D. T. Yazov and V. A. Kryuchkov of 18 September 1989 (attached).
2. Approve the text of the oral response of comrade M. S. Gorbachev to Mengistu Haile Mariam (attached).

    Comrade V. I. Varennikov is to convey the response of the Ethiopian leader and hold a talk with him on the matters raised in the response.
3. During [his] stay in Ethiopia, comrade V. I. Varennikov, after having studied the situation on the ground, is to advise [our] Ethiopian comrades on military questions linked to [any] counteraction against the offensive of the units of the National Front for the Liberation of Tigrai.
4. Forward, for the scrutiny of the USSR Council of Ministers, the practical questions connected with an acceleration of the deliveries to Ethiopia of a certain quantity of ammunition.

CC SECRETARY

18-chv

gd

Re: item 30 of Minutes No. 165

Top secret

CC CPSU

On our moves in connection with the appeals of Mengistu Haile Mariam

[The right-hand edge of this document is missing from most of the photocopy used by the translator.]

ON 4 AND 7 SEPTEMBER 1989, Mengistu Haile Mariam, the General Secretary of the Central Committee of the Workers' Party of Ethiopia and President of the People's Democratic Republic of Ethiopia (PDRE), sent appeals to comrade M. S. Gorbachev expressing concern at the worsening of the internal political situation in the PDRE, as a result of the activization of the armed struggle of anti-governmental forces, and expressing the hope that the USSR, on a par with [its] assistance to the efforts of the Ethiopian leadership to settle the Ethiopian problem, will also provide support for the actions of the Ethiopians at the front.

The military and political situation in Ethiopia has indeed worsened considerably. At the end of August and beginning of September 1989, the oppositional People's Front for the Liberation of Tigrai (PFLT) began a series of sweeping offensive actions in the north of the country (in the areas [close to? —Trans.] Eritrea), threatening to surround and rout the Third Army of the Ethiopian armed forces, which is stationed [in those parts?]. According to available information, this was preceded by a series of military operations carried out by the governmental forces themselves, during the last ten days of August, including aerial bombardments against units of the PFLT.

If the detachments of the PFLT manage to build on their military successes, the main road between Addis Ababa and the port of As[mara?], the only transport artery currently functioning and linking the center of the country with the Red Sea, could be cut off; the Second [Army?], which is based in Eritrea, would [then] also be cut off. In the conditions of general political instability in the country and the continuing ferment in the armed forces after the attempted coup in May, such a turn of events would be fraught with the most negative consequences for the regime of Mengistu.

The worsening of the situation in the north of Ethiopia is creating dangers for the incipient political dialogue between Addis Ababa and the oppositional groupings. It cannot be excluded that reverses for the governmental troops might lead to a toughening of the positions of the People's Front for the Liberation of Eritrea (PFLE), at the meeting of its representatives with representatives of the Ethiopian government, opening in Atlanta (United States) on [October?] 7, 1989, and even impel this Eritrean organization, with which the PFLT is coordinating its moves, to resume military operations in its turn (at the same time the General Secretary of the PFLE, Isaiah Afeworke, assured a Soviet representative during a meeting in Washington on 4 September 1989, that the PFLE was in the mood for negotiations and was not launching any retaliatory operations, despite the fact that the Ethiopians were shelling [and approaching?] the areas where its units were billeted). A breakdown in the negotiating [process], for the smooth running of which considerable efforts were ex-pended by our side, would once again put back the task of [iso]lating Eritrea.

In the circumstances that prevail, it is important for us to support the leadership and to try to firm up its stance on continuing the dialogue with oppositional groupings. To this end, it would be advisable to send Mengistu an oral response from comrade M. S. Gorbachev, containing an assurance to the leader of the PDRE that the Soviet Union will not abandon Ethiopia at a difficult moment, simultaneously stressing the need to stabilize the negotiating process that has now begun, in spite of the growing complexity of the internal situation. This response could be conveyed by a Deputy Minister of Defense of the USSR, comrade V. I. Varennikov, who is going out to Addis Ababa as the head of a Soviet military delegation in compliance with a Resolution of the CC of the CPSU of 12 August 1989 (P164/101).

Instruct comrade V. I. Varennikov, when he has studied the situation on the ground, to advise the Ethiopians on military questions linked to [any] counteraction against the offensive of the NFLT. In Addis Ababa [he is] also to discuss the question of withdrawing all Soviet military experts from the areas of operational activities in the north of Ethiopia, and in general of reducing their number in that country, as is envisaged in the above-mentioned Resolution of the CC of the CPSU.

Bearing in mind that in accordance with the Resolution of the CC of the CPSU of 5 May 1989 (P157/28), we have moved the planned deliveries of tanks from 1990 to 1989, and that in September 1989 we are supplying ammunition, of which the Ethiopians are in particular need, to the value of 18,000,000 rubles; the additional dispatch of weaponry to Ethiopia by us, over and above that which is already being carried out, appears to be inadvisable. In order to speed up the planned delivery of cartridges, it would be possible to send them in by plane.

E. Shevardnadze   A. Yakovlev   D. Yazov   V. Kryuchkov

18 September 1989

No. 782/OS

9 copies

Re: item 30 of Minutes No. 165

TO COMRADE MENGISTU HAILE MARIAM,
GENERAL SECRETARY OF THE CENTRAL COMMITTEE
OF THE WORKERS' PARTY OF ETHIOPIA,
PRESIDENT OF THE PEOPLE'S DEMOCRATIC
REPUBLIC OF ETHIOPIA
Addis Ababa

Dear comrade Mengistu,

I have perused your messages of 4 and 7 September 1989, with the greatest attention.

I should like to confirm that the Soviet Union was and remains a loyal and sincere friend of the Ethiopian revolution. We are very concerned about its fate.

In every possible way the Soviet Union supports the peace initiative of the National Assembly of the PDRE on the question of Eritrea. The Soviet government has announced this publicly. In conformity with this, concrete moves have been undertaken on our part to assist its practical implementation. You know about them. The meeting of representatives of the Ethiopian leadership and of the Popular Front for the Liberation of Eritrea (PFLE) in Atlanta is in our view called upon to mark the beginning of serious and businesslike negotiations on a settlement for Eritrea. It is exceptionally important for the dialogue beginning there to take on a stable character.

Naturally, the Soviet Union will also be ready in the future to provide you with all possible assistance in the political settlement of the Eritrean problem. We shall also work further with Western and Arab countries to create a favorable political background for the negotiating process. New meetings will also be required between our representatives and the leaders of Eritrean organizations in order to bring influence to bear on them from positions which have been agreed between you and us, in the interests of helping them to display a sense of realism.

The latest worsening of the situation in the north of your country has caused us serious anxiety. A similar turn of events, which has already led to the breakdown of incipient contacts with the Popular Front for the Liberation of Tigrai, could also exert a negative impact on the burgeoning dialogue with the NFLE and give rise to a hardening of the positions of this grouping as well. I think that you will agree with me that the violation of the negotiating process, for the smooth running of which considerable efforts were expended, would again put back the task of settling and ending the fratricidal war and solving the complex problems of the north of Ethiopia at the negotiating table.

Of course, we are not going to abandon Ethiopia at this difficult moment for her. You can be assured of our support.

Comrade V. I. Varennikov, with whom we are sending this message, has been tasked with studying closely the situation which is taking shape in the north of Ethiopia and, should there be any need of this, advising [our] Ethiopian comrades on military questions.

We are confident that the wisdom and patience of which you, comrade Mengistu, speak in your message, and the fortitude, which the Ethiopian leadership has exhibited on more than one occasion when defending the supreme interests of the Motherland, will help [you] to get the better of the current difficult period and go forth to the stage of peace, to which the Ethiopian people are so looking forward.

With very best wishes and comradely greetings,

M. GORBACHEV

19 September 1989

19 copies

APPENDIX M

DOCUMENTS FOR CHAPTER 37

———✦———

DOCUMENT 1
Speech by Brezhnev Regarding Poland

31 October 1980
Hoover Archives

2. On the results of the visit of the First Secretary of the Polish United
    Workers' Party, comrade S. Kania, and the Chairman of the Council of
    Ministers of the Polish People's Republic, comrade J. Pinkowski, to the
    USSR

BREZHNEV. We can say with complete certainty that our meeting with
the new Polish leaders was timely. Events in Poland are taking on such a turn
[for the worse] that if we lose time and fail to correct the stance of [our] Polish
comrades, we won't have time to say "knife" before we find ourselves staring
in the face of a critical situation, which will require extreme and, it could be
said, painful decisions.

[Our] Polish comrades did not hide their anxieties concerning the activization of anti-socialist forces. But when it came down to the measures [to
be taken] in the struggle against the counterrevolution, indecisiveness could be
sensed in the views that they were putting forth.

They stated that Poland is bound hand and foot by debts. All imports
from the West—and the functioning of many enterprises and the state of the
internal market are dependent on them—are currently conducted on credit.
The economy of Poland has turned out to be in thrall to the West. In such
conditions, as [our] Polish comrades understand it, any aggravation of the situation in the country could give the capitalists a reason for refusing any further postponement of [the repayment of] credits, and Poland, as Kania put it,

will be brought to its knees.

We asked Kania directly if the Party had a plan for an emergency situation when there was an open threat to the power of the people. He said that there was a plan for such an eventuality and that they knew whom it would be necessary to arrest and how to utilize the army. But everything goes to show that for the present, they are not ready for such a step and are putting it off until some unspecified time in the future.

I will not give you a full account of the contents of our talks. A transcript of the negotiations has been distributed, and [my] comrades can familiarize themselves with it if they have not already had time to do so.

As we were saying at the previous session, the purpose of the meeting with [our] Polish comrades was two-pronged: on the one hand, to help them to realize the full extent of the danger and prod [them] into more decisive actions, and on the other hand, to raise their morale and increase their confidence in their powers and their abilities. I think that the negotiations were useful in the one respect, as in the other.

As I have already said, Kania demonstrated a certain reticence only on the question of introducing a state of emergency. As for the other measures we suggested, he declared that he agreed with us. There was also complete agreement between us when we were weighing up the causes of the crisis and the dimensions of the counterrevolutionary threat.

Kania assured [us] that on his return to Warsaw, he would acquaint the Politburo of the Central Committee of the Polish United Workers' Party with our point of view. They carefully wrote down everything we said. Admittedly, Kania made the proviso that he would not give some members of the Politburo this intelligence in its entirety, because he feared a leakage of information to the West. And it is important for the Polish leadership not to countenance any talk to the effect that they are acting at the behest of Moscow.

As for Kania and Pinkowski personally, both of them made not a bad impression on me and, apparently, on the other comrades who took part in the negotiations; they [Kania and Pinkowski] are serious, thinking people. Obviously, their caliber as political leaders can only be judged by their future deeds.

Most likely, [my] comrades will agree that as of today we have done everything on the Polish question that was required of us. But, of course, we shall have to remain on our guard—the atmosphere in Poland is literally explosive.

What ought to be speeded up is the provision of whatever economic assistance is feasible; this will allow the Poles to hold out at this difficult time. No matter how burdensome this is for us, we have to get at it. Let us agree to this: all the necessary proposals must be tabled by the next session of the Politburo.

Perhaps Nikolai Aleksandrovich [Tikhonov] and other comrades would like to add something to my account?

If not, then let us approve the results of the negotiations we have conducted.

ANDROPOV, SUSLOV, KIRILENKO, CHERNENKO, and TIKHONOV speak to the point that the invitation of the leaders of Poland to talks at the Central Committee of the CPSU was timely and extremely necessary.

BREZHNEV. There is a proposal to approve the talks.

ALL. Correct.

TIKHONOV. The economic situation of Poland is very difficult. They have high indebtedness. Right now it's necessary to return debts of about 500,000,000 dollars. Apart from that, they are now asking for 150,000,000 [dollars] to put into circulation. We will prepare some proposals.

BREZHNEV. Have those proposals ready by the next session of the Politburo.

TIKHONOV. All right.

ARKHIPOV. We will prepare some proposals for providing help to Poland, together with an appeal with your signature, Leonid Ilich, to the leaders of fraternal countries.

BREZHNEV. I don't think there's any need to link these two things. The appeal should be sent off as soon as possible.

GROMYKO. I think that there's absolutely no point in linking these two things. Incidentally, I'll say a few words about the way the negotiations went. During the course of the negotiations, comrades Kania and Pinkowski said nothing about policies in the past, about the policies of Gierek. They spoke about what there is now and what they need.

ANDROPOV. Thanks to these talks, [our] Polish comrades have started to understand their own situation better. On his arrival in Warsaw, comrade Kania said at the airport that he was very pleased with the meeting with Leonid Ilich and that Leonid Ilich had shown exceptional consideration for the needs of Poland.

BREZHNEV. They are afraid to mention the word "counterrevolutionary." But just listen to what comrade Semenov reports from Bonn. He is passing on neither more nor less than a conversation with one of the Polish [political] figures. Here, as you see, he's talking bluntly about an armed uprising in the Polish People's Republic. How is it that [our] Polish comrades can't understand the simple truth that the counterrevolution in their country is completely off the leash?

ANDROPOV. This is indeed a serious observation, which will have to be carefully checked out.

USTINOV. In any event, we will have to be very vigilant.

CHERNENKO. The talks with [our] Polish comrades have helped them to open their eyes to the real state of affairs which exists in Poland and weigh up the situation that has come about in a genuine and Party manner. Naturally, this will help them to be more energetic in the actions which they are planning to carry out against the anti-socialist elements and to safeguard the achievements of the socialist system.

DOCUMENT 2
Transcript of Politburo Session, April 1981

Hoover Archives
Top secret
Only copy
(Working transcript)
SESSION OF THE POLITBURO OF THE CC OF THE CPSU
9 April 1981

IN THE CHAIR: comrade K. U. CHERNENKO
PRESENT: comrades Yu. V. Andropov, M. S. Gorbachev, V. V. Grishin,
    A. A. Gromyko, A. P. Kirilenko, M. A. Suslov, D. F. Ustinov,
    P. N. Demichev, V. V. Kuznetsov, M. S. Solomentsev,
    I. V. Kapitonov, V. I. Dolgikh, M. V. Zimyanin

1.   On the draft of the Appeals of the CC of the CPSU for the First of May, 1981
[Not translated.]
2.   On the arrangements for the First of May demonstration of representatives of the working people of the city of Moscow
[Not translated.]
3.   On the results of the meeting of comrades Yu. V. Andropov and D. F. Ustinov with [our] Polish friends

CHERNENKO. In line with the decision of the Politburo, comrades Andropov and Ustinov held a meeting with comrades Kania and Jaruzelski. Perhaps we will listen to [our] comrades.

ANDROPOV. In line with the understanding with [our] Polish comrades, comrade D. F. Ustinov and I went out to Brest, and there, in the vicinity of Brest, our meeting took place in a [railway] carriage. The meeting began at nine o'clock in the evening and ended at three o'clock at night, on the assumption that [our] Polish comrades wouldn't be spotted as having gone away anywhere.

The task that we had been set was to listen to [our] Polish comrades closely and give [them] our elucidations accordingly, as we had agreed at a session of the Politburo.

The overall impression from the meeting with our comrades was that they were in a very tense [psychological] condition; they felt nervous, and it was obvious that they were near the end of their tether. Comrade Kania said bluntly that they are finding it very difficult to govern the country, and that "Solidarity" and anti-socialist forces are pressing them hard. But at the same time, they stated that the situation in Poland is moving along the road towards stabilization after the Twenty-Sixth Congress of the CPSU. Kania said that they had held meetings to hear reports and elect new officials in the majority of local Party organizations, and he noted that it was characteristic of them that not a single person belonging to "Solidarity" had ended up as one of the delegates, in other words that our [i.e., the Polish authorities'—Trans.] candidates had got through to the [Polish Party] Congress. Then comrade Kania was compelled to say that subsequent events, and in particular the warning strike and the events in Bydgoszcz, had shown that the counterrevolution was stronger than we [i.e., they] are. They were particularly frightened by the warning strike and even more afraid of a general strike and were doing everything they could to avert a general strike.

What are the tasks that are facing us, said comrade Kania. Above all, they concern restoring the people's trust in the Party, getting the economy to run smoothly and liquidating strikes and [involuntary] idle periods at the enterprises. Naturally, [our] Polish comrades don't have any experience of struggling against negative phenomena like these, and so for the moment, they don't know what methods to apply, and they're lurching in one direction and then another. As for sending in troops, they said straight out that it's completely impossible, and it's equally out of the question to bring in martial law. They said that they wouldn't be understood and they would be powerless to do anything. [Our Polish] comrades stressed in the talks that they will introduce proper order without any outside help. What they mean is that the Ninth Congress, that they are now making the preparations for, won't give "Solidarity" the chance to get its candidates selected as delegates. In the Party organizations, they're electing good workers as delegates to the Congress.

During the talks, comrade Kania also observed that the Polish people are very sensitive to truthful information. For instance, they had announced the Congress, then they had started giving the impression that the Congress was going to be postponed, and then they had said again that the Congress would take place. And this sort of hiccup over the timing of the Congress had a very considerable impact on the state of affairs in the country, in the sense that confidence in the Party had been shaken even further. For our part, we told [our] Polish comrades robustly that the adversary was attacking them, he has [certain] advantages, and you [i.e., the Polish authorities] are on the retreat and, moreover, you've lost valuable time. You could have dealt a serious blow to the adversary in September 1980. You didn't do anything, however; you didn't take any measures, either political or, still less, administrative ones. We particularly emphasized that there's no need to set up a dividing line between political measures and measures of a military and administrative character. Everything needs to be combined in a rational way.

As for martial law, it could have been introduced a long time ago. After all, what does the introduction of martial law mean? It would have helped you to break the onslaught of the counterrevolutionary elements and all manner of trouble-makers and put an end once and for all to the strikes and the anarchy in economic life. A draft document on bringing in martial law has been prepared with the help of our [i.e., Soviet] comrades and these documents need to be signed. [Our] Polish comrades said: how on earth are we going to sign these documents when they [first] have to go through the Sejm, and so on. We said that there's no need for them to go through the Sejm, this is a document in line with which you will act when you are bringing in martial law, whereas right now you, comrades Kania and Jaruzelski, need to give your personal signatures so that we know that you agree with this document and so that you know what it will be necessary to do during the period of martial law. If martial law has to be introduced, there will be no time then to work out what measures to take to bring in martial law; they need to be prepared in advance. That's what it's all about.

Then, after our clarification, comrades Kania and Jaruzelski said that they would look through this document on 11 April and sign it.

Next we asked what comrade Jaruzelski's address to the Sejm would contain. Jaruzelski spoke at length and rambled on and on. He explained that he would talk about banning strikes for two months. We asked what he meant by two months—what's going to happen after two months? Two months will quickly go by and then the strikes will start again. You [the Polish authorities] make a lot of promises to your workers, but then you don't keep them, and thereby you provide additional grounds for the lack of trust in the government and the PUWP [Polish United Workers' Party].

Right now the question of carrying out a wide range of political measures is a particularly serious one. Let us just take the clarification of the question as to why you [in Poland] don't have enough bread and other products. How has this come about? Why, because the strikes going on all the time really do disrupt the whole economy, that's why you haven't got enough. A huge number of billions of zloties are lost as a result of each strike, but the workers don't know about this and it's all blamed on the government, and it's the government, the CC [Central Committee] of the Party and the Politburo that are guilty, whereas the ringleaders and the organizers of the strikes stand to one side and it's they—hang it—who look like the defenders of the interests of the workers. But if you get to the root of the matter, we said, [you realize] that the main perpetrators of all the economic difficulties are "Solidarity" and the organizers of the strikes. That's what it's all about. So, why can't you get all this across to the workers?

There's a lot of talk in your country about setting up a national front for the salvation of Poland. Discussions about that are going on in a number of districts. The idea is to include veterans of the revolutionary movement and military leaders—for example, people like Rolia Zymerski and others—in this front for the national salvation of Poland. You could make a note of that too. Or let's take the FRG, for instance, where they're now talking about Silesia and Gdansk as territories that were annexed to Poland and [should be] given back to the FRG. Why don't you get all the mileage you can out of that? I think the [Polish] people could be rallied around things like that. You need to rouse the people.

We said that we don't have any objections to setting up a national front for the salvation of Poland. But this front mustn't be a substitute for the Party and the government.

There's a special question about the struggle for the cohesion of the Party and the unity of the nation. A very great deal was said about the unity of the Party. We also want to suggest [,we said,] that you ought to take all the measures necessary to rally the Party and create the unity of the nation. You yourselves know better what steps should be undertaken. But there are many questions. We have already told you the ones around which it would be possible to rally the nation and foster the unity of the Party. [Our] Polish comrades spoke about bringing three workers [i.e., members of the working class] into the Politburo. They referred to Lenin, who suggested bringing some workers into the Politburo. We said that we had never had a situation when there were any workers in the Politburo. But if you really do feel such a need at the present time, you could introduce [this] in the Politburo, but not necessarily three workers, maybe [just] one. In addition you could select a certain number of workers for the Central Committee, i.e., these are all measures which will contribute to the cohesion and unity of the Party. For instance, you were talking about bringing some workers into the membership of the People's Control body. Not a bad step. Of course, that could be implemented.

Next, the unity of the Party could be enhanced by implementing measures like speeches at Party meetings being given by well-qualified and properly prepared comrades. We gave our own examples of when we, up to and including members of the Politburo, made speeches at meetings of workers. They [Kania and Jaruzelski] agreed with these proposals.

Next, we said that there's no need, comrades, for you to take on the responsibility for extravagant programs, just adopt more modest programs, but carry them out. All the members of the [Polish] Politburo should give speeches at major enterprises. Right now comrade Kania is going to Gdansk, and not only comrade Kania, but comrade Jaruzelski and all the other members of the Politburo and candidate members of the Politburo will go to other towns to speak at enterprises amongst the workers; in other words, it's necessary to speak out against organized "Solidarity," contrasting it with our solidarity. What makes "Solidarity" strong? It's strong because of its demagogy. Demagogically it promises the workers an increase in wages, and as you see it's done that. It's also trying to get [proper] protection of the workers' interests, and it gains authority by announcing strikes when you [the Polish leaders] arrest a few workers or other "Solidarity" activists. We told Kania to his face that you are [i.e., he was] giving ground and going on giving ground every day, whereas you need to act, you need to sanction military measures, sanction emergency measures.

Now there's the special question of holding [a session of] the Sejm. What is "Solidarity" doing? Right now it's working on each member of the Sejm. It's

suggesting to the workers who are members of the Sejm that they should address the Sejm with absolutely down-to-earth speeches targeted against the
PUWP [Polish United Workers' Party] and the socialist system. It's necessary to
smash these plans of "Solidarity." For instance, why not tie each member of
the Sejm to one or another member of the Politburo and tell each Politburo
member that he has to answer for his member of the Sejm and get them ready
for the session? After all, things have come to a pretty pass. For example, one
worker who's a member of the plenum [*sic*—Trans.] of the PUWP got a
telegram about what he had to say at the plenum in line with the instructions
that he'd been given. The speech of this worker at the plenum was delayed; in
other words, he didn't want to take the floor. He then got another telegram
saying the following: "For some reason we didn't hear your speech." This
worker again failed to make an intervention, the plenum came to an end, and
he got the following telegram: "No need for you to come back again." You see
here how "Solidarity" is terrorizing this worker and intimidating him. That's
how "Solidarity" operates.

Regarding support for the Politburo. Who can it lean on? They've got a
400,000-strong army, 100,000 in the Ministry of Internal Affairs and 300,000
reservists, in other words, 800,000 men. Kania said that the tension at the moment has eased off a bit and they had managed to prevent a general strike.
But how long this period of calm will last is an open question.

What have they been doing since our meeting? It has to be said that
they have been doing something. For instance, Kania has been out to
Gdansk. Comrade Jaruzelski has been reworking his speech for the Sejm.
But it has to be said that there are many differences between the views of
Kania and Jaruzelski on specific questions. Comrade Jaruzelski again submitted a request to be released from the post of Prime Minister. We explained to him in easy-to-understand terms that it's imperative [for him] to
remain in this post and to fulfill in a dignified manner the obligations that
have been entrusted to him. We stressed that the adversary is gathering his
forces in order to seize power.

On the other hand, some other members of the Politburo—comrades Olszowski and Grabski—are adopting a somewhat different stance, a firmer one
than that of the leadership. We need to work with them. In particular they are
proposing to organize an underground Politburo and carry out work. It turns
out that they got this idea as a result of advice they were offered by comrade
Zhivkov. I don't know whether this is true or not, but they are saying that

comrade Zhivkov gave them some advice of this sort. We also need to draw a conclusion from this, that if leaders of fraternal Parties are going to give this kind of advice to [our] Polish friends, then we won't gain anything from this, of course; we'll only lose.

SUSLOV. Perhaps we ought to prepare some information sheets [on Poland] for the fraternal Parties.

GROMYKO. Under no circumstances should there be any reference to the fact that a meeting has taken place.

ANDROPOV. It's absolutely out of the question to talk about a meeting.

USTINOV. Yu. V. Andropov has covered everything very well, so I would like to talk briefly about the following. The first thing that really hits you is the dispirited condition of our interlocutors. But it seems to me that in spite of this, we ought to retain this couple—Kania and Jaruzelski—and strengthen the relationship between them. The point is that even in their Politburo there are differences. Naturally, they are shaken first and foremost by the strikes; they are very frightened about them. We asked why you [i.e., they] changed their decision about Bydgoszcz. As you know, they didn't want to give way on the Bydgoszcz conflict, and then they did give way. They assert that the threat of a general strike was hanging over them. Then we were telling them, Why do you pay the workers for the time when they were on strike? They said that "Solidarity" was demanding this. So that means you are being led along by "Solidarity," we said in reply. They haven't taken a decision on rural "Solidar-ity," but to all intents and purposes they have already recognized the existence of this organization.

Yury Vladimirovich [Andropov] and I stressed particularly strongly the question of the imperative necessity for unity in the Politburo. There's no need to bring three workers into the Politburo, as they were saying. That won't strengthen the Politburo. As for the CC, it is necessary to bring in some [more] workers. But in the usual, properly regulated way, in conformity with the Statutes. We told [our] Polish friends that it's particularly necessary to get down to some real work with the members of the Sejm. Next point. They are holding what they call teleconferences. What these amount to are open telephone conversations. Everything that's said immediately becomes known to a broad circle of people, even people who work in "Solidarity." What a carry-on, holding conferences like that. We gave an example [of how to work properly], of how Leonid Ilich has conversations all the time in our country with secretaries of regional [Party] committees, territorial [Party] committees, the Central

Committees of the Communist Parties of the Union Republics, but he talks with each one [separately,] on specifics, referring to the situation in the particular area in question.

In order to dispel their fears about introducing a state of emergency or martial law, we used the example of many countries that announce a state of emergency or martial law the minute an uprising flares up or some sort of chaos breaks out. Take Yugoslavia. There were some demonstrations in Kosovo; they declared martial law, and nobody said a word to them about it. Why the Poles are [so] frightened of announcing a state of emergency is something we can't understand.

Yury Vladimirovich [Andropov] spoke well about the plans for bringing in a state of emergency. We said that it was necessary to sign the plan drawn up by our comrades.

Then I told them straight, as we agreed at the Politburo, what will happen in Poland if there's a really messy situation there and what an economic state it will be in. You know, right now Poland gets absolutely all its oil practically at half price from the Soviet Union. It also gets cotton, iron ore and many other commodities. And if it doesn't get that, what then? Why is a fact like this not being explained, why doesn't it get through to the minds of the workers? This [argument] is a powerful weapon. It's necessary to talk about this to the workers; it's necessary to talk to "Solidarity" as well. Now "Solidarity" has dug in at the most important factories. It's necessary to win these factories back from "Solidarity. You [Poles] have some good factories where the workers are standing up for the leadership. For instance, the factory that makes television sets. You can and you must support branch trade unions and carry out active work with them. Jaruzelski told me again later when I was alone that he can't work, he's got no strength left, and he was begging to be relieved of his post.

ZIMYANIN. When we were in Bulgaria at the Congress, we had some meetings with Grabski. [The text of] these talks has been distributed and [my] comrades are acquainted with it. It makes it clear that the situation in their [the Polish] Politburo really is very difficult; there's no unity, and Yury Vladimirovich and Dmitry Fedorovich were right when they said that it's necessary to work on strengthening unity in the Politburo.

It was resolved:

1. To approve the talks that comrades Yu. V. Andropov and D. F. Ustinov held with comrade S. Kania, the First Secretary of the CC of the PUWP,

and comrade W. Jaruzelski, the Chairman of the Council of Ministers of the PPR [Polish People's Republic] and Minister of National Defense.

2. To instruct the Commission on Poland of the CC Politburo to follow the development of the situation in the PPR closely and to prepare the appropriate proposals as and when necessary.

4. On the results of the talks with H.[-D.] Genscher, the Deputy Federal Chancellor and Minister of Foreign Affairs of the FRG [not translated]

5. On the participation of the delegation of the CPSU in the work of the Twelfth Congress of the Bulgarian Communist Party [not translated]

DOCUMENT 3

Working Transcript of Politburo Session, September 1981

Hoover Archives
Top Secret
Only copy
(Working transcript)
SESSION OF THE POLITBURO OF THE CC OF THE CPSU
10 September 1981

IN THE CHAIR: comrade L. I. BREZHNEV
PRESENT: comrades M. S. Gorbachev, V. V. Grishin, A. A. Gromyko,
N. A. Tikhonov, K. U. Chernenko, P. N. Demichev, M. S. Solomentsev,
I. V. Kapitonov, V. I. Dolgikh, M. V. Zimyanin

9. Exchange of opinions on the Polish question

BREZHNEV. Yesterday I perused the "Appeal to the Peoples of Eastern Europe," which has been adopted by the Congress of the Polish "Solidarity." A dangerous and provocative document. It doesn't contain many words, but all of them are hammering the same point home. Its authors would like to make trouble in the socialist countries and stir up little groups of all manner of renegades.

I don't think we can limit ourselves to criticism in the press of this impudent escapade. How about the collectives of our major enterprises, like, say, the Kirov Factory [in Leningrad—Trans.], Magnitka [in Magnitogorsk], the Kama Automobile Works [near Kazan] and others, giving a rebuff to these demagogues? Their letters to the Congress of "Solidarity" will certainly be hard to pass over in silence [even] there. All the more so, as we will give them the place they deserve in our mass media.

If [my] comrades are in agreement, let us instruct the Commission on Poland to choose three or four production collectives and help them to prepare a highly qualified riposte to "Solidarity."

GROMYKO. The state of affairs in Poland is getting worse all the time. If one can put it this way, hardly anything of the power structures still remains. The positions of the Central Committee of the PUWP [Polish United Workers' Party] and the Council of Ministers are being lost, day in day out. As for a conversation with comrade Kania, maybe now it really would be better not to talk with him, since there was a conversation not long ago.

As for using the leverage that a telephone conversation can provide, this shouldn't be excluded, because it's not a bad way of exerting pressure.

BREZHNEV. Speaking frankly, it seems to me that there's no desire to talk with comrade Kania at the moment, and anyway, no good of any sort could come of it.

CHERNENKO. In their time there were conversations, good instructions were given and there were talks in the Crimea. And what was the use of them? Comrades Kania and Jaruzelski do everything as they see fit.

GRISHIN. They themselves don't deny any longer now that they're giving up one position after another.

ZIMYANIN. I want to tell the Politburo what publications are being scheduled in connection with the Congress of "Solidarity." One can say that the Congress demonstrates the further worsening of the situation in Poland. As is well known, they appealed to the parliaments and peoples of certain countries, including even socialist ones, with their program of "renewal." Consequently, the appropriate pieces are now being prepared for use in our press and by TASS [news agency]. The activities of the "Solidarity" trade union are going to be exposed to the light of day in these materials. I consider that Leonid Ilich's suggestion that several collectives of major leading enterprises be given the opportunity to have their say is completely correct. We will try to get that ready as well.

TIKHONOV. All the same we shall have to react in some way, and react unambiguously, to these escapades of hooligan elements which are taking place in Poland and against which the [Polish] government isn't taking any measures of any sort. As you know, apart from the fact that memorials to our

soldiers are being desecrated there, they are drawing various sorts of carica-
tures of the leaders of our Party and government, insulting the Soviet Union
in every way possible and so on. In other words, that means that they're
laughing at us. It seems to me that we can't hold our peace any longer, and either through [official] state channels or through some other channel, we have
to lodge a protest with the Polish government in connection with this. Not to
react, in my opinion, is absolutely impossible.

GROMYKO. This needs to be thought over carefully. It's a matter of a
country that is friendly towards us.

GORBACHEV. I consider that Leonid Ilich made a completely correct
suggestion about collectives at major enterprises publishing statements on the
pages of the press and exposing the activities of "Solidarity."

GRISHIN. It's necessary to organize such publications both in "Pravda"
and in other newspapers. We will work to ensure that collectives like the
"Likhachev Automobile Works," the "Sickle and Hammer," and other major
factories [in Moscow—Trans.] come out with some statements.

BREZHNEV. I think that it would be possible to instruct the USSR Ministry of Foreign Affairs and a Department of the Central Committee to prepare the draft of a declaration to the government of the Polish Republic in
connection with the hooligan escapades of representatives of "Solidarity"
against the Soviet Union. At the same time, as [my] comrades here were already saying, it is necessary to come out in the press with a number of materials exposing the activities of "Solidarity" and the resolutions of its Congress.

After discussing the matters on the agenda, the Politburo listened to information from comrade M. S. Gorbachev about the course of the harvesting and
of state procurements of agricultural products, and also about the course of
the autumn sowing and the state of affairs regarding the laying-in of fodder.

DOCUMENT 4
Telegram from the Soviet Ambassador to East Berlin

15 September 1981
Hoover Archives

8. Telegram of 15 September 1981 from the Soviet ambassador to [East]
    Berlin (spec. No. 598)

BREZHNEV. Regarding my telephone conversation with comrade Kania on 11 September 1981, to which we agreed at the last session of the Politburo, I sent some information to our ambassadors for briefing comrades Honecker, Kadar, Zhivkov, and Husak.

The ambassadors carried out this assignment and have reported on the results. The leaders of [these] fraternal Parties completely and entirely agreed with what was said to comrade Kania in the telephone conversation and consider that comrade Kania is exhibiting inadmissible liberalism and that it is necessary to apply a good deal of pressure on him.

In his talks with comrade Abrasimov, about which, as you know, he reported by telegram, comrade Honecker put forward this proposal: the leaders of fraternal Parties gather in Moscow, invite comrade Kania, and tell him to resign, and instead of him recommend comrade Olszowski as First Secretary of the CC of the PUWP [Polish United Workers' Party].

In connection with this, I would like to exchange ideas on what we should do. Naturally, it is difficult for us at the moment to take a clear-cut decision on this matter. We don't know the view yet of other comrades, leaders of the socialist countries. All this needs to be thought about in detail.

Perhaps we will instruct the USSR Ministry of Foreign Affairs, the Ministry of Defense, and a Department of the Central Committee to examine the question set out in the telegram and, taking the exchange of opinions in the Politburo into consideration, to draft the appropriate proposals and submit them to the Central Committee.

If there are no objections, perhaps we could take such a decision right away.

Members of the Politburo and candidate members of the Politburo say that the proposal of Leonid Ilich is completely correct and that it ought to be adopted. One should merely include the KGB among the organizations which are instructed to examine these questions.

The proposal is adopted.

DOCUMENT 5
Rusakov's Visit to the GDR, Czechoslavakia, Hungary and Bulgaria

Hoover Archives

2. <u>On the results of the visits of comrade K. V. Rusakov to the German
   Democratic Republic, the Czechoslovak Socialist Republic, the Hungarian People's Republic, and the People's Republic of Bulgaria</u>

BREZHNEV. All the comrades present here know that on the instructions of the CC CPSU Politburo, comrade Rusakov went out to the GDR,
Czechoslovakia, Hungary, and Bulgaria to inform our friends about certain
matters and in particular about the measures which we have been taking and
are going to take in connection with the events in Poland.

Comrade Rusakov has been to these countries and reported to the Politburo on the results of his visits in the memorandum of which you have a copy.

Perhaps Konstantin Viktorovich has something to add to what he set out
in the memo. In which case I ask [him to speak].

RUSAKOV. I held talks with the leaders of four fraternal states, as I had
been instructed to do by the Politburo. The negotiations concerned two questions—the first question related to Poland. In the memorandum, the course of
the talks with the leaders of these fraternal countries on the Polish question is
set out in detail. It can be said that all the leaders of these fraternal Parties are
heart and soul with us regarding the measures which we are taking with regard to Poland, and also with regard to the situation which has now come
into being in Poland. In a word, one can say that here we have a complete
identity of views.

During the course of the negotiations, the leaders of the fraternal countries also touched on economic questions as well. The main one was the question of reducing supplies of energy carriers, above all of oil. Although
comrades Kadar, Husak, and Zhivkov said that this will be difficult for them;
nonetheless, they regarded our proposal, our request, with understanding and
said that they would find a way out of the situation and accepted what we
proposed. To clarify the matter further, I put the following question to [our]
comrades: Can I report to the Politburo that you are in agreement with the
point of view that I have put forward? [Our] comrades answered Yes, you can
report that.

The conversation with comrade Honecker went differently. He said right away that a cutback in oil supplies on that scale was unacceptable to the GDR, that it would do serious damage to the economy and to the GDR as a whole, that it would hit the GDR economy hard and that there would be no way they could make ends meet. He even put it in such a way, that they couldn't accept this and were asking for a written answer from comrade Brezhnev to two of their letters that they had sent [to him]. So the question proved to be very complicated, and in essence it wasn't resolved. Moreover, comrade Honecker again produced as proof [of his argument] that they were supplying us with bismuth and uranium, that they were maintaining a contingent of [Soviet] troops, and that matters were getting especially complicated in their country because the Polish People's Republic wasn't delivering the coal that was supposed to be coming according to our agreements. As a result of this, as Honecker put it, the standard of living of the German population would drop sharply and they didn't know how to explain this. They would have to review all the rough drafts of the plan.

BREZHNEV. I think we ought to approve the talks that comrade Rusakov held with comrades Honecker, Husak, Kadar, and Zhivkov and in [our] subsequent practical work bear in mind the views expressed by [our] comrades on the question of Poland.

As is well known, we decided to cut back oil deliveries to our friends. They all took this badly, and as you see comrade Honecker, for example, is still waiting for an answer to the letters which he has been sending us. The others are not waiting for a reply, but in their hearts, of course, they are thinking about whether we might not somehow alter our decision.

Perhaps at the next meeting with [our] friends we ought somehow to say on this question that we are going to take every measure to fulfill and over-fulfill the plan for oil, and that we hope that we'll manage to do this. In that event, we could adjust the preliminary plans for the supply of energy carriers, on no account, of course, giving [our friends] to understand right off that we are backing away from our decision.

It's obvious that comrade Tikhonov will have to look carefully at this question yet again, and if [even] the smallest opportunity shows up to reduce the tension, [he should] put forward the appropriate proposals to the Central Committee.

GROMYKO. Regarding Poland, I would like to say that I have just had a conversation with [our] ambassador, comrade Aristov. He reported that the one-hour strike was extremely impressive. At many enterprises it is "Solidarity" that is, in effect, running the show. Even those who want to work can't work because the extremists in "Solidarity" are blocking those who wish to work, threatening them in all sorts of ways, and so on.

As for the plenum, comrade Aristov reported that it went off normally; they selected two additional secretaries. At the Sejm, which begins its work on 30 October, they are going to raise the question of limits on strikes. It's hard to say at the moment what this law will lead to, but at any rate they're making attempts to limit strikes by means of the law. I would say that comrade Jaruzelski's speech at the plenum was not bad.

BREZHNEV. I don't believe that comrade Jaruzelski did anything constructive. It seems to me that he's an insufficiently courageous man.

ANDROPOV. Jaruzelski hasn't done anything that's essentially new, although a fair amount of time has already elapsed. Barczikowski and Kubiak are a great nuisance in the Politburo. There have been conversations about this, and advice has even been given about removing Barczikowski and Kubiak from membership of the Politburo. However, Jaruzelski, to all intents and purposes, has refused [to take] such a step. Moreover, he explains this by saying that he doesn't have any personnel who could take the place of these people.

The question as to who will be the Prime Minister of Poland puts one very much on one's guard. Jaruzelski clearly has a liking for Olszowski and Rakowski. Neither the one nor the other, of course, is suitable to be a Prime Minister.

BREZHNEV. In one of our talks, Schmidt even let it slip out that a very dangerous situation is being created in Poland and that this situation could get more complicated and have an impact on my visit to the FRG, which might not take place.

ANDROPOV. The Polish leaders are talking about military assistance from fraternal countries. However, we need to keep firmly to our line, not to send our troops into Poland.

USTINOV. In general, it's necessary to say that it's impossible to send our troops into Poland. They—the Poles—are not ready to receive our troops. People in Poland who have completed their period of [military] service are currently being demobilized. Moreover, demobilized men are being allowed to go home to get their civilian clothes and then go back again and serve out another two months doing physical labor. But at the same time, they are being worked on by "Solidarity." As we know, Jaruzelski has organized some operational squads made up of about three men. But so far these squads haven't done anything. It's obvious that a meeting with the leadership of Poland is required, in particular with Jaruzelski. But who will be at the meeting—that's also a question.

RUSAKOV. Tomorrow sees the opening of the Sejm, at which the question of giving the government some sort of extraordinary powers to deal with a number of matters is on the agenda. Jaruzelski really would like to come to Moscow. In view of this, it's imperative to prepare our position paper on this question.

BREZHNEV. But who will be getting the materials ready for [any] conversations with Jaruzelski?

RUSAKOV. I think we ought to instruct the Commission on Poland to prepare the papers for possible talks with Jaruzelski, in case he expresses such a wish [to visit Moscow].

BREZHNEV. Have we sent Poland the meat about which we took a decision, and have we told Jaruzelski about that?

RUSAKOV. Jaruzelski has been told of this; he even named a figure, 30,000 tons.

ARKHIPOV. We are going to send meat from our state reserves to Poland.

BREZHNEV. After my telegram, are there any improvements in the deliveries of meat from the [other Soviet] Republics to the Union stocks?

ARKHIPOV. For the moment, Leonid Ilich, there are no improvements of any sort in the deliveries of meat. Admittedly, not enough time has passed. But I have talked this over with all the Republics and I can report that steps are being taken everywhere that should make it possible to fulfill the plan for meat deliveries to the state. In particular, measures of this sort have been worked out in Estonia, Belorussia and Kazakhstan. Up to now, the Ukrainians haven't given any instructions to the[ir] regions.

CHERNENKO. But we have sent out our telegram to all the regions in Ukraine.

ARKHIPOV. We will have the data by Monday, and then we'll report how matters will stand.

GORBACHEV. Leonid Ilich, your telegram has played an important role. Above all, all the Republics and regions are seriously considering steps that ought to guarantee fulfillment of the plan. At any event, according to the data that we have as a result of telephone conversations with regional [Party] committees, territorial [Party] committees and the Central Committees of the Communist Parties of the Union Republics, this question has been discussed everywhere by the [Polit- or Party] buros [bureaus]. We will draw up a summary of meat deliveries as of 1 January.

BREZHNEV. I keep on thinking that even though we gave Poland 30,000 tons of meat, our meat will hardly help the Poles. At any rate, we are not at all clear what is going to happen with Poland. Comrade Jaruzelski isn't showing any initiative. Perhaps we ought to ready ourselves for talks with him.

As for the talks about oil deliveries, I am especially worried about the GDR. In general, I want to say that the socialist countries have taken this proposal of ours badly. They are dissatisfied with this decision, if not openly, then in their hearts. And some of them, as is evident from comrade Rusakov's presentation, are expressing their dissatisfaction openly. Comrade Honecker is particularly dissatisfied. He is saying straight out that for them this decision is unacceptable, and he's even asking for a written answer. What decision we are going to come to, I simply don't know.

ANDROPOV, SUSLOV, and KIRILENKO speak to the point that it is necessary to agree with the view that you [i.e., Brezhnev] have just expressed.

ARKHIPOV. We are still having difficulties with fuel. The coal miners are going to fall short of 30,000,000 tons of coal. How can this [shortfall] be covered? The oil industry won't overfulfill the plan, so somehow we'll have to try to cover these 30,000,000 tons. Apart from that, we are 1,500,000 tons short of sugar, which will also have to be bought and paid for, and 800,000 tons of vegetable oil, without which it's impossible to live at the present time.

As for the answer to comrade Honecker, I think that the suggestion that comrade Rusakov made is the correct one. It's necessary to confirm that we can't change the decision of which comrade Honecker was informed.

As for the deliveries of uranium that comrade Honecker refers to, the uranium supplied from the GDR doesn't solve the problem; it comprises only 20 percent of the total quantity of uranium that we utilize. Comrade Honecker also fails to take into account that we are building nuclear power stations for the GDR, and that is no small item.

RUSAKOV. I also want to say that the Poles are asking for oil and gas supplies to be held at the same level that they are on this year.

ARKHIPOV. We are holding negotiations with the Poles and consider that we need to conduct economic relations with them on the principle of balancing out [our respective] plans. Of course, this will lead to a significant reduction of [our] oil deliveries, to the extent that they do not supply us with coal and other products. However, if all goes well, we are keeping [the figures for our next year's] oil deliveries in [our] computations at the same level as we are supplying them [to Poland] now.

BAYBAKOV. All the socialist countries are now feeling us out and, moreover, they are taking their cue from the GDR and watching how we deal with the GDR. If Honecker manages to open up a breach, they will try to do the same thing as well. At any rate no one so far has given any written answers. Over the last few days, I have been holding talks with the chairmen of the State Planning Agencies of all the socialist countries. All of them want to maintain the overall total of oil deliveries, with a breakdown for each year. Some of them are suggesting that oil could be replaced by other energy carriers.

A resolution is adopted:

1. Approve the talks held by comrade K. V. Rusakov with comrades Honecker, Husak, Kadar, and Zhivkov.
2. Ask the Politburo's commission on Poland to prepare the papers necessary for possible talks with comrade Jaruzelski.
3. Instruct comrades Tikhonov, Rusakov, and Baybakov to undertake an additional examination of the question of oil deliveries to these countries, with due regard for the exchange of views which took place at the session of the CC Politburo.

Document 6

Extract from Politburo Session, November 1981,
Including Communication from Brezhnev and Jaruzelski

21 November 1981
Hoover Archives

To Comrades Brezhnev, Tikhonov, Andropov, Gromyko, Suslov, Ustinov, Ponomarev, Rusakov, Arkhipov, Baybakov, Zamyatin, and Smirtyukov.
Extract from Minutes No. 37 of the Session of the Politburo
of the CC of the CPSU on 21 November 1981

On the reception of a Party and state delegation from the PPR [Polish People's Republic] in the USSR and the oral communication from comrade L. I. Brezhnev to comrade W. Jaruzelski

1. Approve the text of the oral communication from comrade L. I. Brezhnev, instructing the Soviet ambassador to the PPR to deliver it to comrade W. Jaruzelski (attached).

2. Recognize the desirability of receiving a Party and state delegation from the PPR, headed by comrade W. Jaruzelski, in the USSR on 14–15 December 1981.

   Approve the composition of the Soviet delegation at the negotiations with the delegation from the PPR: comrades L. I. Brezhnev (head of delegation), M. A. Suslov, Yu. V. Andropov, A. A. Gromyko, N. A. Tikhonov, D. F. Ustinov, K. U. Chernenko and K. V. Rusakov.

3. Before 1 December 1981, a Department of the CC of the CPSU, the USSR Ministry of Foreign Affairs, the Ministry of Defense, the USSR KGB, and the State Planning Agency of the USSR are to prepare the necessary materials for the negotiations with the Polish Party and state delegation, including the draft of a Communique for the press.

   A Department of the CC of the CPSU and the USSR Ministry of Foreign Affairs are to submit proposals for the organizational arrangements connected with the reception of the Polish delegation in the USSR.

CC SECRETARY
Re. item 21 of Minutes No. 37
Secret
WARSAW
SOVIET AMBASSADOR
Visit comrade W. Jaruzelski and, referring to instructions, convey to him the following oral communication from comrade L. I. Brezhnev:

"Respected comrade Jaruzelski!

We have carefully examined your proposal to visit Moscow at the head of a Party and state delegation, which would also include leaders of parties allied with the PUWP [Polish United Workers' Party], and are in agreement with it [the proposal]. As for the timing of the visit, it could take place on December 14–15 if, of course, this is convenient for you.

In addition, as there is still time before the visit, I have decided to convey to you through comrade Aristov some thoughts on current questions concerning the situation in Poland, which remains the subject of our serious concern.

I shall not be revealing a secret when I say that your election as First Secretary of the CC of the PUWP was linked by us with great expectations. We assumed that earlier in the struggle against the anti-socialist forces you, as Chairman of the Council of Ministers, had evidently been constrained by the absence of political decisions coming from the leadership of the Party. Now this sort of obstacle was a thing of the past. The fourth plenum of the CC of the PUWP associated the change of First Secretary directly with the need for immediate measures for the salvation of socialism in Poland.

When I congratulated you by telephone, I was pleased to hear that the confidence that you feel our side has in you played a certain role in persuading you to agree to take on the responsible post of leader of the PUWP in so critical a situation. I told my comrades about this, and it strengthened our hope that in you we would have a kindred spirit and ally in one of the most crucial sectors of the struggle against imperialism, which is what Poland has now become.

I recall that in our telephone conversation, I expressed the hope that now people in Poland and abroad would feel that things in the country would move in a different direction. We spoke then about the key prerequisites for a fundamental improvement in the situation, and you agreed that it was necessary for you to select some reliable assistants from among the dedicated and unwavering communists, activate the entire Party, instilling into it a spirit of struggle, and move on without brooking any delay to active measures against the counterrevolution.

It is obvious that the fundamental question now is the question of the struggle for the masses. However, the impression is building up that here, up to the present time, no breakthrough has been achieved. Anti-socialist forces are not only ruling the roost in many major industrial enterprises, they are also continuing to spread their influence on ever broader sections of the population. Not a day passes without the leaders of "Solidarity" and counterrevolutionaries appearing at all manner of gatherings of the riffraff and making openly inflammatory speeches directed against the PUWP and socialism and stirring up nationalistic passions. A direct consequence of these hostile activities is the dangerous growth of anti-Sovietism in Poland.

It appears to us that now it is necessary to mobilize the entire Party for a struggle for the minds of the people, to go to the very midst of the masses with a precise and clear program for getting out of the crisis, and to try to convince everyone of the correctness of this program. In other words, to win the trust of the working people, to do the work all over again that was carried out by the communists in the years when the power of the people was being established. In this respect, it would be very important to arrange regular meetings of the leaders and the other most active members of the PUWP with work collectives, especially at the major enterprises—and not only in the capital—that the enemy has managed to turn into its bastions. And of course the struggle for the masses will not produce the required results unless real Party control over the media is ensured, and if the adversary, as hitherto, continues to step up his hostile propaganda unimpeded.

I would like to touch on another matter as well. Much has been written and said of late in Poland about your meeting with Glemp and Walensa. Some people are calling it historic and see it as the beginning of a shift away from chaos and towards social peace. As we know, the results of the meeting have been given a positive appraisal by the Politburo and the government of the PPR [Polish People's Republic].

We realize, of course, that when you put forward as a key question at this meeting the establishment of a "National Reconciliation Front," you were pursuing a number of tactical goals and, in the first instance, the broadening of the base of public support for the authorities and the splitting of the leading clique within "Solidarity." But how far is it possible to go along the road of agreements before the danger arises of losing control over the situation? After all, [our] class opponents will certainly try to give the "National Reconciliation Front" a political content that will as a minimum spell out in writing their idea of dividing power up among the PUWP, "Solidarity," and the Roman Catholic Church, with the ensuing dismantling of socialism. In addition, it cannot be doubted that they will utilize their current influence on the masses to secure for themselves a majority at the forthcoming elections to the people's councils and to pave the way for themselves to seize power in the country by legal means.

Hence, as it appears to me, the fundamental importance of spelling out in a clear-cut way the leading role of the PUWP in the "National Reconciliation Front" and the recognition on the part of its participants of the Constitution of the PPR [Polish People's Republic], of socialism and of the international alliances of Poland. Will this be done in the Statutes and other documents of the Front, and, most important, will it be guaranteed in practice? How do you propose to act in connection with the elections to the local organs of power, bearing in mind the risk that does exist of the Party's being defeated?

Another fundamental question is connected with this. In numerous talks, one and the same idea has continually been emphasized by our side: We are not opposed to agreements. But they must not contain concessions to the opponents of socialism. And the main thing—this must not simply be reduced to a matter of agreements: together with measures to win the broad masses of the people and a variety of political forces over to one's own side, decisive actions against the overt enemies of the regime of the people are imperative. You agreed with the problem being formulated in such a way and spoke yourself of your intention to struggle for the working people and simultaneously to smash the class antagonist.

But now the impression is being created that you are banking only on the first part of this intrinsically two-part formula. We know that there are people in your Party leadership who are resting all their aspirations on a continuation of the bankrupt line of Kania. It would be dangerous to yield to their persuasions. It has become absolutely clear by now that without a resolute struggle against the class opponent, it will be impossible to save socialism in Poland. In essence the question is not whether there will be a confrontation or not, but who will start it, what methods will be used to conduct it, and who will retain the initiative.

I would like to stress that when we speak of confrontation, we bear in mind that this presumes a struggle to win over to the side of the PUWP those workers, the working masses, who [currently] find themselves under the influence of "Solidarity" or who are adopting a passive attitude, waiting to see who is going to get the upper hand.

Wojcech Wladyslawovich, you and I have slogged along the roads of war, and we know that the strategy of struggle brings to the forefront the question of timing. This is entirely relevant to the critical situation that has now come about in Poland. The leaders of the anti-socialist forces, who have long been surreptitiously, and here and there even openly, preparing for the decisive encounter, are trying to put it off only until such time as they have an overwhelming advantage. In particular, they are banking heavily on the fact that a new intake, which has been worked on by "Solidarity," will [before long] be called up for military service. Does this not mean that, by failing to take firm measures against the counterrevolution right now, you are losing precious time?

The key question here is the isolation of the overt enemies of socialism. Until this is done, everything will go on as before. More than that, an openly counterrevolutionary organization like the "Confederation for an Independent Poland" is recruiting new supporters and functioning to all intents and purposes legally. It is obvious that this became possible because the Party is in effect losing control over the organs of justice, as is evidenced by the entire history of the trial of Moczulski and other leaders of the CIP [Confederation for an Independent Poland].

I want to share with you some thoughts on one other current question. It is obvious that measures to defend socialism in the first instance require an energetic struggle for the Marxist-Leninist character of the PUWP and an increase in its fighting ability. After the fourth plenum of the CC of the PUWP, signs of revivification in the Party organizations could be discerned. As we understand it, this was also a purpose of the letter of the Politburo to the primary organizations of the PUWP. It is important to [continue to] prioritize such work and not to permit a situation where grassroots communists again drift into a state of passivity and lose all heart. And for this, what is needed above all else is for Party members to believe that words will no longer be at variance with deeds and that the leadership intends to implement firmly and consistently the decisions that it takes.

The consolidation of the PUWP also depends on a clear-cut policy toward the various trends within its ranks. Some people in your country are contending that there are now three tendencies in the Party—leftist, rightist and centrist—and advice is being given to cut off the leftists and the rightists, to deal out equally strong blows to each of them. This is dangerous advice. Who, in reality, are being called "leftists" or "die-hards"? Communists, who base themselves firmly on the positions of Marxism-Leninism, in no way denying the need to rectify the mistakes and distortions that have been allowed to happen. But who are the rightists? They are people who are propagating revisionist views and, in the final analysis, closing ranks with "Solidarity." It is clear that any actions against steadfast communists would be suicidal for the PUWP as a Communist Party. And it is equally clear that until you rid yourselves of the revisionists, including those in the Party leadership, who are attempting to continue the former capitulatory line, they will be a heavy burden hanging on your feet.

It appears to me that these thoughts also provide a key to the solution of personnel questions, for which the time is more than ripe. I am certain that if you work together with comrades who are regarded as "leftists" and provide them with support, you will find precisely in these people a solid foundation for the struggle to overcome the crisis.

Respected Wojcech Wladyslawovich! Raising before you a number of questions which are of concern to us and sharing my ideas with you, I am naturally leaving out a variety of problems which it will be possible to discuss during a personal meeting.

L. BREZHNEV."

Telegraph on implementation.

DOCUMENT 7
Politburo Session Regarding Instituting Martial Law in Poland

10 December 1981
Hoover Archives
Top secret
Only copy
(Working record)
SESSION OF THE POLITBURO OF THE CC OF THE CPSU
10 December 1981

IN THE CHAIR: comrade L. I. BREZHNEV
PRESENT: comrades Yu. V. Andropov, V. V. Grishin, A. A. Gromyko, A. P.
                 Kirilenko, A. Ya. Pelshe, M. A. Suslov, D. F. Ustinov, K. U.
Chernenko,   P. N. Demichev, B. N. Ponomarev, M. S. Solomentsev, I. V.
Kapitonov,   V. I. Dolgikh, K. V. Rusakov.

1.   On the question of the situation in Poland

BREZHNEV. This question doesn't feature on our agenda. But I think that [we] ought to start the session of the Politburo with this question, inasmuch as we sent comrades Baybakov and Kulikov on a special mission to Poland to discuss some urgent questions, which have now come to a head, with [our] Polish comrades. On 8 December comrade Kulikov informed [us] about the talks that he had had in Warsaw, and yesterday, 9 December, comrade Baybakov reported from Warsaw that he had been having a talk with comrade Jaruzelski. It's clear from these and the subsequent talks of comrade Baybakov that [our] Polish comrades are hoping to receive additional deliveries of raw materials and products from the USSR and other socialist countries in the first quarter of next year, to a value of about 1½ [1.5] milliard [in American English: billion] dollars. This includes iron ore, nonferrous metals, fertilizers, oil, tyres, grain, and other things.

At the same time, as you see, [our] Polish comrades assume that deliveries of goods from the USSR to Poland in 1982 will be maintained on the same level as in 1981. Comrade Baybakov informed his interlocutors that all their requests would be reported to Moscow.

Perhaps we ought to instruct comrades Tikhonov, Kirilenko, Dolgikh, Skachkov, and Arkhipov right away, without waiting for any final agreement, to go on studying this question, bearing in mind the exchange of opinions.

And now let's listen to comrade Baybakov.

BAYBAKOV. In accordance with instructions from the Politburo, I went out to Warsaw. I had meetings there with all the comrades with whom it was necessary to talk over the questions which had been entrusted to me.

First of all I had a talk with a deputy chairman of the Council of Ministers, comrade Obodowski. In this talk [our] Polish comrades raised the question of economic aid. I sent a message here in cipher about this request of Poland.

It has to be said that the list of goods which they are including in the category of assistance by our side to the Polish People's Republic comprises 350 items to a value of 1.4 milliard [billion] rubles. This includes commodities like 2 million tons of grain crops, 25,000 tons of meat, 625,000 tons of iron ore, and many other articles. Taking into account what we were intending to give Poland in 1982, the overall amount of aid to the Polish People's Republic will come to approximately 4.4 milliard [billion] rubles, if we add in the requests voiced by [our] Polish comrades.

The time is now approaching for Poland to repay its credits to West European countries. To do this, Poland will require a minimum of 2,800,000 hard currency rubles. When I was listening to [our] Polish comrades as they were making their requests [and thinking about] what the sum total of all this help would come to, I posed the question as to whether we should not conduct our economic relations on a balanced basis. Moreover, in this context I remarked that Polish industry was not by a long chalk fulfilling its planned targets. The coal industry, which is the major source of hard currency earnings, is in essence disorganized, and the appropriate measures are not being taken; strikes are continuing. And now, when there aren't any strikes, the output of coal is also at a very low ebb.

Or, for example, let's say, the peasants are producing things; there is grain, meat products, vegetables and so on. But they [the peasants] aren't giving the state anything; they are just playing a waiting game. In the private markets, trading is fairly active and the prices are very high.

I said to [our] Polish comrades quite bluntly that they need to take more decisive measures in view of the situation that has come into existence. Perhaps they [ought to] bring in something like the requisitioning of farm produce.

For instance, if it's a question of grain reserves, Poland harvested 2 million tons more this year. The people aren't starving. Town dwellers go to the markets and to the villages and buy up all the products they need. And the produce is there.

It's well known that in accordance with a decision of the Politburo and at the request of [our] Polish comrades we are providing them with assistance by supplying 30,000 tons of meat. 16,000 tons of these 30,000 tons have already been sent abroad. It should be said that produce, in this case meat, is delivered in dirty, unsanitized goods wagons, used for transporting ore, with a very unappetizing appearance. When this produce is unloaded at Polish stations, genuine sabotage takes place. Poles come out with the most indecent words about the Soviet Union and Soviet people, refuse to clean out the wagons, and so on. It would be impossible to enumerate all the insults which rain down on our heads.

Sensing the position with the balance of payments situation, the Poles want to introduce a moratorium on the repayment of their indebtedness to Western countries. If they announce a moratorium, all Polish ships located in the waters or berthed at the wharves of any of the states, and all the other assets in countries with which Poland is in arrears will be arrested. So the Poles have now given instructions to the captains of vessels to leave port and lie in neutral waters.

Now I'll say a few words about the talk with comrade Jaruzelski. He confirmed the request which had been submitted by Obodowski regarding the delivery of commodities. Then, in the evening, together with the ambassador and comrade Kulikov, we went to see Jaruzelski again. Obodowski and the secretary of the CC of the Polish United Workers' Party who deals with these matters were also present at this talk. Jaruzelski was in a highly distressed state of mind. It could be felt that he had been greatly affected by the letter of the head of the Polish Catholic Church, Archbishop Glemp, who, as is well known, had promised to declare a holy war against the Polish authorities. True, Jaruzelski had immediately replied that if there were a demonstration by "Solidarity" they would isolate all the hostile elements.

As for the Party organizations, in the provinces they have in essence collapsed and are not functioning. And on the whole Jaruzelski said about the

Party that in essence it didn't exist. The country is falling apart, and the local centers are not receiving any sort of underpinning because the Central Committee and the government are not issuing any firm and clear-cut instructions. Jaruzelski himself has turned into a man who is highly unbalanced and lacking in confidence in his own powers.

RUSAKOV. Comrade Baybakov has given us a correct picture of the situation regarding the state of the Polish economy. What now ought we to do? It seems to me that we should supply Poland with those commodities that are specified in the economic agreement, and these supplies should not exceed the quantity of goods that we delivered in the first quarter of last year.

BREZHNEV. But can we give that right away?

BAYBAKOV. Leonid Ilich, we can only give it out of the state reserves or at the cost of cutting supplies to the internal market.

RUSAKOV. The day before yesterday they had a conference of secretaries of [Party] committees of the Provinces. As comrade Arestov reported, the secretaries of the Province committees simply cannot understand the speech of comrade Jaruzelski, who failed to spell out a clear, precise course of action. Nobody knows what on earth will happen during the next few days. There was talk of Operation "X." At first it was said that it would be during the night from the 11th to the 12th, then from the 12th to the 13th. And now they're already saying that it will be on about the 20th. What they have in mind is that the Chairman of the Council of State, Jablonski, will go on radio and television and announce the introduction of martial law. At the same time, Jaruzelski stated that the law on the introduction of martial law can only be introduced after it is discussed in the Sejm, and the session of the Sejm has been fixed for the 15th of December. Consequently, everything is getting very complicated. The agenda for the session of the Sejm has been published. The question of introducing martial law isn't on it. But at any event "Solidarity" knows full well that the government is preparing to introduce martial law, and in its turn it ["Solidarity"] is undertaking all the necessary measures to introduce martial law [*sic*].

Jaruzelski himself says that he is proposing to address an appeal to the Polish people. However, he will not speak about the Party in his appeal, but rather appeal to the people by laying special stress on their patriotic feelings. Jaruzelski talks about the need to proclaim a military dictatorship of the sort that existed under Pilsudski, pointing out in this context that the Polish people will understand this better than anything else.

As for such figures as Olszanski, he has recently been acting more decisively, and it has to be said that at the session of the Politburo, the decision to introduce martial law and take more decisive measures against the extremist figures in "Solidarity" was taken unanimously; nobody raised any objections at all. At the same time Jaruzelski intends to get in touch with [his] allies on this matter. He says that if the Polish forces cannot cope with the resistance of "Solidarity," [his] Polish comrades are hoping for help from other countries, up to and including the entry of armed forces onto the territory of Poland. In this context, Jaruzelski refers to a speech of comrade Kulikov, who supposedly said that help for Poland from the armed forces of the USSR and allied states will be forthcoming. However, so far as I know, comrade Kulikov did not say [this] explicitly; he simply repeated the words that on one occasion were spoken by L. I. Brezhnev, to the effect that we would not leave the Polish People's Republic in the lurch.

If we are to speak about what is going on in the Polish provinces, it's necessary to say bluntly that the power of the Party organizations cannot be felt out there in the least. To some extent, one can still feel the authority of the [state] administration. In essence, all power is located in the hands of "Solidarity." As for what Jaruzelski is saying, it looks as though he's pulling the wool over our eyes, because you don't feel when you're listening to him that he's making the correct analysis. If they don't organize themselves quickly, right away, and pull themselves together and take action against the onslaught of "Solidarity," there won't be any success in improving the situation in Poland.

ANDROPOV. From the talks with Jaruzelski, it's clear that they haven't so far taken a firm decision to introduce martial law, and even in spite of the unanimous decision of the Politburo of the CC of the Polish United Workers' Party (PUWP) on the introduction of martial law, we don't see any concrete measures for the time being on the part of the leadership. The extremists in "Solidarity" are stepping on the throat of the leadership of the Polish People's Republic. Within the last few days, the Catholic Church has also voiced its clear position. In essence, it has gone over to the side of "Solidarity."

Naturally, in these conditions [our] Polish comrades need to get ready quickly for movement "X" and carry through this operation. At the same time, Jaruzelski announces that we'll launch operation "X" [only] when "Solidarity" forces it on us. This is a very worrisome symptom. All the more so, as the last session of the CC PUWP Politburo and the decision it took on the introduction of martial law testifies to the fact that the Politburo is behaving more decisively. All the members of the Politburo spoke out in favor of resolute action. This decision has put Jaruzelski on the spot, and now he's compelled somehow or other to get off the hook. I was talking to Milewski yesterday and I asked him what measures were being contemplated and for when. He answered that he didn't know about operation "X" or about a precise time for carrying it out. We have a situation, therefore, where either Jaruzelski is hiding a plan for concrete actions from his comrades or he's simply moving away from carrying through this operation.

Now I would like to note that Jaruzelski is rather persistently presenting us with economic demands and making the execution of operation "X" conditional on our economic help and, I would go even further, he's posing the question, albeit not in so many words, of military assistance.

Now, if we take a look at the list of goods that [our] Polish comrades are asking for, then, to put it bluntly, serious doubts arise as to the need for the supply of these products. For instance, where is the link between the successful execution of operation "X" and the delivery of fertilizers and certain other commodities? In this connection, I would like to spell it out that our position, as it was formulated earlier at the last session of the Politburo, and as it has been spelled out repeatedly by Leonid Ilich, is absolutely correct, and we should not retreat from it. In other words, we adopt a policy of international help, we are concerned about the situation that has come about in Poland, but as for the execution of operation "X," that must be fully and completely the decision of [our] Polish comrades; as they decide, so it will be. We will not insist on this and we will not try to dissuade them.

As for economic aid, then naturally it will be difficult for us to do this in the dimensions that they have asked for. Evidently something ought to be given. But I want to say again that the formulation of the question about the allocation of commodities in the form of economic aid has an air of impudence about it, and all this is being done so that if we don't supply something, then later on they will be able to lump the blame on us. If comrade Kulikov really did speak about the dispatch of troops, then I consider that he was wrong to do so. We can't take any chances. We don't intend to send troops into Poland. That is the correct position, and we need to observe it to the end. I don't know how things will go in Poland, but even if Poland is governed by "Solidarity," that will be one thing. But if the capitalist countries fall upon the Soviet Union, and they already have the relevant agreements on various sorts of economic and political sanctions, then things will be very difficult for us. We have to show concern for our country and for the strengthening of the Soviet Union. That is our main political line.

On the whole, it seems to me that our position regarding the situation in Poland has been formulated by Leonid Ilich in his numerous speeches and in decisions which have been put on the record; today at the session of the Politburo a very thorough exchange of opinions is taking place. All this ought indeed to form the basis of the policy which we should adhere to in [our] relations with Poland.

As for the communications which go from the Soviet Union to the German Democratic Republic via Poland, we must of course do something and take [steps] for their protection.

GROMYKO. Today we're discussing the question of the situation in Poland without mincing our words. Earlier, I think, we didn't discuss it so frankly. This can be explained by the fact that at this moment, we ourselves don't know what direction the course of events in the Polish People's Republic (PPR) will take. The leadership in Poland itself has the feeling that power is slipping out of its hands. As you know, Kanja and Jaruzelski staked everything on being able to get the support of the neutrals. But now, in essence, there aren't any, there aren't any neutrals. The situation that has taken shape is fairly clear: "Solidarity" has proclaimed itself to be an explicitly counter-revolutionary organization, laying claim to power and openly announcing the seizure of that power. The Polish leadership has to resolve the question: either it surrenders its position, if it refuses to take decisive measures, or it will take decisive measures, bring in martial law, isolate the extremists in "Solidarity" and establish due order. There is no other way.

What is our attitude to the Polish events? I completely agree with what has been expressed here by [my] comrades. We can say to the Poles that we regard the Polish events with understanding. This is a precise form of wording, and there are no grounds for us to alter it. At the same time, we will somehow have to try to put an end to the attitude of mind of Jaruzelski and other leaders of Poland regarding the dispatch of troops. There can be no dispatch of troops to Poland. I think that on that we can instruct our ambassador to visit Jaruzelski and inform him of this.

In spite of the fairly unanimous decision of the CC PUWP Politburo on the introduction of martial law, Jaruzelski is now taking up a vacillating position once more. At first he cheered up somewhat, but now he's gone soft again. Everything that has ever been said to them remains in force. If they go on wavering any longer in the struggle against the counterrevolution, nothing of socialist Poland will be left for them. Of course, the introduction of martial law would bring it home to the counterrevolution in Poland that the Polish leadership was capable of taking firm decisions. And if the measures that they intend to carry out are implemented, I think it would be possible to expect positive results.

Now regarding the setting up of a new Party that Jaruzelski was talking about. I think it's necessary to tell Jaruzelski flatly that there's absolutely no need to set up any sort of new Party, because that would mean that the Polish leadership was in retreat. It would be an admission of the fact that the PUWP really wasn't a militant political organization, but an organization that had permitted mistakes; it would testify to its weakness and to their own weakness and play into the hands of the extremists in "Solidarity." Then even the population of Poland, which feels a certain sympathy for the PUWP as the leading force, would be completely disillusioned by it.

I consider that we should not at this time permit any sort of strongly worded instructions which would force them into courses of action of one sort or another. I think that we shall adopt the correct position here: the imposition of order in Poland is the task of the Polish United Workers' Party, its Central Committee and Politburo. We have been saying to [our] Polish friends, and we shall go on saying in the future, that it's necessary to adopt firm positions and that it's completely out of the question for them to weaken their grip.

Of course, if the Poles deal a blow to "Solidarity," the West in all probability will refuse them credits and won't give them any help. They [the Poles] realize this, and we too evidently need to take this into consideration. Therefore the proposal of Leonid Ilich is correct: instruct a group of comrades to take a look at this question and provide a certain amount of economic assistance to the Polish People's Republic [PPR], with due regard for the resources at our disposal.

USTINOV. The situation in the PPR is very bad, of course. The situation is getting more and more complicated by the day. There's no firmness, no unity, in the leadership, in particular in the Politburo. And all this has had an impact on the state of affairs. Only at the last session of the Politburo was a unanimous decision taken with regard to the introduction of martial law. Now everything hinges on Jaruzelski. [On] how he will be able to carry out this decision. But for the time being no one can speak frankly about Jaruzelski's behavior. Even we don't know. I had a conversation with Siwicki. He said straight out that even we don't know what the general [Jaruzelski] is thinking. In other words, the man who is currently in effect the acting Minister of Defense of the PPR doesn't know what is going to happen and what actions the Chairman of the Council of Ministers and the Minister will be taking.

As for what comrade Kulikov supposedly said regarding the dispatch of troops to Poland, I can state on full responsibility that Kulikov has not said this. He simply repeated what had been said by Leonid Ilich and me, that we would not leave Poland in the lurch. And he knows full well that the Poles themselves asked [us] not to send in troops.

As for our garrisons in Poland, we are beefing them up. I suppose that I'm also inclined to think that the Poles won't take things to a complete showdown, and maybe they'll get down to serious business only when "Solidarity" has got them by the throat.

The trouble is that the Polish leaders are not displaying any resoluteness. As [my] comrades here have been saying, correctly, there's no need for us to force any sort of our decisions on them, [but rather] to carry out the policy that we have agreed on. In our turn, we ourselves need to be ready and not to provide any evidence of any sort of activity that hasn't been provided for by our decisions.

SUSLOV. I consider that all of us, as is evident from the contributions of [my] comrades, have a single point of view on the situation in Poland. Throughout the entire period of the events in Poland, we have displayed self-control and presence of mind. Leonid Ilich Brezhnev spoke about this at the Plenum. We have said this to the people so that everybody could hear it, and our people have supported this policy of the Communist Party.

We are carrying out a great deal of work for peace, and it is impossible for us to change our position now. World public opinion wouldn't understand us. We have carried out some really large-scale actions at the United Nations to strengthen peace. What results we have from the visit of L. I. Brezhnev to the Federal Republic of Germany and from many other measures in the interests of peace that we have carried out! This has made it possible for all peace-loving countries to realize that the Soviet Union is firmly and consistently upholding a policy of peace. That is why we must not change our position with regard to Poland, [the position] that we adopted from the very beginning of the Polish events. Let [our] Polish comrades themselves determine what actions they should undertake. We ought not to push them into any sort of more decisive actions. But we will go on telling the Poles, as we did earlier, that we regard their actions with understanding.

As it seems to me, Jaruzelski is exhibiting a certain sort of cunning. He wants to fence himself off with the help of the requests which he is presenting to the Soviet Union. Naturally, we are physically incapable of fulfilling these requests, but Jaruzelski can then say later that he appealed to the Soviet Union and asked for help, but he didn't get this help.

At the same time the Poles are stating quite bluntly that they are opposed to the entry of [Soviet] troops. If the troops are sent in, this will mean a catastrophe. I think that all of us here hold the identical view that we can't talk about any sort of dispatch of [our] troops.

As for giving help to Poland, we've given [them] more than a milliard [billion] rubles of it. Not long ago we took a decision to supply 30,000 tons of meat to Poland, and 16,000 tons [of it] have already been delivered. I don't know whether we'll be able to supply the 30,000 tons in full, but, at any rate, we evidently ought to give [them] a certain amount more tons of meat as well, in the form of aid, in accordance with this decision.

As for the Polish United Workers' Party [PUWP] and the setting up of a new Party in its place, I consider that it would be inadvisable to go for the dissolution of the PUWP. It was said here correctly about this, that it would be a completely negative step.

GRISHIN. The situation in Poland is going along the path of further deterioration. The policy line of our Party with regard to the Polish events is completely correct. As for the proposal of Jaruzelski regarding the dissolution of the PUWP and the setting up of a new Party, it's impossible to agree with that. Sending in troops is out of the question. It will be necessary to have a look at the economic problems and give the Poles what we can.

SUSLOV. In the press we need to take the lid off the machinations of "Solidarity" and the other counterrevolutionary forces.

CHERNENKO. I am in complete agreement with what [my] comrades here have been saying. It is indeed the case that the line of our Party and the CC Politburo with regard to the Polish events, as formulated in the statements of Leonid Ilich Brezhnev and in the decisions of the Politburo, is completely correct and should not be changed.

I consider that it would be possible today to adopt the following decision:

1. Take cognizance of the information of comrade Baybakov.
2. In our relations with the Polish People's Republic, to proceed in the future from the general political line of the CC CPSU that has been laid down on this question, and also from the instructions of the CC CPSU Politburo of 8 December 1981 and the exchange of opinions which took place at the session of the CC Politburo of 10 December 1981.
3. Instruct comrades Tikhonov, Kirilenko, Dolgikh, Arkhipov, and Baybakov to continue to study the questions of economic aid to Poland, with due regard for the exchange of opinions which took place at the session of the CC Politburo.

BREZHNEV. What is the opinion of the comrades?

ALL. Comrade Chernenko has formulated all the proposals very correctly; they should be adopted.

The resolution is passed.

APPENDIX N

DOCUMENTS FOR CHAPTER 39

———>•<———

DOCUMENT 1

Extract from Politburo Minutes
Regarding Funding of Communist Parties

30 December 1985
Hoover Archives
Proletarians of all countries, unite!
Communist Party of the Soviet Union. CENTRAL COMMITTEE
TOP SECRET
SPECIAL FILE
[Printed sideways in the left-hand margin:]

FOR INFORMATION

A comrade who receives top secret documents of the CC of the CPSU may neither pass them on to, nor acquaint with them, anyone at all without the express permission to do so of the CC.

Making copies of the said documents or writing out excerpts from them is categorically forbidden.

After acquainting himself with it, the comrade to whom the document is addressed places his personal signature and the date on the document.

PERSONAL
No. P230/51
To Comrade Ponomarev—all
To Comrade Alkhimov—item 2
Extract from Minutes No. 230 of the Session of the Politburo of the CC of the CPSU on 30 December 1985

QUESTION FROM THE International Department of the CC of the CPSU

1. Accept the proposal of the International Department of the CC of the CPSU to sanction an International Fund for the Assistance of Left-Wing Workers' Organizations for 1986 with a budget of 20,350,000 dollars and set the contribution of the CPSU in the amount of 17,000,000 dollars.

2. Instruct the Board of the USSR State Bank (comrade V. S. Alkhimov) to supply comrade B. N. Ponomarev with 17,000,000 dollars for special purposes.

3. Instruct comrade B. N. Ponomarev to inform the leaders of the Communist Parties that are participating in the Fund about the utilization of the assets in 1985 and agree with them on the size of the Fund for 1986 as totaling 20,350,000 dollars and on the contribution of each of the Parties as amounting to the following:

> Socialist Unity Party of Germany—1,200,000 dollars.
> Communist Party of Czechoslovakia—850,000 dollars.
> Hungarian Socialist Workers' Party—750,000 dollars.
> Bulgarian Communist Party—550,000 dollars.

CC SECRETARY

2-gr

ol

Top secret

SPECIAL FILE

[crossed out:] Draft

RESOLUTION of the CC of the CPSU

Question from the International Department of the CC of the CPSU

1. Accept the proposal of the International Department of the CC of the CPSU to sanction an International Fund for the Assistance of Left-Wing Workers' Organizations for 1986 with a budget of 20,350,000 dollars and set the contribution of the CPSU in the amount of 17,000,000 dollars.

2. Instruct the Board of the USSR State Bank (comrade V. S. Alkhimov) to supply comrade B. N. Ponomarev with 17,000,000 dollars for special purposes.

3. Instruct comrade B. N. Ponomarev to inform the leaders of the Communist Parties that are participating in the Fund about the utilization of the

assets in 1985 and agree with them on the size of the Fund for 1986 as totaling 20,350,000 dollars and on the contribution of each of the Parties as amounting to the following:

Socialist Unity Party of Germany—1,200,000 dollars.
Communist Party of Czechoslovakia—850,000 dollars.
Hungarian Socialist Workers' Party—750,000 dollars.
Bulgarian Communist Party—550,000 dollars.

[In handwriting at the foot of the page:]

To comrade Ponomarev—all
To comrade Alkhimov—item 2
P230/51
30. XII. 85
For issuance
30/ XII—85
[indecipherable signature] Top secret
SPECIAL FILE
CC CPSU
Question from the International Department of the CC of the CPSU

The International Fund for the Assistance of Left-Wing Workers' Organizations, sanctioned by the CC of the CPSU and amounting in 1985 to a total of 18,350,000 dollars (P189/68 [or P189/63—Trans.] of December 29, 1984) has been expended to the full.

In 1985 the Socialist Unity Party of Germany, the Communist Party of Czechoslovakia, the Hungarian Socialist Workers' Party, and the Bulgarian Communist Party contributed 3,050,000 dollars to the Fund. Moreover, the fraternal Parties of Czechoslovakia and Bulgaria each contributed 100,000 dollars more than had been envisaged.

During the last few years a number of fraternal Parties (the Chilean, the Portuguese, the Israeli, the Salvadoran, the Iraqi, the Mexican, the Panamanian, and others) have been asking insistently for an increase in the amount of assistance. The requests are motivated by the increasing rise in inflation, the worsening of the political situation in their countries and of the conditions in which the communists operate, [and] by the necessity for the further activization of all forms of struggle.

A proposal is [herewith] tabled to sanction the International Fund for the Assistance of Left-Wing Workers' Organizations for 1986 with a budget of 20,350,000 dollars [and] to instruct the Board of the USSR State Bank (comrade V. S. Alkhimov) to supply comrade B. N. Ponomarev with <u>17,000,000 dollars</u> for special purposes. It is proposed to instruct comrade B. N. Ponomarev to inform the leaders of the Communist Parties that are participating in the Fund about the utilization of the assets in 1985 and agree with them on the size of the Fund for 1986 and on their contributions.

A draft resolution of the CC of the CPSU is attached.

[signature] B. Ponomarev

"29" December 1985.

> [Some ten members of the Politburo have signed this document as being "in favor" of the proposal. The decipherable signatures are those of Ligachev, Gromyko, and Solomentsev.—Trans.]

DOCUMENT 2
Communications Regarding Funding of Left-Wing Workers' Organizations

11 December 1989
Hoover Archives
<u>Fond 89</u>
<u>Finding aid 38</u>
<u>Document 56</u>
Top Secret
No. P175/3

TO COMRADES: FALIN AND GERASHCHENKO
Excerpts from the minutes No. 175 of the *TsK KPSS* Politburo meeting on 11 December 1989.
<u>Concerning the International Department of the *TsK KPSS*.</u>

1. The proposal of the International Department of the *TsK KPSS* to fix the KPSS's contribution to the International Fund for Assistance to Leftist Workers' Organizations at 22 million dollars for the year 1990 is to be accepted.
2. The board of directors of the USSR State Bank (comrade V. V. Gerashchenko) is to be entrusted with paying 22 dollars to comrade V. M. Falin for special purposes.

The *TsK* Secretary

Resolution of the TsK KPSS
Concerning the International Department of the TsK KPSS.
[exactly the same text with a different format including ten signatures (voting record)]
[handwritten:]

To: Comrade Falin—

1. paragraphs 1 and 2
2. personally
3. with the "corner"*

Top Secret
Memorandum of the International Department of the TsK KPSS.

For many years the International Fund for Assistance to Leftist Workers' Organizations received its funding from voluntary contributions of the KPSS and other communist parties of socialist countries. However, since the end of the '70s the Polish and Romanian comrades as well as the Hungarians (in 1987) have dropped out of the Fund's circle of contributors, justifying their decision on the basis of hard currency problems. In 1988 and 1989, the German Socialist Unity Party and the communist parties of Czechoslovakia and Bulgaria did not pay their share, giving no explanation. The contributions of the latter parties had amounted to $2.3 million, i.e., around 13 percent of the total. For the last two years, the Fund has received its funding solely from contributions of the KPSS.

In 1989 the KPSS's contribution to the International Fund for Assistance to Leftist Workers' Organizations was fixed at 13.5 million "hard currency rubles." According to the official exchange rate, this corresponded to $22,044,673.

In 1989 the Fund financially assisted seventy-three revolutionary democratic and communist parties and workers' organizations. 21.2 million dollars was the contribution made to the Fund, out of which 20.5 million dollars have up to this moment been transferred to various communist parties.

Those parties that over a long period of time have regularly received a certain amount highly appreciate this solidarity gesture, and they are convinced that there is no substitute for it. Most of the parties have renewed their well-grounded requests for financial assistance in 1990; some of them have even asked for a considerable increase.

---

*Probably meaning a corner of the page with additional information, like the "Top Secret" stamp, the voting record, etc.—Trans.

It is expedient to have the KPSS contribute $22 million to the International Fund for Assistance to Leftist Workers' Organizations in 1990, which is about the same amount as this year.

A draft of the TsK KPSS resolution is enclosed.

[signed]

V. Falin

Chief of the International Department of the TsK KPSS

5 December 1989

In case the situation with the Socialist Unity Party of Germany and with the communist parties of Czechoslovakia and Bulgaria has stabilized, one could inform them of the state of the Fund and its expenditures in 1988–89. Moreover, one could discuss with them the possibility of renewing their co-operation with the Fund.

Proletarians of all countries, unite!

Communist Party of the Soviet Union. CENTRAL COMMITTEE

TOP SECRET

SPECIAL FILE

[Printed sideways in the left-hand margin:]

A comrade who receives top secret documents of the CC of the CPSU may neither pass them on to, nor acquaint with them, anyone at all without the express permission to do so of the CC.

Making copies of the said documents or writing out excerpts from them is categorically forbidden.

After acquainting himself with it, the comrade to whom the document is addressed places his personal signature and the date on the document.

No. P 175/3

To Comrades Falin and Gerashchenko

Extract from Minutes No. 175 of the Session of the Politburo of the CC of the CPSU on 11 December1989

Question from the International Department of the CC of the CPSU

1. Accept the proposal of the International Department of the CC of the CPSU to set the contribution of the CPSU to the International Fund for the Assistance of Left-Wing Workers' Organizations for 1990 in the amount of 22,000,000 dollars.

2. The Board of the USSR State Bank (comrade V. V. Gerashchenko) is to supply comrade V. M. Falin with <u>22,000,000 dollars</u> for special purposes.

CC SECRETARY

3-lz

vk

SPECIAL FILE

<u>Top secret</u>

<u>Attachment</u> [crossed out]

<u>Draft</u> [crossed out]

RESOLUTION of the CC CPSU

Question from the International Department of the CC of the CPSU

1. Accept the proposal of the International Department of the CC of the CPSU to set the contribution of the CPSU to the International Fund for the Assistance of Left-Wing Workers' Organizations for 1990 in the amount of <u>22,000,000 dollars</u>.
2. The Board of the USSR State Bank [(comrade N. V. Garotovsky) has been crossed out—Trans.] (comrade V. V. Gerashchenko) is to supply comrade V. M. Falin with <u>22,000,000 dollars</u> for special purposes.

CC Secretary

For issuance

[indecipherable signature]

11. 12. 89

<u>To comrade</u> Falin

    1) items 1, 2

    2) personally

    3) with a "corner"

<u>To comrade</u> Gerashchenko

    1) item 2

    2) personally

    3) with a "corner"

[indecipherable signature]

P175/ 3

11. XII. 89

      [Ten indecipherable signatures——presumably of members of the Politburo—all preceded by the term for "in favor," have been added to this document. —Trans.]

SPECIAL FILE
<u>Top secret</u>
CC CPSU

   <u>Question from the International Department of the CC of the CPSU</u>

   Over the course of many years, the International Fund for the Assistance
of Left-Wing Workers' Organizations has been made up from voluntary contributions by the CPSU and a number of other Communist Parties of the socialist
countries. However, since the end of the '70s, [our] Polish and Romanian, and
since 1987 also [our] Hungarian comrades, referring to financial difficulties with
hard currency, have ceased to participate in the Fund. In 1988 and 1989, the Socialist Unity Party of Germany, the Communist Party of Czechoslovakia, and
the Bulgarian Communist Party, without explaining the reasons, avoided paying in the contributions that were expected of them, and the Fund was made up
entirely out of revenues provided by the CPSU. In 1987 the contributions of the
three above-named Parties came to <u>2,300,000 dollars</u>, i.e., about 13 percent of
the total contributed assets.

   The contribution of the CPSU to the International Fund for the Assistance of Left-Wing Workers' Organizations for 1989 was set (P144/129 of 28
December 1989) in the amount of <u>13,500,000 hard currency rubles</u>, which
came to <u>22,044,673 dollars</u> at the official rate of exchange.

   In 1989 the Fund provided help to seventy-three Communist, Workers',
and revolutionary-democratic parties and organizations. The overall total of
the allocated funds amounted to <u>21,200,000 dollars</u>, of which <u>20,500,000 dol-
lars</u> have as of this moment been transferred to the parties.

   Parties which have regularly received certain amounts of money from the
Fund over a prolonged period of time value this form of international solidarity highly, considering that it would be impossible to replace it by any
other types of assistance. Well-founded requests for help in 1990 have by now
been received in the appropriate way from the majority of these parties; some
of them are asking for substantial increases.

   It would seem to be advisable to maintain the contribution of the CPSU
to the International Fund for the Assistance of Left-Wing Workers' Organizations for 1990 at approximately the level of the current year—
<u>22,000,000 dollars</u>.

   A draft resolution of the CC of the CPSU is attached.
   Head of the International Department
   of the CC of the CPSU
   [signature]

(V. Falin)

"5" December 1989.

SPECIAL FILE

In the event of the stabilization of the situation in the Socialist Unity Party of Germany, the Communist Party of Czechoslovakia, and the Bulgarian Communist Party, it would be possible to inform them of the situation which has arisen in the Fund and of the utilization of its assets in 1988–89 and also to hold an exchange of views on the possible continuation of [their] cooperation within the framework of the Fund.

DOCUMENT 3

Request by Argentina CP for Passports and Identity Cards

27 July 1989

Hoover Archives

[rubber stamp:]

CC CPSU

27 JULY 89   1279   OP

TO BE RETURNED TO THE

GENERAL DEPARTMENT

OF THE CC CPSU

SPECIAL FILE

Translation from the Spanish

Top secret

To THE CENTRAL Committee of the CPSU

Taking advantage of the opportunity, I would like to express [our] profound gratitude for the invaluable assistance which you are giving us by manufacturing documents and which is so essential in current conditions.

We are appealing to you to prepare fifteen passports for us and [also fifteen] identity cards for men and for women (forty-five in all).

With fraternal greetings

Amos Fava

Chairman of the Communist

Party of Argentina

21 July 1989

Translated by: [indecipherable signature]

SPECIAL FILE
Top secret
SPECIAL FILE
CC CPSU
No. 1279
2 Sector

On the request of the Chairman of the Communist Party of Argentina, comrade A. Fava

The Chairman of the Communist Party of Argentina, comrade A. Fava, has addressed a request to the CC of the CPSU for assistance in the manufacture of Argentinean passports, identity cards, and receptacles for their transportation and storage. The requirement for the above-mentioned documents and receptacles is explained by the need to carry out illegal work in conditions where the special services are stepping up their activities, and also [by the need] to render assistance to the Paraguayan Communist Party, which is operating in the underground.

[We] would consider it possible to accede to the request of comrade A. Fava, entrusting the manufacture of the documents and receptacles, on request by the International Department of the CC of the CPSU, to the Committee of State Security of the USSR and the USSR Ministry of Defense.

Agreed with comrade L. V. Shebarshin, Deputy Chairman of the Committee of State Security of the USSR and comrade M. A. Moiseev, USSR Deputy Minister of Defense.

Draft resolution of the CC of the CPSU is attached.

Head of the International Department
of the CC of the CPSU
[signature]
V. Falin
"13" September 1989
No. 18-C-1083
No. ST 105/ 114 of 23. IX. 1989
SPECIAL FILE
Top secret
SPECIAL FILE
RESOLUTION
of the Secretariat of the CC of the Communist Party of the Soviet Union

ON THE REQUEST of the Chairman of the Communist Party of Argentina, comrade A. Fava

1. Accede to the request of the Chairman of the Communist Party of Argentina (CPA), comrade A. Fava, and provide assistance to the leadership of the CPA in the manufacture of <u>Argentinean passports, identity cards, and receptacles for</u> their transportation and storage.

2. Instruct the International Department of the CC of the CPSU to examine the requests of the leadership of the CPA <u>to manufacture Argentinean passports, identity cards, and receptacles for their transportation and storage</u>, and instruct the Committee of State Security [KGB] of the USSR and the USSR Ministry of Defense <u>to manufacture them on request by</u> the International Department of the CC of the CPSU.

[signature] Falin

RESULTS OF THE VOTING:
"in favor"—A. Yakovlev
M. Gorbachev [?]
[and four other currently
indecipherable signatures]

FOR ISSUANCE
23. 09. 89   [indecipherable signature]
Excerpts to comrades Kryuchkov, Yazov, Falin
068
15 September 1989 TO BE RETURNED WITHIN THE COURSE OF 3 days to the CC CPSU (General Department, Second Sector)
Proletarians of all countries, unite!
Communist Party of the Soviet Union. CENTRAL COMMITTEE
<u>TOP SECRET</u>
("SPECIAL FILE")
[Printed sideways in the left-hand margin:]
     Rules for handling excerpts from Minutes of the CC CPSU Secretariat
     A comrade who receives top secret documents of the CC of the CPSU may neither pass them on to, nor acquaint with them, anyone at all without the express permission to do so of the CC.

Making copies of the said documents or writing out excerpts from them is categorically forbidden.

After acquainting himself with it, the comrade to whom the document is addressed places his personal signature and the date on the document.

No. St-105/114g

Extract from Minutes of the CC CPSU Secretariat of 23 September 1989

ON THE REQUEST of the Chairman of the Communist Party of Argentina, comrade A. Fava

1. Accede to the request of the Chairman of the Communist Party of Argentina (CPA), comrade A. Fava, and provide assistance to the leadership of the CPA in the manufacture of Argentinean passports, identity cards, and receptacles for their transportation and storage.

2. Instruct the International Department of the CC of the CPSU to examine the requests of the leadership of the CPA to manufacture Argentinean passports, identity cards, and receptacles for their transportation and storage, and the Committee of State Security [KGB] of the USSR and the USSR Ministry of Defense to manufacture them on request by the International Department of the CC of the CPSU.

CC SECRETARY

SENT TO: comrades Kryuchkov, Yazov, Falin.

3ze

DOCUMENT 4
Request by Sudanese CP for Military Training

June 1988

Hoover Archives

SPECIAL FILE

Top secret

SPECIAL FILE

No ST 86/265 gs of 24.VI 1988

RESOLUTION
of the Secretariat of the CPSU of the Communist Party of the Soviet Union

---

ON THE REQUEST of the leadership of the Sudanese Communist Party

1. Comply with the request of the leadership of the Sudanese Communist Party (SCP) regarding the enrollment of twenty members of the SCP in two groups for military training in the USSR in 1988–1989 for a period of up to three months
2. The enrollment, maintenance, material well-being, military training, and expenditures (including those in foreign currency) on the travel of the members of the SCP to the city of Moscow and back to their place of destination is to be entrusted to the USSR Ministry of Defense.

K. Brutents

RESULTS OF THE VOTING: In favor A. Dobrynin
[and eleven additional indecipherable signatures—Trans.]

FOR ISSUANCE
24. 06. 88
[signature]

Excerpts to comrades Yazov, Dobrynin, Gostev
063
14 Jun [sic], 1988 TO BE RETURNED WITHIN THE COURSE OF
3 days to the CC CPSU (General Department, II Sector)
Proletarians of all countries, unite!
Communist Party of the Soviet Union. CENTRAL COMMITTEE
TOP SECRET
("Special file")
[Printed sideways in the left-hand margin:]

RULES FOR THE handling of extracts from the minutes of the CC CPSU Secretariat

A comrade who receives top secret documents of the CC of the CPSU may neither pass them on to, nor acquaint with them, any person whatsoever without the express permission to do so of the CC.

Making copies of the said documents or writing out excerpts from them is categorically forbidden.

After acquainting himself with the document, the comrade to whom it is addressed places his personal signature and the date on the document.

No. St-86/265 gs

Extract from Minutes No. 86 of the Session of the CC CPSU Secretariat
    on 24 June 1988

ON THE REQUEST of the leadership of the Sudanese Communist Party

1. Comply with the request of the leadership of the Sudanese Communist Party (SCP) regarding the enrollment of twenty members of the SCP in two groups for military training in the USSR in 1988–1989 for a period of up to three months.
2. The enrollment, maintenance, material well-being, military training, and expenditures (including those in foreign currency) on the travel of the members of the SCP to the city of Moscow and back to their place of destination is to be entrusted to the USSR Ministry of Defense.

CC SECRETARY

SENT TO: comrades Yazov, Dobrynin, Gostev.

Top secret

SPECIAL FILE

[stamp:] CC CPSU

2 sector

14. JUN 88 1320 OP

TO BE RETURNED TO

THE GENERAL DEPARTMENT

OF THE CC CPSU

CC CPSU

ON THE REQUEST of the leadership of the Sudanese Communist Party

A Resolution of the CC of the CPSU of 22 May 1987 (St-50/46 gs OP) provides for the enrollment of twenty members of the Sudanese Communist Party (SCP) for military training in the Soviet Union in the course of the year. However, as a result of complications in the situation in Sudan, the leadership of the SCP was not able to send them to the USSR in 1987.

The General Secretary of the CC of the SCP, M. I. Nugud, is asking [us] to enroll this group of Sudanese comrades for military training in the USSR in 1988–1989 (cipher telegram from the city of Khartoum, Special No. 230, of 3 June 1988).

[We] would consider it possible to comply with this request and enroll twenty Sudanese comrades in two groups for military training for a period of up to three months in the USSR in 1988–1989.

The enrollment, maintenance, material well-being, military training, and expenditures (including those in foreign currency) on the travel of the members of the SCP to the city of Moscow and back to their place of destination could be entrusted to the USSR Ministry of Defense.

This has been agreed with the Head of the Main Intelligence Directorate [GRU—Trans.] of the General Staff of the Armed Forces of the USSR, comrade V. M. Mikhaylov.

The draft of the Resolution of the CC of the CPSU is attached.
Deputy Head of the International Department
of the CC of the CPSU
K. Brutents
"14" June 1988
No. 18-S-1394

DOCUMENT 5
Consent to Iraq to Sell Soviet Aircraft to Third Countries

24 December 1989
[AS]
Communist Party of the Soviet Union. CENTRAL COMMITTEE
TOP SECRET
SPECIAL FILE
No. P175/52

To Comrades Gorbachev, Ryzhkov, Kryuchkov, Shevardnadze, Yakovlev, Yazov, Baklanov, I. Belousov, Katushev, Belyakov, Falin, Shkabardnya.

Extract from Minutes No. 175 of the Session of the Politburo of the CC of the CPSU on 24 December 1989

Question from the USSR Ministry of Defense, the State Commission of the USSR Council of Ministers on Military-Industrial Problems, and the USSR Ministry of Foreign Economic Relations.

1. Agree with the proposal set out in the memorandum of comrades D. T. Yazov, I. S. Belousov and K. F. Katushev of December 13, 1989 (attached).
2. Approve the text of the instructions to the Soviet ambassador to the Iraqi Republic (attached).

CC SECRETARY
18-ie
nd
2578
Iraq
Re: item 52 of minutes No. 175
Top secret
CC CPSU
On the agreement for the supply by the Iraqi Republic to third countries
of aircraft and aircraft engines of Soviet manufacture
The Government of the Iraqi Republic has submitted a request [to us] to examine the possibility of the purchase by the Soviet side of aircraft previously delivered to Iraq by the USSR—the SU-7 (24 in number), the MIG-21FL (6), the MIG-21F13 (5), the TU-22BU (6)—and of aircraft engines for the MIG-23MF, the MIG-23MC (25 in number) and the MIG-23BN (25), or the replacement of the above-mentioned aircraft and engines by more up-to-date ones, and, in the event of a refusal, to agree to their sale to third countries. The Iraqi side motivates its request by saying that the aforesaid number of aircraft and engines exceeds the requirements of the Iraqi air force.

Bearing in mind that these aircraft and aircraft engines have been fully paid for by the Iraqi side and that their purchase by the Soviet Union would be pointless, the State Commission of the USSR Council of Ministers for Military-Industrial Problems, the USSR Ministry of Defense, and the USSR

Ministry of Foreign Economic Relations submit a proposal to give [our] consent to Iraq to supply the aforesaid special assets to socialist and friendly developing countries that are armed with these types of aircraft and engines.

Agreed with the relevant ministries and departments.

D. Yazov   I. Belousov   K. Katushev

13 December 1989

No. 01/ 5-4/ 22247

2578 Re. item 52 of minutes No. 175

Secret

BAGHDAD

SOVIET AMBASSADOR

Visit A. Shenshal, the Minister of Defense of the Iraqi Republic, and, referring to instructions, inform [him] that his request for the replacement of SU-7, MIG-21FL, MIG-21F13 and TU-22B,U aircraft and also of aircraft engines for MIG-23MF, MIG-23MS and MIG-23BN aircraft by more up-to-date [models] or, in the event of refusal, for permission to sell them to third countries, has been examined closely.

Consent has been given by the Soviet Government for the supply by Iraq of the above-listed aircraft and engines to socialist countries and to developing countries that are friendly to Iraq and the Soviet Union and that are armed with these types of aircraft and engines. In this connection, it is to be borne in mind that questions of supplying these aircraft with spare parts and ammunition will be resolved without the participation of the Soviet side.

Telegraph on implementation.

DOCUMENT 6

Documents Regarding the Supply of Assets to the
People's Republic of Congo, March 1990

7 March 1990

Hoover Archives

Communist Party of the Soviet Union. CENTRAL COMMITTEE

TOP SECRET

[Printed sideways in the left-hand margin:]

To be returned within a 7-day period to the CC

of the CPSU (General Department, First Sector)

No. P181/20

To COMRADES GORBACHEV, Ryzhkov, Kryuchkov, Shevardnadze,
        Yakovlev, Baklanov, I. Belousov, Bakatin, Katushev, Belyakov, Falin—
in conformity with the appendix
    To SHKABARDNYA—*in toto.*
Extract from Minutes No. 181 of the Session of the Politburo of the Central
    Committee of the CPSU on 7 March 1990

On the supply of special assets to the People's Republic of Congo
    Approve the draft of the Dispensation of the USSR Council of Ministers
on this question (attached).
    CC SECRETARY
    21-lz
    vk
Re: item 20 of Minutes No. 181
Secret
Draft
USSR COUNCIL OF MINISTERS
DISPENSATION
of March 1990, Moscow, Kremlin

1. In connection with the request of the President of the People's Republic
    of Congo, give consent:
        to the delivery of special assets and equipment, and also of automo-
    bile technology in accordance with the appendix, to Congo in 1990, with
    payment of costs, including the cost of delivery, in the year when supplied
    and in freely convertible currency;
        to the enrollment of Congolese specialists in 1990 for study in educa-
    tional establishments of the USSR Ministry of Internal Affairs, in spe-
    cializations and in numbers and for periods of time to be agreed by the
    [High Contracting] Parties, with reimbursement by the Congolese Side of
    the instruction costs incurred by the Soviet Side in freely convertible cur-
    rency in the year in which the services are rendered, including the travel
    of the Congolese specialists from Brazzaville to their places of training in
    the USSR and back, as well as the transport of their personal luggage.
        In the event of a pressing request by the Congolese Side, give consent
    to the payment by the Soviet Side of the instruction costs of the Con-
    golese specialists, except for their travel and the transport of their lug-

gage from Brazzaville to their places of training in the USSR and back, including trips while on leave.

2. The USSR Ministry of Foreign Affairs is to inform the Congolese Side of the decision set out in clause 1 of the present dispensation. Instructions to the Soviet ambassador to the People's Republic of Congo are attached.

3. The USSR Ministry of Foreign Economic Relations and the USSR Ministry of Internal Affairs are to conduct negotiations with the Congolese Side, guided by clause 1 of the present dispensation. Once an understanding is achieved, the USSR Ministry of Foreign Economic Relations is to sign the relevant agreement.

4. On signing the Agreement obligate:

   a) the Ministries enumerated in the appendix, in conjunction with the Ministries and departments with which cooperation has been established, to produce the special assets and automobile technology in accordance with the appendix and with the necessary documentation, and to ship them, in line with the orders and commissions of the USSR Ministry of Foreign Economic Relations, for delivery to the People's Republic of Congo.

   b) the USSR Ministry of Internal Affairs:

      to ship the special assets from its own stocks for delivery to the People's Republic of Congo, in accordance with the appendix on shipping requisites which will be supplied by the USSR Ministry of Foreign Economic Relations;

      to provide the Congolese specialists who are enrolled for instruction at educational establishments of the USSR Ministry of Internal Affairs with living accommodation, training materials, and instructional and classroom appurtenances, consumer and medical services, fitting out with uniforms and special clothing for practical training sessions and also, in case of need, with civilian equipment as per the standards established for specialists working in the organs of internal affairs of developing countries and studying at educational establishments of the USSR Ministry of Internal Affairs. Each Congolese specialist enrolled for training is to be given a grant for sustenance and personal expenses of 120 rubles a month.

5. On submissions from the USSR Ministry of Internal Affairs, the USSR Ministry of Transport is to ensure the top-priority provision of rolling-stock for the transportation of consignments whose supply to Congo is stipulated in the present dispensation.

6. On submissions from the USSR Ministry of Foreign Economic Relations, the USSR Ministry of the Marine Fleet is to ensure the delivery of consignments whose supply to Congo is stipulated in the present dispensation, with settlement against the limits allocated to the USSR Ministry of Foreign Economic Relations for payments to Soviet organizations.

7. Permit the USSR Ministry of Internal Affairs to utilize the entire freely convertible currency revenue received for the special equipment, whose delivery is stipulated by the present dispensation, for the purpose of taking urgent measures to implement the resolution of the USSR Supreme Soviet of 4 August 1989, "On the all-out intensification of the struggle against crime."

8. The expenses incurred in connection with the provision of uncompensated assistance, in accordance with the present dispensation, are to be debited in Soviet rubles from the appropriations of the USSR state budget for providing uncompensated aid to foreign states.

Chairman of the USSR Council of Ministers
N. Ryzhkov

THE APPENDIX IS not being distributed.
25-chv
vv
Secret
BRAZZAVILLE
SOVIET AMBASSADOR

Visit the President of the People's Republic of Congo, D. Sassu-Ngesso, or, on his instructions, another person and, referring to [your] instructions, report that the Soviet government has carefully considered the request of the President for the supply of special equipment for the needs of the Command of the Forces of Public Security of Congo and for the training of Congolese specialists in the USSR.

At the present time, as a result of the limited nature of [our] financial and material resources, and also because of additional expenditures caused by the need for urgent measures in the struggle against crime in our country, in accordance with the Resolution of the USSR Supreme Soviet, it unfortunately does not appear to be possible to comply with the request of the Congolese Side in its entirety.

Nonetheless, bearing in mind the friendly nature of Soviet-Congolese relations, an opportunity has been traced which would make it possible to offer for delivery in 1990: five GAZ-53-12 lorries, five VAZ-2106 limousines, sixteen "Dnieper" MT-16 motorcycles with sidecars, thirty standardized suitcases, 160 gas masks, photographic, film, and audio equipment, and other equipment and materials, in all to a value of some 500,000 rubles.

From 1990 the Soviet Side would in addition be prepared to enroll Congolese specialists in educational establishments of the USSR Ministry of Internal Affairs, in specializations and numbers and for periods of time to be agreed by the [High Contracting] Parties.

The Soviet Side proposes to supply Congo with the above-listed assets against payment of their entire costs in freely convertible currency in the year when delivered, and additionally to implement the training of Congolese specialists in the USSR against reimbursement by the Congolese Side of all expenditures by the Soviet Side in freely convertible currency.

In the event of agreement by the Congolese Side, the conduct of negotiations and the signing of the contractual documents will be entrusted to the Trade Representative of the USSR in Congo.

(For Your Information Only. In the event that the Congolese press to be provided with uncompensated assistance, say that the Soviet Side would be able to consider this question only as it applies to the training of Congolese specialists in the USSR. However, even in this eventuality we proceed from the assumption that payments for the travel of the specialists and for the transport of their personal luggage will be disbursed by the Congolese Side. Express the hope that our reasons will be received by the Congolese Side with understanding.)

Telegraph on implementation.

APPENDIX O

DOCUMENTS FOR CHAPTER 40

※

DOCUMENT 1
Session of Politburo with Gromyko and Andropov

10 March 1983
CWIHP Bulletin 8–9 (96/97)
10 March 1983
Session of the CPSU Politburo Chairman Yuri V. Andropov. Those present included Mikhail Gorbachev and A. A. Gromyko

GROMYKO: ON THE WHOLE, the situation in Afghanistan is, as you know, difficult. . . . The number of gangs [i.e., rebels] is not decreasing. The enemy is not laying down its weapons. The negotiations with Pakistan in Geneva are moving slowly and with difficulty. This is why we must do everything to find a mutually acceptable political settlement. In advance, it can already be said that this process will be a lengthy one. . . . For now we cannot give Pakistan consent on concrete time periods for the withdrawal of our troops from the country.

Yes, the situation is stabilizing. It is good that the Afghan Army has grown to 140,000. But the main trouble is that the central authorities have not yet reached the countryside: [they] rarely interact with the masses, about one third of the districts are not under the control of the central authority, and one can feel the fragility of the State government.

. . . It seems that it will be necessary to hold a meeting with Karmal and a group of officials of the People's Democratic Party of Afghanistan sometime in April. It seems that it would also be expedient for Yu. V. Andropov to meet personally with Babrak Karmal.

ANDROPOV: . . . This is a feudal country, where tribes have always been in charge of their territories, and the central authority was far from always able to reach each Kishlak [an Afghan district—Trans.]. The problem is not in Pakistan's position. We are fighting against American imperialism, which well understands that in this part of international politics it has lost its position. That is why we cannot back off.

Miracles don't happen. Sometimes we are angry at the Afghans because they act illogically and work slowly. But let us remember our fight with basmatchism [banditry]. Why, back then, almost the entire Red Army was concentrated in Central Asia, yet the fight with basmatchi continued until the mid-1930s. And so in our relations with Afghanistan, there must be both demands and understanding.

. . . Evidently we do need these talks with Karmal. It will probably be advantageous to hold them in two rounds; moreover, my discussion with Karmal should be organized last.

DOCUMENT 2
Discussion Regarding Fighting in Afghanistan, November 1986

13 November 1986
CWIHP Bulletin 8–9 (96/97)
<u>Top Secret</u>
CPSU Politburo, 13 November 1986; Chairman: Mikhail Gorbachev
Present included A. A. Gromyko

GORBACHEV: I have an intuition that we should waste no time. Najib needs our support. He objectively evaluates the situation and understands the difficulty of the existing problems.

. . . . Karmal is stalling. [Translator's note: Gorbachev here uses an idiomatic Russian expression, *"Karmal vydelyvnet Krendelya,"* which literally means, "Karmal is walking like a pretzel." The expression, derived from a term for the weaving and unsteady gait of a drunkard, in this case signifies Gorbachev's assertion that Karmal is not behaving in a straightforward manner.]

We have been fighting in Afghanistan for already six years. If the approach is not changed, we will continue to fight for another twenty to thirty years. This would cast a shadow on our abilities to affect the evolution of the situation. Our military should be told that they are learning badly from this war. What, can it be that there is no room for our General Staff to maneuver?

In general, we have not selected the keys to resolving this problem. What, are we going to fight endlessly, as a testimony that our troops are not able to deal with the situation? We need to finish this process as soon as possible.

GROMYKO. It is necessary to establish a strategic target. Too long ago we spoke on the fact that it is necessary to close off the border of Afghanistan with Pakistan and Iran. Experience has shown that we were unable to do this in view of the difficult terrain of the area and the existence of hundreds of passes in the mountains. Today it is necessary to say precisely that the strategic assignment concludes with the carrying of the problem towards ending the war.

GORBACHEV. It is necessary to include in the resolution the importance of ending the war in the course of one year—at maximum two years.

GROMYKO. It should be concluded, so Afghanistan becomes a neutral country. Apparently, on our part there was an underestimation of difficulties, when we agreed with the Afghan government to give them our military support. The social conditions in Afghanistan made the resolution of the problem in a short amount of time impossible. We did not receive domestic support there. In the Afghan army the number of conscripts equals the number of deserters.

. . . We can sign under practically everything that Najib suggests. But we should not sharply cut off Karmal, as he serves as a symbol to his people. [Najib's recommendations] deserve attention . . . draw in the peasant masses in supporting the government power . . . negotiations with Islamic parties and organizations inside Afghanistan and beyond . . . relations with the former king. I think that we should not spurn them. Right now a more concrete stage of discussions with [Najib] concerning these questions is needed. . . . Here, it seems, our participation is needed, in particular, through . . . our contacts with Pakistan.

Concerning the Americans, they are not interested in the settlement of the situation in Afghanistan. On the contrary, it is to their advantage for the war to drag on.

GORBACHEV. That's right.

GROMYKO. It should be considered how to link India into the settlement.

DOCUMENT 3

Extract from Politburo Minutes Regarding Troop Withdrawal Strategies

24 January 1989
Hoover Archives
No. P146/VI

To COMRADES GORBACHEV, Ryzhkov, Slyunkov, Chebrikov, Shevardnadze, Yakovlev, Maslyukov, Yazov, Murakhovsky, Kryuchkov, Boldin, Falin—*in toto;* Gostev—item 2.6; Volkov— item 5; Katushev—item 6.
Extract from Minutes No. 146 of the Session of the Politburo of the CC of the CPSU on 24 January 1989

ON MEASURES IN connection with the forthcoming withdrawal of Soviet troops from Afghanistan

1. Agree with the views set out in the memorandum of comrades E. A. Shevardnadze, V. M. Chebrikov, A. N. Yakovlev, D. T. Yazov, V. S. Murakhovsky and V. A. Kryuchkov of 23 January 1989 (attached).

2. Proceed from the need to ensure the functioning of the Hairaton–Kabul highway and to render [our] Afghan comrades comprehensive assistance in organizing the guarding of this highway by their own forces, including, if necessary, putting these Afghan subunits on our payroll for a limited period of time. The State Planning Agency of the USSR and the USSR Finance Ministry, together with the USSR Ministry of Foreign Affairs, the USSR Ministry of Defense, and the KGB of the USSR are to submit the appropriate proposals by 1 February 1989.

3. Instruct comrade D. T. Yazov to pay a visit to Kabul to make an additional assessment of the ongoing military situation and to give practical assistance to the Afghan Side in resolving matters pertaining to defense, including those affecting the protection of the Kabul–Hairaton strategic highway.

4. The USSR Ministry of Defense is to provide assistance to the President of the Republic of Afghanistan in working out a variety of plans for announcing the introduction of martial law in Afghanistan.

5. The USSR Ministry of Defense and the USSR Ministry of Civil Aviation are to study the question of the possibility of using Soviet pilots, on a voluntary basis and with the appropriate financial remuneration, on aircraft of the Afghan transport fleet or on Soviet transport aircraft which could be leased out to the Afghan Side.

6. Before 10 February 1989, the State Planning Agency of the USSR, the USSR Finance Ministry, and the USSR Ministry of Foreign Economic Relations are to submit, in accordance with the established procedures, [their] views on the provision of additional economic aid to Afghanistan.

   In this connection, provision is to be made for a visit to Kabul by comrades Yu. D. Maslyukov, B. I. Gostev, and K. F. Katushev.

7. <u>For protocol purposes</u>. The Commission on Afghanistan of the CC CPSU Politburo, with the participation of the General Department of the CC, is to submit to the CC of the CPSU a selection of materials based on documentary sources on all the stages in the development of events in Afghanistan, beginning with the decision to dispatch Soviet troops to that country, and also its [the Commission's] views on possible scenarios of the further development of the situation in Afghanistan and the consequences for us that ensue from this.

CC SECRETARY
18-tv
zp Re. item VI of Minutes No. 146
<u>Top secret</u>
SPECIAL FILE
CC CPSU
<u>On measures in connection with the forthcoming withdrawal of Soviet troops from Afghanistan</u>

IN THE COMPLICATED situation that characterizes the state of affairs in Afghanistan, there is an ever-increasing sensation of internal tension connected with the forthcoming withdrawal of the remaining units of the Soviet armed forces. The attention of the regime and of the opposition forces is focused entirely on the date of 15 February, when, in accordance with the Geneva Agreements, the presence of our military contingent is due to come to an end. Moreover, for Kabul [itself] the deadline is even closer, because the last Soviet military units have to leave the Afghan capital at the beginning of February.

Military operations between government troops and the opposition are continuing virtually throughout the entire country; on the whole, the government is managing to hold its positions, but [only] with the help of the Soviet air force. Despite his efforts, the adversary has not been able to take possession of Jalalabad, Kunduz, and Kandahar. However, everyone realizes that the main struggle is still ahead. At the moment, the opposition has even somewhat reduced its military activity, building up its forces for the next stage [in the struggle]. Comrade Najibullah considers that after the withdrawal of Soviet troops, it [the opposition] intends to resume large-scale operations in several key sectors simultaneously.

It should be emphasized that [our] Afghan comrades are seriously worried about how the situation will develop. On the whole, their resolve to resist their opponents is on the increase, to which end they are undertaking a series of special measures and attempting to position the forces at their disposal in the most rational manner. They are also counting to a certain extent on continuing their contacts with a fairly sizable number of commanders of the armed detachments of their opponents, on the strong disagreements that continue to exist within the opposition, and on the mutual incompatibility of some of its leading political groupings, in particular the "Islamic Society of Afghanistan" (Rabbani) and the "Islamic Party of Afghanistan" (Hekmatyar). Armed clashes between detachments of these and other opposition groupings are not only not stopping, but are taking on larger dimensions.

The President is also considering in real earnest the possibility of declaring martial law or a state of emergency in the country, thinking that this might make it easier to take and implement difficult decisions in the forthcoming decisive period of time. At first, he was inclined to have martial law introduced while we were still present, but in the course of talks which were held with him, he came to the conclusion that it would be better to do this after Soviet troops have moved out of Afghanistan.

[Our] Afghan comrades are expressing their understanding of the decision to withdraw Soviet troops and are reaffirming it, but at the same time, assessing the situation in a sober light, they observe that they will not be able to manage completely without our military assistance. Such assistance, in their opinion, could be provided in ways that differ from the present ones and be on a limited scale, but all the same it would be an important boost on the practical and psychological levels. [Our] Afghan comrades think that if the opposition fails to seize the main centers in lightning attacks [shortly] after the withdrawal of Soviet troops, the Peshawar "alliance of the seven," and the

Teheran "union of the eight" will have to enter into negotiations with Kabul to work out the future state system of Afghanistan, something which at present they stubbornly refuse to do. The most important thing, as [our] Afghan friends emphasize, is to hold out for at least the first three or four months after the departure of Soviet troops, after which the situation might gradually start to change in their favor. This view is also corroborated by a number of remarks which have been made by representatives of the opposition in the course of contacts with Soviet representatives in Islamabad. It has been emerging from these remarks that if the government of Najibullah holds on to power, they will review their current position on refusing to recognize him as a partner in negotiations.

A number of far from simple points arise for us in this situation. On the one hand, our failure to comply with decisions that have been taken and publicized to complete the withdrawal of [our] troops on 15 February could result in complications on the international level that would be very highly undesirable for us. On the other hand, there can be no certainty that shortly after our departure there will not be some extremely serious threats to the regime, which all over the world is associated with us. This is all the more the case in that the opposition precisely at this decisive juncture may be able for a certain period of time to coordinate its actions, as the Americans and Pakistani military circles are insistently urging it to do. Certain apprehensions also arise in connection with the fact that genuine unity has still not been achieved in the NDPA [National Democratic Party of Afghanistan?—Trans.]; there are still disagreements which run along factional, clan, and other lines. In the arguments of certain Afghan leaders, impulsiveness and memories of bygone "injustices" become apparent. M. Kh. Shark, the Prime Minister, and many of the ministers in his Cabinet are performing weakly, to put it mildly.

An extremely serious factor is that Islamabad's violations of the Geneva Agreements have taken on not just an overt, but a demonstrative, character. Pakistani frontier guards are participating directly in military activities on Afghan territory. Firing on nearby districts of Afghanistan from Pakistan is taking place, weaponry is flowing in continuously, and armed gangs are being sent across the border. The headquarters of Afghan opposition parties and their training centers and depots are continuing to function as hitherto, without hindrance, in Peshawar and other towns. All this results from the inertia which set in during the time of [Pakistani President] Zia Al Haq.

B. Bhutto will hardly be able to change this situation in the immediate future.

These activities of the Pakistani authorities have been and are being condemned continually, resolutely and by citing concrete facts by our and by the Afghan Side. It is the intention to continue to pursue this policy in the future as well, including the UN Security Council, and also in contacts with the Pakistani leadership itself.

1. The fundamental question on which the further development of the situation depends comes down to whether the authorities will be able to hold on to Kabul and the other major towns in the country, but in the first instance specifically the capital. The situation in Kabul is complicated, and moreover, it is not even the military but the economic aspects that occupy the foreground. One can see perfectly clearly that the plan of the opposition is to organize an economic blockade of Kabul, cut off deliveries to it of food and petroleum products, and provoke the discontent and even direct action of the population. In effect a blockade of this sort, relating to goods being transported to the capital in Afghan vehicles by road, is already in place in the form of robberies, intimidation and bribery of the drivers by opposition forces. It should be noted that the current difficulties with flour and with food supplies in general, in Kabul is, to a great extent, connected to the fact that the directive to inflict a defeat on Ahmad Shah, whose detachments present the greatest danger to the road between Kabul and Hairaton, was simply not implemented in good time.

   At present the monthly requirements of Kabul for flour alone are in the region of 15,000 tons. In the very recent past several thousand tons of flour have been delivered by Soviet road and air transport. However, it is imperative to have sizable reserves, at least for [one word missing; it is the first word on p. 5 of the text; the word must be either "two" or "three"—Trans.] months, which would be at the disposal of the President and which would give [our] Afghan friends the opportunity to feel more relaxed in this respect.

   Insofar as it is possible to build up such large reserves only with the help of motor transport, the question here is of the delivery of flour and other foodstuffs along the route from Hairaton to Kabul. In the words of comrade Najibullah, if this road is securely protected so that it can function approximately until May, the preservation of [his] regime can be guaranteed. It is evident that [our] Afghan friends will not be able to ensure the normal functioning of this road without our assistance. The starting point must be that it is impermissible to allow the functioning of the main road between Hairaton and Kabul to be brought to a halt. In this connection, it will be necessary to devote special attention to the most vulnerable section of the road, i.e., the Salang Pass, with its more than three-kilometer-long tunnel.

By way of preparing the conditions to enable such help to be provided, it is imperative to use the remaining time to step up even further the condemnation through all possible channels of the actions of the opposition, which is hampering the delivery of food supplies to Kabul and the other major Afghan towns, and in doing so [we must] put the stress not on the fate of the present regime, but on the situation of the population of these towns, which is suffering grievously from the consequences of such barbaric actions.

One could in principle envisage the following scenarios.

Scenario No. 1. Referring to the difficult situation in which the civilian
   population finds itself, leave one division, i.e., about 12,000 men, on
   the main highway between Hairaton and Kabul. This scenario is
   hardly desirable, as it could lead to a question being asked in the UN
   as to why we had not withdrawn our troops *in toto*. Despite the fact
   that Pakistan is not carrying out its obligations under the Geneva
   Agreements, it can be assumed that the majority of countries at the
   UN will fail to support us, since for many of them the question of
   the troops lies at the center of the problem.

Scenario No. 2. Referring to the threat of famine in Kabul and other
   towns, call on the UN urgently to guarantee the delivery of food supplies and petroleum products to the towns and send in UN troops to
   keep the highway in operation. Until the approach of the UN forces,
   leave our army subunits in these positions to carry out purely humane functions——supplying the population with foodstuffs and petroleum products. At the same time it would be officially recognized
   that the withdrawal of the Soviet military contingent had taken
   place. There would be an announcement to the effect that after the
   approach of the UN forces, our subunits would immediately return
   to the Soviet Union.

   However, this scenario is virtually unrealizable, since a resolution of the Security Council would be required before UN troops
   could be sent in, and it is impossible to count on this.

Scenario No. 3. Withdraw all the troops by 15 February, as indeed is
   planned, and have this officially registered at the international level

by statements of the governments of the USSR and the Republic of Afghanistan. Then, at the Afghan government's request, which will be addressed to [all] the countries of the world, begin the dispatch of columns with civilian goods, assigning Soviet military units to guard them. The pilotage of such columns could begin about a fortnight after the withdrawal of Soviet troops. By this time, widespread public opinion would be created to denounce the activities of the opposition, which is condemning the population of Afghan towns to death from famine. Against the background of this sort of public opinion, the passage of columns with our participation would look like a natural and humane act. At the same time, on this scenario, a number of sections of the road would have to be taken on each occasion by force of arms.

Scenario No. 4. Withdraw almost all Soviet troops by 15 February. Register the withdrawal of the Soviet military contingent officially in an appropriate declaration. However, on the pretext of handing over some of the posts on the Hairaton–Kabul highway to the Afghan Side, leave some Soviet sub-units at certain of the most important points, including the Salang Pass. On our initiative, this action is not to be given widespread publicity; it could just be noted that this is a matter of a small number of Soviet servicemen who have been slightly held up as a result of the fact that the Afghan side has not yet taken over the aforesaid posts from them. Some time later, as in Scenario No. 3, the movement of columns to Kabul gets under way with our military escorts.

The initial assumption in all these scenarios would be that it is our regular units that would take part in operations, but they should be made up of volunteers, primarily from servicemen who are now serving in Afghanistan or who have completed their tour of duty [there] and are now in the Soviet Union. In this connection, the pay for a private soldier is to be set in the region of 800–1,000 rubles a month, part of which is to be paid in Afghan currency, and the pay for officers is also to be considerably increased.

International observers are to be given the right—and this is to be widely publicized——to verify that we really are escorting convoys of goods for the population. Negotiations should take place in the nearest future with the Aga Khan, the Special Coordinator of UN programs, for providing Afghanistan with humanitarian and economic aid, in order to utilize these programs and the facilities of the Special Coordinator to counteract the plans of the extremists to throttle Kabul and the other major Afghan towns in an economic blockade.

In talks with the Aga Khan, it would be proposed that UN caravans with food, petroleum products, and medical supplies should be routed not only through Pakistan, but also, to a significant extent, via the Soviet Union.

In all the four scenarios listed above, it is envisaged that at least an insignificant number of Soviet troops will be left in Afghanistan after 15 February 1989.

One could also examine a further scenario, <u>No. 5</u>. Soviet troops are completely withdrawn by 15 February, but we offer the Afghan Side additional assistance, including financial assistance, to organize the guarding of the Hairaton–Kabul highway by its own forces, up to and including putting these Afghan subunits on our payroll for a limited period of time—although this would undoubtedly involve major difficulties, especially in providing reliable protection for the columns on their way through.

As for Kabul airport, considering its importance, it would be desirable to have a team of up to one hundred of our own civilian air traffic controllers there, concluding the appropriate contracts with the Afghan Side.

2. The Afghan leadership is raising the question of continuing, even after the departure of Soviet troops, the low-flying bombing raids, carried out by the Soviet air force from our territory, on the armed forces of the opposition. The whole complexity of this question is being explained to [our] Afghan comrades, and they are being advised to think about how, in the new conditions, they could make better use of the potential of their own aircraft. On the whole, our explanations are being taken on board with understanding, but at the same time they are saying that in certain—the most critical—situations, the use of Soviet aircraft could be simply essential. It would appear that this question can not be examined without taking into consideration the entire aggregate of internal and external factors.

3. The Afghan Side attaches considerable importance to having at its disposal powerful types of weaponry, such as the R-300 missiles and the "Hurricane" volley-fire launchers. A differentiated approach to the vari-

ous kinds of weaponry is evidently called for in this area, but the general line is to hold out for the fullest possible compliance with the appeals of [our] Afghan friends. It should be borne in mind that the very fact of possessing such types of armaments provides our friends with a great psychological boost and gives them confidence in their own powers. With due regard for this, batteries of "Hurricane" launchers have already been set up at the Special Purpose Guards Unit and in the army of the Republic of Afghanistan. The R-300 missile launchers, which are now at the disposal of the Soviet military contingent, could also be transferred to the Afghan Side after they are upgraded to export model standards and after training Afghan personnel to service and operate these launchers, which [training] should be carried out without delay on our territory.

4.   It would be desirable to respond positively to questions relating to the utilization of the resources of the USSR frontier guards in the Afghan border zone, bearing in mind, however, that the Soviet mobile motorized frontier groups operating there now will be withdrawn.

5.   We have done more than a little of late to render assistance to [our] Afghan friends in the economic sphere, keeping in view the special circumstances in which Afghanistan finds itself. This aid, in spite of all conceivable difficulties which both we and the Afghans encountered when delivering and distributing it, undoubtedly prevented many undesirable shifts in the development of the situation.

Nonetheless, in view of the complexity of the Afghan situation and the exceptional significance that the ongoing economic developments have for the internal political situation, it is imperative for us to look into these questions yet again and with great attention. It is necessary to come out and declare what more can be done for the Afghan economy, which is in a state of crisis, to all intents and purposes on the edge of collapse, and to provide emergency help to solve the acute problems that are arising, in particular by means of deliveries of essential goods and foodstuffs to Kabul and various provinces of the country, including Badakhshan.

6.   In parallel with all these measures, it is essential, as before, to continue to provide the Afghan Side with assistance in arranging and improving contacts with the opposition in Pakistan, Iran, and Western Europe. We need to follow closely all the nuances in the attitude of the opposition and discern the most suitable moments for exerting the necessary influence on it, inducing it to split and prising the "moderates" away from the extremists. At the moment it is important, in particular, to support the mission of

B. Sevan, the representative of the Secretary General of the UN, who has become involved in implementing the idea of setting up a consultative council to work out the future state framework of Afghanistan.

7. Through our diplomatic channels it will be essential to undertake further measures to work with all the states that are involved in one way or another in the conflict in Afghanistan.

    Special attention should be paid to maintaining contacts with the Pakistani Side, for which purpose use should be made of the forthcoming negotiations in Islamabad of the Minister of Foreign Affairs of the USSR.

8. It is imperative to make [our] propaganda work on Afghanistan even more graphic, for which purpose all the scenarios of the possible development of the situation in connection with Afghanistan should be analyzed in advance. Of particular importance will be the propaganda back-up for the decision to introduce martial law in Afghanistan, should this [decision] be taken by President Najibullah.

E. Shevardnadze	V. Chebrikov	A. Yakovlev	D. Yazov
V. Murakhovsky	V. Kryuchkov		

23 January 1989
No. 65/OS
20 copies

DOCUMENT 4
Extract from Politburo Minutes Regarding
Urgent Assistance to Afghanistan

12 March 1989
Proletarians of all countries, unite!
Communist Party of the Soviet Union. CENTRAL COMMITTEE
TOP SECRET
SPECIAL FILE
No. P149/23

TO COMRADES GORBACHEV, Ryzhkov, Zaykov, Shevardnadze, Yakovlev,
    Maslyukov, Yazov, Baklanov, I. Belousov, Voronin, Murakhovsky,
    B. Belousov, Gostev, Katushev, Kryuchkov, Systsov, Finogenov,

Kurochkin, Belyakov, Falin, Smirtyukov.
Extract from Minutes No. 149 of the Session of the Politburo of the CC of
the CPSU on 12 March 1989

ON ADDITIONAL MEASURES for providing urgent assistance to the Republic of Afghanistan

1. Agree with the views of comrades L. N. Zaykov, E. A. Shevardnadze,
   D. T. Yazov, O. D. Baklanov, V. L. Koblov and V. A. Kryuchkov as set out
   in the memorandum on this matter of 12 March 1989 (attached).

2. The USSR Ministry of Defense, the USSR Ministry of Foreign Economic
   Relations, and the USSR Ministry of the Aviation Industry are to carry
   out the necessary modifications and ensure the delivery to the Afghan
   side of twenty-four export model SU-22 and MIG-21 aircraft by the following
   deadlines: eight aircraft by 14 March, eight aircraft by 16 March,
   and eight aircraft by 18 March this year.

3. The USSR Ministry of Defense, the USSR Ministry of Foreign Economic
   Relations, the USSR Ministry of the Defense Industry, and the USSR
   Ministry of the Radio Communications Industry are to ensure the
   refitting of eight R-17 export model missile launchers by the following
   deadlines: four launching platforms before 25 March and four launching
   platforms before 5 April this year.

4. The USSR Ministry of the Defense Industry and the USSR Ministry of
   the Machine Building Industry are to ensure the manufacture of twenty-
   five high-explosive warheads for R-17 missiles, and the USSR Ministry of
   Defense is to ensure their delivery by the following deadlines: seven units
   by 14 March, five units by 18 March, five units by 21 March, and eight
   units by 25 March this year.

5. Agree to increase the wages fund for the defenders of Jalalabad by 15
   million rubles. The USSR Finance Ministry is to release the required resources out of the reserve fund of the USSR Council of Ministers.

6. Within a ten-day period the USSR Ministry of the Defense Industry, the
   USSR Ministry of the Machine Building Industry, the USSR Ministry of
   the Radio Communications Industry, and the USSR Ministry of Defense
   are to draw up, and the State Commission of the USSR Council of Ministers for USSR Military-Industrial Matters is to approve, the schedule for
   the modification during 1989 of two hundred R-17 missiles for their

deployment in non-nuclear weaponry and the production of two hundred high-explosive warheads (WH). Also to make provision for the possible production and dispatch of four hundred missiles with high-explosive WHs in the first half of 1990.

The USSR State Planning Committee, the USSR State Committee on Material-Technical Supply, and the USSR Finance Ministry are to prioritize the allocation of additional material resources in response to applications by the USSR Ministry of the Defense Industry, the USSR Ministry of the Machine Building Industry, and the USSR Ministry of the Radio Communications Industry.

7. The USSR Ministry of Defense is to ensure the delivery of two R-17 missile launchers to the city of Kabul before March 16 this year.

8. The USSR Ministry of Defense and the KGB of the USSR, in conjunction with the Afghan Side, are to make provision for the additional upgrading of the fighting detachments of the R-17 missile complexes at 720 Training Center of the Turkistan Military District.

9. The USSR Ministry of Defense, the USSR Ministry of Foreign Economic Relations, and the KGB of the USSR are to work with the Afghan side on questions pertaining to the additional top-priority delivery of tanks and other military technology and armaments.

10. The USSR Ministry of Foreign Economic Relations and the USSR Ministry of Defense are to conduct the appropriate negotiations with the Afghan side and draw up agreements on the basis of the existing terms of settlement.

11. The USSR Ministry of Foreign Affairs is to inform comrade Najibullah of the decisions taken.

12. Within the forthcoming ten days the USSR Ministry of Defense, the USSR Ministry of Foreign Affairs, and the KGB of the USSR are to complete work on various scenarios of the possible development of further [sic] events in the Republic of Afghanistan and prepare their positions on the appropriate steps [to be taken] in the military sphere.

CC SECRETARY
27-vt
nb
2578 Re: item 23 of Minutes No. 149
Top secret
CC CPSU

On additional measures for providing urgent assistance to the Republic of Afghanistan

In connection with the complication of the situation caused by the attack in the region of the town of Jalalabad by the armed opposition, which is receiving military support out of Pakistan, there is an urgent need to take additional measures to render assistance in the military sphere to [our] Afghan friends.

Practical steps are being undertaken to comply with certain requests in this area from comrade President Najibullah.

At the same time the military-political situation that is taking shape in Afghanistan and the likelihood of its development require on our part some additional urgent measures aimed at providing assistance to the Afghan Side.

The working group established at the Negotiations Commission of the CC CPSU Politburo for the speedy resolution of the military-political and technical questions of providing aid to the Republic of Afghanistan has examined such measures, concerning, in the first instance, the transfer to the Afghan Side of SU-22 and MIG-21 aircraft, the refitting and transfer in the shortest possible time of the R-17 missile launchers, and the speeding up of the transfer of the warheads for these missiles.

L. Zaykov, E. Shevardnadze, D. Yazov, O. Baklanov, V. Kryuchkov, V. Koblov

12 March 1989

28-tv

nb

2578

DOCUMENT 5
Extract from Politburo Minutes Regarding
Measures for Influencing Afghan Situation

13 May 1989

Hoover Archives

Proletarians of all countries, unite!

Communist Party of the Soviet Union. CENTRAL COMMITTEE

TOP SECRET

SPECIAL FILE

No. P158/6

To COMRADES GORBACHEV, Ryzhkov, Zaykov, Chebrikov,
   Shevardnadze, Yakovlev, Yazov, Baklanov, Belousov, Kryuchkov,
   Belyakov, A. Pavlov, Falin.
Extract from Minutes No. 158 of the Session of the Politburo of the CC of
the CPSU on 13 May 1989

ON ADDITIONAL MEASURES for influencing the Afghan situation.

1. Agree with the views of comrades L. N. Zaykov, E. A. Shevardnadze,
    D. T. Yazov, and V. A. Kryuchkov as set out in the memorandum of 12
    May 1989 (attached).
2. The USSR Ministry of Defense, the Committee of State Security of the
    USSR, and the USSR Ministry of Foreign Affairs are to take the measures
    necessary for the implementation of the proposals contained in the mem-
    orandum.
3. As a matter of urgency, the State Commission of the USSR Council of
    Ministers for military-industrial matters and the USSR Ministry of De-
    fense, together with the relevant ministries and departments, are to ex-
    amine the possibility of increasing deliveries of R-17 missiles and their
    warheads to Afghanistan to reach a total of ten to twelve units a day, and
    to take the necessary measures to achieve this.

CC SECRETARY
19—ri
nsh
Re: item 6 of Minutes No. 158
Top secret
CC CPSU
On additional measures for influencing the Afghan situation
   During the course of the almost three months which have passed since
the withdrawal of Soviet troops from Afghanistan, the armed forces of the
Republic [of Afghanistan] have managed to stand up to the opposition, which is
being supported by Pakistan, the United States, and Saudi Arabia. However,
the enemy, seeing that its plans to overthrow the government of Najibullah
might be in jeopardy, is doing everything to step up its military pressure. It
[the enemy] is continuing to count primarily on the capture of Jelalabad, with

the aim of setting up its "transitional government" there and getting ready for the siege of Kabul.

In connection with the preparations for a new, concentrated attack on Jelalabad with even more assistance from the Pakistanis, up to and including the dispatch there of army formations disguised as *malishes,* the USSR Ministry of Foreign Affairs has issued a Statement, and other measures of a preventive nature have been taken, including the use of closed [i.e., secret—Trans.] channels.

Bearing in mind the development of the situation, it would appear to be advisable to carry out a series of measures for the continued support of the government of the Republic of Afghanistan and to exert a restraining influence on the Afghan opposition and on Pakistan.

1. In the present circumstances it is particularly important to bring constant, massive fire-power to bear against the enemy, further increasing it and utilizing the most effective types of weaponry. In this context, it is essential to procure additional ways to speed up deliveries to Afghanistan of arms and ammunition, particularly such items as R-17 missiles, air defense facilities and others.

2. The question of carrying out low-flying bombing raids by the Soviet air force from USSR territory requires further study.

3. It would be desirable to continue to carry out the demonstrative redeployment of our aviation at Soviet airports close to the border with Afghanistan, bearing in mind that these relocations should be executed without any camouflage on the assumption that they will be noted by the Pakistanis and the opposition. [It would also be advisable] to continue even further the flights of Soviet military reconnaissance aircraft over Afghanistan, especially in the areas of the towns of Jelalabad and Host, possibly at lower altitudes, with the aim of obtaining data from aerial photography about the concentration of enemy forces.

4. In connection with the idea suggested by comrade Najibullah of bringing in foreign volunteers to Afghanistan to provide help to the government of the Republic in repelling aggression, it would be possible not to object to [our] Afghan friends carrying out work with a number of countries, especially Muslim ones.

5. It is intended that political and diplomatic work will be carried out continuously with the aim of exerting influence, so far as the Afghan problem

is concerned, on the United States, Pakistan, Iran, and Saudi Arabia, and also in the area of utilizing the opportunities presented by India and the Non-Aligned Movement. In particular, the Afghan theme will also in the future occupy one of the central places in Soviet-American contacts. It would seem to be desirable to accept the proposal of Saudi Arabia to perform the role of intermediary between ourselves and the Afghan opposition. It is assumed that the anti-Afghan policy line of Pakistan will be borne in mind in the development of bilateral relations with that country.

L. Zaykov   E. Shevardnadze   D. Yazov   V. Kryuchkov
12 May 1989
No. 390/os

DOCUMENT 6
*Extracts from Minutes Regarding Negotiations in Kabul
for Assistance to Afghanistan*

16 August 1989
Hoover Archives
Communist Party of the Soviet Union. CENTRAL COMMITTEE
TOP SECRET
SPECIAL FILE
[Printed sideways in the left-hand margin:]

FOR INFORMATION
A comrade who receives top secret documents of the CC of the CPSU may neither pass them on to, nor acquaint with them, any person whatsoever without the express permission to do so of the CC.

Making copies of the said documents or writing out excerpts from them is categorically forbidden.

After acquainting himself with the document, the comrade to whom it is addressed places his personal signature and the date on the document.

PERSONAL
No. P164/117

To Comrades Gorbachev, Ryzhkov, Zaykov, Shevardnadze, Yakovlev, Yazov, Baklanov, I. Belousov, Katushev, Kryuchkov, Belyakov.

Extract from Minutes No. 164 of the Session of the Politburo of the CC of the CPSU on 16 August 1989

On the negotiations in Kabul and our possible further steps in the Afghan sector

1. Agree with the views set out in the memorandum by comrades E. A. Shevardnadze and V. A. Kryuchkov of 11 August 1989 (attached).
2. The USSR Ministry of Defense, the State Commission of the USSR Council of Ministers on military and industrial questions, the USSR Ministry of Foreign Economic Relations, and the USSR Committee of State Security [KGB], together with the USSR Ministry of Foreign Affairs and the Defense Department of the CC of the CPSU, are to examine the list of requests from comrade Najibullah of 6 August 1989, on questions of military cooperation and submit their proposals in accordance with the established procedures.

CC SECRETARY

16-lz

vv

Annex—14 pp.

Re. item 117 of Minutes No. 164

Top secret

SPECIAL FILE

CC CPSU

On the negotiations in Kabul and our possible further steps in the Afghan sector

In accordance with instructions, [we] left on 6 August 1989, on a working visit to Afghanistan, where we held meetings with President comrade Najibullah; the Chairman of the Executive Committee of the Council of Ministers, S. A. Keshtmand; the Minister of Foreign Affairs, A. Vakil; the Minister of Defense, S. Tanai; the Minister of State Security, G. F. Yakubi; and the Minister of Internal Affairs, M. A. Vatandzhar. The most detailed talks were those with comrade Najibullah, which to all intents and purposes went on for an entire day, with a few intermissions.

1. Having already in principle sufficient information at our disposal on the course of events in Afghanistan during the almost six months since the departure of Soviet troops, we strove above all in our talks and in our personal dealings with the Afghan leaders to get the feel of their state of mind and to hear at first hand their assessments of the current situation in the country and of the prospects for the future. [Our] general impression is that much that is new has appeared in the conduct and actions of our Afghan friends over the past six months. Beyond all doubt they require, as hitherto, large-scale and especially material support from us, without which it would simply be impossible for them to hold out until the end of this fairly lengthy period. At the same time, one can clearly observe a growth in self-dependence, self-confidence, and the ability to evaluate the situation correctly, i.e., in everything that they were deficient in at the time of our military presence in Afghanistan.

   This trend is of course developing not without problems; they have to overcome difficulties caused by the absence of real experience and by the habit, now ingrained after many long years, of receiving ready-made decisions from our advisers. But the first and in this respect most critical period, when a transition was in progress from one way of doing things to another, is over, and now [our] Afghan friends are more and more making their mark as people who are themselves answerable for the situation.

2. The sum total of information available at the present time, including the views and assessments of the Afghan leadership and the Soviet representatives in Kabul, indicates that the impact of factors working in favor of the regime is on the increase. During the period when Soviet troops were present in Afghanistan, these factors to a significant extent were, so to speak, away from the limelight. The major factor here is the growth of patriotic feelings and the strengthening of the sense of national identity of the Afghans, the thrust of which is being directed more and more against the interference of Pakistan, the United States, and Saudi Arabia in the internal affairs of Afghanistan. Earlier these sentiments were muted because of the Soviet military presence, and to a certain extent as a result of the propaganda of our opponents, they [these sentiments] were directed against this presence. Together with this, a positive impact results from the government's increased responsibility for the state of affairs in specific areas, which is aided by the self-dependence that has finally come into being in decision-making, including decisions on key questions. The NDPA [National Democratic Party of Afghanistan?] has discov-

ered within itself the strength to put the "factional disagreements" in its highest echelon into the background and to get its work organized under the leadership of comrade Najibullah. As a result, in spite of the fact that the Afghan military formations of the Republic are experiencing great difficulties in replenishing their ranks and are suffering from desertions, the Republic's authorities have not yielded their positions to any real extent and have even strengthened them in individual sectors.

On a par with the fortitude of the Guards and other units, one of the decisive factors is the active utilization of the R-17 E and "Hurricane" missile systems and the concentrated low-flying bombing raids, which have become possible only thanks to the large-scale deliveries of missiles, bombs, and other types of weaponry with increased strike power from the USSR to Afghanistan, in the first instance via the "airlift" to Kabul.

In the economic sphere the Afghan leadership is managing for the time being, and with our help, to solve the most essential problems of sustaining life in Kabul and the adjoining districts by preventing units of the opposition from blockading the capital, but this threat has not yet been completely eliminated. The transit of freight from the Soviet border to Kabul is not being implemented on a sufficiently regular basis.

3. Banking on the internal weakness of the regime and the chance of a military victory, as did the opposition and also the like-minded circles in Pakistan, the United States and a number of other countries, is not paying dividends; that, at least, is how things stand today. Government troops are parrying attempts by the adversary to achieve success in the main sectors, paving the way for a stable defensive system, and ensuring the functioning of vitally important transport routes, such as those between Kabul and Hairaton, Kabul and Jalalabad, Turgundi–Herat–Lashkargah, and Mazari-Sharif and Meimene. Events near Jalalabad have shown that our Afghan friends can not only defend themselves but also carry out individual offensive operations successfully. On the other hand, it has become obvious that the opposition's military capacities have been artificially inflated both by the opposition itself and in Pakistan and the West. The serious disagreements amongst the opposition and its lack of coordination after the withdrawal of Soviet troops are on the increase. Military pressure is being applied mainly by the forces of the most extreme, "irreconcilable" wing of the Afghan opposition, which is receiving material, military and advisory assistance from the United States, Pakistan, and Saudi Arabia, and also by detachments of mercenaries from

Arab countries. Evidence of military activity by this wing is to be found predominantly in districts on or near the Afghan-Pakistani border. Other gang-units operating on three-quarters of the territory of Afghanistan are for the time being playing a waiting game.

4. In the current situation, the important role that the Geneva Agreements, legalizing the withdrawal of Soviet troops from Afghanistan, have played and are continuing to play, is being confirmed. No one is saying that the Soviet army was "on the run." Thanks to Geneva and the ensuing foreign policy measures of the Afghan government, which we supported, Pakistan and the United States have found themselves at a disadvantage in the eyes of world public opinion: They are being held responsible for the continuing war in Afghanistan. This made itself felt in particular during the course of the UN Security Council session on Afghanistan in April 1989. The international authority of the Republic of Afghanistan has risen markedly, and this, in its turn, has prevented the opposition's so-called "transitional government" from gaining wide recognition by other states.

    An extremely important factor is presented by the, in many respects, individual stance of Iran, which has of late been taking a more constructive line in Afghan affairs. To a considerable extent, this is the result of efforts to develop Soviet-Iranian relations. As has been shown by the negotiations between M. S. Gorbachev and A. A. Hashemi-Rafsandzhani in Moscow, and also by the latest talks in Teheran, the Iranians are moving closer to an acceptance of the idea that the present republican regime should participate in the settlement of the Afghan situation.

5. At the same time it is essential to put it on record that the situation of the government of Afghanistan has not yet stabilized, in which respect the next few months will be of particular importance. [Our] Afghan friends are having to overcome great difficulties of a material, political and military nature. Despite a certain sobering up, which set in as a result of some military set-backs, the opposition is still not giving up its idea of seizing power by force and overthrowing the government and President of Afghanistan. It is obvious that the opposition's leaders and the Americans, Pakistanis, and Saudis who are backing them will closely analyze the reasons for the frustration of their plans to seize power in Kabul, draw [the appropriate] conclusions from the lessons they have been taught, and try to find new ways of stepping up military pressure. In particular, reports are coming in of the gradual massing of detachments of the op-

position on the near and the distant approaches to Kabul. Deliveries of more modern American equipment for the "alliance of the Seven" are starting up, and the active political and military involvement of the Pakistanis in the conflict taking place in Afghanistan is continuing.

On the diplomatic and propaganda levels, attempts are being made to persuade us to renounce our support of President Najibullah and remove him from the political arena, supposedly in the interests of setting up a broadly based government with the participation of "Muslims from Kabul."

6. In these conditions, it is important for the government of Afghanistan to continue to strive for a political settlement of the Afghan problem and in this context to put forward ever new initiatives, the essence of which, as before, will come down to a cease-fire and the setting-up of an intra-Afghan dialogue. At the moment these proposals are being rejected by the opposition virtually "on the spot." However, there are signs that this attitude may gradually change in the event that in the future as well the government in Kabul displays tenacity, stands up against the armed onslaughts of the opposition, and keeps up the tempo and aggressive character of its political initiatives. The opposing side no longer retains its earlier certainty of military victory. More realistic assessments have begun to be heard in certain Pakistani and American circles and in the Western press. But, of course, time will be needed for such attitudes to develop into a consistent tendency and for the awareness to dawn that a dialogue must be conducted from positions of reasonable compromise, not from a position of strength.

7. In principle the course of events in Afghanistan can proceed in the future along several basic lines.

With our help, the regime that now exists in Afghanistan will continue to hold on to its positions and even, perhaps, consolidate them. In this event, its transformation is also possible, with the creation of a broadly based coalition-type power structure in which the NDPA [National Democratic Party of Afghanistan?] will remain as one of the leading players who are in a position to determine the internal and foreign policy of the country.

In the event that our Afghan friends are nevertheless unable to consolidate their positions, one of the most likely scenarios is the coming to power of Islamic fundamentalists; moreover, here there can be a variety of "secondary scenarios," especially if one bears in mind the whole mass of contradictions within the camp of the fundamentalists themselves. A very serious complicating factor could also come into being if things do move in this direction, it will be more probable that at some stage the interests of Iran, which for the moment is to some extent neutralized, will coincide with the interests of Pakistan. Naturally, there are also factors working in the opposite direction: both the apprehensions of certain circles in the United States concerning the possibility of the appearance in this part of the world of a new fundamentalist state, and the position of B. Bhutto, who does not harbor any sympathies for the fundamentalists.

In principle it is impossible to exclude even the possibility that the so-called "moderates," perhaps under the aegis of Zahir Shah, the former Afghan king, could take up a position center stage. However, this scenario is less probable today, both because of the existing correlation of forces within the opposition and because of the irresolute attitude of Zahir Shah who, as a result of his age, is becoming ever more inactive and prefers not to put at risk his present way of life in Rome on a Saudi subsidy.

Thus, in the event of a setback for [our] Afghan friends, the most likely result is the coming to power in Afghanistan of the Islamic fundamentalists.

8. Apart from all the consequences that this will bring for our Afghan friends and for our own positions in Afghanistan, such a turn of events will also have a negative impact on the situation in Soviet Central Asia, where even today Islamic sentiments of a fundamentalist nature are on the rise. With the help of Afghan opposition groupings, the Pakistani special services are trying to expand [their] anti-Soviet pro-Islamic propaganda on the territory of the USSR. At the same time, ideas are even being mooted of reconstituting an Islamic state with a capital in Bukhara. The situation could become even more complex if Iran, at any rate for the short-term future, is preserved as a fundamentalist state. Fundamentalist sentiments are strong in Pakistan, and a certain increase in them can also be noted in Turkey.

In talks which we had in Tashkent on the way to and back from Kabul with comrade I. A. Karimov and other Uzbek leaders, they expressed genuine apprehension regarding the possible development of the situation in Uzbekistan and other [Soviet] republics in Central Asia, if Islamic fundamentalism gets the upper hand in Afghanistan. Extremist elements in Uzbekistan, they said, are watching what is going on in that neighboring country with great attention. In the opinion of [our] Uzbek comrades, such a turn of events in Afghanistan must not be permitted to happen.

9. There is also one other serious matter, which will evidently come to the fore in the event of a fundamentalist victory. Finding themselves in power, they will undoubtedly try to lodge an official complaint at state level concerning the "atrocities" allegedly committed by us. The first indications of this are [already] appearing: In the vicinity of Gardez, the opposition has unearthed a grave with the remains of some four hundred people who were executed under Amin, and an attempt is now being made to put the blame for this on the Soviet side.

10. Bearing in mind all the factors of a long-term nature, the inference for our attitude to the events taking place in Afghanistan could evidently be the following: the preservation in some, perhaps even in a very different, form of the present regime accords with our interests of state. It will not be easy to achieve this. It will require the most serious exertions, not only of the Afghans themselves but also of ourselves. However, it can already be said that this task is reasonably realistic. The policy of consolidating the viability of the present regime takes it for granted that wide-ranging and many-sided support, including material support, for the government and President of Afghanistan, will continue to be provided in the future. At the same time, it will undoubtedly be necessary to keep in mind that our assistance, by helping to foster the stability of the regime, thereby reduces the chances of possible victory for the opposition and consequently increases the probability of achieving a political settlement. After all, a protracted war in Afghanistan is not in our interests.

11. The availability of a variety of missiles, strike aircraft, and artillery systems at the disposal of the Afghan leadership will enable it to react quickly and effectively to attempts by the adversary to take Kabul and other key towns in the country by storm. In these conditions, it will be possible to increase the strength of the land forces for the long-term retention of the positions they have taken up and for the execution of more active fighting operations.

Our concrete assistance should consist of building up the fighting strength of the branches of the armed forces of the Republic of Afghanistan that have shown themselves to the best advantage and have the greatest potential for the future—the missile troops and the air force. It is imperative to set up a powerful missile strike force in Kabul itself, adding to the R-17 E and "Hurricane" missiles, which are already there—some missiles with an operational range of up to 70 kilometers. At the same time, the air force of the Republic should be strengthened by supplying aircraft and helicopters over and above what has already been agreed. A start should be made to the training courses for the air crews of the Afghan air force in new types of equipment. Once training is completed and conditions are created for housing ground-based technology, it is to be delivered to the Republic of Afghanistan. A particularly urgent task is the supply of artillery and aircraft ammunition, facilities necessary for intelligence gathering and heavy-load motor vehicles.

On 6 August 1989, comrade Najibullah sent a number of requests to the Soviet leadership concerning our military supplies (attached).

12. It will also be necessary to assist [our] Afghan friends with foodstuffs, especially wheat, for the requirements of the armed forces and the population of Kabul. In this connection, since the stocks of wheat held in Hairaton are coming to an end, 15,000 tons of wheat are to be sent there urgently as part of our aid package to Afghanistan. Direct links between Soviet republics, regions, and cities and their Afghan twins should become a more important conduit. Conditions are being created for the resumption of work on several economic cooperation projects in the northern districts of the Republic of Afghanistan.

13. The ongoing policy of forming a well-functioning coalition government on the broadest possible base in Afghanistan should be pursued consistently, striving to ensure, as the optimal solution, the cooperation of all the national-patriotic, democratic and progressive forces of the country with the NDPA [National Democratic Party of Afghanistan] at the center. At the practical level, one should evidently start from the assumption that despite the continuing stubborn resistance to this policy by the United States, Pakistan and the "irreconcilable" grouping in the Peshawar contingent, the creation of grassroots coalitions and regional understandings might prove to be reasonably feasible at the present stage; later on this could develop into a system of contractual relations between the center (the Najibullah government in Kabul) and the semi-autonomous and self-dependent formations in the provinces (as is currently the case with the Ismailite grouping, as is taking shape in the center of the country with the Hazarites, and as the government in Kabul is planning [to arrange] with the "Panshir leader" Ahmad Shah Masud).

14. At the diplomatic level, active work should continue to be carried out

with Iran and Pakistan, and also with the United States and Saudi Arabia, with the aim of ending military operations in Afghanistan and bringing about an intra-Afghan dialogue. In bilateral contacts with a variety of countries and at international forums, the proposal to put an end to arms deliveries should be pressed home, simultaneously, of course, with a cease-fire and under strict international control.

In order to bring our influence to bear on the Saudis, whose role in providing assistance to the Afghan opposition is not on the decline, direct contacts with them through the Saudi Embassy in Washington should continue to be used, as should the opportunities provided by other Arab states.

It is important also to press on further with our policy of an Afghan settlement through the UN. Our propaganda work on exposing the violations of the Geneva Agreements by Pakistan must not be relaxed. Well-targeted work with Iran is to be continued. The idea that the center of gravity for a political solution of the Afghan problem is shifting more and more to Teheran, this being facilitated by the more realistic stance of the new Iranian leadership, is to be conveyed in the appropriate way in our propaganda, including the use of closed [i.e., black propaganda?—Trans.] channels.

15. Our mass media should draw the attention of the Soviet public to the great significance for our national interests of ensuring that Afghanistan remains well disposed towards us, and to the fact that, in contrast to the past, in order to achieve these important aims of ours, we are now using not any direct involvement in Afghan affairs, but the method of effective assistance to our friends in a neighboring country for the defense and stabilization, through the efforts of the Afghans themselves, of a regime which is well-intentioned so far as we are concerned. It should be explained that the forces of reaction are interested in using the territory of Afghanistan as a base from which to carry out destructive activities aimed at creating an atmosphere of instability in areas adjacent to the USSR.

E. Shevardnadze, V. Kryuchkov
11 August 1989
No. 0703/os
16 copies

APPENDIX P

DOCUMENT FOR CHAPTER 50

———⪼●⪻———

DOCUMENT 1
Extract from Minutes Regarding Arms to Cuba

7 February 1989
Hoover Archives

Communist Party of the Soviet Union. CENTRAL COMMITTEE
TOP SECRET
SPECIAL FILE
No. P147/84

To COMRADES GORBACHEV, Ryzhkov, Zaykov, Shevardnadze, Yakovlev,
    Yazov, Baklanov, I. Belousov, Kryuchkov, Katushev, Falin.
Extract from Minutes No. 147 of the Session of the Politburo of the CC of
the CPSU on 7 February 1989

ON THE QUESTION of compensation in the form of deliveries from the
Soviet Union to the Republic of Cuba of arms [the Russian word also means
"equipment"—Trans.] which may be left behind by Cuban troops in the People's
Republic of Angola

1. Agree with the proposal set out in the memorandum from comrades E.
    A. Shevardnadze, A. N. Yakovlev, D. T. Yazov, V. A. Kryuchkov, and K. F.
    Katushev of 31 January 1989 on this subject (attached).
2. Approve the texts of the instructions to the Soviet ambassadors to the
    People's Republic of Angola and the Republic of Cuba (attached).

CC SECRETARY

16-an

tk

Attachments 4 pp

Re: item 84 of Minutes No. 147

SPECIAL FILE

Top secret

CC CPSU

On the question of compensation in the form of deliveries from the Soviet Union to the Republic of Cuba for the arms, which may be left behind by the Cuban troops in the People's Republic of Angola

---

THE PRESIDENT OF the People's Republic of Angola, J. E. dos Santos, has made a request to the General Secretary of the CC of the CPSU, comrade M. S. Gorbachev, to compensate, in the form of deliveries from the Soviet Union to the Republic of Cuba, for the arms [the wording here is one letter different from the otherwise identical formulation on the previous page and earlier on this page—Trans.] which may be left behind on the withdrawal of the Cuban troops from the People's Republic of Angola.

J. E. dos Santos has also sent M. S. Gorbachev a message with which he conveyed, in pursuance of the development of talks in Moscow in October 1988, [the Russian in the above line is most peculiar—Trans.] an application for the additional delivery to Angola of arms, ammunition, and military technology.

Since 1976, over the period of cooperation, the Soviet Union has supplied Angola with arms and military technology to a value of more than 3.7 milliard rubles. This has permitted the national armed forces, in cooperation with the Cuban troops (armed with over 1,000 tanks, 200 combat vehicles for the infantry, more than 500 pieces of ordnance and missile installations for the artillery, 70 anti-aircraft missile complexes, and 44 military aircraft), to fulfill the task of guaranteeing the independence and territorial integrity of Angola.

Before the end of the current five-year plan and in accordance with signed agreements, provisions have been made to supply Angola with 65 tanks, 18 artillery pieces, 150 mobile anti-aircraft missile complexes, 12 military aircraft, 5 helicopters, ammunition and other assets, with an overall value of some 600 million rubles.

At the same time, there is a need to take additional measures to prevent the weakening of Angola's defensive capability in conjunction with the withdrawal of the Cuban troops from that country.

In connection with what has been outlined, it is proposed to hold trilateral (the USSR, Cuba, and Angola) consultations in Moscow in February–March 1989 on the question of the transfer [of arms and military technology] to Angola by the Cubans and of compensation [for this] in the form of deliveries of arms and military technology to Cuba from the USSR. Proceed in this from the possibility of the aforesaid partial compensation.

Taking account of the results of the consultations, a position is also to be taken on additional deliveries of arms and military technology to Angola in connection with the request of J. E. dos Santos, and proposals are to be presented in accordance with established procedures.

E. Shevardnadze   A. Yakovlev   D. Yazov   V. Kryuchkov   K. Katushev

31 January 1989

No. 318/ 3/ 3-00144

17 copies

Re: item 84 of Minutes No. 147

Top secret

LUANDA

SOVIET AMBASSADOR

Together with the Chief Military Adviser, visit the President of Angola, J. E. dos Santos, or another person who will be instructed to receive you, and, referring to instructions, inform [him] of the following.

The requests for compensation, in the form of deliveries to Cuba from the Soviet Union, for arms which may be left behind by the Cuban troops when they withdraw from Angola, and [requests] also for the additional supply of arms, ammunition, and military technology to Angola, have been closely studied by the Soviet government.

In our opinion, it would be advisable to hold trilateral (the USSR, Angola, and Cuba) consultations in Moscow in February–March 1989 on the question of the transfer [of arms and military technology] to Angola by the Cubans and of compensation in the form of deliveries of arms and military technology to Cuba from the USSR. Taking account of the results of the consultations, a position is also to be taken on additional deliveries of arms and military technology to Angola in connection with the request of J. E. dos Santos.

The precise time and level of these consultations could be decided by mutual agreement between the [High Contracting] Parties.

Telegraph on implementation.

18 copies

Re: item 84 of Minutes No. 147

Top secret

HAVANA

SOVIET AMBASSADOR

Together with the Chief Military Adviser, visit the First Secretary of the CC of the Communist Party of Cuba, F. Castro, or another person who will be instructed to receive you, and, referring to instructions, inform [him] of the following.

The President of the People's Republic of Angola, J. E. dos Santos, has made a request for compensation, in the form of deliveries to Cuba from the Soviet Union, for the arms which may be left behind by the Cuban troops on their withdrawal from Angola.

The request has been closely studied by the Soviet government.

In our opinion, it would be advisable to hold trilateral (the USSR, Cuba, and Angola) consultations in Moscow in February–March 1989 on the question of the transfer of and compensation for the arms and military technology in connection with the request of J. E. dos Santos.

The precise time and level of the consultations could be decided by mutual agreement between the [High Contracting] Parties.

Telegraph on implementation.

18 copies

NOTES

CHAPTER 1   LENIN SEIZES HIS MOMENT

1. Richard Pipes, *The Russian Revolution, 1899–1919* (New York: Alfred A. Knopf, 1990). See ch. 9, "Lenin and the Origins of Bolshevism."
2. Dmitri Volkogonov, *Lenin: Life and Legacy,* trans. and ed. by Harold Shukman (London: HarperCollins, 1995), p. 182.
3. *Ibid.,* p. 181. The theme of Lenin's terror is also developed in Volkogonov's book, *The Rise and Fall of the Soviet Empire: Political Leaders from Lenin to Gorbachev* (London; HarperCollins, 1998), pp. 10, 76, 77, 94, 102. Published in the United States under the title *Autopsy of an Empire.*
4. For further details, see Pipes, *Revolution,* ch. 11, "The Bolshevik Bid for Power," p. 411.
5. George Leggett, *Cheka: Lenin's Political Police* (Clarendon Press, Oxford, 1981), p. 191.

CHAPTER 2   THE RECONQUEST

1. Jan Librach, *The Rise of the Soviet Empire* (New York: Praeger, 1966; and London: Pall Mall, 1965), pp. 11–12.
2. *Communist Takeover and Occupation of the Ukraine,* Special Report No. 4 of Select Committee on Communist Aggression, 83rd Congress, 2d session (Washington, D.C.: Government Printing Office, 1954), p. 8.
3. Lenin, *The Aims of Revolution.*
4. Richard Pipes, *The Formation of the Soviet Union: Communism and Nationalism 1917–1923* (Cambridge, Mass.: Harvard, 1964), pp. 75–99.
5. Hugh Seton-Watson, *The New Imperialism* (London: Bodley Head, 1961), pp. 42 et seq.
6. Pipes, *Formation,* p. 151.
7. Letter from Karl Marx, April 12, 1871, to Dr. Kugelmann, in *Pis'ma k.L.Kugelmanu* (Petrograd, 1920). See also Richard Pipes, *Russia under the Bolshevik Regime 1919–1924* (New York: Alfred A. Knopf, and London: HarperCollins, 1994), p. 6.

8. Cited by N. Sukhanov in *Novaia zhizn'*; see Pipes, *Bolshevik*, p. 6, n. 3.

9. Iu. I. Korablev in *Revoliutsionnyi Voennyi Sovet Respubliki* (Moscow: Military Council of the Soviet Republic, 1991), p. 36; quoted in Pipes, *Bolshevik*, p. 53.

10. Volkogonov, *Lenin*, pp. 220 et seq; also pp. 410 et seq.

11. Quoted in C. H. Ellis, *The Transcaspian Episode* (London: Bodley Head, 1963), App. I, p. 163. This work puts the Transcaspian part of the Civil War in the context of a well-intended but ultimately ineffectual British intervention.

12. The Kokand episode is covered briefly in Ellis, *Transcaspian*, p. 19; in Seton-Watson, *Imperialism*, p. 47; and more fully, in Pipes, *Bolshevik*, pp. 153–58.

13. George Stewart, *The White Armies of Russia* (New York, 1933), pp. 346–47.

14. Pipes, *Bolshevik*, p. 188.

15. For a fuller analysis, see ibid., pp. 9–14.

CHAPTER 3   WORLD REVOLUTION ADJOURNED

1. Radek's recollections of his German mission are in *Krasnaia Nov'* 10 (Moscow, October 1926). See also Pipes, *Bolshevik*, p. 168.

2. *Petrogradskaya Pravda* 255, November 7, 1919.

3. *Protokoll des Zweiten Welt-Kongresses der Kommunistischen Internationale,* July 23–August 7, 1920 (Hamburg, 1921).

4. For a detailed account of the Kronstadt rising, see Pipes, *Bolshevik,* pp. 379–86.

5. Volkogonov, *Lenin,* pp. 423 et seq.

6. *Ibid.,* p. 426, quoting a "Strictly secret" letter from Stalin to the Politburo, dated March 11, 1923. As Volkogonov observes, however, it seems unlikely that Lenin, reduced to monosyllabic speech or unintelligible sounds, could have asked for "potassium chloride." "Perhaps using sign language?" he adds.

7. Albert Weeks, in a review of Volkogonov, *Lenin* in the *Washington Inquirer,* August 26, 1994.

8. Hugh Seton-Watson, *The New Imperialism* (London: Bodley Head, 1961), pp. 52–53.

9. *Yearbook on International Communist Affairs* (Stanford, Calif.: Hoover Institution, 1966).

CHAPTER 4   THE COMINTERN AT WORK, 1921–1939

1. For an account of this troubled period, see Brian Crozier, *The Man Who Lost China: The First Full Biography of Chiang Kai-shek* (New York: Scribner, 1976; and London: Angus & Robertson, 1977), ch. 4, "Chaos and Treachery."

2. Jacques Guillermaz, *A History of the Chinese Communist Party 1921–1949* (London: Methalin, 1972); French original, *Histoire du parti communiste chinois* (Paris: Payot, 1968), pp. 61–62.

3. Crozier, *Chiang,* p. 61.

4. Chiang Kai-shek, *Soviet Russia in China: A Summing-Up at Seventy* (New York: Farrar Straus, 1957), ch. 1, "Beginnings."
5. Jean Lacouture, *Hô Chi Minh* (Paris, 1967), p. 12.
6. *Ibid.*, p. 16.
7. Robert F. Turner, *Vietnamese Communism: Its Origins and Development* (Stanford, Calif.: Hoover Institution, 1975), p. 6. The fullest treatment of the subject available.
8. *Ibid.*, pp. 8–9. See also P. J. Honey, *Communism in North Vietnam* (Cambridge, Mass.: MIT Press, 1963), p. 4.
9. Brian Crozier, *The Rebels: A Study of Post-War Insurrections* (London: Chatto & Windus, 1960), p. 32.
10. Turner, *Vietnamese Communism*, p. 12.
11. See *M. N. Roy's Memoirs*, ed. by G. D. Perrikh (Bombay: Allied Publishers Private, 1964), pp. 228–36.
12. Burnett Bolloten, *The Spanish Revolution: The Left and the Struggle for Power during the Civil War* (Stanford, Calif.: Hoover Institution, 1979). See, in particular, ch. 8, "The Communists Strive for Hegemony." This revised and expanded version of Bolloten's *The Grand Camouflage: The Communist Conspiracy in the Spanish Civil War* (London: Hollis & Carter, 1961) is the most authoritative account of this theme and one of the most important of the thousands of works on the Civil War.
13. Brian Crozier, *Franco: A Biographical History* (Boston: Little, Brown; and London: Eyre & Spottiswoode, 1967), ch. 8, "Franco Blends a Government," pp. 259 et seq. For a fuller version of events, see Bolloten, *Grand Camouflage*, chs. 25–30.
14. Boris Ponomarev, "Outstanding Event in the History of the Communist Movement," *World Marxist Review* (February 1969); Dolores Ibarruri et al., "Fighting Side by Side with Spanish Patriots against Fascism," *Novosti* (Moscow 1986), quoted by Herbert Romerstein, in *Heroic Victims: Stalin's Foreign Legion in the Spanish Civil War* (Washington, D.C.: Council for the Defense of Freedom, 1994), p. 3.
15. Crozier, *Franco*, p. 301.
16. Hugh Thomas, *The Spanish Civil War* (London: Penguin, 1965, 1977), pp. 469, 855–56, and 982.
17. Alexander Orlov, *The Secret History of Stalin's Crimes* (1953), pp. 235–36.
18. Romerstein, *Heroic Victims*, p. 8.
19. *Ibid.*, p. 90.
20. Bolloten, *Grand Camouflage*, pp. 142–44.

CHAPTER 5 "TOTALIST" RIVALRIES

1. For a fuller discussion of this issue, see Brian Crozier, *Socialism: Dream and Reality* (London: 1987), ch. 3.

2. Robert Conquest, *Stalin: Breaker of Nations* (London: Weidenfield & Nicolson, 1991), pp. 217–21. Also, Roy Medvedev, *Let History Judge: The Origins and Consequences of Stalinism* (New York: Columbia University, and Oxford: Oxford University, 1989), pp. 723–32. See also Boris Souvarine, *Staline, Aperçu historique du bolchévisme* (Paris: Champ Libre, 1977).

3. This particular batch of Top Secret archives had been kept in a "Special Dossier" at the offices of the Communist Party's Central Committee in Moscow, and are quoted extensively by former Red Army officers General Oleg Sarin and Colonel Lev Dvoretsky, *Alien Wars: The Soviet Union's Aggressions against the World, 1919 to 1989* (Novato, Calif.: Presidio Press, 1996). These archives included Secret Protocols to the Nazi-Soviet Pact of August 23, 1939.

4. Sarin, *Alien Wars*, p. 40.

5. *Ibid.*, p. 50.

6. *Ibid.*, pp. 26–38.

7. Conquest, *Stalin*, pp. 226–27.

8. Medvedev, *Stalinism*, pp. 730–31.

9. Nikolai Tolstoy, *Stalin's Secret War* (London: Jonathan Cape, 1981), p. 112. A work of outstanding value.

10. *Ibid.*, p. 112. See also Francis Beckett, *Enemy Within: The Rise and Fall of the British Communist Party* (London: Jonathan Murray, 1995), pp. 90–101.

11. For a revealing account of the penetration of Nazi Germany during the war, by the OSS (forerunner of the CIA), see Joseph E. Persico, *Piercing the Reich* (New York, 1979). The author obtained the release of previously censored CIA files.

12. A. Rossi, *Les Communistes français pendant la drôle de guerre* ("The French Communists during the phony war," Paris: Iles d'or, 1951): the fullest treatment of this shameful period. See especially pp. 295 et seq.

13. Tolstoy, *War*, pp. 194–95.

14. Quoted in Tolstoy, *War*, p. 179, from Louis FitzGibbon, *Katyn: A Crime Without Parallel*, pp. 183–84; and Harold Nicolson, *Diaries and Letters 1939–1945*, respectively.

15. Medvedev, *Stalinism*, p. 738. Surprisingly, Conquest, in *Stalin*, does not mention Richard Sorge in his account of Stalin's misjudgment of Hitler's intentions.

16. Tolstoy, *War*, p. 238.

CHAPTER 6   THE EXPANSIONIST MACHINE

1. Quoted from Winston Churchill, *The Second World War*, Vol. 12 (London: Cassell, 1955), ch. 4, "Yalta Finale."

2. J. H. Brimmell (a former British Intelligence officer), *Communism in South-East Asia* (Oxford: Oxford University, 1959), part V, pp. 249 et seq.

3. For a detailed account of the activities of the International Department, see Brian Crozier, "Subversion and the USSR," in *Annual of Power and Conflict 1974–75* (London: Institute for the Study of Conflict-ISC, 1975). See also Brian Crozier, *Strategy of Survival* (London: Temple Smith; and New Rochelle, N.Y.: Arlington, 1978), pp. 141–47.

4. Brian Crozier, *The Gorbachev Phenomenon* (London: Claridge, 1990), p. 86, and in general, part II.

5. Brian Crozier, *Free Agent: The Unseen War 1941–1991* (London: HarperCollins, 1993), pp. 1–2.

6. For a fuller description of postwar international front organizations, see Brian Crozier, *The Future of Communist Power* (London: Eyre & Spottiswoode, 1970; U.S. ed.: *Since Stalin: An Assessment of Communist Power,* New York: Coward McCann, 1970), Appendix. For a later and more detailed account, see Clive Rose, *The Soviet Propaganda Network: A Directory of Organizations Serving Soviet Foreign Policy* (London: Pinter; and New York: St. Martin's, 1988).

7. Michael Bialoguski, *The Petrov Story* (Melbourne, London: Heinemann, 1955), pp. xiii–xiv and 235 et seq.

8. For further details, see Crozier, *Gorbachev*, part II, p. 6, "The Terror Network." See also *Terroristic Activity: International Terrorism* (Washington, D.C.: Hearings of the U.S. Senate Committee on the Judiciary, May 14, 1975: Testimony of Brian Crozier, Director of the Institute for the Study of Conflict, London).

9. Fond 89 references: Finding Aid (Opis 18), Docs. 30, 31.

10. Fond 89 reference: Opis 51, Doc. 22.

11. Fond 89 reference: Opis 51, Doc. 23.

Chapter 7 Transitional Accretions

1. David Martin, *The Web of Disinformation: Churchill's Yugoslav Blunder* (New York: Harcourt Brace, 1990), p. 23.

2. Martin, *Web* p. xviii

3. Churchill, *Second World War,* Vol. 11, ch. 6, "Italy and the Riviera Landing."

4. Christopher Hibbert, "Mussolini," *Encyclopaedia Britannica*, Macropaedia, Vol. 12, pp. 751–52.

5. C. M. Woodhouse, *Apple of Discord: A Survey of Recent Greek Politics in their International Setting*, 3d ed. (London, New York, 1948; 1951), pp. 59 et seq; and pp. 84 et seq.

6. James Burnham, *The Struggle for the World* (New York: The John Day Company, 1947), ch. 1.

7. Librach, *Soviet Empire,* pp. 185–89. Also Tolstoy, *War*, p. 350.

8. David Rees, *The Soviet Seizure of the Kuriles* (New York: Praeger, 1985), p. 82 (quoting from *Pravda*, September 3, 1945).

9. *Foreign Relations of the United States: The Conferences at Malta and Yalta, 1945* (U.S. Government Printing Office, Washington, D.C., 1955), pp. 894–97. See also Rees, *Kuriles,* p. 82 and pp. 60–65.

10. Brian Crozier, Drew Middleton, and Jeremy Murray-Brown, *This War Called Peace* (London: Sherwood, 1984), p. 55.

CHAPTER 8   SATELLIZATION BEGINS, 1945–1948

1. Biographical entry on Kim Il Sung in *Who's Who in North Korea:* confidential material compiled by British Foreign and Commonwealth Office Information Research Department (IRD), updated in 1971.

2. *War/Peace,* pp. 91–92.

3. *Ibid.,* p. 91. See also entry on Kim Il Sung in *Grand Larousse Encyclopédique* (Paris, 1968).

4. The biographical notes on Enver Hoxha are mainly drawn from the appropriate volume of IRD, *Who's Who* (revised in 1973).

5. William L. Shirer, *The Rise and Fall of the Third Reich* (London: Seeker & Warburg, 1963), p. 193.

6. See "Dimitrov" in Jeanne Vronskaya and Vladimir Chuguev, eds., *The Biographical Directory of the Former Soviet Union* (London: Bowker-Saur, 1992), p. 103. An indispensable reference book for Sovietologues.

7. *Nazi-Soviet Relations, 1939–1941* (Washington, D.C.: Documents from the Archives of the German Foreign Office, Department of State), p. 155.

8. Librach, *Empire,* p. 164.

9. *Ibid.* See also "Communist Takeover and Occupation of Romania," *Special Report* 11, Select Committee on Communist Aggression, 83d Congress (Washington, D.C.: Government Printing Office), pp. 5–6.

10. Librach, *Empire.*

CHAPTER 9   THE CZECHOSLOVAK TRAGEDY

1. Librach, *Empire,* p. 155.

2. For a fuller examination of the postwar situation, see Crozier, *Survival,* especially ch. 6, pp. 101 et seq.

3. Librach, *Empire,* p. 175.

4. "Cold War International History Project," *Working Paper 9* (Washington, D.C.: Woodrow Wilson International Center for Scholars, March 1994), p. 19.

5. *Ibid.,* p. 26.

6. "Communist Takeover and Occupation of Czechoslovakia," *Special Report* 8, Select Committee on Communist Aggression, 83d Congress (Washington, D.C.: Government Printing Office), p. 23.

7. See Frantisek August and David Rees, *Red Star over Prague* (London: Sherwood, 1984), pp. 40–43. August took refuge in London after serving as a senior officer

in the StB (the Czech equivalent of the NKVD-KGB). His translated memoirs were edited and rewritten by David Rees, author of *Kuriles*, and a specialist on Communist affairs.

8. Eugen Loebl and Dusan Polorny, *Stalinism in Prague* (New York: Grove Press, 1969), quoted in Medvedev, *Stalinism*, pp. 795–96.

CHAPTER 10   HUNGARY'S "SALAMI" REVOLUTION

1. "Communist Occupation and Takeover of Hungary," *Special Report* 10, Select Committee on Communist Aggression, 83d Congress (Washington, D.C.: Government Printing Office), 1954. In particular, see testimony of Mgr. Varga, p. 8.

2. Librach, *Empire*, p. 158.

CHAPTER 11   STALIN'S GERMAN PLOY

1. James Byrnes, *Speaking Frankly* (New York: Harper, 1947), p. 25.

2. Librach, *Empire*, p. 132.

3. David Pryce-Jones, *The War That Never Was: The Fall of the Soviet Empire, 1985–1991* (London: Weidenfield & Nicolson, 1995), pp. 65 et seq.

4. Hermann Rauschning, *Hitler Speaks* (London: T. Butterworthy, 1939), p. 134. (Rauschning was a former Nazi leader in Danzig: see Shirer, *Third Reich*, p. 169.)

5. Eliot B. Wheaton, *Prelude to Calamity: The Nazi Revolution 1933–35* (Garden City, NY: Doubleday, 1968), p. 436. See also Nikolai Tolstoy, *Stalin's Secret War* (London: J. Cape, 1981), pp. 86–87.

6. Kurt L. Shell in *The Politics of Postwar Germany,* ed. Walter Stahl (1963), p. 85.

7. Shell, *Postwar Germany*, p. 86.

CHAPTER 12   THE FIRST INDOCHINA WAR, 1946–1954

1. See Brian Crozier, *South-East Asia in Turmoil*, 3d ed. (London: Penguin, 1968), pp. 46 et seq.

2. Crozier, *Rebels*, pp. 35–37. For Jean Sainteny's own (honest and well-written) account, see his book *Histoire d'une paix manquée* (*Story of a Peace That Failed*, [Paris: 1953]).

3. See John Colvin, *Giap: Volcano under Snow* (New York: Soho Press, 1996), p. 91.

4. Crozier, *South-East Asia*, p. 56.

5. Donald Lancaster, *The Emancipation of French Indochina* (Oxford: Oxford University Press, 1961), pp. 336–37. See also Crozier, *Agent*, pp. 22–23.

CHAPTER 13   OTHER ASIAN VENTURES, 1947–1954

1. Brimmell, *Communism*, p. 257. Brimmell drew, in part, from a Special Bulletin published in April 1948 by the Colonial Bureau of the International Union of Students in Prague.

2. Crozier, *South-East Asia*, p. 76.

3. Brimmell, *Communism,* p. 117.

4. Brimmell, *Communism,* pp. 198 et seq.

CHAPTER 14   CHINA: THE TEMPORARY SATELLITE, 1946–1950

1. For a fuller account, see Eric Chou, *Mao Tse-tung: The Man and the Myth* (London: Cassell, 1982), pp. 175 et seq. An accurate and fascinating biography, published posthumously.

2. *Ibid.,* pp. 179–80.

3. "The Cold War in Asia," Wilson, *Bulletin* (Winter 1995–1996).

4. Dmitri Volkogonov, *Stalin: Triumph and Tragedy* (London: Weidenfield & Nicolson, 1991), p. 539.

5. "Mao's Conversation with Yudin," Top Secret document, March 31, 1956; Wilson, *Bulletin* (Winter 1995–1996), pp. 164–67.

6. See Stuart Schram, *Mao Tse-tung* (London, 1966), pp. 254–57; and Harold M. Vinacke, *Far Eastern Politics in the Postwar Period* (London, 1956), pp. 170–71.

CHAPTER 15   KOREA: THE SATELLITE WAR

1. Specific details of Stalin's commitments in advance of and during the Korean War are given by Sarin and Dvoretsky in *Alien Wars.* Their revelations appear in ch. 4 of their book, *Stalin's Last Military Adventure,* and are based on: the USSR Central State Historic Archive 11/87, Vol. 203, p. 7 and p. 92; the USSR Central State Archive of the October Revolution and Socialist Construction of the USSR, 12/72, Vol. 211, p. 90; and the Russian Affairs Ministry Archive, 245/4542, Vol. 16, pp. 86–88.

2. On a state visit to South Korea in June 1994, President Boris Yeltsin of Russia presented to President Kim Young Sam a collection of high-level documents on the Korean War, which in turn reached the Woodrow Wilson Center, some of which were published in *Bulletin 5* (Spring 1995). Some 1,200 pages of further documents were declassified by the Presidential Archive in Moscow. A detailed analysis by Dr. Kathryn Weathersby appeared in *Bulletin 6–7* (Winter 1995–1996), along with translations of a selection of the documents, also discussed in this chapter.

3. Quoted in David Rees, *Korea: The Limited War* (London: MacMillan; New York: St. Martin's, 1964), p. 6. This work, the earliest of the full histories of the Korean War, remains in some respects the most authoritative. A new history, Michael Hickey's *The Korean War: The West Confronts Communism* (London: John Murrey, 1999), also is of high quality and incorporates Soviet archival material.

4. Wilson, *Bulletin 6–7,* p. 43.

5. See "The Sino-Soviet Alliance and China's Entry into the Korean War," the first Working Paper of the Woodrow Wilson Center in the Cold War Project (June 1992), pp. 24 et seq. The author, Chen Jian, a graduate of Fudan University in

China, took a further degree in history at Southern Illinois University, and remained in the United States.

6. Sarin and Dvoretsky, *Alien Wars,* pp. 78–79.

7. *Ibid.,* p. 77, quoting from Central Committee CPSU Archive, 654/21426, Vol. 24, pp. 45–47.

CHAPTER 16   THE BERLIN RISING, 1952–1955

1. Christian F. Ostermann, "Cold War International History Project," Working Paper 11 (Washington, D.C.: Woodrow Wilson International Center for Scholars, December 1994), pp. 4 et seq. (See footnote * of ch. 16, p. 161 of current volume.)

2. James B. Conant to Secretary of State, February 27, 1953 (Washington, D.C.: National Archives), quoted in Ostermann, Wilson Paper 11, pp. 9–10.

3. James B. Conant to Secretary of State, May 4, 1953, in Ostermann, Wilson Better Paper 11, p. 11).

4. Summary of discussion, March 12, 1953, 136th meeting of the National Security Council (NSC), in Ostermann, Wilson Paper 11, p. 11.

5. Quoted in Walt W. Rostow, *Europe after Stalin* (Austin, Tex.; University of Texas Press, 1982), App. C, p. 108.

6. See also Klaus W. Larres, *Politik der Illusionen: Churchill, Eisenhower und die deutsche Frage 1945–1955* (Göttingen, Lower Saxony, 1995); and M. Steven Fish, "After Stalin's Death: The Anglo-American Debate over a New Cold War," *Diplomatic History* (Journal of Society for Historians of American Foreign Relations) 10, (1986): 335.

7. Special meeting of National Security Council, March 13, 1953 (Abilene, Kans.: Dwight D. Eisenhower Library), Ann Whitman File, NSC Series, Box 4.

8. Wallace Carroll and Hans Speier, "Psychological Warfare in Germany: A Report to the United States High Commissioner for Germany and the Department of State," December 1, 1950 (National Archives), in Ostermann, Wilson Paper 11, p. 13.

9. *Die Rolle des feindlichen Rundfunks bei den Ereignissen in Berlin* (The Role of Enemy Broadcasts During the Events in Berlin), June 21, 1953, *Stiftung "Archiv der Parteien und Massenorganisationen der ehemaligen DDR" im Bundesarchive* (Foundation: "Archives of the Party and Mass Organizations of the Former GDR").

10. *Abteilung Leitende Organe der Partei und Massenorganisationen, "Analyse über die Vorbereitunbg, den Ausbruch und die Niederschlagung des faschistischen Abenteurs vom 16.-22.6, 1953,"* July 20, 1953 (Classified Leading Organs of the Party and Mass Organizations), "Analysis of the Preparations for the Outbreak and the Suppression of the Fascist Adventure of 16-22.6.1953" (SED Party Archives).

11. *Zusammenfassung der Stimmung, Vorschläge und Kritik der Werktätigen zur Erklärung des ZK vom 22.6.53* (Summary of the Workers' Opinions, Suggestions,

and Criticism on the Central Committee Declaration of June 22, 1953), in Ostermann, Wilson Paper 11, p. 28.

12. High Commissioner in Occupied Germany (HICOG) to Secretary of State, August 4, 1953, in Ostermann, Wilson Paper 11, p. 30.

13. High Commissioner in Occupied Germany (HCIOG) to Secretary of State,
July 16, 1953 in Ostermann, Wilson Paper 11, p. 30.

14. Memorandum to Secretary of State, September 24, 1953 in Ostrmann, Wilson
Paper 11, p. 37.

CHAPTER 17   THE GHETTO WALL, 1961

1. Hope M. Harrison, *Ulbricht and the Concrete "Rose": New Archival Evidence
on the Dynamics of Soviet–East German Relations and the Berlin Crisis, 1958–
1961,* Wilson Working Paper 5 (Washington, D.C.: Woodrow Wilson International Center for Scholars, May 1993).

2. Quoted on p. 313 of Arthur M. Schlesinger, Jr., *A Thousand Days: John F. Kennedy in the White House,* paperback ed. (London: Mayflower Dell, 1967), in a
detailed account of the Kennedy-Khrushchev meeting in Vienna.

3. *Keesing's Contemporary Archives* (Bristol, UK: Keesing's Publications, June
24–July 1, 1961), Vol. XIII, pp. 18163–18167.

4. *Ibid.,* July 22–29, 1961, pp. 18223 *et seq.*

5. *Ibid.*

6. *Ibid.*

7. *Ibid.,* August 19–26, pp. 18274 *et seq.*

8. Dennis L. Bark, *Agreement on Berlin: A Study of the 1970–72 Quadripartite Negotiations* (Washington, D.C. and Stanford, Calif.: American Enterprise Institute
for Public Policy Research, 1974), p. 22.

9. Eleanor Lansing Dulles, *The Wall: A Tragedy in Three Acts* (Columbia, S.C.: University of South Carolina, 1972), pp. 32–33.

10. *Ibid.,* pp. 44–45.

11. *Ibid.,* pp. 46–49.

12. Schlesinger, *Thousand Days,* pp. 681–82.

13. *Ibid.*

14. The unfortunate "sausage" connection, though widely reported in the news
media, is not mentioned in Schlesinger's book.

15. Annex II to the Agreement. For a full account of the Berlin negotiations and text
of the Agreement, see Bark, *Berlin.*

CHAPTER 18   UNREST IN POLAND, 1956–1957

1. For a general assessment of Gomulka's character and career, see Nicholas Bethell,
Gomulka: His Poland, His Communism (New York: Holt, Rinehart and Winston, 1969). See also Neal Ascherson, *The Polish August: What Has Happened in*

Poland (New York and London: Penguin, 1981). Although the main theme of Ascherson's book is the later crisis of 1980, he covers earlier history in considerable detail.

2. Ascherson, pp. 53–54.
3. Vronskaya and Chuguev, *Biographical Directory*, p. 437.
4. Nikita Khrushchev, *Khrushchev Remembers: The Last Testament*, trans. and ed. by Strobe Talbott (Boston: Little, Brown, 1974), pp. 199–200.
5. *Ibid.*
6. Nikita Khrushchev, *Khrushchev Remembers: The Glasnost Tapes*, trans. and ed. by Jerrold L. Schecter, with Vyacheslav W. Luchkov (Boston: Little, Brown, 1990), p. 115.

CHAPTER 19   UPRISING IN HUNGARY

1. Librach, *Empire*, pp. 157 et seq.
2. Carlile A. Macartney, in *Encyclopaedia Britannica 1976*, Vol. 9, p. 42.
3. For a lively and accurate account of these events, see *Chronicle of the Twentieth Century* (London: Longman, 1988), pp. 790–79.
4. *Chronicle*, p. 791.
5. John Barron, *KGB: The Secret Work of Soviet Secret Agents* (New York: Reader's Digest, 1974), p. 72.
6. David Pryce-Jones, *The Hungarian Revolution* (New York, 1970), p. 110.
7. Librach, *Empire,* pp. 182–83.

CHAPTER 20   THE SINO-SOVIET RIFT BEGINS, 1955–1962

1. For a fuller account of the AAPSO, see Rose, *Propaganda Network*, pp. 80–86. See also Crozier, *Since Stalin*, pp. 122–23.
2. A substantial summary of the speech was carried in *Keesing's Contemporary Archives*, July 21–28, 1956. The most penetrating commentary, together with the full text (in French) is by the Yugoslav-born Sovietologist Branko Lazitch: *Le Rapport Khrouchtchev et Son Histoire* (Paris: Sevil, 1976).
3. "From the Journal of P. F. Yudin, Top Secret, April 5, 1956," Wilson, *Bulletin* (Winter 1995–1996): 164–67.
4. *Ibid.*, pp. 153–54.
5. *Ibid*, pp. 155–59.
6. Chou, *Mao,* pp. 196–97.
7. Mark Kramer, "The USSR Foreign Ministry's Appraisal of Sino-Soviet Relations on the Eve of the Split, September 1959," *Bulletin* (Winter 1995–1996): p. 173.
8. *Ibid.*
9. Edward Crankshaw, *The New Cold War: Moscow v. Pekin* (London: Penguin, 1963), pp. 69–70.

10. Many accounts of the "Hundred Flowers" episode have been published. The most succinct is in Chou, *Mao,* pp. 193–95.

11. Many descriptions of the Great Leap Forward and the communes have been written. See Chou, *Mao,* pp. 197–200. See also Brian Crozier, *The Morning After: A Study of Independence* (London: Methuen, 1963), pp. 241–53.

12. See David Floyd, *Mao against Khrushchev: A Short History of the Sino-Soviet Conflict* (1964), pp. 66–67; also Crozier, *Since Stalin,* pp. 64–66, and *The Masters of Power* (Boston: Little, Brown, 1969), pp. 176–78.

13. The full text of the Soviet statement appears in Floyd, *Mao against Khrushchev,* p. 261.

CHAPTER 21   THE RISE OF FIDEL CASTRO, 1953–1962

1. For a full account of the CIA role in the Guatemalan crisis, see David Wise and Thomas B. Ross, *The Invisible Government* (London: Jonathan Cape, 1965), pp. 165–83. See also Crozier, *Masters,* pp. 307–8.

2. See Crozier, *Rebels,* pp. 69–75 and 155–57. For a fuller account, see Tad Szulc, *Fidel: A Critical Portrait* (New York: William Morrow, 1986), pp. 262–79. Despite the subtitle, this massive biography of Fidel Castro (703 pages) is in reality a hagiography, with only minor critical passages. For a critical evaluation of the "Critical Portrait," see Daniel James, "'Fidel: A Critical Portrait Which Is Far from Critical," in *Human Events* (April 4, 1987).

3. Szulc, *Fidel,* pp. 445 et seq.

4. *Ibid.,* p. 62.

5. James, "Fidel"; also his book, *Cuba: The First Soviet Satellite in the Americas* (New York: Avon, 1961).

6. Aleksandr Fursenko and Timothy Naftali, *One Hell of a Gamble: The Secret History of the Cuban Missile Crisis* (New York: W. W. Norton; London: John Murray, 1997), the fullest account of the crisis available, p. 45, quoting Alekseyev's reports to Moscow on March 12, 1960 (Folio 3, List 65, File 871, Archive of the President of the Russian Federation; ditto, March 7, 1960, and June 8, 1960, File 78825; p. 299, Files of SVR [Russian Foreign Intelligence Service]).

7. The nuclear superiority of the United States was first revealed in the *Economist's* confidential bulletin *Foreign Report* (April 5, 1962), in an article headed "Burial of the Missile Gap." The tip came from a senior MI-6 officer, but the original source (not mentioned in the article for security reasons at that time) was Oleg Penkovsky. See Crozier, *Agent,* pp. 46–47. For a detailed account of Penkovsky's crucial contribution to U.S. intelligence on the alleged "missile gap," see Jerrold L. Schecter and Peter S. Deriabin, *The Spy Who Saved the World: How a Soviet Colonel Changed the Course of the Cold War* (New York: Scribner, 1992), a major contribution to the story of the intelligence rivalry between the KGB and the CIA.

8. For a more detailed account of the Cuba crisis, see Crozier, *War/Peace*, pp. 170–74. See also Barron, *KGB*, pp. 147–52.

9. Wilson, *Bulletin* (Spring 95).

10. *Ibid.*, p. 109.

CHAPTER 22   THE TAMING OF FIDEL, 1963–1972

1. For further details, see Oleg Gordievsky and Christopher Andrew, *KGB: The Inside Story of its Foreign Operations from Lenin to Gorbachav* (London: Hodder & Stoughton, 1990), pp. 423–27.

2. Orlando Castro Hidalgo, *Spy for Fidel* (Miami: E. A. Seemann, 1971), p. 61.

3. *The Role of Cuba in International Terrorism and Subversion:* Hearings before the Subcommittee on Security and Terrorism, Committee on the Judiciary, United States Senate, Testimony of Gerardo Peraza, February 26, March 4, 11, 12, 1982; p. 6.

CHAPTER 23   AFRICAN VENTURES, 1954–1964

1. See Brian Crozier, *The Struggle for the Third World* (London: Bodley Head, 1966), part II, "The New Scramble for Africa," p. 49. This short work was written, largely on the basis of then-secret dispatches, entirely in offices provided by the Information Research Department (IRD) of Britain's Foreign Office.

2. *Ibid.*, p. 69.

3. Barron, *KGB*, pp. 252–53.

4. Crozier, *Survival*, pp. 60–66.

5. See Brian Cozier, "Aid for Terrorism," *Annual of Power and Conflict*, (1973–1974).

6. See Neil Bruce, "Portugal's African Wars," *Conflict Studies* 34 (March 1973).

7. *Ibid.*

8. Hugh Kay, "Portugal: Revolution and Backlash," *Conflict Studies* 61 (September 1975).

9. First reported in Pierre Andibert and Daniel Brignon, *Portugal: les Nouveaux Centurions* (Paris, 1974).

10. Moscow Radio, quoting TASS, February 23, 1974.

11. *Guardian* (London), September 6, 1975. For further details, see *APC* (1975–1976): 20–21.

CHAPTER 24   THE RIVAL SUNS, 1960–1972,

1. *Daily Nation* (Nairobi), February 4, 1961.

2. For fuller accounts of Chinese subversion in Africa, see Brian Crozier, "The Struggle for the Third World," *International Affairs* (July 1964); and Crozier, *Struggle*, pp. 57–66 and pp. 115 et seq. See also Crozier, *Since Stalin*, especially the chapter entitled "Competitive Subversion."

CHAPTER 25   VIETNAM II BEGINS, 1958–1962

1. See Crozier, *South-East Asia,* p. 136.
2. Quotations in ibid, pp. 138–39.
3. For a fuller description of relations among Diem, Collins, and Lansdale, see Robert Shaplen, *The Lost Revolution: Vietnam 1945–65* (London: Deutsch, 1966), pp. 118 et seq.
4. Crozier, *War/Peace,* pp. 177–78.

CHAPTER 26   POSTWAR THIRD WORLD SETBACKS

1. *Foreign Report* ("confidential" bulletin of the *Economist),* July 24, 1958; also, July 17 and August 14, 1958.
2. *Yearbook on International Communist Affairs* (Stanford, Calif.: Hoover Institution, 1969).
3. *Annual of Power and Conflict,* 1971, pp. 29–30. For a detailed account of the Marighella phenomenon, see Robert Moss, *Urban Guerrillas: The New Face of Political Violence* (London: Temple Smith, 1972), pp. 190–209.
4. The essential facts are in *APC* 1971, pp. 31–32.
5. For a detailed critique of the American intervention, see Theodore Draper, *The Dominican Revolt: A Case Study in American Policy* (New York, 1968). The author's book is essentially an expanded version of articles he wrote for the magazine *Commentary,* the *New Leader,* and the *New Republic* in 1965–1966.
6. For a detailed account of the background, see "Quebec: The Challenge from Within," *Conflict Studies* 20 (February 1972) by "A Canadian Correspondent" who, in fact, was a recently retired member of the Royal Canadian Mounted Police, better known as "the Mounties."
7. See Rowland Mans, "Canada's Constitutional Crisis: Separatism and Subversion," *Conflict Studies* 98 (August 1978).
8. For fuller accounts of the 1965 and later crises in Indonesia, see Crozier, *South-East Asia,* pp. 178–85; and *A Theory of Conflict* (London: Hamish Hamilton, 1974), pp. 188–89. For essential background, see Arnold C. Brackman, *Indonesian Communism: A History* (New York: Praeger, 1963).
9. For a full account of the coup and its consequences, see Arnold C. Brackman, *The Communist Collapse in Indonesia* (New York: W. W. Norton, 1969). See also Tarzie Vittachi, *The Fall of Sukarno* (London: Mayflower Dell, 1967).

CHAPTER 27   1968: THE PRAGUE SPRING AND BEYOND

1. The full text of this important letter was first revealed by Mark Kramer, "New Source on the 1968 Soviet Invasion of Czechoslovakia" Wilson, *Bulletin* 35 (Fall 1992). The circumstances, including the meeting in a lavatory, were covered by Kramer in "The Prague Spring and the Soviet Invasion of Czechoslovakia," Wilson, *Bulletin* 3 (Fall 1993).

2. *Yearbook on International Communist Affairs* (Stanford, Calif.: Hoover Institution, 1969), pp. 226 et seq.

3. Quoted in ibid., p. 230.

4. Josef Josten, "Czechoslovakia: From 1968 to Charter 77: A Record of Passive Resistance," *Conflict Studies* 86 (August 1977). The author, a well-known Czechoslovak dissident, twice took refuge in London: in 1938 when the Nazis took over, and in 1968 when the Warsaw Pact armies marched in.

5. *Ibid.*, p. 6.

6. A detailed account of this move was published by the U.S. Congress, under the title: *Aspects of Intellectual Ferment and Dissent in Czechoslovakia.* See Josten, "Czechoslovakia," p. 8.

7. August, *Red Star,* p. 147.

8. See Crozier, *War/Peace,* pp. 202 et seq.

9. For details, see August, *Red Star,* pp. 122 et seq.

10. Wilson, *Bulletin* (Fall 1992): 8 et seq.

CHAPTER 28   AFRICAN CLIENT-STATES, 1971–1977

1. See Thierry Desjardins, *Sadate: Pharaon d'Egypte* (Paris: Marcel Valtat, 1981), pp. 359 et seq.; and Malcolm Mackintosh in *APC* 1971, p. 97.

2. See Desjardins, *Sadate,* pp. 369 et seq.; and *APC* 1971, p. 98.

3. Desjardins, *Sadate,* p. 372.

4. This account of Soviet pressures on Somalia is largely based on Brian Crozier, "The Soviet Presence in Somalia," *Conflict Studies* 54 (February 1975), which drew heavily on material provided by the CIA on a confidential basis, and subsequently confirmed.

CHAPTER 29   THE SECOND INDOCHINA WAR, 1958–1975

1. See John Dornberg, *Brezhnev: The Masks of Power* (London: André Deutsch, 1974), pp. 172–76.

2. *Ibid.*, p. 182.

3. Mikhail Gorbachev, *Perestroika* (London, New York: Harper Row, 1987), ch. 1 in particular.

4. For full details of Soviet arms shipments to North Vietnam, see Sarin, *Alien Wars,* ch. 5.

5. See *Television and Conflict* (ISC Special Report, November 1978), p. 10.

6. Jonathan Aitken, *Nixon: A Life* (London: Weidenfield & Nicolson; 1993), pp. 385 et seq. An important work.

7. *Ibid.*, p. 385.

8. Richard Nixon, *The Real War* (New York: Warner, 1980), p. 108.

9. Aitken, *Nixon,* p. 386.

10. Nixon, *Real War,* p. 109.

11. Aitken, *Nixon*, p. 410.
12. For a full account of the North Vietnamese offensive, see Ian Ward, "Why Giap Did It: Report from Saigon," *Conflict Studies* 27 (October 1972). (Ward was at the time Southeast Asia correspondent of the London *Daily Telegraph*.) See also Brian Crozier, "Revolutionary War: Fact *versus* Theory," *Conflict Studies* 27 (October 1972). For an in-depth analysis of the political and ideological background, see Dennis J. Duncanson, "Indo-China: the Conflict Analyzed," *Conflict Studies* 39 (October 1973).
13. Richard Nixon, *The Memoirs of Richard Nixon* (New York: Grosset & Dunlap; London: Sidgwick & Jackson, 1978), pp. 754–55.

CHAPTER 30   LIBYA, THE MAVERICK "ALLY"

1. William Gutteridge,"Libya: Still a Threat to Western Interests," *Conflict Studies* 160 (1983).
2. *APC* 1977, pp. 14–15.
3. Claire Sterling, in her book, *The Terror Network: The Secret War of International Terrorism* (London: Weidenfeld & Nicolson, 1981), has interesting insights into Ghaddafi's role, but her calculation of the per capita value of the Soviet arms deal is mathematically flawed (pp. 258 et seq).
4. Sterling, *Terror Network*, p. 259. For further insights into Libyan aid to terrorists, see Albert Parry, *Terrorism: From Robespierre to Arafat* (New York: Vanguard, 1976); and Paul Wilkinson, *Terrorism and the Liberal State* (London: Macmillan, 1977).

CHAPTER 31   THIRD TIME LUCKY IN AFGHANISTAN, 1978–1979

1. Vladimir Kuzichkin, *Inside the KGB: Myth and Reality* (London: André Deutsch, 1999), p. 312. The author, a former high-ranking KGB officer, gives the fullest and most authoritative account of the three coups in Afghanistan.
2. Entry on Afghanistan in *APC, 1978–1979*.
3. Wilson *Bulletin* (Fall 1994): 70–75.
4. Kuzichkin, *KGB*, p. 315.

CHAPTER 32   THE ETHIOPIAN SATELLITE, 1974–1989

1. For a full account of the Ethiopian revolt, see David Hamilton, "Ethiopia's Embattled Revolutionaries," *Conflict Studies* 82 (April 1977). See also Colin Legum, *Ethiopia: The Fall of Haile Selassie's Empire* (London, 1975). Further details from entry on Ethiopia in APC 1977–78, pp. 181–186.
2. Hamilton, "Ethiopia," pp. 12–13.
3. Peter Janke, "Marxist Statecraft in Africa: What Future?" *Conflict Studies* 95 (May 1978).

4. *Ibid.*, p. 5.
5. *APC* 1978–1979, p. 6.
6. *New York Times,* December 6, 1978 (quoted in *APC,* 1978–1979).
7. *Wilson Bulletin* (Winter 96/97): 58–61.
8. These figures, compiled from various sources, first appeared in *APC* 1978–1979, p. 5
9. Paul B. Henze, "Ethiopia: The Fall of the Derg and the Beginning of Recovery under the EPRDF, March 1990–March 1992," in *Africa Contemporary Record* 23 (1998). A detailed and illuminating account of the collapse of the Mengistu regime.
10. The ensuing details, provided by a high-level defector, were originally carried in three issues of *Notes and Analysis* (August–September, October, and November 1985).

CHAPTER 33   ARAB UPHEAVALS

1. For a fuller analysis of Moscow geopolitical concerns, see *Soviet Objectives in the Middle East* (London: ISC Special Report, March 1974).
2. For a comprehensive analysis of the obstacles to Soviet plans in the Middle East, see Robert O. Freedman, *Soviet Policy toward the Middle East Since 1970* (New York: Praeger, 1975). See also Ivo J. Lederer and Wayne S. Vucinich (eds.), *The Soviet Union and the Middle East: The Post–World War II Era* (Stanford, Calif.: Hoover Institution Press, 1974).
3. *APC* 1978–1979, pp. 374–75.
4. For more detailed coverage of the rival presidential assassinations, see J. E. Peterson, *Conflict in the Yemens and Superpower Involvement* (Washington, D.C.: Georgetown University, 1981), pp. 15–21.
5. *APC* 1972–1973, p. 72.
6. *APC* 1973–1974, p. 68.
7. *APC* 1974–1975, pp. 121–23.
8. *APC* 1975–1976, p. 174.

CHAPTER 34   REDS AGAINST REDS, 1976–1979

1. Fritz Sitte, a German journalist, gives the higher figures of between 2 and 3 million Khmers massacred in his interesting book, *Die Roten Khmer: Völkermord im Fernen Osten* (*The Red Khmers: Genocide in the Far East*; Graz, Vienna, and Cologne: Verlag Styria, 1982, p. 9). He attributes the motivation of the Khmer Rouge to "an enigmatic and mysterious political doctrine and ideology, designed to build a fictitious 'Stone Age communism'": "*aufgrund einer rätselhaften und mysteriösen politischen Doktrin und Ideologie, eine fiktiven 'Steinzeitkommunismus' zu schaffen. . . .* "
2. Richard Evans, *Deng Xiaoping and the Making of Modern China* (London: Hamish Hamilton, 1993).

3. For a detailed account, see Edouard Sablier, *L'École française du terrorisme* (Paris: Rocher, 1993), ch. 10, *"À Phnom Penh aussi, c'est la faute à Rousseau."* ("In Phnom Penh too, it's Rousseau's fault.")

CHAPTER 35   TROUBLE IN PARADISE, 1977–1987

1. James R. Mancham, *Paradise Raped: Life, Love and Power in the Seychelles* (London: Methuen, 1983), p. 9.
2. René broadcast on June 5, 1977: BBC Summary of World Broadcasts (SWB), (ME/5531), June 8, 1977; TASS commentary: SWB (SU/5514), June 11, 1977.
3. Private source, in *Notes and Analysis* (January 1983).
4. Private source, in *Transnational Security* (January 1980).
5. René's speech in September 1979 is reproduced in full, along with other speeches of his in a book entitled *Seychelles: The New Era* (Victoria, Seychelles: Ministry of Education and Information, 1982).
6. Private sources, recorded in *Notes and Analysis* (January and June 1983).
7. *White Paper on Aggression of November 25th 1981 against the Republic of Seychelles* (*Livre Blanc: l'agression du 25 novembre 1981 contre la République des Seychelles* (Victoria, Seychelles: Department of Information, 1982), pp. 12 et seq.).
8. Sol W. Sanders, *Businessweek*, November 19, 1984.
9. Tony Hodges, in "Democratic Republic of São Tomé and Principle," *World Encyclopaedia of Political Systems* Hodges (pp. 1252–53, goes on to aver that "the party is not Marxist." Perhaps not, but by its own definition it must be classed, more relevantly, as *Leninist.*
10. French intelligence source, used in *Notes and Analysis* (July–August 1980).

CHAPTER 36   THE CHILEAN CRISIS AND BEYOND, 1970–1982

1. For a fuller analysis of the Chilean Communist Party, see William E. Ratliff in *Yearbook on International Communist Affairs* (Stanford, Calif.: Hoover Institution, 1973), pp. 305–14.
2. The best account of the Allende regime is Robert Moss, *Chile's Marxist Experiment* (London: World Realities, 1973). See also Crozier, *Survival*, pp. 133–36; and *War/Peace,* pp. 190–91.
3. James Whelan, "Augusto Pinochet: A Twentieth-Century Hero," *Human Events* (November 6, 1998).
4. There is a broad academic consensus in support of this interpretation. For instance: "Beyond occasionally associating themselves with Marxism-Leninism in public, the FSLN consistently offered unequivocal allegiance to the Soviet Union and Cuba and supported Soviet and Cuban foreign policy objectives." (Sharyl Nicolette Cross, *The Soviet Union and the Nicaraguan Revolution* (Los Angeles: University of California, 1990), p. 311. On ideology: "The FSLN 'Marxist-Leninist organisation' was to be

come 'an iron-hard Leninist party', as the platform states." (*Conflict in Nicaragua: A Multidimensional Perspective,* ed. by Jiri Valenta and Esperanza Durán; London: Allen & Unwin for the Royal Institute of International Affairs/Chatham House, p. 11.) The satellization theme is developed with appropriate examples in G. W. Sand, *Soviet Aims in Central America: The Case of Nicaragua* (New York and London: Praeger, 1989). For a divergent view: "Nicaragua's revolution offered a model of 'democratic socialism' where a 'popular hegemony' would operate in a system of political pluralism and a mixed economy." (Mary B. Vanderlaan, *Revolution and Foreign Policy* (Boulder, Colo., and London: Westview Press, 1986), p. 32.

5. For further details, see Eduardo Crawley, *Nicaragua: Key to Regional Peace, Conflict Studies* 166 (1984), the first of three linked studies on Central America.

6. Revelations by Miguel Bolaños Hunter, as recorded in *Hydra of Carnage: International Linkages of Terrorism—The Witnesses Speak* (collated by Uri Ra'anan; Lexington, Massachusetts: D. C. Health, 1986), pp. 309–32.

7. Timothy Ashby, *The Bear in the Backdoor: Moscow's Caribbean Strategy* (Lexington, Mass.,1987), p. 113.

8. See Sand, *Central America*, pp. 32–34. Also Crozier, *War/Peace*, p. 236.

9. Quoted in Stephen Clissold, ed., *Soviet Relations with Latin America, 1918–1968,* Documentary Survey (Oxford: Oxford University Press, 1970), p. 15, quoting Blanca Luz, *Contra la Corriente Against the Current* (Santiago: Ediciones Ercilla, 1936).

10. Quoted in Jiri and Virginia Valente's comprehensive survey, "Sandinistas in Power," *Problems of Communism* (September–October 1989).

11. *Ibid.*

12. For details of Pastora's views, see Hunter, *Hydra,* pp. 321 et seq.

13. *Yearbook on International Communist Affairs* (Stanford, Calif.: Hoover Institution, 1982), p. 125.

14. Peter Calvert, *Guatemalan Insurgency and American Security, Conflict Studies* 167 (1984).

15. For further details, see *Yearbook*; the American political weekly *Human Events* (September 12, 1981); and *La Prensa Gráfica* (San Salvador), (August 17, 1981).

CHAPTER 37   THE POLISH TURNING POINT, 1980–1982

1. Quoted in Timothy Garton Ash, *The Polish Revolution: Solidarity* (New York: Scribner, 1983).

2. Crozier, *Agent*, pp. 196–97.

3. Ronald W. Reagan, *An American Life* (New York: Simon & Schuster; London: Hutchinson, 1990), pp. 301–7.

4. Crozier, *Agent*, pp. 260–62.

5. *Ibid.*, pp. 197–98.

6. Gordievsky, *KGB*, p. 486.

7. Pryce-Jones, *Fall of Empire*, pp. 214 et seq.
8. Gordievsky and Andrew, *KGB*, p. 486.
9. Reagan, *Life*, p. 303.
10. *Notes and Analysis* (January 1982).
11. Pryce-Jones, *Fall of Empire*, p. 196, quoting Andrzej Swidlicki, historian of the Polish repression.
12. *Ibid.*

CHAPTER 38   GRENADA: THE FIRST STRATEGIC DEFEAT, 1983

1. See Indira Jhappan, "Grenada," *World Encyclopaedia of Political Systems*, (New York: Facts on File), Vol. 1, pp. 394–95.
2. For a full account of the key meetings of the New Jewel Movement (Plenary, Central Committee, and Political Bureau), see Paul Seabury and Walter A. McDougall, eds., *The Grenada Papers: The Inside Story of the Grenadian Revolution and the Making of a Totalitarian State—As Told in Captured Documents* San Francisco: Institute for Contemporary Studies, 1984).
3. Gregory Sandford and Richard Vigilante, *Grenada: The Untold Story* (New York: Madison Books, 1984), p. 173. An interesting analysis.
4. *Ibid.*, p. 174.
5. *Ibid.*, p. 175. The authors describe the Soviet reaction as "completely supportive." Another interpretation appears in *Yearbook on International Communist Affairs* (Stanford, Calif.: Hoover Institution, 1984), p. 126: "Cuba condemned Bishop's killing in strong terms; Soviet criticism was less vociferous." For geographical reasons, Grenada's relations with Cuba were perhaps closer than with the Soviet Union, the Soviet Communist Party enrolled fourteen Grenadian party members for scholarships at the Lenin Institute in Moscow in May 1983. For a fuller discussion of New Jewel Movement relations with Moscow and Havana, see Jiri Valenta and Herbert J. Ellison, eds., *Grenada and Soviet/Cuban Policy: Internal Crisis and Us/Oecs Intervention: A Special Study of the Kennan Institute for Advanced Russian Studies, the Wilson Center,* (Boulder, Colo., and London: Westview Press, 1986).
6. A Spanish language translation of Indira Gandhi's letter appeared in Fidel Castro's denunciatory account of the U.S. intervention: *La Invasión a Granada* (Havana: Realidad Social, 1983), pp. 100–101. In a speech on November 14, 1983, Castro delivered a detailed attack on the American action, published later under the title: *Una Victoria militar pírrica y una profunda derrota moral (A Pyrrhic military victory and a profound moral rout).* For a critical American view of the U.S. intervention in Grenada, see Reynold A. Burrowes, *Revolution and Rescue in Grenada: An Account of the U.S.-Caribbean Invasion* (New York: Greenwood Press, 1988).

7. Most of the facts about the international aspects of the Grenada crisis, especially its relations with the Soviet Bloc, together with the quotations or summaries of captured secret documents are drawn from Brian Crozier, ed., *The Grenada Documents* (London: Sherwood, 1987). For a detailed history of the island, see Kai P. Schoenhals and Richard A. Melanson, *Revolution and Intervention in Grenada: The New Jewel Movement, the United States, and the Caribbean* (Boulder, Colo., and London: Westview, 1985). As always, the background narrative draws heavily on the relevant issue of *Keesings Contemporary Archives,* Vol. 30, (January 1984).

CHAPTER 39 THE INTERNATIONAL MACHINE AT WORK

1. Crozier, *Agent*, p. 295.
2. Fond 89 identification: Opis 51, File 31.
3. Opis 46, File 118.
4. Opis 51, File 31.
5. Opis 27, File 34.
6. Opis 43, File 1.
7. Opis 43, File 5.
8. Opis 13, File 8
9. Opis 13, File 10.
10. Opis 11, File 144.
11. Opis 13, File 15.
12. Opis 13, File 16.
13. Opis 10, File 20.
14. Crozier, *Agent,* p. 258.
15. For a detailed account of these events, see Crozier, *Agent,* pp. 239–50.

CHAPTER 40 DEFEAT IN AFGHANISTAN, 1986–1989

1. For a perceptive and fuller account of the military and political situation in 1984—halfway through the war—see Anthony Hyman, "Afghan Resistance: Danger from Disunity," *Conflict Studies* 161 (1984). See also Appendix O: Document 1 to this volume.
2. Alexander R. Alexiev, "The Soviet Strategy in Afghanistan," *Global Affairs* (Winter 1987): 75–77.
3. Brian Crozier, "Afghan Rebels Armed with Sam-7 Rockets," *NOW!* (London), June 13, 1980 and several reports in the *Independent* (London), May 1987. The factual material for this article was provided by the CIA. For these and further details about the Stinger and other weapons, see Alex Alexiev. "US Policy and War in Afghanistan," in *Global Affairs* (at that time the organ of the International Security Council, New York), Winter 1988.
4. Tom Rogers, "Afghans in Exile: Refugees—A Threat to Stability," *Conflict Studies* 202 (1987).

5. Alexiev, "Soviet Strategy."

6. Captain Kenneth L. Davison, Jr., USAF, "The Geopolitics of the Soviet With-drawal from Afghanistan," *Strategic Review* (Winter 1990).

CHAPTER 41   THE GLASNOST FACTOR, 1985–1991

1. For a fuller account, see Brian Crozier, *The Gorbachev Phenomenon* (London: Claridge, 1990), pp. 16–18 and 23. Source: Donald Jameson, formerly CIA's top Sovietologist, later Deputy Director, Jamestown Foundation, Washington, D.C.; supplemented by Friedrikh Neznansky, ex-head of Moscow's Criminal Investigation Department before defecting to the West, as published in *Sunday Telegraph* (London), March 6, 1988.

2. Arkady N. Shevchenko, a former Soviet ambassador to the United Nations who defected to the United States, in his book, *Breaking with Moscow* (New York: Alfred A. Knopf, 1985), p. 185.

3. Statistics collected by Françoise Thom in a book coauthored with David Regan, *Glasnost, Gorbachev and Lenin: Behind the New Thinking* (London: Policy Research Publications, 1988).

4. Michael Voslensky, *Nomenklatura: Anatomy of the Soviet Ruling Class* (London: Bodley Head, 1980): a key exposé of the doctrinal cynicism of the 1970s.

5. *Literaturnaya Gazeta*, December 3, 1986.

6. *USSR News Brief*, December 3, 1986.

7. *Radio Liberty Research Bulletin*, June 3, 1987.

8. Françoise Thom, *Le Moment Gorbachev* (Paris, 1989).

9. Mikhail Gorbachev, *Perestroika: New Thinking for our Country and the World* (New York, London: Harper Row, 1987), pp. 18–19.

10. *Ibid.*, p. 26.

11. *Ibid.*, p. 40.

12. Robert Conquest gives this figure in his definitive study, *The Harvest of Sorrow: Soviet Collectivisation and the Terror Famine* (London: Hutchinson, 1986).

13. The *Nedelya* details were quoted in Angus Roxborough from Moscow, "Soviets Admit Stalin Killed 50 m" in *Sunday Times,* April 17, 1988. The admission was made by Professor Igor Bestuzhev-Lada.

14. For further details see Crozier, *Phenomenon,* part II, ch. 1, pp. 81–92. Original sources included *Counterpoint,* a monthly bulletin edited by two leading Soviet defectors, Stanislav Levchenko and Peter Deryabin; *Soviet Analyst,* a privately financed British fortnightly bulletin with which this author was associated; a private French bulletin entitled *Désinformation;* and, during the Reagan and Bush years in the United States, a number of reports issued by the CIA, the State Department, the U.S. Information Agency, the Justice Department, and various Congressional committees.

15. *Pravda*, July 1, 1987.

16. BBC, *Summary of World Broadcasts, Soviet Union/9469*, May 30, 1989.
17. *Wall Street Journal*, October 25, 1989.

CHAPTER 42   CRACKS IN THE EMPIRE, 1986–1990

1. Archie Brown, *The Gorbachev Factor* (Oxford: Oxford University Press, 1996), p. 252.
2. Brown, *Gorbachev*, p. 260, quoting Kolvin interview, *The Second Russian Revolution* transcripts (London: BBC Books, 1991).
3. Mikhail Gorbachev, *Memoirs* (London, New York, 1996), p. 331. In the earlier German version (Gorbatschow, *Erinnerungen;* Berlin, 1995), p. 480, he is slightly more self-critical and confesses to "a big mistake" (*ein grosser irrtum*).
4. For a fuller account of these events, see Brown, *Gorbachev*, pp. 262–64.
5. Pierre Ibéri, "La nuit de la Saint Barthélemy géorgienne" in *Est & Ouest* (Paris), May 1989. Ibéri quotes the French news agency Agence France Presse (AFP), for the figure of seven hundred poisoned by gas.
6. *Ibid.*, and Brown, *Gorbachev*, pp. 265–66.
7. Eduard Shevardnadze. *The Future Belongs to Freedom* (London: Sinclair-Stevenson, 1991), p. 193.
8. *Ibid.*, p. 194.
9. Brown, *Gorbachev*, p. 266.
10. George Schöpflin, "The Polish Dilemma," *Soviet Analyst* (London), June 14, 1989.
11. As reported in *The Times* (London, October 28, 1989), and the *Guardian* (London, December 5, 1989).
12. Markus Wolf (with Anne McElvoy), *Man Without a Face: The Memoirs of a Spymaster* (London: Jonathan Cape, 1997), pp. 324–25. See also David Pryce-Jones, *The War that Never Was* (London: Weidenfield & Nicolson, 1995), pp. 239 et seq.
13. Wolf, *Face*, pp. 325–26.

CHAPTER 43   MORE CRACKS IN THE EMPIRE, 1990

1. Brian Crozier, *The Gorbachev Phenomenon* (London: Claridge, 1990), part I, ch. 3 and part II, ch. 1.
2. Gorbachev, *Memoirs*, p. 344.
3. Brown, *Gorbachev*, p. 199.
4. For a fuller discussion of the presidential options and other constitutional questions, see ibid., pp. 195–205.
5. Boris Yeltsin, *Against the Grain,* trans. by Michael Glenny (London: Jonathan Cape, 1990); Boris Yeltsin, *The View from the Kremlin,* trans. and anno. by Catherine A. Fitzpatrick (London: HarperCollins, 1994). Both accounts are vivid if undisciplined records, respectively, of Yeltsin's years in the political wilderness, and the collapse of the Soviet system.

6. Yeltsin, *Grain,* p. 142.

7. *Ibid.,* p. 153–154.

8. Yeltsin, *View,* p. 16.

9. *Grain,* p. 199.

10. *Ibid.,* p. 201.

11. *View,* p. 17.

CHAPTER 44   COUP AND COUNTER-COUP, 1991

1. Gorbachev, *Memoirs, pp.* 578 et seq.

2. Yeltsin, *View,* p. 25.

3. *Ibid.,* p. 36.

4. Mikhail Gorbachev, *The August Coup: The Truth and the Lessons* (London: HarperCollins, 1991).

5. Gorbachev, *Memoirs,* p. 631.

6. *Ibid.,* p. 632.

CHAPTER 45   BIRTH OF THE CIS, 1991

1. Yeltsin, *View,* p. 47.

2. *Ibid.,* p. 72.

3. *Ibid.,* pp. 106–8. Although Yeltsin's description of events is colorful and convincing, his chronology is vague, and it is not clear to the reader when his nighttime telephone call was made.

4. For a fuller account of Western reactions to the August coup, see Brian Crozier, "Getting It Wrong about Gorby," *National Review,* September 23, 1991.

5. Gorbachev, *Memoirs,* p. 644.

6. Boris Pankin, *The Last Hundred Days of the Soviet Union,* trans. by Alexei Pankin (London and New York: I. B. Jarvis, 1996), p. 238. The final chapter, "The Last Days of the Soviet Union," is a lively account of the Fifth Extraordinary Congress of People's Deputies, at which Pankin, a former journalist, assisted in his capacity as the last foreign secretary of the Soviet Union, and of the first session of the new State Council.

7. The quoted passages are all from Pankin, *Last Hundred Days,* pp. 240–43.

CHAPTER 46   CHAOS AND REBIRTH IN THE EX-USSR

1. *European Security and the Soviet Problem* (London: ISC Special Report, January 1972), p. 1.

2. For a fuller account and analysis of the new Communist parties, see *Russia Briefing* (a London-based monthly "political and economic service" edited by Charles Meynell and Sergei Novikov) 2: 3 (March 23, 1994).

3. Yeltsin, *View,* pp. 241 et seq.

4. *Ibid,* p. 247.

CHAPTER 47   RED NAME CHANGES

1. I first drew attention to this post-Communist pattern in *Freedom Today* (London, April 1994).
2. *Economist*, October 8, 1997, p. 62.
3. *Eastern Europe Newsletter* (London), April 14, 1995.
4. For further details, see *Hoover Yearbook* (1985), pp. 250 et. seq.
5. *Hoover Yearbook* (1988).

CHAPTER 48   SEMI-SURVIVAL IN ASIA

1. For a fuller discussion of this argument, see Brian Crozier, "What Went Wrong in Moscow and Beijing," *The World and I* (October 1989). For a detailed analysis of perestroika and glasnost, see Crozier, *Phenomenon*.
2. Walter Ellis in *The European* (London), March 30, 1998.
3. *Wall Street Journal Europe*, May 22, 1997.
4. David Tracey, "Inside North Korea's Gulag," *Reader's Digest* (February 1994).
5. *Financial Times* (London), October 29, 1997.
6. Radio Australia on March 20, 1996, citing "a party insider."
7. *Wall Street Journal Europe*, October 24–25, 1997.
8. Extracted from Sam Rainsy, Cambodia's Finance Minister from 1993 to 1994, and leader of the opposition Khmer Nation Party, in *Wall Street Journal Europe*, April 21, 1998.

CHAPTER 49   CHAOTIC CHANGE IN AND AROUND AFRICA

1. During and after the traumatic events of 1989–1998, two major sources about South Africa were the highly factual (and confidential) *Roca Report* and the hard-hitting *Aida Parker Newsletter*, which placed its coverage in the context of international Communism. During the first eight months of 1994, another important source was the "Strictly Private and Confidential" *South Africa Assessment*.
2. Keith Campbell, *ANC: A Soviet Task Force?* (London: Institute for the Study of Terrorism, 1986), App. II.

CHAPTER 50   FIDEL ON HIS OWN

1. These figures appeared in a serious analysis of the annual costs of the Soviet Empire, compiled by the Jamestown Foundation in Washington, D.C., a think tank partly staffed by Soviet defectors.
2. A full account of Castro's unpublicized purge, by Juan Benemelis, a high-level DGI defector, appeared in the April 1988 issue of *Analysis,* the "Restricted" newsletter of the private sector action agency, The 61. See Crozier, *Agent*.
3. Most of this chapter is an adaptation of the author's own chapter on the same themes in *Le Phénix rouge* (Paris: Rocher, 1995). Coauthors: Hans Huyn, Constantine Menges, and Édouard Sablier.

CHAPTER 51   REFLECTIONS: THE EXORBITANT PRICE OF
                         LENIN'S UTOPIA

1. The authors were the editor and coordinator of the project, Stéphane Courtois, editor of the review *Communisme*; Nicolas Werth, researcher at the *Institut d'histoire du temps présent*; Jean-Louis Panné, contributor to the *Dictionnaire biographique du mouvement ouvrier français (1914–1939)*; Andrzej Paczkowski, assistant director of the *Institut d'études politiques de l'Académie polonaise des sciences*; Karel Bartosek, Czech-born editor of the review *La Nouvelle Alternative*; and Jean-Louis Margolin, lecturer at the *Université de Provence*. All are authors of books on themes related to Communism.

2. *Salisbury Review* (London, Summer 1998).

SELECTED BIBLIOGRAPHY

—————

Abramovitch, Raphael R. *The Soviet Revolution, 1917–1939*. New York: International Universities Press,1962.

Alvarez, Luis H. *Nicaragua Sandinista o el Refinamiento del Engaño (Sandinista Nicaragua or the Refinement of Deception)*. Prologue by Alvaro C. Alsogaray. Buenos Aires: Instituto Democracia y Libertad, 1985. The author attacks Sandinista atrocities.

Annual of Power and Conflict. (APC), Edited by Brian Crozier. Published annually, between 1971 and 1984, London: Institute for the Study of Conflict (ISC). Covers terrorism world-wide, with strategic analyses.

Ascherson, Neal. *The Polish August*. London: Allen Lane, 1981.

Bacevich, A. J., James D. Hallums, Richard H. White, and Tomas F. Young. *American Military Policy in Small Wars: The Case of El Salvador.* Washington and London: Pergamon-Brassey's/Institute for Foreign Policy Analysis, 1987.

The Birth of Solidarity: The Gdansk Negotiations, 1980. Translated and introduced by A. Kemp-Welch in association with St. Antony's College, Oxford. New York: St. Martin's, 1983. Comprehensive and enlightening coverage.

Browder, R. P., and A. F. Kerensky. *The Russian Government 1917: Documents and Material*. 3 vols. Stanford, Calif.: Hoover Institution, 1961.

Bunyan, J., and H. H. Fisher. *The Bolshevik Revolution, 1917–8, Documents and Materials*. Stanford, Calif.: Hoover War Library, 1934; reprinted 1965.

Carr, E. H. *A History of Soviet Russia, 9* vols. London: Pelican, 1950–1971 Factually accurate but biased in favor of the Soviet regime.

Chamberlain, W. H. *The Russian Revolution, 1917–1921*. 2 vols. 1935; paperback ed. 1965.

Deutscher, Isaac. *The Prophet Armed: Trotsky 1879–1921*. New York: Oxford University Press, 1954.

————. *The Prophet Outcast: Trotsky 1929—1940*. Oxford, New York: Oxford University Press, 1980.

————. *The Prophet Unarmed: Trotsky 1921—1929.* London, New York: Oxford University Press, 1980.

Dobb, Maurice. *Soviet Economic Development since 1917.* New York: International Publishers, 1966.

Fainsod, M. *How Russia Is Ruled.* 2d ed. Cambridge, Mass.: Harvard University Press, 1963.

Fauriol, Georges, ed., *Latin American Insurgencies.* Washington, D.C.: National Defense University Press, 1985.

Held, Joseph. *Dictionary of East European History since 1945: Vol. 32, Poland.* Compiled by Richard C. Lewanski. Oxford: Clio Press, 1984.

Holstein, William J., Mark D'Anastasio, and Boyd France. "Gorbachev Raises the Ante in Afghanistan; Threatens Pakistan to Cut Aid to Afghan Rebels." *Business Week,* May 20, 1985.

Indian Ocean Newsletter/La lettre de l'Océan Indien. 1986. Published in French and English in Paris.

Karp, Craig M. "The War in Afghanistan." *Foreign Affairs* (Summer 1986).

Keesing's Contemporary Archives. I have drawn extensively from the issues of February 3 and October 27, 1978; February 23, April 6, May 25, and October 12, 1979.

Kerensky, A. F. *The Kerensky Memoirs: Russia and History's Turning Point.* London: Cassell, 1966.

Leggett, G. *The Cheka: Lenin's Political Police.* Oxford: Clarendon, 1981.

Lockhart, R. H. Bruce. *Memoirs of a British Agent.* London and New York: Putnam, 1932.

Lockhart, R. H. Bruce, with John Keep, *The Two Revolutions: An Eye-Witness Study of Russia 1917.* London: Bodley Head, 1967.

Los Sandinistas. Bogota, Colombia: Editorial La Oveja Negra ("The Black Sheep"), 1979. Calls for a Sandinista popular revolution.

MacShane, Denis. *Solidarity: Poland's Independent Trade Union.* Nottingham: Spokesman, 1981. A penetrating analysis.

Manwaring, Max G., and Court Prisk, eds. *El Salvador at War.* With a preface by Ambassador Edwin G. Corr. Washington, D.C.: National Defense University Press, 1988. In a foreword, Lieutenant-General Bradley C. Hosmer deals with the clash between totalism and democracy.

Mouvement pour la Résistance. 1984. A dissident newspaper produced (or claiming to be produced) on Mahé Island.

Nolan, David. *The Ideology of the Sandinistas and the Nicaraguan Revolution.* Coral Gables, Fla.: University of Miami, 1984. The author (rightly) points to the Cuban revolution as the catalyst for the FSLN.

Ortega, Daniel. *La Revolución no se Detiene (The Revolution Hasn't Stopped)*. Three speeches by President Ortega after the 1990 elections, which the Sandinistas lost. In one of the speeches, at the Olof Palme Center in Managua, on February 28, 1990, Ortega claimed, with justification, that although the Sandinistas would have liked to win, the fact that they accepted the outcome confirmed that they are democrats.

Ortega Saavedra, Huberto, *50 Años de Lucha Sandinista*. Havana: Ciencias Sociales, 1980. A text of pure Marxism.

Pipes, Richard. *The Formation of the Soviet Union: Communism and Nationalism, 1917–1923*. Cambridge, Mass.: Harvard, 1954; rev. ed. 1964.

Poland under Jaruzelski: A Comprehensive Sourcebook on Poland during and after Martial Law. Edited by Leopold Labedz with the staff of *Survey* magazine. New York: Scribner, 1983.

History of the Communist Party of the Soviet Union. 2d rev. ed. Edited by B. N. Ponomarev, et al. Moscow: Foreign Languages Publishing House, 1962.

Rauch, Georg von. *Geschichte des bolschewistischen Russland*. 1955. Eng. trans., *A History of Soviet Russia*, 5th rev. ed., New York: Praeger, 1967. Translated by Peter and Annette Jacobson.

Reed, J. *Ten Days That Shook the World*. paperback ed, Harmondsworth: Penguin, 1966.

Sandino, Augusto C. and Carlos Fonseca Amador. *Nicaragua: La Estrategia de la Victoria*, Mexico: Nuestro Tiempo, 1980. Prologue by Fernando Carmona, who proclaims the class war and condemns Yankee imperialism.

Schapiro L. B. *The Origin of the Communist Autocracy*, London: University of London, 1955; paperback ed. 1965.

———. *The Communist Party of the Soviet Union*. London: Eyre & Spottiswoode, 1960; paperback ed. 1964.

Seton-Watson, H. *The Decline of Imperial Russia, , 1855–1914*, London: Methuen, 1953; 2d ed. 1964.

Seychelles Democratic Party. 1986, 1987. Dissident newspaper produced in London.

Seychelles Freedom Herald. 1986, 1987. Dissident newspaper produced in London.

Seychelles Nation. 1983. Organ of the René government.

Sheerman, Peter, and Phil Williams. *The Superpowers, Central America and the Middle East*. London: Brassey's, 1988. The authors praise Soviet moderation under Gorbachev.

Snarr, Neil, et al. *Sandinista Nicaragua*. Ann Arbor, Mich.: Pierian Press, 1989. Chapter 2, by Rhonda L. Neugebauer, sings the praises of Sandino.

Shub, D. *Lenin: A Biography*. Harmondsworth: Penguin, 1966.

Souvarine, Boris. *Staline: aperçu historique du Bolchévisme*. Paris: Plon, 1935; Engl. trans. 1939).

Trotsky, L., *History of the Russian Revolution, 1932–1933,* abridged ed. by F. W. Dupee, Garden City, New York: Doubleday, 1959.

Turner, Robert F. *Nicaragua v.United States: A Look at the Facts*. Washington and London: Pergamon-Brassey's/Institute for Foreign Policy Analysis, 1987.

Ulam, Adam B. *The Bolsheviks*. Cambridge, Mass.: Harvard University Press, 1998.

Volkogonov, Dmitri. *Autopsy for an Empire,* edited and translated by Harold Shukman. New York and London: HarperCollins, 1998. The London edition appeared under the same title, but it is, in fact, a collection of biographies of all Soviet leaders from Lenin to Gorbachev.

———. *Stalin: Triumph and Tragedy,* edited and translated by Harold Shukman, London: Weidenfield & Nicolson, 1991.

———. *Lenin: Life and Legacy*. Edited and translated by Harold Shukman. London: HarperCollins, 1995.

———. *Trotsky: The Eternal Revolutionary.* Edited and translated by Harold Shukman. New York: Free Press, 1996.

Wolfe, B. D. *Three Who Made a Revolution*. New York: Dial Press, 1948; rev. paperback ed., 1964. The "three" in the title are Lenin, Trotsky, and Stalin.

Yearbook on International Communist Affairs. Stanford, Calif.: Hoover Institution. Useful interpretative analyses are found in *Yearbook,* specifically the entries on Cambodia (Peter A. Poole) and on the Socialist Republic of Vietnam (Douglas Pike) in the 1977 edition; and the corresponding entries in the editions of 1978, 1979, and 1980.

INDEX